THE CHARLES BABBAGE INSTITUTE

REPRINT SERIES FOR THE HISTORY OF COMPUTING

TITLES IN SERIES

1. *The Preparation of Programs for an Electronic Digital Computer* (1951), by Maurice V. Wilkes, David J. Wheeler, and Stanley Gill, 1984.

2. *Babbage's Calculating Engines: A Collection of Papers* (1889), by Henry Prevost Babbage, 1984.

3. *Handbook of the Napier Tercentenary Celebration or Modern Instruments and Methods of Calculation* (1914), edited by E. M. Horsburgh, 1984.

4. *High-Speed Computing Devices* (1950), by Engineering Research Associates, Inc., 1984.

5. *Punched Card Methods in Scientific Computation* (1940), by W. J. Eckert, 1984.

6. *Calculating Machines: Recent and Prospective Developments and Their Impact on Mathematical Physics* (1947) and *Calculating Instruments and Machines* (1949), by Douglas R. Hartree, F.R.S., 1984.

7. *Proceedings of a Symposium on Large-Scale Digital Calculating Machinery* (1947), jointly sponsored by The Navy Department Bureau of Ordnance and The Harvard University Computation Laboratory, 1985.

8. *A Manual of Operation for the Automatic Sequence Controlled Calculator* (1946), by The Harvard University Computation Laboratory, 1985.

9. *The Moore School Lectures* (1946), edited by Martin Campbell-Kelly and Michael R. Williams, 1985.

A MANUAL OF OPERATION
FOR THE AUTOMATIC SEQUENCE CONTROLLED CALCULATOR

VOLUME 8

IN THE

CHARLES BABBAGE INSTITUTE

REPRINT SERIES FOR THE

HISTORY OF COMPUTING

THE CHARLES BABBAGE INSTITUTE REPRINT SERIES FOR THE HISTORY OF COMPUTING

This volume is one of a series of works selected for reprinting by an editorial board of the Charles Babbage Institute. The Charles Babbage Institute for the History of Information Processing was founded in late 1977 to promote study of the technical and socioeconomic aspects of the development of information processing. To this end, the Institute serves as an archive of the history of information processing; as a clearinghouse for information about historical material and interested persons; and as a foundation that fosters research and writing in the field of information processing through the use of historical materials. In 1980 the Institute moved to its permanent home at the University of Minnesota.

The principal aim of the reprint series has been to make the key literature of the history of computing more accessible. Until now, the scarcity of many significant works has been a handicap to serious study. Reprinted items include classic textbooks, influential reports, and conference proceedings that have proved to be significant steps in the development of the subject. If original editing or print quality now seems unsatisfactory, new editions of some works are to be offered. In addition, non-English works are translated. Most volumes are provided with an authoritative introduction to afford insight and context for the present-day reader.

In selecting works for reprinting, the editorial board has consciously endeavored to produce a balanced collection of material that is representative of the full spectrum of the history of computing. The complete series will thus form a sound basis for studies in the history of computing, and will be of value both to active historians and to computer practitioners interested in the origins of their subject.

Howard Hathaway Aiken (1900–1973)

A MANUAL OF OPERATION FOR THE AUTOMATIC SEQUENCE CONTROLLED CALCULATOR

by the Staff of the Computation Laboratory

---

with a new foreword by
I. Bernard Cohen

and a new introduction by
Paul Ceruzzi

The MIT Press
Cambridge, Massachusetts
London, England

and

Tomash Publishers
Los Angeles/San Francisco

PUBLISHER'S NOTE

This book is a photographically reproduced facsimile of the original edition of the book, entitled *A Manual of Operation for the Automatic Sequence Controlled Calculator*, by the staff of The Computation Laboratory and published by Harvard University Press in 1946.

Printed and bound in the United States of America

Library of Congress Cataloging in Publication Data

Main entry under title:

A Manual of operation for the Automatic Sequence Controlled Calculator.

(The Charles Babbage Institute reprint series for the history of computing; v. 8)
Reprint. Originally published: Cambridge, Mass.: Harvard University Press, 1946.
Bibliography: p.
Includes index.
1. Mark I (Calculator) 2. Computers—History.
I. Harvard University. Computation Laboratory.
II. Series.
QA75.M348 1985 510'.28'53 84-28901

ISBN: 978-0-262-51379-1

FOREWORD

The machine known as the Harvard Mark I, or the IBM Automatic Sequence Controlled Calculator (ASCC), is a monument in the development of the art of computing. The product of Howard Hathaway Aiken's seminal ideas and the engineering know-how of the International Business Machines Corporation, it proved to the world at large that full-scale, rapid, automatic sequenced numerical calculation was possible and could be reliable. Most experts would agree with the judgment expressed in the *Encyclopedia of Computer Science and Engineering* (1983, p. 916) that the Mark I "marked the beginning of the era of modern computing." In a review of the *Manual of Operation* reprinted here, L. J. Comrie (*Nature* 158 (1946): 567–568) wrote that "Babbage's Dream Comes True." Other machines had been designed, imagined, or built, for which a claim of predecessor can be made (for example, those of John V. Atanasoff, George Stibitz, or Konrad Zuse), but the Mark I was the one that put the actuality of computers into general ken. Many pioneers were introduced to computers through the Mark I (in its successive modifications). In part, this unique role derived from the fact that it was so great a success and did such important work, especially during wartime; but there was also the plain and obvious fact that there was wide press coverage of the dedication ceremony, followed by many magazine articles.

In the history of computers and of information processing, Aiken has three separate claims to fame. The first, and most obvious, was his pioneering achievement in the development of machines (the Mark I and its successors, the Marks II, III, and IV) and the art and science of computers, together with methods of numerical analysis. Second, Aiken established the pioneering school of advanced computer science: the roster of his Harvard students reads like a Who's Who of the computer world. Third, by his lectures and articles, and especially by the series of computer conferences that he organized in the years following World War II, Aiken aroused worldwide interest in the new science and conveyed his vision of a computer world which we have come to accept today but which was then often considered far-out and unreal.

Aiken's great achievements were recognized by many honorary doctorates, medals and awards, and memberships in honorary scientific societies all over the world, including the AFIPS prestigious Harry Goode Memorial Award. And yet Aiken and the Mark I do not today always receive the degree of recognition to which they are entitled. The reason is that the Mark I, like the Mark II, was not electronic, a fact which often masks its pioneering ability to operate automatically and sequentially in relation to a set of instructions or program.

Why was the Mark I electromechanical? I raised this question some ten years ago, on 24 February 1973, when Henry Tropp and I conducted a taped interview with Aiken at his home in Fort Lauderdale, Florida. Since the occasion for designing a machine was Aiken's thesis on electronics, or vacuum tube circuits, naturally I was curious about how the Mark I came to be electromechanical rather than electronic, and so I asked Aiken why this was so. He replied: "I never had any preconceived notion about what kind of components you should use to build a computing machine: mechanical, relays, vacuum, or what. The thing to do was to get the machine built and running so that it would make numbers." He elaborated: "What it comes down to is this: If Monroe had decided to pay the bill, this thing would have been made out of mechanical parts. If RCA had been interested, it might have been electronic. And it was made out of tabulating machine parts because IBM was willing to pay the bill."[1]

The realization of Aiken's dream by a team of IBM engineers involved not merely money but many hours of invention, innovation, and trial. In the end, the Mark I required more than the mere assemblage of existing IBM components; it embodied many new inventions as basic units. Among the novelties was a newly designed tape assembly that was described by Comrie as "really the brains of the machine," and the Bryce divider. J. W. Bryce, chief scientist at IBM, was, according to Aiken, "a very astute inventor." He repeated, "a very astute inventor," then added: "a valuable senior adviser. If you started down a road that didn't look very practical, he could put his finger on it, just about that quick!"

On his shelf at home, Aiken had two copies of Charles Babbage's *Passages from the Life of a Philosopher* (London, 1864). One had been a gift from Bryce. It originally belonged to Charles H. Pillamer and is inscribed "from W. M. C., February 1889." Underneath are two signatures: "J. W. Bryce" and "Howard H. Aiken." The other copy bears the inscription, "From one admirer of Babbage to another, L. J. Comrie to Howard H. Aiken, 1946 March 8."[2]

Although Aiken had made frequent and regular trips to Endicott to keep the work going and to ensure that the engineering development would embody his fundamental ideas, he did not contribute significantly to the design and use of hardware. Aiken told us about the difficulty encountered with dividing: He had spent the whole of a night in a hotel room in Endicott (or Binghampton) inventing "the technique of dividing by computing by reciprocals," using essentially the method of Newton and Raphson. In the end, Aiken's idea was rejected because it required too many machine cycles and the design suggested by Bryce was used instead. The chief members of the design team at IBM were Clair D. Lake, Francis E. Hamilton, and Benjamin M. Durfee (see figure 1). Aiken's own description of the relative contributions made by himself and the IBM engineers, taken from his talk at the formal dedication of the Mark I in August 1944, are quoted in part in James B. Conant's foreword to the original edition of the *Manual*. Conant specified the contributions of IBM and of Thomas J. Watson, Sr., even to the point of calling the machine "the IBM Automatic Sequence Controlled Calculator." There is only one other reference to IBM and Mr. Watson in the volume. At the end of Aiken's preface, he expresses his "appreciation to Thomas J. Watson . . . for his support" and "to C. D. Lake, F. E. Hamilton, and B. M. Durfee, engineers of the company, who together with the writer are the coinventors of the machine."[3]

Looking back at this machine from the perspective of history, it seems slow, crude, and mammoth—like a dinosaur of some distant age of the past. It was, in fact, slow by comparison to the first electronic machine, built shortly afterward, the ENIAC (designed by John Mauchly and J. Presper Eckert). Aiken often complained that the operation of the Mark I was limited by the speed of the output machine, the pair of IBM electric typewriters. Whoever had conversations with Aiken in those early days, or who heard him lecture about the new device, will remember that for him the key word was always "reliability." I believe that if it would ever have been a choice between speed and reliability, Aiken would have opted for the latter.

In our interview Aiken recalled that he always tried to find "an identity or some kind of algorithm in the mathematics so that when you compute the number x, you can subject the number x to mathematical scrutiny to show that it's right." As an example, he recalled the computation of trigonometric tables "for our own use." "We wanted sine x," but "we computed cosine x too, and we squared and added them to make sure they were

Figure 1 The inventors of the ASCC (the Mark I): left to right, Frank Hamilton, Clair Lake, Howard Aiken, Benjamin Durfee.

equal to one." Even when the Mark I was tabulating results for internal use, that is, for direct storage on tape or cards, the same results were also typed out so that the operators could see the results and make a check. Aiken also noted, "We had a check counter, and if you subtracted two numbers in that check counter, and the absolute value of the difference was greater than the preassigned counters, the machine stopped." In a somewhat boastful vein, he told us how Comrie had come to see the Mark I in action soon after receiving the first published tables: "Comrie was a very quizzing individual. He didn't believe everything he was told. He had to see it for himself completely." Aiken recalled that Comrie had received an advance copy of the tables and "he differenced those tables to see if he could find some errors." In my innocence, I asked Aiken whether Comrie had stopped at second and third differences. Oh, no, he replied, Comrie went on to "seventh or eighth differences . . . looking for errors." Aiken proudly concluded that Comrie had been forced to report ("grudgingly almost") that "he had found no errors."[4]

The Mark I was constructed at the IBM facility at Endicott, New York, and was set up in the old "battery room" in the basement of Harvard's Cruft Laboratory, where it was officially dedicated on 7 August 1944, seven years after Aiken's first contact with Bryce at IBM. In 1944 the United States was still in the throes of a major war; Aiken, as a reserve officer, had been called to active service as School Officer of the Naval Warfare School at Yorktown. In our interview, Aiken recalled receiving a telephone call from an "influential person in the Navy," who asked why he was not running the computer. Aiken replied, "I've got orders." Aiken told us that this situation was corrected within hours. "I had new orders to pack up and go back to Harvard to become officer in charge of the United States Navy Computing Project." With typical wry humor, he then commented, "I guess I'm the only man in the world who was ever commanding officer of a computer." The Mark I ran as a Navy project during the war years, then worked for the Atomic Energy Commission and for Harvard. It was the first of four machines associated with Aiken.

To any visitor, the most striking aspect of the Mark I was its outer face, which gave the machine a truly modern or twentieth-century appearance. This gleaming creation of stainless steel and polished aluminum was especially commissioned by Watson from the industrial designer Normal Bel Geddes. Aiken would have preferred to have the machine be bare, so that its functioning parts would be plainly visible and easy to get at in case of repair. But Watson wanted the machine he had sponsored to have the look of the future, to declare openly and at once to every beholder that something new had come into being. When the switch was thrown and the machine turned on, the computer age had begun.

I. Bernard Cohen
Victor S. Thomas Professor
of the History of Science Emeritus
Harvard University

1. Some further extracts from this interview are published in my introduction to George C. Chase's "History of mechanical computing machinery," *Annals of the History of Computing 2* (1980): 198–200.

2. I have written a separate study of Aiken and Babbage for publication in the *Annals of the History of Computing*.

3. The relations between Aiken and Watson became strained after the formal dedication. A news release, prepared at Harvard, seems not to have given the IBM engineers sufficient credit for their inventions. On 14 January 1948, a letter (signed by Paul H. Buck, Provost, Harvard University) was published in *The Wall Street Journal*. This letter spelled out in a detailed list the devices used in the Mark I, together with the dates of invention and the name of the inventor. The letter stated that the new machine "was invented by engineers of IBM following the basic theory of Professor Howard H. Aiken of Harvard." Further, "Full credit for the invention should go to four engineers of IBM: Clair D. Lake, Frank E. Hamilton, Benjamin M. Durfee, and James V. Bryce. The machine was built to their specifications after six years of laboratory work in the IBM plant at Endicott, N. Y., with Mr. Lake in charge of the inventive work." A discussion of the relations between Aiken and Harvard and Watson and IBM will appear in a book about Aiken which I am editing, and which will be published by The MIT Press in their new History of Computing series.

4. An edited transcript of the interview with Aiken will be featured in the book mentioned at the end of note 3 supra.

INTRODUCTION

The Automatic Sequence Controlled Calculator (ASCC), later known as the Harvard Mark I, was the first of the large-scale digital computing machines to be well publicized. Completed in 1943, its existence remained quite secret for a year; then it was moved to the basement of Cruft Laboratory at Harvard, when in August 1944 the IBM Corporation presented it to the university in a public dedication ceremony.[1] News of the dedication touched off an unexpected interest in the Harvard Computation Laboratory and its new machine (which I shall refer to hereafter as the Mark I, as it is known today). Howard Hathaway Aiken, whose idea it was to build such a machine, had already told some of his colleagues about the machine as it was being built at IBM's plant in Endicott, New York. By July 1944 several had responded with five or six problems they felt the Mark I could solve (the first was a problem in lens design for James Baker of the Harvard Observatory). But after the dedication, the Harvard Computation Lab found many others interested in using it. Clearly a latent need for automatic computing had been building up throughout the United States. In response, Aiken and his staff (figure 1) prepared the *Manual of Operation* reprinted here, which was published in the spring of 1946 as volume 1 of the Annals of the Harvard Computation Laboratory. What began as a set of mimeographed notes for the staff's own use grew into a 500-page volume that both explained how to set up the machine to solve problems and gave a general outline of the operating principles of computing machines, prefaced by a thorough treatment of the history of such devices.

This manual was a milepost that marked the state of the art of machine computation at one of its critical places: where, for the first time, machines could automatically evaluate arbitrary sequences of arithmetic operations. Most of this volume (pp. 98–337 and 406–557) consists of descriptions of the Mark I's components, its architecture, and operational codes for directing it to solve typical problems. In developing those codes, Aiken's staff was breaking new ground. Prior work in digital computing, like that done by Wallace Eckert at Columbia University, had used standard punched card machines that computed in "parallel."[2] That is, if one wanted to evaluate a polynomial function over a range of values, the

Figure 1 The staff of the Harvard Computation Laboratory (August 1944).
Top, left to right: C. Bissel, Calvin Verdonck, H. Livingston, unidentified, unidentified.
Bottom: Richard Bloch, Hubert Arnold, Howard Aiken, Grace Hopper, Robert Campbell.

punched card machines would first compute the first term of the polynomial for all values of the independent variable, then the next term, and so on. By contrast, the Mark I, being an Automatic Sequence Controlled Calculator, evaluated the terms of the polynomial in *sequence* for each input value, one at a time. (Aiken said his machine computed "lines" instead of "columns.") Aiken recognized that sequential operation, directed by paper tape, would endow his machine with much more flexible and general powers than any practical configuration of punched card equipment could have. By modern standards the Mark I was not truly automatic—it needed human intervention and judgment at several steps in a typical computation. But in comparison to computing installations as they existed in 1944, it took the first necessary step toward fully automatic program execution.

The *Manual* is one of the first places where sequences of arithmetic operations for the solution of numeric problems *by machine* were explicitly spelled out. It is furthermore the first extended analysis of what is now known as computer programming since Charles Babbage's and Lady Lovelace's writings on the Analytical Engine a century earlier.[3] The instruction sequences, which one finds scattered throughout this volume, are thus among the earliest examples anywhere of digital computer programs.

Although no author's name appeared on the title page of the *Manual*, the preface makes it clear that Captain Grace Murray Hopper (then Lieutenant, USNR) was primarily responsible for writing up chapters 1–3 and the appendices. Chapters 1 and 2 drew in large measure from Aiken's "old notes, many of which were written before work on the calculator was begun," while chapter 3 was written by Hopper with the collaboration of other staff members. Chapters 4 and 5 were written up by Aiken and Robert Campbell, and Aiken especially singled out the "contributions to these chapters" made by Richard M. Bloch. All the chapters reflect Aiken's personal philosophy of computing.

Since the Navy contributed about half the money for the Mark I, most of the staff held commissions in the U.S. Naval Reserve. Campbell and Bloch had the rank of Lieutenant (jg). Campbell and Bloch, along with Hopper, were the Mark I's first programmers. Grace Hopper, who in 1943 had taken leave from her post as associate professor of mathematics at Vassar College to attend the Navy's Midshipmen's School at Northhampton, Massachusetts, had been ordered to the Computation Lab in 1943. Twenty-five years later, she recounted her introduction to the world of computing, including her first encounter with Aiken. It is worth quoting at length:

Until 1944, I had been a thoroughly respectable mathematician. I had never met a digit, and I wanted nothing to do with digits. I came into the computer business in a unique fashion. I was ordered to the Navy Liaison Officer at Harvard. I left Midshipmen School on Friday, and on Monday morning, 2nd July 1944, I reported to the Navy Liaison Officer, Harvard. He took me by the hand, and led me to an underground laboratory. I had just acquired one-and-a-half stripes. There stood a large object, with three stripes, who took one look at me and said, "Where the hell have you been?" I spluttered, and said that I had had two days' travel time. He said, "For the last three months." I said "Midshipmen's School," and he said he had told them it was not necessary. By this time I was practically cowering, of course, but with one-and-a-half stripes, I would stand up straight and listen to three stripes. He waved his hand and said: "That's a computing machine." I said, "Yes, Sir." What else could I say? He said he would like to have me compute the coefficients of the arc tangent series, for Thursday. Again, what could I say? "Yes, Sir." I did not know what on earth was happening, but that was my meeting with Howard Hathaway Aiken.[4]

The *Manual* begins with a historical introduction that stresses the long tradition of constructing aids to calculation that preceded the Mark I, such as the abacus, logarithms, the slide rule, and Pascal's adding machine. This quick survey was well researched and is still useful though somewhat dated. The introduction quickly moves to a discussion of the principal problems of mechanizing arithmetic: carry and carry propagation during addition, subtraction by the use of complements, and machine multiplication. This discussion takes place in the context not of the Mark I, but of the life and work of Charles Babbage a hundred years earlier. Babbage's work was not well known in America in 1944. For Howard Aiken, however, the successful completion of the Mark I represented the fulfillment of Babbage's unrealized plans. Indeed, Aiken chose to introduce this chapter with a dramatic quote from Babbage. There were many differences between Aiken's and Babbage's machines, but the only difference that really mattered to Aiken was that his machine worked. It succeeded where Babbage had failed, showing finally that one could build a practical and useful automatic digital calculator.

Chapter 2 offers a brief description of the calculator and its principal components, with detailed photographs accompanying the text. The appearance of the Mark I was unique, not at all like other machines of its day or like any computer built since then. Because it was powered and synchronized by a central drive shaft, it was long and slender—fifty-one feet wide and eight feet high (and only a foot or two deep). Just before its public unveiling, IBM engineers covered it with a gleaming shell of stainless steel and glass (in spite of what must have been war-time shortages of such materials). The photographs show it a handsome machine indeed; there was little of the chaotic tangle of cables typical of some other computers of the 1940s.

Aiken did not want the machine enclosed, especially since right up to the day of its commissioning he and his staff were busy tracking down wiring errors, broken relays, dirty switch contacts, and other "bugs." But he relented after encountering strong pressure from IBM, whose position was that a public view of the uncovered machine (see figure 2) with its wires, relays, and drive shafts was not consistent with its image as a supplier of commercial business equipment. One may speculate how the image of the Mark I as a "mechanical brain" (as the popular press often described it) might have been inspired by its physical appearance. The Mark I certainly was not a commercial product but rather an experimental device, and the photographs that show it neat and polished belie the fact that it was constantly being modified in one way or another.

Chapter 2 starts with a review of the ways that had been used to obtain numerical solutions to mathematics problems, with a somewhat misleading focus on the history of interpolation rather than numerical analysis in general. By this roundabout way Aiken introduces the method of finite differences as a method of evaluating polynomials. The polynomials, in turn, may be chosen so as to approximate whatever function one desires, to any desired accuracy. The point Aiken is trying to make in this passage is that a relatively simple machine, which can do little more than addition and subtraction, can nonetheless solve very general problems throughout numerical analysis. That was of course the starting point for Babbage's work a century earlier.

But after noting the power of finite difference methods, Aiken then says that "from a practical standpoint" it is better to have a machine with a wider range of powers. So after this recapitulation of Babbage's (and Aiken's?) steps to the concept of a general-purpose computer, Aiken concludes that a practical computing machine should be able to perform the

Figure 2   Left to right: Robert Hawkins, Howard Aiken, Richard Bloch.

five primitive operations: addition, subtraction, multiplication, division, and reference to tables, from which all other numerical processes may be derived. Thus he justifies the existence of the Mark I, a machine which executes those fundamental operations in any arbitrary combination or sequence.

Most of the chapter discusses how those operations are coded onto a sequence tape and how the machine then carries them out. The chapter also discusses how the calculator generates the values of the log, antilog, and sine functions out of sub-sequences of elementary operations. Much thought must have gone into having the Mark I generate those values with an optimum balance of circuit complexity, memory requirements, and speed. (Some of these techniques, described on pp. 27–38, were rediscovered in the early 1970s when cheap, four-function pocket calculators first became available, but when transcendental functions were still relatively expensive.)[5]

The architecture of the Mark I was unlike that of any modern computer. Its basic units were a set of seventy-two accumulators that could both store and add 23-digit signed decimal numbers. There was no clear separation of the storage and arithmetic functions. Besides the accumulators there were sixty constant registers whose contents could be read but not altered during a program run, a multiply-divide unit, and paper tape readers for reading numbers and sequences of operations.

Of the four fundamental operations of arithmetic, the structure of the Mark I clearly favored addition (and subtraction) over the rest. It had seventy-two places where it could perform addition and subtraction but only one place for multiplication and division. (The consulting of previously computed values could be done in a variety of ways.) That was due in part to the fact that standard IBM punched card equipment used accumulators and the Mark I's counters were derived from that design. But it was also due to Aiken's own familiarity with existing numerical methods. In the past, the practical difficulties of machine multiplication had led numerical analysts to techniques that evaluated functions using only addition and subtraction—techniques like the method of finite differences that Babbage had sought to mechanize. So while the Mark I could perform each of the arithmetic operations automatically, it's architecture lay somewhere between Babbage's Difference Engine, which only accumulated sums and differences, and his Analytical Engine, which had a clear separation between its "Store" and "Mill."

By current standards the 23-digit word length seems excessive (it would correspond to a binary word length of over eighty bits). It was over twice as long as that used in punched card machines or in desk calculators. In practice, though, the machine made good use of that word length in computing tables of functions to a high degree of accuracy. Some of the sample problems given in chapter 6 show how useful such a word length was. Despite the 23-digit register size, deciding where to set the decimal point was always an important and carefully considered part of planning a computation. The position of the decimal point was set by plugging cables on the relevant accumulators before a program run. The Mark I did have what might be called a rudimentary floating point ability (see pp. 24 & 159), but as with its use of accumulators, the use of fixed decimal arithmetic reflected its business-machine ancestry.

The sixty Constant Registers were really just banks of 10-position rotary switches on which 23-digit signed numbers could be set and retained through a computation. These roughly correspond to the programmable read-only-memory (ROM) of a modern computer, but one should not take the analogy too literally. Today's computers make extensive use of ROMs more for the storage of programs than data. The Mark I's Constant Registers supplied only numerical constants, never sequence codes, although it conceivably could have stored sequence codes, as the ENIAC's function tables did after 1947. As it turned out, this part of the computer saw little use. Because of the tedium and risk of error in setting all those switches by hand, numerical constants were more frequently entered by punched cards or Value Tapes instead.

A decimal calculator may perform multiplication by two methods: by repeated addition and shifts or by looking up digit products in an internal table. The Mark I used an internal table, using an arrangement first developed by IBM a decade earlier for the 601 multiplying punch. The multiplier, a divider, an interpolator, and special units for sine, log and antilog (to base ten) contained special control units that stepped through a fixed sub-sequence of simpler operations like addition and reference to internal tables whenever the main sequence tape set them in motion. Those operations tended to be time-consuming, and those who wrote the codes for the Mark I spent a good part of their time minimizing their use. Since the multiplier took at least several machine cycles to multiply two numbers, the machine could do other operations in the accumulators in the meantime, as long as those operations did not require that product. So the Mark I, despite its being an Automatic Sequence Controlled Calculator, was not entirely a sequential calculator—it was capable of a modest amount of parallel computing whenever it was engaged in operations like multiplication. (Apparently that ability was not consciously designed into the machine but was discovered soon after its installation at Harvard.)

Besides the Sequence Tape Reader, there were three Value Tape readers that supplied numerical values of a function instead of operations. Physically all four tape readers were identical, but they interpreted the tapes quite differently. One line of a function tape had twenty-four columns, divided into three fields of eight holes each: "out," "in," and "misc." The Value Tape also was twenty-four columns wide (for the twenty-three digits and sign of a number), but it took four lines of code to represent that number. The illustration on page 46 of the hole patterns shows a mixed-weight, four-bit code.

That the units were physically identical suggests, with hindsight, that the Mark I's designers might have recognized that in some sense numbers and operations are equivalent. Probably they did not. Long after the stored program concept became the guiding principle of computer design, Aiken resisted any mixing of instructions and data in a computer's memory.[6]

In addition to the Value Tape readers, standard IBM card readers could feed in function values, and there was a specially designed mechanism that could interpolate those function values to a high order.

The Mark I's principal output devices were two "electromatic" typewriters (see figure 3). These seem inadequate by today's standards, but their speed was a good match for the speeds of the Mark I's computing circuits. Note that elaborate circuits allowed for the formatting of typed output (p. 43). For much of the Mark I's lifetime it computed and printed tables of Bessel and other similar functions. By plugging the formatting circuits appropriately, these tables could be printed by offset lithography from typed pages without having to retype them manually. This eliminated a major source of error in the preparation of tables. The first of these tables was that of the "Modified Hankel Functions of Order One-Third" (published as volume 2 of the Annals of the Harvard Computation Laboratory, 1945). Its preparation, incidentally, did require manual retyping of the Mark I's output, because the Mark I was being used for other war-related projects of higher priority, which prevented its operators from having a

Figure 3 Left to right: Unidentified, Robert Campbell, Howard Aiken, inspecting the output of one of the Mark I's printing devices.

long enough run to justify the special setup of the typewriters. (The tables of Bessel Functions of the First Kind appeared between 1947 and 1951 as volumes 3 through 14 of the Annals of the Harvard Computation Laboratory. The nearly 8,000 pages of these tables were printed without any retyping.)

Besides the automatic typewriters there was also a standard card punch that served as an output device. This punch gave the calculator a temporary store for problems requiring more than the calculator's internal storage units. Intermediate results would be punched onto cards and then reentered when needed via one of two card readers. The punch could also be used to prepare tables of functions as decks of punched cards, for use in other computation laboratories.

Chapter 3 describes the electrical circuits and their operation by introducing a "miniature" ASCC. The modern reader unaccustomed to electromechanical technology might find this section hard to follow. The Laboratory staff realized that one ought to know how the calculator's circuits worked in order to exploit its powers effectively; this section introduces the reader to those circuits, while the appendix gives their full description.

The basic computing element was a multipole rotary switch, connected by a clutch to a drive shaft, by which decimal units, carry, and timing information were stored. Banks of twenty-four switches (holding twenty-three decimal digits and the sign of a number), made up one accumulator. The drive shaft rotated continuously; electrically activated clutches engaged the wheels of an accumulator whenever a number was to be transferred. The clutches were in turn driven by double-throw relays. The Mark I was an electromechanical calculator: it held numbers in mechanical elements (the rotary switches), which were electrically controlled (by the clutch relays). Electrical pulses traveling along a common bus conveyed numbers to and from the accumulators.

Like a nineteenth-century New England textile mill, the Mark I's components took their power and control from a rotating shaft running the full length of the machine (see figure 4). It was a simple, direct, and effective way of ensuring that its thousands of individual parts all worked in synchrony with one another.

Getting the Mark I to execute a desired sequence of operations involved a combination of two processes: preparing a sequence tape fed into the Sequence Control Unit (coding), and plugging cables into plugboards located at several places on the machine (setup). Each activity was given a separate chapter. It is interesting to compare the relative importance of coding and setup here with their counterparts on a modern computer: for the Mark I, both were an important part of solving a problem. Since then there has been a steady trend toward eliminating setup, though a vestigial amount of setup still remains in the modern computer.

The listing of the numeric codes for the calculator's basic operations of storage and arithmetic (pp. 99–104) offer an interesting contrast with Babbage's plans for controlling his Analytical Engine. Babbage envisioned two sets of cards: Operation Cards specifying the arithmetic operation to be performed, and Variable Cards giving the locations of the data on which those operations would be performed. But the Sequence Control tapes of the Mark I do not distinguish arithmetic operations from storage locations. Specifying a certain register in the "in" field meant that whatever number was sent to that register would automatically be added to its current contents. There was no need for the command "add." (Though there was a command for the machine to continue to the next line of coding. This was done by punching a hole in the seventh column of the "misc." field.) The sample sequences shown in chapter 6 show that by far the most common line of code is a set of two registers in the "out" and "in" fields, followed by a "7" in the "misc." field. That concept was carried over to the other operations as well, including multiplication and division. When one wanted to multiply two numbers, for example, two lines of code were used to direct each operand, whose addresses were coded in successive "out" fields, to a register that was part of the Multiplier Unit, as given in the "in" field. The table of codes shows that commands for multiplication, division, log, and sine were also punched into the "in" field; only a few operations were coded into the "misc." field of the tape.

The Sequence Tape reader had no provision for backing up the tape or for skipping steps. This meant that the Mark I executed only simple, linear sequences of instructions. Sequence (and Value) Tapes could be cemented into endless loops, however, and this was frequently done. After 1947 a Subsidiary Sequence mechanism was attached to the Calculator that allowed such endless loops of tape to supply sub-sequences to the main sequence control.[7] Note that sub-sequence controls were already wired into the machine's log, antilog, and sine units.

So the Mark I not only was made of different physical components but also had a different structure from Babbage's Analytical Engine. From the

Figure 4 Robert Hawkins making an adjustment shortly before the public unveiling of the Mark I in 1944. Note the drive shaft running the length of the machine.

emphasis Aiken gave to finite difference methods at the beginning of chapter 2, it appears he may not have understood that Babbage's Analytical Engine was a major advance over his earlier Difference Engine in its design. The *Manual* at least gives some clues as to what kind of an influence Babbage had on Aiken, but that question remains unanswered.

Codes appear as decimal numbers in each of three columns corresponding to the three fields of the Sequence Tape. Note that the fields are not labeled as they might be on a modern computer: the "out" field gives the locations of values taken from the accumulators, constant registers, or value tapes, while the codes directing the machines output to a typewriter or punch are given in the "in" field. Note also that the decimal numbers listed are *not* the decimal equivalents of the tape codes. They indicate only which columns of that field have holes. For example, the code "732" in one of the address fields means that the tape has holes in columns 7, 3, and 2. That represents the binary value 01000110, or counter 70. (Numbers higher than seventy-two refer to constant registers and other units. The location codes follow a straight binary sequence, but the authors do not explicitly identify it as such.)

Chapter 5 shows that getting the Mark I to solve a problem involved quite a bit of cable plugging: setting the position of the decimal point was perhaps the most important detail. Another important feature controlled by plugging was the operation of registers 70 and 72 in such a way as to give the Mark I a measure of conditional branching capability. By today's standards, the Mark I did not have the ability to choose among sequences of operations depending on the results of a previous calculation. This criterion is frequently offered as the divide marking true computers from lesser machines, but the line is often not that sharp, as is revealed here.

Register 72 was a "check" register that caused the machine to stop whenever its contents fell below a specified tolerance value. Its main use was to check the machine's accuracy. Selected parts of a computation would be repeated using different accumulators or different arithmetic sequences (including finite-difference methods), and the two results would be checked against one another in register 72. If they did not agree to the operator's satisfaction, the machine stopped. These checks were automatically performed at regular intervals during a long computation, thereby ensuring that the calculator was not printing out a list of incorrect numbers. The staff used many ways, including hand computation of selected values, to check the machine's output, but the judicious use of register 72 was probably the most important method.

Register 70, the "choice" register, could be set up to prefix its algebraic sign to the absolute value of any number stored in one of the other registers. Its primary use was to simplify the computing of functions symmetrical about the origin, where $f(-x) = -f(x)$, but Bloch noted that it could also "permit the choice of one function if the value of the independent variable is less than a given quantity and the choice of a different function if the independent variable equals or exceeds the given quantity."[8] But the properties of register 70 could hardly have provided for more than a primitive kind of choice.

The most fascinating part of the manual itself is chapter 6, where the authors describe sample problems, showing for each the mathematical method, together with instructions for coding, plugging, and setup. The problems themselves are for illustration only; they are really too simple to require a large-scale computer. But they do illustrate the same techniques used for the day-to-day computation that the Mark I performed throughout its life. It is especially interesting to read how the Computation Laboratory faced the problem of detecting and minimizing machine and human errors—the pioneering nature of their work is clearly evident.

The *Manual* never really fulfilled its purpose of being an actual operating manual. By the time it appeared in print, the machine itself had already been modified, rendering many of the codes and plugging instructions obsolete.[9] But the examples given in chapter 6, showing the simplified coding and plugging for problems typical of the kind the machine routinely solved, reveal the calculator's power in a way that a simple description of its innards cannot do. The modern reader will enjoy following the attacks taken by the Harvard staff on numerical problems. Many of the sample codes given here can be rewritten for a small computer or programmable calculator, an exercise I strongly recommend to get a better sense of how the Mark I worked.

It is in this chapter where the method of finite differences finally comes into play. Several examples include codes that allow the checking of the values of polynomials computed by direct evaluation with those computed by building up a table of differences. The difference method appears to have been used only as a check, not as a method of producing tables as Babbage had proposed for his Difference Engine.

The *Manual* concludes with an extensive bibliography of numerical analysis. The numerical methods described by the items listed are especially interesting because they mark the state of numerical analysis as it was practiced just before the advent of the digital computer. D. H. Lehmer remarked that this extensive bibliography was "perhaps the most useful part of the volume, for the general reader."[10]

An appendix ends the volume with a complete description of the machine's sequence codes and circuits for sequencing, register storage, multiplication, and division. Chapter 3, as already mentioned, gives an abridged description of the machine, but this section was probably the one that the Laboratory staff itself most heavily relied on. Like some other parts of the manual, its usefulness was diminished by modifications made to the machine before 1946.

The primary use envisioned for the Mark I was the sequential evaluation of polynomial functions, either to be published in tables or to solve ordinary differential equations by iterative numerical methods. It was a machine for "making numbers," as Aiken often said. In that sense his vision was more restricted than Babbage's, despite his familiarity with at least some of Babbage's writings on the Analytical Engine. Comrie noticed that deficiency in his review of the *Manual* in *Nature*, where his enthusiasm seems dampened by the fact that the machine did not seem to "open up new fields in numerical and mathematical analysis."[11] While commending the ability to compute and print tables of functions, Comrie suggested that an automatic computing machine ought to be exploring regions of mathematics where, unlike the preparation of tables, there exist no practical manual methods whatsoever. The Mark I probably did explore such territory, in doing classified work for the Navy and later the Air Force. Although the existence of the calculator itself, and its design, were not kept secret after August 1944, most of the problems it worked on were. As Aiken said in 1951, "the computation of these tables of Bessel Functions has always been treated as a low-priority problem to be used as a filler between the solution of shorter problems on the Automatic Sequence Controlled Calculator."[12] But although those tables did fill a need, there were several sets of tables of Bessel functions available from other sources by 1944.[13]

According to Philip and Emily Morrison, "Babbage once said that he would gladly give up the remainder of his life if he could be allowed to live three days five-hundred years hence and be provided with a scientific guide to explain the discoveries made since his death."[14] Had he been granted his wish and returned in the 1980s, the high speeds and non-numeric applications of microprocessor-based systems might have overwhelmed him. But if he could have returned to Cruft Laboratory in 1944, with Howard Aiken as his guide, he would have felt right at home. The Mark I, working round the clock computing and printing mathematical tables, was doing just the work that Babbage's engines were planned to do. By 1950 the power of the Mark I was already eclipsed by the stored program electronic computers and by Harvard's own Mark II and Mark III. Its programmers called the Mark I "Bessie"—from the Bessel functions whose evaluation kept "her" busy. That year, a cover story on "The Thinking Machine" appeared in *Time* magazine, in which its place in history was affirmed: "Compared to her children . . . she is dim-witted and slow. But Bessie is a progenetrix, a sort of mechanical Eve. By proving what computing machines could do, she started one of the liveliest developments in modern science."[15]

The Mark I was dismantled in 1959, having served a useful life "making numbers." Its *Manual* remains an important volume, marking as it does the transition from an age when computing was something humans did (with mechanical assistance of varying degrees), to one where the machines themselves do most of the work. The Mark I straddled both ages.

Paul Ceruzzi
National Air and Space Museum
Washington, D.C.

1. Despite wartime censorship, the popular press reported the dedication: for example, Volta Torrey, "Robot Mathematician Knows All the Answers," *Popular Science Monthly* 145 (October 1944): 86–89, 222, 226, 230; "Mathematical Robot," *Time* (August 14, 1944): p. 72; "Giant New Calculator," *Science News Letter* (August 12, 1944): cover and p. 111; and finally, "Superbrain," *Nation's Business* (September 1944): 8–9. Each of these articles gave a brief description of the calculator and of its computing elements.

2. Wallace Eckert, *Punched Card Methods in Scientific Computation* (New York: Columbia University, 1940), reprinted as volume 5 in the Charles Babbage Reprint Series (Cambridge: The MIT Press, 1984); see also Eckert's remarks to George Stibitz, "The Organization of Large-Scale Calculating Machinery," in *Proceedings of a Symposium on Large-Scale Digital Calculating Machinery* (Cambridge: Harvard University Press, 1949), pp. 98–100, reprinted as volume 7 in The Charles Babbage Institute Reprint Series (Cambridge: The MIT Press, 1985).

3. Konrad Zuse and Helmut Schreyer were probably the first, after Babbage and Lovelace, to describe sequential programming of a digital computer. See Brian Randell, ed., *The Origins of Digital Computers, Selected Papers*, 2nd ed. (New York, Heidelberg, Berlin: Springer Verlag, 1975), pp. 155–186; also Paul Ceruzzi, "The Pioneering Computers of Konrad Zuse," *Annals of the History of Computing* 3 (July 1981): 241–262 for a listing of comparable codes Zuse wrote, ca. 1941.

4. Grace M. Hopper, "Computer Software," in *Computers and Their Future: Speeches Given at the World Computer Pioneer Conference, Llandudno, July 1970* (Llandudno, Wales: Richard Williams and Partners), pp. 7/3–7/4.

5. See, for example, W. C. Elmore, "Calculation of Elementary Functions with a Simple Electronic Calculator," *Am. J. Phys.* 41 (1973): 44–45; also Grover Martin, "Algorithm Derives Logs with Four-function Calculator, *EDN* (January 20, 1974): 78–80.

6. Grace Hopper, "Keynote Address," in Richard L. Wexelblat, ed., *History of Programming Languages* (New York: Academic Press, 1981), p. 21.

7. Richard M. Bloch, "Mark I Calculator," in *Proceedings of a Symposium on Large-Scale Digital Calculating Machinery*, pp. 23–30.

8. Ibid. Bloch may have been referring to the ASCC as modified by 1947.

9. D. H. Lehmer, *Mathematical Tables and Other Aids to Computation* 2 (1946–7), 185–187.

10. Ibid., p. 187.

11. L. J. Comrie, "Babbage's Dream Comes True," *Nature* 158 (1946): 567–568.

12. Aiken, in the preface to volume 14 of the Annals of the Harvard Computation Laboratory, 1951.

13. See the guide to such tables published in *Mathematical Tables and Other Aids to Computation*, vol. 1 (1944), 205–308.

14. Philip and Emily Morrison, eds., *Charles Babbage and His Calculating Engines* (New York: Dover, 1961), p. xxxi.

15. *Time* (January 23, 1950): cover and pp. 54–60.

THE ANNALS OF THE COMPUTATION LABORATORY OF HARVARD UNIVERSITY

VOLUME I

A MANUAL OF OPERATION FOR THE AUTOMATIC SEQUENCE CONTROLLED CALCULATOR

BY

THE STAFF OF THE COMPUTATION LABORATORY.

WITH A FOREWORD BY

JAMES BRYANT CONANT

CAMBRIDGE, MASSACHUSETTS

HARVARD UNIVERSITY PRESS

1946

The opinions or assertions contained herein are the private ones of the writers and are not to be construed as official or reflecting the views of the Navy Department or the naval service at large.

Printed in the United States of America

STAFF OF THE COMPUTATION LABORATORY

Comdr. Howard H. Aiken, USNR
Officer in Charge

Lt. Comdr. Hubert A. Arnold, USNR
Lt. Harry E. Goheen, USNR
Lt. Grace M. Hopper, USNR
Lt(jg) Richard M. Bloch, USNR
Lt(jg) Robert V. D. Campbell, USNR
Lt(jg) Brooks J. Lockhart, USNR
Ens. Ruth A. Brendel, USNR

William A. Porter, CEM
Frank L. Verdonck, Y1/c
Delo A. Calvin, Sp(I)1/c
Hubert M. Livingston, Sp(I)1/c
John F. Mahoney, Sp(I)1/c
Durward R. White, Sp(I)1/c
Geary W. Huntsberger, MMS2/c
John M. Hourihan, MMS3/c

Kenneth C. Hanna
Joseph O. Harrison, Jr.
Robert L. Hawkins
Ruth G. Knowlton
Eunice H. MacMasters
Frederick G. Miller
John W. Roche
Robert E. Wilkins

FOREWORD

No combination of printed words can ever do justice to the real story of an undertaking in which coöperation between men of capacity and genius is of the essence. The development of the IBM Automatic Sequence Controlled Calculator is such a story, with many fascinating chapters. To understand the significance of this fruitful collaboration between the International Business Machines Corporation and Harvard University one would have to trace the history of this company, which for many years has been collaborating with leading universities and research organizations and continuously developing and adapting its equipment for use in the fields of scientific computations. Harvard University's need for a machine such as the IBM Automatic Sequence Controlled Calculator has long been a matter of discussion in several of the scientific departments of the University. Because of the well-known policy of the International Business Machines Corporation, Professor Aiken of our staff turned to this company to discuss the possibility of building a calculating machine. To quote from Mr. Aiken's own words,

"Our first contact with that company was with Mr. J. W. Bryce. Mr. Bryce for more than thirty years has been an inventor of calculating machine parts, and when I first met him he had to his credit over four hundred fundamental inventions — something more than one a month. They involved counters, multiplying and dividing apparatus, and all of the other machines and parts which I have not the time to mention, which have become components of the Automatic Sequence Controlled Calculator. . . .

"With this vast experience in the field of calculating machinery, our suggestion for a scientific machine was quickly taken and quickly developed. Mr. Bryce at once recognized the possibilities. He at once fostered and encouraged this project, and the multiplying and dividing unit included in the machine is designed by him.

"On Mr. Bryce's recommendation, the construction and design of the machine were placed in the hands of Mr. C. D. Lake, at Endicott, and Mr. Lake called into the job Mr. Frank E. Hamilton and Mr. Benjamin M. Durfee, two of his associates.

"The early days of the job consisted largely of conversations — conversations in which I set forth requirements of the machine for scientific purposes, and in which the other gentlemen set forth the properties of the various machines which they had developed, which they had invented, and based on those conversations the work proceeded until the final form of the machine came into being."

It is not my function in this brief foreword to attempt to summarize the detailed history of the development of the IBM Automatic Sequence Controlled Calculator; this has been done admirably in a little booklet published by the International Business Machines Corporation. The readers of this and subsequent volumes will, however, be interested in the fact that a whole series of inventions by IBM engineers are incorporated in the machine as basic units; the names of Mr. Bryce and Mr. Lake appear frequently on such a list. Here is a striking example of the way in which the accomplishments of engineers of a great corporation may enrich many fields of human endeavor. While the public has frequently been told of the ways in which advances in pure science benefit industry, all too little is known of the way in which advances in industry benefit science. I hope the story of the IBM Automatic Sequence Controlled Calculator may to some degree right the balance.

On August 7, 1944, Mr. Thomas J. Watson, on behalf of the International Business Machines Corporation, presented Harvard University with the IBM Automatic Sequence Controlled Calculator. Since that date the machine has been in constant use by the Navy Department on confidential work. Therefore, Mr. Watson's gift came at a time when the new instrument his company had created was able to serve the country in time of war, before being used for the peaceful advance of knowledge. It will serve in the future as a focal point for certain types of mathematical work which the machine is unique in handling. I am told it is already clear that highly significant discoveries in pure and applied science will be possible through its use. Therefore, I cannot refrain from concluding this brief foreword by paying tribute to Mr. Watson. Harvard is indebted to him for a most generous gift; far more important, the scientific world is indebted to him for the development by his company of new tools which he has ever been ready to put at the disposal of the scientific and learned world.

James Bryant Conant

PREFACE

In May 1944, the Staff of the Computation Project began operations with the Automatic Sequence Controlled Calculator as an activity of the Bureau of Ships. One of the first tasks undertaken was the preparation of a report setting forth the coding procedures of the calculator. This was followed by detailed plugging instructions, which unfortunately were hardly completed before the code book was out of date. In the succeeding months, computing techniques were developed so rapidly that stabilized operating instructions could not be prepared.

At the same time, many mathematicians, physicists, and engineers requested copies of such data on operating techniques as were available in the laboratory. This general and widespread interest encouraged the Staff to publish this Manual of Operation as the first volume of the Annals of the Computation Laboratory, rather than as a mimeographed compilation of notes as originally intended. Thus the Manual is unusual in that it is an outgrowth of notes prepared by the Staff primarily for their own use. The Manual is also exceptional in that it represents the work of a great many people whose efforts have been closely integrated as is necessary in the operation of large-scale calculating machines. Chapters I and II represent extensions and revisions by Lt. Grace Murray Hopper, USNR, of the writer's old notes, many of which were written before work on the calculator was begun. Chapter III was written by Lieutenant Hopper with the collaboration of other members of the Staff. Chapters IV and V represent the outgrowth of the original code book and plugging instructions prepared by the writer and Lt(jg) Robert V. D. Campbell, USNR. Nearly every member of the Staff has made contributions to these chapters, but Lt(jg) Richard M. Bloch, USNR, especially should be mentioned. Chapter VI is made up of the solutions of elementary examples chosen from those assigned by the Officer in Charge to new members of the Staff as part of their instruction in the use of the calculator. Those given in Chapter VI were largely the work of Lt(jg) Brooks J. Lockhart, USNR.

The bibliography of numerical analysis is the result of the library work of the Staff in connection with the problems assigned to the project. Work on the bibliography was begun by Lt. Comdr. Hubert A. Arnold, USNR, and completed by Lt. Harry E. Goheen, USNR, assisted by Ens. Ruth A. Brendel, USNR.

PREFACE

The appendices were prepared by Lieutenant Hopper with the assistance of Ensign Brendel, Robert L. Hawkins, and Eunice H. MacMasters. Mrs. MacMasters drew all the figures and diagrams in the book. Ruth G. Knowlton and Frank L. Verdonck, Y1/c, USNR, are responsible for the typography. The photographs of the calculator and the films from which the plates for printing the book were made are the work of Paul Donaldson, photographer of Cruft Laboratory. Lieutenant Hopper also acted as general editor, and more than any other person is responsible for the completion of the book.

In less than two years, twenty-three reports were completed for the Bureau of Ships. On the first of January 1946, the project was transferred to the Bureau of Ordnance under whose cognizance it is now functioning. The gratitude of the Staff is extended to the Bureau of Ordnance and to the Bureau of Ships for the privilege of working with the calculator.

This Manual was made necessary by the existence of the calculator itself. The writer therefore takes this opportunity to express his appreciation to Thomas J. Watson, President of the International Business Machines Corporation, for his support during the years the machine was under construction, and to C. D. Lake, F. E. Hamilton, and B. M. Durfee, engineers of the company, who together with the writer are the coinventors of the machine.

Howard H. Aiken
Commander, USNR
Officer in Charge

Cambridge, Massachusetts
March 1946

CONTENTS

LIST OF PLATES

I Calculating Wheels designed by Charles Babbage

CHAPTER I

HISTORICAL INTRODUCTION

"If, unwarned by my example, any man shall undertake and shall succeed in really constructing an engine embodying in itself the whole of the executive department of mathematical analysis upon different principles or by simpler mechanical means, I have no fear of leaving my reputation in his charge, for he alone will be fully able to appreciate the nature of my efforts and the value of their results."

Charles Babbage
"The Life of a Philosopher" (1864)

The desire to economize time and mental effort in arithmetical computation, and to eliminate human liability to error, is probably as old as the science of arithmetic itself. This desire has led to the design and construction of a variety of aids to computation beginning with "groups of small objects such as pebbles, used first loosely, later as 'counters' on ruled boards, and later still as beads mounted on wires fixed in a frame, constituting the abacus".[1]

It seems most likely that the abacus originated in the Tigris-Euphrates valley,[2] and that its use traveled both east and west along the routes of the caravans. Elaboration of the instrument and later development of the techniques of its manipulation made it applicable to multiplication, division, and even to the extraction of square and cube roots, as well as to addition and subtraction for which the instrument was probably originally intended. Indeed, the abacus, despite its ancient origin, is still in use by the oriental peoples. This long period of utility is due not only to the simplicity of the instrument, but also due to two fundamental notions inherent in its construction. Place significance, or the use of zero to signify an empty column, is provided by the several wires on which the beads are strung. Moreover, the principle of carry, whereby the $(n + 1)$st column is increased by one when the nth has become exhausted, is applied in adding.

After the invention of the abacus, five thousand years elapsed before the next computational aid was developed. During this time, gears and pointers were used in the design of clocks. These machine elements, and more especially a wheel which at the end of a complete revolution gave impetus to a second wheel, paved the way for the development of calculating machinery.

In 1617, John Napier, following his invention of logarithms, published an account of his numbering rods, known as "Napier's bones".[3] Various forms of the bones appeared, some approaching the beginning of mechanical computation. Subsequent to the introduction of logarithms, the slide rule[4] was developed by Oughtred (1630), Everard (1755), Mannheim (1850) and others. The slide rule received wide recognition from scientists as early as 1700. Particularly in engineering design, the slide rule has proved an invaluable instrument. It has been increasingly applied to the solution of problems requiring an accuracy of not more than three or four significant figures and where the total bulk of the computation is not extensive. The slide rule is probably the most useful computational aid so far devised; its low cost, ease of construction, and the simplicity of its principle of operation and of its use, make the instrument of primary importance. The slide rule is probably the ancestor of all those calculating devices whose operation is based upon an analogy between numbers and physical magnitudes, in which the computed results are obtained by physical measurements. Many such analogy devices have since been constructed. Examples of these are the planimeter, integraph, Kelvin's tide predicter and finally the differential analyzer. All analogy devices, like the slide rule, are limited to the accuracy of a physical measurement.

It was Blaise Pascal[5] who, in 1642, designed and built the first mechanical adding machine in the modern sense of the term. Incidentally, it should be noted that Pascal's machine was designed not to further scientific research but rather for use in his father's mercantile business. It was an accounting machine and as such was the forerunner of the modern accounting machine and cash register. The design of Pascal's machine depended upon rotating wheels and provided for carry by mechanically turning the wheel of next higher order one position when the lower passed from nine to zero. The direct actuation of a numbered wheel and the secondary feature of effecting carry (which seem to have been first used in an adding machine by Pascal) are the foundation on which nearly all mechanical calculating machines have since been constructed.

Naturally, any machine designed for addition may also perform subtraction by means of complementary numbers. The complement on ten of a number is that second number which must be added to the first in order to obtain a power of ten. The complement on ten of a number may be read off from left to right by taking the complement on nine of each successive digit except the last on the right, of which the complement on ten must be taken. Thus the complement on ten of 7528 is 2472. If it is desired to subtract 7528 from any number, for example, 38421, the work may be written,

$$38421 - 7528 = (38421 - 10000) + (10000 - 7528) = 28421 + 2472 = 30893.$$

This procedure may further be simplified by the use of complements on nine and "end around carry".[6] End around carry implies carry from the highest column of a machine to the lowest column of the machine. The complement on nine of 7528 in a six column machine is 992471. Subtraction now becomes

$$038421 + 992471 + 000001 = 030893,$$

where the third term, 000001, is supplied by end around carry.

If any number, 007364, is added to 999999, operation of the machine will yield,

$$999999 + 007364 + 000001 = 007364,$$

where the third term is again the result of end around carry. Since, under these conditions, 999999 is a number having the properties of zero for machine purposes, the complement on nine of any number may be adopted as the negative of the number. Clearly, an n digit calculating machine must be supplied with (n + 1) columns, the highest being reserved for the algebraic sign, zero and nine being positive and negative respectively.

The next major development in mechanical aids to numerical computation came in 1666 when Samuel Morland[7] built a machine similar to Pascal's, adapted to multiplication by repeated addition. Independently, in 1671, Leibnitz[8] conceived a multiplying machine and finished it in 1694. In Pascal's machine the wheels were set and turned individually by hand; in Leibnitz' machine all wheels were set and turned simultaneously by a crank to a previously determined position. In the "stepped reckoner", Leibnitz added a device which still occurs as a component part of modern calculating machines.

In the years that followed, methods of carrying were refined and calculating machines soon added by a process not used by the human mind. The addition of two numbers, 3279 and 8935, requires the following mental steps:

3279	
8935	
4	add units digits
1	carry
14	add tens digits
1	carry
214	add thousands digits
1	carry
2214	add ten-thousands digits
1	carry
12214	

In adding two numbers, a machine may add all digits simultaneously, store the individual carry numbers and then perform all carrying operations simultaneously. For example,

3279	
8935	
1104	sum without carry
1111	carry numbers
12214	

Thus the machine consumes not more than two steps for any addition, no matter how many significant digits there may be in the terms of the addition.

From the seventeenth century on, it was even more evident that precise and rapid methods of computation were required. The computation of tables of logarithms demanded by Napier's discovery, of tables of sines and cosines, of tables of tides needed by faster and more extensive navigation and of the astronomical tables envisioned by Kepler, accentuated this need. Among many others, Gauss, Cayley, Tchebychev, Maxwell and Kelvin all attempted to devise or improve computational aids.[9] Naturally these men all considered mechanical calculation largely from their own point of view, the desire to further scientific advancement. Despite this widespread interest, the development of modern calculating machinery proceeded slowly until the growth of commercial enterprise and the increasing complexity of accounting made mechanical computation an economic necessity. Thus the ideas of the physicists and mathematicians, who foresaw the possibilities and gave the fundamentals, were turned to excellent purposes, but differing greatly from those for which they were originally intended.

It was not until just before the beginning of the nineteenth century that any attempt was made to build highly specialized calculating machines designed for the mathematical and physical sciences. A Hessian military engineer, J. H. Müller,[10] seems to have had the first idea of a difference engine in 1786. But this idea remained in a purely theoretical state and was without doubt forgotten when, in 1812, it occurred to Charles Babbage and he set about the actual construction of such an engine.[11] This engine was to "perform the whole operation-(the computation and printing of tables of functions) -without any mental attention when once the given numbers have been put into the machine".[12] A first model was built in 1820-22 and consisted of six columns using second differences. In 1823, the construction of an engine using twenty-six significant digits and sixth differences was begun with the aid of a subvention from the British government. The construction continued until 1833 when the government aid was withdrawn. The unfinished machine is preserved in the collections of the Science Museum in South Kensington. It should be borne in mind that the difference engine, although a highly useful scientific instrument, was still a specialized machine being intended for the sole purpose of tabulating the values of a function for equidistant values of the argument.

Having been unable to complete the difference engine, Babbage embarked upon the creation of a far more ambitious concept, an " analytical engine ".[13] Though the terms of the problem proposed were enough to stagger the contemporary imagination, he attempted to design a machine capable of carrying out not just a single arithmetical operation, but whole series of such operations without the intervention of an operator. The numbers in the first part of the machine, called the "store", were to be operated upon by the second part of the machine, called the "mill". A succession of selected operations were to be executed mechanically at the command of a "sequence mechanism" (a term unknown to Babbage). For this latter, he intended to use a variation of the Jacquard cards.[14]

These cards,[15] the precursors of Hollerith's punched cards, were used by the Jacquard weavers to control the looms to produce and reproduce the patterns designed by the artists. The designs were first sketched as they were to appear in the finished product, transferred to squared paper and used as guides for punching the cards. The cards allowed certain needles to be extended through the punched holes, thereby controlling hooks which, in turn, raised particular warp threads to produce the desired pattern. In order to continue the weaving of the same design, the cards were interlaced with twine in an endless sequence so that one card was brought into position immediately after another was used. Holes were punched for the lacings as well as for the pegs which guided the cards over a cylinder.

In adapting these cards for use in his machine, Babbage required two decks: one of variable cards and one of operational cards. The first set was designed to select the particular numbers to be operated upon from the store; the second set, to select the operation to be performed by the mill. The deck of operation cards therefore represented the solution of a mathematical situation independent of the values of the parameters and variables involved. Thus the analytical engine was to have been completely general as regards algebraic operations.

In order to use selected values of transcendental and other functions, the engine was to be equipped with a mechanism to call for such functions. Having stopped and rung a bell, a certain part of the machine would indicate that a particular value of a particular function was required. The attendant would then insert a punched card containing the desired function and its argument. The machine then checked the card to make sure that it was the one requested, by subtracting the argument of the inserted card from the argument standing in the machine. If the difference was zero, the engine would continue its computation. If an incorrect card was supplied, the engine would "ring a louder bell and stop".[16]

As in the difference engines, the analytical engine was to print its own results. Further, a mechanism was to have been added for punching numerical results in blank cards for future use. In this way, the engine could compute the tables required and punch its own cards " entirely free from error ".[17]

In 1852, Charles Babbage said: "At a period when the progress of physical science is obstructed by that exhausting intellectual and mental labor indispensable for its advancement, which it is the object of the Analytical Engine to relieve, I think the application of machinery in aid of the most complicated and abstruse calculations can no longer be deemed unworthy of the attention of the country. In fact there is no reason why mental as well as bodily labor should not be economized by the aid of machinery".[18] He felt most strongly that the time must arrive when no table would ever be calculated or printed except by machine. It was of the utmost importance, he thought, to accelerate the arrival of the time, "when the completion of a calculating engine shall have produced a substitute for-(manual computation, so that)-the attention of the analysts will naturally be directed to simplifying its application by a new discussion of the methods of converting analytical formulae into numbers".[19]

In 1834, George Scheutz,[20] a printer in Stockholm, built a less ambitious difference engine with the aid of a grant from the Swedish government. The machine was completed in 1853 and used for the computation and printing of tables of logarithms, sines and logarithms of sines. It was exhibited at the Paris exposition in 1855 and later became the property of the Dudley Observatory in Albany, New York. From Sweden also came Wiberg's difference machine[21] (1863) which was presented to the Academy of Sciences in Paris by the astronomer Delaunay.

One of the first Americans to build a difference machine was G. B. Grant of Cambridge, Massachusetts, who needed a machine for his " computing for excavation and embankment ".[22] Encouraged

II Front View of the Calculator

III Front View of the Calculator

in his designs by Professor Wolcott Gibbs of the Harvard Mining School, Grant successfully built a small model in 1871 under Professor Benjamin Peirce, then superintendent of the Coast Survey. This machine was designed to contain the usual calculating and printing parts contained in Babbage's and Scheutz' engines, but with considerable improvement in the printing mechanism.[23] Grant's indebtedness for assistance in his study was expressed to John N. Bachelder of Cambridge and to Professors Eustis, Winlock, and Whitney of Harvard.

In 1893, Torres[24] restated Babbage's problem: to construct a purely automatic calculator capable of carrying out any succession of arithmetical operations on any given numbers, without human intervention from the time when the operations have been indicated until the time when the machine sends the results to a printing device. Torres had available electro-mechanical counters and both electrical and mechanical controls. He gave a solution to the problem and proved that such a machine was theoretically possible, although his solution was not free from certain complications due to the multiplicity of the electrical connections assumed.

Despite the partial successes of Scheutz, Wiberg and Grant, the problem of designing calculating machinery was abandoned by the students of science and left in the hands of the inventors. For the purposes of accounting, these men, both in this country and abroad, with the aid of the improved materials and tools created during the industrial revolution, succeeded in bringing key driven calculating machines to a high state of perfection. The use of punched cards as a means of storing numbers and all the associated mechanisms, developed by Bryce, Carrol, Lake, Hamilton, Daly and Durfee of the International Business Machines Corporation brought the possibility of scientific calculating machinery again into a position where the situation could be viewed with some hope of success.

In 1906, H. P. Babbage, son of the philosopher, completed a part of the analytical engine. A table of multiples of π which it computed to twenty-nine significant digits was published as a specimen of its work.[25] Clearly then, Babbage's failure to complete either of his projects himself was not due to a lack of understanding of the principles and purposes of the engines that he designed, but rather to his lack of machine tools, materials of construction and electrical circuits. Of these deficiencies, the first was probably the most important. Also, Babbage was a "natural philosopher".[26] His machines were perforce built by hired engineers.[27] He himself was not " well-acquainted " with the medium in which he chose to work.[28] Therefore, though his principles were theoretically sound and though he was successful to a limited extent, it remained for the twentieth century and the evolution of advanced mechanical and electrical engineering to bring his ideas into being.

References

1. D. Baxandall, Catalogue of the Collections in the Science Museum, South Kensington. Mathematics I Calculating Machines and Instruments (1926), p. 7.

2. F. Cajori, History of Mathematics (1919), p. 7; L. Jacob, Le calcul mécanique (1911), p. 3; C.G. Knott, The calculating machine of the east: the abacus, in Modern Instruments and Methods of Calculation, E. M. Horsburgh, ed. (1914), pp. 136-154; M. d'Ocagne, Le calcul simplifié (1905), p. 7.

3. G. A. Gibson, Napier and the invention of logarithms, in Modern Instruments and Methods of Calculation, E. M. Horsburgh, ed. (1914), pp. 1-16.

4. F. Cajori, History of the Logarithmic Slide Rule (1909); F. Cajori, William Oughtred (1916); A. Galle, Mathematische Instrumente (1912), pp. 1-21; Jacob, op. cit., pp. 96-109; d'Ocagne, ibid., pp. 105-128; G.D.C.Stokes, The slide rule, in Modern Instruments and Methods of Calculation, E. M. Horsburgh, ed. (1914), pp. 155-180.

5. S. Chapman, Blaise Pascal (1623-1662), Nature, 150; 508-509 (1942); d'Ocagne, ibid., pp. 24-31; J. A. V. Turck, Origin of Modern Calculating Machines (1921), pp. 11-13.

6. Crompton Patent, U. S., No. 1514954, claim no. 7.

7. Baxandall, op. cit., pp. 8, 14-16; d'Ocagne, ibid., p. 30.

8. Jacob, op. cit., pp. 39-46; d'Ocagne, ibid., p. 30; M. d'Ocagne, Machines à calculer (1922), pp. 21-23.

9. Baxandall, op. cit.; Jacob, op. cit.; d'Ocagne, ibid.; Modern Instruments and Methods of Calculation, E. M. Horsburgh, ed. (1914).

10. F. Cajori, History of Mathematics (1919), p. 485; Jacob, op. cit., pp. 114-115; d'Ocagne, Le calcul simplifié (1905), p. 82.

11. Charles Babbage, Passages from the Life of a Philosopher (1864), chap. V, "Difference Engine No. I", pp. 41-96; Baxandall, op. cit., pp. 30-34.

12. Babbage, ibid., p. 41.

13. Babbage, ibid., chap. VIII, "Of the Analytical Engine", pp. 112-141; Jacob, op. cit., pp. 188-190; P. E. Ludgate, Automatic calculating machines, in Modern Instruments and Methods of Calculation, E. M. Horsburgh, ed. (1914) pp. 124-127.

14. Babbage, ibid., pp. 116-117.

15. E. A. Posselt, The Jacquard Machine (189-?), pp. 9, 17-20, 85-102.

16. Babbage, ibid., pp. 119-120.

17. Babbage, ibid., p. 122.

18. Babbage, ibid., p. 106.

19. Charles Babbage, Economy of Machinery and Manufactures (1846), p. 195.

20. Charles Babbage, Passages from the Life of a Philosopher (1864), p. 48; Baxandall, op. cit., pp. 32, 34-36; Jacob, op. cit., pp. 115-117; d'Ocagne, ibid., pp. 83-86.

21. Jacob, op. cit., pp. 117-123; d'Ocagne, ibid., pp. 86-87.

22. G. B. Grant, On a new difference engine, American Journal of Sciences and Arts (3) 2; 113-117 (1871).

23. Jacob, op. cit., p. 45.

24. Jacob, op. cit., pp. 165-169, 189-200; d'Ocagne, ibid., p. 95; M. d'Ocagne, Machines à calculer (1922), pp. 49-53.

25. Ludgate, op. cit., p. 127.

26. Cf. the title of his book, "Passages from the Life of a Philosopher".

27. Babbage, ibid., pp. 79-82.

28. Babbage, ibid., p. 92.

CHAPTER II

DESCRIPTION OF THE CALCULATOR

"Interpolation ist die Kunst zwischen den Zeilen einer Tafel zu lesen."

T. N. Thiele
"Interpolationsrechnung" (1909)

Although a method of interpolation bearing some resemblance to modern central difference formulae was used by Briggs[1] in 1624, it was not until 1670 that James Gregory[2] introduced the notion of interpolation based upon the representation of functions by means of approximating polynomials. The use of approximating polynomials reduced the whole problem of the tabulation and subtabulation of functions, over a limited range of the argument, to the arithmetical operations of addition and subtraction alone, once the necessary initial differences were established. Thereby the basic principle was given for the operation of the difference engines briefly mentioned in the foregoing chapter.

Further development of the theory of interpolation by Newton, Stirling and others laid the foundation for the Calculus of Finite Differences set forth as a new branch of mathematics by Taylor in 1715[3]. Since that time the subject has been increasingly developed so that now a variety of techniques are available for numerical differentiation and for the numerical evaluation of definite integrals. The latter include the formulae of Gregory, Cotes, Euler-Maclaurin, Simpson, Weddle, Gauss, Tchebychev and Steffensen[4].

In 1883, Adams and Bashforth[5], using the methods of finite differences, devised a technique for the numerical solution of ordinary differential equations. This has been followed by many other methods, that given by Runge in 1895[6], and improved and extended by Kutta in 1901[7] being, perhaps, the best known. More recently methods have been given for the numerical solution of partial differential equations. The extension and application of these methods present one of the most important problems in mathematics at the present time.

In every case, the effect of the numerical methods has been to reduce the processes of mathematical analysis to a sequence of the five fundamental operations of arithmetic: addition, subtraction, multiplication, division and reference to tables of previously computed results. Thus the calculus of finite differences has become the bridge between mathematical analysis and numerical computation.

IV Rear View of the Storage Counter Unit and the Multiply-Divide Relay Panel

V Rear View of the Multiply-Divide Counters and Relay Panel

DESCRIPTION OF THE CALCULATOR

Unfortunately, the application of numerical methods is attended by a relatively great amount of computational labor, so that while existing types of calculating machinery are sufficient from a theoretical viewpoint, they are entirely inadequate from a practical standpoint. It is for this reason that the Automatic Sequence Controlled Calculator has been constructed.

In 1937, the calculator was visualized "as a switchboard on which are mounted various pieces of calculating machine apparatus. Each panel of the switchboard is given over to definite mathematical operations."[8] It stands today much as originally imagined, in a stainless steel and glass case, fifty-one feet long and eight feet high, (Plates II and III). Two panels, each six feet long, extend at right angles from the back of the machine. Between these two panels is the four horsepower motor which drives the mechanical parts, (Plates IV and V). Altogether the machine weighs about five tons.

The calculator is equipped with a central multiplying and dividing unit together with seventy-two adding-storage registers and sixty constant registers corresponding to the mill and store of Babbage's proposed analytical engine. In addition, the machine is supplied with electro-mechanical tables of $\log_{10} x$, 10^x and sine x. Three non-linear interpolator units are capable of interpolation of any order up to and including the eleventh, on functions supplied to them in the form of perforated paper tape. Other computing elements included are: two card feeds for supplying the machine with empirical or other data, a card punch for punching results in tabulating machine cards, two automatic typewriters for recording computed results and an automatic sequence unit having control of the machine as a whole.

The sequence control unit, shown in Plate VI, consists of a main drive sprocket drum over which runs a perforated paper tape, called a control tape, together with such gears, cams and clutches as are necessary to advance the drum and tape one line of perforations at a time. The tape is strung on racks in back of the machine as shown in Plate VII and held taut by a roller just below the sequence mechanism. The sequence unit is equipped with a set of twenty-four sensing pins, controlled by a crosshead, which are advanced at the end of each forward step of the tape to detect the distribution of holes in one line of the tape and to close electric contacts in the same distribution.

Each horizontal line of the tape has space for twenty-four equidistant holes, these being considered as three groups of eight holes each, known as the A, B and C groups, (Plate VI). The A group of holes controls the "out-relays" by means of which all units in the machine are connected to the central distribution buss over which numbers are transferred from one unit to another with the aid of timed electrical impulses later to be described. The B group of holes controls the "in-relays" of all of the units in the machine. These also connect the units to the central distribution buss, and when closed, permit the egress of numbers from the buss into the units. Finally, the C group of holes represent, in general, an operation to be performed on the number in unit A in connection with the number in unit B.

Each horizontal line of holes perforated in the tape is the equivalent of a single spoken command, "Take the number out of unit A; deliver it to unit B; start operation C." Since the A, B and C groups of perforations each contain eight holes, the maximum number of out, in or miscellaneous operational relays which can be controlled by the machine is $2^8 = 256$ each. The maximum possible number of commands which can be represented by a single line of holes is $2^{24} = (256)^3 = 16,777,216$. Actually, many of these are not used, and many others are invalid because of special features to be made clear in Chapter IV on Coding. The number of combinations of coded perforations in use at present is considerably smaller than the maximum possible number. In any event, a very great many possibilities are available in each line of perforations. Since the number of consecutive lines of holes is in no way limited, it is apparent that control tapes may be provided with great generality. The reiteration of the single command, "Take the number out of unit A; deliver it to unit B; start operation C", permuting A and B over the various units of the machine, while changing the nature of the operation C, is sufficient to guide the machine through any problem of mathematics capable of reduction to the five fundamental operations of numerical analysis.

At the left of the machine, as well as at the left of Fig. 1, are the sixty constant registers. Each constant register consists of twenty-four manually set ten-pole dial switches designed to accommodate twenty-three digits and the algebraic sign. Because of their composition, the constant registers are commonly known as the sixty "switches". Each constant register or switch is connected to the buss through its out-relay, (Plate VIII), and each is connected to the common transfer terminal of the storage register invert relay. The normally closed and normally open contacts of this relay are in turn connected to the direct and invert cam controlled contacts, respectively, which furnish the timed electrical impulses necessary to the transfer of numbers via the buss.

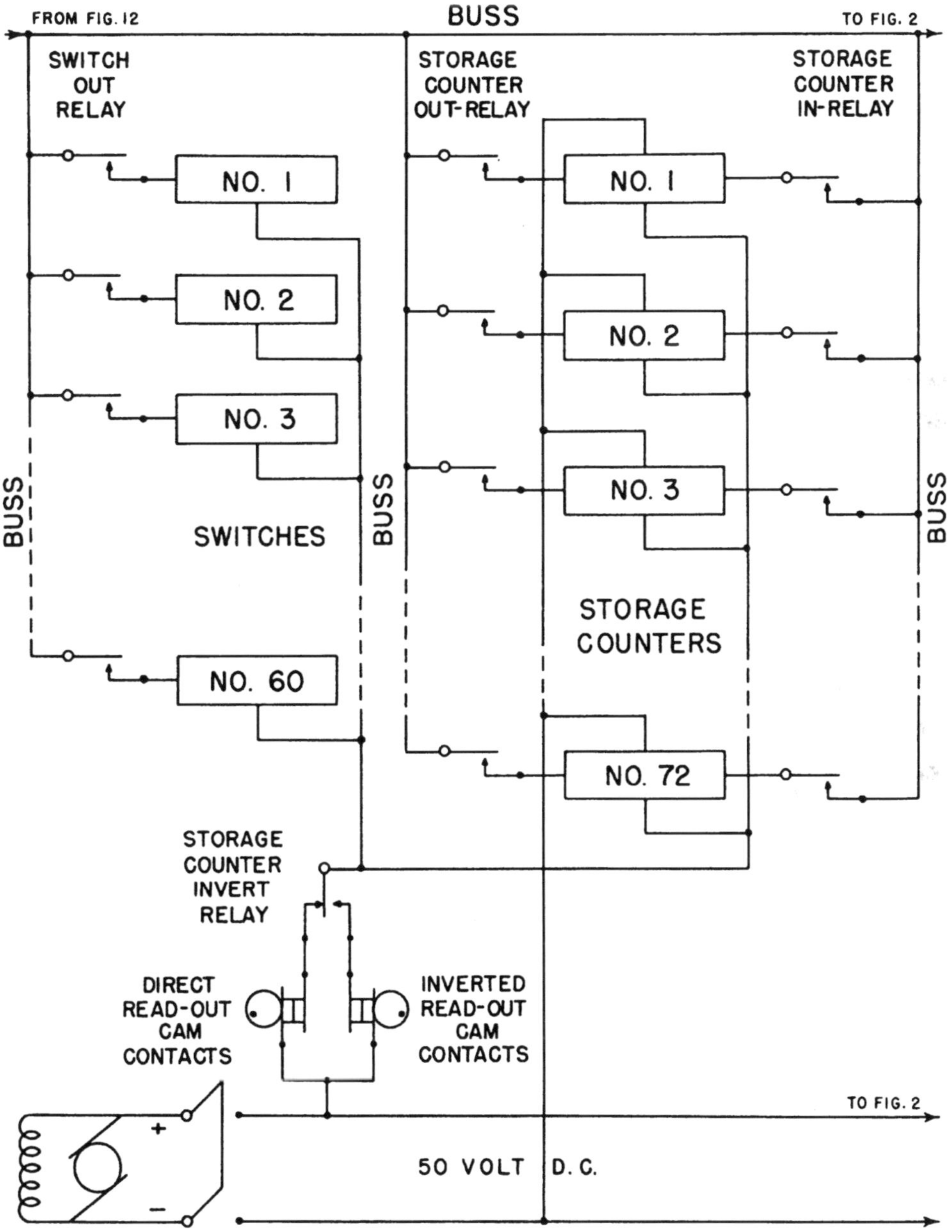
FROM FIG. 12
BUSS
TO FIG. 2
SWITCH OUT RELAY
STORAGE COUNTER OUT-RELAY
STORAGE COUNTER IN-RELAY
NO. 1
NO. 2
NO. 3
NO. 60
SWITCHES
BUSS
BUSS
BUSS
NO. 1
NO. 2
NO. 3
NO. 72
STORAGE COUNTERS
BUSS
STORAGE COUNTER INVERT RELAY
DIRECT READ-OUT CAM CONTACTS
INVERTED READ-OUT CAM CONTACTS
TO FIG. 2
+
−
50 VOLT
D. C.

Figure 1

To the right of the switches, Fig. 1, are shown diagrammatically the seventy-two storage registers. Each storage register consists of twenty-four electro-mechanical counter wheels. The storage registers, usually referred to as "storage counters" or more briefly as "counters", have electrical connections similar to those of the switches. In addition, each storage counter is provided with an in-relay connected to the buss, a complete set of carry controls and a connection to the negative terminal of the generator.

Plate IX shows a close-up view of twelve columns of the storage counters 16 and 17 as seen from the front of the calculator while Plate X shows the relays associated with storage counters in general and mounted at the back of the machine.

Each register in the calculator is provided with a code number. The code numbers of the storage counters 1, 2, 3, ..., 71, 72 are 1, 2, 21, ..., 7321, 74 respectively, while the code numbers of switches 1, 2, 3, ..., 59, 60 are 741, 742, 7421, ..., 821, 83 respectively. Similarly, all operations in the calculator have assigned code numbers. For example, code 32 in the operational or miscellaneous group C controls the storage counter invert relay, and hence is the mathematical equivalent of a minus sign. A complete discussion of all codes will be found in Chapter IV on Coding; the few here given will suffice for present purposes.

Now let it be required that the number x in storage counter number 3, code 21, be added to the number y in storage counter number 71, code 7321. This operation may be written,

Take x from ctr. 3 and add it into ctr. 71.

OUT	IN	MISC.
21	7321	

On the other hand, if it is required to subtract x from y , the coding will be written,

Take x from ctr. 3 and by means of the invert relay add its complement on nine to ctr. 71; i.e., subtract x now in ctr. 3 from y in ctr. 71.

OUT	IN	MISC.
21	7321	32

Returning to Fig. 1, the perforations in the control tape corresponding to code 21 in the Out column, as interpreted by the sequence mechanism, cause the closure of the out-relay of counter 3, while the code 7321 in the In column causes the closure of the in-relay of counter 71. The blank in the Miscellaneous column of the coding is interpreted as a plus sign leaving the storage counter invert

VI Sequence Control Mechanism

VII Tape Racks

relay in its normally closed position. Thus a complete electrical circuit exists beginning at the positive terminal of the generator, passing through the cam contacts; through the normally closed contacts of the storage counter invert relay into counter 3; through counter 3 and its out-relay to the buss; from the buss to counter 71 through its in-relay; through counter 71 and finally back to the negative terminal of the generator. Hence, the timed electrical impulses produced by the cam contacts are enabled to transfer the quantity in counter 3 to counter 71 and bring about addition. The detailed mechanisms by which this is accomplished will be described in Chapter III.

When it is required to subtract x from y, the whole operation is the same except that code 32 in the Miscellaneous column causes the storage counter invert relay to transfer its contacts. This causes the complement on nine of x to be read out into the buss instead of x itself. Since all storage counters are equipped with complete carry controls, including end around carry, addition of the complement on nine completes the process of subtraction as demanded in the example.

Before further considering the functions of the storage counters, it is necessary to discuss briefly the means by which the calculator is kept in continuous operation. Most mechanisms, once started, remain in operation until signalled to stop. By contrast, the calculator continues in operation only so long as the command "continue operation" is repeated, cycle by cycle, and immediately stops on the first occasion on which this command fails of being given. A 7 in the Miscellaneous column of a line of coding instructs the sequence mechanism to continue operation; i.e., to read the next line, act upon it and step to the line beyond. Every line of coding must contain a 7 in the Miscellaneous column or its equivalent in the form of some other automatic continue operation code. Since the storage counter codes are not such "automatic codes", the two examples of coding already cited should read,

	OUT	IN	MISC.
Take x from ctr. 3 and add it to y in ctr. 71.	21	7321	7
Take x from ctr. 3 and subtract it from y in ctr. 71.	21	7321	732

From what has so far been said it should now be clear that the storage counters serve more than one purpose. Each is a complete adding and subtracting machine, and functions as a storage or memory device, thereby providing the calculator with brackets, parentheses and other signs of association as required in mathematical expressions. In addition, relays associated with each counter provide other functions not indicated in the single line diagram, Fig. 1, for reasons of clarity. The nature of these electrical controls will be set forth in Chapter III; however, their mathematical significance may be given here.

The quantity in each storage counter may be read out as either a positive or negative absolute value under the control of the operational codes 2 and 1, respectively, in the Miscellaneous column of the line of coding. For example, if x lies in storage counter number 23, code 5321, and y in counter number 34, code 62, then $|x| + y$ may be obtained in counter number 34 by the line of coding,

	OUT	IN	MISC.
Add $\|x\|$ to y.	5321	62	72

The use of absolute magnitudes provides the calculator with a means of dealing with discontinuous functions. For example,

$$(x + |x|)/2x = 0 \text{ or } 1,$$

according as x is negative or positive.

Each storage counter may be reset to zero by reading into the counter the complement on ten of the quantity standing in the counter while the carry controls are disabled. This is accomplished for any storage counter whose code is A, by the line of coding,

	OUT	IN	MISC.
Reset ctr. A.	A	A	7

Inasmuch as a blank other than 7 in the Miscellaneous column of coding has been defined as a plus sign, the reset coding requires further explanation. The resetting operation is one which occurs with great frequency. To eliminate the necessity of writing and rewriting a special reset code in the Miscellaneous column, special wiring is included in the machine such that the duplication of a storage counter code in both the Out and In columns of a line of coding resets the counter concerned.

Of all the computing elements in the calculator, the storage counters are the simplest. Therefore, it is relatively easy to alter and to add to their electrical circuits in such a way as not to interfere with their normal functioning, but at the same time introduce added possible operations. A number of such special operations have been required in the past, and have been permanently built into the machine.

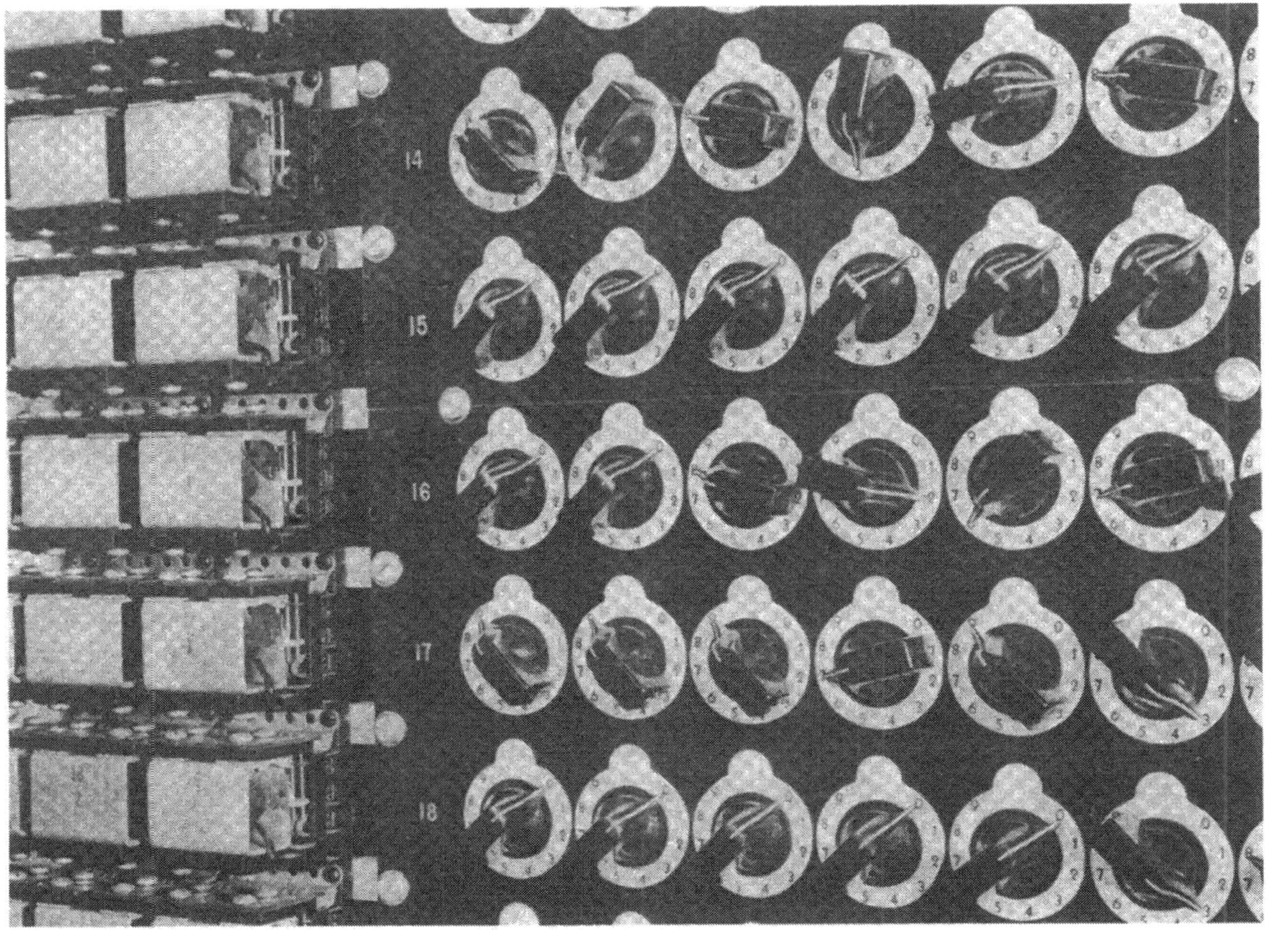

VIII Switches

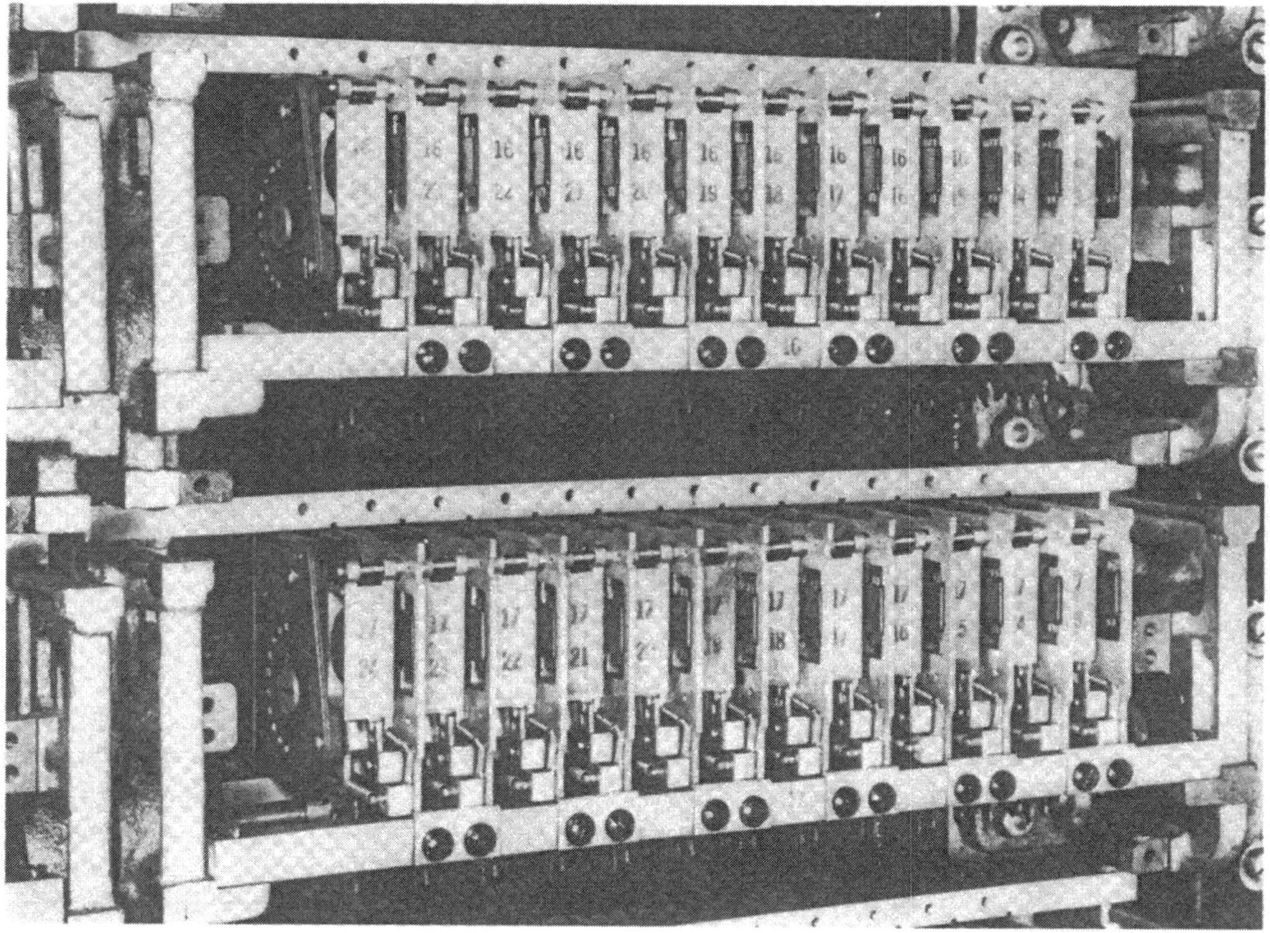

IX Storage Counters

DESCRIPTION OF THE CALCULATOR

Counter 70 has been equipped with relay circuits which prefix the algebraic sign of the quantity in counter 70 to the positive absolute value of the quantity standing in any other storage counter when the latter is read out under the code 432 in the Miscellaneous column. This feature is especially valuable when dealing with the interpolation of odd functions, since it is only necessary to evaluate $f(x)$ in order to have available $f(-x) = -f(x)$. Counter 70 is usually called the choice counter for reasons which are not immediately obvious. For instance, the choice counter makes it possible to use the two identities,

$$\arctan |x| = \pi/2 - \arctan 1/|x|,$$

$$\arctan (-x) = -\arctan x,$$

to reduce the labor of computing $f(x) = \arctan x$, $-\infty < x < +\infty$. If $|x| - 1$ is read into counter 70, and $(1/|x| + |x|)/2$ and $(1/|x| - |x|)/2$ are stored in counters B and C respectively, the addition of C to B under control of counter 70 will give in counter B,

$$z = (1/|x| + |x|)/2 - (1/|x| - |x|)/2 = |x|, \qquad \text{if } |x| \le 1;$$

$$z = (1/|x| + |x|)/2 + (1/|x| - |x|)/2 = 1/|x|, \qquad \text{if } |x| > 1.$$

Thus only $\arctan z$, $0 \le z \le 1$, need be computed by the machine and stored in counter D. If $\pi/4$ and $\pi/4 - \arctan z$ are stored in counters E and F respectively, the addition of F to E under control of the choice counter gives in counter E,

$$u = \pi/4 - \arctan z - \pi/4 = -\arctan z$$

$$= -\arctan |x|, \qquad \text{if } |x| \le 1;$$

$$u = \pi/4 - \arctan z + \pi/4 = \pi/2 - \arctan z$$

$$= \pi/2 - \arctan 1/|x|, \qquad \text{if } |x| > 1.$$

Transferring u to counter G under control of the choice counter gives

$$v = \arctan |x|, \qquad \text{if } |x| \le 1;$$

$$v = \pi/2 - \arctan 1/|x| = \arctan |x|, \qquad \text{if } |x| > 1.$$

It now remains only to prefix the algebraic sign of x; the choice counter is therefore reset and x read in. The read-out of v to counter H under control of the choice counter completes the evaluation of $f(x)$,

$$f(x) = \arctan x = \arctan |x|, \qquad x \ge +0;$$

$$f(x) = \arctan x = -\arctan |x|, \qquad x \le -0.$$

Inasmuch as the manipulation of the choice counter in the computation of arc tan x is typical of many similar applications, the necessary coding will be given in detail.

Let counter A = x, counter B = $(1/|x| + |x|)/2$, counter C = $(1/|x| - |x|)/2$,

switch 1 = 1, switch 2 = $\pi/4$

and counters D, E, F, G, H and 70 be reset and available for computation.

	OUT	IN	MISC.
$\|x\|$ to ctr. 70	A	732	72
- 1 to ctr. 70	741	732	732
ctr. C to ctr. B under control of ctr. 70; ctr. B = z	C	B	7432

The calculator now computes arc tan z and delivers it to counter D.

$\pi/4$ to ctr. E	742	E	7
$\pi/4$ to ctr. F	742	F	7
- arc tan z to ctr. E	D	E	732
ctr. F to ctr. E under control of ctr. 70; ctr. E = u	F	E	7432
ctr. E to ctr. G under control of ctr. 70; ctr. G = v	E	G	7432
reset ctr. 70	732	732	7
x to ctr. 70	A	732	7
arc tan x to ctr. H	G	H	7432

The use of the choice counter to construct discontinuous functions and to choose among two or more functions is treated in detail in Chapter IV.

Associated with counter 71, the " multiple in-out " counter, are a special set of carry controls which make a twelve column storage register out of the twelve high order columns of the counter. This twelve column counter is complete with end around carry, can be independently reset and does not in any way interfere with the normal twenty-four column functioning of counter 71. As shown in Fig. 2, the multiple in-out counter has extra in- and out-relays which connect the upper twelve columns of the counter to either the upper or the lower twelve columns of the buss. Mathematically, this is the equivalent of multiplying by 1 or 10^{12} when numbers are read into the counter and by 1 or 10^{-12} when

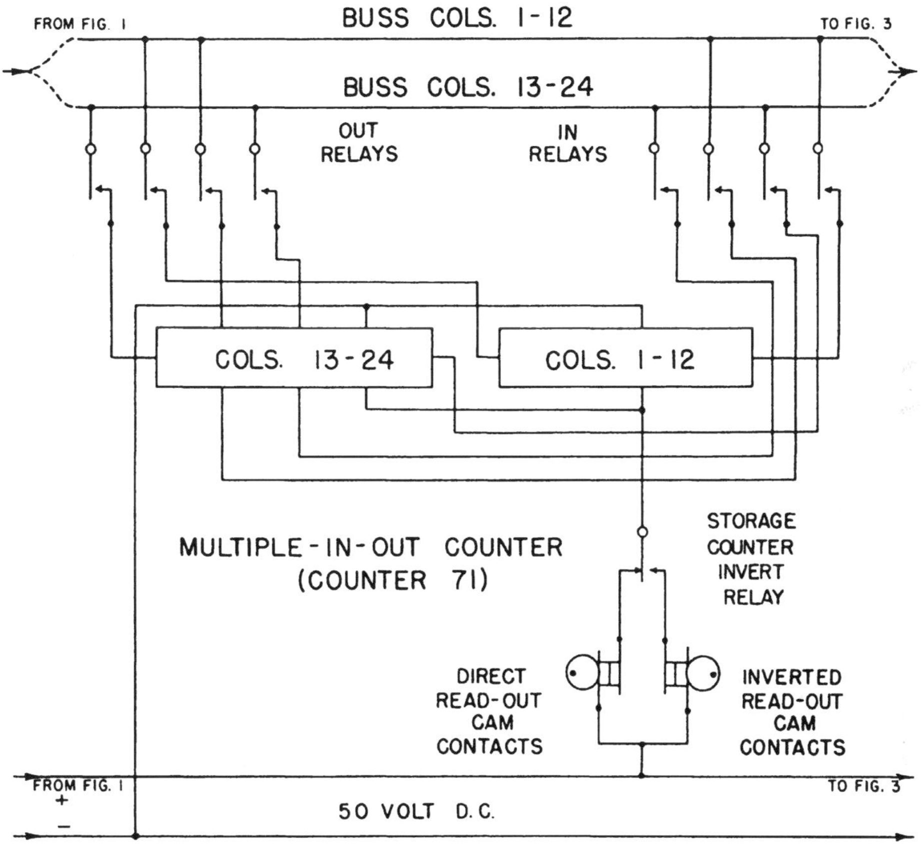

Figure 2

numbers are read out of the counter depending upon the operational codes employed. (See Chapter IV, Coding, Multiple In-Out Counter.) In all problems requiring less than twelve significant digits for computation, the transfer of numbers through counter 71 permits the storage of two quantities in each of the seventy-two storage counters, thus doubling the storage capacity of the machine. The function of the multiple in- out counter is most valuable in statistical computation where the quantities dealt with are large in number and of low accuracy.

Just as the multiple in-out counter doubles the storage capacity of the calculator at the expense of accuracy, so do the "ganged counters", 68 and 69, double the accuracy of the machine at the expense of storage capacity. Counters 68 and 69 are equipped with special carry controls such that they function as a single storage register consisting of forty-six columns and the algebraic sign which is repeated in the two component counters. Since this feature has been proved to be of considerable value in high accuracy computation, counters 64 and 65 have likewise been ganged together. Needless to say, the inclusion of the special carry controls on counters 64, 65, 68 and 69 do not interfere with their normal functions. Two lines of coding are required to make a single forty-six column addition, since the two parts of the number must be added successively. An 8 prefixed to the ordinary read-in codes of the ganged counters picks up the special carry controls. The addition of A + B, a forty-six column quantity lying in counters 35, 34, codes 621, 62, to C + D, standing in counters 69, 68, codes 731, 73, is coded as:

	OUT	IN	MISC.
Add A + B to C + D with special carry controls.	621	8731	7
	62	873	7

The most important of the specialized storage registers is the automatic check counter, 72. Mathematically all checks may be reduced to determining that a given quantity c is less in absolute magnitude than a selected positive tolerance, t; i.e., that $t - |c| > 0$. The use of the check counter is based upon the notion that this inequality will be evaluated in counter 72. Obviously, an end around carry will occur when $-|c|$ is added to t, if and only if the inequality holds. The coding for the check procedure is:

	OUT	IN	MISC.
Check the quantity in ctr. C against the positive tolerance in sw. or ctr. T.	T	74	7
	C	74	71
			64

where the code 64 is an automatic continue operation code if and only if an end around carry takes place in the check counter. If $t - |c| \leq 0$, no end around carry will take place, the machine will receive no command to continue operation and will therefore stop.

X Storage Counter Relays

XI Multiply-Divide and Functional Counters

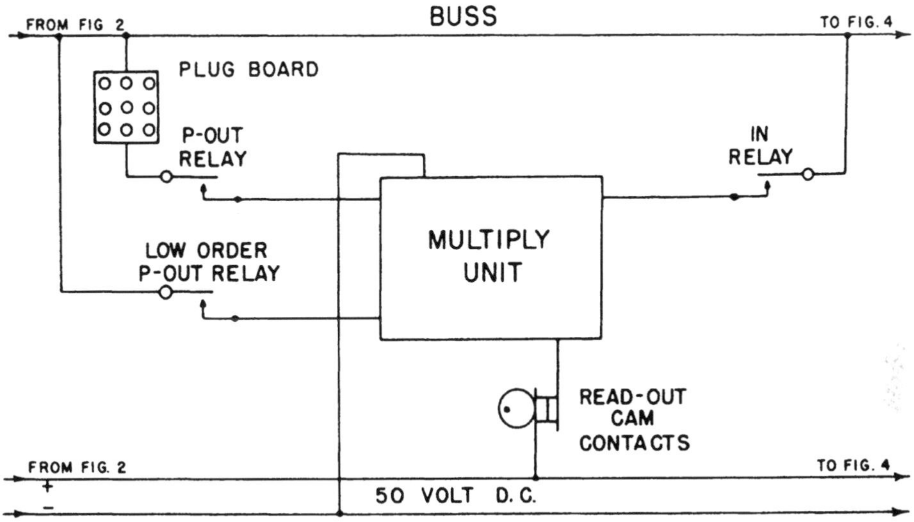

Figure 3

The registers given over to multiplication and division are shown in Plate XI. While the counter wheels and allied controls involved in these two operations are electrically interconnected, in such a way that both multiplication and division cannot be carried on at the same time, the basic mode of operation is better explained in terms of two separate schematic diagrams, Figs. 3 and 4. In the case of multiplication, the multiplicand and the multiplier are read into the unit through in-relays connected to the buss as in the case of the storage counters. The out-relay, however, through which the product is read out of the multiply unit, connects to the buss through a plugboard provided to fix the decimal point relation between the product counter and the buss.

The location of the decimal point is of no importance as far as the operation of the storage counters is concerned. When the operating decimal point is assumed to lie between columns n and n + 1 in the switches and storage counters, the corresponding decimal point in the product counter will lie between columns 2n and 2n + 1. Clearly, the product counter must contain forty-six columns and the algebraic sign. Since only twenty-three of these columns and the algebraic sign may normally be read out into the buss, it is the purpose of the plugboard, previously mentioned, to make a suitable selection of the columns to be read out based upon the location of the operating decimal point. The plugging must be manually adjusted before the machine is placed in operation.

Since the coding for multiplication must select the multiplicand and multiplier and deliver the product, it consists of three lines:

Multiply x in ctr. 56, code 654, by y in ctr. 18, code 52, and deliver the product xy to ctr. 13, code 431.

OUT	IN	MISC.
654	761	
52		
	431	7

There are no 7's in the Miscellaneous column of the lines of coding selecting the multiplicand and multiplier and delivering them to the multiply unit. These are omitted because the code B 761, the multiply code, is an automatic continue operation code and therefore replaces the 7's. No longer does each line of coding correspond to a single operation of the machine. The first line of coding delivers the multiplicand to the multiply unit, and turns over control of the calculator to a subsidiary sequence control within the multiply unit itself. The unit builds up and stores a multiplication table consisting of the nine integer multiples of the multiplicand. The multiply unit then signals the sequence control and calls for the multiplier. The process of multiplication is completed, within the unit, by withdrawing such multiples of the multiplicand as may be indicated by the multiplier and adding them together while shifting them to the proper columnar position. Upon completion of this summation, control of the machine is turned back to the main sequence mechanism and the product delivered as indicated by the third line of multiply coding.

In the event that one or both of the factors involved in a multiplication are negative numbers, this fact is sensed and stored by the multiply unit. The factors are then treated as positive absolute magnitudes for use in the multiplication. Finally the proper algebraic sign is appended to the product and it is read out directly or inverted as required.

The buss is used during the multiplying operation only three times. If properly timed, other operations involving the buss but not involving either multiplication or division may be carried on during multiplication. Such operations are known as " interposed operations " and are considered in detail under Multiplication in Chapter IV. Note that division as well as multiplication is excluded because, as previously mentioned, these operations are electrically interconnected.

When the operating decimal point of the calculator is assumed to lie between columns twenty-three and twenty-four, the corresponding decimal point in the product counter will fall between column forty-six and the algebraic sign. For this case, the multiply unit is equipped with a special out-relay permitting the read-out of columns one through twenty-three of the product counter to the buss. The normal multiplying operation, with suitable plugging, delivers columns twenty-four through forty-six of the product counter to columns one through twenty-three of the buss as usual. The use of the special low order product out-relay in effect provides the machine with forty-six column products as obtained from twenty-three column factors. The coding for this operation is as follows:

Multiply x in ctr. 56, code 654, by y in ctr. 18, code 52, and deliver forty-six columns of the product xy to ctrs. 69, 68, codes 731, 73.

OUT	IN	MISC.
654	761	
52		
	731	7
86	73	7

Note that the line of coding dictating the low order product out must immediately follow the normal product read-out in order to preserve the algebraic sign and deliver it to both counters receiving the product.

One of the two pairs of ganged counters may be used in combination with this special product read-out to build up the product of two quantities, either or both of which may consist of forty-six or fewer digits. The error in such a multiplication will be less than or equal to 2.7×10^{-46}. Thus if the quantity stored across counters A and B is multiplied by the quantity stored across counters C and D, three multiplications, A x C, A x D, B x C, will be performed and the products summed in the ganged counters. The product B x D is neglected since it is below the capacity of the machine. Examples of the coding of such multiplications will be found under High Accuracy Computation in Chapter IV.

Although the organization of the multiply unit is far more complex than that of the storage counters, it is nevertheless possible to alter the multiplying circuits to permit special operations. For example, it is sometimes required to print a function having a very wide range of values. In this case, it is convenient to print a fixed number of significant figures together with an associated power of ten. The "normalizing register", in conjunction with the multiply unit, accomplishes this purpose by shifting a quantity so that its first significant digit appears in column twenty-three and recording the amount of the shift. The amount of shift combined in a storage counter with a constant dependent upon the position of the operating decimal point supplies the exponent required. Further examples of special controls associated with the multiply unit will be described later in connection with the discussion of the electro-mechanical tables of the elementary transcendental functions.

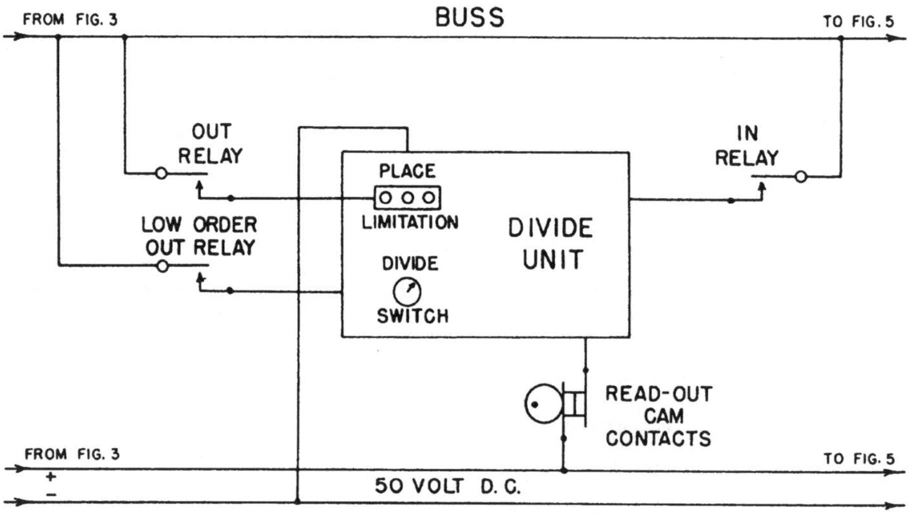

Figure 4

Division like multiplication requires three lines of coding. These read the divisor and dividend into the divide unit and deliver the quotient to its specified destination using the connections shown diagrammatically in Fig. 4.

Divide x in ctr. 3, code 21, by y in ctr. 4, code 3, and deliver the quotient to ctr. 5, code 31.

OUT	IN	MISC.
3	76	
21		
	31	7

After the divisor and dividend are read into the unit, they are shifted and stored so that their first significant digits appear in the highest column of the registers in which they are stored. The number of columns that the dividend was shifted and the complement on nine of the number of columns the divisor was shifted are added together in the " Q-shift " counter. A constant dependent upon the position of the operating decimal point is supplied to the Q-shift counter by a manually preset switch known as the divide switch. Since the Q-shift counter is not equipped with an end around carry circuit, the addition of a one in the units column completes the determination of the number of columns the quotient must be shifted when it is read out into the buss in proper decimal position. A one added into the units column of a counter to compensate for a missing end around carry is commonly known as an "elusive one".

As soon as the divisor is delivered and control of the calculator turned over to the divide unit, a table of the nine integer multiples of the divisor is built up and stored within the unit. When called upon, the main sequence mechanism delivers the dividend. Under the subsidiary sequence control, the multiples of the divisor are compared with the dividend and the largest multiple less than the dividend selected. This multiple is then subtracted from the dividend while the digit defining it is entered in the quotient counter. The process of division is continued in this manner, successively comparing, subtracting and shifting to the right. Since the successive subtractions involve different columnar positions of the dividend counter, an end around carry cannot be provided. The subtractions are accomplished by means of complements on nine together with elusive ones introduced into the units column of each succeeding subtrahend. As the subtractions move to the right, ones appear on the left since the multiples of the divisor consist of at most twenty-four columns and do not have sufficient nines to the left to fill the dividend counter. However, when the digits of the remainders are selected for comparison the extra ones are omitted. Assuming a six column machine, the subtractions appear as follows:

```
             213109                        213109
27400 / 58392000000              274 / 58392000000
        45199
        03591000000                  - 548
         1
        03592000000                    359
        972599
        00851900000                  - 274
          1
        00852000000                     852
         917799
        10029990000                  - 822
           1
        10030000000                     300
         972599
        11002599000                  - 274
            1
        11002600000                      2600
           753399
        11010133990                  - 2466
              1
        11010134000                        134
```

If, upon comparison, the calculator finds that all multiples of the divisor are greater than the dividend or the remainder under consideration, a zero or "no-go" is entered in the quotient counter and a new comparison made one column to the right. When the division is terminated, the dividend counter will contain a series of ones and zeros and the last remainder.

Division may be terminated after any desired number of comparisons, by the place limitation plugging and coding discussed under Division in Chapter IV. The number of significant digits in the quotient will be either equal to the number of comparisons made or to this number less one (if the first comparison yields a no-go). Since the accuracy of the division is thus under control of the main sequence mechanism it may be varied as desired within any given problem.

The quotient is read out into the buss through that part of the out-relay selected by the quantity standing in the Q-shift counter. If a negative number is shifted to the right, the out-relay also supplies the nines at the left required to complete the complement on nine of the quotient. The algebraic sign is determined by the methods employed in the case of multiplication.

Further, as in multiplication, the buss is used only three times during division, and is otherwise free for any interposed operations not involving either multiplication or division. It should now be clear that many of the electro-mechanical operations necessary to multiplication and division are identical. Indeed the calculator as constructed uses the same registers for both operations. These, however, are controlled by two separate subsidiary sequence control systems, one for multiplication, and one for division.

Though it is not immediately evident, division consumes almost four times as many cycles of machine time as does multiplication and uses a great deal more apparatus. Clearly, then, this process is to be avoided whenever possible. Fortunately, an iterative process based on the Newton Raphson rule,

$$x_{n+1} = x_n - f(x_n)/f'(x_n), \qquad n = 0, 1, 2, \ldots \qquad (1)$$

is available for finding reciprocals. Let

$$f(x) = N - 1/x. \qquad (2)$$

Then

$$x_{n+1} = x_n(2 - Nx_n), \qquad (3)$$

defines a sequence, x_n, which converges towards the reciprocal of N. Each succeeding application of the iterative process roughly squares the error of the last preceding approximation.

Suppose that in a given computation the values of the independent variable increase in an arithmetic sequence. Under these circumstances, the reciprocal of the nth value of the variable will furnish a good first approximation to the reciprocal of the (n + 1)st value. Thus the process of division may be avoided with a considerable gain in the speed of computation. The application of equation (3) to the design of calculating machinery was first suggested by Aiken in 1938.[9]

Equation (3) also provides the calculator with a means of dividing to an accuracy of forty-six significant digits. The technique by which this is accomplished together with the techniques for addition, subtraction and multiplication, to the same accuracy, are described in the section on High Accuracy Computation in Chapter IV.

The Newton Raphson rule, by proper choice of f(x), may be made to yield an iterative process for obtaining any fractional power of a given number so long as a suitable first approximation is available. This fact greatly extends the usefulness and speed of operation of the calculator without the inclusion of a single special electrical circuit.

On the other hand, the computation of the elementary transcendental functions may not be disposed of so easily. These require special registers as shown at the right of Plate XI, and make use of the second panel of relays extending to the rear of the calculator.

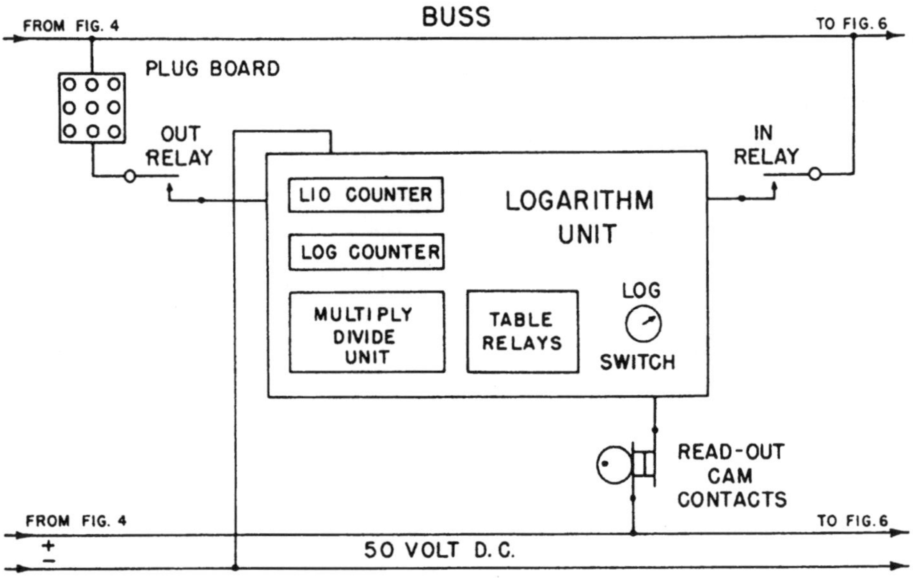

Figure 5

The method of computation of logarithms (Fig. 5) within the calculator depends upon two equations,

$$\log (a \cdot b \cdot c \cdot \ldots) = \log a + \log b + \log c + \ldots, \qquad (4)$$

and

$$\log_e(1 + h) = h - h^2/2 + h^3/3 - h^4/4 + \ldots + (-1)^{n+1}\, h^n/n + \ldots \qquad (5)$$

for $h^2 < 1$. The logarithm unit includes two counters known as the logarithm counter and the logarithm in-out counter, together with a subsidiary sequence control which governs these counters in conjunction with the multiply-divide unit. If it is desired to compute $\log_{10}x$, the coding in the main sequence control tape will read as follows:

x lies in ctr. 39, code 6321, deliver $\log_{10}x$ to ctr. 8, code 4.

OUT	IN	MISC.
6321	762	
831	4	7
		763

At the same time that x is read into the logarithm in-out counter, the code B 762 signals the logarithm subsidiary sequence control to take over the direction of the calculator. From the logarithm in-out counter, x is read to the logarithm counter so shifted that the first significant digit of x appears in the twenty-third column of the logarithm counter. The amount of the shift is recorded and its complement on ten entered in columns twenty-two, twenty-three and twenty-four of the logarithm in-out counter, in which the decimal point is now considered to lie between columns twenty-one and twenty-two. The computation of the characteristic of x is then completed by adding 22 - n into the logarithm in-out counter, the operating decimal point being between columns n and n + 1. This quantity is supplied by a manually preset constant register known as the logarithm switch. For example, if the operating decimal point lies between columns fifteen and sixteen and x = 783.54210 50928 67954, x is shifted five columns to the left on reading from the logarithm in-out counter to the logarithm counter. In this case, 22 - n = 7. Hence, the characteristic of x is computed as 995 + 007 = 002.

Now $\bar{x}$ = 7.83542 10509 28679 54 stands in the logarithm counter with the decimal point following its first significant digit, and it is only necessary to compute the mantissa of $\log_{10}\bar{x}$. This computation is perhaps best explained by a numerical example. Four successive divisions are performed:

$$\bar{x}/7 = 1.11934\ 58644\ 18382\ 79142\ 85\ ;$$

$$\bar{x}/(7)(1.1) = 1.01758\ 71494\ 71257\ 08311\ 68\ ;$$

$$\bar{x}/(7)(1.1)(1.01) = 1.00751\ 20291\ 79462\ 45853\ 14\ ;$$

$$\bar{x}/(7)(1.1)(1.01)(1.007) = 1.00050\ 84698\ 90230\ 84263\ 30\ .$$

Equation (4) becomes

$$\log 7.83542\ 10509\ 28679\ 54 = \log 7 + \log 1.1 + \log 1.01 + \log 1.007 + \log 1.00050\ 84698\ 90230\ 84263\ 30\ . \qquad (6)$$

The logarithm table relays store $\log_{10}N$ accurate to twenty-one decimal places, for N equal to:

1.0	1.1	1.01	1.001
2.0	1.2	1.02	1.002
3.0	1.3	1.03	1.003
4.0	1.4	1.04	1.004
5.0	1.5	1.05	1.005
6.0	1.6	1.06	1.006
7.0	1.7	1.07	1.007
8.0	1.8	1.08	1.008
9.0	1.9	1.09	1.009 .

The internal logarithm sequence controls select the four logarithms called for by the first four terms on the right side of equation (6) and deliver them to the logarithm in-out counter for summation.

The last term of the logarithmic sum in equation (6) is of the form $\log(1 + a\,10^{-4})$ where $a < 10$.

Writing $$(1 + a\,10^{-4}) = 1 + h,$$

then $$h < 10^{-3}.$$

In using equation (5), six terms of the series are employed. Therefore, the remainder of the series will be

$$R < h^7(1 + 7h/8 + 7h^2/9 + 7h^3/10 + \ldots)/7\ ,$$

$$R < h^7(1 + h + h^2 + h^3 + \ldots)/7\ ,$$

$$R < h^7/7(1 - h)\ ,$$

$$R < 10^{-21}/7(0.999)\ .$$

Clearly, the choice of four divisions and six terms of the series puts the error below the lower limit of the capacity of the machine. The series given in equation (5) is used by the machine in the form

$$\log_{10}(1 + h) = (((((hc_6 + c_5)h + c_4)h + c_3)h + c_2)h + c_1)h\ ,$$

where $c_1 = M$, $c_2 = -M/2$, $c_3 = M/3$, $c_4 = -M/4$, $c_5 = M/5$, $c_6 = -M/6$;

$M = \log_{10}e$.

The values of the c's are also stored in relays and supplied to the multiply unit as directed by the logarithm sequence controls. One feature of these controls, not previously mentioned in this discussion, permits the multiplicand, h, and its multiples to remain stored in the multiply-divide unit throughout the evaluation of the series. This saves a considerable amount of machine time.

After summing all terms of equation (6) in the logarithm in-out counter, $\log_{10}x$ is read out into the buss through plugging since it stands with its decimal point between columns twenty-one and twenty-two and must be shifted to conform with the operating decimal position.

The exponential function, or anti-logarithm, is derived by a reversal of the process used to compute logarithms. The method of computation is dependent upon the equations

$$10^x = 10^{10a+b} \cdot 10^{c/10} \cdot 10^{d/100} \cdot 10^{e/1000} \cdot 10^f\ , \tag{7}$$

$$10^f = e^h = 1 + h + h^2/2! + h^3/3! + \ldots, \tag{8}$$

where $$h = f\log_e 10\,.$$

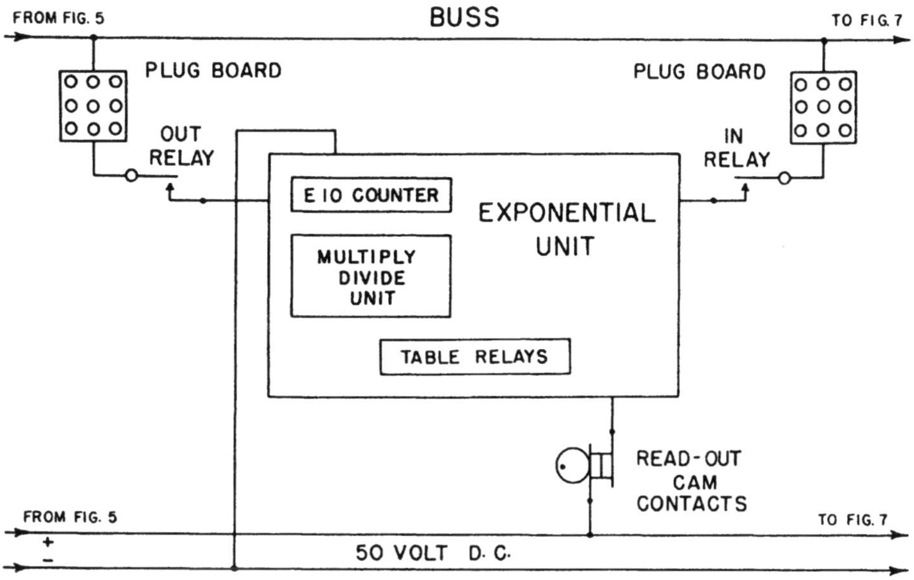

Figure 6

The exponential unit (Fig. 6) includes the exponential in-out counter and a subsidiary sequence control governing this counter in connection with the multiply-divide unit. In order to compute 10^x, the main sequence control tape must read as follows:

x lies in ctr. 27, code 5421; deliver 10^x to ctr. 20, code 53.

OUT	IN	MISC.
5421	7621	
	741	
832	53	
		731

The code B 7621 signals the exponential sequence control to take over command of the calculator. Simultaneously, x is read to the exponential in-out counter via the multiply unit, exponential-in plugging and certain transformation circuits, which accomplish two purposes. First, a zero or nine is read into the twenty-fourth column of the exponential in-out counter according as x is positive or negative; second, the absolute value of x is read into the exponential in-out counter so shifted that the decimal point lies between columns twenty-one and twenty-two. Thus x stands in the exponential in-out counter in the form:

column	24	23	22	21	20	19	18-1
digit	$\pm$	a	b .	c	d	e	f

Columns one through eighteen of x are then multiplied by $\log_e 10$ and delivered to the multiply unit for expansion in the series (8). The coefficients are stored in relays and sent to the multiply unit as required. Again the multiplicand, h, is held constant while expanding the series in order to conserve machine time. Since $h < 2.3 \times 10^{-3}$, the remainder of the series will be

$$R = h^7/7! + h^8/8! + h^9/9! + \dots ,$$

$$R < h^7(1 + h/8 + h^2/8 \cdot 9 + \dots)/7! ,$$

$$R < h^7(1 + h + h^2 + h^3 + \dots)/7! ,$$

$$R < h^7/7!(1 - h) ,$$

$$R < (2.3)^7 \times 10^{-21}/7!(0.997) ,$$

$$R < 10^{-21} .$$

Clearly, the use of seven terms of the series leaves a remainder which is below the capacity of the machine.

The quantities,

$10^{0.0}$	$10^{0.00}$	$10^{0.000}$
$10^{0.1}$	$10^{0.01}$	$10^{0.001}$
$10^{0.2}$	$10^{0.02}$	$10^{0.002}$
$10^{0.3}$	$10^{0.03}$	$10^{0.003}$
$10^{0.4}$	$10^{0.04}$	$10^{0.004}$
$10^{0.5}$	$10^{0.05}$	$10^{0.005}$
$10^{0.6}$	$10^{0.06}$	$10^{0.006}$
$10^{0.7}$	$10^{0.07}$	$10^{0.007}$
$10^{0.8}$	$10^{0.08}$	$10^{0.008}$
$10^{0.9}$	$10^{0.09}$	$10^{0.009}$,

are stored in table relays accurate to twenty-one decimal places. The proper values are called for by columns nineteen, twenty and twenty-one of x as it stands in the exponential in-out counter so that the product,

$$P = 10^{c/10} \cdot 10^{d/100} \cdot 10^{e/1000} \cdot 10^{f} ,$$

may be formed.

This product, P, will stand in the product counter with its decimal point between columns forty-two and forty-three. If x is a positive quantity, the product is read out to a forty-five column plugboard in which the decimal point is assumed to lie between columns twenty-one and twenty-two. This read-out is accomplished through a multiple out-relay, the proper part of which is selected by the quantity 10a + b standing in columns twenty-two and twenty-three of the exponential in-out counter. From the plugboard, the product passes to the buss at the operating decimal position through manually preset plugwires connecting the plugboard to the buss in proper columnar relation, and thence to the storage register indicated by the third line of exponential coding.

If x is a negative quantity, the reciprocal of the product, P, is obtained by the divide unit as ordered by the exponential sequence control. The reciprocal is then read out of the quotient counter to the storage register by circuits equivalent to those employed in the case in which x is positive.

The third electro-mechanical table contained within the calculator is that of the function, sin x. The method of computing sin x is based upon the equations:

$$\sin(-x) = -\sin x\,; \tag{9}$$

$$\sin(x + 2n\pi) = \sin x\,; \tag{10}$$

$$\sin x = \cos(\pi/2 - x)\,; \tag{11}$$

$$\begin{aligned}\sin x &= x - x^3/3! + x^5/5! - x^7/7! + \dots\\ &\quad + (-1)^n x^{2n+1}/(2n+1)! + \dots, \qquad n = 1, 2, 3, \dots, 10\,;\end{aligned} \tag{12}$$

$$\begin{aligned}\cos x &= 1 - x^2/2! + x^4/4! - x^6/6! + \dots\\ &\quad + (-1)^n x^{2n}/(2n)! + \dots, \qquad n = 1, 2, 3, \dots, 10\,.\end{aligned} \tag{13}$$

Since the series (12) and (13) are alternating series the remainder, R, will be less than the first term omitted. Assuming $x \le \pi/4$,

$$|R| < (\pi/4)^{22}/22! \quad .$$

Taking the logarithm of both sides of the inequality,

$$\begin{aligned}\log_{10}|R| &< 22(\log_{10}\pi - \log_{10}4) - \log_{10}(22!)\\ &< 22(0.498 - 0.602) - 21.050 < -23 \quad .\end{aligned}$$

Thus $|R| < 10^{-23}$ and the error in using these series for computation falls below the capacity of the calculator.

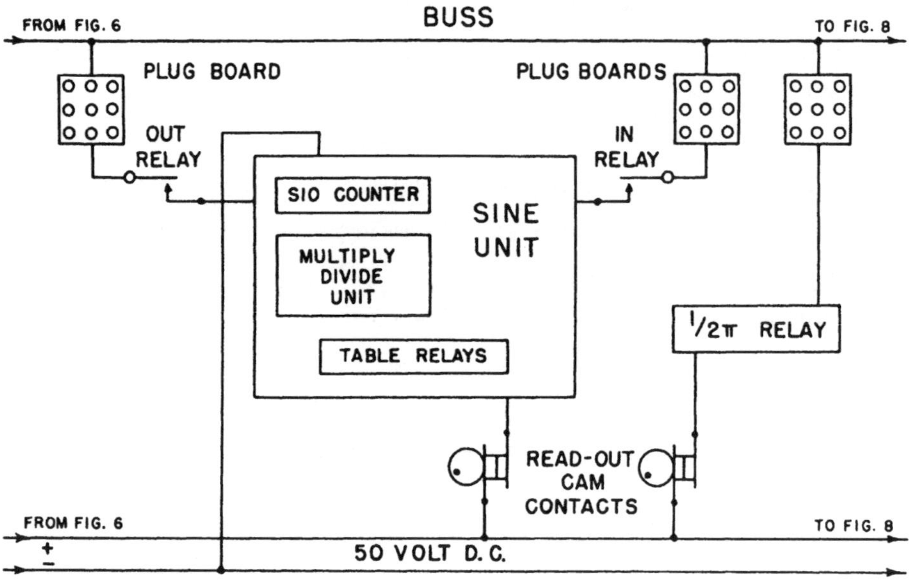

Figure 7

The sine unit (Fig. 7) is composed of the sine in-out counter and subsidiary sequence circuits having control of this counter, the multiply unit and certain table relays providing the coefficients of the series together with other necessary constants such as $\pi/4$, $\pi/2$, $\pm\pi$ and 2π. The main sequence control tape dictates the computation of sin x by the coding:

x lies in ctr. 14, code 432; deliver sin x to ctr. 40, code 64.

OUT	IN	MISC.
432	7631	
84	64	7
		7321

In order to compute sin x, it must first be determined in which quadrant x falls. The first operation in the sine sequence multiplies x by $1/2\pi$ (supplied by a relay through plugging) at the operating decimal position. Then the product $|x|/2\pi$ is read into columns one through twenty-three of the sine in-out counter with decimal point at the operating position. At the same time, the algebraic sign of x is read into the twenty-fourth column of the sine in-out counter. Let $|\bar{x}|/2\pi$ indicate $|x|/2\pi$ with its integral part omitted. This integral part represents multiples of 2π which may be dropped by virtue of equation (10). Through plugging, $|\bar{x}|/2\pi$ is next read from the sine in-out counter to the multiplicand counter so shifted that its decimal point lies between columns twenty-two and twenty-three. The algebraic sign of x remains stored in the sine in-out counter. The integer four, supplied by a table relay, is read to the multiplier counter. The resulting product is read into the sine in-out counter with its decimal point between columns twenty-two and twenty-three. Four cases may now be distinguished:

(α) $0 \leq 2|\bar{x}|/\pi < 1$, $|x|$ in quadrant I, $\sin|x| \geq 0$;

(β) $1 \leq 2|\bar{x}|/\pi < 2$, $|x|$ in quadrant II, $\sin|x| > 0$;

(γ) $2 \leq 2|\bar{x}|/\pi < 3$, $|x|$ in quadrant III, $\sin|x| \leq 0$;

(δ) $3 \leq 2|\bar{x}|/\pi < 4$, $|x|$ in quadrant IV, $\sin|x| < 0$.

Which of these four cases appertain in the case of a specific value of x may be determined by sensing the integer in the twenty-third column of the sine in-out counter. The value of this integer together with the algebraic sign of x previously stored in the twenty-fourth column of the sine in-out counter complete the determination of the sign of sin x.

The procedure by which this is accomplished and by which x is reduced to a first quadrant angle will now be discussed. The quantity $2|x|/\pi$ is multiplied by $\pi/2$ and when this operation is completed, the product, $|\bar{x}|$, is read into the sine in-out counter. During this multiplication, the sensing circuits on column twenty-three of the sine in-out counter order the following operations:

(1) Reset all columns but the twenty-fourth of the sine in-out counter;

(2) Case (α): $0 \leq |\bar{x}| < \pi/2$

$|\bar{x}|$ is read into the sine in-out counter directly;

Case (β): $\pi/2 \leq |\bar{x}| < \pi$

$|\bar{x}|$ is inverted when read into the sine in-out counter,

π is added into the sine in-out counter;

Case (γ): $\pi \le |\bar{x}| < 3\pi/2$

$|\bar{x}|$ is read into the sine in-out counter directly,

$-\pi$ is added into the sine in-out counter,

a nine is added into the twenty-fourth column of the sine in-out counter;

Case (δ): $3\pi/2 \le |\bar{x}| \le 2\pi$

$|\bar{x}|$ is inverted when read into the sine in-out counter,

2π is added into the sine in-out counter,

a nine is added into the twenty-fourth column of the sine in-out counter.

Since the sine in-out counter has no end around carry, and since any digit other than a nine in the twenty-fourth column of this counter is the equivalent of a zero, the final algebraic sign of sin x now stands in the twenty-fourth column of the sine in-out counter. The reduced first quadrant angle, X, corresponding to the given value of x stands in the remaining columns.

Two cases remain to be distinguished:

(a) $0 \le X < \pi/4$;

(b) $\pi/4 \le X \le \pi/2$.

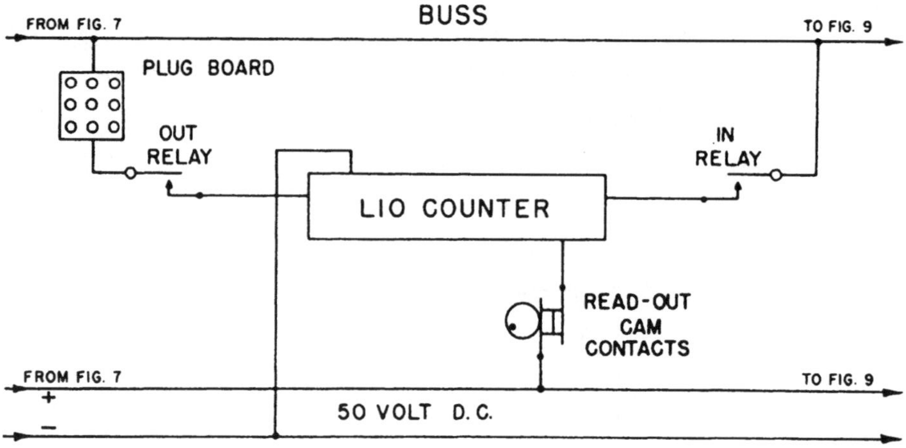

Figure 8

After a sensing circuit has compared the value of X with $\pi/4$, in case (a), the computation proceeds by evaluating the series (12). In case (b), $\pi/2$ - X is formed and the series (13) is evaluated. In either case, the result of the summation of the series is delivered to the sine in-out counter, columns one through twenty-three, with the result that this counter then contains $|\sin x|$ and the appropriate algebraic sign.

The read-out of sin x to the buss for delivery to storage is through plugging, in order to shift the function to conform to the operating decimal position. The read-out is direct or inverted according as zero or eight on the one hand, or a nine on the other hand, stands in the twenty-fourth column of the sine in-out counter.

The logarithm in-out counter and the sine in-out counter are commonly used as "shift counters". These counters are equipped with pluggable and direct read-ins and read-outs as shown in Figs. 8 and 9. They may be used to multiply or divide by powers of ten. In addition, the pluggable read-outs may be manually so adjusted as to permit selective read-out of the shift counters by means of which any

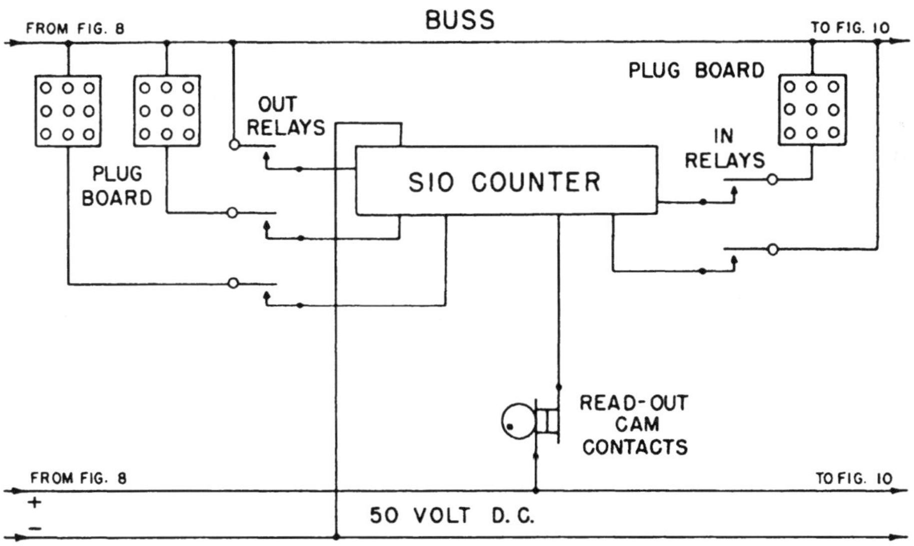

Figure 9

m columns may be delivered to the buss while the remaining 24 - m are suppressed. This selective read-out does not erase any part of the number standing in the shift counter. The read-ins and read-outs of these two counters have been placed under control of the main sequence mechanism by codes which are independent of the codes of the functional units of which the shift counters are themselves a part. Since the logarithm in-out and sine in-out counters do not have complete carry circuits at all times, and have codes and resets which differ materially from those of other registers, they must be used with care. A detailed discussion of these codes and their uses will be found in Chapter IV.

With the aid of the electro-mechanical tables of $\log_{10}x$, 10^x and sin x, all of the elementary transcendental functions, including the hyperbolic functions, may be obtained through the use of the operations of the calculator already described. In order to provide for inverse trigonometric functions, higher transcendental functions and empirical functions defined by tabular data, the calculator is equipped with three mechanical interpolators.

The three interpolator mechanisms and their accompanying switches are shown in Plate XII, to the left of the main sequence mechanism. The three units share in common the interpolation counter and the interpolation check counter, (Fig. 10). A function is introduced into an interpolation mechanism in the form of a perforated paper tape, (Plate XIII). This tape is similar to the main sequence control tape, but in place of commands to the calculator, contains coded successive equidistant values of the argument, each accompanied by the necessary interpolation coefficients. Any order of interpolation up to and including the eleventh may be employed.

The coding for interpolation by unit I as it appears in the main sequence control tape is:

x lies in ctr. 50, code 652; a tape containing f(x) is on Interpolator I; determine f(x) and deliver it to ctr. 51, code 6521.

OUT	IN	MISC.
652	7654	
		62
841		
652	763	
	6521	73
		7

There are a very great many possible variations in this coding as well as in the possible uses of the

XII Sequence Control Mechanism and Interpolators

XIII Interpolator

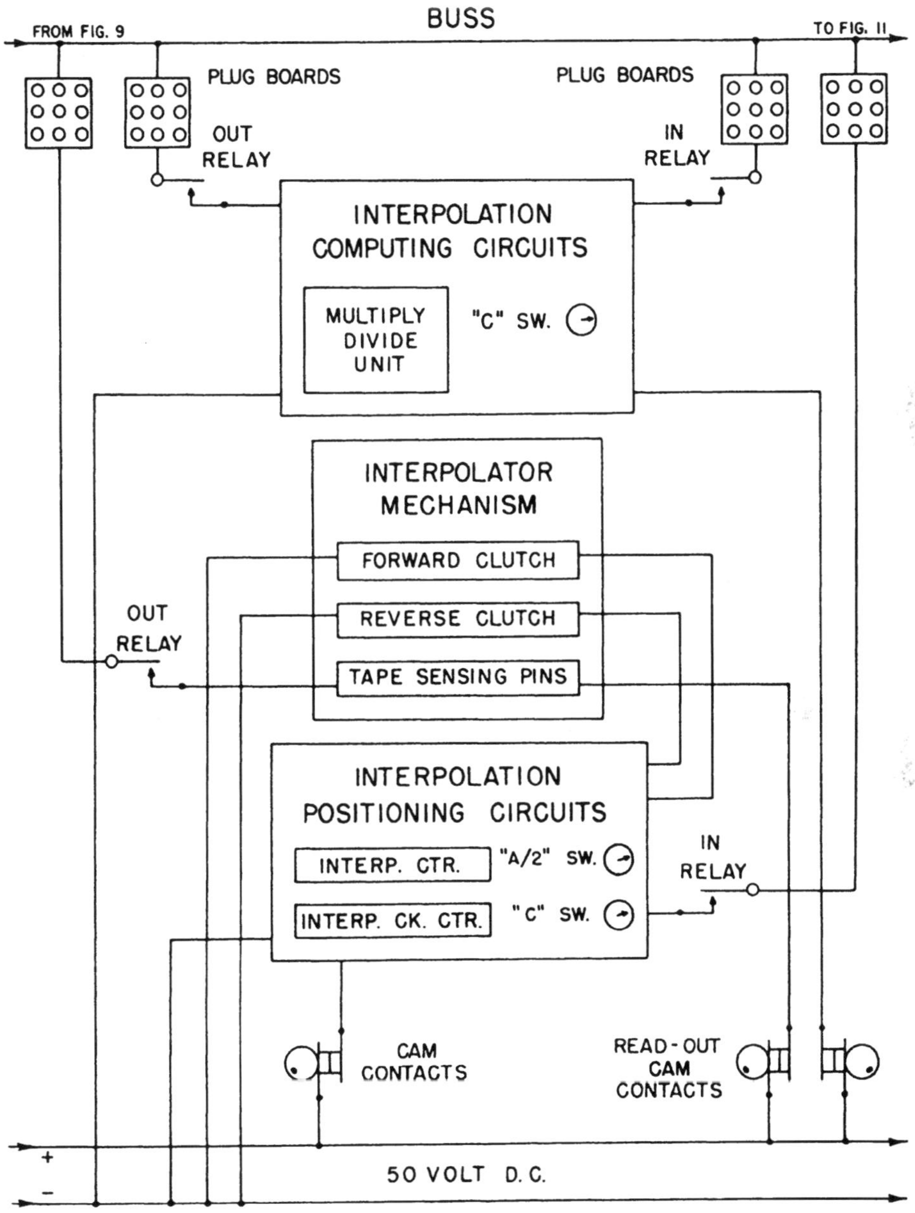
BUSS
FROM FIG. 9
TO FIG. 11
PLUG BOARDS
PLUG BOARDS
OUT
RELAY
IN
RELAY
INTERPOLATION
COMPUTING CIRCUITS
MULTIPLY
DIVIDE
UNIT
"C" SW.
INTERPOLATOR
MECHANISM
FORWARD CLUTCH
REVERSE CLUTCH
TAPE SENSING PINS
OUT
RELAY
INTERPOLATION
POSITIONING CIRCUITS
INTERP. CTR.
"A/2" SW.
INTERP. CK. CTR.
"C" SW.
IN
RELAY
CAM
CONTACTS
READ-OUT
CAM
CONTACTS
+
-
50 VOLT D. C.

Figure 10

interpolator units. All of those which have been developed up to the present time are included in Chapter IV. The present discussion will be confined to the most elementary case, that of interpolation by means of Taylor's series.

A function f(x) is to be determined. The independent variable, x, is considered as consisting of two parts, $x = a + h$, where a is an integral multiple of a power of ten. Since four columns are provided for containing the value of a, it is clear that a functional tape may contain 10^4 arguments.

An interpolation is performed by evaluating the series,

$$\begin{aligned} f(x) &= f(a + h) \\ &= f(a) + f'(a)h + f''(a)h^2/2! + \dots \\ &= c_0 + c_1h + c_2h^2 + c_3h^3 + \dots, \end{aligned} \tag{14}$$

in the form,

$$f(x) = f(a + h) = ((((\dots + c_4)h + c_3)h + c_2)h + c_1)h + c_0 . \tag{15}$$

The interpolation process may be divided into two distinct parts. The first consists of positioning the functional tape and the second of the computation necessary to the interpolation itself. For tape positioning, the argument, a, and the highest order column of h are delivered to the interpolation counter. The interpolator mechanism first reads the tape to discover the position at which the tape is standing. By subtraction in the interpolation counter, the number of arguments the mechanism must pass over in order to arrive at the required argument is determined. To accomplish tape positioning in the shortest possible time, functional tapes are made endless. Suitable sensing circuits aided by manually preset switches direct the mechanism to move the tape in the direction of shorter travel. The highest order column of h is combined with a half-correction in the interpolation counter to insure positioning to the nearest argument. As the tape steps, the number of arguments to be covered (stored in the interpolation counter) is reduced one for each argument passed and is finally reduced to zero.

At the beginning of the positioning operation the required argument, a, is read into the interpolation check counter. At the end of the positioning operation it is transferred to the interpolation counter and used to check the position of the tape. If the tape is not in proper position because an impossible argument has been sent to the interpolation unit or because of faulty mechanical operation, the positioning mechanism will try a second time to find the required argument. The calculator is stopped and a red light turned on in the event that the positioning mechanism fails on this second try.

However, if the tape is found to be in the required position, the interpolation sequence control takes over command of the calculator. The quantity x is again read out of storage into the buss and the h part delivered by plugging to the multiply unit. Suitable corrections of h, such as nines to the left if h is negative, are also made by plugging.

The interpolation sequence control then evaluates series (15), while the multiplicand, h, is held constant as usual to conserve machine time. The coefficients, $c_n, c_{n-1}, ..., c_1, c_0$, are read out of the functional tape and added into the multiplier counter under control of the interpolation sequence circuits.

When a relatively large number of values, such as constants or random values of a variable, are to be used by the calculator, and further when these values are to be used in a prescribed order, they may be supplied to the machine via one of the interpolator mechanisms and a perforated paper tape. Such a tape is known as a "value tape" to distinguish it from a functional tape. Mathematically, the operation of reading from a value tape is the equivalent of zero order interpolation. In order to increase the flexibility of the interpolators when used in this manner, three sequence codes have been assigned to each interpolator mechanism. These require that the tape be stepped forward, stepped back and that the sensing pins read from the tape (Fig. 11), as in the following examples for interpolator I.

	OUT	IN	MISC.
Step the tape forward.			753
Step the tape back.			754
Read the value from the tape to ctr. 34, code 62.	85		7
		62	7

The codes for accomplishing the same purposes in connection with interpolators II and III may be found in the section on Interpolators in Chapter IV.

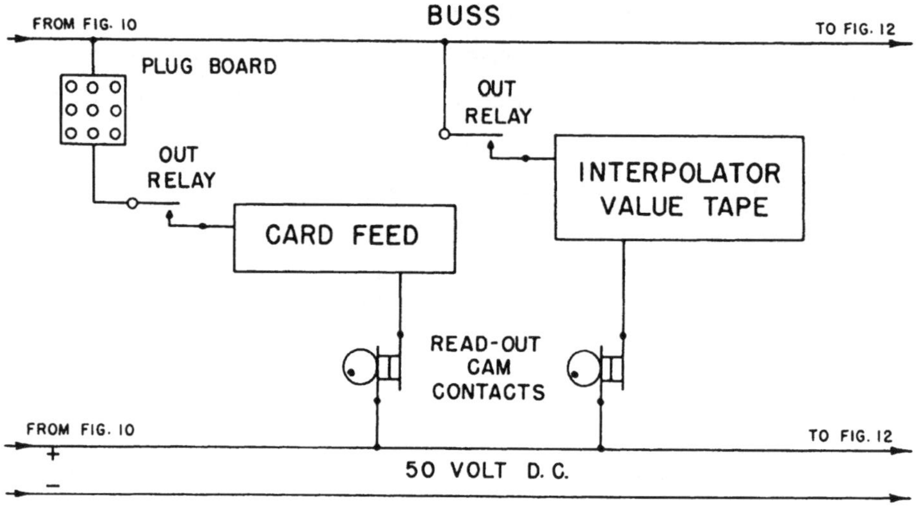

Figure 11

Other means of supplying data to the calculator are the two card feeds shown in Plate XIV and Fig. 11. These employ standard tabulating machine cards and have three advantages over the value tape. First, since tabulating machines are highly standardized, the cards permit the interchange of data from one computation laboratory to another. Second, the devices required in the manual preparation of the cards have been developed to a high degree of perfection. Third, the calculator is itself equipped with a card punching mechanism.

The disadvantage of punched cards as compared to a value tape lies in the fact that the card feeds must accept the cards in the order in which the deck is stacked. No provision is made for retrieving a card once it has passed through the feed. Hence, a second use of the value punched in a card requires the intervention of an operator.

The coding for reading from card feed I is:

	OUT	IN	MISC.
Read the value from the card in feed I to ctr. 3, code 21.		21	7632

When using punched cards and value tapes, the coding must be arranged to synchronize their reading

XIV Typewriters, Card Feeds and Card Punch

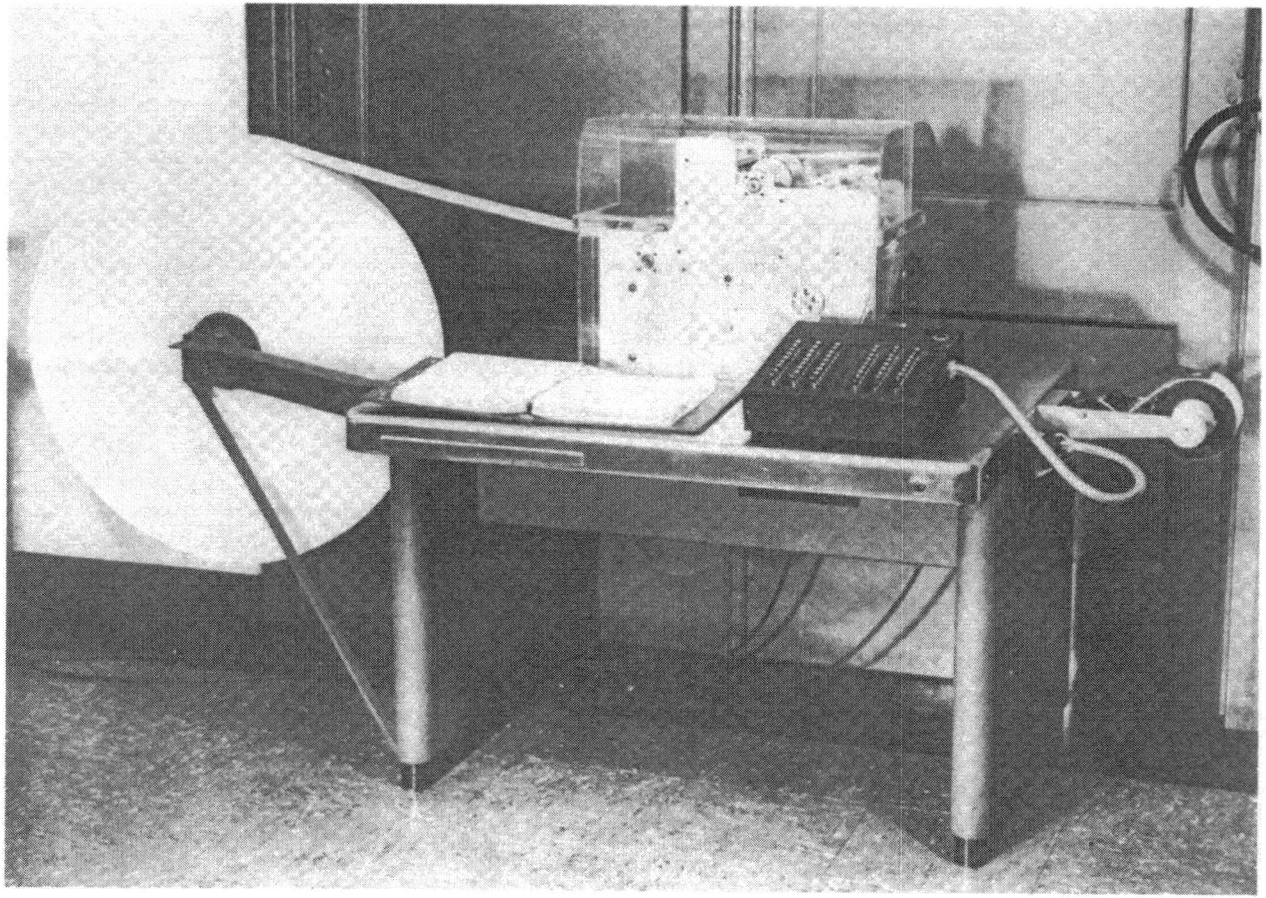

XV Tape Punch

units with the main control tape. This implies that suitable operating instructions must be prepared to insure that cards and value tapes are properly inserted in the calculator.

A control is provided on each card feed to stop the calculator when the cards are exhausted or jammed. The quantities in the cards are read into the buss through plugging and therefore may be shifted to conform with the operating decimal position. This is not true, however, of value tapes.

Occasionally a problem is so voluminous as to tax the facilities of the calculator. In such cases, the main control tapes are so designed that the computation may proceed part way, the intermediate results may be punched into cards and the cards later fed into the calculator for further computation under the direction of a second main control tape.

The card feeds and interpolator mechanisms together with the switches previously described represent the means by which numbers may be introduced into the calculator as a basis for computation. For recording computed results, two methods are available, the card punch mentioned in the previous paragraph and two automatic typewriters, (Plate XV).

The printing and punching of numbers is accomplished with the aid of registers known as the "print" and "punch" counters together with special circuits designed to control the recording devices. The print and punch counters (Fig. 12) are equipped with in- and out-relays and complete carry circuits so that they may function as standard storage counters in addition to performing their special purposes.

The coding for the printing operation consists of two lines, one line to read the quantity to be printed to the print counter and one to initiate the printing operation.

	OUT	IN	MISC.
x lies in ctr. 18, code 52; print x on typewriter I.	52	7432	
		752	7

The controls of the typewriters are very flexible with respect to the number of digits printed, their spacing, columnar position and line spacing. These controls are considered in detail under Printing in Chapters IV and V. The computed results may be reproduced photographically directly from the typewritten sheets. This avoids the possibility of error due to copying, inherent in most computational procedures.

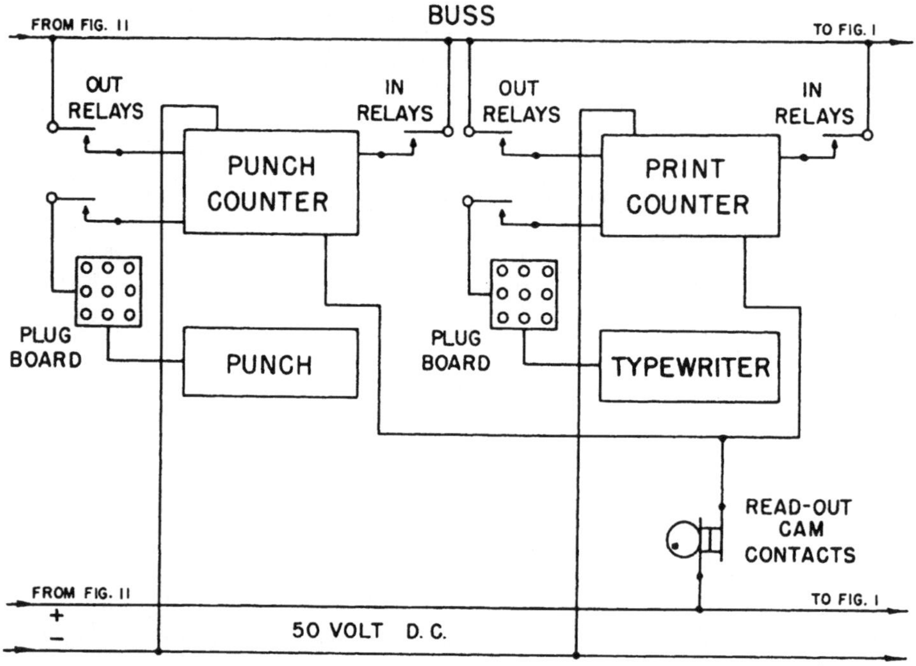

Figure 12

The punch coding also consists of two lines, one line to read into the punch counter and one to initiate the punching operation.

x lies in ctr. 37, code 631; punch x into a card.

OUT	IN	MISC.
631	753	
		75

In order to avoid the loss of computed results, the card punch is equipped with a stop control which prevents a read-in to the punch counter, stops the calculator and lights a red signal light in the event that a blank card is not in the proper punching position at the time the sequence control tape dictates the punching operation.

Not all problems imposed on the calculator require the use of punched cards. Hence, a manual keyboard connected with the punch may be used for the preparation of cards while the calculator is in operation. This punch, however, does not produce any of the tapes used by the machine. It will be recalled that the Jacquard weavers laced their cards together to provide the tapes they required for the control of their looms. The calculator, on the other hand, uses smooth tapes prepared by means of a specially designed manual punch shown in Plate XV.

Two keyboards are used interchangeably to control this punch. The first of these is used in the preparation of functional and value tapes. It has twenty-four columnar positions and perforates the tape in such a way as to represent any one of the ten digits in each column of a twenty-three figure number together with the algebraic sign. A four line code is used as shown in Fig. 13. This figure must be read from the bottom to the top, representing the forward direction in which the tape passes through the reading mechanisms of the interpolator units.

In general, a value tape consists of a tabulation of constants punched into the tape in a given order. A functional tape, in contrast, contains a group of entries associated with each argument. The first entry in each group is the argument itself. This is followed by the interpolational coefficients, c_n, c_{n-1}, ..., c_1, c_0, in this order as shown in Fig. 14.

The argument must be punched in columns fifteen, sixteen, seventeen and eighteen of the tape regardless of the location of either the tape decimal point or the operating decimal point. The negative algebraic sign, if required, must be represented by a nine in the twenty-fourth column. Each argument must be identified by an argument code consisting of a three-four punched in the first column of argument punching. Fig. 14 represents a portion of a tape for fourth order interpolation on $f(x) = \tan x$ with an accuracy of twelve decimal places. The figure illustrates all of the salient features of an interpolation tape.

The main control tapes are punched by the second keyboard, previously mentioned, which appears in Plate XV. It is designed to contain two lines of coding which must be punched simultaneously. This is necessary because the sequence and interpolator mechanisms, though radically different in operation, are in reality made of the same mechanical components. One numerical value in a functional tape occupies the same amount of space as two lines of control tape coding. The device of setting up two lines of control tape coding per punching operation makes it possible to punch sequence control tapes and functional tapes with one and the same manual punch.

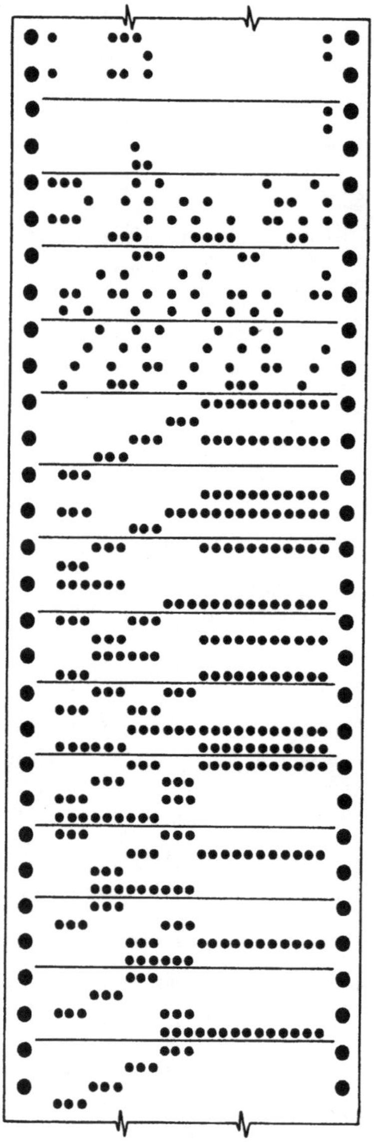
VALUE TAPE
Negative Argument -51
Argument Code in 1st col.
Positive Argument 51
Argument Code in 1st col.
Negative Number
-698 321 576 438 499 013 451
Positive Number
521 328 794 532 605 972 100 28
Diagonal Number
012 345 678 901 234 567 890 123
0 000 111 222 333 999 999 999 99
0 999 000 111 222 888 888 888 88
0 888 999 000 111 777 777 777 77
0 777 888 999 000 666 666 666 66
0 666 777 888 999 555 555 555 55
0 555 666 777 888 444 444 444 44
0 444 555 666 777 333 333 333 33
0 333 444 555 666 222 222 222 22
0 222 333 444 555 111 111 111 11
0 111 222 333 444 000 000 000 00

Figure 13

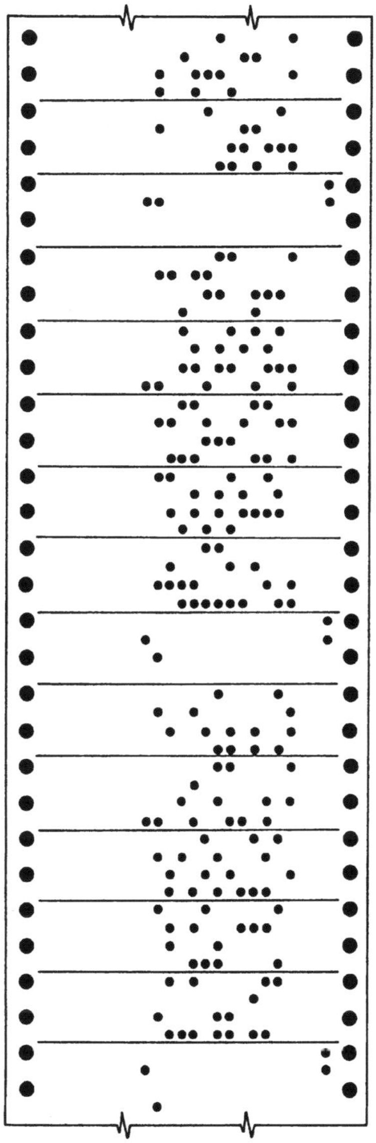

FUNCTIONAL TAPE

C_3 0.503 529 133 009

C_4 0.300 041 586 295

Arg 0.33

C_0 0.331 389 405 224

C_1 1.109 818 937 895

C_2 0.367 782 237 736

C_3 0.491 818 782 980

C_4 0.285 577 613 215

Arg 0.32

C_0 0.320 327 505 078

C_1 1.102 609 710 509

C_2 0.353 196 217 642

C_3 0.480 675 033 370

C_4 0.271 705 506 740

Arg 0.31

Figure 14

CONTROL TAPE

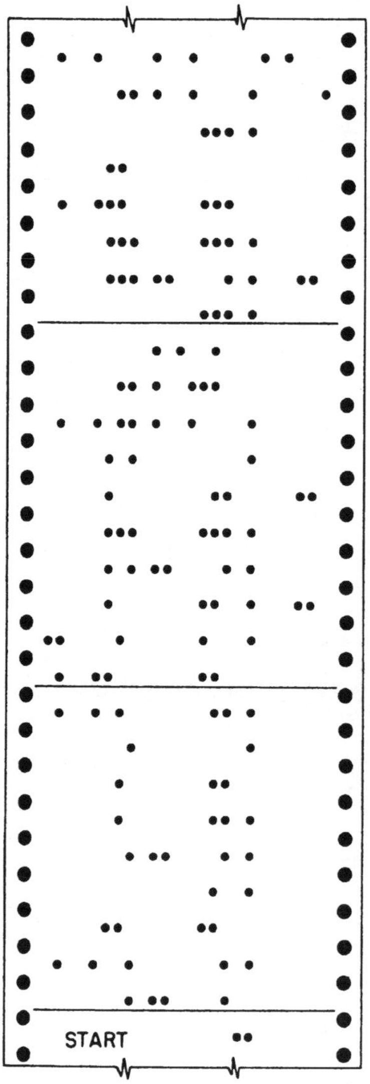

OUT	IN	MISC.
74	74	64
21	74	71
	321	7
32		
7432	321	
321	321	7
321	761	732
	321	7
	752	
21	7432	
7421	74	7
31		7
3	21	32
321	321	7
31	761	7
3	32	732
872	3	7
743	32	
742	21	7
1		7
2	21	
2	21	7
1	761	7
	2	7
32	32	
741	1	7
1	761	
	START	87

Figure 15

CODING SHEET

OPERATION	LINE	OUT	IN	MISC.
x_{n-1} to MC	1	1	761	
Δx to MP and to ctr. 1; ctr. 1 = x_n		741	1	7
reset ctr. 6		32	32	
$x_{n-1}\Delta x$ to ctr. 2			2	7
x_n to MC		1	761	7
$x_{n-1}\Delta x$ to ctr. 3		2	21	7
$x_{n-1}\Delta x$ to ctr. 3		2	21	
x_n to MP		1		7
$(\Delta x)^2$ to ctr. 3		742	21	7
1 to ctr. 6	10	743	32	
x_n^2 to ctr. 4; turn on typewriter I		872	3	7
$-x_n^2$ to ctr. 6; ctr. 6 = $1 - x_n^2$		3	32	732
$1/\sqrt{1 - x_{n-1}^2}$ to MC		31	761	7
reset ctr. 7		321	321	7
$-x_n^2$ to ctr. 3		3	21	32
$1/\sqrt{1 - x_{n-1}^2}$ to MP		31		7
tolerance to check ctr.		7421	74	7
check to print ctr. I		21	7432	
print on typewriter I			752	
$1/(1 - x_{n-1}^2)$ to ctr. 7	20		321	7
$-1/(1 - x_{n-1}^2)$ to MC		321	761	732
reset ctr. 7		321	321	7
3 to ctr. 7		7432	321	
$1 - x_n^2$ to MP		32		
$(1 - x_n^2)/(1 - x_{n-1}^2)$ to ctr. 7			321	7
check to check ctr.		21	74	71
check and reset check ctr.		74	74	64

Figure 16

Figure 15 shows a short section of control tape and Fig. 16, the corresponding coding. As in the case of value and functional tapes, the control tape must be read upwards.

Since the control tapes deal with operations only, they represent the solution of a mathematical situation independent of the values of the parameters involved. Hence, such control tapes as are of general application are preserved in the tape library for future use. Functional and value tapes of general interest are likewise preserved.

When a problem is referred to the Computation Laboratory, the first step in its solution is that taken by the mathematician who chooses the numerical method best adapted to computation by the calculator. This choice is made on the basis of the accuracy desired, the possible checking operations and the speed of computation. Such functional, value and control tapes as are required are then computed, coded and punched. Since the mathematician cannot always be present while the calculator is running, instructions must be prepared to guide the operating staff. These must include switch settings, the list of tapes to be used, plugging instructions, manual resets, information concerning checks, starting, stopping and rerun instructions. The instructions for the plugging of the functional units are usually given in the form of diagrams similar to those in Chapter V. The manual resets may include the clearing of both functional and storage counters. On the functional panel, (Plate XI), may be seen the push-buttons by which all of the functional counters may be reset except the forty-seventh or sign column of the product-quotient counter which is reset at the end of each multiplying or dividing operation. Above the sequence mechanism are the seventy-two push-buttons which permit manual resetting of each of the storage counters. Directly below the reset buttons and above the sequence mechanism, (Plate XII), is a constant register which exactly duplicates one of the sixty switches. Because this register is frequently used to provide the increment of the independent variable, it is known as the independent variable switch. Further, because it is located conveniently near the sequence mechanism, this switch is particularly useful in testing the various units of the calculator.

The start and stop keys are located directly above the sequence mechanism as shown in Plate XII. The use of these keys and their associated electrical circuits will be discussed in Chapter III.

The main sequence control is equipped to advance the tape, step by step, normally at a rate of 200 steps per minute, unless one of the subsidiary sequence controls is directed by the coding to temporarily take over command of the calculator. In this case, the control tape is stopped until the subsidiary sequence control has finished its operation and signals the main sequence control to continue operation.

The normal step rate of the sequence tape, then, does not give a good estimate of the speed of the calculator. This may be better given by citing the time required for various operations. When computing with twenty-three significant digits and operating decimal point between columns fifteen sixteen, the maximum operation times are as shown in the following table.

Operation	Seconds	Cycles
Addition	0.3	1
Subtraction	0.3	1
Multiplication	6.0	20
Division	11.4	38
$\mathrm{Log}_{10}x$	68.4	228
10^x	61.2	204
Sin x	60.0	199

All of the times cited include the time required to transfer the arguments to the functional units and to deliver the results for further computation. The time required for all operations, except addition and subtraction, may be shortened by reducing the accuracy of the computation. Obviously, the only way to state the relative speed of the calculator is to solve a problem first by manual methods and then by use of the machine. Such an estimate has been made and apparently the machine is well nigh one hundred times as fast as a well equipped manual computer. When it is borne in mind that a computer can work little more than six hours a day before fatigue causes him to produce a prohibitive number of errors, it becomes clear that operating on a twenty-four hour schedule, the calculator may produce as much as six months work in a single day.

References

1. E. T. Whittaker and G. Robinson, Calculus of Observations (3rd ed.) (1940), p. 2.

2. Whittaker and Robinson, loc. cit.

3. F. Cajori, History of Matnematics (1919), p. 226.

4. Whittaker and Robinson, op. cit., chap. VII.

5. Whittaker and Robinson, op. cit., p. 363.

6. Whittaker and Robinson, op. cit., p. 367.

7. Whittaker and Robinson, loc. cit.

8. H. H. Aiken, Proposed Automatic Calculating Machine (1937), p. 18, (privately distributed).

9. H. H. Aiken, Harvard Lecture Notes on Applied Mathematics (1938), p. 10.

CHAPTER III

ELECTRICAL CIRCUITS

"Simplicity is Nature's first step, and the last of Art."

Philip James Bailey

In the preceding chapter, means were described by which the Automatic Sequence Controlled Calculator is kept in continuous operation. However, no mention was made of the circuits by which the machine is started and stopped. This subject may best be approached by consideration of the main sequence control.

Figures 17 and 18 show the sequencing circuits of a machine having nine reading pins, three in each of the A, B and C groups, rather than the twenty-four pins of the calculator. The nine reading pins are numbered 6, 7 and 8 in each group in order that the starting and stopping circuits may be presented in a manner consistent not only with the diagrams, but also with the calculator itself. The nine reading pins make available 2^9 possible orders per line of coding and are sufficient to develop all the ideas necessary to a clear understanding of the sequence control. An attempt to draw the actual circuits employed in the calculator would lead to inconveniently large and complex diagrams.

Figure 17 shows the reading contacts controlled by the reading pins and the tape, neither of the latter being shown in the figure. Once the pins have advanced against the tape and closed the reading contacts in positions corresponding to the holes in the tape, an electrical circuit is established to energize the sequence relays. Suppose a line of coding to read (6, 6, 7) corresponding to the reset of counter 32, code 6. Then beginning at the positive terminal of the generator, assuming the cam controlled contact FC-101 to be closed and for the moment further assuming that the four-pole read relay contacts are closed, complete circuits exist through the reading contacts A-6, B-6, C-7, through the corresponding sequence relays to the negative generator terminal. When the sequence relays are picked up, each is held in its energized position through one of its own contacts and the cam controlled contact FC-102.

The sequence relays are multipolar, and in addition to their hold contacts, have "cascade" contacts wired as shown in Fig. 18. These permit the selection of out-, in- and miscellaneous relays

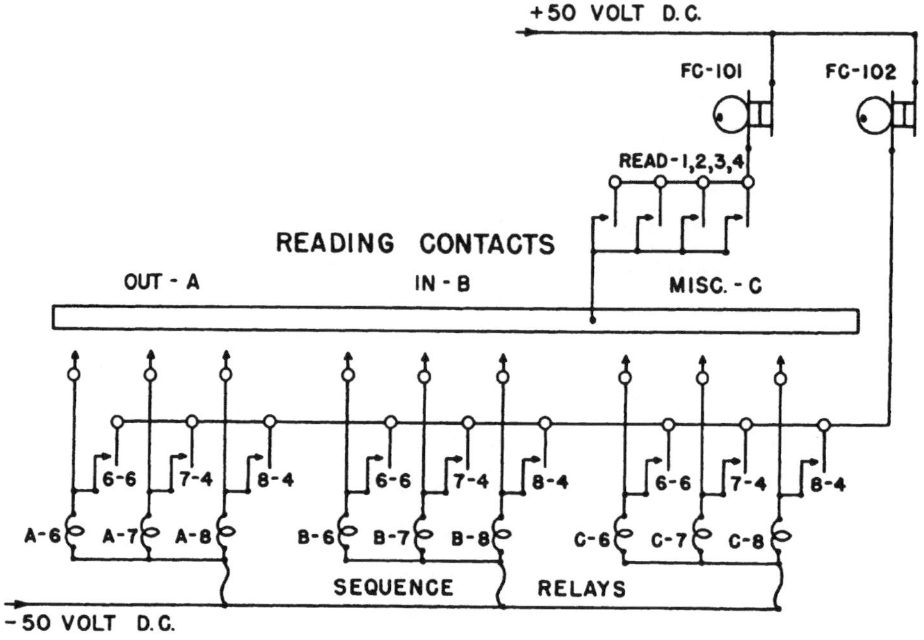

Figure 17

which are picked up by means of cam controlled impulses. The multipole relays are of the double throw variety, having four, six or twelve poles, and may be either single or double coil. They are jack connected and wired with the aid of plug-in wires as shown in Plate XVI. When a relay is not energized, circuits may be completed through its normally closed (NC) contacts. On the other hand, when a relay is picked up, circuits may be completed through its normally open (NO) contacts. Thus any code corresponds to a series of normally open and normally closed sequence relay contacts. For example, as may be seen in Fig. 18, the in-relay of counter 32, code 6, is picked up through B-8-1 NC, B-7-1 NC and B-6-1 NO. A complete tabulation of the cascade contacts for all of the codes at present used by the calculator is given in Appendix I.

The contacts of the out-, in- and miscellaneous relays are not shown in Fig. 18 as these are parts of the circuits to be controlled by these relays rather than of the sequence control circuits.

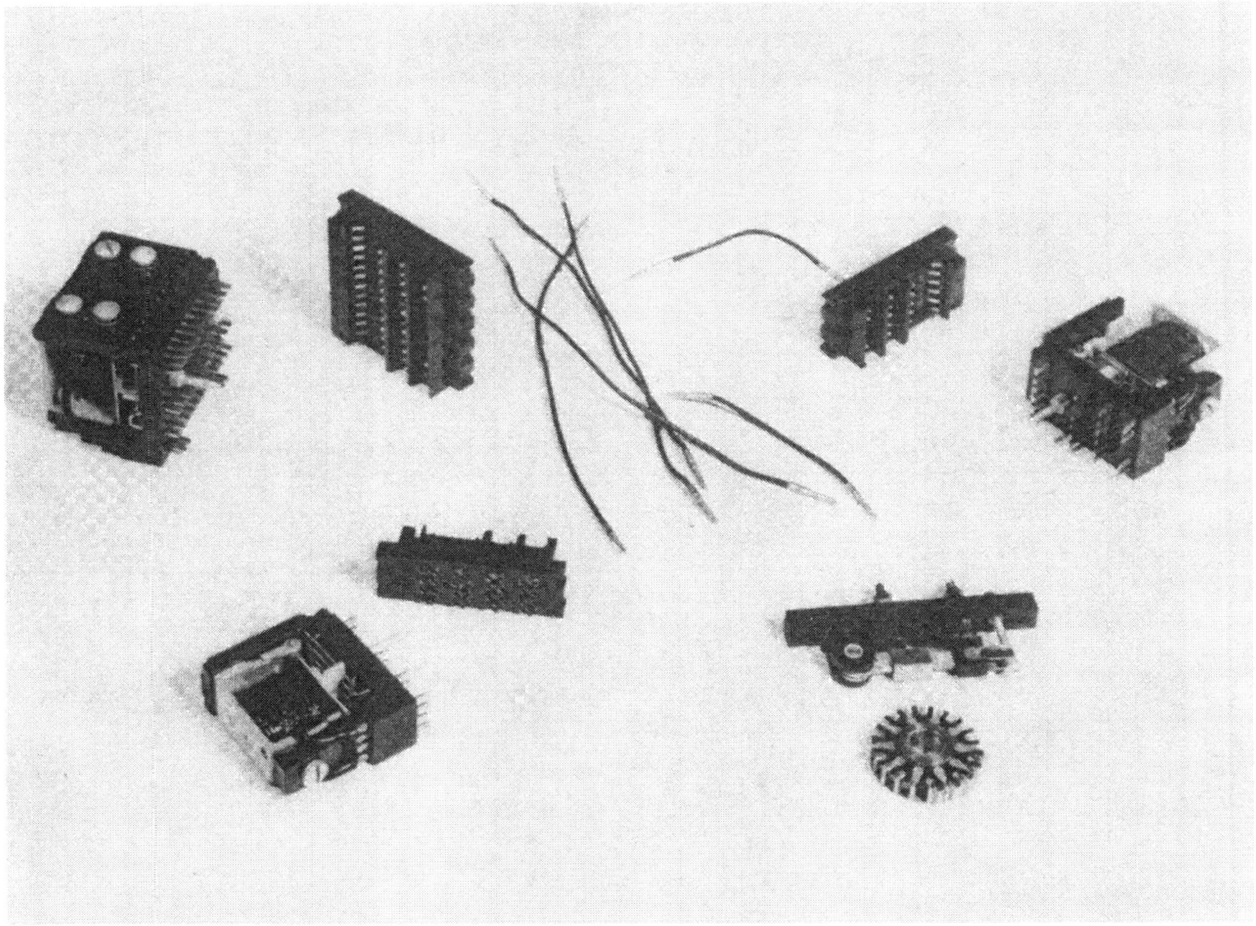

XVI Relays and Cam

XVII Storage Counter

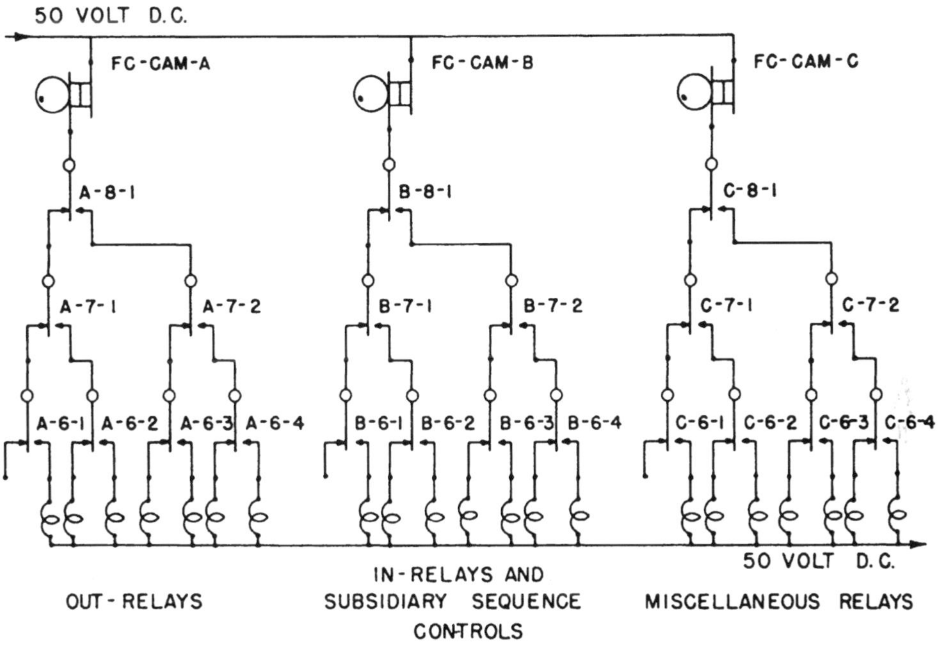

Figure 18

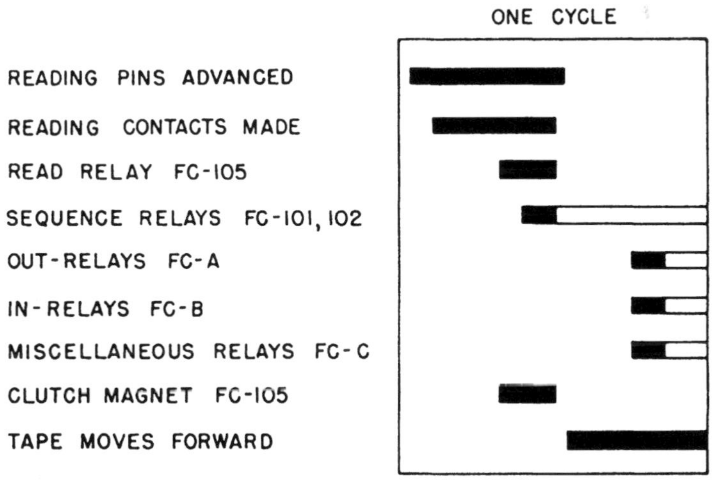

Figure 19

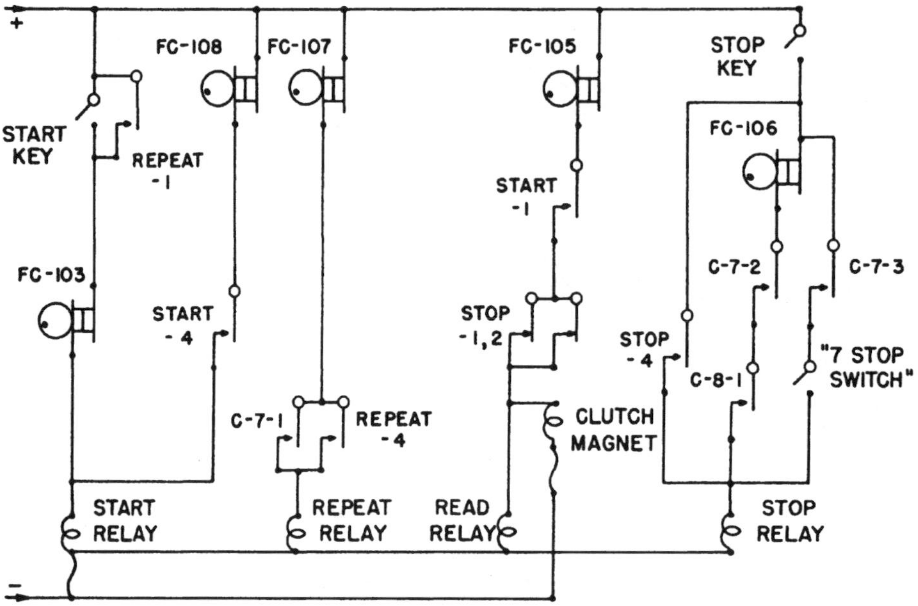

Figure 20

These contacts will be considered in connection with the computing circuits of which they form a part. The timing diagram, Fig. 19, together with the foregoing description should make clear the repetitive operation of the circuits shown in Figs. 17 and 18 insofar as continuous operation of the calculator is concerned.

Figure 20 and the diagram, Fig. 21, show the start and stop circuits and their timing. The depression of the start key completes the circuit through FC-103 to pick up the start relay. The repeat relay, one point of which is shunted across the start key, is controlled by the sequence relay, C-7. This is picked up by the continue operations code, Miscellaneous 7. The transfer of the contacts of the start relay closes the circuit, controlled by FC-105, to the read relay and the clutch magnet. This circuit contains two normally closed contacts of the stop relay. The stop relay is picked up if, and only if, the stop key is depressed and one of two circuits completed. The first of these is completed by FC-106 and relay contacts governed by the code Miscellaneous 87, while the second is governed by the code

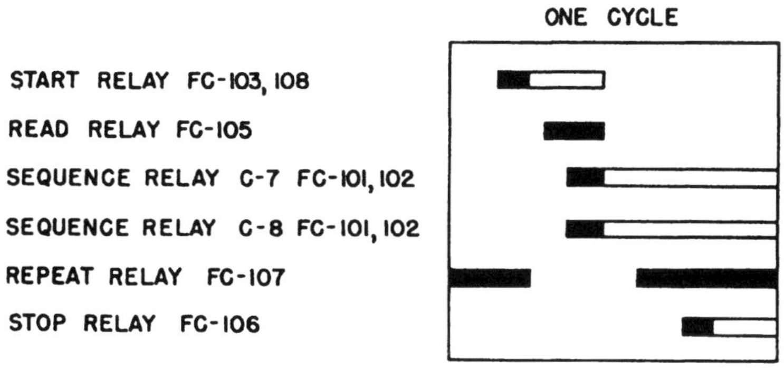

Figure 21

Miscellaneous 7 in combination with the "7 stop switch". The stop relay is held up through one of its own contacts and the stop key. The emergency stop switch is located on the sequence mechanism, (Plate VI). The 87 stop and the 7 stop have decidedly different purposes. The 87 stop may be so coded in a control tape that if the stop key is depressed the machine will stop at a preassigned point in the computation. On the other hand, the 7 stop switch together with the stop key will interrupt the operation of the machine after reading any line of coding containing a Miscellaneous 7. This makes it possible to stop the calculator at the end of any functional operation without interfering with the computation provided that no operations have been interposed. Further discussion of the codes 87 and 7 is contained in Chapter IV.

The relays, relay points and cam controlled contacts in Figs. 17, 18 and 20 have been indicated and numbered as in the calculator itself. For simplicity, one relay, the start interlock relay, has been omitted from these circuits. In the event that the start key is held down too long, the start interlock relay prevents the calculator from receiving more than one starting impulse. The circuits of this relay together with all of the automatic continue operation circuits which may energize the start relay are given in Appendix II.

Unlike the main sequence control, the operations dictated by the subsidiary sequence control are not subject to permutation. Consisting of relay networks and counters, the twenty subsidiary controls at present wired in the calculator direct fixed series of operations. These are largely concerned with the sequences of operations necessary to the control of the functional units. However, it is possible to construct a subsidiary sequence control for any given purpose. For example, the evaluation of a definite integral may be reduced to the computation of values of the integrand for equidistant values of the argument by a short control tape, which also directs a subsidiary sequence control wired to apply a general quadrature formula. In this instance, the coding necessary to the evaluation of definite integrals is greatly reduced. Such specialized subsidiary sequence controls are added to the calculator from time to time as may be desired. These differ only in the sense that some control a greater number of operations and in that their control extends over a longer period of time. Unfortunately, space will not permit the description of all of the sequence controls in the calculator. The fact that those controlling multiplication and division are not only the most simple, but also the more basic in computation, dictates their choice for detailed discussion.

Before entering upon this subject, however, it will be necessary to discuss the use of counters and their drive. Referring to Fig. 22, A is a line shaft extending nearly the full length of the calculator and driven by the four horsepower motor, B. This shaft is contained in the shaft housing shown near the base of the machine in Plates II, III and XII. The main sequence mechanism and the three interpolator mechanisms are supplied with mechanical power by roller chain and sprocket drives, C and D,

MECHANICAL DRIVE SYSTEM

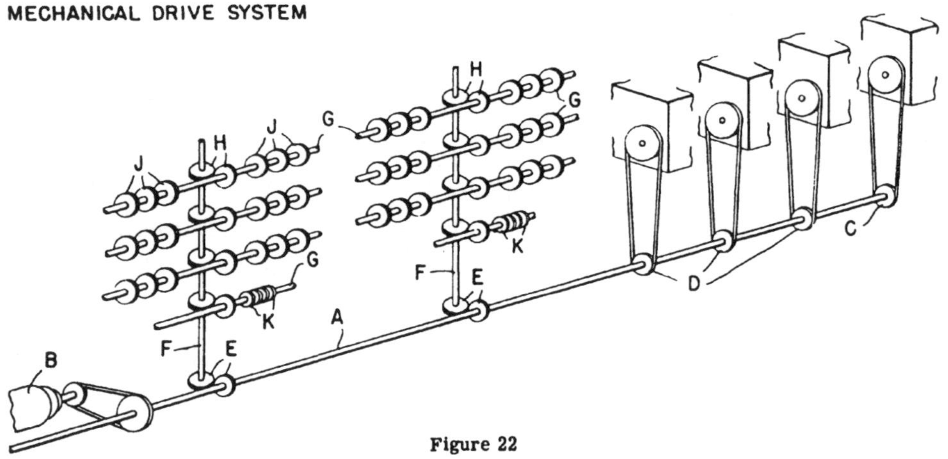

Figure 22

respectively. The spiral gears, E, connect the main drive shaft to the vertical shafts, F. These in turn are connected to the horizontal shafts, G, through smaller spiral gears, H. On the shaft, G, are mounted twelve or fewer gear wheels, J of Fig. 22, E of Plate XVII, each of which supplies mechanical power to a single counter wheel by engaging with the gear shown in the partially assembled counter, A of Plate XVII. Since the sequence and interpolator mechanisms and counter wheels are all driven by a single gear-connected mechanical system, it is clear that all mechanical parts of the machine revolve in synchronism with each other.

Each counter wheel is an electro-mechanical assembly consisting of the following major components shown in Plate XVII: (1) a commutator mounted in a molded plastic part, B and J, commonly called a "molding", having a half slip ring and ten segmental contacts numbered 0 through 9; (2) a pair of stranded wire brushes, C and F, which rotate to connect one of the contact segments with the commutator half slip ring; (3) a magnetically controlled clutch, D, which engages to connect the continuously rotating gear, A, with the sleeve on which the rotating brushes are mounted; (4) a ten's carry contact which operates in conjunction with an external relay circuit to provide carry to the counter wheel in the next higher columnar position when the counter wheel under consideration passes through ten; (5) a nine's carry contact which also operates in conjunction with an external relay circuit to provide carry to the next higher counter wheel when the wheel under consideration stands on nine and the next lower wheel has passed through ten; (6) and finally, a socket, G and K, by which the counter assembly may be jack-connected to the calculator wiring.

The ten segments of the commutator are usually called the number "spots". The time interval necessary for the brush to traverse the distance between two successive spots is one-sixteenth of a cycle, the number spots being so spaced in the commutator as to minimize the ratio of the mechanical backlash to the distance traversed between spots. In order to read, say, a seven into a counter, the counter magnet is picked up at "seven time", thus engaging the clutch. The brushes are spun past six spots and the clutch is mechanically disengaged or knocked off at "zero time". Obviously, nine equally timed and equally spaced impulses must be provided to pick up the counter magnets in order to read in the nine digits and all counters must be knocked off at zero time, (Fig. 23).

The number impulses are supplied by cam controlled contacts. A cam and its follower are shown at the lower right in Plate XVI, and the position in which the cams are mounted is shown in Fig. 22, K. The duration of contact controlled by a cam may be varied by adding or subtracting rollers in the twenty possible sockets in a cam wheel. Several types of followers are used, with variations in the sharpness of the make and break of the contacts they control.

For purposes of cam timing, the fundamental cycle of the calculator, 300 milliseconds, is subdivided into sixteen equal parts commonly referred to as "points". These are numbered:

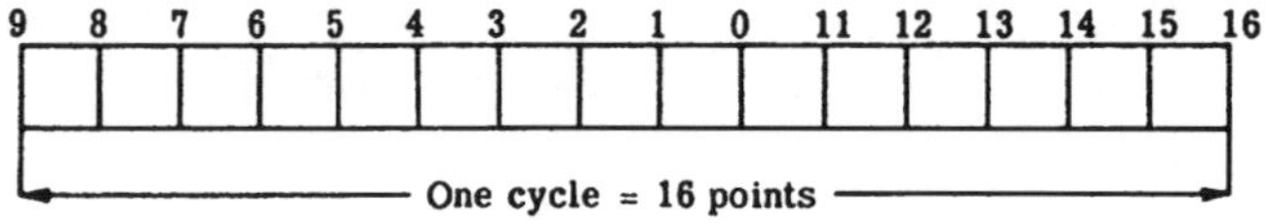

The first nine subdivisions contain the number impulses. The so-called "seven impulse", for example, is delivered by a cam contact making at seven time and breaking half way between seven and six time, commonly called seven and one-half time. The points zero through sixteen are available to supply carry and other control impulses. A timing diagram of the number and carry impulses is given in Fig. 23.

As stated in Chapter II, the transfer of a quantity to a reset counter and the process of addition are one and the same. For instance, a counter stands at zero; a seven impulse picks up the counter magnet at seven time; the counter wheel rotates through six positions, is mechanically knocked off at zero time and comes to rest standing on the seven spot. On the other hand, if a counter stands at

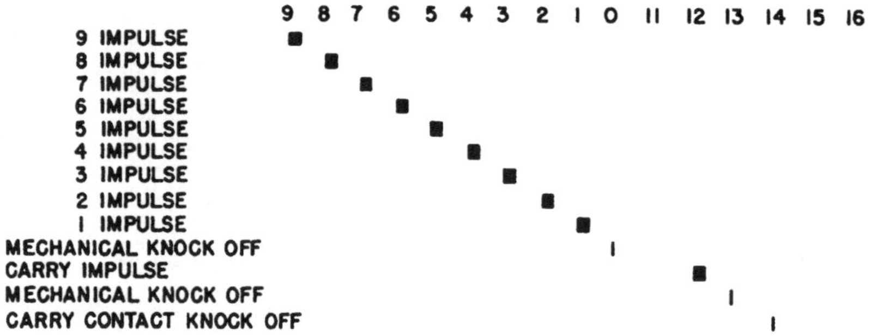

Figure 23

five, a seven impulse picks up the counter magnet at seven time; the counter wheel rotates through six positions, is mechanically knocked off at zero time and comes to rest standing on the two spot, having passed through zero.

As the counter wheel turns, the carry cam, (Fig. 24 and F of Plate XVII), also turns. When the rotating brush touches the nine spot, the follower of the carry cam is dropped and the nine's carry contact is made, (B of Fig. 24). As the counter wheel passes nine and approaches the zero spot, the follower is raised and the ten's carry contact is made, (C of Fig. 24). The ten's carry contact once made is maintained, (D of Fig. 24), until a mechanical knock off returns the carry contact to neutral position, (A of Fig. 24), at fourteen and one-half time. Prior to this, the counter magnet, as shown in Fig. 23, is again picked up at twelve time by the carry impulse if the carry relay circuits are closed and if the ten's carry contact of the next lower counter is made. The counter magnet is also picked up at twelve time by the carry impulse if the carry relay circuits are closed and if the nine's carry contacts of the succeeding lower counters receive a carry impulse due to a still lower ten's carry. The counter wheel moves one position for the carry and is again mechanically knocked off at thirteen time.

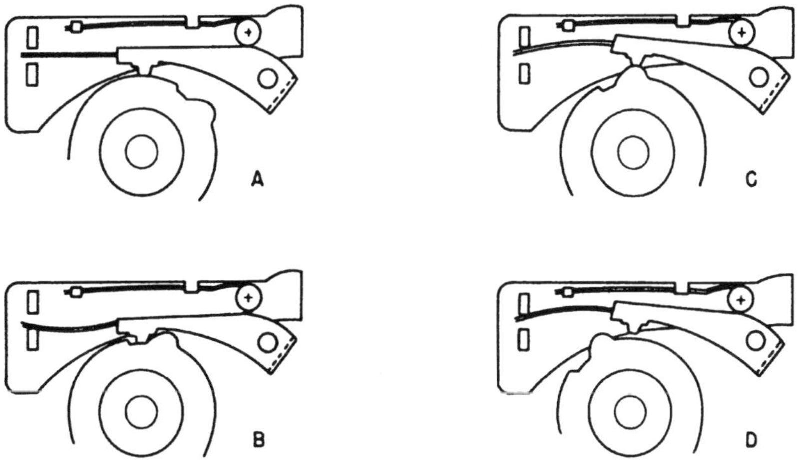

Figure 24

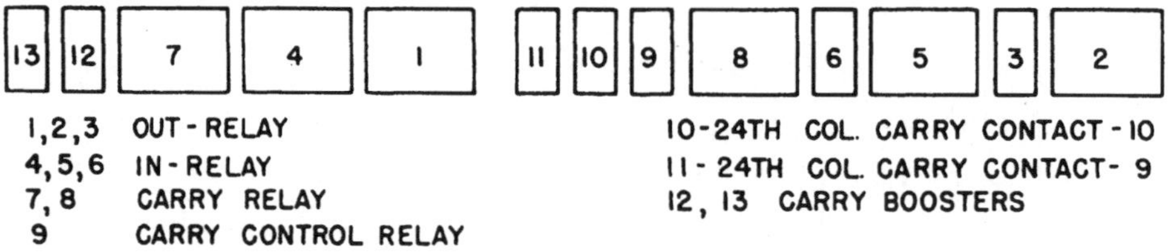

STORAGE COUNTER RELAYS

Figure 25

These operations may be clarified by considering the relay circuits associated with the storage counters. The relays are shown in Plate X, and their usual numbering and position in Fig. 25. There are thirteen individual relays providing the normal circuits for each counter. Some of these are grouped to function as a single relay of more than twelve poles, this being the maximum number of poles available in any single relay as such. Relays 1, 2 and 3 compose the out-relay, while 4, 5 and 6 compose the in-relay. Relays 7 and 8 are the carry relays, with 9 serving as the carry control relay. Also part of the carry circuits are relays 12 and 13, the carry booster relays. The nine's and ten's carry contacts, of the twenty-fourth column counter, control relays 11 and 10 respectively, these being employed in the end around carry circuit.

The storage counter cams, SC-1 through -9, control the number impulses for reading out either from a switch or from a storage counter. Figure 26 shows the circuits for a read-out. The out-relay is energized by a circuit through the sequence relay cascade contacts as previously discussed. Beginning at the positive terminal of the generator, the read-out circuit of a counter is completed to the buss through the reset and invert relays, via the brushes connecting the number spots to the half slip ring and thence through the out-relay. The read-out circuit of a switch is exactly similar except that the commutator of the counter is replaced by the manually preset switch contacts. The wiring by which the energized invert and reset relays provide complements on nine and ten respectively is also shown in Fig. 26.

In order to read into a counter, a circuit is completed through the in-relay connecting the buss to the counter magnets and to the negative terminal of the generator. If a quantity is standing in the

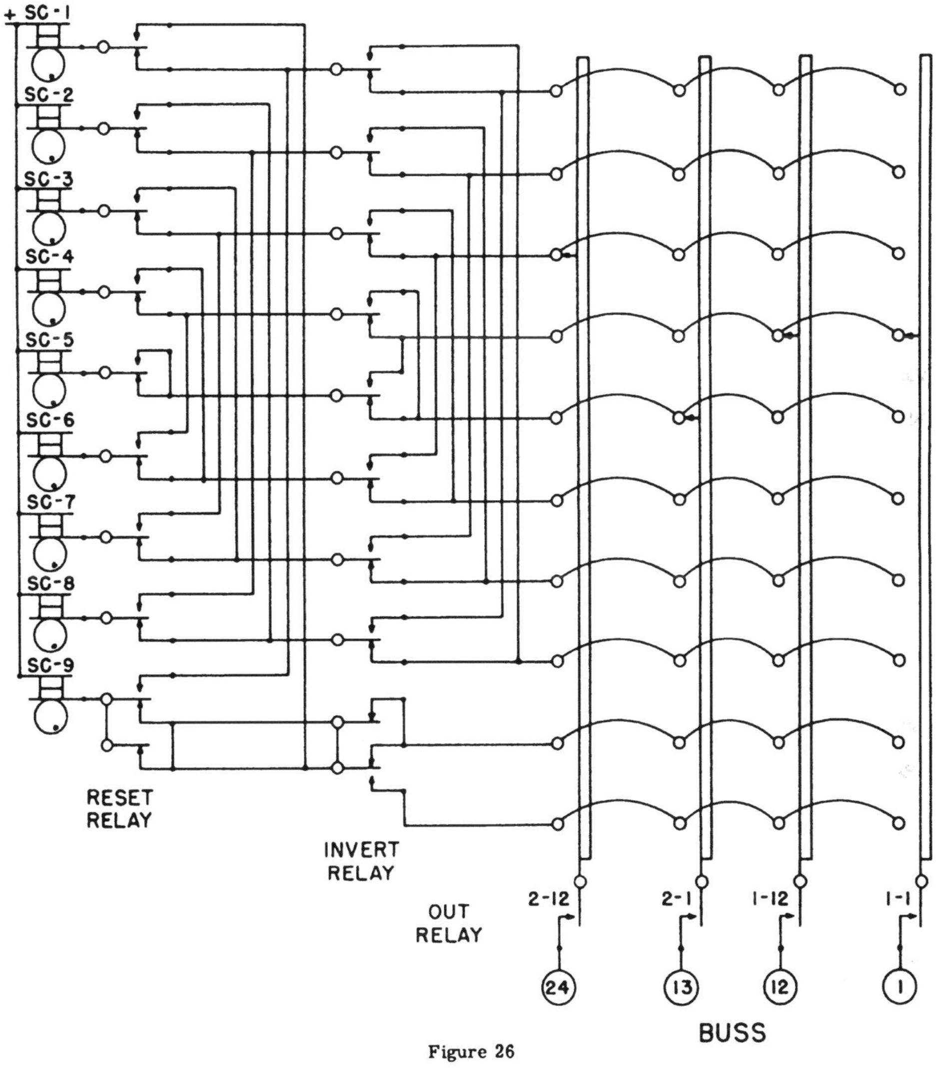

Figure 26

counter at the time of read-in so that addition must be performed, the carry circuits are utilized. As shown in Fig. 27, the carry control relay, 9, is picked up by an impulse, controlled by SC-13, at two time. The first point of this relay, through SC-12, then controls the pick up of the carry relays, 7 and

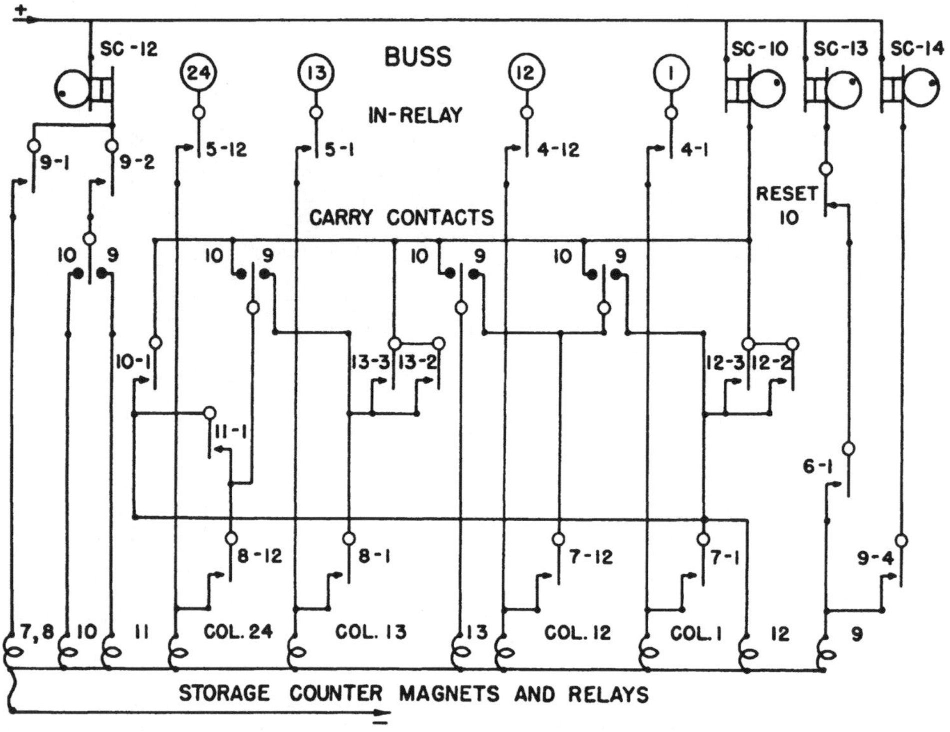

Figure 27

8,at eleven time. The second point of the carry control relay and SC-12 control the pick up circuits of relays 11 and 10. These circuits are completed through the nine's and ten's carry contacts, respectively, of the counter in the twenty-fourth columnar position. The carry circuits are closed on all read-ins except resets, when the carry control relay is not picked up due to the opening of the normally closed contacts of the reset relay. The tenth point of this relay is in the pick up circuit of the carry control relay.

If a counter, other than the twenty-fourth, has passed through ten and its ten's carry contact has been made, the carry impulse, at twelve time, through SC-10 and the appropriate carry relay point, will energize the magnet of the counter in the next higher columnar position. If the twenty-

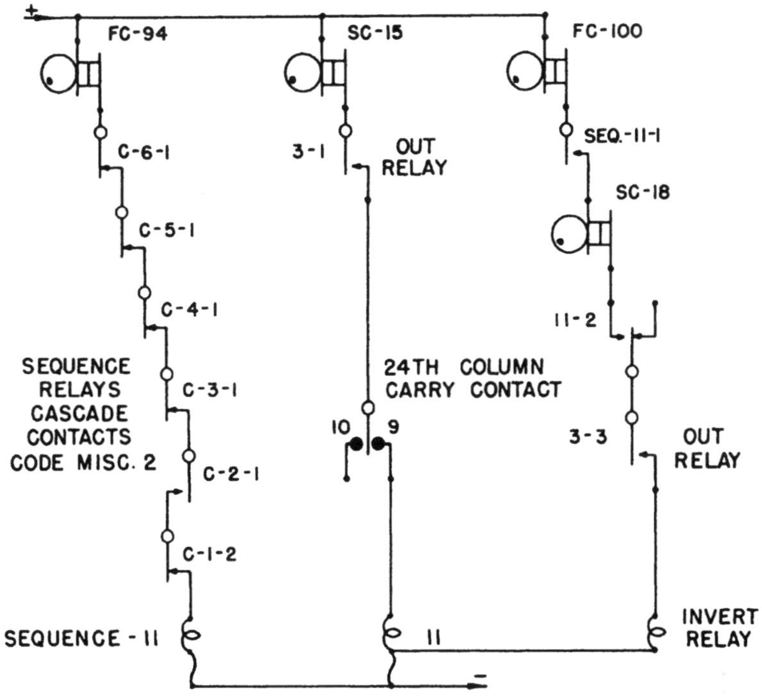

Figure 28

fourth column counter carry contact stands at ten, relay 10 will have been energized at eleven time. Then the carry impulse at twelve time controlled by SC-10 will travel through the first point of the carry relay, 7, and pick up the magnet of the first column counter for an end around carry. Careful study of Fig. 27 will make clear the operation of the circuits when several successive counters stand on nine and a carry impulse is provided by the next lower counter.

The circuits for switches and storage counters including the circuits for all of the specialized storage counters are given in Appendix III. Further, the relay list, Appendix VI, includes all of the normal and special storage counter relays together with specific functions of each of the relay points.

Among others in Appendix III will be found the circuits by means of which it is possible to read positive and negative absolute magnitudes out of any storage counter. The first of these circuits finds

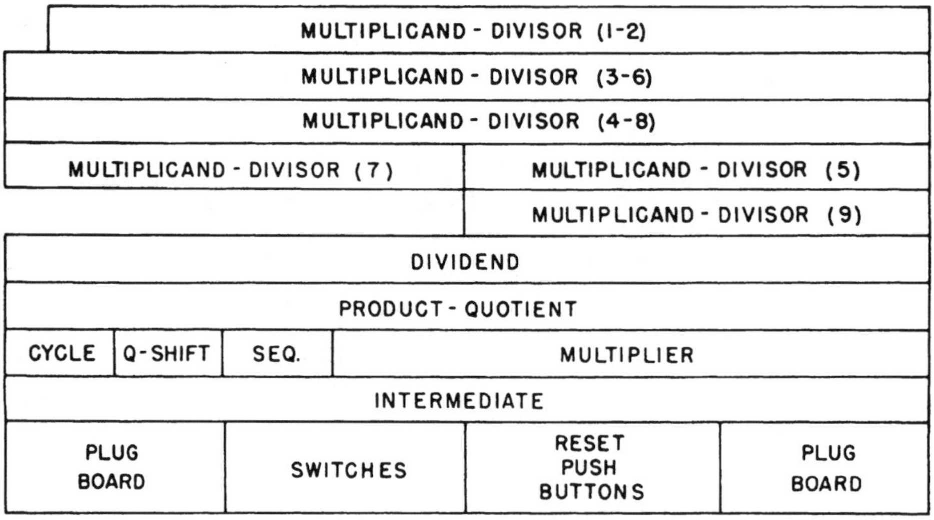

Figure 29

application in connection with the "intermediate" counter through which all quantities must be read in passing into the multiply-divide unit. The operation of the positive absolute magnitude read-out circuit is dependent upon the presence or absence of a nine in the twenty-fourth column. Upon read-out, the presence of a nine brings about the pick up of the invert relay. Figure 28 illustrates the positive absolute read-out as employed in connection with the storage counters. In this figure, C-4-1, for example, refers to the first point of the fourth cascade relay in the C group. The particular C relays shown are those necessary to the pick up of the sequence relay 11 called for by the code Miscellaneous 2; c.f., page 16. The second branch of the circuit in Fig. 28 shows the pick up at thirteen time of storage counter relay 11. This circuit is completed through 3-1, the first point on the third relay composing the storage counter out-relay, and through the nine's carry contact of the twenty-fourth column counter. The third branch circuit at fourteen time picks up the invert relay through the second point of storage counter relay 11 and through the third point of the third relay composing the out-relay. The use of the positive absolute magnitude read-out circuit has been explained here because the application of such a circuit in multiplication and division will reduce the problem to one dealing with positive absolute magnitudes only during these operations.

The counters in the multiply-divide unit and the functional units are not the simple single molding counters that compose the storage registers. The functional counters are equipped with several commutators, each set in a separate molding, and have special wiring which enables these counters to perform operations other than simple addition. The operations of adding into and resetting of the multiple molding counters are, however, the same as in the case of the storage counters. The counters of the multiply-divide unit may be seen in Plate XI and are arranged as shown in Fig. 29. These counters will require individual description. For this purpose, a calculator consisting of six columns, the sixth column being reserved for the algebraic sign, will be assumed. This miniature calculator may perform all of the operations of the calculator itself. The correspondences given in the table below will be valid under this assumption.

Register	Calculator Column	Miniature Machine Column
Switch	24 23 22-1	6 5 4-1
Storage Counter	24 23 22-1	6 5 4-1
Intermediate Counter	24 23-1	6 5-1
MC-DR Counters	24 23-1	6 5-1
MP Counter	23-1	5-1
PQ Counter	47 46-1	11 10-1
DD Counter	45-1	9-1
Q-Shift Counter	2-1	1
Sequence Counter	1	1
Cycle Counter	1	1

ELECTRICAL CIRCUITS

As previously mentioned, the most frequently used of the multiply-divide counters is the intermediate counter. The multiplicand (MC), divisor (DR), multiplier (MP) and dividend (DD) all pass through this counter as they enter the multiply-divide unit. All these quantities are read into the intermediate counter just as they stood in the storage counter from which they were selected. All four values are read out of intermediate to the appropriate counters as positive absolute magnitudes. The MC and MP are transferred without being shifted, but the DR and DD are read out from the intermediate counter so shifted that their first significant digits appear in the twenty-third and forty-fifth columns of the DR and DD counters respectively.

The intermediate counter has twenty-four columns. The twenty-fourth column is a four commutator, usually called "four molding", counter. The first molding is used for ordinary read-outs and resets. The second molding is used to determine whether it is necessary to sense through zeros or through nines to obtain the amount of shift necessary in reading DR and DD to their respective counters. The third molding, if the twenty-fourth column stands at nine, forms a part of the pick up circuit of the relays controlling the entry of a nine into the forty-seventh, or sign counter, of the product-quotient counter (PQ). The fourth molding, if the twenty-fourth column stands at nine, forms a part of the pick up circuits of the intermediate invert relay which delivers the positive absolute value of MC, DR, MP or DD if these quantities were negative when they entered the multiply-divide unit. The remaining twenty-three columns of the intermediate counter are three molding counters. The first moldings are used for ordinary read-outs and resets. The second and third moldings are used when sensing through zeros and nines respectively to determine the amount of DR or DD shift.

The nine integer multiples of the MC and DR are built up in the multiplicand-divisor counters (MC-DR), in the first four cycles of multiplication and division respectively. Six counters, storing the (1-2), (3-6), (4-8), (5), (7) and (9) multiples, are used for this purpose. Of these, the first three are equipped with "doubling" read-outs; i.e., they have extra moldings so wired that they may read out either the number upon which they stand or twice that number. The wiring diagram of a doubling counter is shown in Fig. 30. The number impulses are provided as usual by cam controlled contacts. In the counter shown, the read-out may be through one of four relays; reset, build-up, times one or times two. As shown, the doubling counter requires four moldings. The first molding is used for ordinary read-outs and resets. The second molding is used for the doubling read-out when there is no carry from the next lower column. The third molding is used for the doubling read-out when there is carry from the next lower column. The fourth molding controls the doubling read-out of the counter in the next higher columnar position, selecting its second or third molding according as there is not or is carry from the counter under consideration. All of the MC-DR counters have twenty-four columns except MC-DR (1-2), which has twenty-three, and all are equipped with normal carry circuits but no end around carry. MC-DR (5), (7) and (9) are composed of single molding counters exactly similar to those used in the storage registers.

It is interesting to note that two and five are the only integer multiples which may be obtained from a static reading circuit without using an undue amount of equipment. In the case of the two multiple, the only carry number is unity and hence a carry from the nth column to the (n + 1)st cannot affect a column of still higher order. Therefore, the circuits of a doubling read-out must pass through not more than two counter columns. A similar situation obtains in connection with the five multiple as may readily be seen. Since a quintupling counter is not used in the calculator, no further details of such circuits will be given here.

The MP counter consists of twenty-three double molding counter wheels. The first molding of each is used for resets. The second selects the proper multiples of MC to be read out of the MC-DR counters.

The dividend counter has forty-five single molding columns. During multiplication, the multiples selected by the even columns of the multiplier are added into DD in the proper columnar position. Thus, if the digits in MP are 25137, then 3 x (MC) and 5 x (MC) are read into DD in the following positions.

DD counter column

9 8 7 6 5 4 3 2 1

←—— 3 x (MC)→

←—— 5 x (MC)→

The odd multiples of MC are cared for in the PQ counter which will be described later.

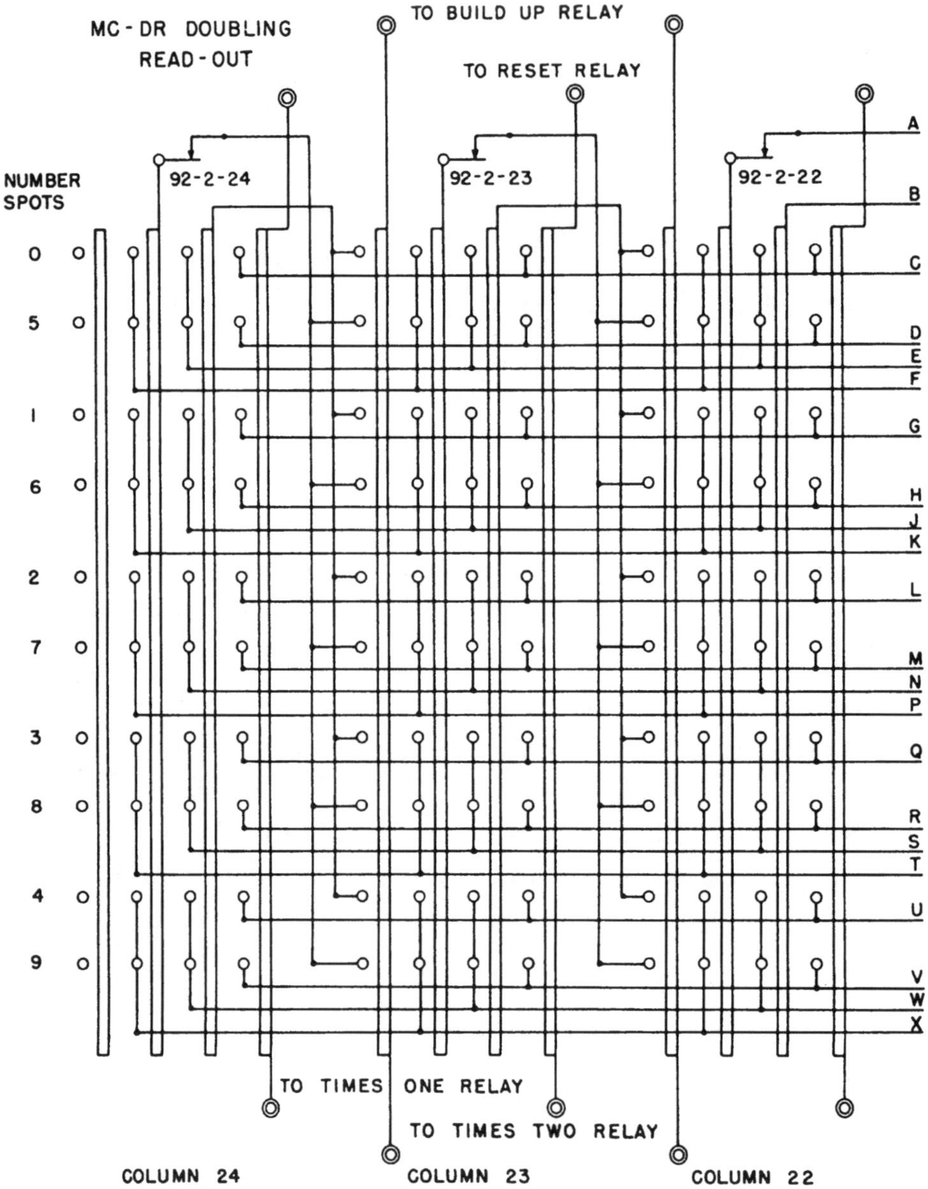
MC - DR DOUBLING
READ - OUT
TO BUILD UP RELAY
TO RESET RELAY
NUMBER
SPOTS
0
5
1
6
2
7
3
8
4
9
92-2-24
92-2-23
92-2-22
A
B
C
D
E
F
G
H
J
K
L
M
N
P
Q
R
S
T
U
V
W
X
TO TIMES ONE RELAY
TO TIMES TWO RELAY
COLUMN 24
COLUMN 23
COLUMN 22

Figure 30 A

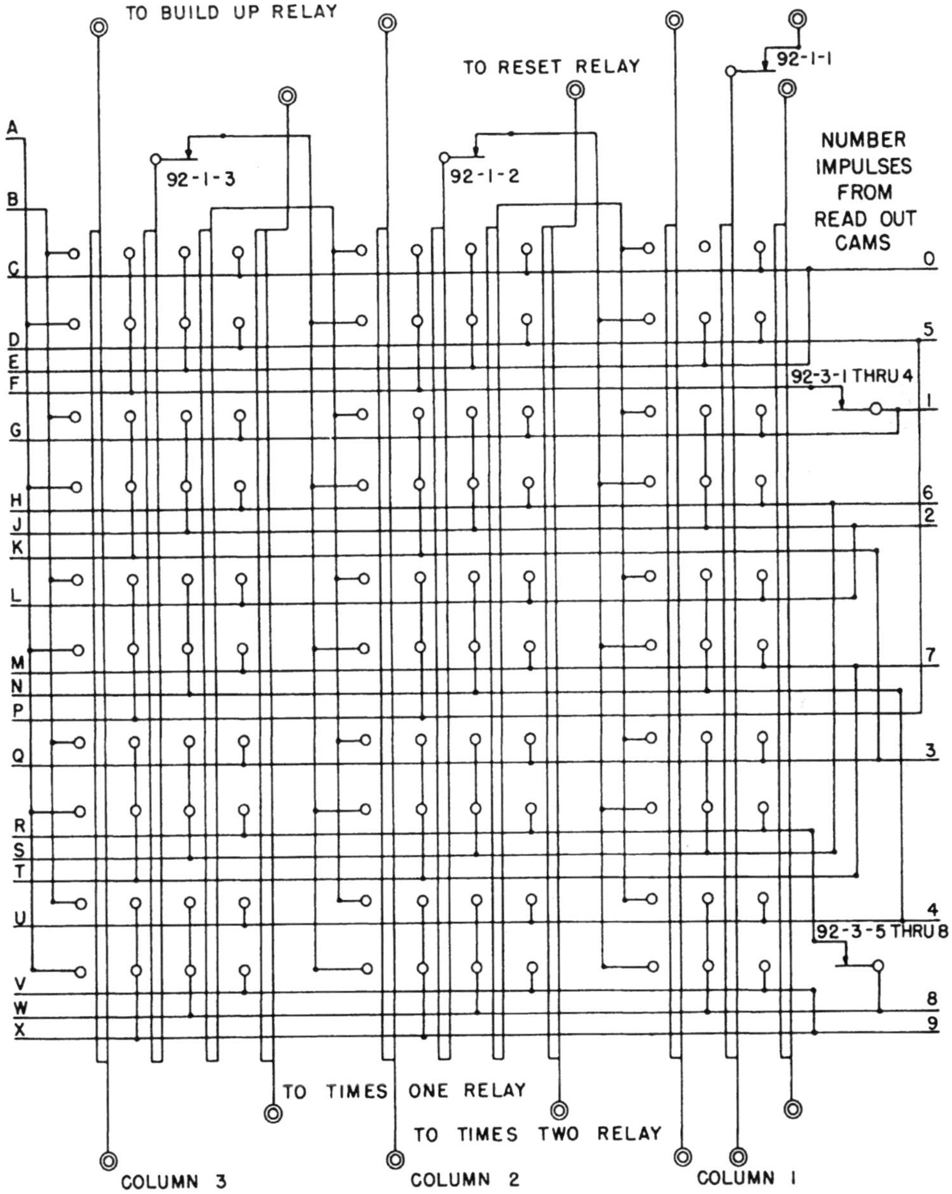
TO BUILD UP RELAY
TO RESET RELAY
92-1-1
92-1-3
92-1-2
NUMBER IMPULSES FROM READ OUT CAMS
A
B
C
D
E
F
G
H
J
K
L
M
N
P
Q
R
S
T
U
V
W
X
0
5
92-3-1 THRU 4
1
6
2
7
3
4
92-3-5 THRU 8
8
9
TO TIMES ONE RELAY
TO TIMES TWO RELAY
COLUMN 3
COLUMN 2
COLUMN 1

Figure 30 B

During division, the successive multiples of DR are subtracted from the dividend in the DD counter. Since these subtractions terminate at least one column to the right with each successive operation, end around carry is replaced by the addition of an elusive one in the lowest order column of each subtrahend.

The product-quotient counter has forty-seven columns. The forty-seventh column of PQ, sometimes called the sign counter, has two moldings. The first of these is used for resets. The second, if the counter stands at nine, forms a part of the circuits picking up the DD-PQ invert relay, in order to read out the negative product or quotient. The sign counter is the only one in the machine which cannot be reset by button. If the machine is stopped before a multiplication or division is terminated, care must be taken to see that this counter is manually reset before continuing operation. This must be accomplished by manipulation of the armature of the counter magnet.

During multiplication, the multiples selected by the odd columns of the multiplier are added into PQ in the proper columnar position. Thus, if the digits in MP are 25137, then 7 x (MC), (MC) and 2 x (MC) are read into PQ in the following positions.

PQ counter column

11 10 9 8 7 6 5 4 3 2 1

←——7 x (MC)→

←(MC)——→

←——2 x (MC)→

At the end of the multiplying operation, the multiples previously added into DD are transferred to PQ and the final product read out from this counter. The device of adding the odd and even multiples of MC into the PQ and DD counters, respectively, doubles the speed of multiplication because two multiples may be added in each machine cycle.

The PQ counter in the case of division receives the digits of the quotient which are read in successively, starting at the forty-sixth column.

The quotient shift counter (QS), as mentioned in Chapter II, is used to calculate the number of columns the quotient must be shifted to the right upon reading out to the buss in order to conform with the operating decimal position. This counter has two columns. The first column is a four molding counter. Of these four moldings, the first is used for reset. The second, third and fourth are used to read out quotient shifts amounting to zero through nine columns, ten through nineteen columns and twenty through twenty-two columns, respectively. The second column of the QS counter has two moldings. The first molding is again used for reset and the second to read out the tens digit of the amount of shift in conjunction with the proper molding of the first column. The quantity standing in the QS counter is not read out in the ordinary manner but rather the combination of number spots in the two columns form a part of the pick up circuit required to select the appropriate section of the Q-shift relay. During each dividing operation the QS counter receives four quantities. These are: (1) the complement on nine of the amount of the DR shift left when reading from the intermediate counter to the MC-DR counters; (2) the amount standing in the divide switch which is equal to 22 - n where the operating decimal point lies between columns n and n + 1; (3) an elusive one in the first column; (4) the amount of the DD shift left when reading from the intermediate counter to the DD counter. The total standing in the Q-shift counter must always be positive, as no provision is made for shifting the quotient to the left because quantities so shifted would be above the capacity of the calculator under the assumed operating decimal position. The shift is counted to the right considering the forty-sixth column of PQ as corresponding to the twenty-third column of the buss.

All of the multiply-divide counters so far described are controlled by a subsidiary sequencing circuit which includes two special counters. The first of these is the sequence counter which has one four molding counter wheel. When the first line of multiply or divide coding has been read, this counter is stepped forward one position. It continues to step once each cycle during the build-up of the integer multiples of MC-DR, for the resets of the intermediate counter and finally for the read-out of the product or quotient. This counter also has the function of signalling the main sequence mechanism to read the line of coding supplying the multiplier or dividend and the line of coding delivering the product or quotient. The first molding of the sequence counter is used for resetting. The functions of the remaining three moldings are best presented in a table which lists the relays whose pick up circuits are governed by each position of the sequence counter. The table includes the relays used both in multiplication and division.

Seq. Ctr.	Second Molding	Third Molding	Fourth Molding
1	Intermediate In	Not used	DD-PQ Reset
2	Shift Pick Up	MC-DR In Q-Shift Invert	Intermediate Invert Control
3	First Build-Up	First and Second Build-Up	Intermediate Reset
4	Intermediate In	First and Second Build-Up	Second Build-Up Add-22
5	Shift Pick Up	MP-In DD-In	Intermediate Invert Control
6	Not used	Not used	Intermediate Reset
7	Sequence Ctr. Reset	MC-DR Reset	Product Out
8	Not used		
9	Not used		

The impulse which steps the sequence counter is not derived from the number impulse cam contacts. This impulse is supplied at zero time by a cam controlled contact, CC-10, and positions the sequence counter fifteen points earlier than all other multiply-divide counters in order to give the associated relay circuits ample time to operate before numbers are transferred.

The second special counter employed by the multiply-divide unit is the cycle counter, which consists of one five molding counter of which the fifth molding is used for resetting. The first four moldings of the cycle counter control the multiplying and dividing operations between sequence counter positions six and seven. During multiplication the cycle counter steps once each cycle and these four moldings determine the columnar positions in DD and PQ to which the multiples of MC are read. During division the cycle counter steps once each subtracting cycle, controlling the columnar positions in DD from which the multiples of DR are subtracted.

The complete circuits for multiplication are given in Appendix IV, and for division in Appendix V. These appendices also include timing diagrams which give the positions of relay and counter magnets as picked up and held by impulses through the cam controlled contacts. The relays used in multiplication and division, including the functions of each wired point, are listed in Appendix VI. Each cam, with the time of make and break of its contact and its function, appears in Appendix VII. The multiply-divide fuses are classified in two ways in Appendix VIII; first, listing the relays and the fuse to which each is connected, and second, listing the fuses and the relays which they serve. Figure 31 shows, cycle by cycle, the transfers of quantities from counter to counter in the multiply-divide unit during the multiplication 0.3461 x 2.5137 = 0.8699. The operation is carried out on the miniature six-column calculator previously mentioned.

Cycle 0

The sequence mechanism reads the first line of multiply coding (A, 761, blank). The sequence counter advances to one.

Cycle 1

The MC is read from storage counter A via the buss to the intermediate counter. The intermediate carry circuits, including end around carry, are energized. The DD, PQ and QS counters are reset. The sequence counter advances to two.

Cycle 2

The positive absolute value of MC is read into MC-DR (1-2), (3-6), (5), (7) and (9) within the multiply unit, (Fig. 32). The sequence counter advances to three.

Cycle 3

If a nine stood in the twenty-fourth column of the intermediate counter (MC ≤ - 0), a nine is read into the forty-seventh column of PQ. The intermediate counter resets. The first build-up takes place; i.e., the first step is taken in building up the nine integer multiples of MC. Twice the MC is read from the doubling moldings of MC-DR (1-2) to MC-DR (3-6), (4-8), (5) and (9) within the multiply unit, (Fig. 32). The sequence counter advances to four. The sequence mechanism reads the second line of multiply coding (B, blank, blank).

Cycle 4

The MP is read from storage counter B via the buss to the intermediate counter. The complete intermediate carry circuits are energized. The second build-up takes place, completing the nine integer

Cyc No.	Storage Counter	Seq Ctr	Intermediate Counter	MC-DR (1-2) Counter	MC-DR (3-6) Counter	MC-DR (4-8) Counter	MC-DR (5) Counter
0	0 0 3 4 6 1 MC	0 1 1	0 0 0 0 0 0	0 0 0 0 0	0 0 0 0 0 0	0 0 0 0 0 0	0 0 0 0 0 0
1	MC to Int	1 1 2	0 0 0 0 0 0 3 4 6 1 0 0 3 4 6 1				
2		2 1 3	MC to MC-DR (1-2),(3-6) (5),(7),(9)	0 0 0 0 0 3 4 6 1 0 3 4 6 1	0 0 0 0 0 0 3 4 6 1 0 0 3 4 6 1		0 0 0 0 0 0 3 4 6 1 0 0 3 4 6 1
3	0 2 5 1 3 7 MP	3 1 4	0 0 3 4 6 1 7 6 4 9 0 0 0 0 0 0	2 times MC to MC-DR (3-6),(4-8) (5),(9)	0 0 3 4 6 1 6 9 2 2 0 1 0 3 8 3	0 0 0 0 0 0 6 9 2 2 0 0 6 9 2 2	0 0 3 4 6 1 6 9 2 2 0 1 0 3 8 3
4	MP to Int	4 1 5	0 0 0 0 0 0 2 5 1 3 7 0 2 5 1 3 7	2 times MC to MC-DR (4-8),(5)	6 times MC to MC-DR (7), (9)	0 0 6 9 2 2 6 9 2 2 0 1 3 8 4 4	0 1 0 3 8 3 6 9 2 2 0 1 7 3 0 5
5		5 1 6	to MP				
6			0 2 5 1 3 7 8 5 9 7 3 0 0 0 0 0 0		to DD		
7				to PQ			to DD
8				to PQ			
9							
10		6 1 7		0 3 4 6 1 7 6 4 9 0 0 0 0 0	0 1 0 3 8 3 9 7 2 7 0 0 0 0 0 0	0 1 3 8 4 4 9 7 2 6 6 0 0 0 0 0 0	0 1 7 3 0 5 9 7 3 5 0 0 0 0 0 0
11	0 0 0 0 0 0 8 6 9 9 0 0 8 6 9 9 P	7 3 0					

Figure 31 A

MC-DR (7) Counter	MC-DR (9) Counter	MP Counter	Cyc Ctr	DD Counter	PQ Counter	Cyc No.
000000	000000	00000	0	329763180	02964153287	0
				329763180 78134792 000000000	02964153287 8146957823 00000000000	1
000000 3461 003461	000000 3461 003461					2
	003461 6922 010383				0 0	3
003461 2 766 024227	010383 2 766 031149					4
		00000 25137 25137	0 1 1			5
to PQ			1 1 2	000000000 1 383 000103830	00000000000 24227 00000024227	6
			2 1 3	000103830 173 5 017408830	00000024227 3461 00000370327	7
			3 1 4		00000370327 6922 00069590327	8
			4 1 5	to PQ	00069590327 883 00069599157	9
024227 86883 000000	031149 79961 000000		5 5 0	to PQ	00069599157 174 00086999157	10
					0 to Storage 0	11

Figure 31 B

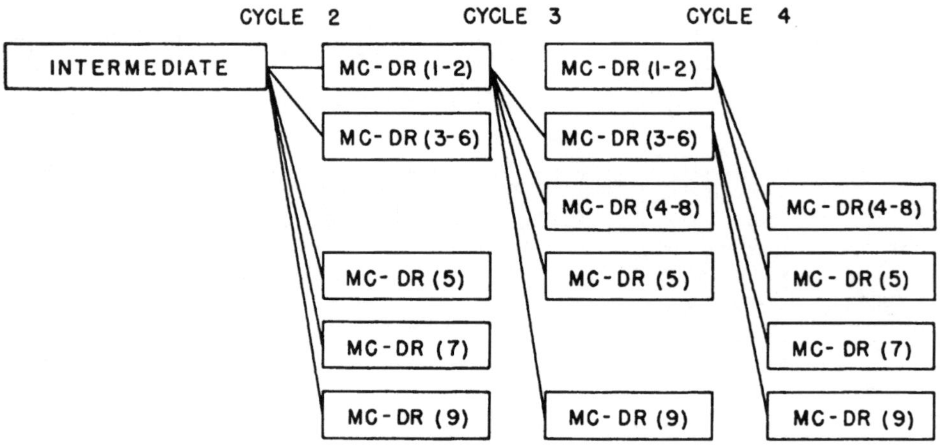

Figure 32

multiples of MC-DR. Twice the MC is read from the doubling moldings of MC-DR (1-2) to MC-DR (4-8) and (5). Six times MC is read from the doubling moldings of MC-DR (3-6) to MC-DR (7) and (9), (Fig. 32). The sequence counter advances to five.

Cycle 5

The positive absolute value of MP is read to the MP counter from the intermediate counter. The sequence counter advances to six. The cycle counter advances to one.

Cycle 6

If a nine stood in the twenty-fourth column of the intermediate counter (MP ≤ - 0), a nine is read into the forty-seventh column of PQ. There is no end around carry from column forty-seven to column one of PQ. The eight spot of column forty-seven of PQ is jumpered to the zero spot. The algebraic sign is, therefore, cared for in the following manner.

$+ \cdot + = +$ corresponds to $0 + 0 = 0$,

$+ \cdot - = -$ corresponds to $0 + 9 = 9$,

$- \cdot + = -$ corresponds to $9 + 0 = 9$,

$- \cdot - = +$ corresponds to $9 + 9 \rightarrow 8 \rightarrow 0$.

If, at the end of multiplication, a nine stands in the forty-seventh column of PQ, the product is inverted as it is read out into the buss, since it stands in PQ as a positive absolute magnitude. The intermediate counter resets and is ready for the next multiplying or dividing operation. Under control of the cycle counter, the multiples corresponding to the digits in the first and second columns of MP are added into PQ and DD respectively. The cycle counter is advanced to two.

The multiples of MC continue to be selected in pairs and added, while the shift circuits advance the columns of entry into PQ and DD under control of the cycle counter. If both of a pair of digits of MP, one in an odd and one in an even column, are zero, the next pair of multiples is immediately properly shifted and added. If the entire MP is zero, cycle 6 is combined with cycle 9. If the MP is not zero, but contains n non-zero digits in either the odd or even numbered columns, whichever is the greater, then n - 1 cycles intervene between cycle 6 and cycle 9 → 6 + n. Thus, in order to increase the speed of multiplication, whenever possible the number having the fewer non-zero digits should be used as the multiplier. If a multiplication is to be performed in which one factor is a constant, this quantity should usually be used as the multiplier because the number of non-zero digits and their positions are known. This makes it possible to interpose a predetermined number of operations during the multiplication. (See Chapter IV, Coding, Multiplication.)

Cycle 7 (4 + n)

A pair of multiples is added into PQ and DD. The cycle counter is advanced.

Cycle 8 (5 + n)

The last pair of multiples is added into PQ and DD. The cycle counter is advanced.

Cycle 9 (6 + n)

The first DD to PQ transfer takes place. The quantity standing in the lower half of DD is added into the lower half of PQ. The cycle counter is advanced for the last time. If MP = 0, this cycle combines with cycle 6.

Cycle 10 (7 + n)

The second DD to PQ transfer takes place. The quantity standing in the upper half of DD is added into the upper half of PQ. The MC-DR, MP and cycle counters are reset in preparation for the next operation. If the multiplying operation is interrupted, these counters together with the intermediate, sequence and PQ sign counters must be manually reset before continuing operation. The sequence counter advances to seven. The sequence mechanism reads the last line of multiply coding (blank, C, 7).

Cycle 11 (8 + n)

The product is read out to storage counter C via the buss and the multiply plugging. (See Chapter V, Plugging Instructions.) The product is inverted if a nine stands in the forty-seventh column of PQ. The sequence counter and the forty-seventh column of PQ, the sign counter, are reset. The sequence mechanism reads the next line of coding.

It may readily be seen from Fig. 31 that the rounding off error in multiplication is less than one in the lowest order column read out; i.e., if the operating decimal point lies, for example, between columns 15 and 16, the rounding off error will be less than 1×10^{-15}.

Included in Appendix IV are the circuits of the low order read-out of PQ and of the normalizing register, both described in Chapter II. The use of these circuits and their coding is considered in detail under High Accuracy Computation and Normalizing Register in Chapter IV.

Division makes use of all of the functional counters used in multiplication except the MP counter. This process does, however, make use of the QS counter, previously described on page 72. The pair of dial switches just to the right of the sequence mechanism must be set to 22 - n where the operating decimal point lies between columns n and n + 1. Division also requires plugging to terminate the operation after the desired number of comparisons have been made. This plugging and the coding controlling it are considered under Division in Chapters IV and V.

Figure 33 shows the transfer, cycle by cycle, of the quantities in the multiply-divide unit during division. Again the miniature six-column calculator is used for purposes of illustration. The division of - 0.375 by + 0.213 to give - 1.760 is performed. The operating decimal point is considered to lie between columns three and four, the divide switch being set at 4 - n = 4 - 3 = 1, since column four of the miniature calculator corresponds to column twenty-two of the actual machine. The division is considered to be plugged for five comparisons.

Cycle 0

The sequence mechanism reads the first line of divide coding (A, 76, blank). The sequence counter advances to one.

ELECTRICAL CIRCUITS

Cycle 1

The DR is read from storage counter A via the buss to the intermediate counter. The intermediate carry circuits, including end around carry, are energized. The DD, PQ and QS counters are reset. The sequence counter advances to two.

Cycle 2

The positive absolute value of DR is read, without traversing the buss, to MC-DR (1-2), (3-6), (5), (7) and (9) so shifted that its highest significant digit appears in the twenty-third column of MC-DR (1-2). The complement on nine of the number of columns the DR is shifted left is read into the QS counter. An elusive one is read into the first column of the QS counter. The sequence counter advances to three.

Cycle 3

If a nine stood in the twenty-fourth column of the intermediate counter (DR $\leq$ - 0), a nine is read into the forty-seventh column of PQ. The intermediate counter resets. The first build-up takes place. Twice the DR is read from the doubling moldings of MC-DR (1-2) to MC-DR (3-6), (4-8), (5) and (9) within the multiply-divide unit. The sequence counter advances to four. The sequence mechanism reads the second line of divide coding (B, blank, blank).

Cycle 4

The DD is read from storage counter B via the buss to the intermediate counter. The complete intermediate carry circuits are energized. The second build-up takes place, completing the nine integer multiples of DR. Twice the DR is read from the doubling moldings of MC-DR (1-2) to MC-DR (4-8) and (5). Six times DR is read from the doubling moldings of MC-DR (3-6) to MC-DR (7) and (9). The quantity standing in the divide switch is read into the QS counter. The sequence counter advances to five.

Cycle 5

The positive absolute value of DD is read into the DD counter so shifted that its highest significant digit appears in the forty-fifth column of DD. The number of columns the DD is shifted left is read into the QS counter, completing the computation of the number of columns the quotient must be shifted to the right when it is read out. The sequence counter advances to six and the cycle counter to one.

Cyc No.	Storage Counter	Seq Ctr	Intermediate Counter	MC-DR (1-2) Counter	MC-DR (3-6) Counter	MC-DR (4-8) Counter	MC-DR (5) Counter
0	0 0 0 2 1 3 DR	0 1 1	0 0 0 0 0 0	0 0 0 0 0	0 0 0 0 0 0	0 0 0 0 0 0	0 0 0 0 0 0
1	DR to Int	1 1 2	0 0 0 0 0 0 2 1 3 0 0 0 2 1 3				
2		2 1 3	DR to MC-DR (1-2),(3-6) (5),(7),(9)	0 0 0 0 0 2 1 3 2 1 3 0 0	0 0 0 0 0 0 2 1 3 0 2 1 3 0 0		0 0 0 0 0 0 2 1 3 0 2 1 3 0 0
3	9 9 9 6 2 4 DD	3 1 4	0 0 0 2 1 3 8 9 7 0 0 0 0 0 0	2 times DR to MC-DR (3-6),(4-8) (5),(9)	0 2 1 3 0 0 4 2 6 0 6 3 9 0 0	0 0 0 0 0 0 4 2 6 0 4 2 6 0 0	0 2 1 3 0 0 4 2 6 0 6 3 9 0 0
4	DD to Int	4 1 5	0 0 0 0 0 0 9 9 9 6 2 4 9 9 9 6 2 4	2 times DR to MC-DR (4-8), (5)	6 times DR to MC-DR (7), (9)	0 4 2 6 0 0 4 2 6 0 8 5 2 0 0	0 6 3 9 0 0 4 2 6 1 0 6 5 0 0
5		5 1 6	to DD				
6			9 9 9 6 2 4 1 1 1 4 8 6 0 0 0 0 0 0	to DR Compare	to DR Compare	to DR Compare	to DR Compare
7				inverted to DD			
8				to DR Compare	to DR Compare	to DR Compare	to DR Compare
9							
10				to DR Compare	to DR Compare	to DR Compare	to DR Compare
11					6 times DR inverted to DD		
12				to DR Compare	to DR Compare	to DR Compare	to DR Compare
13				to DR Compare	to DR Compare	to DR Compare	to DR Compare
14		6 1 7					inverted to DD
15	0 0 0 0 0 0 9 9 8 2 3 9 9 9 8 2 3 9	7 3 0		2 1 3 0 0 8 9 7 0 0 0 0 0	0 6 3 9 0 0 4 7 1 0 0 0 0 0 0	0 8 5 2 0 0 2 5 8 0 0 0 0 0 0	1 0 6 5 0 0 9 4 5 0 0 0 0 0 0

Figure 33 A

MC-DR (7) Counter	MC-DR (9) Counter	QS Ctr	Cyc Ctr	DD Counter	PQ Counter	Cyc No.
000000	000000	2	0	163649670	88532075484	0
		2 8 0		163649670 947461143 000000000	88532075484 22578 35626 00000000000	1
000000 213 021300	000000 213 021300	0 7 1 8				2
	021300 426 063900				0 0	3
021300 1278 149100	063900 1278 191700	8 1 9				4
		9 2 1	0 1 1	000000000 375 375000000		5
to DR Compare	to DR Compare			to DD Compare	0 9 9	6
			1 1 2	375000000 78699 1 162000000	90000000000 1 91000000000	7
to DR Compare	to DR Compare			to DD Compare		8
Inverted to DD			2 1 3	162000000 85 899 1 012900000	91000000000 7 91700000000	9
to DR Compare	to DR Compare			to DD Compare		10
			3 1 4	012900000 872199 1 100120000	91700000000 6 91760000000	11
to DR Compare	to DR Compare			to DD Compare		12
to DR Compare	to DR Compare			to DD Compare		13
			4 1 5	100120000 893499 1 101013500	91760000000 5 91760500000	14
149100 9619 000000	191700 9193 000000		5 5 0		9 1 to Storage 0	15

Figure 33 B

Cycle 6

If a nine stood in the twenty-fourth column of the intermediate counter (DD ≤ - 0), a nine is read into the forty-seventh column of PQ, completing the determination of the algebraic sign of the quotient by the same means as are used in multiplication. The intermediate counter resets and is ready for the next multiplying or dividing operation. The nine integer multiples of the divisor are read to the DR compare relay and the dividend is read to the DD compare relay. A sensing circuit through the compare relays selects the largest multiple of the divisor less than the dividend. If all multiples are greater than DD, the cycle becomes a "no go" cycle and the comparison is made again, shifted one column to the right, in the next succeeding cycle. Since all comparing operations are identical, the comparing circuits and their operation will be illustrated and described in connection with cycle 10.

Cycle 7

The selected multiple of DR is subtracted from DD, with an elusive one added in the first column of the subtrahend. The digit defining the multiple is entered in the PQ counter. The cycle counter is advanced.

Cycles 8 and 9

These two cycles of the example duplicate the compare and subtract operations described in cycles 6 and 7.

Cycle 10

This cycle duplicates the comparing operations performed in cycles 6 and 8. According to Fig. 33, the quantity 012900000 now stands in the DD counter. Since, in the example, cycle 10 makes the third comparison, the quantity 129000 is transferred to the DD compare relay. This transfer is accomplished by circuits of which one column is shown in Fig. 34. In these and following circuits, certain relay and hold points, not necessary to the discussion, have been omitted for the sake of brevity and clarity. The complete circuits will be found in Appendix V.

The quantity 129000 is transferred to the DD compare relay by impulses derived from the cam controlled contacts CC-1 through -9. By impulses derived from the same cam controlled contacts, Fig. 34, each of the nine integer multiples of the divisor is read to the DR compare relay. The compare relays are all provided with hold circuits, not shown in the figure, such that these relays once

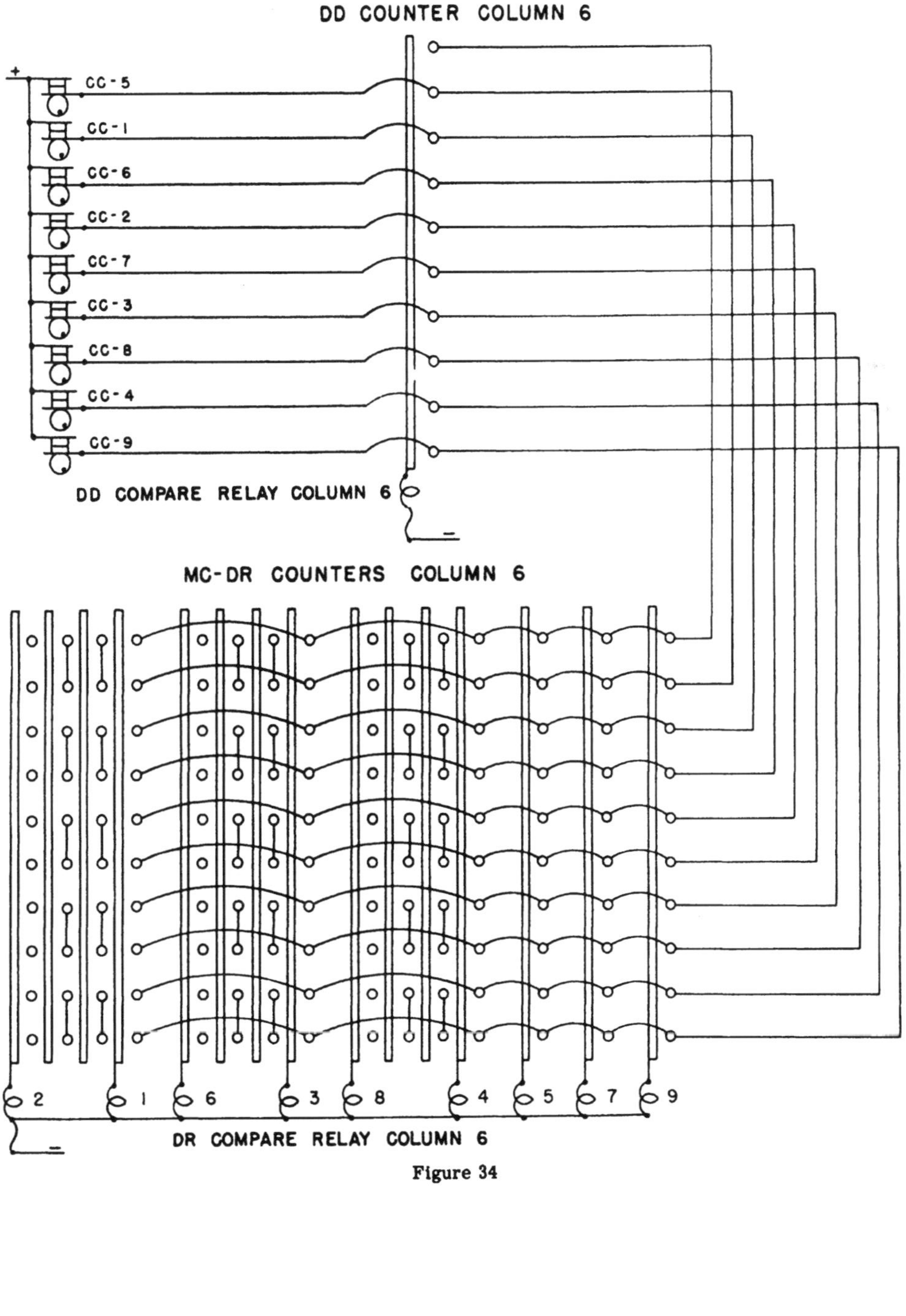
DD COUNTER COLUMN 6
+
CC-5
CC-1
CC-6
CC-2
CC-7
CC-3
CC-8
CC-4
CC-9
DD COMPARE RELAY COLUMN 6
−
MC-DR COUNTERS COLUMN 6
2
1
6
3
8
4
5
7
9
−
DR COMPARE RELAY COLUMN 6

Figure 34

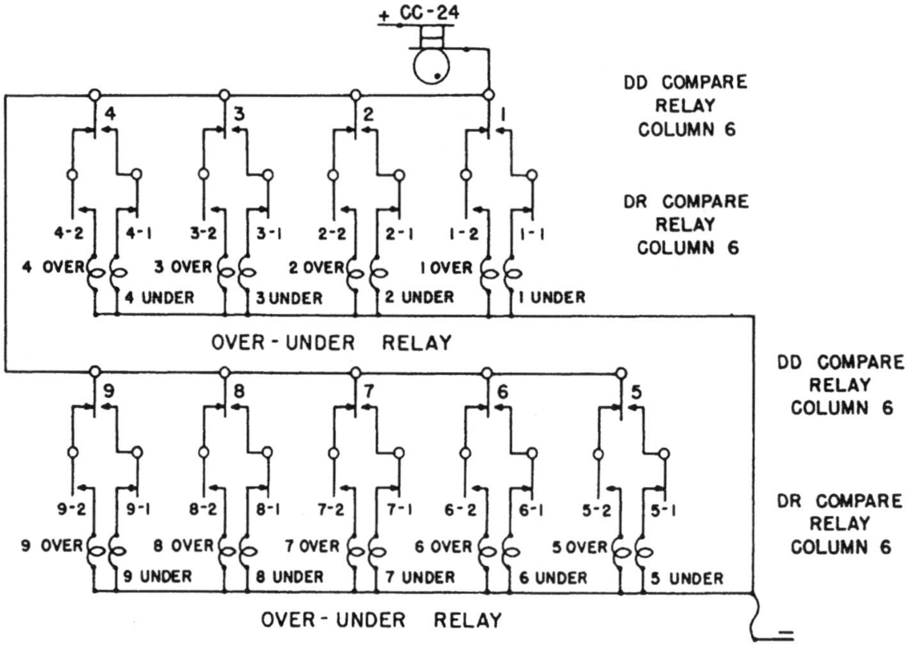

Figure 35

picked up remain energized until twelve time. With the aid of the compare relays, DD is compared with each of the nine integer multiples of DR at one and the same time. How this is accomplished will be explained for the case of the sixth column of the miniature calculator. The integer standing in this column of DD is one. The integers standing in the corresponding columns of the multiples of DR, one through nine, are 0, 0, 0, 0, 1, 1, 1, 1, 1, respectively. At "one time" the DD compare relay is picked up. At the same time, the DR compare relays associated with the five, six, seven, eight and nine multiples are likewise picked up. As previously stated, all these relays are held until twelve time.

The DD and DR compare relays have contacts wired as shown in Fig. 35, known as the over-under circuits. The over and under relays are picked up by impulses supplied by the cam controlled contact, CC-24, which is timed one-quarter impulse later than each of the number impulses derived from CC-1 through -9. Each over relay is picked up through a normally open point of a DR compare relay and a corresponding normally closed contact of the DD compare relay. Similarly, each under relay is picked up through a normally closed point of a DR compare relay and a corresponding normally open contact of the DD compare relay. Three cases must now be distinguished. (1) If the digit of a DR multiple is greater than the digit of DD, the DR compare relay corresponding to the given multiple is picked up before the DD compare relay and a circuit is completed through the normally closed point of the DD compare relay and the normally open point of the DR compare relay to pick up the over relay. (2) If the digit of a DR multiple is less than the digit of DD, the DR compare relay corresponding to the given multiple is picked up after the DD compare relay and a circuit is completed through the normally open point of the DD compare relay and the normally closed point of the DR compare relay to pick up the under relay. This is true of the one, two, three and four multiples in the example under consideration. (3) If the digit of a DR multiple is equal to the digit of DD, the DR and DD compare relays are picked up simultaneously and no circuit is completed to pick up either an over or an under relay. This situation occurs in the case of the five, six, seven, eight and nine multiples in the example.

All of the over-under relays, like the compare relays, are held until twelve time. Recalling that Figs. 34 and 35 are drawn for one column only, it should now be clear that the miniature calculator has six DD compare, fifty-four DR compare and ninety-nine over-under relays corresponding to twenty-four DD compare, 216 DR compare and 423 over-under relays in the calculator itself.

The over-under relays of all columns have contacts connected to form nine identical circuits, called Q control circuits, one of which is shown in Fig. 36. These circuits are supplied with an

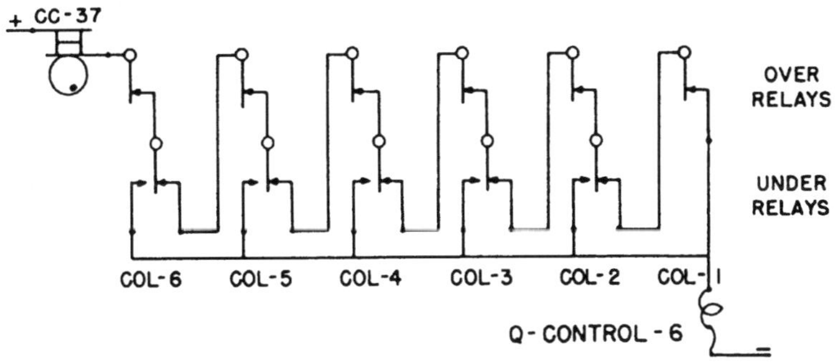

Figure 36

impulse at eleven time by the cam controlled contact CC-37. Each circuit controls the pick up of one of the nine Q control relays. The operation of these circuits may be made clear by a discussion of the relays associated with the two highest columns. Three cases must again be distinguished. (1) If the digit of a DR multiple is greater than the digit of DD in the sixth column, Fig. 36, the normally closed over relay contact of column six will be open. No circuit will be closed to pick up a Q control relay. (2) If the digit of a DR multiple is less than the digit of DD in the sixth column, the over relay contact remains closed, the under relay transfers its contact and the circuit is completed to energize a Q control relay. (3) If the digit of a DR multiple is equal to the digit of DD in the sixth column, neither the over nor the under relay is picked up. In this case the operation of the circuit is controlled by the over-under relays associated with the fifth column and so on.

In the particular case of the example under consideration, the sixth Q control relay is picked up by the normally open under relay contact of column four, since the digits in columns six and five have been found equal. The Q control relays once picked up are held until nine time.

The last step in the comparison cycle consists of the selection of the multiple of the divisor to be subtracted from the DD counter in the next succeeding cycle. This is accomplished by the circuit shown in Fig. 37 made up of contacts of the Q control relays of which there are nine, one for each integer multiple. The Q control relays have, by the over-under relays, been divided into two classes: those not picked up, corresponding to DR multiples greater than DD; those which are energized and correspond to DR multiples less than DD. In Fig. 37, the cam controlled contact CC-31 at twelve and

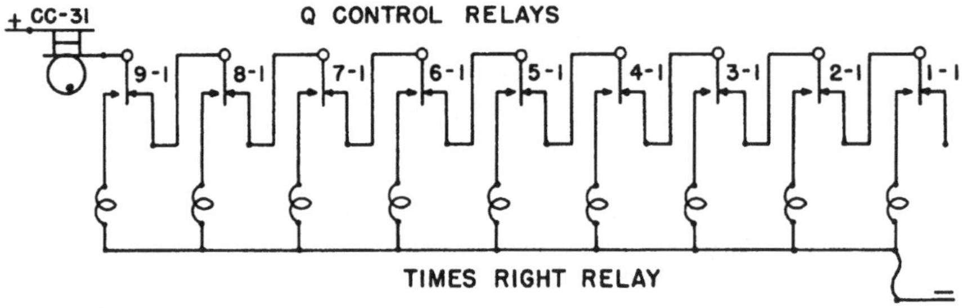

Figure 37

one-half time delivers an impulse to pick up the appropriate part of the "times right" relay corresponding to the positions of the contacts of the Q control relays. In the example, the nine, eight and seven multiples are all greater than DD, while the six multiple is the largest multiple less than DD. Hence, the impulse supplied by CC-31 passes through the normally closed Q control contacts nine, eight and seven, and through the normally open contact, six, to the six times section of the times right relay. In the next cycle this six times section of the times right relay serves as an out relay when reading the selected six multiple to the DD counter for subtraction. The times right relay also controls the entry of the digit defining the multiple into the PQ counter. The simple circuit for accomplishing this is given in Appendix V.

Cycle 11

This is a subtract cycle duplicating the subtracting operation of cycles 7 and 9. The appropriate digit is entered into the PQ counter. The cycle counter is advanced.

Cycle 12

This is a compare cycle which yields a no go in the example.

Cycle 13

This is the fifth compare cycle. The place limitation plugging becomes operative to energize the relay circuits terminating the division under discussion. If the calculator is plugged for n comparisons, a minimum of n + 1 cycles and a maximum of 2n cycles will occur between the reading of the dividend to the DD counter (cycle 5) and the read-out of the quotient (cycle 15).

Cycle 14

The last subtraction is made in the DD counter and the last digit of the quotient entered in the PQ counter. The cycle and sequence counters are advanced for the last time. The sequence mechanism reads the last line of divide coding (blank, C, 7).

Cycle 15

The quotient is read out to storage counter C via the buss and that part of the quotient-shift relay selected by the quantity standing in the QS counter. The quotient is inverted if a nine stands in the forty-seventh column of PQ. The MC-DR, sequence, cycle and sign (forty-seventh column of PQ) counters are reset. The sequence mechanism reads the next line of coding.

It may be seen from Fig. 33 that the rounding off error in division is either less than one in the lowest order column read out, or less than one in the column in which the last comparison is made. If the operating decimal point lies between columns 15 and 16 and division is plugged for n comparisons, the rounding off error is less than 1×10^{-15} or 1×10^{-n}, whichever is the greater.

The discussion of division completes the description of the fundamental computing circuits of the calculator, those of addition, subtraction, multiplication and division. There remain to be discussed the functional units. These consist of subsidiary sequence circuits which control the multiply-divide unit and certain special counters. These counters are mounted to the right of the multiply-divide unit, Plate XI, and are arranged as shown in Fig. 38. Among the special counters are the logarithm in-out counter (LIO), the logarithm counter (LOG), the exponential in-out counter (EIO) and the sine in-out counter (SIO). As described on pages 37 and 38, the LIO and SIO counters are available for arithmetic operations in addition to their normal use in their respective units. The logarithm sequence (LS), logarithm cycle (LC), exponential sequence (ES) and two sine sequence (SS_1 and SS_2) counters are subsidiary sequence controls similar to the sequence and cycle counters of the multiply-divide unit. In addition to the functional counters and the multiply-divide unit, these sequence counters

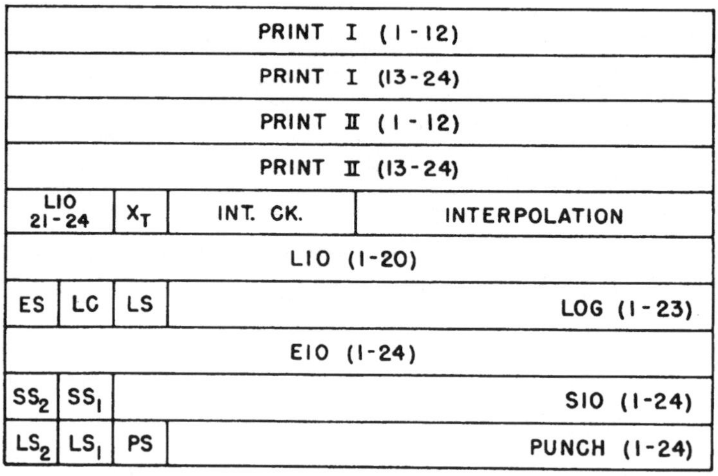

Figure 38

also control certain table relays. The wiring of a table relay (columns thirteen through twenty-four) containing π and reading directly into the buss is shown in Fig. 39. Such a relay is picked up through the subsidiary sequence control and held through one of its own points during that part of a machine cycle given over to the nine number impulses.

Since the computation of the logarithm, exponential and sine is accomplished by the multiply-divide unit operating in conjunction with the functional counters and certain table relays, a complete discussion of the electro-mechanical tables of these functions would further require only a description of the functional sequence circuits. The theory of the methods employed together with the order in which the operations are performed in the computation of the logarithm, exponential and sine was set forth on pages 28 through 37 of Chapter II. The sequence circuits of the functional units are elaborate extensions of the circuits already described under multiplication and division covering a great many cycles. They would require a protracted discussion to set forth their operations cycle by cycle. Since no new ideas of circuit design are introduced, the description would add but little to an understanding of the basic principles of the calculator. Hence, the functional units will receive no further attention here.

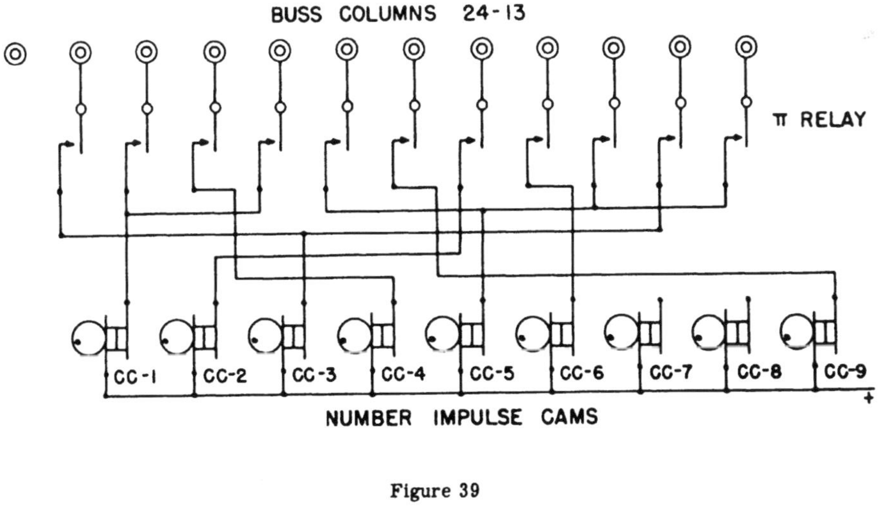

Figure 39

The interpolator units make use of three special counters (Fig. 38), the interpolation, the interpolation check and the X_t counters. All three of these function during tape positioning. As stated in Chapter II, the interpolation counter receives the argument (and the highest order column of h) to which the tape is to be positioned. The interpolation check counter also receives the argument, in order to check the position of the tape when the interpolator mechanism has come to rest. The X_t counter counts the number of coefficients passed over in stepping the tape and signals for a one to be added or subtracted from the interpolation counter for each argument passed over. Once the tape has been positioned, relay networks together with the X_t counter control the computation. The interpolation sequence circuits again are of the same general type as those used in the functional units, dictating the operations to be performed by the multiply unit. The process of interpolation, however, is further complicated by the necessity of reading numerical values from a tape. The reading of a functional or value tape is similar to the reading of a sequence control tape, except that four lines of holes, covering the same space as two lines of coding are read simultaneously, (Figs. 13 and 14). Fig. 40 shows one column of the wiring employed for this purpose. The reading contacts are closed in the distribution demanded by the punching in the tape, not shown in the figure. An impulse supplied by FC-54 passes through the closed reading contacts to energize the value tape relays. These relays are held through their own fourth points and FC-55. The value tape relays, like the sequence relays,

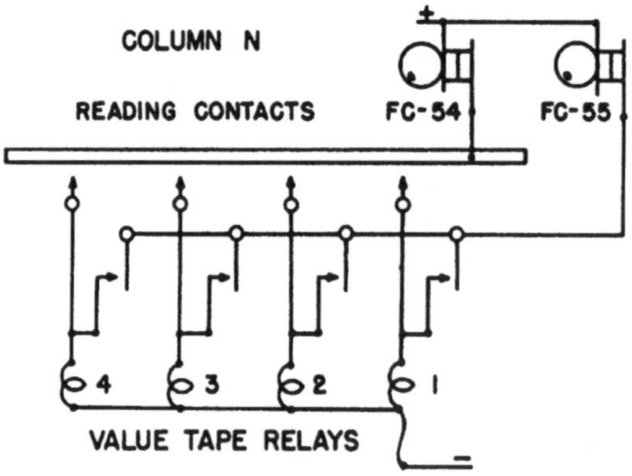

Figure 40

form a cascade. The nine number impulses are read through a cascade (Fig. 41) for each column of the tape to the corresponding column of the buss. Actually, Fig. 41 is drawn for the case of a value tape rather than a functional tape and hence reads directly into the buss without passing through the plugging and relays as required by the process of interpolation. (See Chapter V, Interpolators.)

In addition to the counters given over to the electro-mechanical tables of functions, Fig. 38 also shows the print and punch registers employed in the recording of computed results. The punch register has twenty-four double molding counters and is equipped with complete carry circuits including end around carry. The first moldings are employed for resets and for ordinary read-outs, thus making the punch register available for use as an additional storage counter. The second moldings are used to deliver the quantity standing in the punch register to the punch itself. This is accomplished by means

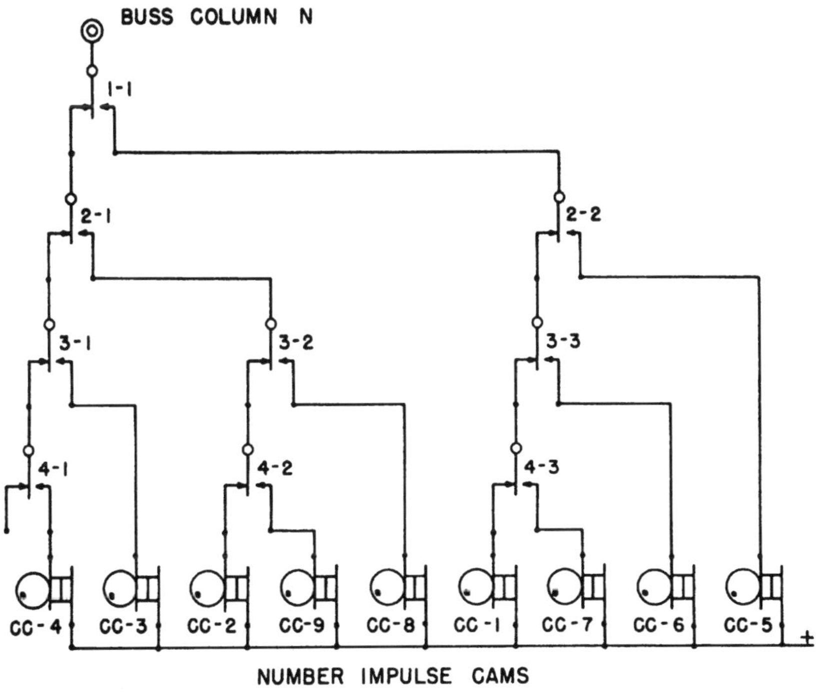

Figure 41

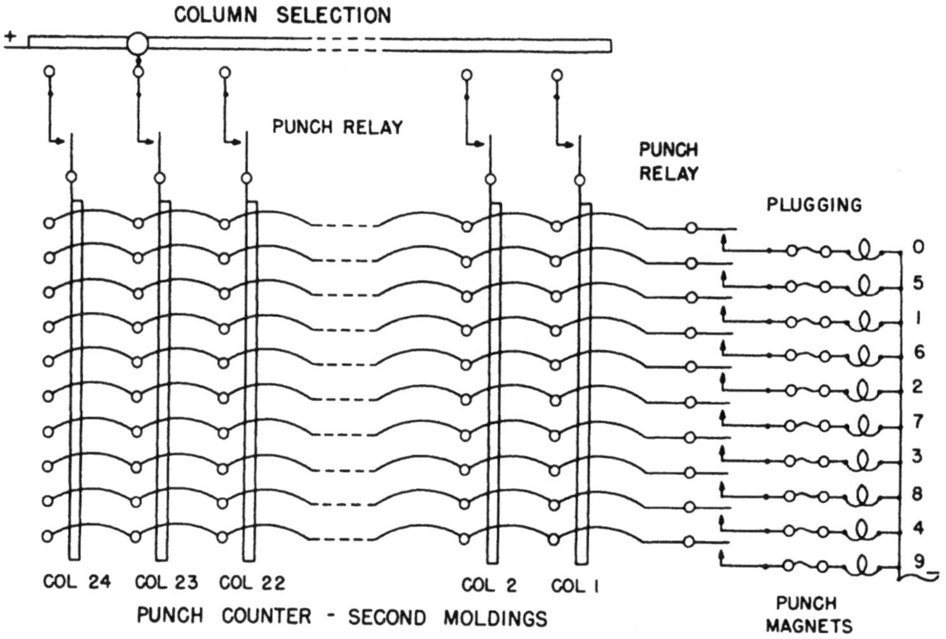

Figure 42

of the circuit shown in Fig. 42. An impulse through the column selection contact of the punch and through the energized punch relay passes to the half slip ring of the twenty-fourth column of the punch counter. From the half slip ring it travels via the brushes to the number spot, through another contact of the punch relay to the punch magnets. The punch magnets control the punches which perforate a standard tabulating machine card as shown in Fig. 43. The quantity e, the base of natural logarithms, and a serial number have been entered in this card. The operation of the punch magnets also completes circuits which control the forward motion of the card to the next column and the movement of the column selection contact to the next lower column of the punch counter. The operation is repeated until the integer in column one has been punched. The card is then skipped out of the punch and stacked. The punch relay is energized and the punching operation initiated by the code Miscellaneous 5. The normally closed contacts of the punch relay, not shown in the diagram, complete the ordinary read-out circuits of the punch counter.

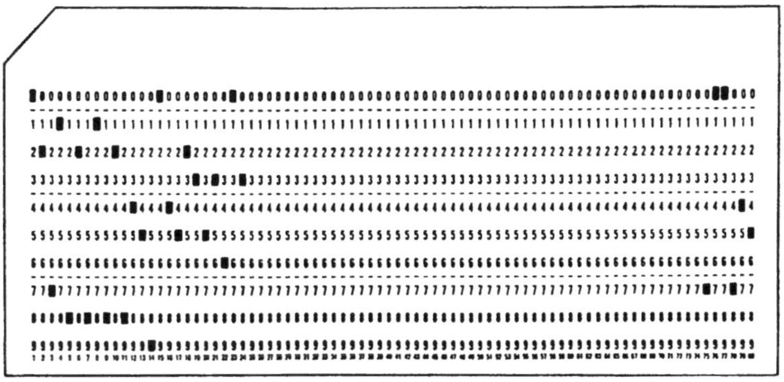

Figure 43

The punch is equipped with a special circuit such that if there is no card in punching position, a stop control prevents punching, stops the calculator and lights a red signal light. Other than this circuit to avoid the loss of computed results, the punch wiring is of the standard type described in the publications of the International Business Machines Corporation.

The moveable column selection contact of the punch is replaced in the print circuit by the print step counter (PS), (Fig. 38). The print circuit is similar to the punch circuit, but considerably more complicated due to the fact that the complements on nine as delivered to the print counters must be inverted and printed in true form. The print circuit is further complicated because of the flexibility required in the printing operation. For example, the typewriter plugboards provide controls by means of which zeros may be dropped off to the right and left, decimal points and minus signs may be printed and the digits of the quantity horizontally spaced as desired. The plugging of the two line step counters (LS_1 and LS_2) controls the vertical spacing of the quantities being printed. All of the plugging necessary to the printing operation is described in detail in Chapter V.

The two print counters (Fig. 38) have complete carry circuits, including end around carry, and may perform all of the operations of normal storage counters. They consist of twenty-four four molding counters. The first molding is used for ordinary operations and resets. However, all four moldings are used to deliver the quantities in the print counter to the magnets which operate the number keys of the typewriters. Except for these magnets the typewriters (Plate XIV) are standard writing machines manufactured by the International Business Machines Corporation and described in detail in that company's publications.

Located just below the typewriters (Plate XIV) are two card feeds. These read quantities from standard tabulating machine cards (Fig. 43) into the calculator under control of the sequence mechanism. Sequence relays control the pick up of the solenoids directing the downward motion of the card through the feed and the pick up of the brush control relay. The nine number impulses, provided by the control cams CC-17, 19, 21 and 23 are routed through a brush to the common roller, (Fig. 44).

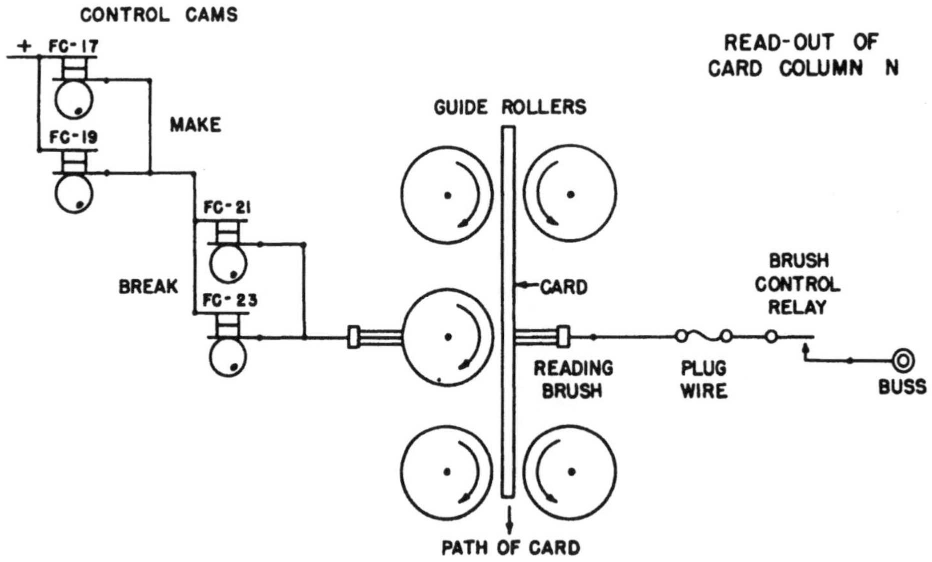

Figure 44

The reading brush of each card column makes contact with the common roller through the perforations in the card. The motion of the card between the brushes and the common roller is so timed that the number impulses and the number perforations in the card are synchronized. From the reading brush, the impulse travels via the plugging and the brush control relay to the buss. The card feeds are equipped with an automatic control such that a card jam or lack of cards in the feeds will stop the calculator and light a red signal light. Like the card punch and the typewriters, descriptions of the card feeds may be found in the publications of the International Business Machines Corporation.

The card feeds are the last of the component parts of the calculator to be described in this chapter. The discussion of electrical circuits here given is far from complete. It is hoped, however, that it will furnish an adequate preparation for the coding and plugging procedures to be discussed in the two following chapters. These, followed by a study of the examples given in Chapter VI, will enable a mathematician to make full use of the calculator, and to exploit its facilities to the greatest possible advantage.

CHAPTER IV

CODING

"These Babes of Grace should be taught by a master well verst in the cant language or slang patter, in which they should by all means excel."
Early Elizabethan. Quoted in "Secret and Urgent" by Fletcher Pratt

The basic codes initiating the various available operations of the calculator may be employed one after another as required in the solution of a problem without further change. However, in order to attain the maximum speed of computation, full advantage must be taken of the methods of interposition. These are governed by a set of rules which can best be made clear by the study of a large number of examples. There are many coding routines, such as that for determining the square root by an iterative process, which occur so frequently as to make standard coding procedures of real value. This chapter includes the following sections containing the basic codes and certain of the longer procedures.

SUMMARY OF OPERATIONAL CODES

The operational codes include all codes except those of the switches and the storage counters. An operational code is defined as automatic if it initiates a process which controls the operation of the machine for one or more succeeding cycles. A code which is non-automatic is read, acted upon and the sequence mechanism steps to the next line of coding but does not read it. A non-automatic code must lie under the control of an automatic code or a Miscellaneous 7 must be added.

Automatic Codes

	OUT	IN	MISC.
Stop code. If the control switch on the sequence mechanism is down and the stop key depressed, the machine will stop on the line following the next 87 code.			87
Read the next line of coding and step to the one beyond. If the control switch on the sequence mechanism is in the up position and the stop key down, the machine will stop on the line following the next 7 code.			7
Punch and complete punching before starting next operation. Stop the machine if there is no card in punching position.			51
Print and complete printing before starting next operation. Used when 752 or 7521 is in the In column.			6
Drop out tape selection relays.			61
Automatic check.			64
Interpolator position tape to the closest lower value of the argument. May replace 61.			641
Read into EIO counter.		741	
Read into print counter I.		7432	
Read into print counter II.		74321	
Read into punch counter. Stop the machine if there is no card in punching position.		753	

CODING

	OUT	IN	MISC.
Divide.		76	
Multiply.		761	
Logarithm.		762	
Exponential.		7621	
Interpolate.		763	
Sine.		7631	
Select interpolator I.		7654	
Select interpolator II.		76541	
Select interpolator III.		76542	
Print counter I half pick-up.		76543	
Print counter II half pick-up.		765431	
Read into SIO counter (read-in II, plugged).		8741	
Read out of EIO counter.	832		
Read "h" correction into intermediate counter.		841	

SUMMARY OF OPERATIONAL CODES

Non-Automatic Codes

	OUT	IN	MISC.
Read out negative absolute value from storage counter.			1
Read out positive absolute value from storage counter.			2
Invert read-out of IVS or switch.			21
Reset IC counter.			3
Reset EIO counter.			31
Invert read-out of any storage counter or switch except IVS.			32
Reset SIO counter.			321
Invert or do not invert read-out of any storage counter or switch (except IVS) under control of counter 70.			432
Punch.			5
Step interpolator I ahead.			53
Step interpolator II ahead.			531
Step interpolator III ahead.			532
Step interpolator I back			54

	OUT	IN	MISC.
Step interpolator II back.			541
Step interpolator III back.			542
Pick up interpolation sequence control relay.			62
Reset LIO counter.			63
Read from card feed I.			632
Read from card feed II.			6321
Place limitation in division.			643
Place limitation in division.			6431
Place limitation in division.			6432
Place limitation in division.			64321
Print on typewriter I.		752	
Print on typewriter II.		7521	
Read into LIO counter.		765421	
Read into normalizing register.		8321	

SUMMARY OF OPERATIONAL CODES

	OUT	IN	MISC.
Special read-in for counter 64 "ganging" carry controls of counters 64 and 65.		87	
Special read-in for counter 65 "ganging" carry controls of counters 64 and 65.		871	
Special read-in for counter 68 "ganging" carry controls of counters 68 and 69.		873	
Special read-in for counter 69 "ganging" carry controls of counters 68 and 69.		8731	
Read into SIO counter (read-in I, direct).		874	
Read out of LIO counter (plugged read-out).	831		
Read out power of ten from normalizing register.	8321		
Read out of SIO counter (read-out II, plugged).	84		
Reset print counter I.	842		
Reset print counter II.	8421		
Reset punch counter.	843		
Read out of IVS.	8431		
Read tape I.	85		
Read tape II.	851		

	OUT	IN	MISC.
Read tape III.	852		
Read out of (into) columns 13-24 of counter 71 into (from) columns 13-24 of the buss.	853	(853)	
Read out of (into) columns 13-24 of counter 71 into (from) columns 1-12 of the buss.	8531	(8531)	
Low order PQ counter read-out. Read out columns 1-23 and the algebraic sign of PQ counter. Must directly follow a high order product-out or a quotient-out.	86		
Read out of print counter I.	862		
Read out of print counter II.	8621		
Read out of punch counter.	863		
Argument control, drops off zeros to the right.	87		
Turn on typewriter II.	871		
Turn on typewriter I.	872		
Turn off typewriter II.	8731		
Turn off typewriter I.	8732		
Read out of SIO counter (read-out I, plugged).	874		
Read out of SIO counter (read-out III, direct).	8741		

TIMING

(1) The unit of time employed by the machine is the cycle; 200 cycles equal one minute.

(2) Except for certain functional operations, one line of coding corresponds to one cycle of machine time.

(3) Multiplication requires 8 + n cycles, where n is the number of non-zero digits in the odd or even columns of the multiplier whichever is the greater. Multiplication consumes a minimum of time when the multiplier is zero: 8 cycles = 2.4 seconds. When the multiplier contains 23 non-zero digits, maximum time is consumed: 20 cycles = 6.0 seconds.

(4) Division requires 6 + 2n cycles, where n is the number of comparisons for which division is plugged. Division covers a minimum of time when the operation contains but one subtract cycle: 7 + n cycles: a maximum of time when it is plugged for 23 comparisons and there are no "no go's": 52 cycles = 15.6 seconds.

(5) Logarithms require 114 + 8n cycles, where n is the number of comparisons for which division is plugged. The divisions, which are a part of the logarithm sequence, are carried through 23 comparisons unless division is plugged for fewer comparisons. If division is plugged for 23 comparisons, the computation of a logarithm requires at most 298 cycles = 1.49 minutes = 89.4 seconds.

(6) Exponentials require 172 + 2n cycles, where n is the number of comparisons for which division is plugged. The division, which is part of the negative exponential sequence, is carried through 23 comparisons unless division is plugged for fewer comparisons. If division is plugged for 23 comparisons, the computation requires at most 218 cycles = 1.09 minutes = 65.4 seconds. If x is known to be positive, the exponential computation is reduced to 167 cycles = 0.835 minutes = 50.1 seconds.

(7) Sines require 199 cycles = 1.0 minutes = 60 seconds.

(8) Interpolation of order k

(a) Positioning time for any tape is

$$P = 8 + N(k + 2)/2 \text{ cycles, maximum}$$

where N = the number of arguments in the tape

k + 1 = the number of interpolational coefficients including C_0.

(b) Computation time is

$$C = 7 + k(4 + n') \text{ cycles}$$

where k + 1 = the number of interpolational coefficients including C_0.

If the maximum number of digits in any interpolational coefficient is 2d; i.e., even, then n' = d.

If the maximum number of digits in any interpolational coefficient is 2d + 1; i.e., odd, then n' = d + 1.

(9) Punching a card through 24 columns and resetting the punch counter requires 10 cycles.

(10) Printing and resetting the print counter requires $(10c/27) + 4$ cycles, where c is the number of column selection plughubs up to and including the reset. An allowance of 23 cycles between prints is sufficient for any printing.

SWITCHES

No.	Code	No.	Code	No.	Code
1	741	21	75431	41	7651
2	742	22	75432	42	7652
3	7421	23	754321	43	76521
4	743	24	76	44	7653
5	7431	25	761	45	76531
6	7432	26	762	46	76532
7	74321	27	7621	47	765321
8	75	28	763	48	7654
9	751	29	7631	49	76541
10	752	30	7632	50	76542
11	7521	31	76321	51	765421
12	753	32	764	52	76543
13	7531	33	7641	53	765431
14	7532	34	7642	54	765432
15	75321	35	76421	55	7654321
16	754	36	7643	56	8
17	7541	37	76431	57	81
18	7542	38	76432	58	82
19	75421	39	764321	59	821
20	7543	40	765	60	83

Independent Variable Switch, IVS, Code 8431

(1) In order to check the quantities inserted in switches, these should be printed out before a computation is begun.

(2) Negative numbers are inserted in switches as complements on nine, or inserted positively and read out using the invert code.

(3) The number in any switch may be read into any storage counter or, under the operational codes, into a functional counter.

(4) To invert the read-out of any switch (except IVS), it is preferable to use the operational code 32 instead of the code 21 in the Miscellaneous column. To invert the read-out of the IVS, it is necessary to use the operational code 21 in the Miscellaneous column.

(5) Since the read-out codes of switches are non-automatic, they require a 7 in the Miscellaneous column unless they are under the control of a preceding automatic code.

1. Read out sw. A into ctr. B; i.e., add sw. A into ctr. B.

OUT	IN	MISC.
A	B	7

2. Add minus sw. A (except IVS) into ctr. B.

A	B	732

or

A	B	721

3. Add IVS to ctr. B.

8431	B	7

	OUT	IN	MISC.
4. Add minus IVS to ctr. B.	8431	B	721
5. Invert the read-out of sw. A (except IVS) under control of ctr. 70, and read into ctr. B. See Choice Counter.	A	B	7432

(6) If the number of constants desired for a problem exceeds the number of switches, the constants may be read into storage counters not used in the problem by means of the IVS.

(7) If the number of constants in a problem exceeds the number of switches, they may be placed in a value tape (see Interpolation) or if all three interpolators are in use, they may be placed in card feeds or in counters as suggested in note (6).

(8) If a column of a switch is set on either of the blank positions between "0" and "9", numbers will not be read out of that switch column either normally or with an invert code. For example of use, see Logarithm In-Out Counter, example 6.

STORAGE COUNTERS

No.	Code	No.	Code	No.	Code
1	1	25	541	49	651
2	2	26	542	50	652
3	21	27	5421	51	6521
4	3	28	543	52	653
5	31	29	5431	53	6531
6	32	30	5432	54	6532
7	321	31	54321	55	65321
8	4	32	6	56	654
9	41	33	61	57	6541
10	42	34	62	58	6542
11	421	35	621	59	65421
12	43	36	63	60	6543
13	431	37	631	61	65431
14	432	38	632	62	65432
15	4321	39	6321	63	654321
16	5	40	64	64	7
17	51	41	641	65	71
18	52	42	642	66	72
19	521	43	6421	67	721
20	53	44	643	68	73
21	531	45	6431	69	731
22	532	46	6432	70	732
23	5321	47	64321	71	7321
24	54	48	65	72	74

(1) The number in any storage counter may be read into any other storage counter or, under the operational codes, into a functional counter.

(2) It is good practice to reset a storage counter just before using it. This frequently avoids the necessity of starting tapes and preserves quantities in the machine as long as possible.

(3) Counters 64, 65, 68, 69, 70, 71 and 72 are wired for special operations. These extra uses do not invalidate their use as normal storage counters. The details of these extra functions will be dealt with in sections concerning these counters.

(4) The LIO and SIO counters may be used as normal storage counters and as special counters for the addition of positive quantities and the shifting of quantities to the right or left. In any case, they require special codes and plugging. See Logarithm In-Out Counter and Sine In-Out Counter.

(5) Since the read-out and read-in codes of the storage counters are non-automatic, they require a 7 in the Miscellaneous column unless they are under the control of a previous automatic operational code.

(6) Since the print and punch counters have complete sets of carry controls, including end around carries, quantities may be read into them as into any storage counter except that their read-in codes are automatic and must not be followed by a 7 in the Miscellaneous column. The read-in to the punch counter must not be interposed in multiplication or division. See Printing and Card Punch.

	OUT	IN	MISC.
1. Add ctr. A to ctr. B.	A	B	7

	OUT	IN	MISC.
2. Add minus ctr. A to ctr. B.	A	B	732
3. Invert the read-out of ctr. A under control of ctr. 70 and read into ctr. B. See Choice Counter.	A	B	7432
4. Add absolute value of ctr. A to ctr. B.	A	B	72
5. Add minus absolute value of ctr. A to ctr. B.	A	B	71
6. Reset ctr. A.	A	A	7

MULTIPLICATION

(1) Multiplication requires plugging to care for the decimal point. See Plugging Instructions.

(2) Numbers may not be read into the multiplying unit from card feeds.

(3) The multiplicand, MC, and the multiplier, MP, may be interchanged without affecting the value of the product. The number having the fewer non-zero digits should be used as the multiplier.

(4) The read-out of a product may not be inverted. In order to read out a negative product, invert either the multiplicand or the multiplier.

(5) The product may be read out to a print counter or to the punch counter.

(6) Two lines of coding, not involving the intermediate counter, may be interposed between the read-in of MC and the read-in of MP. When operations are thus interposed, a 7 is required in the Miscellaneous column of the line containing the read-in of MC.

If only one line is interposed between MC and MP, it must not contain an automatic code (or a 7 in the Miscellaneous column).

If two lines are interposed between MC and MP, the first must and the second may contain an automatic code (or a 7 in the Miscellaneous column).

(7) 3 + n lines of coding, not involving the intermediate counter, may be interposed between the read-in of MP and the read-out of the product. Here n is equal to the number of non-zero digits in the odd or even columns of MP, whichever is the greater. Where operations are thus interposed, a 7 is required in the Miscellaneous column of the line containing the read-in of MP.

If only one line is interposed between MP and the read-out of the product, it must not contain an automatic code (or a 7 in the Miscellaneous column).

If two or more lines are interposed between MP and the read-out of the product, all but the last line must contain automatic codes (or 7's in the Miscellaneous column). The line preceding the read-out of the product must not contain an automatic code.

(8) If a zero MP is possible, no more than three cycles may be interposed between the read-in of MP and the read-out of the product.

(9) Card feeding, reading into the punch counter or the check procedure may be interposed in multiplication only when the coding is specially arranged. See Interposition of Machine Stops.

(10) "Print and complete printing" or "punch and complete punching" should in general not be interposed in multiplication.

1. Multiply sw. or ctr. A by sw. or ctr. B and deliver the product to ctr. C.

OUT	IN	MISC.
A	761	
B		
	C	7

2. Multiply minus sw. (except IVS) or ctr. A by sw. or ctr. B and deliver the product to ctr. C.

OUT	IN	MISC.
A	761	32
B		
	C	7

3. Multiply sw. or ctr. A by minus sw. (except IVS) or ctr. B and deliver the product to ctr. C.

A	761	
B		32
	C	7

4. Multiply the absolute value of ctr. A by sw. or ctr. B and deliver the product to ctr. C.

A	761	2
B		
	C	7

5. Multiply sw. or ctr. A by minus IVS and deliver the product to ctr. C.

A	761	
8431		21
	C	7

6. Multiply sw. or ctr. A by sw. or ctr. B, read the product to print ctr. I and print on typewriter I.

A	761	
B		
	7432	
	752	7

7. Multiply sw. or ctr. A by sw. or ctr. B and deliver the product to ctr. C. Interpose one addition between MC and MP.

A	761	7
D	E	
B		
	C	7

8. Multiply sw. or ctr. A by sw. or ctr. B and deliver the product to ctr. C. Interpose one subtraction between MC and MP.

OUT	IN	MISC.
A	761	7
D	E	32
B		
	C	7

9. Multiply sw. or ctr. A by sw. or ctr. B and deliver the product to ctr. C. Interpose two additions between MC and MP.

A	761	7
D	E	7
F	G	
B		
	C	7

10. Multiply minus sw. (except IVS) or ctr. A by sw. or ctr. B and deliver the product to ctr. C. Interpose an addition and a subtraction between MC and MP. Turn on typewriter I.

A	761	732
D	E	7
F	G	32
B		
872	C	7

11. Multiply the absolute value of ctr. A by sw. or ctr. B and deliver the product to ctr. C. Read from ctr. D to print ctr. I and print on typewriter I with argument control between MC and MP.

A	761	72
D	7432	
87	752	
B		
	C	7

12. Multiply the negative absolute value of ctr. A by minus sw. (except IVS) or ctr. B and deliver the product to ctr. C. Step and read from value tape on interpolator I to ctr. D, between MC and MP. Turn on typewriter I and turn off typewriter II.

A	761	71
85		753
872	D	

Continued on next page

12. (continued)

OUT	IN	MISC.
B		32
8731	C	7

13. Multiply sw. or ctr. A by sw. or ctr. B and deliver the product to ctr. C. Step the value tape on interpolator I twice between MC and MP. Step and read from the tape to ctr. D and then step twice more between MP and the read-out of the product. Turn off typewriter I.

A	761	7
		753
		53
B		7
85		753
	D	7
8732		753
		53
	C	7

14. Multiply sw. or ctr. A by sw. or ctr. B and deliver the product to ctr. C. Interpose one addition between MP and read-out of product.

A	761	
B		7
D	E	
	C	7

15. Multiply sw. or ctr. A by sw. or ctr. B, reset ctr. C and deliver the product to ctr. C.

A	761	
B		7
C	C	
	C	7

16. Multiply sw. or ctr. A by sw. or ctr. B and deliver the product to ctr. C. Interpose two additions and two subtractions between MP and read-out of product.

A	761	
B		7
D	E	7

Continued on next page

16. (continued)

OUT	IN	MISC.
F	E	7
G	H	732
G	J	32
	C	7

17. Multiply sw. or ctr. A by sw. or ctr. B and deliver the product to ctr. C. Interpose a step and read from a value tape on interpolator I between MC and MP. Interpose a step and read from a value tape on interpolator I and an addition and a reset between MP and read-out of product.

A	761	7
85		753
	D	
B		7
85		753
	E	7
F	G	7
C	C	
	C	7

18. Multiply plus or minus the quantity in sw. (except IVS) or ctr. A under control of ctr. 70 by sw. or ctr. B and deliver the product to ctr. C. Interpose two additions between MC and MP. Interpose a print, reset of ctr. 70 and addition of an absolute value to ctr. 70 between MP and read-out of product.

A	761	7432
D	E	7
D	F	
B		7
G	7432	
	752	7
732	732	7
H	732	2
	C	7

19. Multiply sw. or ctr. A by the absolute value of ctr. B and deliver the product to ctr. C. Interpose read-in and read-out of LIO between MC and MP. Interpose reset of LIO, a print and addition of negative absolute value between MP and read-out of product.

OUT	IN	MISC.
A	761	7
D	765421	7
831	E	
B		72
		763
E	7432	
	752	7
F	G	1
	C	7

20. Multiply sw. or ctr. A by sw. or ctr. B and deliver the product to ctr. C. Interpose a print between MC and MP. Interpose reset of ctr. C and read-in, read-out and reset of SIO between MP and read-out of product.

A	761	7
D	7432	
	752	
B		7
C	C	7
E	8741	7
8741	F	7
		321
	C	7

(11) If necessary, the blank In column of the line of coding reading the MP may be used to read the MP simultaneously to a storage counter, to a print counter or to initiate printing.

21. Multiply sw. or ctr. A by sw. or ctr. B, simultaneously reading B to C and read the product to D. Note that this may not be used to reset ctr. B. Print G between reading of A and B. Interpose 4 cycles between read-in of MP and read-out of product.

OUT	IN	MISC.
A	761	7
G	7432	
	752	

Continued on next page

21. (continued)

OUT	IN	MISC.
B	C	7
85		753
	E	7
85		753
	F	
	D	7

22. Multiply sw. or ctr. A by B + C, print G and deliver the product to ctr. D. Interpose other operations.

A	761	7
C	B	7
G	7432	
B	752	7
85		753
	E	7
85		753
	F	
	D	7

23. Multiply sw. or ctr. A by sw. or ctr. B, print B and deliver the product to ctr. C. Reset ctr. C during multiplication. Interpose other operations.

A	761	7
D	D	7
E	E	
B	7432	
	752	7
C	C	7
F	D	32
	C	7

24. Multiply sw. or ctr. A by B which is read from a value tape. Simultaneously read B to ctr. B and deliver the product to ctr. C. Reset ctr. C during multiplication. Note line containing reset of D must be included if only as line (blank, blank, 7).

OUT	IN	MISC.
A	761	7
D	D	7
85		
	B	7
C	C	
	C	7

25. Multiply sw. or ctr. A by B which is read from a value tape. Deliver the product to ctr. C. Turn on both typewriters. Interpose other adding and reset cycles.

A	761	7
D	D	7
85		
871		7
G	G	7
E	D	7
E	G	
872	C	7

(12) If necessary, the blank Out column of the line of coding reading out the product may be used to select a value tape from which the value is read on the next line, or for turning typewriters on and off.

26. Multiply sw. or ctr. A by sw. or ctr. B and deliver the product to ctr. C. Read the value from a tape on interpolator I to ctr. D.

OUT	IN	MISC.
A	761	
B		
85	C	7
	D	7

27. Multiply sw. or ctr. A by sw. or ctr. B and deliver the product to ctr. C. Read D from a tape on interpolator I and multiply it by sw. or ctr. E and deliver this product to ctr. F. Turn off both typewriters.

A	761	
B		

Continued on next page

27. (continued)

OUT	IN	MISC.
85	C	7
8731	761	
E		
8732	F	7

(13) If necessary, the codes for punching and for stepping an interpolator may be placed in the Miscellaneous column of the lines of coding reading the MP and MC if these lines do not already contain an invert or other operational code. These codes may also be added in the line of coding reading out the product.

28. Multiply sw. or ctr. A by the absolute value of ctr. B. Add A to C and print C with half pick-up on typewriter I. Step the tape on interpolator I four times and read the value to D. Step the tape twice more. Reset ctr. C. Deliver the product to ctr. P and punch out the quantity in the punch ctr. Turn on typewriter II.

OUT	IN	MISC.
A	761	753
A	C	753
C	7432	53
B	76543	72
85	752	753
	D	753
C	C	53
871	P	75

DIVISION

(1) Division does not require plugging to care for the decimal point.

(2) The "Divide N minus Decimal" switch must be set to the value,

$$N = 22 - K$$

where K is the number of columns to the right of the decimal point. If the decimal point lies between columns 23 and 24, division may be performed by setting the "Divide N minus Decimal" switch to zero and shifting the quotient one column to the left via LIO counter or SIO counter. There will, however, be no more than 22 decimal places in the result.

(3) The first number read to the dividing unit in the first line of division coding is the divisor, DR.

(4) Numbers may not be read into the dividing unit from the card feeds.

(5) The read-out of a quotient may not be inverted. In order to read out a negative quotient, invert either the divisor, DR, or the dividend, DD.

(6) The quotient may be read out to a print counter or to the punch counter.

(7) The degree of accuracy in division may be controlled by operational codes and plugging. See Plugging Instructions. The accuracies available vary with the plugging from one to twenty-three columns. For a given problem five different accuracies may be selected in this range. If only one accuracy is needed in a given problem, no code need be used; i.e., the Miscellaneous column is "blank". The operational codes of the accuracies are placed in the Miscellaneous column with either DR or DD read-in or on the lines interposed between them. The codes are 643, 6431, 6432, 64321 and "blank". These codes may not be used in combination with an invert or other operational code. The degree of accuracy of division within the logarithm and exponential units is controlled by the plugging of the "blank" code. Not more than 23 digits of any quotient, including the first "no go" if any, can be read out of the PQ counter.

(8) Two lines of coding, not involving the intermediate counter, may be interposed between the read-in of DR and the read-in of DD. When operations are thus interposed, a 7 is required in the Miscellaneous column of the line containing the read-in of DR.

If only one line is interposed between DR and DD, it must not contain an automatic code (or a 7 in the Miscellaneous column).

If two lines of coding are interposed between DR and DD, the first must and the second may contain an automatic code (or a 7 in the Miscellaneous column).

(9) It is possible to interpose n + 1 lines of coding, not involving the multiply-divide unit, between the read-in of DD and the read-out of the quotient. Here n is equal to the number of comparisons for which division is plugged. Where operations are thus interposed, a 7 is required in the Miscellaneous column of the line containing the read-in of DD.

If only one line is interposed between DD and the read-out of the quotient, it must not contain an automatic code (or a 7 in the Miscellaneous column).

If two or more lines are interposed between DD and the read-out of the quotient, all but the last line must contain automatic codes (or 7's in the Miscellaneous column). The line preceding the read-out of the quotient must not contain an automatic code.

(10) Card feeding, reading to the punch counter or the check procedure may be interposed in division only when the coding is specially arranged. See Interposition of Machine Stops.

DIVISION

(11) "Print and complete printing" or "punch and complete punching" should in general not be interposed in division.

1. Divide sw. or ctr. A by sw. or ctr. B and deliver the quotient to ctr. C.

OUT	IN	MISC.
B	76	
A		
	C	7

2. Divide minus sw. (except IVS) or ctr. A by sw. or ctr. B and deliver the quotient to ctr. C.

B	76	
A		32
	C	7

3. Divide sw. or ctr. A by minus sw. (except IVS) or ctr. B and deliver the quotient to ctr. C.

B	76	32
A		
	C	7

4. Divide the absolute value of ctr. A by sw. or ctr. B and deliver the quotient to ctr. C.

B	76	
A		2
	C	7

5. Divide sw. or ctr. A by minus IVS and deliver the quotient to ctr. C.

8431	76	21
A		
	C	7

6. Divide sw. or ctr. A by sw. or ctr. B with accuracy 6431 and deliver the quotient to ctr. C.

B	76	6431
A		
	C	7

or

B	76	
A		6431
	C	7

OUT	IN	MISC.

7. Divide minus sw. (except IVS) or ctr. A by sw. or ctr. B with accuracy 6432 and deliver the quotient to ctr. C.

OUT	IN	MISC.
B	76	6432
A		32
	C	7

8. Divide sw. or ctr. A by minus sw. (except IVS) or ctr. B with accuracy 64321 and deliver the quotient to ctr. C.

B	76	32
A		64321
	C	7

9. Divide sw. or ctr. A by sw. or ctr. B and read the quotient to print ctr. I and print on typewriter I.

B	76	
A		
	7432	
	752	7

10. Divide sw. or ctr. A by sw. or ctr. B with accuracy 643 and deliver the quotient to ctr. C. Interpose one addition between DR and DD. Turn on typewriter I.

B	76	7643
D	E	
A		
872	C	7

11. Divide sw. or ctr. A by sw. or ctr. B and deliver the quotient to ctr. C. Interpose one subtraction between DR and DD.

B	76	7
D	E	32
A		
	C	7

12. Divide sw. or ctr. A by sw. or ctr. B and deliver the quotient to ctr. C. Interpose two additions between DR and DD.

B	76	7
D	E	7
F	G	

Continued on next page

DIVISION

12. (continued)

OUT	IN	MISC.
A		
	C	7

13. Divide minus sw. (except IVS) or ctr. A by sw. or ctr. B with accuracy 6431 and deliver the quotient to ctr. C. Interpose an addition and a subtraction between DR and DD.

B	76	76431
D	E	7
F	G	32
A		32
	C	7

14. Divide the absolute value of ctr. A by sw. or ctr. B and deliver the quotient to ctr. C. Read from ctr. D to print ctr. I and print on typewriter I between DR and DD.

B	76	7
D	7432	
	752	
A		2
	C	7

15. Divide the negative absolute value of ctr. A by minus sw. (except IVS) or ctr. B and deliver the quotient to ctr. C. Step and read from value tape on interpolator I to ctr. D between DR and DD.

B	76	732
85		753
	D	
A		1
	C	7

16. Divide sw. or ctr. A by sw. or ctr. B with accuracy 6432 and deliver the quotient to ctr. C. Step the value tape on interpolator I twice between DR and DD, read from the tape and step twice more between DD and the read-out of the quotient.

B	76	76432
		753
		53
A		7
85		7

Continued on next page

16. (continued)

OUT	IN	MISC.
	D	7
		753
		53
	C	7

17. Divide sw. or ctr. A by sw. or ctr. B with accuracy 64321 and deliver the quotient to ctr. C. Interpose one addition between DD and the read-out of the quotient.

B	76	64321
A		7
D	E	
	C	7

18. Divide sw. or ctr. A by sw. or ctr. B and deliver the quotient to ctr. C. Reset ctr. C between DD and the read-out of the quotient.

B	76	
A		7
C	C	
	C	7

19. Divide sw. or ctr. A by sw. or ctr. B and deliver the quotient to ctr. C. Interpose eight adding and resetting operations between DD and the read-out of the quotient.

B	76	
A		7
D	E	7
D	F	7
D	G	7
H	H	7
I	I	7
J	J	7
D	H	72
A	H	2
	C	7

DIVISION

20. Divide plus or minus the quantity in ctr. A under control of ctr. 70 by sw. or ctr. B, with accuracy 643, and deliver the quotient to ctr. C. Interpose two additions between DR and DD. Interpose a print of ctr. A under control of ctr. 70, reset of ctr. 70, addition of an absolute value to ctr. 70 and addition of ctr. G to ctr. 70 between DD and read-out of quotient.

OUT	IN	MISC.
B	76	7643
D	E	7
D	E	
A		7432
A	7432	432
	752	7
732	732	7
F	732	72
G	732	
	C	7

21. Divide sw. or ctr. A by the absolute value of ctr. B with accuracy 6431 and deliver the quotient to ctr. C. Interpose a print of ctr. A between DR and DD. Interpose a read-in, read-out and reset of LIO and additions into LIO between DD and read-out of quotient.

B	76	72
A	7432	
	752	
A		76431
D	765421	7
831	E	7
		763
F	765421	7
G	765421	
	C	7

(12) If necessary, the blank In column of the line of coding reading the DD may be used to read the DD simultaneously to a storage counter, to a print counter or to initiate printing.

22. Divide sw. or ctr. A by sw. or ctr. B, with accuracy 6432, simultaneously reading A to C and deliver the quotient to ctr. D. Note that this may not be used to reset A.

OUT	IN	MISC.
B	76	6432
A	C	

Continued on next page

22. (continued)

or

OUT	IN	MISC.
	D	7
B	76	
A	C	6432
	D	7

23. Divide sw. or ctr. A by sw. or ctr. B and deliver the quotient to ctr. C. Print A with half pick-up between DR and DD. This operation may also be coded by omitting the first 7 and the second A.

B	76	7
A	7432	
	76543	
A	752	
	C	7

24. Divide sw. or ctr. A by sw. or ctr. B and deliver the quotient to ctr. C. Print A. Reset ctr. C during division. The number of cycles interposed between the read-in of DD and the read-out of the quotient is dependent upon the division accuracy plugging.

B	76	
A	7432	
	752	7
D	E	7
C	C	7
F	E	732
G	E	7
A	G	
	C	7

25. Divide A, which is read from a value tape, by sw. or ctr. B and deliver the quotient to ctr. C. Simultaneously read A to ctr. A. Reset ctr. C between DR and DD. The number of cycles interposed between the read-in of DD and the read-out of the quotient is dependent upon the division accuracy plugging.

B	76	7
C	C	7
85		
	A	7
D	D	7

Continued on next page

25. (continued)

OUT	IN	MISC.
E	D	
	C	7

26. Divide A, which is read from a value tape, by sw. or ctr. B and deliver the quotient to ctr. C. The number of cycles interposed between the read-in of DD and the read-out of the quotient is dependent upon the division accuracy plugging.

B	76	7
D	D	7
85		
		7
G	G	7
E	D	7
E	G	
	C	7

27. Divide A, which is read from a value tape, by minus ctr. B with accuracy 6432 and deliver the quotient to ctr. C. The number of cycles interposed between the read-in of DD and the read-out of the quotient is dependent upon the division accuracy plugging.

B	76	732
D	D	7
85		
		76432
G	G	7
E	D	7
E	G	7
F	G	
	C	7

(13) If necessary, the blank Out column of the line of coding reading out the quotient may be used to select a value tape from which the value is read on the next line or for turning typewriters on and off.

28. Divide sw. or ctr. A by sw. or ctr. B and deliver the quotient to ctr. C. Read value from tape on interpolator I to ctr. D.

OUT	IN	MISC.
B	76	
A		

Continued on next page

OUT	IN	MISC.
85	C	7
	D	7

28. (continued)

29. Divide sw. or ctr. A by sw. or ctr. B and deliver the quotient to ctr. C. Read D from a tape on interpolator I and multiply it by sw. or ctr. E, deliver this product to ctr. F. Turn off typewriter I.

B	76	
A		
85	C	7
	761	
E		
8732	F	7

(14) If necessary, the codes for punching and for stepping an interpolator may be placed in the Miscellaneous column of the lines of coding reading the DR and DD if these lines do not already contain an invert or other operational code. These codes may also be added in the line of coding reading out the quotient.

30. Divide minus sw. (except IVS) or ctr. B by sw. or ctr. A with accuracy 643, deliver the quotient to ctr. C and punch out the quantity in the punch ctr. Turn on typewriter I.

OUT	IN	MISC.
A	76	643
B		32
872	C	75

CHOICE COUNTER

Counter 70

(1) The special controls on counter 70 make it possible to reverse the algebraic sign of a quantity if and only if some second quantity standing in counter 70 is negative (including the quantity minus zero).

1. Invert the read-out of sw. (except IVS) or ctr. A to ctr. B if and only if the quantity standing in ctr. 70 is negative.

OUT	IN	MISC.
A	B	7432

(2) Counter 70 may be used to round off numbers to n places of accuracy by addition or subtraction of $5 \times 10^{-(n+1)}$ according as the given number is positive or negative. The resulting number may then be printed with the (n + 1)st, (n + 2)nd, ... places cut off by typewriter plugging. This may substitute for the half pick-up discussed under Printing.

2. Round off the number in ctr. A to n places, where $5 \times 10^{-(n+1)}$ is in sw. B and print on typewriter I.

OUT	IN	MISC.
A	732	7
B	732	7432
732	7432	
	752	7

(3) For punched cards not to be fed to the machine for further computation, counter 70 may be used to round off to n places of accuracy as in note (2). The extra places are cut off by punch plugging. If the cards are to be fed to the machine for further computation, $5 \times 10^{-(n+1)}$ must be added in all cases. See Multiple In-Out Counter, note (6).

(4) Any computation involving an odd function $f(x) = -f(-x)$, may be simplified by use of counter 70. For example, if sin x is to be computed by interpolation, the functional tape need only be punched for positive arguments, the quantity x read to counter 70 and the result of interpolation read out of a storage counter under control of counter 70. See Interpolators.

(5) The choice counter may be used to compute various types of discontinuous functions and functions with discontinuous derivatives. Suppose it is desired to compute

$$F(x) = f_1(x), \qquad x \leq a,$$

$$F(x) = f_2(x), \qquad a < x.$$

Calculate

$$g_1 = f_2 + f_1$$

$$g_2 = f_2 - f_1$$

and store x - a in counter 70.

Compute $2F(x) = g_1 \pm g_2$ under control of counter 70.

Thus if $x \leq a$, $x - a \leq -0$,

$$F(x) = f_1(x) = (g_1 - g_2)/2 .$$

If $x > a$, $x - a > 0$,

$$F(x) = f_2(x) = (g_1 + g_2)/2.$$

Repetition of this process will care for functions with any desired number of discontinuities, or discontinuities of their derivatives.

Suppose

$$F(x) = f_1(x), \qquad x \le a,$$

$$F(x) = f_2(x), \qquad a < x \le b,$$

$$F(x) = f_3(x), \qquad b < x.$$

Calculate

$$g_1 = f_2 + f_1$$

$$g_2 = f_2 - f_1$$

and store $x - a$ in counter 70.

Compute $2F_1(x) = g_1 \pm g_2$ under control of counter 70.

Calculate

$$g_3 = f_3 + F_1$$

$$g_4 = f_3 - F_1$$

and store $x - b$ in counter 70.

Compute $2F(x) = g_3 \pm g_4$ under control of counter 70.

While this is the basic coding for such functions, in many cases it is possbile to shorten the calculation depending upon the form of the functions.

AUTOMATIC CHECK COUNTER

Counter 72

(1) The special controls on this counter insure that the absolute value of a given number is less than another given positive number or tolerance. If this condition is not satisfied, the machine is stopped.

1. To check the absolute value of the quantity in ctr. A against the positive tolerance in sw. or ctr. B.

OUT	IN	MISC.
B	74	7
A	74	71
74	74	64

2. To insure that $+0 \leq A < B$, check the quantity in ctr. A against the positive tolerance in sw. or ctr. B.

B	74	7
A	74	732
74	74	64

(2) The first line of the check coding may be separated from the other two.

(3) The last two lines of the check coding may not be separated. The machine stops on the line following a 64 code unless in the preceding cycle there is an end around carry in counter 72.

(4) The last line of the check coding includes the reset of the check counter as well as the 64 code for the check operation. It is possible in case of necessity to omit the reset of the check counter and use this space for another reset or an addition. In this eventuality the check counter must be reset before using it again.

(5) It is always desirable to print out the quantity being checked before it is routed through the check counter. Thus in case of failure to check, the magnitude and type of error readily may be observed.

(6) If possible, all essential parts of a computation should be preserved in the machine until the check has been made. Thus in case of machine error, the elements can be read out and manual computation used to aid in detecting the error.

(7) The consumption of machine time must enter into the choice of checking methods. If a final check can be devised for an entire computation when the time is half an hour or less per run, intervening check computations may well be omitted. If each element of out-put is independent, each should be checked. If a run continues more than half an hour, checks should be inserted at intermediate points.

(8) The most commonly used methods of checking are:

(a) <u>Inverse Operation</u>
If $y = f(x)$ is computed, then a check of $x - x'$, where $x' = f^{-1}(y)$, against a preassigned tolerance will in general give an adequate check. If $y = x^{1/n}$ is computed by iteration or logarithms, n being an integer, then $x - x'$, where $x' = y^n$ as computed by multiplication, is a check making use of distinct machine processes.

(b) <u>Independent Calculation</u>
In some cases it is possible to derive two independent methods of computing f(x) which may be checked against each other.

(c) Interchange of Counters
If no brief method of check can be devised, the computation may be repeated using different storage or functional counters. In checking multiplication, the multiplier and multiplicand may be interchanged. The problem may be rerun with a different decimal point or with certain values multiplied or divided by powers of ten. This will shift digits into different columns of the storage and functional counters.

(d) Identities
In many cases functions satisfy certain identities or recursion formulae which may be used as checks. For example, the computation of sin x and cos x may be checked by:

$$\sin^2 x + \cos^2 x - 1 = 0.$$

It should be noted, however, that this particular identity will not detect compensating errors.

(e) Differences
Standard differencing techniques provide a basic method of checking. If one of the higher differences of a function conforms to a certain pattern, a check is provided. Naturally, the use of differencing techniques depends upon the amount of information available concerning the function and its differences.

(f) Gross Checks
Observation of the trend of a function and rough differencing, together with graphing, will in many cases provide gross checks.

(9) The checking of value and functional tapes, cards and printed data is considered in their respective sections. See Design of Functional Tapes, Card Feeds, Card Punch and Printing.

(10) If the choice counter is used in conjunction with the check procedure, it is possible to determine whether or not two given quantities having the same sign differ by not more than one in a given significant digit.

3. If the quantities A, 10000 > A ≥ 1, and B, lying in ctrs. A and B, are of the same sign, the following coding will insure that A and B differ by less than one in the fifth significant digit. Ctrs. C, 70 and 72 are reset and available for computation.
Switch ST = 10
SU = 90
SV = 900
SW = 0.05005
SX = 0.00045
SY = 0.0045
SZ = 0.045

OUT	IN	MISC.
A	732	71
ST	732	732
SW	C	7
SX	C	7432
SU	732	732
SY	C	7432
SV	732	732
SZ	C	7432
A	B	732
C	74	7
B	74	71
		64

MULTIPLE IN-OUT COUNTER

(1) This counter is equipped with multiple in-out relays as follows:

(a) From columns 1-24 of the buss into columns 1-24 of the counter in normal position, code 7321 in the In column.

(b) From columns 1-24 of the counter into columns 1-24 of the buss in normal position, code 7321 in the Out column.

(c) From columns 13-24 of the buss into columns 13-24 of the counter, code 853 in the In column.

(d) From columns 13-24 of the counter into columns 13-24 of the buss, code 853 in the Out column.

(e) From columns 1-12 of the buss into columns 13-24 of the counter, code 8531 in the In column.

(f) From columns 13-24 of the counter into columns 1-12 of the buss, code 8531 in the Out column.

(2) Columns 13-24 of the MIO counter may be reset using the code 853 in the Out and In columns.

(3) The effect of this counter is to double the number of storage counters in the machine, each storage counter having a capacity of 12 columns. Essentially, only the upper half is used in this process, since there is no special read-out of the lower 12 columns. The lower half of MIO may not be used for adding negative numbers, since there is no carry from column 12 to column 1. All adding which involves any negative numbers must be done in the upper half of the counter, which is supplied with a special carry from column 24 to column 13.

(4) If both of the numbers stored in a counter by means of the MIO counter are positive, they may be simultaneously multiplied by a third positive quantity. This process is frequently of use in dealing with statistical data.

(5) The special controls on counter 71 do not invalidate its use in the normal manner, when the code 7321 is used.

1. Sw. A and sw. B each contain two numbers, one in cols. 1-12, and the other in cols. 13-24, cols. 12 and 24 containing the algebraic sign. It is required to add together the numbers in corresponding columns of the two switches and deliver the two sums to ctr. C in corresponding columns. Both sums are to be printed in cols. 1-12 by typewriter I.

OUT	IN	MISC.
7321	7321	7
A	853	7
B	853	7
853	C	7
8531	7432	
	752	6
7321	7321	7
A	8531	7

Continued on next page

1. (continued)

OUT	IN	MISC.
B	8531	7
8531	C	7
8531	7432	
	752	6

(6) The MIO counter may be used to round off numbers to be punched in cards. The number is shifted by the LIO counter so that the columns to be punched appear in columns 13-24 of the MIO counter. Two cases then arise depending on whether the cards are to be used in further calculations or not.

(a) If the cards are not to be used in further calculations in the machine, but simply printed out or used for checking purposes, a five is added or subtracted from the 12th column according as the number is positive or negative under the control of counter 70. Columns 13-24 of the MIO counter are read to the punch counter.

2. The number in ctr. A is to be rounded off and punched in cols. 1-12 of a card. Sw. B contains a five in col. 12.

OUT	IN	MISC.
A	732	7
A	765421	7
831	7321	7
B	7321	7432
853	753	
		51

(b) If the cards are to be fed to the machine for use in further calculations, a five is added in the 12th machine column. Columns 13-24 of the MIO counter are read to the punch counter.

3. The number in ctr. A is to be rounded off and punched in cols. 1-12 of a card for further computation. Sw. B contains a five in col. 12.

OUT	IN	MISC.
A	765421	7
831	7321	7
B	7321	7
853	753	
		51

(7) The MIO counter may be used to produce serial numbers for sorting punched cards. A deck is to be punched with values of several functions; e.g., $f(x)$, $g(x)$, $h(x)$, in the order $f(x_{n-1})$, $g(x_{n-1})$, $h(x_{n-1})$, $f(x)$, $g(x)$, $h(x)$, $f(x_{n+1})$, $g(x_{n+1})$, $h(x_{n+1})$, etc. The cards are later to be

sorted according to the magnitude of the first four digits of f(x). There are not more than eleven significant digits in each of the functions to be punched. The functions are sent to columns 13-24 of the MIO counter. The first four columns of f(x) are selected by routing through the LIO counter to columns 6-9 of the MIO counter. The serial numbers within the group are delivered from an accumulation counter to the low order columns of the MIO counter. Columns 1-24 of the MIO counter are then delivered to the punch counter. Thus if

f(x) = 23.137 564 76
g(x) = 0.249 301 24
h(x) = 1.656 837 96,

the three cards punched will read,

0 023 137 564 760 002 313 000 01
0 000 247 301 240 002 313 000 02
0 001 656 837 960 002 313 000 03.

4. Read g(x) from ctr. A to cols. 13-24 of MIO. Read the first four digits of f(x) from ctr. B via LIO to cols. 6-9 of MIO. Read the serial number within the group from ctr. C and punch the cards.

OUT	IN	MISC.
A	853	7
B	765421	7
831	7321	7
C	7321	7
7321	753	
		51

(8) The MIO counter may be used to drop off digits to the left; i.e., columns 1-12 of a number may be retained. See also Logarithm In-Out Counter, note (4), and Sine In-Out Counter, note (4).

(a) If the number is positive, read it into the MIO counter with the columns to be dropped in columns 13-24. Reset columns 13-24 of MIO.

5. Read the number in ctr. A to MIO. Reset cols. 13-24 of MIO. Read result to ctr. B.

OUT	IN	MISC.
A	7321	7
853	853	7
7321	B	7

(b) If the sign of the number A is unknown, read it into the MIO counter with the columns to be dropped in columns 13-24. Reset columns 13-24 of MIO. Read columns 1-12 of MIO direct to B. Supply nines when needed with negative numbers by reading columns 13-24 of MIO to B under control of counter 70.

6. Read the number in ctr. A to MIO. Reset cols. 13-24 of MIO. Read result to ctr. B. Supply nines when needed with negative numbers by reading cols. 13-24 of MIO to ctr. B under control of ctr. 70.

OUT	IN	MISC.
A	7321	7
853	853	7

Continued on next page

6. (continued)

OUT	IN	MISC.
7321	B	7
A	732	7
853	B	7432

LOGARITHM IN-OUT COUNTER

(1) The logarithm in-out counter, LIO counter, may be used as a storage counter if necessary. It requires certain special codes, and plugging. See Plugging Instructions.

1. Read from ctr. A into LIO.

OUT	IN	MISC.
A	765421	7

2. Read from LIO into ctr. B. Plugged read-out.

831	B	7

3. Reset LIO.

		763

(2) The LIO counter may not be used for addition unless all of the numbers involved are positive, since this counter has no end around carry.

(3) The LIO counter may be used to shift numbers to the right or left, since it has a pluggable read-out to the buss. If negative numbers are involved, they may not be shifted more than ten columns to the right on reading out, since only ten nines are available to be plugged in at the left. See Plugging Instructions.

(4) The LIO counter may be used to drop off digits to the right or left, since it has a pluggable read-out. Care must be taken to supply nines in dropping digits from negative numbers. See Plugging Instructions.

(5) If it is desired to superpose numbers, the LIO counter may be used to shift one of them. See Plugging Instructions. A and B are two arguments with the same decimal point. Superpose B on A to prepare for printing both arguments in one typing operation. If A = 27 and B = 32, the combination is printed as 32000027 in one typing operation.

4. Shift the number in ctr. B and superpose it on the number in ctr. A. Print on typewriter I.

OUT	IN	MISC.
B	765421	7
831	A	7
A	7432	63
	752	7

(6) The LIO counter may be used as a "doubling" counter to build up simple multiples of a positive quantity, especially products by powers of two. These operations may be interposed in other multiplications or in division.

5. x lies in ctr. A. Read 8x to ctr. B.

OUT	IN	MISC.
A	765421	7
831	765421	7

Continued on next page

5. (continued)

OUT	IN	MISC.
831	765421	7
831	765421	7
831	B	7

(7) The LIO counter reset does not involve the buss.

(8) If more than ten nines are needed for reading out negative numbers from the LIO counter they may be supplied from a switch under control of the choice counter. If 13 nines are needed in columns 11-23, ten of them are supplied by plugging to ten columns, say 14-23, and three are supplied from a switch to columns 11-13.

6. Read x from ctr. A to ctr. B, shifting 13 columns to right. Sw. P has 000 in cols. 11-13. The other columns of sw. P (cols. 1-10 and 14-24) are set on the blank position (not zero). Nines are plugged to cols. 14-23. The algebraic sign, col. 24, is bottle-plugged as usual.

OUT	IN	MISC.
A	765421	7
831	B	7
B	732	7
P	B	7432

SINE IN-OUT COUNTER

(1) The sine in-out counter, SIO counter, may be used as a storage counter if necessary. It requires certain special codes and plugging. See Plugging Instructions.

(2) The SIO counter should not be used independently of the sine computation unless the "85-1 P.U." switch is in the off position. This switch is at the left hand end of row 21 of the Multiply-Divide relay panel. If the switch is thrown off, it should be entered in the log, since it is necessary that the relay be in operation for a sine computation.

	OUT	IN	MISC.
1. Read out of ctr. A into SIO. Direct read-in I, no carry; may not be used for doubling.	A	874	7
2. Read out of ctr. A into SIO. Plugged read-in II, with carry in all columns except from col. 23 to col. 24 and col. 24 to col. 1. Automatic Code.	A	8741	

(3) If the "SIO-OUT-2 Invert Control" switch is in the on position, a nine in the 24th column will pick up nines from the ten left hand plughubs of row 40 of the functional plugboard and will invert the read-out of those columns of SIO which are plugged to the buss. If the "SIO-OUT-2 Invert Control" switch is in the off position, a nine in the 24th column will pick up nines from the plugboard, but the read-out from the SIO will be direct.

	OUT	IN	MISC.
3. Read out of SIO into ctr. B. Plugged read-out II.	84	B	7

(4) The plugged read-out I reads directly from the SIO counter, through the plug wires, into the buss and will not pick up nines from row 40 of the plugboard.

	OUT	IN	MISC.
4. Read out of SIO into ctr. B. Plugged read-out I, no nines.	874	B	7

(5) The direct read-out III is completely independent of all plugging.

	OUT	IN	MISC.
5. Read out of SIO into ctr. B. Direct read-out III.	8741	B	7

(6) The SIO counter reset, a Miscellaneous code, does not involve the buss and may therefore be added to any line of coding not already containing a Miscellaneous code.

	OUT	IN	MISC.
6. Reset SIO.			7321

(7) The SIO counter may not be used for addition unless all of the quantities involved are positive and plugged read-in II is used, since this counter has no carry into the 24th column and no end around carry.

(8) The SIO counter may be used to shift positive numbers to the right or left, since it has a pluggable read-in from the buss and two pluggable read-outs to the buss.

7. Shift the positive quantity standing in cols. 13, 14, 15 and 16 of ctr. A to cols. 3, 4, 5 and 6 of ctr. B.

OUT	IN	MISC.
A	874	7
84	B	7

or

A	874	7
874	B	7

or

A	8741	
8741	B	7

(9) The SIO counter may be used to drop off digits to the right or left of quantities, since it has a pluggable read-out which supplies nines.

8. The last five digits of the quantity standing in ctr. A contain the code numbers controlling the punched cards. It is desired to read the function to ctr. B and the code to ctr. C.

OUT	IN	MISC.
A	874	7
874	B	7
84	C	7

(10) The SIO counter may be used as a "doubling" counter to build up simple multiples of a positive quantity, especially products by powers of two, if plugged read-in II is used. These operations may be interposed in other multiplications or in divisions.

9. x lies in ctr. A. Read 4x to ctr. B.

OUT	IN	MISC.
A	8741	
8741	8741	
8741	8741	
8741	B	7

SINE IN-OUT COUNTER

(11) The SIO may be used with the normalizing register to shift quantities from the standard position in the machine to read out of columns 20 and up. This must be done to facilitate the printing of the argument of a function in the required columns to conform with the read-out of the exponent computed in the normalizing register.

10. Ctr. A contains the argument x with decimal point in the operating position between cols. 15 and 16. Shift x so that it will be printed with decimal point between cols. 19 and 20, and print on typewriter I.

OUT	IN	MISC.
A	874	7
874	7432	
	752	7

HIGH ACCURACY COMPUTATION

Counters 64 and 65
Counters 68 and 69

(1) It is possible to carry on computations covering 46 columns and the algebraic sign.

(2) Special controls are available on the pairs of counters (65, 64) and (69, 68) which make possible their use as two single adding counters. Counters 65 and 69 contain the high order columns 24-46; 64 and 68, the low order columns 1-23. All additions and subtractions of 46 column numbers must be performed in one of these pair of "ganged" counters.

(3) Such numbers are stored across two switches, for example A and B. The algebraic sign is stored in the 24th column of both switches. Columns 1-23 of the number are stored in columns 1-23 of switch B and columns 24-46 of the number in columns 1-23 of switch A.

(4) If such numbers are to be fed to the machine from cards or a value tape, two entries are required similar to those used in storing in switches.

(5) 46 column numbers are stored across two storage counters A and B with the algebraic sign in the 24th column of both counters, columns 1-23 of the number in columns 1-23 of counter B, and columns 24-46 of the number in columns 1-23 of counter A.

(6) The numbers are stored across any pair of storage counters by reading in each half separately to the two counters. These read-ins are subject to any of the usual operational codes.

1. A quantity lies across sws. or ctrs. (A,B); read it across ctrs. (C,D).

OUT	IN	MISC.
A	C	7
B	D	7

2. Invert the read-out of the quantity across sws. or ctrs. (A,B) into ctrs. (C,D).

A	C	732
B	D	732

3. Invert the read-out of the quantity across sws. or ctrs. (A,B) into ctrs. (C,D) under control of ctr. 70.

A	C	7432
B	D	7432

4. Read the absolute value of the quantity across ctrs. (A,B) into ctrs. (C,D).

A	C	72
B	D	72

5. Read minus the absolute value of the quantity across ctrs. (A,B) into ctrs. (C,D).

A	C	71
B	D	71

OUT	IN	MISC.

6. A quantity lies across ctrs. (A,B); reset the ctrs.

OUT	IN	MISC.
A	A	7
B	B	7

7. A quantity is stored across two cards, high order columns in feed I and low order columns in feed II; read the quantity into ctrs. (C,D).

	C	7632
	D	76321

8. A quantity is stored across two cards in feed I, high order column card preceding low order column card; read the quantity into ctrs. (C,D).

	C	7632
	D	7632

9. A quantity is stored in two entries in a value tape on interpolator I, high order columns preceding low order columns; read the quantity into ctrs. (C,D).

85		7
85	C	753
	D	753

(7) The special carry controls of the "ganged" counters are such that column 23 of the low order counter will carry to column 1 of the high order counter. Column 23 of the high order counter will carry to column 24 of both of the counters. Column 24 of the high order counter has an end around carry to column 1 of the lower order counter. The special codes operating these carry controls are an 8 combined with the normal read-in codes of the counters in the In columns.

(8) The special controls on counters 64, 65, 68 and 69 do not invalidate their use as normal storage counters. For usual operations, read-ins, read-outs and resets, the codes 7, 71, 73 and 731 of the respective counters apply.

10. Add the quantities stored across sws. or ctrs. (A,B), (C,D) and (E,F), deliver the sum to ctrs. (G,H). Use "ganged" ctrs. (69,68) for addition.

OUT	IN	MISC.
A	731	7
B	73	7
C	8731	7
D	873	7
E	8731	7
F	873	7
731	G	7
73	H	7

11. Subtract the quantity across sws. or ctrs. (C,D) from the quantity across sws. or ctrs. (A,B) and deliver the difference to ctrs. (E,F). Use "ganged" ctrs. (65,64) for subtraction.

OUT	IN	MISC.
A	71	7
B	7	7
C	871	732
D	87	732
71	E	7
7	F	7

(9) In order to use counter 70 as a sign control counter either the high order columns or the low order columns of the 46 column number may be read into counter 70, since both are prefixed by the algebraic sign.

12. Read the quantity stored across sws. or ctrs. (C,D) to ctrs. (E,F) under control of the algebraic sign of the number stored across ctrs. (A,B).

OUT	IN	MISC.
A	732	7
C	E	7432
D	F	7432

(10) In using the "ganged" counters in multiplication, the operating decimal point of the machine must lie between columns 46 and 47; i.e., between columns 23 and 24 of the high order counter. Therefore, computations in most cases must be normalized.

(11) The automatic check counter may be used in high accuracy computation if comparisons are made with known tolerances.

(a) If the tolerance is greater than or equal to 10^{-23} it is necessary to check the high order columns only.

13. Check the quantity across ctrs. (A,B) against a tolerance $\geq 10^{-23}$ in sw. P.

OUT	IN	MISC.
P	74	7
A	74	71
74	74	64

(b) If the tolerance is less than 10^{-23} it is necessary to check that the high order columns are all zero and that the low order columns are less than the tolerance.

14. Check the quantity stored across ctrs. (A,B) against a tolerance $< 10^{-23}$ in sw. Q. Sw. P $= 10^{-23}$.

OUT	IN	MISC.
P	74	7
A	74	71
74	74	64
Q	74	7
B	74	71
74	74	64

(12) To read a 46 column product out of the PQ counter special plugging is required. See Plugging Instructions.

(13) In general, all products involving 46 column numbers must be accumulated in one of the pairs of "ganged" counters using the special carry controls and the special product read-out. The error of this product is not more than 3 in the lowest order column.

(14) The code 873 or 87 in the In column of the line of coding reading out the product reads columns 24-46 of PQ to columns 1-23 of counter 68 or 64, and the sign column of PQ to column 24 of counter 68 or 64 respectively.

(15) The code 8731 or 871 in the In column of the line of coding reading out the product, followed immediately by the line (86, 873, 7) or (86, 87, 7), reads the sign column of PQ to column 24 of both counters 68 and 69 or 64 and 65, columns 24-46 of PQ to columns 1-23 of counter 69 or 65 and columns 1-23 of PQ to columns 1-23 of counter 68 or 64 respectively.

(16) The special carry controls operate throughout these processes, permitting the accumulation of the product.

(17) Let (A, B) and (C, D) indicate two 46 column numbers stored across these pairs of counters (high order columns in A and C).

(a) If all the numbers in a computation are known to be positive, the product (A, B) x (C, D) is built up as follows:

Columns 1-46 of A x C to columns 1-23 of the high order and 1-23 of the low order "ganged" counters under the special product read-out.

Columns 24-46 of A x D to columns 1-23 of the low order "ganged" counter under the special carry controls.

Columns 24-46 of B x C to columns 1-23 of the low order "ganged" counter under the special carry controls.

15. Multiply (A,B) by (C,D) and deliver the product to ctrs. (69,68). All values positive. Lines where operations may be interposed are left clear. 7's required if operations are interposed are given as (7).

OUT	IN	MISC.
A	761	(7)
C		(7)
	8731	7
86	873	7
A	761	(7)
D		(7)
	873	7
B	761	(7)
C		(7)
	873	7

(b) If some of the numbers in a computation may be negative, the product (A,B) x (C,D) is built up as follows:

Columns 1-46 of A x C to columns 1-23 of the high order and 1-23 of the low order "ganged" counters under the special product read-out.

Columns 24-46 of A x D to columns 1-23 of the low order "ganged" counter under the special carry controls, according as A x C is positive or negative and plus or minus zero to columns 1-23 of the high order "ganged" counter under the special carry controls and under control of counter 70.

Columns 24-46 of B x C to columns 1-23 of the low order "ganged" counter under the special carry controls, according as A x C is positive or negative and plus or minus zero to columns 1-23 of the high order "ganged" counter under the special carry controls and under control of counter 70.

16. Multiply (A,B) by (C,D) and deliver the product to ctrs. (65,64). Sw. P contains plus zero. Factors may be positive or negative. Lines where operations may be interposed are left clear. 7's required if operations are interposed are given as (7). In general, no quantities should be read into ctr. 65 before storing the algebraic sign in the choice counter.

OUT	IN	MISC.
A	761	(7)
C		(7)
	871	7
86	87	7
A	761	7
732	732	7
71	732	
D		7
P	871	7432
P	871	(7)432
	87	7
B	761	(7)

Continued on next page

16. (continued)

OUT	IN	MISC.
C		(7)
	87	7

(18) When one of the two factors of a product is known to be less than 10^{-23}, it is of the form (0,D). Only one multiplication need be performed and the product may be stored in any pair of counters E and F.

(a) If all numbers are known to be positive, columns 24-46 of A x D are read to columns 1-23 of counter F and counter E remains reset to zero.

(b) If some numbers may be negative, columns 24-46 of A x D are read to columns 1-23 of counter F and plus or minus zero to counter E under control of counter 70, according as A x D is positive or negative.

17. Multiply (A,B) by (0,D) and deliver the product to (E,F). Factors are positive. Spaces where operations may be interposed are left clear. 7's required if operations are interposed are given as (7).

OUT	IN	MISC.
A	761	(7)
D		(7)
	F	7

18. Multiply (A,B) by (0,D) and deliver the product to (E,F). Sw. P contains plus zero. Factors may be positive or negative. Spaces where operations may be interposed are left clear. 7's required if operations are interposed are given as (7). In general, no quantities should be read into ctr. F before storing the algebraic sign in the choice counter.

A	761	7
732	732	(7)
D		(7)

Continued on next page

18. (continued)

OUT	IN	MISC.
	F	7
F	732	7
P	E	7432

(19) When one of the two factors of a product has only 23 decimal places, only two multiplications need be performed and the factors are of the form (A,B) and (C,0).

(a) If all the numbers are known to be positive:

Columns 1-46 of A x C are read to columns 1-23 of the high order and 1-23 of the low order "ganged" counters.

Columns 24-46 of B x C are read to columns 1-23 of the low order "ganged" counter.

19. Multiply (A,B) by (C,0) and deliver the product to (69,68). All values are positive. Lines where operations may be interposed are left clear. 7's required if operations are interposed are given as (7).

OUT	IN	MISC.
A	761	(7)
C		(7)
	8731	7
86	873	7
B	761	(7)

Continued on next page

19. (continued)

OUT	IN	MISC.
C		(7)
	873	7

(b) If some numbers may be negative:

Columns 1-46 of A x C are read to columns 1-23 of the high order and 1-23 of the low order "ganged" counters.

Columns 24-46 of B x C are read to columns 1-23 of the low order "ganged" counter and plus or minus zero to the high order "ganged" counter under control of counter 70 according as A x C is positive or negative.

20. Multiply (A,B) by (C,0) and deliver the product to (69,68). Sw. P contains plus zero. Factors may be positive or negative. Lines where operations may be interposed are left clear. 7's required if operations are interposed are given as (7). In general, no quantities should be read into ctr. 69 before storing the algebraic sign in the choice counter.

OUT	IN	MISC.
A	761	7
732	732	(7)
C		(7)
	8731	7
86	873	7
B	761	7
731	732	7
P	8731	432
C		(7)

Continued on next page

20. (continued)

OUT	IN	MISC.
	873	7

(20) Division in high accuracy computation may be performed by dividing by the high order columns of the divisor to obtain a first approximation to the reciprocal, iterating once for the reciprocal and multiplying. Since the operating decimal point lies between columns 23 and 24, division should be plugged for 24 comparisons and the "Divide N minus Decimal" switch must be set at zero. If the absolute value of the divisor is such that $1 > |DR| > 10^{-n}$, in place of 1, 10^{-n} must be used as the dividend in obtaining the reciprocal. Thus after division the Q-shift counter stands at zero and the first approximation to the reciprocal is delivered as $Q \times 10^{-n-1}$. This quotient is then routed through either the LIO or the SIO counter and shifted to the left.

21. Divide (A, B) by (C, D), where either or both of the quantities may be negative, $1 > |C| > 0.1$, and deliver the quotient to (65, 64). The LIO-OUT is plugged to shift one column to the left. The SIO-OUT II is plugged to shift positive quantities one column to the left. The SIO-OUT I is plugged to read the 23rd column of SIO to the first column of the buss.

Sw. P = 1 in the 23rd column.
Sw. Q = 5 in the 2nd column.
Sw. R = minus zero.
Sw. S = 2 in the 23rd column.
Sw. T = 1 in the 1st column.

Counters G, H, 64, 65, 68, 69, 70, LIO and SIO are available for computation but are not reset.

The equations used in the computation are

$$x_0 = 1/|C|$$

$$N = |(C,D)|$$

$$x_1 = x_0(2 - Nx_0) .$$

After the iteration, five is added in column 3 to obtain the best result. Errors at various stages are as follows:

$$x_0/10 = 1/10N \pm 10^{-22}$$

$$x_1/10 = 1/10N \pm 51 \times 10^{-45}$$

Final result = $(A,B)/10(C,D) \pm 512 \times 10^{-46}$

An additional iteration will gain very little accuracy, the errors then being as follows:

$x_2/10 = 1/10N \pm 3 \times 10^{-45}$

Final result = $(A,B)/10(C,D) \pm 32 \times 10^{-46}$

The quotient as delivered to (65,64) is (A,B)/10(C,D). (7)'s must be omitted if no operations are interposed.

	OUT	IN	MISC.
$\lvert C\rvert$ to DR	C	76	72
reset ctr. G, reset SIO	G	G	7321
reset ctr. H, reset LIO	H	H	63
1 in 23rd col. to DD	P		7
reset ctr. 64	7	7	7
reset ctr. 65	71	71	7
reset ctr. 68	73	73	7
reset ctr. 69	731	731	7
reset ctr. 70	732	732	(7)
18 cycles free for interposed operations			
$1/(100\lvert C\rvert)$ to ctr. H		H	7
$1/(100\lvert C\rvert)$ to SIO	H	874	7
$1/(10\ \lvert C\rvert)$ to ctr. G = $x_0/10$	84	G	7
$-\lvert C\rvert$ to MC	C	761	71
reset ctr. H	H	H	(7)
$x_0/10$ to MP	G		(7)
$-\lvert C\rvert x_0/10$ to (69,68)		8731	7
	86	873	7

Continued on next page

21. (continued)	OUT	IN	MISC.
$-\|D\|$ to MC	D	761	71
-0 to (69,68)	R	8731	(7)
$x_0/10$ to MP	G		7
2 in 23rd col. to (69,68)	S	8731	(7)
$-\|D\|x_0/10$ to (69,68); (69,68) = $(2 - Nx_0)/10$		873	7
HO $(2 - Nx_0)/10$ to MC	731	761	(7)
$x_0/10$ to MP	G		(7)
$x_0(2 - Nx_0)/100$ to (65,64)		871	7
	86	87	7
LO $(2 - Nx_0)/10$ to MC	73	761	7
C to ctr. 70	C	732	7
5 in 2nd col. to ctr. 64	Q	87	
$x_0/10$ to MP	G		7
reset ctr. 68	73	73	7
reset ctr. 69	731	731	7
reset ctr. G	G	G	7

Continued on next page

21. (continued)

	OUT	IN	MISC.
reset SIO			321
$x_0(2 - Nx_0)/100$ to (65,64)		87	7
HO $x_0(2 - Nx_0)/100$ to LIO	71	765421	7
HO $x_0(2 - Nx_0)/10$ to ctr. G	831	G	7
LO $x_0(2 - Nx_0)/100$ to SIO	7	874	7
1st col. SIO to ctr. G; reset LIO; G = HO $x_1/10$	874	G	763
LO $x_0(2 - Nx_0)/10$ to ctr. H; H = LO $x_1/10$	84	H	7
A to MC under control of ctr. 70	A	761	7432
reset ctr. 64	7	7	7
reset ctr. 65	71	71	
HO $x_1/10$ to MP	G		(7)
$(A,B)x_1/10$ to (65,64)		871	7
	86	87	7
A to MC under control of ctr. 70	A	761	(7)432
LO $x_1/10$ to MP	H		(7)
$(A,B)x_1/10$ to (65,64)		87	7
B to MC under control of ctr. 70	B	761	7432
reset ctr. 70	732	732	7

Continued on next page

21. (continued)

	OUT	IN	MISC.
-HO $(A,B)x_1/10$ to ctr. 70	71	732	32
HO $x_1/10$ to MP	G		7
±0 to (65,64) under control of ctr. 70	R	871	7432
±0 to (65,64) under control of ctr. 70	R	871	7432
1 in 1st col. to ctr. 64	T	87	
$(A,B)x_1/10$ to (65,64)		87	7

(21) If 46 column numbers are to be punched in cards, they must be punched in two cards, one containing the high order columns and the algebraic sign, and the second, the low order columns and the algebraic sign.

	OUT	IN	MISC.
22. Punch out the number (A,B).	A	753	
			51
	B	753	
			75

(22) To print 46 column numbers, the high order columns may be printed on one typewriter and the low order columns on the other. If the low order columns are printed with several spaces after the decimal point, the algebraic sign and the decimal point may be cut off and the strips joined side by side.

	OUT	IN	MISC.
23. Print the number (A,B).	A	7432	
		752	6
	B	74321	
		7521	7

(23) If numbers have been normalized for high accuracy computation, they may usually be printed with their decimal points in true position by suitable typewriter plugging. See Plugging Instructions.

(24) The following is an example of the building up of a series in high accuracy computation.

24. Determine $Ax^2 + Bx + C$, where no information is given of any algebraic sign, store the result in (E, F), and print it on typewriter I. A, B and C are 46 column numbers stored in switches (A_1, A_2), (B_1, B_2) and (C_1, C_2). Sw. P = plus zero. x is stored in ctrs. (x_1, x_2).

Counters E, F, 64, 65, 68, 69 and 70 are available for computation. (7)'s must be omitted if no operations are interposed.

24. (continued)	OUT	IN	MISC.
A_1 to MC	A_1	761	7
reset ctr. 69	731	731	7
reset ctr. 68	73	73	
x_1 to MP	x_1		7
reset ctr. 70	732	732	7
reset ctr. 65	71	71	7
reset ctr. 64	7	7	
HO A_1x_1 to ctr. 69		8731	7
LO A_1x_1 to ctr. 68	86	873	7
A_1 to MC	A_1	761	7
A_1x_1 to ctr. 70	731	732	7
±0 to (69,68) under control of ctr. 70	P	8731	432
x_2 to MP	x_2		7
±0 to (69,68) under control of ctr. 70	P	8731	7432
B_1 to ctr. 69	B_1	8731	7
B_2 to ctr. 68	B_2	873	
A_1x_2 to (69,68)		873	7
A_2 to MC	A_2	761	(7)
x_1 to MP	x_1		(7)
A_2x_1 to (69,68)		873	7
x_1 to MC	x_1	761	7

Continued on next page

24. (continued)

	OUT	IN	MISC.
reset ctr. 70	732	732	(7)
HO (Ax + B) to MP	731		(7)
HO $(Ax + B)x_1$ to ctr. 65		871	7
LO $(Ax + B)x_1$ to ctr. 64	86	87	7
x_1 to MC	x_1	761	7
HO $(Ax + B)x_1$ to ctr. 70	71	732	(7)
LO (Ax + B) to MP	73		7
±0 to (65,64) under control of ctr. 70	P	871	7432
±0 to (65,64) under control of ctr. 70	P	871	(7)432
$(Ax + B)x_1$ to (65,64); turn on typewriter I	872	87	7
x_2 to MC	x_2	761	7
reset ctr. E	E	E	7
reset ctr. F	F	F	
HO (Ax + B) to MP	731		7
C_1 to ctr. 65	C_1	871	7
C_2 to ctr. 64	C_2	87	(7)
$(Ax + B)x_2$ to (65,64)		87	7
ctr. 65 to ctr. E	71	E	7
ctr. 64 to ctr. F	7	F	7

Continued on next page

24. (continued)

Instruction	OUT	IN	MISC.
print value in ctr. 65 on typewriter I	71	7432	
		752	6
print value in ctr. 64 on typewriter I	7	7432	
		752	6

NORMALIZING REGISTER

(1) Any positive quantity may be shifted so that its first significant digit stands in the 23rd machine column. This is done within the machine by multiplying the given quantity by a one in such a position that the first significant digit will fall in the 23rd column of the PQ counter. The product is then read out of the first 23 columns of the PQ counter by means of the low order product read-out (86 in the Out column). The number of columns shifted is recorded in a counter and a predetermined number of significant digits and a power of ten are read out. For example, if

0000 35296 73145 89740 28715
0000 00000 00000 27557 68214

stand in the machine, operating with decimal point between columns 15 and 16, they may be read out as

3529 1 ; i.e., 3529 x 10
2755 -9 ; i.e., 2755 x 10^{-9}.

Thus the second quantity printed indicates the power of ten by which the first quantity is to be multiplied.

(2) The number of significant digits printed and the position of the decimal point, if printed, are determined by the typewriter plugging.

(3) The power of ten recorded is determined by the position of the final decimal point and the operating decimal point of the machine.

A constant K is placed in a switch in columns 20 and 21. Here K = 23 - n - d, where d is equal to the number of digits to the left of the final decimal point and the operating decimal point of the machine lies between columns n and n + 1.

The power of ten recorded lies in columns 20 and 21 and must be read out or printed out of those columns.

(4) Negative quantities must be routed through this procedure as positive absolute values. The algebraic sign is stored in counter 70 and the final read-out of the quantity must be under control of counter 70.

(5) The code 8321 in the In column shifts the quantity under consideration into the first 23 columns of PQ. The code 8321 in the Out column reads the amount of the shift to the counter indicated. These codes are not independent and must be used in conjunction with the multiplication coding as shown below.

(6) The special coding requires nine cycles of computation time. Counter A contains the quantity to be treated. Counters B, C, D and E are reset and available for computation. Switch SC contains the constant K. At the end of the process, counter B contains the power of ten, counter D contains the quantity under consideration with its first significant digit in the 23rd column and counter E contains the "one" multiplier selected by the shift circuit. Note that the line of coding reading the normal product-out may not be used for any other operation.

1. The operating decimal point lies between cols. 15 and 16. The final decimal point is to lie between cols. 19 and 20. Thus K = 4 is placed in col. 20 of sw.SC. The quantity in ctr.A is shifted and printed together with its power of ten.

OUT	IN	MISC.
A	761	7
SC	B	7

Continued on next page

1. (continued)

This line of coding may contain any of the codes normally interposed in multiplication. (A second such line may also be interposed if it is known that the quantity to be shifted does not equal zero.)

OUT	IN	MISC.
A	8321	
	E	7
8321	C	7
		7
C	B	32
		7
86	D	7
D	7432	
	752	6
B	7432	
	752	7

(7) It is advisable to check the multiplication involved in this process by interchanging multiplier and multiplicand. Thus the "one" multiplier, read into storage counter E, is used as the multiplicand in the second multiplication. The product is again read out under the special low order read-out.

2. The operating decimal point lies between cols. 15 and 16. The final decimal point is to lie between cols. 19 and 20. The tolerance of one in the first column lies in sw. SB.

OUT	IN	MISC.
A	761	7
SC	B	7
A	8321	
	E	7
8321	C	7
		7
C	B	32
		7
86	D	7
E	761	7
74	74	7
SB	74	

Continued on next page

2. (continued)

OUT	IN	MISC.
A		7
D	F	(7)32
		7
86	F	7
F	74	71
		64

LOGARITHM UNIT

(1) The logarithmic function delivered by the machine is $\log_{10}x$. Logarithms to other bases may be obtained by multiplying by a suitable constant.

$$\log_a N = \frac{\log_{10}N}{\log_{10}a} = \log_{10}N \cdot \log_a 10$$

In particular

$$\log_e N = \log_{10}N \cdot \log_e 10$$

where

$$\log_e 10 = 2.302\ 585\ 092\ 994\ 045\ 684\ 017\ 991.$$

(2) If the operating decimal point lies between columns 21 and 22, the error in this function is less than 5×10^{-21}. If the decimal point lies between columns n and n + 1, n< 21, the error is less than $10^{-n} + 5 \times 10^{-21}$. If desired, for log x > 0, a coded half pick-up may be added and the error reduced to $1/2(10^{-n} + 10^{-20})$ as shown in example 4 below.

(3) The range of arguments covered is 10^{-22} to $10^{23} - 1$.

(4) Logarithms with negative characteristics may not be computed directly if there are ten or fewer operating decimal places. For exception, see note (10).

(5) The two dial switches labeled "Log N value" to the right of the sequence mechanism must be set at 22 - n, where the operating decimal point is between columns n and n + 1.

(6) The logarithm unit requires plugging of the LIO counter to care for the decimal point. See Plugging Instructions.

(7) The LIO counter may be used as a storage counter, for the addition of positive quantities, and to shift numbers, since it has a pluggable read-out. See Logarithm In-Out Counter and Plugging Instructions.

(8) Before using the logarithm unit it should be tested on known values:

$$e = 2.718\ 281\ 828\ 459\ 045\ 235\ 360\ 287,$$

$$\log_{10}e = 0.434\ 294\ 481\ 903\ 251\ 827\ 651\ 129.$$

(9) Any operation not using the buss may be carried on during the logarithm computation time. This requires a 7 in the Miscellaneous column of the first line of logarithm coding and no automatic (no 7 in the Miscellaneous column) in the last line of interposed coding. This coding is shown in example 5.

1. x lies in sw. or ctr. A. Determine $\log_{10}x$ and deliver it to ctr. B.

OUT	IN	MISC.
A	762	
831	B	7
		763

LOGARITHM UNIT

2. x lies in sw. or ctr. A. Determine $\log_{10}|x|$ and deliver it to ctr. B.

OUT	IN	MISC.
A	762	2
831	B	7
		763

3. x lies in sw. or ctr. A. Determine $\log_e x$ and deliver it to ctr. B. $\text{Log}_e 10$ lies in sw. P.

A	762	
831	B	7
		763
B	761	
P		7
B	B	
	B	7

4. Log x > 0. x lies in sw. or ctr. A. Determine $\log_{10} x$ and deliver it to ctr. B. If the operating decimal point lies between columns n and n + 1, sw. P must contain a 5 in the (21 - n)th column.

A	762	
P	765421	7
831	B	7
		763

5. Print the quantities in ctrs. C and D. Punch the quantity in ctr. E. Step the value tape on interpolator I ahead twice. x lies in sw. or ctr. A. Determine $\log_{10} x$ and deliver it to ctr. B.

	C	7432	
	D	74321	
	E	753	
	A	762	75
		752	753
			753
(repeat this line 23 times)			7
		7521	
	831	B	7
			763

(10) If negative logarithms are computed when there are ten or fewer operating decimal places, more nines will be required for the read-out of the complementary figure than the ten that are available by plugging. The additional nines required may be supplied from a switch under control of the choice counter. If the operating decimal point is between columns 8 and 9, 13 nines are needed in columns 11-23. Ten of them are supplied by plugging to ten columns, say 14-23, and three are supplied from a switch to columns 11-13.

6. The operating decimal point lies between cols. 8 and 9. x lies in sw. or ctr. A. Sw. P has 000 in cols. 11-13. The other columns of sw. P (cols. 1-10 and 14-24) are set on the blank position (not zero). Nines are plugged to cols. 14-23. The algebriac sign, col. 24, is bottle-plugged as usual. Determine $\log_{10} x$ and deliver it to ctr. B.

OUT	IN	MISC.
A	762	
831	B	7
B	732	763
P	B	7432

EXPONENTIAL UNIT

(1) The exponential function delivered by the machine is 10^x. Exponential functions of other bases may be obtained by multiplication.

$$a^x = 10^{x \log_{10} a}$$

In particular

$$e^x = 10^{x \log_{10} e}$$

where

$$\log_{10} e = 0.434\ 294\ 481\ 903\ 251\ 827\ 651\ 129.$$

(2) If the operating decimal point lies between columns 21 and 22, the error in this function is less than 5×10^{-21}. If the decimal point lies between columns n and n + 1, n < 21, the error is less than $10^{-n} + 5 \times 10^{-21}$. A half pick-up maybe added and the error reduced, as shown in example 5 below, to $1/2(10^{-n} + 10^{-20})$.

(3) The range of arguments covered is - 20 to 23 - 10^{-n} where the operating decimal point lies between columns n and n + 1.

(4) Any operation not using the buss may be carried on during the exponential computation time. This requires a 7 in the Miscellaneous column of the first line of exponential coding and no automatic (no 7 in the Miscellaneous column) in the last line of interposed coding. This is shown in example 6.

(5) The exponential unit requires plugging of the EIO counter to care for the decimal point. See Plugging Instructions.

(6) If an exponential is preceded by a multiplication or a division, at least one line of coding (blank, blank, 7) or some other operation not involving a functional unit must be inserted between the operations.

(7) If an exponential is preceded by an interpolation, at least one line of coding (blank, blank, 7) or some other operation not involving a functional unit must be inserted between the operations. This with the last line of interpolation coding makes two such lines intervening.

(8) The hyperbolic functions may be obtained from the exponential functions by algebraic operations.

(9) Before using the exponential unit in a computation, it should be tested on known values.

$$10^{\log_{10} e} = e$$

$$\log_{10} e = 0.434\ 294\ 481\ 903\ 251\ 827\ 651\ 129$$

$$e = 2.718\ 281\ 828\ 459\ 045\ 235\ 360\ 287$$

1. x lies in sw. or ctr. A. Compute 10^x and deliver it to ctr. B.

OUT	IN	MISC.
A	7621	
	741	
832	B	
		731

2. x lies in sw. (except IVS) or ctr. A. Compute 10^{-x} and deliver it to ctr. B.

OUT	IN	MISC.
A	7621	32
	741	
832	B	
		731

3. x lies in IVS. Compute 10^{-x} and deliver it to ctr. B.

8431	7621	21
	741	
832	B	
		731

4. x lies in sw. or ctr. A. Ctr. C is available for computation. $\text{Log}_{10}e$ lies in sw. P. Compute e^x and deliver it to ctr. B.

A	761	
P		
	C	7
		7
C	7621	
	741	
832	B	
		731

5. x lies in sw. or ctr. A. Sw. P contains a 5 in the (21 - n)th column, where the operating decimal point lies between columns n and n + 1. Compute 10^x and deliver it to ctr. B.

A	7621	
	741	
P	741	
832	B	
		731

6. Print the quantities in ctrs. C and D. Punch the quantity in ctr. E. Step the tape on interpolator II back three times. x lies in ctr. A. Compute 10^x and deliver it to ctr. B.

C	7432	

Continued on next page

6. (continued)

	OUT	IN	MISC.
	D	74321	
	E	753	
	A	7621	75
		752	7541
			7541
(repeat this line 22 times)			7
		7521	541
		741	
	832	B	
			731

7. x lies in sw. or ctr. A. Ctr. C is available for computation. Sw. P = 1. Sw. Q = 1/2. Sw. R = $\log_{10} e$. Compute sinh x and deliver it to ctr. B. If x is known to be positive, bracketed codes and lines may be omitted.

A	761	(2)
R		
	C	7
		7
C	7621	
	741	
832	B	
		731
B	76	32
P		
	B	7
B	761	(7)
(732)	(732)	(7)
(A)	(732)	(7)
Q		7(432)
B	B	
	B	7

8. x lies in sw. or ctr. A. Ctr. C is available for computation. Sw. P = 1. Sw. Q = 1/2. Sw. R = $\log_{10}e$. Compute cosh x and deliver it to ctr. B.

OUT	IN	MISC.
A	761	
R		
	C	7
		7
C	7621	2
	741	
832	B	
		731
B	76	
P		
	B	7
B	761	
Q		7
B	B	
	B	7

9. x lies in sw. or ctr. A. Sw. P = 1. Sw. Q = $\log_{10}e$. Ctrs. C and D are available for computation. Compute tanh x and deliver it to ctr. B. If x is known to be positive, bracketed codes and lines may be omitted.

A	C	7(2)
A	C	7(2)
C	761	(7)
(732)	(732)	(7)
(A)	(732)	(7)
Q		
	D	7
		7
D	7621	
	741	
832	B	

Continued on next page

9. (continued)

OUT	IN	MISC.
		731
P	B	7
B	76	7(432)
P	B	732
P	B	32
B		7
B	B	
	B	7

SQUARE ROOTS AND OTHER ITERATIVE PROCESSES

(1) Roots and reciprocals of roots may be found by using logarithms and exponentials. However, if a good first approximation is available, the method of iteration is not only faster, but is also self-corrective.

(2) Square roots may be found using logarithms and exponentials by

$$N^{1/2} = 10^{(\log_{10}N)/2}$$

1. N lies in ctr. A. $N^{1/2}$ is to be delivered to ctr. B. Ctrs. C and D are available for computation. Sw. P = 1/2.

OUT	IN	MISC.
A	762	
831	C	7
		763
C	761	
P		
	D	7
		7
D	7621	
	741	
832	B	
		731

(3) The Newton-Raphson method of determining the roots of an equation f(x) = 0 requires that $f'(x) \neq 0$ and $f''(x) \neq 0$ between the first approximation, x_0, to the root of f(x) and $\bar{x}$, the root sought, and that $f(x_0) \cdot f''(x_0) > 0$. Then

$$\text{(A)}\quad x_{n+1} = x_n - \frac{f(x_n)}{f'(x_n)}, \quad n = 0, 1, 2, \ldots$$

gives successive approximations to $\bar{x}$. If successive iterations involving division are performed, the accuracy of division should be successively increased. This method may after further investigation be applied in some cases when the function does not satisfy all of the above conditions.

In some cases the computation may be simplified by using

$$\text{(B)}\quad x_{n+1} = x_n - \frac{f(x_n)}{f'(x_0)}, \quad n = 0, 1, 2, \ldots$$

for the successive iterations, though this does not converge as rapidly as (A).

(4) If the method of iteration is used to obtain the positive square root of N, then

$$x_{n+1} = (x_n + N/x_n)/2\,.$$

In performing the successive iterations, the accuracy of division should be successively increased. The error, e_{n+1}, of x_{n+1} is given by:

$$e_{n+1} = x_{n+1} - N^{1/2}$$

$$= e_n^2 / 2(e_n + N^{1/2}) \quad \text{and}$$

$$e_{n+1} < e_n^2 / 2N^{1/2}, \qquad n > 0.$$

(5) Since most machine computation is repeated for values of N which change by small amounts, the root or reciprocal calculated for the preceding value of N will in general be available for use as a first approximation when starting the next iterative process.

2. N lies in ctr. A. The approximation to $N^{1/2}$ lies in ctr. B. Read the next approximation to ctr. B. Sw. P = 1/2.

OUT	IN	MISC.
B	76	
A		
	B	7
B	761	
P		7
B	B	
	B	7

(6) If two successive iterations are to be made in finding $N^{1/2}$, machine time may be saved by using the following coding which involves two divisions, one multiplication and four additions instead of two divisions and two multiplications. Usually it will be possible to interpose the four adding cycles, thus reducing the time for two iterations to 81 cycles.

3. N lies in ctr. A. The approximation x_0 to $N^{1/2}$ lies in ctr. B. Read the approximation x_2 to ctr. B. Sw. P = 1/4. (7)'s are to be omitted if no operations are interposed. Ctr. C is available for computation.

	OUT	IN	MISC.
x_0 to MC	B	761	7
reset ctr. C	C	C	7
x_0 to ctr. C	B	C	
1/4 to MP	P		7
x_0 to ctr. C	B	C	7
x_0 to ctr. C	B	C	7

Continued on next page

3. (continued)

	OUT	IN	MISC.
x_0 to ctr. C; $C = 4x_0$	B	C	7
reset ctr. B	B	B	
$x_0/4$ to ctr. B		B	7
$4x_0$ to DR; place limitation	C	76	76432
reset ctr. C	C	C	(7)
N to DD	A		(7)
$n + 1$ cycles free for interposed operations where n is the number of significant digits (including the first "no go") for which the Misc. 6432 code is plugged.			
$N/4x_0$ to ctr. B; $B = x_0/4 + N/4x_0 = x_1/2$		B	7
$x_1/2$ to ctr. C	B	C	7
$x_1/2$ to ctr. C	B	C	7
$x_1/2$ to ctr. C	B	C	7
$x_1/2$ to ctr. C; $C = 2x_1$	B	C	7
$2x_1$ to DR	C	76	(7)
N to DD	A		(7)
$n + 1$ cycles free for interposed operations where n is the number of significant digits (including the first "no go") in the quotient.			
$N/2x_1$ to ctr. B; $B = x_1/2 + N/2x_1 = x_2$		B	7

(7) If other computations are being carried on in which operations may be interposed, the time for three successive iterations may be reduced from three divisions and three multiplications to three divisions, one multiplication and 13 adding cycles, which may be interposed.

(8) To find the cube root of N by iteration

$$x_{n+1} = 2x_n/3 + N/3x_n^2 \quad \text{and}$$

$$e_{n+1} < e_n^2/(e_n + N^{1/3}).$$

4. N lies in ctr. A. The approximation to $N^{1/3}$ lies in ctr. B. Read the next approximation to ctr. B. Ctr. C is available for computation and sw. P = 1/3. (7)'s must be omitted if no operations are interposed.

n cycles free for interposed operations where n is the number of significant digits (including the first "no go") in the quotient.

OUT	IN	MISC.
B	761	7
C	C	(7)
B		(7)
	C	7
C	76	7
C	C	7
B	C	
A		7
B	C	(7)
	C	7
C	761	7
C	C	7
B	B	
P		(7)
	B	7

(9) The cube root of N may also be found by iteration by

$$x_{n+1} = \frac{x_n^3 + 2N}{2x_n^3 + N}\, x_n$$

This involves three multiplications and a division but in most cases converges much more rapidly than the method given in note (8), so that fewer iterations need be used for the desired accuracy. If two successive approximations x_n and x_{n+1} agree in the first i significant digits, then x_{n+1} will be correct to 3i - 2 digits. The error e_{n+1} is given by:

$$e_{n+1} = \frac{e_n^3 (e_n + 2N^{1/3})}{2(e_n + N^{1/3})^3 + N}$$

5. N lies in ctr. A. The approximation to $N^{1/3}$ lies in ctr. B. Read the next approximation to ctr. B. Ctrs. C and D are available for computation. (7)'s must be omitted if no operations are interposed.

	OUT	IN	MISC.
	B	761	7
	C	C	7
	D	D	
	B		(7)
		C	7
	C	761	7
	C	C	7
	A	D	
	B		(7)
Ctr. C $= x_0^3$		C	7
	C	D	7
Ctr. D $= 2x_0^3 + N$	C	D	7
	D	76	7
	A	C	7
Ctr. C $= x_0^3 + 2N$	A	C	
	C		7
	C	C	7

Continued on next page

5. (continued)

n - 1 cycles free for interposed operations where n is the number of significant digits (including the first "no go") in the quotient.

Ctr. C = $(x_0^3 + 2N) / (2x_0^3 + N)$

Ctr. B = $x_0(x_0^3 + 2N) / (2x_0^3 + N) = x_1$

OUT	IN	MISC.
D	D	(7)
	C	7
C	761	(7)
B		7
B	B	7
C	C	(7)
	B	7

(10) The reciprocal of N may be found by iteration using

$$x_{n+1} = x_n(2 - Nx_n) ,$$

$$e_{n+1} = -Ne_n^2 .$$

In high accuracy computation, it is necessary to use this process for division.

6. N lies in ctr. A. The approximation to 1/N lies in ctr. B. Ctr. C is available for computation. Sw. P = 2. (7)'s must be omitted if no operations are interposed. The new approximation to the reciprocal of N is to be delivered to ctr. B.

OUT	IN	MISC.
A	761	732
C	C	7
P	C	
B		(7)

Continued on next page

6. (continued)

OUT	IN	MISC.
	C	7
B	761	(7)
C		7
C	C	7
B	B	
	B	7

(11) In many applications of the process of iteration the choice of the function f(x) can be so made as to conserve much machine time. This is evident in iterating for $1/N^{1/p}$. f(x) may be written either as

(1) $f(x) = 1/x^p - N$

or (2) $f(x) = 1 - Nx^p$.

(1) leads to

(1a) $x_{n+1} = x_n \left[\frac{p+1}{p} - \frac{N}{p} x_n{}^p \right]$

which requires p + 2 multiplications, unless N/p is available, in which case only p + 1 multiplications are required.

(2) leads to

(2a) $x_{n+1} = \frac{1 + (p-1)Nx_n^p}{pNx_n^{(p-1)}}$

which requires p + 1 multiplications and a division. Obviously, the former requires less machine time than the latter and should be used for all roots of reciprocals. If (1a) is used to obtain $1/N^{1/2}$, the error after each iteration is

$$e_{n+1} = -\frac{3e_n^2 N^{1/2}}{2} .$$

7. N lies in ctr. A. The approximation to $N^{-1/2}$ lies in ctr. B. Read the next approximation to ctr. B. Ctr. C is available for computation. Sw. P = 1/2. Sw. Q = 3. (7)'s must be omitted if no operations are interposed.

OUT	IN	MISC.
B	761	7
C	C	(7)

Continued on next page

7. (continued)

OUT	IN	MISC.
B		(7)
	C	7
C	761	732
C	C	7
Q	C	
A		(7)
	C	7
C	761	7
C	C	(7)
B		(7)
	C	7
C	761	7
C	C	(7)
P		7

Continued on next page

7. (continued)

OUT	IN	MISC.
B	B	
	B	7

8. N/2 lies in ctr. A. The approximation to $N^{-1/2}$ lies in ctr. B. Read the next approximation to ctr. B. Ctr. C is available for computation. Sw. P = 3/2. (7)'s must be omitted if no operations are interposed. The computation of example 7 may be modified so that the method of example 8 may be used for each successive iteration after the first, thereby requiring four multiplications for the first iteration and three for each thereafter. In this case, Sw. Q = 3/2, and N/2 is computed directly and retained, rather than computing each iteration in the form

$$x_{n+1} = x_n(3/2 - x_n^2 \, N/2).$$

B	761	7
C	C	(7)
B		(7)
	C	7
C	761	7
C	C	7
P	C	
A		(7)32
	C	7
C	761	(7)
B		7
C	C	7

Continued on next page

8. (continued)

OUT	IN	MISC.
B	B	(7)
	B	7

(12) The Rule of False Position

If f(x) is continuous in the interval $a \leq x \leq b$ and f(a) and f(b) are of opposite sign, then

$$a' = a - \frac{(b - a)\, f(a)}{f(b) - f(a)}$$

is a first approximation to the root of f(x) lying between a and b. Since f(a') and either f(a) or f(b) are of opposite sign, either

$$a'' = a - \frac{(a' - a)\, f(a)}{f(a') - f(a)} \quad \text{or} \quad a'' = b - \frac{(a' - b)\, f(b)}{f(a') - f(b)}$$

is a second approximation.

9. If counter A = a
   counter B = b
   counter C = f(a)
   counter D = f(b)
   switch P = 1/2

and counters E through L and counter 70 are available for computation, the following coding will deliver:

a or b depending on the sign of f(a') to counter A,
a' to counter B,
f(a) or f(b) depending on the sign of f(a') to counter C,
f(a') to counter D.

The coding may be repeated to obtain the desired accuracy and the accuracy of division should be increased with the repetitions.

	OUT	IN	MISC.
reset ctr. F.	F	F	7
a to ctr. F	A	F	7
- b to ctr. F; F = a - b	B	F	732
f(a) to MC	C	761	7
reset ctr. I	I	I	7

Continued on next page

9. (continued)	OUT	IN	MISC.
f(a) to ctr. I	C	I	
- (b - a) to MP	F		7
- f(b) to ctr. I; I = f(a) - f(b)	D	I	732
reset ctr. 70	732	732	7
reset ctr. K	K	K	
- (b - a) f(a) to ctr. K		K	7
f(b) - f(a) to DR	I	76	732
reset ctr. E	E	E	7
a to ctr. E	A	E	
- (b - a) f(a) to DD	K		7
reset ctr. K	K	K	7
a to ctr. K	A	K	7
b to ctr. E; E = a + b	B	E	7
reset ctr. H	H	H	7
f(a) to ctr. H	C	H	7
f(b) to ctr. H; H = f(a) + f(b)	D	H	7
reset ctr. G	G	G	7
f(a) to ctr. 70	C	732	7
(a - b) or - (a - b) to ctr. G	F	G	7432
reset ctr. J	J	J	7
[f(a) - f(b)] or - [f(a) - f(b)] to ctr. J	I	J	432
a' in ctr. K		K	7

f(a') is computed and stored in ctr. L; during the computation, ctr. 70 is reset	732	732	7
- f(a') to ctr. 70	L	732	732
2a or 2b to ctr. E under control of ctr. 70	G	E	7432

Continued on next page

9. (continued)

	OUT	IN	MISC.
2f(a) or 2f(b) to ctr. H under control of ctr. 70	J	H	7432
2a or 2b to MC	E	761	7
reset ctr. B	B	B	7
a' to ctr. B	K	B	7
1/2 to MP	P		7
reset ctr. D	D	D	7
f(a') to ctr. D	L	D	7
reset ctr. A	A	A	
a or b to ctr. A		A	7
2f(a) or 2f(b) to MC	H	761	(7)
1/2 to MP	P		7
reset ctr. C	C	C	
f(a) or f(b) to ctr. C		C	7

SINE UNIT

(1) If the operating decimal point lies between columns 22 and 23, the error in this function is less than 5×10^{-22}. If the decimal point lies between columns n and n + 1, n < 22, the error is less than $6.5 \times 10^{-n} + 5 \times 10^{-22}$. A half pick-up may be added and the error reduced to less than $6 \times 10^{-n} + 5 \times 10^{-22}$ as shown in example 5 below.

(2) Any positive or negative argument in radians may be used, except that sines of third and fourth quadrant angles cannot be computed directly if there are eleven or fewer operating decimal places. For exception, see note (10).

(3) The sine unit requires plugging of the SIO counter and the read-out of $1/2\,\pi$ to care for the decimal point. See Plugging Instructions.

(4) The SIO counter may be used as a storage counter, for the addition of positive quantities and to shift or split numbers, since it has pluggable read-in and read-outs. See Sine In-Out Counter and Plugging Instructions.

(5) Before using the sine unit in a computation it should be tested on known values.

sin 0 = 0

sin 0.584 073 464 102 067 615 3736 = 0.551 426 681 241 690 550 6611

sin 1.867 258 771 281 654 092 2989 = 0.956 375 928 404 503 013 4325

sin π = sin 3.141 592 653 589 793 238 4626 = - 0

sin 3.867 258 771 281 654 092 2989 =-0.663 633 884 212 967 502 1510

sin 4.867 258 771 281 654 092 2989 =-0.988 031 624 092 861 789 9878

The unit should also be tested for sines of negative arguments.

(6) Any operation not using the buss may be carried on during the sine computation time. This requires a 7 in the Miscellaneous column of the first line of sine coding and no automatic (no 7 in the Miscellaneous column) in the last line of interposed coding. This is shown in example 6 below.

(7) Two sines may not be computed successively. At least one line of coding, (blank, blank, 7) or some other operation not involving the functional units must be inserted.

(8) The cosine may be computed by the sine unit by means of the relation

$$\cos x = \sin(\pi/2 - x).$$

(9) The remaining trigonometric functions may be computed by the usual algebraic operations.

1. x lies in sw. or ctr. A. Compute sin x and deliver it to ctr. B.

OUT	IN	MISC.
A	7631	
84	B	7
		7321

SINE UNIT

	OUT	IN	MISC.
2. x lies in sw. (except IVS) or ctr. A. Compute sin (-x) and deliver it to ctr. B.	A	7631	32
	84	B	7
			7321
3. x lies in IVS. Compute sin (-x) and deliver it to ctr. B.	8431	7631	21
	84	B	7
			7321
4. x lies in sw. or ctr. A. $\pi/2$ lies in sw. P. Ctr. C is available for computation. Compute cos x and deliver it to ctr. B.	P	C	7
	A	C	732
	C	7631	
	84	B	7
			7321
5. x lies in sw. or ctr. A. Compute sin x and deliver it to ctr. B. Sw. P contains a 5 in the (22 - n)th column when the operating decimal point lies between columns n and n + 1.	A	7631	
	P	874	7
	84	B	7
			7321
6. Print the quantities in ctrs. C and D. Punch the quantity in ctr. E. Step the value tape on interpolator III back twice. x lies in sw. or ctr. A. Compute sin x and deliver it to ctr. B.	C	7432	
	D	74321	
	E	753	
	A	7631	75
		752	7542
(repeat this line 23 times)			7
		7521	542

Continued on next page

6. (continued)

OUT	IN	MISC.
84	B	7
		7321

(10) If negative sines are computed when there are eleven or fewer operating decimal places, more nines will be required for the read-out of the complementary figure than the ten that are available by plugging. The additional nines required may be supplied from a switch under control of the choice counter. If the operating decimal point is between columns 9 and 10, 13 nines are needed in columns 11-23. Ten of them are supplied by plugging to ten columns, say 14-23, and three are supplied from a switch to columns 11-23.

7. The operating decimal point lies between cols. 9 and 10. x lies in sw. or ctr. A. Sw. P has 000 in cols. 11-13. The other columns of sw. P (cols. 1-10 and 14-24) are set on the blank position (not zero). Nines are plugged to cols. 14-23. The algebraic sign, col. 24, is bottle-plugged as usual. Compute sin x and deliver it to ctr. B.

OUT	IN	MISC.
A	7631	
84	B	7
B	732	7321
P	B	7432

(11) Before using the sine unit, the "85-1 P.U." switch and "SIO-OUT-2 Invert Control" switch must both lie in the on position.

INTERPOLATORS

(1) If an interpolator has not been in use for some time, it should be tested before being used in a computation. Diagonal numbers should be read out. If interpolation is to be carried on, several values should be computed.

(2) A tape containing a set of numerical values, arbitrary constants or random values of a function is called a value tape rather than a functional tape.

(3) Before using a functional tape, two switch settings must be made. One half the number of arguments is set up in the push button switches labeled "Value Tape set up 1/2 "A" values in tape" above the interpolator. The number of interpolational coefficients (including C_0) is set in each of the dial switches labeled "Set up number of "C" values on each switch" above the interpolator. See note (28) for special use of the dial switches.

(4) The tape decimal point, the "highest order 'h' " and the interval of the argument must be specified for proper plugging of the interpolators. If the tape contains negative C values, the decimal point may not be shifted to the right. See Plugging Instructions.

(5) It is desirable that functional tapes be designed with the tape decimal point between columns 15 and 16 unless more decimal places are needed for the desired accuracy.

(6) A functional tape positions to the closest value of the argument if the Miscellaneous column of the first line of interpolation coding is blank or 61. It positions to the closest lower value of the argument if the Miscellaneous column of the first line of coding contains 641 or if the first column of the interpolation counter is not plugged.

(7) If an argument which is not in the range of the tape is sent to the interpolator, a red light is switched on above interpolator I and the machine is stopped.

(8) Interpolators I, II and III are distinguished by the operational codes 7654, 76541 and 76542 respectively in the In column.

1. x lies in sw. or ctr. A. The functional tape is on interpolator I. Determine f(x) and deliver it to ctr. B.

OUT	IN	MISC.
A	7654	
		62
841		
A	763	
	B	73
		7

2. x lies in sw. (except IVS) or ctr. A. The functional tape is on interpolator II. Determine f(-x) and deliver it to ctr. B.

A	76541	32
		62
841		
A	763	32

Continued on next page

2. (continued)

OUT	IN	MISC.
	B	73
		7

3. x lies in ctr. A. The functional tape is on interpolator III. Determine f(|x|) and deliver it to ctr. B.

A	76542	2
		62
841		
A	763	2
	B	73
		7

(9) An addition, reset, reading to a print counter or any other operation not involving the multiply-divide unit or the interpolators may be inserted in the last line of interpolation coding. The typewriters may be turned on or off in the next to the last line of interpolation coding (line resetting the interpolation check counter).

4. x lies in ctr. A. The functional tape is on interpolator I. Determine f(-|x|) and deliver it to ctr. B. Reset ctr. C in the last line. Turn off typewriter II.

OUT	IN	MISC.
A	7654	1
		62
841		
A	763	1
8731	B	73
C	C	7

(10) Occasionally when the interpolator positioning time is very short (the same or the next argument) it may be desirable to use the computation time to cover one or more prints. The quantity to be printed must be read to the print counter before the interpolation is initiated as shown below.

5. Print the quantity in ctr. C on typewriter I during computation time. x lies in ctr. A. The functional tape is on interpolator II. Determine f(x) and deliver it to ctr. B.

OUT	IN	MISC.
C	7432	
A	76541	
		62
841		
A	763	7

Continued on next page

5. (continued)

OUT	IN	MISC.
	752	
	B	73
		7

6. Print the quantities in ctrs. C and D on typewriters I and II. x lies in ctr. A. The functional tape is on interpolator III. Determine f(x) and deliver it to ctr. B.

C	7432	
D	74321	
	752	7
A	76542	
		62
841		
A	763	7
		7
Repeat this line (blank, blank, 7) a sufficient number of times so that the positioning time plus these lines cover 23 cycles.		
		7
	7521	
	B	73
		7

(11) It may be desirable to carry on calculations not involving the interpolators after interpolation is initiated and during tape positioning time. In this case sufficient cycles must be inserted to cover more than the maximum tape positioning time of the given problem. The maximum tape positioning time for interpolation of order k is

$$P = 8 + N(k + 2)/2$$

where
N = the number of arguments to be covered
k + 1 = the number of interpolational coefficients including C_0 .

(12) If operations are inserted during tape positioning time, the read-in of the argument to the interpolator in the first line of coding may not be altered by any operational code such as the invert code.

7. x lies in sw. or ctr. A. The functional tape is on interpolator I. Determine f(x) and deliver it to ctr. B. Insert other operations during tape positioning time.

OUT	IN	MISC.
A	7654	61
		762
Other computations inserted here must cover tape positioning time.		
841	7654	
A	763	
	B	73
		7

8. x lies in sw. or ctr. A. Ctr. C is available for computation. The functional tape is on interpolator II. Determine f(-x) and deliver it to ctr. B. Insert other operations during tape positioning time.

A	C	732
C	76541	61
		762
Other computations inserted here must cover tape positioning time.		
841	76541	
C	763	
	B	73
		7

(13) If operations are inserted during tape positioning time, a 641 code in the Miscellaneous column will insure that the tape will position to the closest lower value of the argument rather than to the closest value of the argument. The positioning of the tape to the closest lower value may be used to select data as in zero order interpolation.

9. A tape is punched x_1, $f(x_1)$, x_2, $f(x_2)$, ... x lies in sw. or ctr. A. It is required to determine $f(x_n)$ where $x_n \le x < x_{n+1}$ and deliver it to ctr. B. Insert other operations during tape positioning time. The tape is on interpolator I.

OUT	IN	MISC.
A	7654	641
		762
Other computations inserted here must cover tape positioning time.		
		73
85		753
	B	7

(14) A tape designed for an odd function need only be punched for positive values of the argument and counter 70 may be used to determine the sign of the result.

10. A tape for f(x) = - f(-x) is on interpolator II. x lies in ctr. A. It is required to determine f(x) and deliver it to ctr. B. Ctrs. 70 and C are reset and available for use.

OUT	IN	MISC.
A	732	7
A	76541	2
		62
841		
A	763	2
	C	73
C	B	7432

(15) All functional tapes and value tapes should be checked as described in the section on the design of functional tapes before being used in a computation.

(16) No switch setting or plugging is required for the use of a value tape since the values are read directly into the buss. If the decimal point of a value tape is not the same as the operating decimal point of the machine, the values must be routed through either the LIO or SIO counter to shift them to the proper position.

(17) Selected coefficients may be read out of a functional tape as if it were a value tape. The arguments cannot be read out because of the argument code punched in the first column.

(18) Since the sequence control tape may contain coding to step the interpolators ahead or back and to read values from the tape, the value tape must be synchronized with the control tape. Therefore, the starting position of a value tape must be clearly indicated.

(19) The codes selecting the interpolator from which values are to be read are 85, 851 and 852 in the Out column for interpolators I, II and III respectively.

(20) The codes stepping the interpolators ahead are 753, 7531 and 7532 in the Miscellaneous column for interpolators I, II and III respectively.

(21) The codes stepping the interpolators back are 754, 7541 and 7542 in the Miscellaneous column for interpolators I, II and III respectively.

11. Step interpolator I ahead.

OUT	IN	MISC.
		753

12. Step interpolator II back.

		7541

13. Read the value from interpolator III to ctr. B.

852		7
	B	7

OUT	IN	MISC.
85		753
	A	7

14. Step interpolator I ahead and read the value to ctr. A.

851		7541
	A	7

15. Step interpolator II back and read the value to ctr. A.

852		7
	A	7532

16. Read the value from interpolator III to ctr. A, and step ahead.

85		7
	A	754

17. Read the value from interpolator I to ctr. A, and step back.

(22) If it is desired to read successive values, n + 1 cycles are necessary to read out n values.

18. Read five successive values from a tape on interpolator II, supposing the tape to be standing on the first value, to ctrs. A, B, C, D and E, and step the tape to the next value.

OUT	IN	MISC.
851		7
851	A	7531
851	B	7531
851	C	7531
851	D	7531
	E	7531

(23) A function f(n), such as a series of constants, is punched in a tape where n is the number of the entry in the tape. The following examples illustrate the selection of data from such a tape.

19. Assuming the tape is on interpolator III and standing on f(n), read f(n - 2), 2f(n), f(n + 1), f(n + 2) to ctrs. A, B, C and D respectively and leave the tape on f(n + 2).

OUT	IN	MISC.
		7542
852		7542
	A	7532
852		7532

Continued on next page

19. (continued)

OUT	IN	MISC.
852	B	7
852	B	7532
852	C	7532
	D	7

20. Assuming the tape is on interpolator I and standing on f(n - 2) read f(n), f(n + 1) and f(n + 2) to ctrs. A, B and C respectively and leave the tape on f(n).

		753
85		753
85	A	753
85	B	753
	C	754
		754

(24) The coefficients may be read from a functional tape using these codes.

21. Position the tape on interpolator II to the argument next lower than x in ctr. A and read the three interpolational coefficients to ctrs. B, C and D.

OUT	IN	MISC.
A	76541	641
		762
Other computations inserted here must cover tape positioning time.		
		73
851		7531
851	B	7531
851	C	7531
	D	7

(25) Several values at known intervals may be read out in zero order interpolation. The tape is punched x_1, $f(x_1)$, x_2, $f(x_2)$, ...

22. If the tape is on interpolator III, and $x_n \leq x < x_{n+1}$, x lies in ctr. A, read $f(x_{n-1})$, $f(x_n)$, $f(x_{n+1})$ to ctrs. C, D and E respectively. Insert sufficient operations to cover tape positioning time. Leave the tape standing on an argument.

OUT	IN	MISC.
A	76542	641
		762

Continued on next page

22. (continued)

OUT	IN	MISC.
Other computations inserted here must cover tape positioning time.		
		73
852		7542
	C	7532
852		7532
	D	7532
852		7532
	E	7532

(26) The interpolators may be used to evaluate any function of the form

$$f(x) = C_0 + C_1 g(x) + C_2 (g(x))^2 + C_3 (g(x))^3 \ldots$$

where g(x) is any function of x computed in the machine. The functional tape is punched as usual with the argument and the coefficients $C_k, C_{k-1}, \ldots, C_0$, in that order. Plugging must be checked for the complete read-in to the intermediate counter. This saves the build-up time in each multiplication of the computation of the series. If the C_k are functions of x, then x would usually have to be an integral multiple of the tape interval, Δx. If the C_k are constants, the argument line is not punched except for the argument code.

23. x lies in ctr. A. g(x) lies in ctr. B. The tape is on interpolator I. Evaluate f(x) as defined above and deliver f(x) to ctr. C. Omit (A) in the first line if the C_k are constants.

OUT	IN	MISC.
(A)	7654	
		62
B	763	
	C	73
		7

(27) If it is not desirable to cover tape-positioning time and if it is necessary to initiate operations other than the usual interpolation sequence as soon as the proper argument is located, the tape selection relays may be dropped out by the two lines of coding (blank, blank, 761; blank, blank, 762) immediately following the first two normal lines of coding.

24. From the value tape on interpolator I read out two functions associated with the argument x, which lies in ctr. A. Store the functions in ctrs. B and C. Leave the tape on an argument.

OUT	IN	MISC.
A	7654	
		62

Continued on next page

24. (continued)

OUT	IN	MISC.
		761
		762
		73
85		753
85	B	753
	C	753

(28) The two dial switches above an interpolator need not be set alike. The right dial switch must be set to the number of values accompanying an argument in the tape in order to position the tape. The left dial must be set to the number of these values to be used in the interpolation computation.

25. On interpolator I there is a functional tape with seven coefficients to be used on a problem where five coefficients will give the necessary accuracy. Set the right dial switch to seven and the left dial switch to five. After locating the argument, drop out the tape selection relays, step twice to eliminate C_6 and C_5 from the computation, and proceed to interpolate using C_4 to C_0. Ctr. A contains x. Deliver f(x) to ctr. B.

OUT	IN	MISC.
A	7654	
		62
		761
		762
		753
		753
841	7654	
A	763	
	B	73
		7

(29) Special problems may require unusual applications of the interpolators. For example, "h" correction-2 or "h" correction-3 may be stored in counter C by the line of coding (841, C, blank) in conjunction with special wiring. See Plugging Instructions. The interpolator sequence can be used for shifting or clipping numbers by plugging the intermediate counter for the proper shift and using a tape punched with three repeated lines reading (a) argument code only, (b) unity, (c) blank. In this case no Out code is used on the first line and on the third line the Out code is for the counter containing the number to be shifted.

<u>Multiple Use of Interpolators</u>

(30) When two or three functions have the same range of the independent variable and can be represented to the desired accuracy with the same interval of the argument and the same number of interpolational coefficients punched with the same decimal point, the functional tapes will be

identical except for the numerical values of the coefficients. Under these circumstances, it may be desirable to position two or three tapes simultaneously. Only one tape positioning is coded in the main sequence tape and the "Interpolator gang-positioning switches" control the positioning of the one or two remaining tapes.

(31) This coding involves the operational code 61 in the Miscellaneous column. Therefore the read-in of the argument may not be subject to an operational code and sufficient cycles must be inserted to cover maximum tape positioning time.

(32) Other calculations may be performed between the computations of the several interpolations or not as desired.

(33) It should be noted that the number of interpolational coefficients may be made identical by including zero coefficients. See Design of Functional Tapes. (Such zero coefficients consume only four cycles of machine time.)

26. x lies in sw. or ctr. A. Read f(x), g(x) and h(x) from interpolators I, II and III to ctrs. B, C, and D respectively. Use interpolator I as a control for positioning the three tapes simultaneously.

OUT	IN	MISC.
A	7654	61
		762
Other computations inserted here must cover tape positioning time.		
841	7654	
A	763	
	B	7
		7
Other computations of any length, if desired.		
841	76541	
A	763	
	C	7
		7
Other computations of any length, if desired.		
841	76542	
A	763	
	D	73
		7

DESIGN OF FUNCTIONAL TAPES

(1) The interpolators are designed for all orders of interpolation up to and including the eleventh order.

(2) Interpolation is carried out by means of the interpolational polynomial:

$$f(a + h) \cong C_0 + C_1h + C_2h^2 + \ldots$$

where

$x = a + h$, the amount standing in a given storage counter for which $f(x)$ is to be computed,

a = the argument in the tape which most closely approximates x and for example:

$$C_0 = f(a), \ldots, C_k = f^k(a)/k! \ .$$

(3) Numbers are punched in a functional tape in accordance with a four row code discussed in the physical description of the machine.

(4) Negative arguments and coefficients are punched as complements on nine. It is desirable that tapes be designed with the decimal point between columns 15 and 16 unless the accuracy desired requires more decimal places.

(5) The punched arguments are distinguished from all other values by the argument code punched in the lowest order machine column.

(6) The values of the argument, a, must be punched in columns 15, 16, 17, 18 and 24 (for the algebraic sign), the lowest order column of the argument being punched in the fifteenth column. The maximum range of the argument must be encompassed in four powers of ten. The interval of the argument must be a power of ten, positive or negative; i.e., $\Delta a = 10^n$. Hence the maximum value of h is 0.5×10^n. A tape must include an even number of arguments. When using a functional tape, one half the number of arguments, N/2, must be set up in the push button switches labeled "Value tape set up 1/2 "A" values in tape" above the interpolator.

(7) For each value of the argument the values punched in the tape in order are:

the argument and the argument code in the first column,

the coefficient C_k,

the coefficient C_{k-1},

... ...

the coefficient C_1,

the coefficient C_0.

The number of interpolational coefficients (including C_0), k + 1, is set in the dial switches labeled "Set up number of "C" values on each switch".

(8) The interpolators require plugging to care for the argument, the decimal point, the "h" correction and the "C" values. If the tape contains negative "C" values, the decimal point may not be shifted to the right. The highest order "h"; i.e., the number of the column containing 10^{n-1}, must be specified for the proper plugging of functional tapes.

(9) The maximum tape positioning time (one half the length of the tape) for interpolation of order k is

$$P = 8 + N(k + 2)/2 \quad \text{cycles},$$

where
N = number of arguments punched in tape,
k + 1 = number of interpolational coefficients including C_0.

(10) The computation time for interpolation of order k is

$$C = 7 + k(4 + n') \quad \text{cycles},$$

where
k + 1 = number of interpolational coefficients including C_0,
n' = n if the maximum number of digits in any interpolational coefficient is even, 2n,
or n' = n + 1 if the maximum number of digits in any interpolational coefficient is odd, 2n + 1.

(11) The design of a functional tape for interpolation of order k involves the specification of:

1. the accuracy of the tape,
2. the range of the argument and any special coding devices by which the range may be increased,
3. the interval of the argument,
4. the number of arguments, N,
5. the number of interpolational coefficients, k + 1,
6. the tape decimal point.

(12) For any specific range of the argument and any predetermined accuracy, a function may be represented by a functional tape in several different ways. Many interpolational coefficients may be used with large intervals of the argument, giving a short tape, brief positioning time, but long computation time. On the other hand, a small interval of the argument with few interpolational coefficients will result in short computation time but longer positioning time. In general, a tape should be so designed that the sum of the mean positioning time and the computation time will be a minimum. If, however, it is known that the successive arguments for which interpolation is to be performed differ but little from one another, the positioning time is small in any case, and it will be more effective to design the tape for minimum computation time. If the variable is random and expected to vary by large increments, it is desirable to design the tape so that positioning time is a minimum and spend a longer time on computation. Thus the design of a functional tape is governed in the main by three factors: accuracy, tape positioning time and computation time.

(13) In computing the accuracy of a tape, if k is the index of the last interpolational coefficient, k is determined by

$$r = \sum_{k+1}^{\infty} C_i \, (h \max)^i$$

where the remainder, r, must be less than one half unit in the lowest order column required to give the desired accuracy. When Taylor's series is used, k is determined by

$$r \leq C_{k+1} \, (h \max)^{k+1}$$

taking for C_{k+1} its maximum value as a function of x in the range under consideration.

DESIGN OF FUNCTIONAL TAPES

1. As an example of the design of a functional tape consider $f(x) = \arctan x$ (principal values). By a coding device employing the identities

$$\arctan(-x) = -\arctan x$$

and

$$\arctan|x| = \pi/2 - \arctan 1/|x|,$$

a tape covering the arguments $0 \leq x \leq 1$ may be extended to cover interpolation for $-\infty \leq x \leq +\infty$. Using Taylor's series, the coefficients of the interpolational polynomial are

$$C_0 = f(a) = \arctan a$$

$$C_1 = f'(a) = \frac{1}{1 + a^2}$$

$$C_2 = \frac{f''(a)}{2!} = \frac{-a}{(1 + a^2)^2}$$

$$C_3 = \frac{f'''(a)}{3!} = \frac{3a^2 - 1}{3(1 + a^2)^3}$$

$$C_4 = \frac{f^{iv}(a)}{4!} = \frac{a - a^3}{(1 + a^2)^4}$$

$$C_5 = \frac{f^{v}(a)}{5!} = \frac{1 - 10a^2 + 5a^4}{5(1 + a^2)^5}$$

The absolute value of all coefficients is less than or equal to one.

The following table shows the calculations for accuracy, tape positioning time in cycles and computation time in cycles. The accuracy desired is an error of not more than 5×10^{-8} and the tape is punched with decimal point between columns 9 and 10.

Calculations for Tape for $f(x) = \arctan x$

Tape number	I	II	III
Interval of argument	0.1	0.01	0.001
Range of arguments	$0 \leq x \leq 1.1$	$0 \leq x \leq 1.01$	$0 \leq x \leq 1.001$
Number of arguments = N	12	102	1002
C_1 (h max)	5×10^{-2}	5×10^{-3}	5×10^{-4}
C_2 (h max)^2	8.125×10^{-4}	8.125×10^{-6}	8.125×10^{-8}

Calculations for Tape for f(x) = arc tan x (continued)

Tape number	I	II	III
C_3 (h max)^3	4.2×10^{-5}	4.2×10^{-8}	4.2×10^{-11}
C_4 (h max)^4	2.5×10^{-6}	2.5×10^{-10}	2.5×10^{-14}
C_5 (h max)^5	6.3×10^{-8}	6.3×10^{-13}	6.3×10^{-18}
Number of coefficients = k + 1	6	3	3
Tape positioning time in cycles...			
Maximum	50	212	2012
Mean	29	110	1010
Computation time in cycles	52	25	25
Interpolation time in cycles...			
Maximum	102	237	2037
Mean	81	135	1035
Error of tape	4×10^{-8}	4.3×10^{-8}	4.3×10^{-11}

(14) Since the number of coefficients required for the desired accuracy varies with the argument, computation time may be saved by punching zeros in place of the higher coefficients for values of the argument not requiring as many terms of the series. Since the MC is held constant during the computation, a multiplication by zero consumes only four cycles in such cases.

2. For example, consider f(x) = arc sin x. The tape is to be punched for $0 \leq x \leq 0.9$, the intervals of the argument being 0.01.

Calculations for Tape for f(x) = arc sin x				
arg	C_4 (h max)^4	C_5 (h max)^5	C_6 (h max)^6	C_7 (h max)^7
0	0	2.35×10^{-13}	0	
0.1	2.45×10^{-11}	2.65×10^{-13}	5.30×10^{-16}	
0.2	5.56×10^{-11}	3.73×10^{-13}	1.36×10^{-15}	
0.3	1.04×10^{-10}	6.24×10^{-13}	3.07×10^{-15}	
0.4	1.91×10^{-10}	1.21×10^{-12}	7.34×10^{-15}	
0.5	3.74×10^{-10}	2.71×10^{-12}	2.02×10^{-14}	
0.6	8.31×10^{-10}	7.38×10^{-12}	6.97×10^{-14}	
0.7	2.30×10^{-9}	2.70×10^{-11}	3.37×10^{-13}	
0.8	9.56×10^{-9}	1.68×10^{-10}	3.12×10^{-12}	6.20×10^{-15}
0.9	1.09×10^{-7}	3.81×10^{-9}	1.32×10^{-10}	5.62×10^{-11}

Thus a tape with an error of $e \leq 6 \times 10^{-11}$ due to the termination of the Taylor's series would be punched with the following coefficients:

$0 \leq a \leq 0.2$	a, 0, 0, 0, C_3, C_2, C_1, C_0
$0.2 < a \leq 0.7$	a, 0, 0, C_4, C_3, C_2, C_1, C_0
$0.7 < a \leq 0.8$	a, 0, $C_5, C_4, C_3, C_2, C_1, C_0$
$0.8 < a \leq 0.9$	a, $C_6, C_5, C_4, C_3, C_2, C_1, C_0$

Thus for random values of x, Tape I is the most effective. If, however, it were known that the values of x were increasing and that in no case was $\Delta x \geq 0.1$, the positioning time of Tape II would be reduced to 48 cycles or less, giving a maximum interpolation time of only 76 cycles and making Tape II the more efficient. For the desired accuracy, Tape III is obviously inefficient.

(15) With the possible exception of very elementary functional tapes, the values of the interpolation coefficients should be computed on the calculator itself. Hence the design of a functional tape involves the coding of a sequence tape for its preparation.

(16) To facilitate punching of the functional tape, the sequence tape calculating the coefficients should be so coded that it prints the argument, followed by the coefficients in the order $C_k, C_{k-1}, \ldots, C_1, C_0$. Negative numbers should be printed as complements on nine.

(17) Before the functional tape is used in a calculation, there are two checks which should be made using the calculator. The interpolator should be required to position on each argument and to print out the successive coefficients (the argument cannot be printed from the tape because of the argument code in the first column). This set of coefficients should then be proof-read against the computed coefficients. The coding for the sequence tape to accomplish this, if the functional tape has three interpolational coefficients, is given in example 3.

3. Test arguments and read out three coefficients. Functional tape on interpolator I.

	OUT	IN	MISC.
			87
accumulate argument in ctr. 1	8431	1	7
position tape	1	7654	
			62
drop out tape selection relays			761
			762
reset interpolation check counter			73
print argument on typewriter I	1	7432	
		752	6
step ahead, read and print C_2	85		753
		7432	
		752	6

Continued on next page

3. (continued)

Description	OUT	IN	MISC.
Step ahead, read and print C_1	85		753
		7432	
		752	6
Step ahead, read and print C_0	85		753
		7432	
		752	6
			87

The operating instructions for this tape must include plugging instructions for interpolator I and typewriter I, as well as the following instructions:

A. Reset counter 1 before starting.

B. Set IVS for first value of the argument.

C. Start machine and press 87 stop key.

D. If interpolator does not position, check tape to see that first argument and argument code are in proper position. If these are correct, test interpolator.

E. When machine stops on 87, reset IVS to 1×10^n where $\Delta a = 10^n$. Restart machine.

F. For each argument the interpolator may fail to position. If the interpolator does not position, check tape to see that the appropriate argument and argument code are in proper position.

The interpolator should also be required to interpolate on assigned values of x which can be checked against tables. In general, it is wise to check the mid-values, since these give rise to approximately the maximum error. The coding for such a tape is given in example 4.

4. Test interpolation. Tape on interpolator I.

Description	OUT	IN	MISC.
			87
reset ctr. 2	2	2	7
accumulate argument in ctr. 1	8431	1	7
position and interpolate	1	7654	
			62
	841		
	1	763	

Continued on next page

4. (continued)

	OUT	IN	MISC.
read f(x) to ctr. 2		2	73
			7
print x on typewriter I	1	7432	
		752	6
print f(x) on typewriter I	2	7432	
		752	6
			87

The operating instructions for this tape must include plugging instructions for interpolator I and typewriter I, as well as the following instructions:

A. Reset counter 1 before starting.

B. For the first round of sequence tape set IVS equal to the first value to be checked, then change to Δx. If it is desired to interpolate on mid-values on a tape starting with argument zero, set IVS = $5 \times 10^{n-1}$ for the first round and IVS = 10^n thereafter, where $\Delta a = 10^n$.

(18) One interpolator can be made to serve for several functions by subjecting the arguments to a linear transformation and punching them in a single tape. In this case, the interval of the transformed arguments and the number of interpolational coefficients must be equal for all functions. The number of interpolational coefficients may of course be made identical by using zero coefficients which consume only four cycles of machine computation time.

A tape is to be designed for

$y = f(x)$ $\quad\quad$ $0 \leq a \leq x < b$

$y = g(x)$ $\quad\quad$ $0 < c < x \leq d.$

The tape must be punched for

$F(z)$ $\quad\quad$ $0 \leq a \leq z \leq bd/c$

where

$F(z) = f(x)$ $\quad\quad$ $a \leq z < b$

$F(z) = 0$ $\quad\quad$ $z = b$

$F(z) = g(cz/b)$ $\quad\quad$ $b < z \leq bd/c$

For $y = f(x)$, the argument is read directly to the interpolator.
For $y = g(x)$, $z = bx/c$ is read to the interpolator as the argument.

Care must be taken in selecting the limits a, b, c and d of the functions, so that the interpolator is not required to position to the argument $z = b$.

METHODS OF DIFFERENCING

(1) In calculating the successive differences of a function, three schemes for the use of counters are available. To calculate nth differences, the first method consumes 3n cycles and uses n counters. The second or "round-robin" method covers n + 2 cycles, uses n + 1 counters, and must be repeated n + 1 times. The third method covers 2n + 2 cycles and uses n + 1 counters.

(2) If a computation includes sufficient multiplication and division so that many lines are free for interposed operations, and if there is a shortage of counters, the first method is appropriate.

(3) If the coding is tight and if the computation is brief so that repetition will not make too long a tape, the second method is more efficient.

(4) In most other cases except first order differencing, the third method is most useful. Note that this method provides a simple check on the result.

(5) The first method is coded to compute and print fifth differences.

1. The value u_0 lies in ctr. P and may therefore be inverted when read out, and

counter A = u_{-1}
counter B = Δu_{-2}
counter C = $\Delta^2 u_{-3}$
counter D = $\Delta^3 u_{-4}$
counter E = $\Delta^4 u_{-5}$.

	OUT	IN	MISC.
$-u_0$ to ctr. A; $A = -\Delta u_{-1}$	P	A	732
$-\Delta u_{-1}$ to ctr. B; $B = -\Delta^2 u_{-2}$	A	B	7
$-\Delta^2 u_{-2}$ to ctr. C; $C = -\Delta^3 u_{-3}$	B	C	7
$-\Delta^3 u_{-3}$ to ctr. D; $D = -\Delta^4 u_{-4}$	C	D	7
$-\Delta^4 u_{-4}$ to ctr. E; $E = -\Delta^5 u_{-5}$	D	E	7
print $\Delta^5 u_{-5}$ on typewriter I	E	7432	32
		752	6
reset ctr. E	E	E	7
$\Delta^4 u_{-4}$ to ctr. E	D	E	732
reset ctr. D	D	D	7
$\Delta^3 u_{-3}$ to ctr. D	C	D	732
reset ctr. C	C	C	7
$\Delta^2 u_{-2}$ to ctr. C	B	C	732
reset ctr. B	B	B	7

Continued on next page

1. (continued)	OUT	IN	MISC.
Δu_{-1} to ctr. B	A	B	732
reset ctr. A	A	A	7
u_0 to ctr. A	P	A	7

2. The value u_0 lies in a value tape or arises from any sources from which the read-out cannot be inverted, and

counter A = $-u_{-1}$
counter B = $-\Delta u_{-2}$
counter C = $-\Delta^2 u_{-3}$
counter D = $-\Delta^3 u_{-4}$
counter E = $-\Delta^4 u_{-5}$.

	OUT	IN	MISC.
u_0 to ctr. A; $A = \Delta u_{-1}$	P	A	7
Δu_{-1} to ctr. B; $B = \Delta^2 u_{-2}$	A	B	7
$\Delta^2 u_{-2}$ to ctr. C; $C = \Delta^3 u_{-3}$	B	C	7
$\Delta^3 u_{-3}$ to ctr. D; $D = \Delta^4 u_{-4}$	C	D	7
$\Delta^4 u_{-4}$ to ctr. E; $E = \Delta^5 u_{-5}$	D	E	7
print $\Delta^5 u_{-5}$ on typewriter I	E	7432	
		752	6
reset ctr. E	E	E	7
$-\Delta^4 u_{-4}$ to ctr. E	D	E	732
reset ctr. D	D	D	7
$-\Delta^3 u_{-3}$ to ctr. D	C	D	732
reset ctr. C	C	C	7
$-\Delta^2 u_{-2}$ to ctr. C	B	C	732
reset ctr. B	B	B	7
$-\Delta u_{-1}$ to ctr. B	A	B	732
reset ctr. A	A	A	7
$-u_0$ to ctr. A	P	A	732

(6) The "round-robin" method is coded to compute and print third differences.

3. **Successive values of the function are delivered from a value tape, card feed or ctr. P and**

counter A $= -\Delta^3 u_{-4}$
counter B $= \Delta^2 u_{-3}$
counter C $= -\Delta u_{-2}$
counter D $= u_{-1}$.

	OUT	IN	MISC.
reset ctr. A	A	A	7
u_0 to ctr. A	P	A	7
$-u_0$ to ctr. D; $D = -\Delta u_{-1}$	A	D	732
Δu_{-1} to ctr. C; $C = \Delta^2 u_{-2}$	D	C	732
$-\Delta^2 u_{-2}$ to ctr. B; $B = -\Delta^3 u_{-3}$	C	B	732
print $\Delta^3 u_{-3}$	B	7432	32
		752	6
reset ctr. B	B	B	7
u_1 to ctr. B	P	B	7
$-u_1$ to ctr. A; $A = -\Delta u_0$	B	A	732
Δu_0 to ctr. D; $D = \Delta^2 u_{-1}$	A	D	732
$-\Delta^2 u_{-1}$ to ctr. C; $C = -\Delta^3 u_{-2}$	D	C	732
print $\Delta^3 u_{-2}$	C	7432	32
		752	6
reset ctr. C	C	C	7
u_2 to ctr. C	P	C	7
$-u_2$ to ctr. B; $B = -\Delta u_1$	C	B	732
Δu_1 to ctr. A; $A = \Delta^2 u_0$	B	A	732
$-\Delta^2 u_0$ to ctr. D; $D = -\Delta^3 u_{-1}$	A	D	732
print $\Delta^3 u_{-1}$	D	7432	32
		752	6
reset ctr. D	D	D	7
u_3 to ctr. D	P	D	7

Continued on next page

3. (continued)

	OUT	IN	MISC.
$-u_3$ to ctr. C; $C = -\Delta u_2$	D	C	732
Δu_2 to ctr. B; $B = \Delta^2 u_1$	C	B	732
$-\Delta^2 u_1$ to ctr. A; $A = -\Delta^3 u_0$	B	A	732
print $\Delta^3 u_0$	A	7432	32
		752	6

(7) The third method is coded to compute and print fifth differences.

4. Successive values of the function are delivered from a value tape, card feed or ctr. P and

counter A $= u_{-1}$
counter B $= \Delta u_{-2}$
counter C $= \Delta^2 u_{-3}$
counter D $= \Delta^3 u_{-4}$
counter E $= \Delta^4 u_{-5}$
counter F $= \Delta^5 u_{-6}$.

	OUT	IN	MISC.
reset ctr. F	F	F	7
$-\Delta^4 u_{-5}$ to ctr. F	E	F	732
$-\Delta^3 u_{-4}$ to ctr. F	D	F	732
$-\Delta^2 u_{-3}$ to ctr. F	C	F	732
$-\Delta u_{-2}$ to ctr. F	B	F	732
$-u_{-1}$ to ctr. F	A	F	732
u_0 to ctr. F; $F = \Delta^5 u_{-5}$	P	F	7
print $\Delta^5 u_{-5}$ on typewriter I	F	7432	
		752	6
$\Delta^5 u_{-5}$ to ctr. E; $E = \Delta^4 u_{-4}$	F	E	7
$\Delta^4 u_{-4}$ to ctr. D; $D = \Delta^3 u_{-3}$	E	D	7
$\Delta^3 u_{-3}$ to ctr. C; $C = \Delta^2 u_{-2}$	D	C	7
$\Delta^2 u_{-2}$ to ctr. B; $B = \Delta u_{-1}$	C	B	7
Δu_{-1} to ctr. A; $A = u_0$	B	A	7

Note that an excellent check on the accuracy of the differencing process can be made in three additional cycles by checking u_0 in A against P.

CENTRAL-DIFFERENCE INTERPOLATION

(1) "A central-difference formula terminating at a mean difference of the entry u_0 is more accurate than a formula which is curtailed at the corresponding difference of $u_{-1/2}$, and it is less accurate than a formula which is curtailed at the corresponding difference of $u_{1/2}$." Whittaker and Robinson, The Calculus of Observations, 3rd ed., London, 1940, p. 49.

Thus the Newton-Bessel formula is more accurate as far as mean differences of even order when further terms are neglected than the corresponding Newton-Stirling formula. In the same way Newton-Stirling is more accurate as far as mean differences of odd order.

If interpolation is being performed on third differences, the Newton-Stirling formula is the more accurate since it terminates in mean third differences. Since operations are inserted during tape positioning time and interposed during multiplication, the cost of including the term containing the fourth difference is but one multiplication. Because of this gain in accuracy, the formula has been coded to include the fourth difference term. The computations of the coefficient, fourth difference and the completed term have been underlined so that they may easily be omitted if desired. For even differences the same considerations apply to the use of the Newton-Bessel formula.

(2) It is assumed in this section that a table of some function, f, is given, and that a value tape has been punched with an argument of the form $a + kw$, followed by the value of the function $f(a + kw)$, for $k = 0, 1, ..., 9$, and all values of a required. The integer n and the parameters a and w are fixed, for a particular case, and are connected by the relations $w = 10^{-n}$, $n \lesseqgtr 0$, $\Delta a = 10w$. It is now desired to compute f(y) by interpolation, where y is within the range of the arguments on the tape. The coding first puts the argument y in the form $a + xw$, where x is now not necessarily an integer, and where $0 < x < 10$.

(3) The value y is sent to the interpolator to position the tape to the tape argument, a, immediately below it; i.e., such that $0 \leq y - a < 10w$. The tape positioning time, which must be covered, since the tape is being positioned to the next lower value of the argument, is used to determine x and the coefficients involving x. If the tape positioning time cannot be covered, the usual coding is used and the first column of the interpolation counter is not plugged. See Plugging Instructions.

(4) The method of computation of x during tape positioning time, when a is still unknown and w is a power of ten, is shown below.

(a) If $w = 10^{-n}$, n a positive integer or zero, then $a + xw$ is shifted n columns to the left by passing it through the LIO counter. The LIO counter is plugged for such a shift except that the plugging is omitted in the columns above one to the left of the decimal point and nines are plugged into the first n machine columns of the buss. This will finally give x if y is positive, and $x - 10^{-p}$ if y is negative, where the position of the decimal point is between columns p and p + 1. A correction is made by adding five in column 24 and then subtracting five in column 24 under control of the choice counter. Thus x is the result in either case.

1. $a + xw$ lies in ctr. A; sw. P contains 5 in col. 24. Deliver x to ctr. B.

	OUT	IN	MISC.
reset LIO ctr.			763
a + xw to LIO ctr.	A	765421	7
reset ctr. B	B	B	7

Continued on next page

CENTRAL-DIFFERENCE INTERPOLATION

1. (continued)

	OUT	IN	MISC.
x to ctr. B	831	B	7
reset ctr. 70	732	732	7
- (a + xw) to ctr. 70	A	732	732
5 in 24th column to ctr. B	P	B	7
5 in 24th column to ctr. B under control of ctr. 70	P	B	7432

(b) If $w = 10^n$, n a positive integer, it is in most cases better to normalize the units of the argument and of the function to include this in the previous case.

(5) In the coding which follows it is assumed that $\Delta a = 0.1$ in the tape, and that the tape is on interpolator I. It is also assumed that the successive values of a + xw appearing in the computation do not differ by more than one unit. If they differ by more than one unit more cycles must be added to cover tape positioning time. If it is known that the values of a + xw occur in close succession, it might be profitable to defer at least a part of the computation of the coefficients until the tape has positioned, and use these multiplications to cover the differencing. This is particularly true of computations involving the higher order differences.

(6) For interpolation extending through third or fifth differences, the Newton-Bessel formula was used:

$$f(a + xw) = 1/2\left[f(a) + f(a + w)\right] + (x - 1/2)\Delta f(a) + \frac{x(x-1)}{2!}\,1/2\left[\Delta^2 f(a - w) + \Delta^2 f(a)\right]$$
$$+ \frac{x(x-1)(x-1/2)}{3!}\Delta^3 f(a - w) + \frac{(x+1)x(x-1)(x-2)}{4!}\,1/2\left[\Delta^4 f(a - 2w) + \Delta^4 f(a - w)\right]$$
$$+ \frac{(x+1)x(x-1)(x-2)(x-1/2)}{5!}\Delta^5 f(a - 2w) + \ldots$$

2. a + xw lies in ctr. A. f(a + xw) is to be delivered to ctr. L. Ctrs. B through L, 70 and LIO are available for computation, but not reset. Switches are set as follows:

Switch SP = 1/2
Switch SQ = 1.0
Switch SR = 1/4
Switch SS = 2/3
Switch ST = 5 in machine column 24 .

Coefficients for and computation of third differences which may be omitted are underlined. (7)'s must be omitted if no operations are interposed.

	OUT	IN	MISC.
(a + xw) to interpolator I	A	7654	641
interpolator I positions			762

Continued on next page

2. (continued)

	OUT	IN	MISC.
reset LIO ctr.			763
(a + xw) to LIO ctr.	A	765421	7
reset ctr. B	B	B	7
x to ctr. B	831	B	7
reset ctr. 70	732	732	7
- (a + xw) to ctr. 70	A	732	732
5 in column 24 to ctr. B	ST	B	7
$\mp$ 5 in column 24 to ctr. B under control of ctr. 70	ST	B	7432
reset ctr. M	M	M	7
x to ctr. M	B	M	7
x to MC	B	761	7
- 1 to ctr. B	SQ	B	732
reset ctr. C	C	C	
(x - 1) to MP	M		7
1/2 to ctr. P	SP	P	7
reset ctr. D	D	D	7
reset ctr. E	E	E	7
reset ctr. F	F	F	
x(x - 1) to ctr. C		C	7
x(x - 1) to MC	C	761	7
reset ctr. N	N	N	7
reset ctr. G	G	G	
1/4 to MP	SR		7
reset ctr. H	H	H	7
reset ctr. I	I	I	7
reset ctr. J	J	J	7

Continued on next page

CENTRAL-DIFFERENCE INTERPOLATION

2. (continued)	OUT	IN	MISC.
reset ctr. K	K	K	
x(x - 1)/4 to ctr. N		N	7
x(x - 1)/4 to MC	N	761	7
- 1/2 to ctr. P	SP	P	732
x to ctr. P	B	P	
(x - 1/2) to MP	P		(7)
x(x - 1)(x - 1/2)/4 to ctr. D		D	7
x(x - 1)(x - 1/2)/4 to MC	D	761	7
reset ctr. L	L	L	7
reset ctr. Q	Q	Q	
2/3 to MP	S		(7)
x(x - 1)(x - 1/2)/3! to ctr. Q		Q	7

A check should be made to see that sufficient cycles have been inserted to cover interpolation positioning time.

interpolator I has positioned; reset IC			73
select interpolator I and step ahead	85		753
f(a) to ctr. E and step ahead		E	753
select interpolator I and step ahead	85		753
f(a + xw) to ctr. F and step back		F	754

Continued on next page

2. (continued)

	OUT	IN	MISC.
1/2 to MC, step back	SP	761	754
f(a) to ctr. K, step back	E	K	754
f(a + w) to ctr. K, step back	F	K	54
$[f(a) + f(a + w)]$ to MP	K		7
f(a + w) to ctr. G.	F	G	7
- f(a) to ctr. G; $G = \Delta f(a)$	E	G	732
select interpolator I	85		7
f(a - w) to ctr. H, step ahead		H	53
$[f(a) + f(a + w)]/2$ to ctr. L, step ahead		L	753
(x - 1/2) to MC, step ahead	P	761	753
- f(a) to ctr. H; $H = -\Delta f(a - w)$	E	H	732
$\Delta f(a)$ to ctr. H; $H = \Delta^2 f(a - w)$, step ahead	G	H	53
$\Delta f(a)$ to MP, step ahead	G		753
select interpolator I, step ahead	85		753
f(a + 2w) to ctr. I		I	7
- f(a + w) to ctr. I; $I = \Delta f(a + w)$	F	I	732
- $\Delta f(a)$ to ctr. I; $I = \Delta^2 f(a)$	G	I	32
$(x - 1/2)\Delta f(a)$ to ctr. L		L	7
x(x - 1)/4 to MC	N	761	7
$\Delta^2 f(a - w)$ to ctr. J	H	J	7
$\Delta^2 f(a)$ to ctr. J	I	J	
$[\Delta^2 f(a - w) + \Delta^2 f(a)]$ to MP	J		7
$-\Delta^2 f(a - w)$ to ctr. I; $I = \Delta^3 f(a - w)$	H	I	(7)32

Continued on next page

2. (continued)

	OUT	IN	MISC.
$x(x-1)\left[\Delta^2 f(a-w) + \Delta^2 f(a)\right]/4$ to ctr. L		L	7
<u>$x(x-1)(x-1/2)/3!$ to MC</u>	Q	761	(7)
<u>$\Delta^3 f(a-w)$ to MP</u>	I		(7)
<u>$x(x-1)(x-1/2)\Delta^3 f(a-w)/3!$ to ctr. L.</u> $f(a+xw)$ lies in ctr. L.		L	7

(7) For interpolation extending through fourth differences, the Newton-Stirling formula was used:

$$f(a+xw) = f(a) + x\left[\Delta f(a) + \Delta f(a-w)\right]/2 + x^2/2!\,\Delta^2 f(a-w)$$

$$+ x(x^2 - 1^2)/3!\left[\Delta^3 f(a-w) + \Delta^3 f(a-2w)\right]/2 + x^2(x^2 - 1^2)/4!\,\Delta^4 f(a-2w) + \ldots$$

3. $a + xw$ lies in ctr. A. $f(a+xw)$ is to be delivered to ctr. L. Ctrs. B through N, 70 and LIO are available for computation but not reset. Switches are set as follows:

Switch SP = 1/2
Switch SQ = 5 in machine column 24
Switch SR = 1.0
Switch SS = 1/6
Switch ST = 1/12.

Coefficients for and computation of fourth differences which may be omitted are underlined. (7)'s must be omitted if no operations are interposed.

	OUT	IN	MISC.
(a + xw) to interpolator I	A	7654	641
interpolator I postion			762
reset LIO ctr.			763
(a + xw) to LIO ctr.	A	765421	7

Continued on next page

3. (continued)

	OUT	IN	MISC.
reset ctr. B	B	B	7
x to ctr. B	831	B	7
reset ctr. 70	732	732	7
- (a + xw) to ctr. 70	A	732	732
5 in first column to ctr. B	SQ	B	7
$\mp$ 5 in first column to ctr. B under control of ctr. 70	SQ	B	7432
x to MC	B	761	7
reset ctr. C	C	C	7
reset ctr. D	D	D	
x to MP	B		7
- 1 to ctr. D	SR	D	732
reset ctr. E	E	E	7
reset ctr. F	F	F	7
reset ctr. G	G	G	
x^2 to ctr. C		C	7
x to MC	B	761	7
x^2 to ctr. D; $D = x^2 - 1$	C	D	7
reset ctr. H	H	H	
1/2 to MP	SP		7
reset ctr. I	I	I	7
reset ctr. J	J	J	7
reset ctr. K	K	K	7
reset ctr. P	P	P	
x/2 to ctr. P		P	7
x^2 to MC	C	761	7
reset ctr. L	L	L	7

Continued on next page

3. (continued)	OUT	IN	MISC.
reset ctr. M	M	M	
1/2 to MP	SP		7
reset ctr. N	N	N	(7)
reset ctr. Q	Q	Q	
$x^2/2!$ to ctr. Q		Q	7
$(x^2 - 1)$ to MC	D	761	(7)
x/2 to MP	P		(7)
$x(x^2 - 1)/2$ to ctr. E		E	7
$x(x^2 - 1)/2$ to MC	E	761	(7)
1/6 to MP	SS		7
reset ctr. U	U	U	
$x(x^2 - 1)/(2)(3!)$ to ctr. U		U	7
$\underline{x^2/2 \text{ to MC}}$	$\underline{\text{Q}}$	$\underline{761}$	$\underline{(7)}$

Continued on next page

3. (continued)

	OUT	IN	MISC.
$(x^2 - 1)$ to MP	D		7
reset ctr. R	R	R	
$x^2(x^2 - 1)/2$ to ctr. R		R	7
$x^2(x^2 - 1)/2$ to MC	R	761	(7)
1/12 to MP	ST		7
reset ctr. S	S	S	
$x^2(x^2 - 1)/4!$ to ctr. S		S	7

A check should be made to see that sufficient cycles have been inserted to cover interpolation positioning time.

	OUT	IN	MISC.
interpolator I has positioned, reset IC			73
select interpolator I and step ahead	85		753
f(a) to ctr. F, step ahead		F	753
select interpolator I and step ahead	85		753
f(a + w) to ctr. G, step back		G	754
f(a + w) to ctr. H, step back	G	H	754
- f(a) to ctr. H; H = Δf(a)	F	H	732
f(a) to ctr. L, step back	F	L	754
select interpolator I and step back	85		754

Continued on next page

3. (continued)	OUT	IN	MISC.
$f(a - w)$ to ctr. I, step back		I	754
$- f(a - w)$ to ctr. F; $F = \Delta f(a - w)$	I	F	732
$x/2$ to MC, step back	P	761	754
$\Delta f(a)$ to ctr. M	H	M	7
$\Delta f(a - w)$ to ctr. M	F	M	
$\Delta f(a) + \Delta f(a - w)$ to MP	M		7
select interpolator I	85		7
$f(a - 2w)$ to ctr. J, step ahead		J	753
$- f(a - 2w)$ to ctr. I; $I = \Delta f(a - 2w)$	J	I	732
$- \Delta f(a - w)$ to ctr. I; $I = - \Delta^2 f(a - 2w)$	F	I	32
$x/2 \left[\Delta f(a) + \Delta f(a - w)\right]$ to ctr. L, step ahead		L	753
$x^2/2!$ to MC, step ahead	Q	761	753
$- \Delta f(a)$ to ctr. F; $F = - \Delta^2 f(a - w)$	H	F	732
$\Delta^2 f(a - w)$ to ctr. K	F	K	32
$\Delta^2 f(a - w)$ to MP	F		732
$- \Delta^2 f(a - 2w)$ to ctr. K; $K = \Delta^3 f(a - 2w)$, step ahead	I	K	753
step ahead			753
step ahead			753
reset ctr. T, step ahead	T	T	53
$(x^2/2!)\Delta^2 f(a - w)$ to ctr. L, step ahead		L	753
select interpolator I	85		7
$f(a + 2w)$ to ctr. T		T	
$- f(a + w)$ to ctr. T; $T = \Delta f(a + w)$	G	T	732
$- \Delta f(a)$ to ctr. T; $T = \Delta^2 f(a)$	H	T	732
$- \Delta^2 f(a - w)$ to ctr. T; $T = \Delta^3 f(a - w)$	F	T	7
$x(x^2 - 1)/12$ to MC	E	761	7
$\Delta^3 f(a - 2w)$ to ctr. N	K	N	7

Continued on next page

3. (continued)

	OUT	IN	MISC.
$\Delta^3 f(a - w)$ to ctr. N	T	N	
$\left[\Delta^3 f(a - 2w) + \Delta^3 f(a - w)\right]$ to MP	N		7
$- \Delta^3 f(a - 2w)$ to ctr. T; $T = \Delta^4 f(a - 2w)$	K	T	(7)32
$x(x^2 - 1)/3! \left[\Delta^3 f(a - 2w) + \Delta^3 f(a - w)\right] /2$ to ctr. L		L	7
$x^2(x^2 - 1)/4!$ to MC	S	761	(7)
$\Delta^4 f(a - 2w)$ to MP	T		(7)
$x^2(x^2 - 1)/4! \, \Delta^4 f(a - 2w)$ to ctr. L. $f(a + xw)$ lies in ctr. L.		L	7

INTERPOLATION BY NEWTON-GREGORY DIFFERENCE FORMULA

(1) In certain cases the Newton-Gregory formula of interpolation is found convenient. It may be used in the form

$$f(a + xw) = f(a) + x\,\Delta f(a) + \frac{x(x-1)}{2!}\Delta^2 f(a) + \frac{x(x-1)(x-2)}{3!}\Delta^3 f(a)$$
$$+ \frac{x(x-1)(x-2)(x-3)}{4!}\Delta^4 f(a) + \frac{x(x-1)(x-2)(x-3)(x-4)}{5!}\Delta^5 f(a) \ldots$$

(2) It is assumed that a functional tape has been punched with the values

$$\ldots, (a-2w), f(a-2w), (a-w), f(a-w), a,$$

$$f(a), (a+w), f(a+w), (a+2w), f(a+2w), \ldots$$

(3) In the coding which follows, it is assumed that the interval of the arguments is 0.1 and that the tape is on interpolator I. See Central-Difference Interpolation, note (5).

1. (a + xw) lies in ctr. A. f(a + xw) is to be delivered to ctr. I. Ctrs. B through P, 70 and LIO are available for computation but not reset. Switches are set as follows:

   Switch SP = 5 in machine column 24
   Switch SQ = 1/2
   Switch SR = 1/3
   Switch SS = 1/4
   Switch ST = 1/5
   Switch SU = 1/6
   Switch SV = 1.0

   The computation is carried to sixth differences.

	OUT	IN	MISC.
(a + xw) to interpolator I	A	7654	641
interpolator I positions			762
reset LIO ctr.			763
(a + xw) to LIO ctr.	A	765421	7
reset ctr. B	B	B	7
x to ctr. B	831	B	7
reset ctr. 70	732	732	7
- (a + xw) to ctr. 70	A	732	732
5 in first col. to ctr. B	SP	B	7
∓ 5 in first col. to ctr. B under control of ctr. 70	SP	B	7432
reset ctr. C	C	C	7

Continued on next page

1. (continued)

	OUT	IN	MISC.
x to MC	B	761	7
x to ctr. C	B	C	7
- 1 to ctr. C; C = x - 1	SV	C	32
x - 1 to MP	C		7
reset ctr. D	D	D	7
reset ctr. E	E	E	7
reset ctr. F	F	F	
x(x - 1) to ctr. D		D	7
ctr. D to MC	D	761	7
reset ctr. Q	Q	Q	7
- 1 to ctr. C; C = x - 2	SV	C	32
1/2 to MP	SQ		7
reset ctr. G	G	G	7
reset ctr. H	H	H	7
reset ctr. I	I	I	
x(x - 1)/2 to ctr. Q		Q	7
ctr. Q to MC	Q	761	7
reset ctr. J	J	J	7
reset ctr. K	K	K	
(x - 2) to MP	C		7
reset ctr. L	L	L	7
reset ctr. M	M	M	7
reset ctr. N	N	N	
x(x - 1)(x - 2)/2! to ctr. E		E	7
ctr. E to MC	E	761	7
reset ctr. R	R	R	7

Continued on next page

INTERPOLATION BY NEWTON-GREGORY DIFFERENCE FORMULA

1. (continued)	OUT	IN	MISC.
- 1 to ctr. C; C = x - 3	SV	C	32
1/3 to MP	SR		7
reset ctr. O	O	O	7
reset ctr. P	P	P	(7)
x(x - 1)(x - 2)/3!		R	7
ctr. R to MC	R	761	(7)
x - 3 to MP	C		(7)
x(x - 1)(x - 2)(x - 3)/3! to F		F	7
ctr. F to MC	F	761	7
reset ctr. S	S	S	7
- 1 to ctr. C; C = x - 4	SV	C	32
1/4 to MP	SS		(7)
x(x - 1)(x - 2)(x - 3)/4! to ctr. S		S	7
ctr. S to MC	S	761	(7)
x - 4 to MP	C		(7)

Continued on next page

CODING

1. (continued)

	OUT	IN	MISC.
x(x - 1)(x - 2)(x - 3)(x - 4)/4! to ctr. G		G	7
ctr. G to MC	G	761	7
reset ctr. T	T	T	7
- 1 to ctr. C; C = x - 5	SV	C	32
1/5 to MC	ST		(7)
x(x - 1)(x - 2)(x - 3)(x - 4)/5! to ctr. T		T	7
ctr. T to MC	T	761	(7)
reset ctr. V	V	V	
	C		(7)
x(x - 1)(x - 2)(x - 3)(x - 4)(x - 5)/5! to ctr. H		H	7
ctr. H to MC	H	761	7
reset ctr. U	U	U	(7)
1/6 to MP	SU		(7)

Continued on next page

1. (continued)

	OUT	IN	MISC.
$x(x-1)(x-2)(x-3)(x-4)(x-5)/6!$ to ctr. U		U	7
reset IC			73
select interpolator I and step ahead	85		753
f(a) to J, step ahead		J	753
f(a) to V	J	V	7
select interpolator I and step ahead	85		753
f(a + w) to K, step ahead		K	753
x to MC, step ahead	B	761	753
f(a) to I	J	I	7
- f(a + w) to J; $J = -\Delta f(a)$	K	J	32
$\Delta f(a)$ to MP	J		732
select interpolator I	85		7
f(a + 2w) to L, step ahead		L	753
- f(a + 2w) to K; $K = -\Delta f(a+w)$	L	K	732
$\Delta f(a+w)$ to J; $J = \Delta^2 f(a)$	K	J	32
x $\Delta f(a)$ to I, select interpolator I and step ahead	85	I	753
f(a + 3w) to M, step ahead		M	753
$x(x-1)/2!$ to MC, step ahead	Q	761	753
- f(a + 3w) to L; $L = -\Delta f(a+2w)$	M	L	732
$\Delta f(a+2w)$ to K; $K = \Delta^2 f(a+w)$	L	K	32
$\Delta^2 f(a)$ to MP	J		7
$-\Delta^2 f(a+w)$ to J; $J = -\Delta^3 f(a)$	K	J	732
select interpolator I	85		7
f(a + 4w) to N, step ahead		N	753
- f(a + 4w) to M; $M = -\Delta f(a+3w)$	N	M	32

Continued on next page

1. (continued)	OUT	IN	MISC.
$x(x-1)/2!\,\Delta^2 f(a)$ to I, step ahead		I	753
$x(x-1)(x-2)/3!$ to MC	R	761	7
$\Delta f(a+3w)$ to L; $L = \Delta^2 f(a+2w)$	M	L	732
$-\Delta^2 f(a+2w)$ to K; $K = -\Delta^3 f(a+w)$	L	K	32
$\Delta^3 f(a)$ to MP	J		732
$\Delta^3 f(a+w)$ to J; $J = \Delta^4 f(a)$	K	J	732
select interpolator I	85		7
$f(a+5w)$ to O, step ahead		O	753
$-f(a+5w)$ to N; $N = -\Delta f(a+4w)$	O	N	32
$x(x-1)(x-2)/3!\,\Delta^3 f(a)$ to I, step ahead		I	753
$x(x-1)(x-2)(x-3)/4!$ to MC	S	761	7
$\Delta f(a+4w)$ to M; $M = \Delta^2 f(a+3w)$	N	M	732
$-\Delta^3 f(a+3w)$ to L; $L = -\Delta^3 f(a+2w)$	M	L	32
$\Delta^4 f(a)$ to MP	J		7
$\Delta^3 f(a+2w)$ to K; $K = \Delta^4 f(a+w)$	L	K	732
$-\Delta^4 f(a+w)$ to J; $J = -\Delta^5 f(a)$	K	J	732
select interpolator I	85		7
$f(a+6w)$ to P		P	
$x(x-1)(x-2)(x-3)/4!\,\Delta^4 f(a)$ to I		I	7
$x(x-1)(x-2)(x-3)(x-4)/5!$ to MC	T	761	7
$-f(a+6w)$ to O; $O = -\Delta f(a+5w)$	P	O	732
$\Delta f(a+5w)$ to N; $N = \Delta^2 f(a+4w)$	O	N	32
$\Delta^5 f(a)$ to MP	J		732
$-\Delta^2 f(a+4w)$ to M; $M = -\Delta^3 f(a+3w)$	N	M	732
$\Delta^3 f(a+3w)$ to L; $L = \Delta^4 f(a+2w)$	M	L	732
$-\Delta^4 f(a+2w)$ to K; $K = -\Delta^5 f(a+w)$	L	K	732

Continued on next page

INTERPOLATION BY NEWTON-GREGORY DIFFERENCE FORMULA

1. (continued)	OUT	IN	MISC.
$\Delta^5 f(a + w)$ to J; $J = \Delta^6 f(a)$	K	J	32
$x(x - 1)(x - 2)(x - 3)(x - 4)/4!\,\Delta^5 f(a)$ to I		I	7
$x(x - 1)(x - 2)(x - 3)(x - 4)(x - 5)/6!$ to MC	U	761	(7)
$\Delta^6 f(a)$ to MP	J		7
product to I		I	7

SUBTABULATION

(1) If a table exists giving values of a function for a certain interval of the argument, the process of calculating the values of the function for a smaller interval of the argument is called subtabulation.

(2) Subtabulation is carried out by differencing the given function, then either interpolating on these differences for the intervening functions or determining a new difference table for the smaller tabular interval from which to build the functions.

(3) If interpolation is to be used, the selection of a particular formula should be determined by the following considerations:

(a) formulae which proceed to constant differences are exact,
(b) formulae which stop short of constant differences are not exact, but are approximate,
(c) approximate formulae terminating in the same difference are identical,
(d) approximate formulae terminating in distinct differences of the same order are not identical,
(e) central difference formulae terminating in a mean difference of order r are more exact than formulae which terminate in a single difference of order r.

(4) For purposes of machine computation, the central difference formulae are usually more convenient. In particular, to subtabulate to tenths, the Newton-Bessel central difference formula is well adapted to machine computation. See note (6) of the previous section.

If $y(x_0 + d)$ is the desired value of the function $(0 < d < h$ and $h = x_n - x_{n-1})$

$$y(x_0 + d) = A_0(y_0 + y_1) + A_1\Delta y_0 + A_2(\Delta^2 y_{-1} + \Delta^2 y_0)$$
$$+ A_3\Delta^3 y_{-1} + A_4(\Delta^4 y_{-2} + \Delta^4 y_{-1}) + A_5\Delta^5 y_{-2}$$
$$+ A_6(\Delta^6 y_{-3} + \Delta^6 y_{-2}) + A_7\Delta^7 y_{-3} + A_8(\Delta^8 y_{-4} + \Delta^8 y_{-3}) + \ldots$$

This form of the Newton-Bessel formula has the following advantages:

(a) the A_i are short, terminating decimal fractions, thus reducing multiplication time and eliminating errors arising from non-terminating coefficients,
(b) the values of the function for $d/h = 0.6, 0.7, 0.8, 0.9$ can be evaluated directly from the computations for $d/h = 0.4, 0.3, 0.2, 0.1$, respectively, by appropriate reversals of sign, thus almost halving the number of multiplications required,
(c) every second term in the function is zero when the value of the function for the half interval $d/h = 0.5$ is computed.

(5) The numerical values of the A_i, for $i = 0$ through 8, are given in Table 1.

(6) The Newton-Bessel formula should never be used without a careful examination of the error introduced by neglecting the remainder. For references on this, see Bibliography, Subtabulation.

(7) The error due to the neglect of the remainder does not include the errors inherent in machine computation; e.g., cutting off digits in products. These errors must be evaluated for the particular problem.

(8) Table 2 gives an example of the high accuracy which can be obtained using the Newton-Bessel formula as given in note (4). In Table 2 the correct values of the function are given to 23 places of decimals, eighth differences were used, ten values of the function from 7.94 to 8.04 were used to subtabulate. The maximum error is but a few units in the 23rd decimal place.

TABLE 1

d/h	0.1	0.2	0.3
A_0	0.5	0.5	0.5
A_1	-0.4	-0.3	-0.2
A_2	-0.022 5	-0.04	-0.052 5
A_3	0.006	0.008	0.007
A_4	0.003 918 75	0.007 2	0.009 668 75
A_5	-0.000 627	-0.000 864	-0.000 773 5
A_6	-0.000 795 506 25	-0.001 478 4	-0.002 001 431 25
A_7	0.000 090 915	0.000 126 72	0.000 114 367 5
A_8	0.000 171 744 117 187 5	0.000 321 024	0.000 436 383 492 187 5

d/h	0.4	0.5
A_0	0.5	0.5
A_1	-0.1	The A_i, i odd, equal zero for d/h = 0.5 .
A_2	-0.06	-0.062 5
A_3	0.004	
A_4	0.011 2	0.011 718 75
A_5	-0.000 448	
A_6	-0.002 329 6	-0.002 441 406 25
A_7	0.000 066 56	
A_8	0.000 509 184	0.000 534 057 617 187 5

d/h = 0.6

The A_{2k}, k = 0, 1, 2, 3, 4, are identical with the corresponding values for d/h = 0.4 .
The A_{2k+1}, k = 0, 1, 2, 3, are the negatives of the corresponding values for d/h = 0.4 .

d/h = 0.7

The A_{2k}, k = 0, 1, 2, 3, 4, are identical with the corresponding values for d/h = 0.3 .
The A_{2k+1}, k = 0, 1, 2, 3, are the negatives of the corresponding values for d/h = 0.3 .

d/h = 0.8

The A_{2k}, k = 0, 1, 2, 3, 4, are identical with the corresponding values for d/h = 0.2 .
The A_{2k+1}, k = 0, 1, 2, 3, are the negatives of the corresponding values for d/h = 0.2 .

d/h = 0.9

The A_{2k}, k = 0, 1, 2, 3, 4, are identical with the corresponding values for d/h = 0.1 .
The A_{2k+1}, k = 0, 1, 2, 3, are the negatives of the corresponding values for d/h = 0.1 .

TABLE 2

x	Correct Value of f(x)	Subtabulated Values of f(x)
7.980	1.763 147 388 660 678 723 1763	1.763 147 388 660 678 723 1763
7.981	1.760 829 249 550 966 677 1468	1.760 829 249 550 966 677 1464
7.982	1.758 509 640 161 486 144 7192	1.758 509 640 161 486 144 7188
7.983	1.756 188 562 959 490 626 2892	1.756 188 562 959 490 626 2887
7.984	1.753 866 020 413 355 311 2638	1.753 866 020 413 355 311 2633
7.985	1.751 542 014 992 574 599 4059	1.751 542 014 992 574 599 4057
7.986	1.749 216 549 167 759 621 3753	1.749 216 549 167 759 621 3753
7.987	1.746 889 625 410 635 758 4682	1.746 889 625 410 635 758 4683
7.988	1.744 561 246 194 040 161 5585	1.744 561 246 194 040 161 5586
7.989	1.742 231 413 991 919 269 2417	1.742 231 413 991 919 269 2418

INVERSE INTERPOLATION

(1) The values of an argument in arithmetical sequence and the corresponding values of a function are given in tabular form. Inverse interpolation is the process of finding the value of the argument corresponding to a value of the function intermediate between two tabular values.

(2) The inversion of a functional table may conveniently be accomplished by iteration. One of several iterative procedures is the following:

Let f(x) be a function tabulated for equal intervals of x. It is desired to retabulate this function for equal intervals h of the variable y.

Assume that

$$x_{-2} = f^{-1}(y_0 - 2h)$$

and

$$x_{-1} = f^{-1}(y_0 - h)$$

are two values of x previously found to correspond to $(y_0 - 2h)$ and $(y_0 - h)$. It is required to find

$$x_0 = f^{-1}(y_0) .$$

A first approximation $x_0^{(1)}$ to x_0 may be found from

$$x_0^{(1)} = x_{-1} + kh$$

where

$$k = \frac{x_{-1} - x_{-2}}{h} .$$

A second approximation $x_0^{(2)}$ to x_0 may be found by first computing

$$y_0^{(1)} = f\left[x_0^{(1)}\right]$$

by direct interpolation. If a polynomial interpolation tape for use in direct interpolation is not available, difference interpolation may be used here. Then

$$x_0^{(2)} = x_0^{(1)} + k\left[y_0 - y_0^{(1)}\right] .$$

Successively better approximations to x_0 may be found by the repeated application of the last two equations.

1. In the following example, the tape for direct interpolation is on interpolator III. Switch P contains 1/h and y_0 is in ctr. A. Ctr. C contains x_{-1} and ctr. D contains x_{-2}. Ctrs. B, E, F and G are available for computation of $x_0^{(2)}$.

	OUT	IN	MISC.
reset ctr. E	E	E	7
x_{-1} to ctr. E	C	E	7
$- x_{-2}$ to ctr. E; E = kh	D	E	732

Continued on next page

1. (continued)

	OUT	IN	MISC.
kh to MC	E	761	7
x_{-1} to E; E = $x_0^{(1)}$	C	E	7
reset ctr. F	F	F	
1/h to MP	P		7
reset ctr. B	B	B	7
reset ctr. G	G	G	7
y_0 to ctr. G	A	G	
kh/h to ctr. F; F = k		F	7
read $x_0^{(1)}$ to interpolator III and compute $y_0^{(1)} = f\left[x_0^{(1)}\right]$	E	76542	
			62
	841		
	E	763	
ctr. B = $y_0^{(1)}$		B	73
			7
k to MC	F	761	7
$-y_0^{(1)}$ to ctr. G; G = $y_0 - y_0^{(1)}$	B	G	(7)32
$y_0 - y_0^{(1)}$ to MP	G		(7)
$k\left[y_0 - y_0^{(1)}\right]$ to ctr. E; E = $x_0^{(2)}$		E	7

(3) The tabular interval h of the function must be examined in order to determine the rapidity of convergence before using this iterative process.

CARD FEEDS

(1) Before a problem involving card feeding is started, the feeds must be coupled to the machine. They should be uncoupled when the problem does not involve card feeding.

(2) Cards are fed under an automatic control which will light a red light and stop the machine if the cards run out, or if a card jam occurs. In order to use the card feed automatic safety control, the switch on the card feed control panel must be thrown to the On position. When cards run out, this switch must be thrown to the Off position in order to restart the machine.

(3) Card feeds may only be used to read into counters, not into functional units.

(4) The read-out of a number from a card feed may not be inverted. Negative numbers should be punched as complements on nine.

(5) By plugging, numbers may be shifted to the right or left. If numbers are shifted to the left, negative numbers should either be punched as complements on 10 or sufficient nines should be plugged to the right. If numbers are shifted to the right, negative numbers require sufficient nines plugged to the left. Plugging from any of the eighty card columns into any buss column is possible. See Plugging Instructions.

(6) The card feeds may not be used in interposed operations during multiplication or division.

(7) If a control tape is coded to use card feed I, card feed II may be used by throwing the card feed reverse switch. A similar comment holds for card feed II. The plugging is not carried over by the switch.

(8) It is frequently necessary to check decks of cards to see that a certain group is used in a certain run, to see that cards are in their proper order and that cards from the two feeds are properly paired or grouped. Serial numbers are used to denote the order of groups of cards. Classification numbers usually follow serial numbers and denote the order of cards within the group. If classification and serial numbers are punched in the cards, the classification numbers may be checked through the automatic check counter. The serial numbers may be checked against a value tape, an accumulation counter or another deck of cards.

(9) All decks of cards should be clearly labeled with the run in which they are to be used, the feed in which they are to be placed and necessary information about their classification and serial numbers.

	OUT	IN	MISC.
1. Read out of card feed I into ctr. A.		A	7632
2. Read out of card feed II into ctr. A.		A	76321
3. Read out of card feed I into print ctr. I and print.		7432	632
		752	7
4. Read out of card feed II into punch ctr. and punch.		753	6321
			75

5. Read successive cards out of card feed I into print ctr. I and print.

OUT	IN	MISC.
	7432	632
	752	6
	7432	632
	752	6

(10) If necessary, the blank Out column of the card feed coding may be used to select a value tape from which the value is read on the next line, or to turn on or off typewriters.

6. Read out of card feed I into ctr. A. Select the value tape on interpolator I and read the value to ctr. B and step the tape.

OUT	IN	MISC.
85	A	7632
	B	753

7. Read out of card feed I into ctr. A. Turn on typewriter II.

871	A	7632

CARD PUNCH

(1) Before a problem involving punching is started, the punch cable connection must be closed. This connection should be open when the problem does not involve punching to allow for manual punching.

(2) Cards are fed into the punch under an automatic control such that lack of a card in punching position will automatically stop the machine. This control operates with the codes 753 in the In column and 51 in the Miscellaneous column, stopping the machine on the line following these codes. If a card jam occurs, the direct current should be turned off and a card placed in punching position. The machine may then be started and the computation continued. Since this control may stop the machine, the codes 753 in the In column and 51 in the Miscellaneous column must not be interposed in multiplication or division.

(3) Numbers may be shifted to the right or left by suitable plugging. See Plugging Instructions.

(4) Negative numbers are punched as complements on nine.

(5) Since the punch counter has a complete set of carry controls, including end around carry, quantities may be accumulated in it. It may be read into as into any storage counter except that its read-in code is automatic, must not be followed by a 7 in the Miscellaneous column and may be interposed in multiplication or division only when the coding is specially arranged.

(6) If a half pick-up is desired on values punched in cards, see Multiple In-Out Counter.

(7) Two punching operations are available. In the first, the punching operation is completed before the machine starts the next operation, and in the second, the machine starts the next operation as soon as punching is initiated.

(8) Ten cycles for punching must intervene between the start of one punching operation and the initiation of another. Hence if it is necessary to perform a succession of punching operations, the "punch and complete punching" code must be used.

(9) In the operating instructions of any problem it should be stated how cards punched are to be labeled and stored.

	OUT	IN	MISC.
1. Read the quantity in sw. or ctr. A into punch ctr. If no card is in punching position the machine will stop on the next line of coding.	A	753	
2. Read minus the quantity in sw. (except IVS) or ctr. A into the punch ctr.	A	753	32
3. Read minus IVS to the punch ctr.	8431	753	21
4. Punch out the number lying in the punch ctr. Start next operation before punching is completed.			5
or			75
5. Punch out the number lying in the punch ctr. and complete punching before starting next operation.			51

OUT	IN	MISC.

6. Reset the punch ctr.

843		

7. Read out of the punch ctr.

863		

8. Punch out the quantity lying in sw. or ctr. A.

A	753	
		75

9. Accumulate the quantities lying in sws. or ctrs. A, B, C and D and punch out the sum.

A	753	
B	753	
C	753	
D	753	
		75

10. Punch successively the quantities lying in sws. or ctrs. A and B.

A	753	
		51
B	753	
		75

(10) The blank Out and In column of the line of coding initiating punching may be used to code any operation not requiring an operational code in the Miscellaneous column. The code which initiates punching may not be combined with the invert code or any other operational code in the Miscellaneous column. That is, the 5 or 75 in the Miscellaneous column initiating punching may be inserted in any Miscellaneous column not already containing an operational code other than 7.

(11) The blank Miscellaneous column of the line of coding reading into the punch counter (if not used for an invert or other such operational code), may be used to code the stepping of a tape on an interpolator.

11. Print and punch the quantity in sw. or ctr. A. Typewriter I.

OUT	IN	MISC.
A	753	
A	7432	
	752	75

12. Multiply sw. or ctr. A by sw. or ctr. B. Deliver the product to ctr. C. Punch out the quantity standing in the punch ctr. Turn off typewriter I.

OUT	IN	MISC.
A	761	5
B		
8732	C	7

or

OUT	IN	MISC.
A	761	
B		5
8732	C	7

or

OUT	IN	MISC.
A	761	
B		
8732	C	75

13. Multiply minus sw. (except IVS) or ctr. A. by the absolute value of ctr. B. Deliver the product to ctr. C and punch out the quantity in the punch ctr. Turn on typewriter I.

A	761	32
B		2
872	C	75

14. Multiply minus sw. (except IVS) or ctr. A. by sw. or ctr. B. Deliver the product to ctr. C, punch out the quantity in the punch ctr. and step and read the value from the tape on interpolator I to ctr. D. Turn on typewriter II.

A	761	32
B		5
85	C	753
871	D	7

15. Punch the quantity in sw. or ctr. A, print it with half pick-up on typewriter I, multiply minus sw. (except IVS) or ctr. B by ctr. A, deliver the product to ctr. C, step the value tape on interpolator II three times, and read the value to ctr. D.

A	753	531
B	761	32
A	7432	531
	76543	531
	752	5
851	C	7
	D	7

(12) In order to check the values punched in cards, summations of the quantities punched may be employed. Suppose $f(x_n)$ is computed and punched, the quantities $f(x_n)$ are accumulated in the

machine and the summations printed out.

The difference

$$\sum_{0}^{k} f(x_i) - \sum_{0}^{k-1} f(x_i) = \overline{f(x_k)}$$

is computed and subjected to a check procedure.

The cards are later summed on a tabulator or fed to the machine and summed. If the independent summations are compared, this process insures that $f(x_k)$ has been correctly punched. Note that if the check is made directly on $f(x_k)$ as computed, the cards are not checked since the read-outs to the accumulation and punch counter could be incorrect.

(13) Cards may be punched containing a function in the first n card columns and a code number in the last columns of the card. After the first n columns are punched, a duplicating card and skip bar control the punch. The punch counter resets and the code number is added into the punch counter. The code number is then punched in the columns fixed by the skip bar.

16. Punch the 24 columns of the function f(x) standing in ctr. A in card columns 1-24. Punch the code number accumulated in ctr. E from ctrs. B, C and D in card columns 70, 73, 74, 75, 76 and 79. The duplicating card contains an R in column 25. The punch is plugged as shown below.

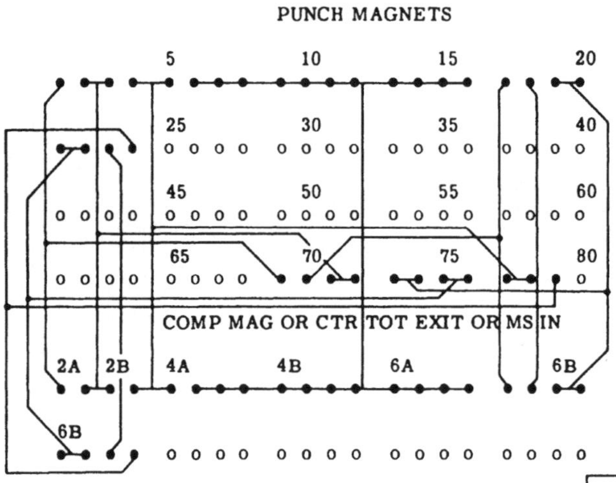

	OUT	IN	MISC.
reset ctr. E	E	E	7
accumulate the code number in ctr. E	B	E	7
	C	E	7

Continued on next page

CARD PUNCH

16. (continued)

	OUT	IN	MISC.
	D	E	7
f(x) to punch ctr.	A	753	
punch out f(x)			51
code number to punch ctr.	E	753	
punch out code number			51

PRINTING

(1) The decimal point, vertical spacing, horizontal spacing, half pick-up and argument control all require plugging. See Plugging Instructions.

(2) The typewriters should be turned on at least two cycles before they are required to print. The typewriters may be turned off as soon as printing operations are completed; i.e., 20 to 23 cycles after the initiation of the last print or immediately after a "print and complete printing" code.

(3) There are three parts of the printing operation, the read-in to the print counters, the half pick-up which may be used or not as desired and the initiation of the printing operation.

(4) Negative numbers may be printed as such or as complements on nine if the print complement switch is thrown.

(5) Since the print counters have complete sets of carry controls including end around carry circuits, quantities may be accumulated in them. They may be read into as into any storage counter except their read-in codes are automatic and must not be followed by a 7 in the Miscellaneous column.

(6) Two printing operations are available. In the first, the printing operation is completed before the machine starts the next operation, and in the second, the machine starts the next operation as soon as printing is initiated.

(7) The operation "print and complete printing" must not be interposed in multiplication or division.

(8) Approximately 23 cycles for printing must intervene between the start of one printing operation and the beginning of another. Hence if it is necessary to perform a succession of printing operations, the "print and complete printing" code must be used. See Timing.

(9) The half pick-up may be used if a number is to be rounded off to fewer digits than the machine capacity. Its effect is to add one in the lowest order column retained if the next lower column contains five or more. Actually the half pick-up adds or subtracts five in the column to which it is plugged, in the print counter for which it is coded, according as the number in the print counter is positive or negative. A half pick-up may also be added in from a switch under control of counter 70. See Choice Counter.

(10) If a control tape is coded to use print counter I and typewriter I, print counter II and typewriter II may be used by throwing one of the typewriter reverse switches. A similar comment holds for typewriter II. Note that this does not change over the half pick-up which is not reversed and continues to add into the print counter for which it is coded.

(11) Numbers from print counter I may only be printed on typewriter I. Numbers from print counter II may only be printed on typewriter II.

(12) There is available a special control on printing, the "argument control", which will cause the typewriter not to print zeros to the right of the point to which it is plugged. This code, an 87 in the Out column, is placed on the line of coding initiating printing.

	OUT	IN	MISC.
1. Turn on typewriter II.	871		
2. Turn on typewriter I.	872		

PRINTING

	OUT	IN	MISC.
3. Turn off typewriter II.	8731		
4. Turn off typewriter I.	8732		
5. Read the quantity in sw. or ctr. A to print ctr. I.	A	7432	
6. Read minus the quantity in sw. (except IVS) or ctr. A to print ctr. I.	A	7432	32
7. Read minus the quantity in IVS to print ctr. I.	8431	7432	21
8. Read the quantity in sw. or ctr. A to print ctr. II.	A	74321	
9. Read minus the quantity in sw. (except IVS) or ctr. A to print ctr. II.	A	74321	32
10. Reset print ctr. I. Cannot be used while either typewriter is printing.	842		
11. Reset print ctr. II. Cannot be used while either typewriter is printing.	8421		
12. Read out of print ctr. I.	862		
13. Read out of print ctr. II.	8621		
14. Multiply sw. or ctr. A by sw. or ctr. B and deliver the product to print ctr. I.	A	761	
	B		
		7432	
15. Print the quantity in print ctr. I on typewriter I and complete printing before starting other operations.		752	6

	OUT	IN	MISC.
16. Print the quantity in print ctr. II on typewriter II and complete printing before starting other operations.		7521	6
17. Print the quantity in print ctr. I on typewriter I and start other operations.		752	7
18. Print the quantity in print ctr. II on typewriter II and start other operations.		7521	7
19. Read the quantity in sw. or ctr. A to print ctr. I and print on typewriter I.	A	7432	
		752	7
20. Read minus the quantity in sw. (except IVS) or ctr. A to print ctr. II and print on typewriter II.	A	74321	32
		7521	7
21. Print the quantity in print ctr. I on typewriter I omitting zeros to the right.	87	752	7
22. Print the quantity in print ctr. II on typewriter II omitting zeros to the right.	87	7521	7
23. Add half pick-up to print ctr. I.		76543	
24. Add half pick-up to print ctr. II.		765431	
25. Print the quantity in sw. or ctr. A with half pick-up on typewriter I.	A	7432	
		76543	
		752	7
26. Print minus the quantity in sw. (except IVS) or ctr. A with half pick-up on typewriter II.	A	74321	32
		765431	
		7521	7

27. Multiply sw. or ctr. A by sw. or ctr. B. Deliver the product to print ctr. I and print.

OUT	IN	MISC.
A	761	
B		
	7432	
	752	7

28. Step and read the value from the tape on interpolator I to print ctr. I and print.

85		753
	7432	
	752	7

29. Print successively the quantities lying in sws. or ctrs. A and B on typewriter I.

A	7432	
	752	6
B	7432	
	752	7

30. Print the quantity lying in sw. or ctr. A on typewriter I and the quantity in sw. or ctr. B on typewriter II.

A	7432	
	752	6
B	74321	
	7521	7

31. Multiply sw. or ctr. A by sw. or ctr. B. Deliver the product to ctr. C and print B on typewriter I with half pick-up.

A	761	
B	7432	
	76543	
	752	
	C	7

(13) The blank Miscellaneous column of the lines of coding reading into the print counter (if not used for an invert or other such operational code), reading in the half pick-up, or initiating printing, may be used for punching or stepping an interpolator.

(14) The blank In column of the lines of coding reading in the half pick-up or initiating printing may be used to select a value tape from which the value is read on the next line.

32. Print the quantity in sw. or ctr. A with half pick-up. Step the tape on interpolator III back three times and read the value to ctr. B.

OUT	IN	MISC.
A	7432	542
	76543	542
852	752	7542
	B	7

33. Multiply minus ctr. A by the value from the tape on interpolator II after stepping ahead once, deliver the product to ctr. C, print the quantity in sw. or ctr. B with half pick-up, and punch out the quantity in the punch ctr.

A	761	732
B	7432	5
851	76543	531
	752	
	C	7

34. Punch and print with half pick-up the absolute value of the quantity in ctr. A on typewriter I, multiply it by minus sw. or ctr. B and deliver the product to ctr. C.

A	753	2
A	761	72
A	7432	2
	76543	5
B	752	32
	C	7

(15) Printed data may be checked by printing quantities on both typewriters or by simultaneously printing and punching and later checking the punched cards against the printed results.

(16) Quantities or groups of quantities may be printed simultaneously on both typewriters. This requires special wiring in the machine and that the typewriters be plugged identically, except for the read-out control. It is necessary to read into both print counters, but only one code to initiate printing need be used, since the wiring "gangs" the codes 752 and 7521.

(17) As an added precaution for greater accuracy of the typewriters, half-time printing may be used. For half-time printing only every other column selection plughub is plugged to a digit from the print counter read-out. The intervening plughubs are left blank or may be filled by the argument control, the decimal point or spaces if desired. This may be of particular advantage when printing on both typewriters at the same time, if the column selection plughubs of the two typewriters are plugged alternately and provided that the number of digits in each printed quantity is small enough. See Plugging Instructions.

(18) When there are many prints in a computation, so that it is desired to print as rapidly as possible, the code 76 in the Miscellaneous column may be used instead of the usual 7 or 6 with 752 or 7521. This will allow other operations to be interposed during the printing time, but does not permit a print to be initiated until the previous print is completed. As in other interposed operations, the automatic (7 in the Miscellaneous column) must be omitted from the last interposed line.

INTERPOSITION OF MACHINE STOPS

(1) It is possible under specialized codings for the machine to choose the time at which certain operations will be performed. This possibility of a choice is inherent in the nature of the automatic codes controlling the functional units. In particular, the choice of the time at which the product is read out makes it possible to interpose in multiplication and division certain codes which may stop the machine.

(2) The check procedure and the read-in to the punch counter may be interposed in multiplication or division only when the coding is specially arranged. This special coding prevents the loss of the multiplication or division if the check fails or if there is no card in punching position. The saving of time is but two cycles, but if checking and punching are frequent operations in a tape, the time saved may become proportionately large per revolution. The coding must be used with extreme caution.

(3) It is necessary to code the read-in to the punch counter or the check procedure immediately before the read-out of the product and to duplicate the product read-out. The first coding of the product-out must not have a 7 code in the Miscellaneous column. If the procedure fails, the machine stops on the first product-out. The automatic from the completed multiplication will cause the sequence mechanism to read the first product-out line. The product will be delivered to the designated storage counter. The sequence mechanism will step to the next line of coding and stop, since there was no Miscellaneous 7 on the product-out line. It should be noted that if there were a Miscellaneous 7 on the product-out line, the machine would continue operation as if the check had not failed. If the check or punch read-in does not fail, the automatic from the procedure will cause the sequence mechanism to read the first product-out as if it were the last line of interposed coding and step to the next line. No transfer will take place since there is no code in the Out column. The automatic from the completed multiplication will cause the sequence mechanism to read the second product-out line which has a 7 in the Miscellaneous column, the product will be delivered to the designated storage counter and the machine will continue operation.

1. Multiply the quantity in sw. or ctr. A by the quantity in sw. or ctr. B and deliver the product to ctr. C. Interpose a read-in from ctr. D to the punch ctr. Lines reading (blank, blank, 7) or (blank, blank, blank) may be used for interposed operations.

OUT	IN	MISC.
A	761	7
		7
B		7
		7
		7
D	753	
	C	
	C	7

2. Multiply the quantity in sw. or ctr. A by the quantity in sw. or ctr. B and deliver the product to ctr. C. Interpose

A	761	7

Continued on next page

2. (continued)

a check of the quantity in ctr. D against the tolerance in sw. W during the multiplication. Lines reading (blank, blank, 7) or (blank, blank, 64) may be used for interposed operations.

OUT	IN	MISC.
		7
74	74	
B		7
SW	74	7
D	74	71
		64
	C	
	C	7

3. Multiply the quantity in sw. or ctr. A by the quantity in sw. or ctr. B and deliver the product to ctr. C. Interpose a "ganged" print from ctrs. B and E and a check of the quantity in ctr. D against the tolerance in sw. W during the multiplication.

A	761	7
74	74	7
SW	74	
B	74321	
E	7432	
D	74	71
	752	64
	C	
	C	7

(4) If both the read-in to the punch counter and the check procedure are to be interposed, there must be at least two non-zero digits in either the odd or the even columns of the multiplier. The product-out line of coding must appear three times. First, immediately after the check procedure, it appears with a 7 in the Miscellaneous column; secondly, immediately after the read-in to the punch counter, it appears without a 7 in the Miscellaneous column; thirdly, in the following line, it appears with a 7 in the Miscellaneous column.

If the check procedure fails, the machine will stop on the first product-out line. The automatic from the completed multiplication will signal the sequence mechanism to read this first product-out line and step to the next. The product will be delivered to the designated storage counter. The 7 in the Miscellaneous column will order the sequence mechanism to read the next line of coding and step to the next. There will be a read-in to the punch counter. The automatic from the punch counter read-in will order the sequence mechanism to read the next line. This line (blank, C, blank) will effect no transfer and the sequence control will remain on the last line of coding.

If there is no card in punching position, the machine will stop on the second product-out line. The automatic from the completed multiplication will signal the sequence mechanism to read the second product-out line and step. The product will be delivered to the designated storage counter and the machine will remain on the last line of coding.

If the check fails and there is no card in punching position, the machine will stop on the first product-out line. The automatic from the completed multiplication will signal the sequence mechanism to read the first product-out line and step. The product will be delivered to the designated storage counter. The 7 in the Miscellaneous column will order the sequence mechanism to read the next line of coding and step. Since there is no card in punching position, the sequence mechanism will remain on the second product-out line.

If neither the punch counter read-in nor the check procedure fails, the automatic from the check will cause the sequence mechanism to read the first product-out line as if it were merely a line of interposed coding. No transfer will take place, since there is no code in the Out column. The 7 in the Miscellaneous column will order the sequence mechanism to read the next line of coding and step. There will be a read-in to the punch counter. The sequence mechanism will read the second product-out as if it were the last line of interposed coding. No transfer will take place since there is no code in the Out column. The automatic from the completed multiplication will cause the machine to read the third product-out line. The product will be delivered to the designated storage counter. The machine will continue operation.

(5) Similar codings may be applied to division. There will of course be more interposed lines during the division, and the check or punch procedure will immediately precede the read-out of the quotient.

4. Multiply the quantity in sw. or ctr. A by the quantity in sw. or ctr. B and deliver the product to ctr. C. Interpose a check of the quantity in ctr. E against the tolerance in sw. W and a read-in from ctr. D to the punch ctr. Line reading (blank, blank, 64) may be used for an interposed operation.

OUT	IN	MISC.
A	761	7
74	74	7
SW	74	
B		7
E	74	71
		64
	C	7
D	753	
	C	
	C	75

5. Divide the quantity in ctr. A by the quantity in ctr. B and deliver the quotient to ctr. C. Division must be plugged to at least ten digits. Interpose a check of the quantity in ctr. E against the tolerance in sw. W

B	761	7
74	74	7

Continued on next page

5. (continued)

and a read-in from ctr. D to the punch ctr. Lines reading (blank, blank, 7) and (blank, blank, 64) may be used for interposed operations.

OUT	IN	MISC.
SW	74	
A		7
		7
		7
		7
		7
		7
		7
E	74	71
		64
	C	7
D	753	
	C	
	C	75

CHAPTER V

PLUGGING INSTRUCTIONS

"One deviates to the right, another to the left; the error is the same with all, but it deceives them in different ways." Horace.

Once the tapes necessary to the solution of a problem have been prepared, the appropriate switches set and the plugging completed, the calculator may be started. The machine will then continue in operation, hour after hour, completely checking its own results until either the problem has been solved or until a breakdown occurs. Experience has shown that the calculator will operate approximately ninety percent of the time without failure of any kind, and on occasion has run as long as four weeks without interruption. At such times it is necessary for the operator only to exercise minor supervision such as checking the bearing temperatures, keeping the typewriters supplied with paper and the feeds with cards. However, the accuracy of all computed results is dependent not only upon the accurate operation of the calculator itself but also upon the accuracy with which the manual adjustments were made prior to starting the problem. Herein lies the only opportunity for error which is not automatically checked by the machine itself. The calculator is far more nearly infallible than the personnel in charge of its operation. The setting of the switches and the plugging of the functional units provide the two possible sources of human error. It cannot be too strongly emphasized that these two operations must be carried out with the greatest of care and thoroughly checked before a problem is started. For example, if two neighboring wires in the typewriter plugging are interchanged, two digits in the printed results will be interchanged. The entire computation will have been automatically checked by the calculator, but the results will be incorrectly printed. If two card feed plugwires are interchanged, the calculator will compute on incorrect input data, check its computation and the error will not be detected. It is essential therefore that the plugging be checked by reading in known values, such as diagonal numbers, and printing them out before a computation is begun.

The plugging of a particular unit, though tedious, is not difficult once the underlying principles and the labeling of the plugboards are understood. In order to simplify the plugging diagrams, a wiring convention will be employed. Whenever n successive plughubs in any one row of the plugboard are to be plugged in one to one correspondence with n other plughubs in another row, the n plugwires will be represented by a single connection as shown in the following diagram.

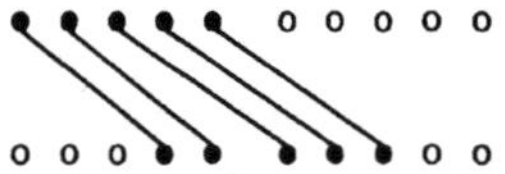

Actual wiring

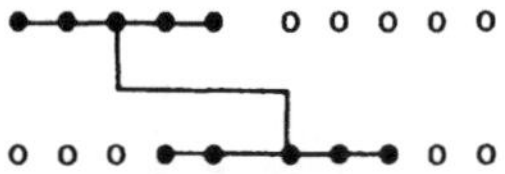

Convention

For convenient reference the plugging instructions have been divided into sections corresponding to the various units of the machine and to the sections of the chapter on coding.

MULTIPLICATION

(1) The multiply unit requires plugging for the read-out of the PQ counter into the buss.

(2) If the operating decimal point of the machine lies between columns n and n + 1, the decimal point of the PQ counter lies between columns 2n and 2n + 1. From the PQ counter, 23 columns and the algebraic sign are read into the buss (P-OUT plughubs). The P-OUT plughubs are so plugged that the decimal point of the quantity standing in the PQ counter is shifted to conform with the operating decimal point; i.e.,

2n + 1st plughub of PQ to n + 1st plughub of P-OUT,
2nth plughub of PQ to nth plughub of P-OUT,
sign plughub of PQ to 24th plughub of P-OUT.

The plugging is continued to the right and left until the P-OUT plughubs are filled.

(3) The PQ counter plughubs lie in rows 2 and 3 of the MP-DIV plugboard. The P-OUT plughubs lie in the 4th row of the same board. The sign plughub of the PQ counter is the 24th plughub in the 3rd row.

1. Plug the multiply unit for operating with the decimal point between columns 15 and 16.

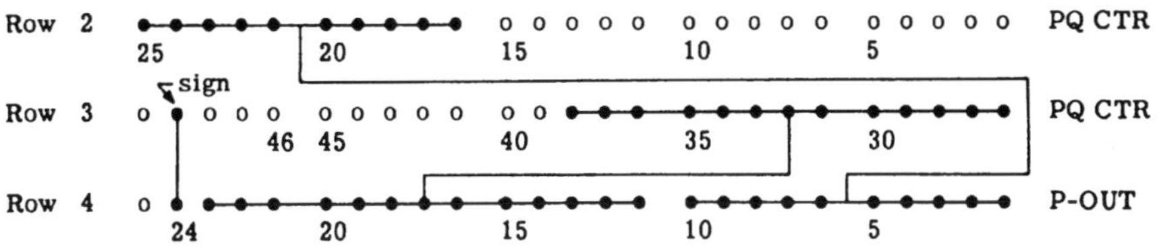

(4) The omission of plugging to some of the low-order P-OUT plughubs increases the speed of computation at the expense of accuracy, since fewer non-zero digits are carried to the next step in the computation.

2. The operating decimal point lies between columns 19 and 20. Plug the multiply unit to read no more than twelve decimal places from the PQ counter.

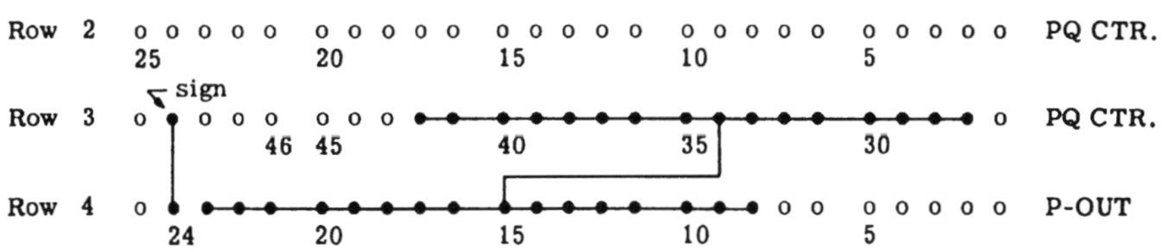

(5) For high accuracy computation, the operating decimal point is assumed to lie between columns 23 and 24.

3. Plug the multiply unit for high accuracy computation.

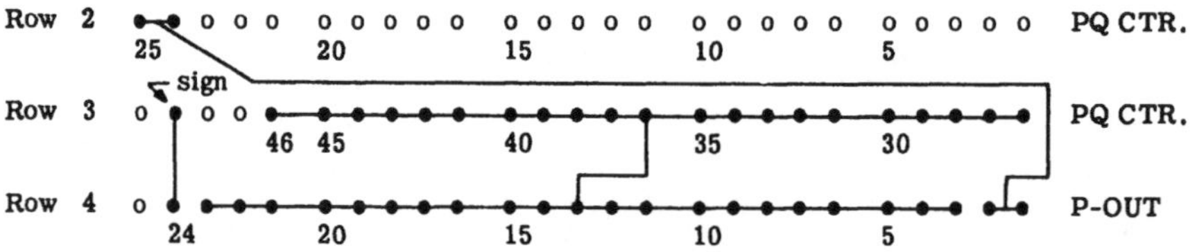

(6) Table 1 shows the necessary plugging for the read-out from the PQ counter to the buss (P-OUT plughubs) for each position of the operating decimal point. The number at the top of each column refers to the P-OUT plughub. The numbers in the body of the table refer to the PQ counter plughubs. Note that the sign plughub of the PQ counter is connected to the 24th P-OUT plughub.

TABLE 1 MULTIPLICATION: PQ COUNTER TO P-OUT

	P-OUT COLUMNS																							
Operating Decimal Position	24	23	22	21	20	19	18	17	16	15	14	13	12	11	10	9	8	7	6	5	4	3	2	1
1/0	S	23	22	21	20	19	18	17	16	15	14	13	12	11	10	9	8	7	6	5	4	3	2	1
2/1	S	24	23	22	21	20	19	18	17	16	15	14	13	12	11	10	9	8	7	6	5	4	3	2
3/2	S	25	24	23	22	21	20	19	18	17	16	15	14	13	12	11	10	9	8	7	6	5	4	3
4/3	S	26	25	24	23	22	21	20	19	18	17	16	15	14	13	12	11	10	9	8	7	6	5	4
5/4	S	27	26	25	24	23	22	21	20	19	18	17	16	15	14	13	12	11	10	9	8	7	6	5
6/5	S	28	27	26	25	24	23	22	21	20	19	18	17	16	15	14	13	12	11	10	9	8	7	6
7/6	S	29	28	27	26	25	24	23	22	21	20	19	18	17	16	15	14	13	12	11	10	9	8	7
8/7	S	30	29	28	27	26	25	24	23	22	21	20	19	18	17	16	15	14	13	12	11	10	9	8
9/8	S	31	30	29	28	27	26	25	24	23	22	21	20	19	18	17	16	15	14	13	12	11	10	9
10/9	S	32	31	30	29	28	27	26	25	24	23	22	21	20	19	18	17	16	15	14	13	12	11	10
11/10	S	33	32	31	30	29	28	27	26	25	24	23	22	21	20	19	18	17	16	15	14	13	12	11
12/11	S	34	33	32	31	30	29	28	27	26	25	24	23	22	21	20	19	18	17	16	15	14	13	12
13/12	S	35	34	33	32	31	30	29	28	27	26	25	24	23	22	21	20	19	18	17	16	15	14	13
14/13	S	36	35	34	33	32	31	30	29	28	27	26	25	24	23	22	21	20	19	18	17	16	15	14
15/14	S	37	36	35	34	33	32	31	30	29	28	27	26	25	24	23	22	21	20	19	18	17	16	15
16/15	S	38	37	36	35	34	33	32	31	30	29	28	27	26	25	24	23	22	21	20	19	18	17	16
17/16	S	39	38	37	36	35	34	33	32	31	30	29	28	27	26	25	24	23	22	21	20	19	18	17
18/17	S	40	39	38	37	36	35	34	33	32	31	30	29	28	27	26	25	24	23	22	21	20	19	18
19/18	S	41	40	39	38	37	36	35	34	33	32	31	30	29	28	27	26	25	24	23	22	21	20	19
20/19	S	42	41	40	39	38	37	36	35	34	33	32	31	30	29	28	27	26	25	24	23	22	21	20
21/20	S	43	42	41	40	39	38	37	36	35	34	33	32	31	30	29	28	27	26	25	24	23	22	21
22/21	S	44	43	42	41	40	39	38	37	36	35	34	33	32	31	30	29	28	27	26	25	24	23	22
23/22	S	45	44	43	42	41	40	39	38	37	36	35	34	33	32	31	30	29	28	27	26	25	24	23
24/23	S	46	45	44	43	42	41	40	39	38	37	36	35	34	33	32	31	30	29	28	27	26	25	24

DIVISION

(1) Division requires:

A. plugging for the number of comparisons to be made during the dividing operation,
B. a switch setting to control the amount of shift to the right of the read-out of the quotient from the PQ counter to the buss.

(2) The number of comparisons through which the dividing operation is carried is determined by the Miscellaneous codes controlling the place limitation plugging. The number of comparisons in a dividing operation may vary from 1 to 24. Five orders of accuracy may be selected in this range by non-automatic operational codes in the Miscellaneous column. The codes are associated with the 25th plughubs of rows 1, 3, 4, 5 and 6 of the MP-DIV plugboard.

Code	25th plughub in row	
643	6	minimum accuracy
6431	5	
6432	4	
64321	3	
blank	1	maximum accuracy

The number of comparisons is controlled by the plughubs of the first row of the MP-DIV plugboard. The number of comparisons includes a first no go if such occurs. This implies that if d significant digits are desired in the PQ counter, the dividing operation must be plugged for d + 1 comparisons. At most, 23 columns are read out of the PQ counter unless the low order read-out is used.

1. Plug the place limitations of division to provide 4, 9 and 15 significant digits in the PQ counter, using codes 643, 6431 and blank respectively.

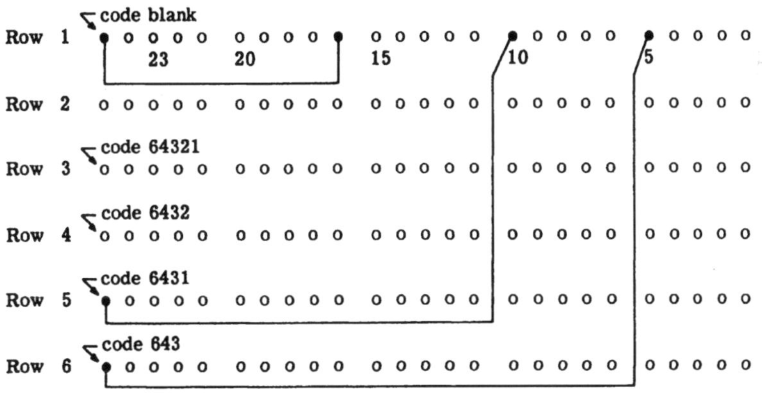

2. Plug the place limitation of division to provide 18 significant digits in the PQ counter, using the blank code.

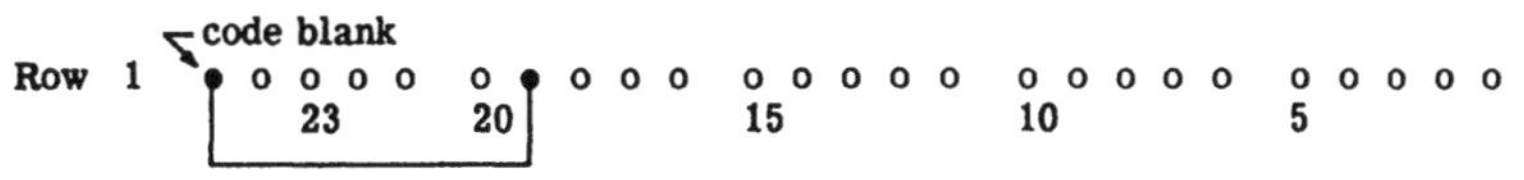

PLUGGING INSTRUCTIONS

3. Plug the place limitation of division to provide 23 significant digits in the PQ counter, using the blank code.

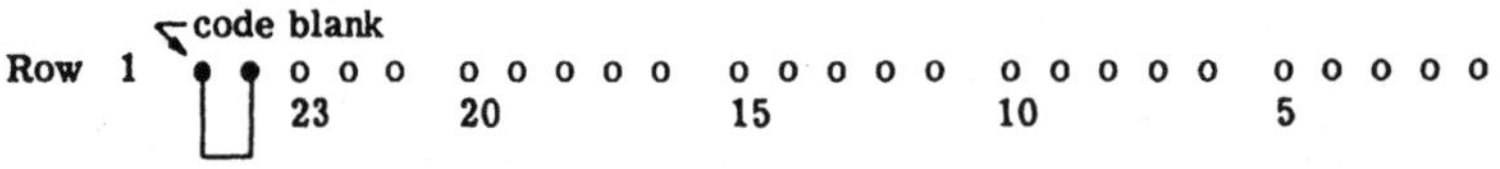

(3) The amount of shift to the right of the read-out of the quotient from the PQ counter to the buss is controlled by a pair of manually set switches. These two dial switches, located to the right of the sequence mechanism, are labeled "Divide N minus decimal". The switches must be set to the value 22 - n, where the operating decimal point lies between columns n and n + 1. For high accuracy computation, the switches must be set to 00.

LOGARITHM IN-OUT COUNTER

(1) The LIO counter has a pluggable read-out from the counter into the buss.

(2) The LIO-OUT plughubs lie in row 26 and the corresponding buss plughubs in row 25 of the functional plugboard. The auxiliary nines, necessary in plugging for negative numbers, lie in the ten plughubs of the right side of the bottom row of the board.

(3) The LIO counter may be used to shift quantities to the right or left; i.e., to multiply by a power of ten.

1. Plug the LIO counter to shift quantities 5 columns to the left; i.e., to multiply by 10^5.

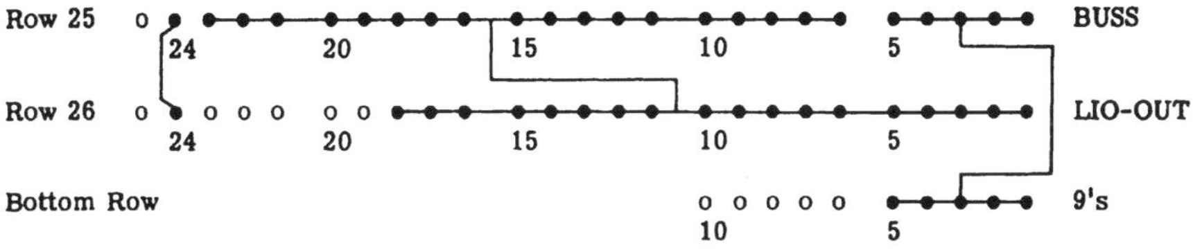

2. Plug the LIO counter to shift quantities 8 columns to the right; i.e., to multiply by 10^{-8}.

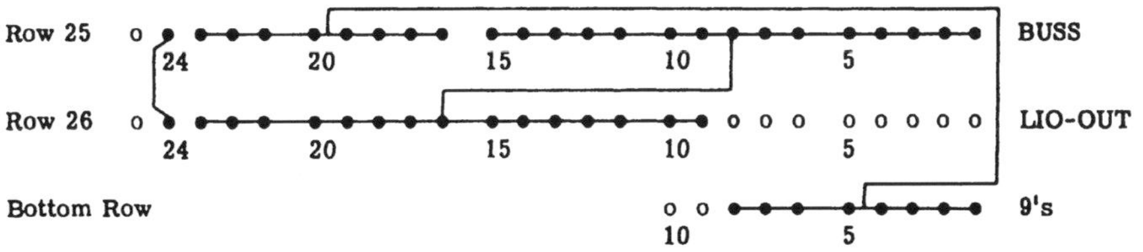

(4) The LIO counter may be used to drop off digits from any quantity.

3. The operating decimal point lies between columns 15 and 16. Plug the LIO counter to read out only the decimal part of a quantity.

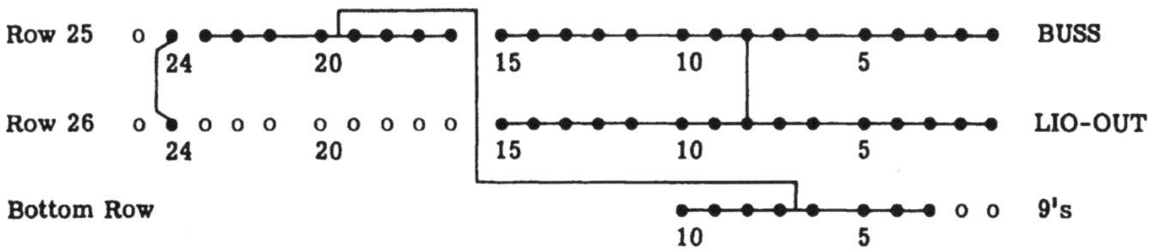

4. The first five columns of a quantity constitute a serial number. Plug the LIO counter to drop off the serial number.

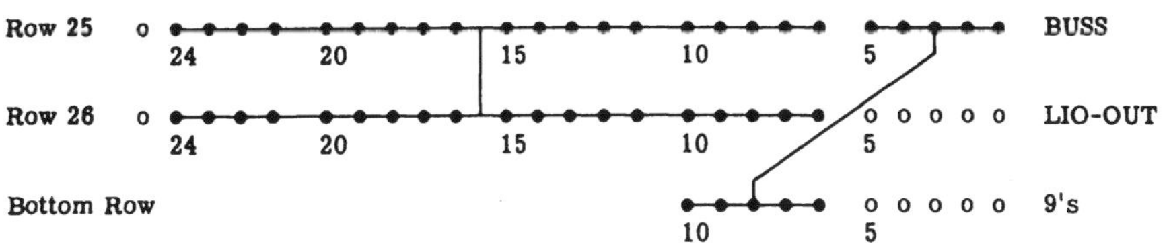

SINE IN-OUT COUNTER

(1) The SIO counter has a pluggable read-in, SIO-IN II, and two pluggable read-outs, SIO-OUT I and SIO-OUT II. The "85-1 PU" switch must be in the off position when the SIO counter is used for any operation not a part of the sine computation.

(2) The SIO-IN II plughubs lie in row 32 and the corresponding buss plughubs in row 33 of the functional plugboard. This read-in is associated with the automatic code 8741 in the In column.

(3) The SIO-OUT I plughubs lie in row 35 and the corresponding buss plughubs in row 34 of the functional plugboard. This read-out is associated with the code 874 in the Out column.

(4) If negative quantities are to be routed via SIO-IN II and SIO-IN I, auxiliary nines must be supplied from a switch under control of the choice counter.

(5) The SIO-OUT II plughubs lie in row 36 and the corresponding buss plughubs in row 37 of the functional plugboard. The auxiliary nines, necessary in plugging for negative numbers, lie in the ten plughubs of the left side of the bottom row of the board. This read-out is associated with the code 84 in the Out column.

(6) If the "SIO-OUT-2 Invert Control" switch is in the on position, a nine in the 24th column will pick up the plugged auxiliary nines and will invert the read-out of the plugged columns of SIO. If the switch is in the off position, a nine in the 24th column will pick up the plugged auxiliary nines but the read-out of the plugged columns of SIO will be direct.

(7) The SIO counter may be used to shift quantities to the right or left; i.e., to multiply by a power of ten.

1. Plug SIO-IN II to shift positive quantities 2 columns to the left; i.e., to multiply by 100.

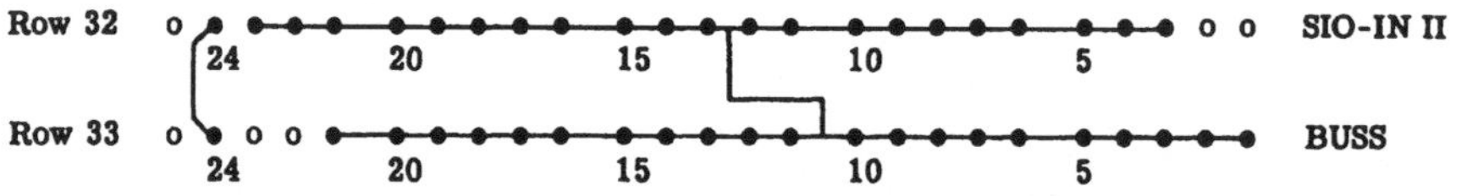

2. Plug SIO-OUT I to shift positive quantities 3 columns to the right; i.e., to multiply by 10^{-3}.

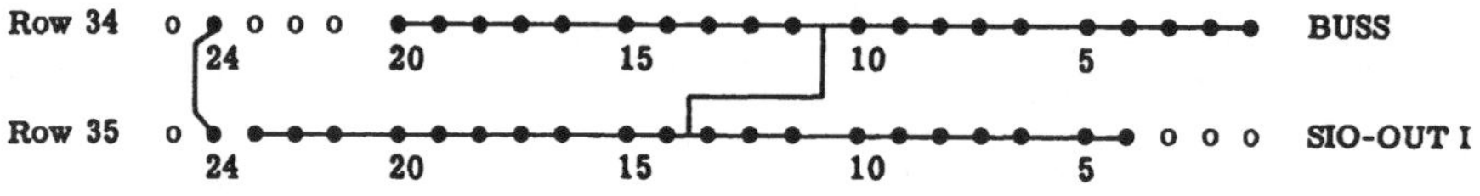

3. Plug SIO-OUT II to shift quantities 2 columns to the right; i.e., to multiply by 10^{-2}.

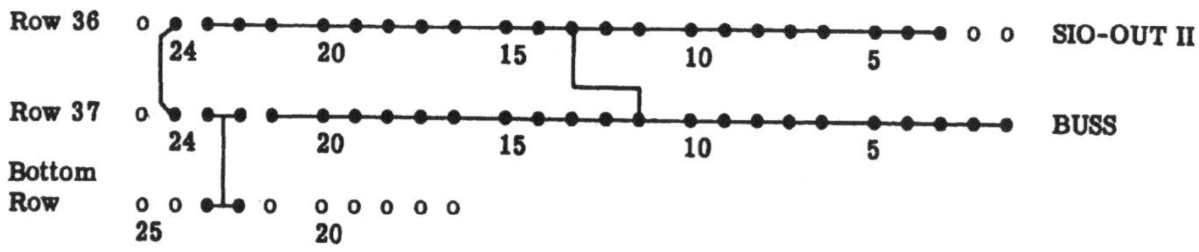

SINE IN-OUT COUNTER

(8) The SIO counter may be used to drop off digits from any quantity.

4. Plug SIO-OUT I to shift the 23rd column of a quantity to the 1st column of the buss. Plug SIO-OUT II to shift columns 1-22 of a quantity one column to the left. This plugging is used in high accuracy division.

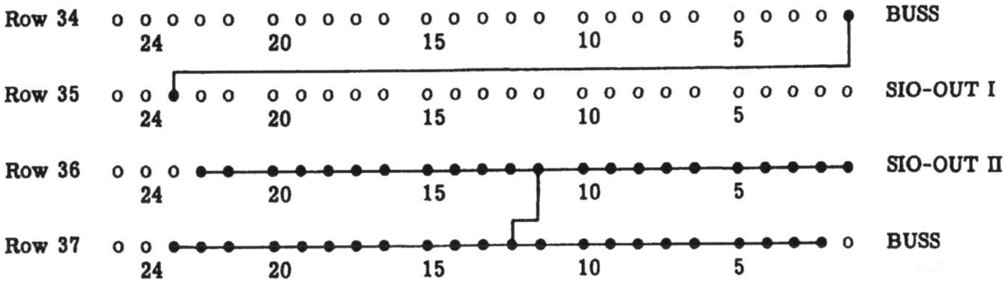

5. The operating decimal point lies between columns 15 and 16. Plug SIO-OUT I to read the integral part of a positive quantity to the buss. Plug SIO-OUT II to read the decimal part of a positive quantity to the buss.

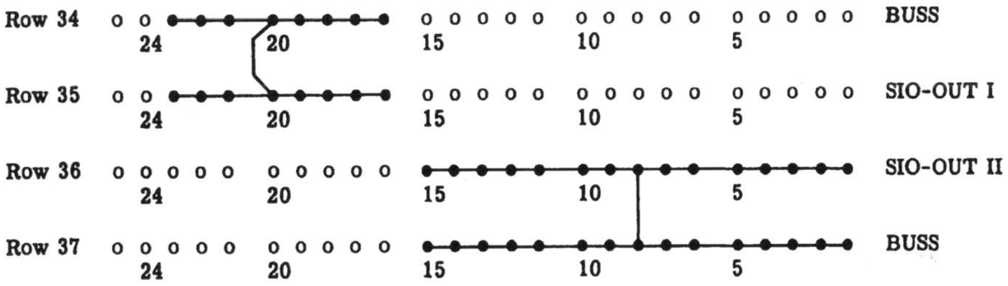

LOGARITHM UNIT

(1) The logarithm unit requires:

A. plugging to read the logarithm from the LIO counter into the buss,

B. a switch setting used in the determination of the characteristic,

C. plugging to terminate division; see Division.

(2) At the end of the computation, the logarithm stands in the LIO counter with decimal point between columns 21 and 22. The LIO-OUT must be plugged to read the logarithm into the buss with decimal point at the operating position.

(3) The LIO-OUT plughubs lie in row 26 and the corresponding buss plughubs in row 25 of the functional plugboard. The auxiliary nines, necessary if the logarithm has a negative characteristic, lie in the ten plughubs of the right side of the bottom row of the board. Since only ten such auxiliary nines are available, special provisions must be made for computing logarithms when there are ten or fewer operating decimal places. See Coding, Logarithm Unit.

(4) Table 2 shows the necessary plugging of LIO-OUT for each position of the operating decimal point. The number at the top of each column refers to the buss plughub. The numbers in the body of the table refer to the LIO-OUT plughubs, except that "9's" refers to any of the ten plughubs at the right side of the bottom row of the functional plugboard.

TABLE 2 LOGARITHMS: LIO-OUT TO BUSS

	BUSS COLUMNS																							
Operating Decimal Position	24	23	22	21	20	19	18	17	16	15	14	13	12	11	10	9	8	7	6	5	4	3	2	1
1/0	24																						23	22
2/1	24																					23	22	21
3/2	24																				23	22	21	20
4/3	24																			23	22	21	20	19
5/4	24																		23	22	21	20	19	18
6/5	24																	23	22	21	20	19	18	17
7/6	24																23	22	21	20	19	18	17	16
8/7	24															23	22	21	20	19	18	17	16	15
9/8	24														23	22	21	20	19	18	17	16	15	14
10/9	24													23	22	21	20	19	18	17	16	15	14	13
11/10	24												23	22	21	20	19	18	17	16	15	14	13	12
12/11	24	9's	9's	9's	9's	9's	9's	9's	9's	9's	9's	23	22	21	20	19	18	17	16	15	14	13	12	11
13/12	24	3's	9's	9's	9's	9's	9's	9's	9's	9's	23	22	21	20	19	18	17	16	15	14	13	12	11	10
14/13	24	9's	9's	9's	9's	9's	9's	9's	9's	23	22	21	20	19	18	17	16	15	14	13	12	11	10	9
15/14	24	9's	9's	9's	9's	9's	9's	9's	23	22	21	20	19	18	17	16	15	14	13	12	11	10	9	8
16/15	24	9's	9's	9's	9's	9's	9's	23	22	21	20	19	18	17	16	15	14	13	12	11	10	9	8	7
17/16	24	9's	9's	9's	9's	9's	23	22	21	20	19	18	17	16	15	14	13	12	11	10	9	8	7	6
18/17	24	9's	9's	9's	9's	23	22	21	20	19	18	17	16	15	14	13	12	11	10	9	8	7	6	5
19/18	24	9's	9's	9's	23	22	21	20	19	18	17	16	15	14	13	12	11	10	9	8	7	6	5	4
20/19	24	9's	9's	23	22	21	20	19	18	17	16	15	14	13	12	11	10	9	8	7	6	5	4	3
21/20	24	9's	23	22	21	20	19	18	17	16	15	14	13	12	11	10	9	8	7	6	5	4	3	2
22/21	24	23	22	21	20	19	18	17	16	15	14	13	12	11	10	9	8	7	6	5	4	3	2	1
23/22	24	22	21	20	19	18	17	16	15	14	13	12	11	10	9	8	7	6	5	4	3	2	1	23
24/23	This decimal position cannot be used.																							

LOGARITHM UNIT

1. The operating decimal point lies between columns 15 and 16. Plug the LIO-OUT.

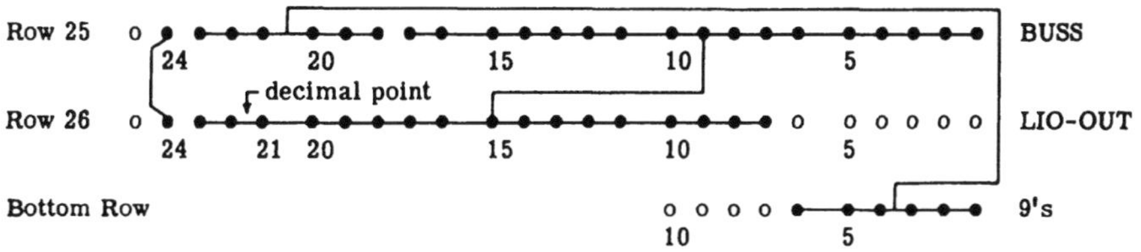

(5) The determination of the characteristic of the logarithm is controlled by a pair of manually set switches. These two dial switches, located to the right of the sequence mechanism, are labeled "log N value". The switches must be set to the value 22 - n, where the operating decimal point lies between columns n and n + 1.

EXPONENTIAL UNIT

(1) The exponential unit requires:
- A. plugging to read x from the buss into the EIO counter,
- B. plugging to read the exponential function from the EIO counter into the buss,
- C. plugging to terminate division; see Division.

(2) At the start of the exponential computation, x stands with its decimal point at the operating position. The EIO-IN must be plugged to read x from the buss into the EIO counter with decimal point between columns 21 and 22.

(3) The EIO-IN plughubs lie in row 27 and the corresponding buss plughubs in row 28 of the functional plugboard.

(4) Table 3 shows the necessary plugging of EIO-IN for each position of the operating decimal point. The number at the top of each column refers to the buss plughub. The numbers in the body of the table refer to the EIO-IN plughubs.

TABLE 3 EXPONENTIAL: BUSS TO EIO-IN

Operating Decimal Position	BUSS COLUMNS 24	23	22	21	20	19	18	17	16	15	14	13	12	11	10	9	8	7	6	5	4	3	2	1
1/0	24																						23	22
2/1	24																					23	22	21
3/2	24																				'23	22	21	20
4/3	24																			23	22	21	20	19
5/4	24																		23	22	21	20	19	18
6/5	24																	23	22	21	20	19	18	17
7/6	24																23	22	21	20	19	18	17	16
8/7	24															23	22	21	20	19	18	17	16	15
9/8	24														23	22	21	20	19	18	17	16	15	14
10/9	24													23	22	21	20	19	18	17	16	15	14	13
11/10	24												23	22	21	20	19	18	17	16	15	14	13	12
12/11	24											23	22	21	20	19	18	17	16	15	14	13	12	11
13/12	24										23	22	21	20	19	18	17	16	15	14	13	12	11	10
14/13	24									23	22	21	20	19	18	17	16	15	14	13	12	11	10	9
15/14	24								23	22	21	20	19	18	17	16	15	14	13	12	11	10	9	8
16/15	24							23	22	21	20	19	18	17	16	15	14	13	12	11	10	9	8	7
17/16	24						23	22	21	20	19	18	17	16	15	14	13	12	11	10	9	8	7	6
18/17	24					23	22	21	20	19	18	17	16	15	14	13	12	11	10	9	8	7	6	5
19/18	24				23	22	21	20	19	18	17	16	15	14	13	12	11	10	9	8	7	6	5	4
20/19	24			23	22	21	20	19	18	17	16	15	14	13	12	11	10	9	8	7	6	5	4	3
21/20	24		23	22	21	20	19	18	17	16	15	14	13	12	11	10	9	8	7	6	5	4	3	2
22/21	24	23	22	21	20	19	18	17	16	15	14	13	12	11	10	9	8	7	6	5	4	3	2	1
23/22	24	22	21	20	19	18	17	16	15	14	13	12	11	10	9	8	7	6	5	4	3	2	1	--
24/23	24	21	20	19	18	17	16	15	14	13	12	11	10	9	8	7	6	5	4	3	2	1	--	--

1. The operating decimal point lies between columns 15 and 16. Plug the EIO-IN.

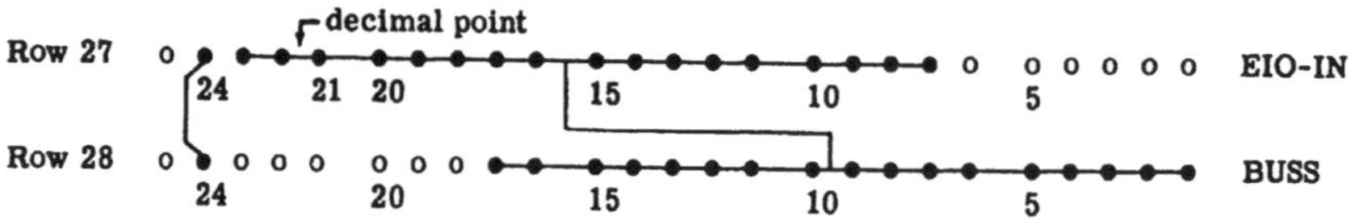

(5) At the end of the computation, the exponential function stands with its decimal point between plughubs 21 and 22. The EIO-OUT must be plugged to read the exponential function into the buss with decimal point at the operating position.

(6) The EIO-OUT plughubs lie in rows 30 and 31 and the corresponding buss plughubs in row 29 of the functional plugboard.

(7) Table 4 shows the necessary plugging of EIO-OUT for each position of the operating decimal point. The number at the top of each column refers to the buss plughub. The numbers in the body of the table refer to the EIO-OUT plughubs.

TABLE 4 EXPONENTIAL: EIO-OUT TO BUSS

	BUSS COLUMNS																							
Operating Decimal Position	24	23	22	21	20	19	18	17	16	15	14	13	12	11	10	9	8	7	6	5	4	3	2	1
1/0	--	44	43	42	41	40	39	38	37	36	35	34	33	32	31	30	29	28	27	26	25	24	23	22
2/1	--	43	42	41	40	39	38	37	36	35	34	33	32	31	30	29	28	27	26	25	24	23	22	21
3/2	--	42	41	40	39	38	37	36	35	34	33	32	31	30	29	28	27	26	25	24	23	22	21	20
4/3	--	41	40	39	38	37	36	35	34	33	32	31	30	29	28	27	26	25	24	23	22	21	20	19
5/4	--	40	39	38	37	36	35	34	33	32	31	30	29	28	27	26	25	24	23	22	21	20	19	18
6/5	--	39	38	37	36	35	34	33	32	31	30	29	28	27	26	25	24	23	22	21	20	19	18	17
7/6	--	38	37	36	35	34	33	32	31	30	29	28	27	26	25	24	23	22	21	20	19	18	17	16
8/7	--	37	36	35	34	33	32	31	30	29	28	27	26	25	24	23	22	21	20	19	18	17	16	15
9/8	--	36	35	34	33	32	31	30	29	28	27	26	25	24	23	22	21	20	19	18	17	16	15	14
10/9	--	35	34	33	32	31	30	29	28	27	26	25	24	23	22	21	20	19	18	17	16	15	14	13
11/10	--	34	33	32	31	30	29	28	27	26	25	24	23	22	21	20	19	18	17	16	15	14	13	12
12/11	--	33	32	31	30	29	28	27	26	25	24	23	22	21	20	19	18	17	16	15	14	13	12	11
13/12	--	32	31	30	29	28	27	26	25	24	23	22	21	20	19	18	17	16	15	14	13	12	11	10
14/13	--	31	30	29	28	27	26	25	24	23	22	21	20	19	18	17	16	15	14	13	12	11	10	9
15/14	--	30	29	28	27	26	25	24	23	22	21	20	19	18	17	16	15	14	13	12	11	10	9	8
16/15	--	29	28	27	26	25	24	23	22	21	20	19	18	17	16	15	14	13	12	11	10	9	8	7
17/16	--	28	27	26	25	24	23	22	21	20	19	18	17	16	15	14	13	12	11	10	9	8	7	6
18/17	--	27	26	25	24	23	22	21	20	19	18	17	16	15	14	13	12	11	10	9	8	7	6	5
19/18	--	26	25	24	23	22	21	20	19	18	17	16	15	14	13	12	11	10	9	8	7	6	5	4
20/19	--	25	24	23	22	21	20	19	18	17	16	15	14	13	12	11	10	9	8	7	6	5	4	3
21/20	--	24	23	22	21	20	19	18	17	16	15	14	13	12	11	10	9	8	7	6	5	4	3	2
22/21	--	23	22	21	20	19	18	17	16	15	14	13	12	11	10	9	8	7	6	5	4	3	2	1
23/22	--	22	21	20	19	18	17	16	15	14	13	12	11	10	9	8	7	6	5	4	3	2	1	--
24/23	--	21	20	19	18	17	16	15	14	13	12	11	10	9	8	7	6	5	4	3	2	1	--	--

2. The operating decimal point lies between columns 15 and 16. Plug the EIO-OUT.

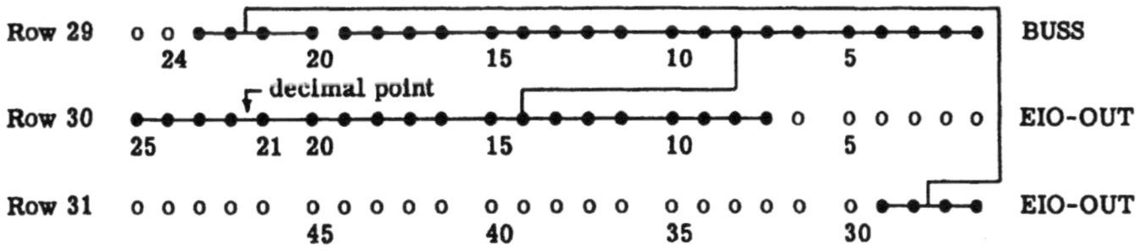

SINE UNIT

(1) The sine unit requires plugging to:
- A. read $1/2\pi$ from the table relays into the buss,
- B. read $x/2\pi$ from the buss into the SIO counter,
- C. read the decimal part of $x/2\pi$ from the SIO counter into the buss,
- D. read sin x from the SIO counter into the buss,
- E. multiply at the operating decimal position; see Multiplication.

(2) In the table relays, $1/2\pi$ stands with its decimal point between columns 22 and 23. The read-out of the table relays must be plugged to read $1/2\pi$ into the buss with decimal point at the operating position.

(3) The $1/2\pi$ plughubs lie in row 20 and the corresponding buss plughubs in row 19 of the MP-DIV plugboard.

(4) Table 5 shows the necessary plugging of the read-out of $1/2\pi$ for each position of the operating decimal point. The number at the top of each column refers to the buss plughub. The numbers in the body of the table refer to the $1/2\pi$ plughubs.

TABLE 5 SINE: $1/2\pi$ TO BUSS

BUSS COLUMNS

Operating Decimal Position	24	23	22	21	20	19	18	17	16	15	14	13	12	11	10	9	8	7	6	5	4	3	2	1
1/0	This decimal position cannot be used.																							
2/1																								22
3/2																							22	21
4/3																						22	21	20
5/4																					22	21	20	19
6/5																				22	21	20	19	18
7/6																			22	21	20	19	18	17
8/7																		22	21	20	19	18	17	16
9/8																	22	21	20	19	18	17	16	15
10/9																22	21	20	19	18	17	16	15	14
11/10															22	21	20	19	18	17	16	15	14	13
12/11														22	21	20	19	18	17	16	15	14	13	12
13/12													22	21	20	19	18	17	16	15	14	13	12	11
14/13												22	21	20	19	18	17	16	15	14	13	12	11	10
15/14											22	21	20	19	18	17	16	15	14	13	12	11	10	9
16/15										22	21	20	19	18	17	16	15	14	13	12	11	10	9	8
17/16									22	21	20	19	18	17	16	15	14	13	12	11	10	9	8	7
18/17								22	21	20	19	18	17	16	15	14	13	12	11	10	9	8	7	6
19/18							22	21	20	19	18	17	16	15	14	13	12	11	10	9	8	7	6	5
20/19						22	21	20	19	18	17	16	15	14	13	12	11	10	9	8	7	6	5	4
21/20					22	21	20	19	18	17	16	15	14	13	12	11	10	9	8	7	6	5	4	3
22/21				22	21	20	19	18	17	16	15	14	13	12	11	10	9	8	7	6	5	4	3	2
23/22			22	21	20	19	18	17	16	15	14	13	12	11	10	9	8	7	6	5	4	3	2	1
24/23	Use this decimal position with caution.																							

1. The operating decimal point lies between columns 15 and 16. Plug the read-out of $1/2\pi$.

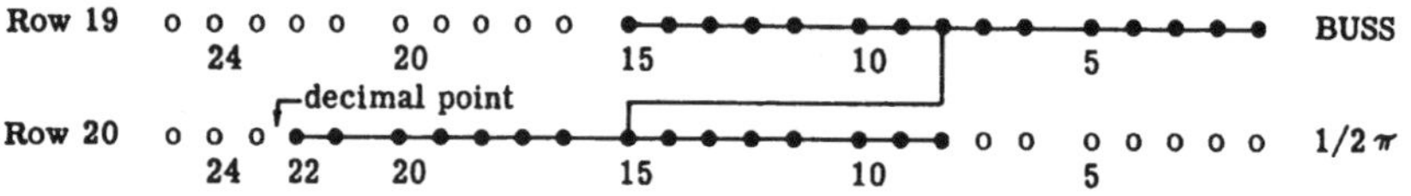

(5) In the buss, $x/2\pi$ stands with its decimal point at the operating position. The SIO-IN II must be plugged to read $x/2\pi$ into the SIO counter at the same decimal position; i.e., the plugging is direct.

(6) The SIO-IN II plughubs lie in row 32 and the corresponding buss plughubs in row 33 of the functional plugboard.

2. Plug SIO-IN II.

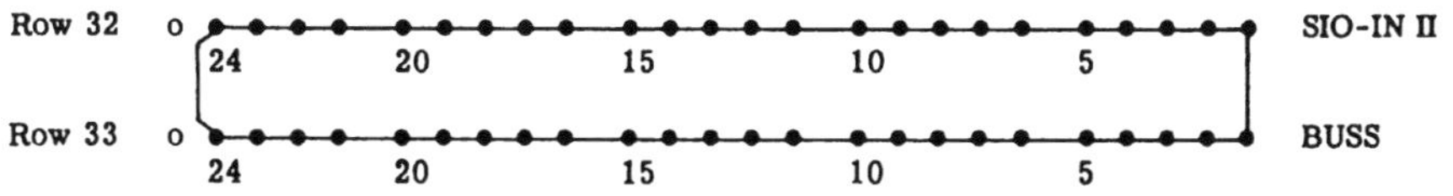

(7) In the SIO counter, $x/2\pi$ stands with its decimal point at the operating position. The SIO-OUT I must be plugged to read $x/2\pi$ into the buss with its decimal point between columns 22 and 23.

(8) The SIO-OUT I plughubs lie in row 35 and the corresponding buss plughubs in row 34 of the functional plugboard.

(9) Table 6 shows the necessary plugging of SIO-OUT I for each position of the operating decimal point. The number at the top of each column refers to the buss plughub. The numbers in the body of the table refer to the SIO-OUT I plughubs.

TABLE 6 SINE: SIO-OUT I TO BUSS

Operating Decimal Position	BUSS COLUMNS 24	23	22	21	20	19	18	17	16	15	14	13	12	11	10	9	8	7	6	5	4	3	2	1
1/0	This decimal position cannot be used.																							
2/1	--	--	1																					
3/2	--	--	2	1																				
4/3	--	--	3	2	1																			
5/4	--	--	4	3	2	1																		
6/5	--	--	5	4	3	2	1																	
7/6	--	--	6	5	4	3	2	1																
8/7	--	--	7	6	5	4	3	2	1															
9/8	--	--	8	7	6	5	4	3	2	1														
10/9	--	--	9	8	7	6	5	4	3	2	1													
11/10	--	--	10	9	8	7	6	5	4	3	2	1												
12/11	--	--	11	10	9	8	7	6	5	4	3	2	1											
13/12	--	--	12	11	10	9	8	7	6	5	4	3	2	1										
14/13	--	--	13	12	11	10	9	8	7	6	5	4	3	2	1									
15/14	--	--	14	13	12	11	10	9	8	7	6	5	4	3	2	1								
16/15	--	--	15	14	13	12	11	10	9	8	7	6	5	4	3	2	1							
17/16	--	--	16	15	14	13	12	11	10	9	8	7	6	5	4	3	2	1						
18/17	--	--	17	16	15	14	13	12	11	10	9	8	7	6	5	4	3	2	1					
19/18	--	--	18	17	16	15	14	13	12	11	10	9	8	7	6	5	4	3	2	1				
20/19	--	--	19	18	17	16	15	14	13	12	11	10	9	8	7	6	5	4	3	2	1			
21/20	--	--	20	19	18	17	16	15	14	13	12	11	10	9	8	7	6	5	4	3	2	1		
22/21	--	--	21	20	19	18	17	16	15	14	13	12	11	10	9	8	7	6	5	4	3	2	1	
23/22	--	--	22	21	20	19	18	17	16	15	14	13	12	11	10	9	8	7	6	5	4	3	2	1
24/23	Use this decimal position with caution.																							

3. The operating decimal point lies between columns 15 and 16. Plug SIO-OUT I.

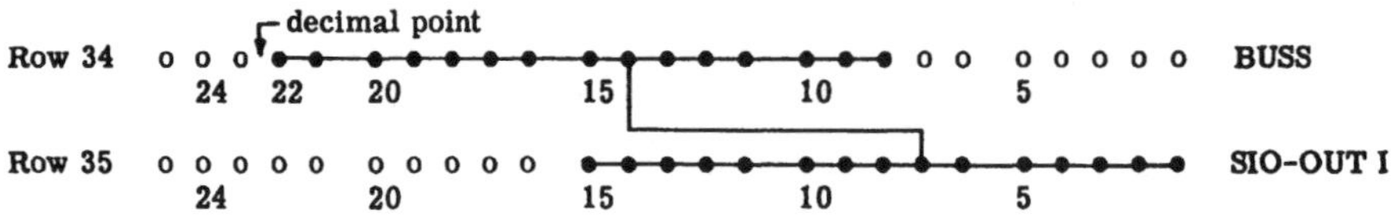

(10) At the end of the computation, sin x stands in the SIO counter with decimal point between colums 22 and 23. The SIO-OUT II must be plugged to read the sine into the buss with decimal point at the operating position.

(11) The SIO-OUT II plughubs lie in row 36 and the corresponding buss plughubs in row 37 of the functional plugboard. The auxiliary nines, necessary if the sine is negative, lie in the ten plughubs of the left side of the bottom row of the same board. Since only ten such auxiliary nines are available, special provisions must be made for computing the sines of third and fourth quadrant angles if there are eleven or fewer operating decimal places. See Coding, Sine Unit.

(12) Table 7 shows the necessary plugging of SIO-OUT II for each position of the operating decimal point. The number at the top of each column refers to the buss plughub. The numbers in the body of the table refer to the SIO-OUT II plughubs, except that "9's" refers to any of the ten plughubs at the right side of the bottom row of the functional plugboard.

TABLE 7 SINE: SIO-OUT II TO BUSS

	BUSS COLUMNS																							
Operating Decimal Position	24	23	22	21	20	19	18	17	16	15	14	13	12	11	10	9	8	7	6	5	4	3	2	1
1/0	This decimal position cannot be used.																							
2/1	24																						23	22
3/2	24																					23	22	21
4/3	24																				23	22	21	20
5/4	24																			23	22	21	20	19
6/5	24																		23	22	21	20	19	18
7/6	24																	23	22	21	20	19	18	17
8/7	24																23	22	21	20	19	18	17	16
9/8	24															23	22	21	20	19	18	17	16	15
10/9	24														23	22	21	20	19	18	17	16	15	14
11/10	24													23	22	21	20	19	18	17	16	15	14	13
12/11	24												23	22	21	20	19	18	17	16	15	14	13	12
13/12	24	9's	9's	9's	9's	9's	9's	9's	9's	9's	9's	23	22	21	20	19	18	17	16	15	14	13	12	11
14/13	24	9's	9's	9's	9's	9's	9's	9's	9's	9's	23	22	21	20	19	18	17	16	15	14	13	12	11	10
15/14	24	9's	9's	9's	9's	9's	9's	9's	9's	23	22	21	20	19	18	17	16	15	14	13	12	11	10	9
16/15	24	9's	9's	9's	9's	9's	9's	9's	23	22	21	20	19	18	17	16	15	14	13	12	11	10	9	8
17/16	24	9's	9's	9's	9's	9's	9's	23	22	21	20	19	18	17	16	15	14	13	12	11	10	9	8	7
18/17	24	9's	9's	9's	9's	9's	23	22	21	20	19	18	17	16	15	14	13	12	11	10	9	8	7	6
19/18	24	9's	9's	9's	9's	23	22	21	20	19	18	17	16	15	14	13	12	11	10	9	8	7	6	5
20/19	24	9's	9's	9's	23	22	21	20	19	18	17	16	15	14	13	12	11	10	9	8	7	6	5	4
21/20	24	9's	9's	23	22	21	20	19	18	17	16	15	14	13	12	11	10	9	8	7	6	5	4	3
22/21	24	9's	23	22	21	20	19	18	17	16	15	14	13	12	11	10	9	8	7	6	5	4	3	2
23/22	24	23	22	21	20	19	18	17	16	15	14	13	12	11	10	9	8	7	6	5	4	3	2	1
24/23	Use this decimal position with caution.																							

4. The operating decimal point lies between columns 15 and 16. Plug SIO-OUT II.

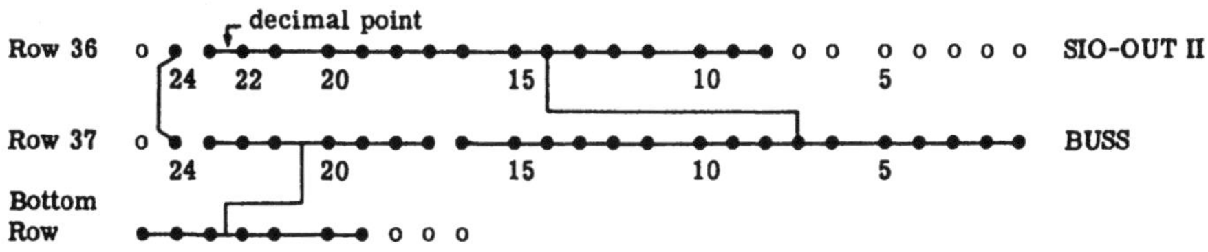

INTERPOLATORS

(1) The plugging of each interpolator unit is complete and independent. In order to plug an interpolator unit, the following quantities must be specified:

A. the interval of the argument or the highest order "h",
B. the tape decimal point,
C. the number of arguments in the tape,
D. the number of interpolational coefficients (including C_0) accompanying each argument,
E. the operating decimal point.

(2) An interpolator unit requires:

A. plugging to read the argument from the buss into the interpolation counter,
B. plugging to read "h correction-2" into the intermediate counter,
C. plugging to read "h correction-3" into the intermediate counter,
D. plugging to read "h" from the buss into the intermediate counter,
E. plugging to read the interpolational coefficients from the buss to the intermediate counter,
F. a switch setting of one half the number of arguments in the tape,
G. a switch setting of the number of interpolational coefficients (including C_0) accompanying each argument,
H. plugging to multiply at the operating decimal position; see Multiplication.

(3) In order to position a functional tape to the nearest value of the argument, six columns of the buss must be plugged to the interpolation counter. These six columns include the algebraic sign column, the four argument columns and the highest order "h" column. In order to position a functional tape to the next lower value of the argument, only five columns of the buss are plugged to the interpolation counter. The plugging from the highest order "h" column to the first column of the interpolation counter is omitted.

(4) The interpolation counter plughubs and the corresponding buss plughubs lie in the following rows:

Interpolator I - functional plugboard, row 15 INTERPOLATION-IN-1, row 16 BUSS;
Interpolator II - MP-DIV plugboard, row 12 I-IN-1-2, row 11 BUSS;
Interpolator III - MP-DIV plugboard, row 13 I-IN-1-3, row 14 BUSS.

(5) Table 8 shows the necessary plugging for the read-in of the argument to the interpolation counter for each highest order "h" column. The number at the top of each column refers to the interpolation counter plughub. The numbers in the body of the table refer to the buss plughubs.

1. The operating decimal point lies between columns 15 and 16. Plug the interpolation counter for the following values of Δa and highest order "h".

Interpolator	Δa	Highest Order "h"
I	0.1	14
II	0.01	13
III	0.001	12

FUNCTIONAL PLUGBOARD

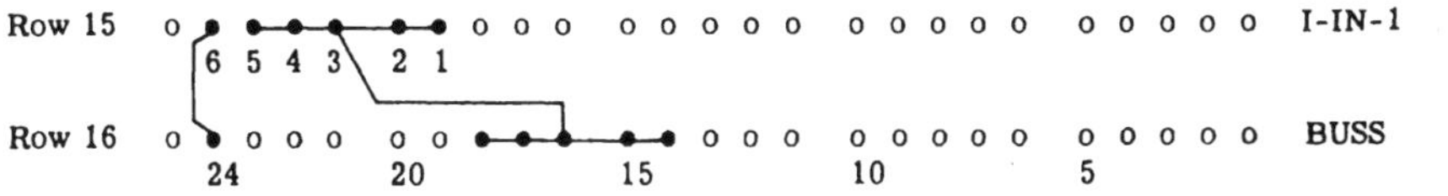

MP-DIV PLUGBOARD

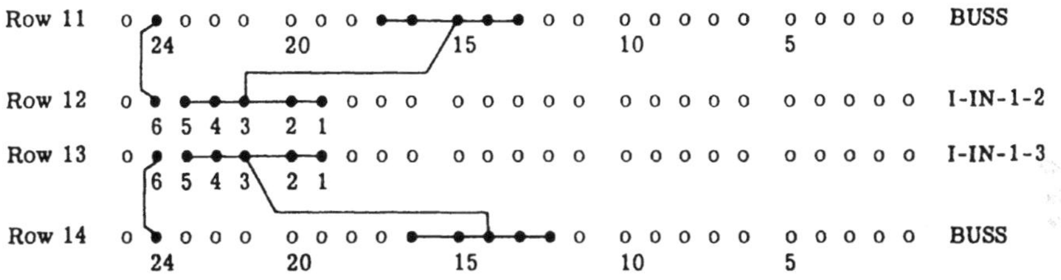

(6) If h is negative, the "h" correction-2 reads auxiliary nines into the columns of the intermediate counter to the left of the highest order "h" column. If it is desired to read these auxiliary nines into a storage counter A under control of the line of coding (841, A, blank), the "h" correction-2 plughubs should be plugged to any available row of buss plughubs instead of to the intermediate plughubs.

TABLE 8 INTERPOLATION: BUSS TO INTERPOLATION COUNTER

	INTERPOLATION COUNTER COLUMNS 6	5	4	3	2	1
Highest Order "h" Column 1	24	5	4	3	2	1
2	24	6	5	4	3	2
3	24	7	6	5	4	3
4	24	8	7	6	5	4
5	24	9	8	7	6	5
6	24	10	9	8	7	6
7	24	11	10	9	8	7
8	24	12	11	10	9	8
9	24	13	12	11	10	9
10	24	14	13	12	11	10
11	24	15	14	13	12	11
12	24	16	15	14	13	12
13	24	17	16	15	14	13
14	24	18	17	16	15	14
15	24	19	18	17	16	15
16	24	20	19	18	17	16
17	24	21	20	19	18	17
18	24	22	21	20	19	18
19	24	23	22	21	20	19
20	24	--	23	22	21	20
21	24	--	--	23	22	21
22	24	--	--	--	23	22

(7) The "h" correction-2 plughubs and the corresponding intermediate counter plughubs lie in the following rows:

Interpolator I - functional plugboard, row 19 H-CORR-2, row 20 INTERMED-IN-2;
Interpolator II - MP-DIV plugboard, row 21 H-CORR-2-2, row 22 INT;
Interpolator III - MP-DIV plugboard, row 25 H-CORR-3-2, row 26 INT.

(8) Table 9 shows the necessary plugging for reading the "h" correction-2 auxiliary nines to the intermediate counter for each highest order "h" column. The number at the top of each column refers to the intermediate plughub. The numbers in the body of the table refer to the "h" correction plughubs.

TABLE 9 INTERPOLATION: "h" CORRECTION-2 TO INTERMEDIATE COUNTER

Highest Order "h" Column	INTERMEDIATE COUNTER COLUMNS																							
	24	23	22	21	20	19	18	17	16	15	14	13	12	11	10	9	8	7	6	5	4	3	2	1
1	24	23	22	21	20	19	18	17	16	15	14	13	12	11	10	9	8	7	6	5	4	3	2	
2	24	23	22	21	20	19	18	17	16	15	14	13	12	11	10	9	8	7	6	5	4	3		
3	24	23	22	21	20	19	18	17	16	15	14	13	12	11	10	9	8	7	6	5	4			
4	24	23	22	21	20	19	18	17	16	15	14	13	12	11	10	9	8	7	6	5				
5	24	23	22	21	20	19	18	17	16	15	14	13	12	11	10	9	8	7	6					
6	24	23	22	21	20	19	18	17	16	15	14	13	12	11	10	9	8	7						
7	24	23	22	21	20	19	18	17	16	15	14	13	12	11	10	9	8							
8	24	23	22	21	20	19	18	17	16	15	14	13	12	11	10	9								
9	24	23	22	21	20	19	18	17	16	15	14	13	12	11	10									
10	24	23	22	21	20	19	18	17	16	15	14	13	12	11										
11	24	23	22	21	20	19	18	17	16	15	14	13	12											
12	24	23	22	21	20	19	18	17	16	15	14	13												
13	24	23	22	21	20	19	18	17	16	15	14													
14	24	23	22	21	20	19	18	17	16	15														
15	24	23	22	21	20	19	18	17	16															
16	24	23	22	21	20	19	18	17																
17	24	23	22	21	20	19	18																	
18	24	23	22	21	20	19																		
19	24	23	22	21	20																			
20	24	23	22	21																				
21	24	23	22																					
22	24	23																						

2. The operating decimal point lies between columns 15 and 16. Plug "h" correction-2 for the following values of Δa and highest order "h".

Interpolator	Δa	Highest Order "h"
I	0.1	14
II	0.01	13
III	0.001	12

FUNCTIONAL PLUGBOARD

MP-DIV PLUGBOARD

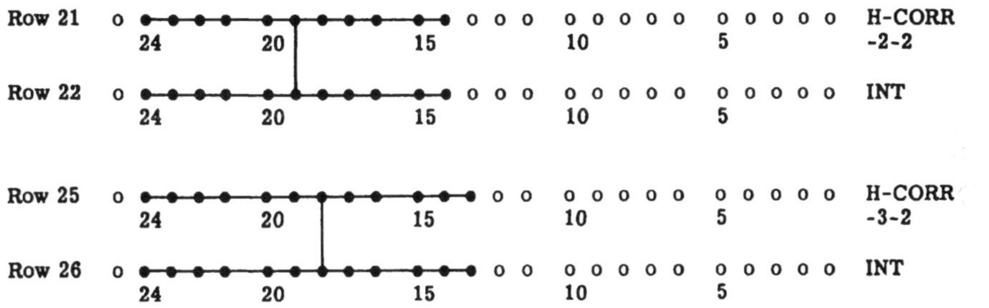

(9) In order to read minus one to lowest order "a" column, columns 1-23 of the "h" correction-3 plughubs provide nines and the 25th plughub provides an eight. The "8" plughub is connected to the lowest order "a" column of the intermediate counter. The nine plughubs are connected to the remaining 23 columns of the intermediate counter. If it is desired to read the minus one of "h" correction-3 into a storage counter A under control of the line of coding (841, A, blank), the "h" correction-3 plughubs should be plugged to any available row of buss plughubs instead of to the intermediate plughubs.

(10) The intermediate counter plughubs and the corresponding "h" correction-3 plughubs lie in the following rows:

Interpolator I - functional plugboard, row 21 INTERMED-IN-2, row 22 H-CORR-3;
Interpolator II - MP-DIV plugboard, row 23 INT, row 24 H-CORR-2-3;
Interpolator III - MP-DIV plugboard, row 27 INT, row 28 H-CORR-3-3.

(11) Table 10 shows the necessary plugging for reading "h" correction-3; i.e., minus one, to the intermediate counter for each highest order "h" column. The number at the top of each column refers to the intermediate counter plughub. The numbers in the body of the table refer to the "h" correction-3 plughubs, except that '8' refers to the 25th plughub of the "h" correction-3 row.

3. The operating decimal point lies between columns 15 and 16. Plug "h" correction-3 for the following values of Δa and highest order "h".

Interpolator	Δ a	Highest Order "h"
I	0.1	14
II	0.01	13
III	0.001	12

PLUGGING INSTRUCTIONS

FUNCTIONAL PLUGBOARD

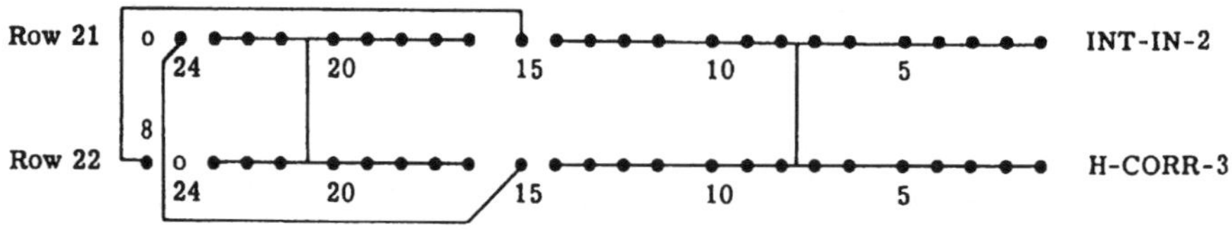

MP-DIV PLUGBOARD

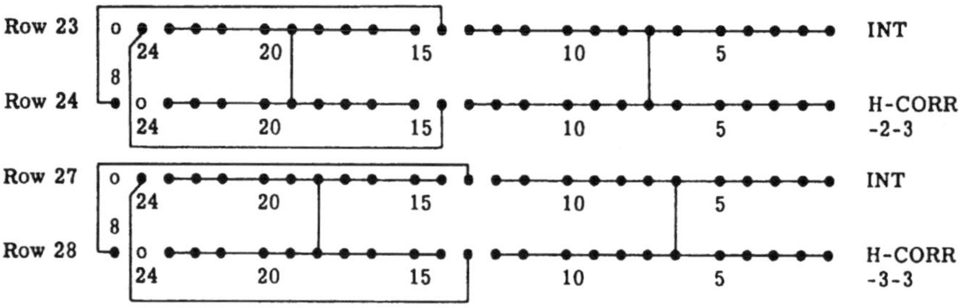

TABLE 10 INTERPOLATION: "h" CORRECTION-3 TO INTERMEDIATE COUNTER

Highest Order "h" Column	INTERMEDIATE COUNTER COLUMNS 24	23	22	21	20	19	18	17	16	15	14	13	12	11	10	9	8	7	6	5	4	3	2	1
1	2	23	22	21	20	19	18	17	16	15	14	13	12	11	10	9	8	7	6	5	4	3	'8'	1
2	3	23	22	21	20	19	18	17	16	15	14	13	12	11	10	9	8	7	6	5	4	'8'	2	1
3	4	23	22	21	20	19	18	17	16	15	14	13	12	11	10	9	8	7	6	5	'8'	3	2	1
4	5	23	22	21	20	19	18	17	16	15	14	13	12	11	10	9	8	7	6	'8'	4	3	2	1
5	6	23	22	21	20	19	18	17	16	15	14	13	12	11	10	9	8	7	'8'	5	4	3	2	1
6	7	23	22	21	20	19	18	17	16	15	14	13	12	11	10	9	8	'8'	6	5	4	3	2	1
7	8	23	22	21	20	19	18	17	16	15	14	13	12	11	10	9	'8'	7	6	5	4	3	2	1
8	9	23	22	21	20	19	18	17	16	15	14	13	12	11	10	'8'	8	7	6	5	4	3	2	1
9	10	23	22	21	20	19	18	17	16	15	14	13	12	11	'8'	9	8	7	6	5	4	3	2	1
10	11	23	22	21	20	19	18	17	16	15	14	13	12	'8'	10	9	8	7	6	5	4	3	2	1
11	12	23	22	21	20	19	18	17	16	15	14	13	'8'	11	10	9	8	7	6	5	4	3	2	1
12	13	23	22	21	20	19	18	17	16	15	14	'8'	12	11	10	9	8	7	6	5	4	3	2	1
13	14	23	22	21	20	19	18	17	16	15	'8'	13	12	11	10	9	8	7	6	5	4	3	2	1
14	15	23	22	21	20	19	18	17	16	'8'	14	13	12	11	10	9	8	7	6	5	4	3	2	1
15	16	23	22	21	20	19	18	17	'8'	15	14	13	12	11	10	9	8	7	6	5	4	3	2	1
16	17	23	22	21	20	19	18	'8'	16	15	14	13	12	11	10	9	8	7	6	5	4	3	2	1
17	18	23	22	21	20	19	'8'	17	16	15	14	13	12	11	10	9	8	7	6	5	4	3	2	1
18	19	23	22	21	20	'8'	18	17	16	15	14	13	12	11	10	9	8	7	6	5	4	3	2	1
19	20	23	22	21	'8'	19	18	17	16	15	14	13	12	11	10	9	8	7	6	5	4	3	2	1
20	21	23	22	'8'	20	19	18	17	16	15	14	13	12	11	10	9	8	7	6	5	4	3	2	1
21	22	23	'8'	21	20	19	18	17	16	15	14	13	12	11	10	9	8	7	6	5	4	3	2	1
22	23	'8'	22	21	20	19	18	17	16	15	14	13	12	11	10	9	8	7	6	5	4	3	2	1

(12) The "h" columns must be plugged to read from the buss into the intermediate counter; i.e., the highest order "h" column and the columns to its right are plugged. Since the multiplications necessary to interpolation are carried on at the operating decimal position, this plugging is direct.

(13) The intermediate counter plughubs and the corresponding buss plughubs lie in the following rows:

Interpolator I - functional plugboard, row 23 INTERMED-IN-2, row 24 BUSS;
Interpolator II - MP-DIV plugboard, row 16 INT-IN-3, row 15 BUSS;
Interpolator III - MP-DIV plugboard, row 17 INT-IN-4, row 18 BUSS.

(14) Table 11 shows the necessary plugging for the read-in of "h" from the buss to the intermediate counter for each highest order "h" column. The number at the top of each column refers to the buss plughub. The numbers in the body of the table refer to the intermediate counter plughubs.

TABLE 11 INTERPOLATION: BUSS TO INTERMEDIATE-IN-2, 3, OR 4

Highest Order "h" Column	BUSS COLUMNS 24	23	22	21	20	19	18	17	16	15	14	13	12	11	10	9	8	7	6	5	4	3	2	1
1																								1
2																							2	1
3																						3	2	1
4																					4	3	2	1
5																				5	4	3	2	1
6																			6	5	4	3	2	1
7																		7	6	5	4	3	2	1
8																	8	7	6	5	4	3	2	1
9																9	8	7	6	5	4	3	2	1
10															10	9	8	7	6	5	4	3	2	1
11														11	10	9	8	7	6	5	4	3	2	1
12													12	11	10	9	8	7	6	5	4	3	2	1
13												13	12	11	10	9	8	7	6	5	4	3	2	1
14											14	13	12	11	10	9	8	7	6	5	4	3	2	1
15										15	14	13	12	11	10	9	8	7	6	5	4	3	2	1
16									16	15	14	13	12	11	10	9	8	7	6	5	4	3	2	1
17								17	16	15	14	13	12	11	10	9	8	7	6	5	4	3	2	1
18							18	17	16	15	14	13	12	11	10	9	8	7	6	5	4	3	2	1
19						19	18	17	16	15	14	13	12	11	10	9	8	7	6	5	4	3	2	1
20					20	19	18	17	16	15	14	13	12	11	10	9	8	7	6	5	4	3	2	1
21				21	20	19	18	17	16	15	14	13	12	11	10	9	8	7	6	5	4	3	2	1
22			22	21	20	19	18	17	16	15	14	13	12	11	10	9	8	7	6	5	4	3	2	1

4. The operating decimal point lies between columns 15 and 16. Plug the read-in of "h" for the following values of Δa and highest order "h".

Interpolator	Δa	Highest Order "h"
I	0.1	14
II	0.01	13
III	0.001	12

FUNCTIONAL PLUGBOARD

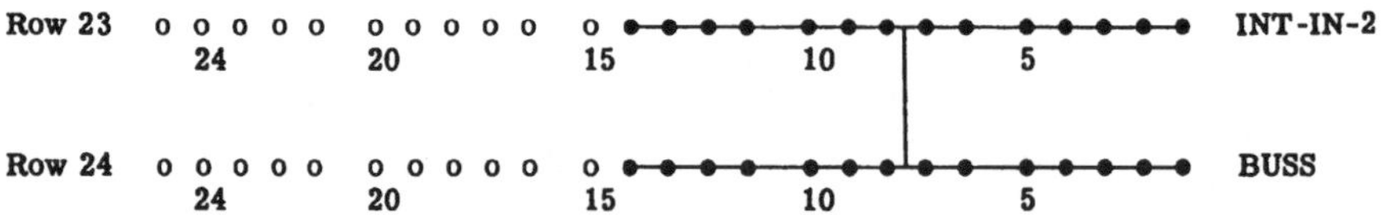

MP-DIV PLUGBOARD

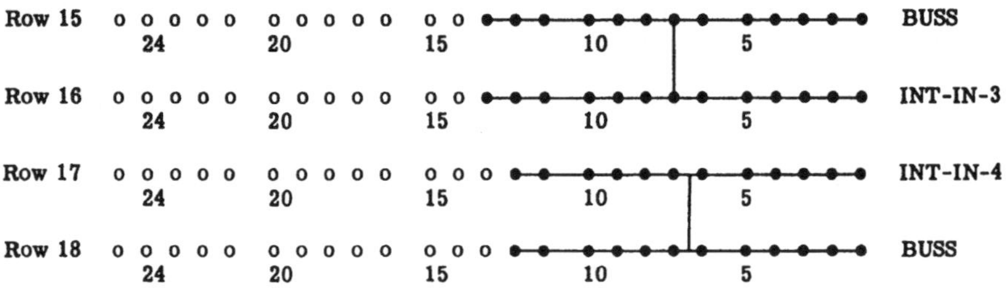

(15) The interpolator units read the interpolational coefficients from the functional tape into the buss with decimal point at the tape decimal position. The coefficients must be read from the buss into the intermediate counter (C-value plughubs) for computation at the operating decimal position. Negative coefficients may not be shifted to the right, since no auxiliary nines are available to fill in at the left.

(16) The intermediate counter (C-value) plughubs and the corresponding buss plughubs lie in the following rows of the MP-DIV plugboard:

Interpolator I, row 5 C-VALUE-1, row 6 BUSS;
Interpolator II, row 8 C-VALUE-2, row 7 BUSS;
Interpolator III, row 9 C-VALUE-3, row 10 BUSS.

5. The operating decimal point lies between columns 15 and 16. Plug interpolators I and III for tape decimal point between columns 15 and 16. Plug interpolator II for tape decimal point between columns 9 and 10, $|C_k| < 10^9$.

MP-DIV PLUGBOARD

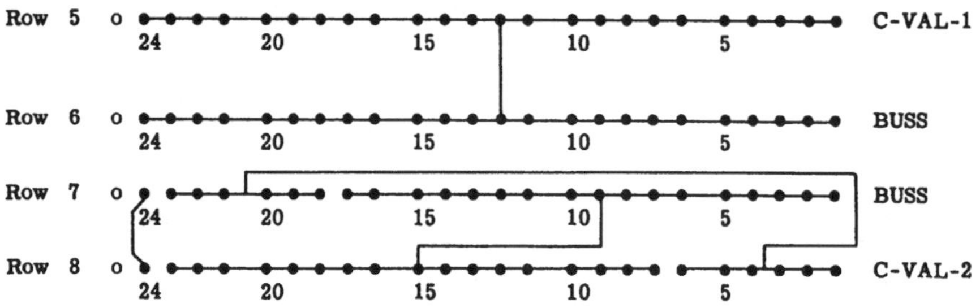

MP-DIV PLUGBOARD

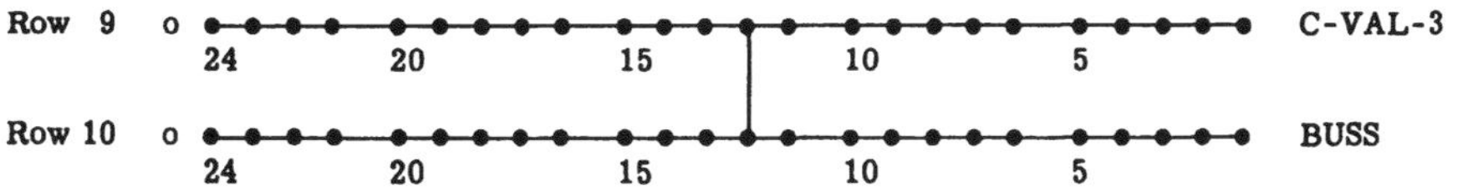

6. The operating decimal point lies between columns 15 and 16. In the functional tape, $\Delta a = 0.1$ and highest order "h" = 14. The tape decimal point lies between columns 15 and 16. Plug interpolator I.

FUNCTIONAL PLUGBOARD

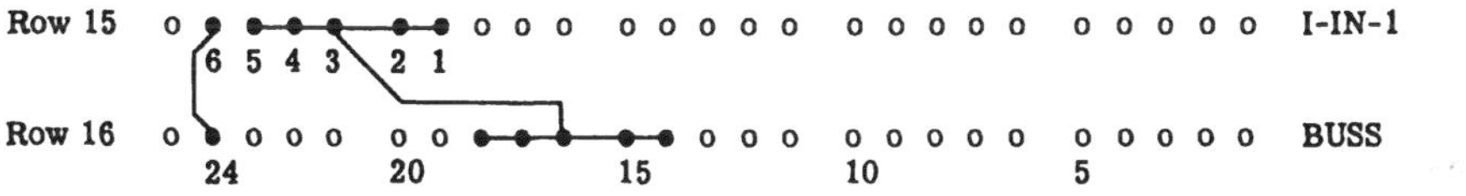

Rows 17 and 18 not used.

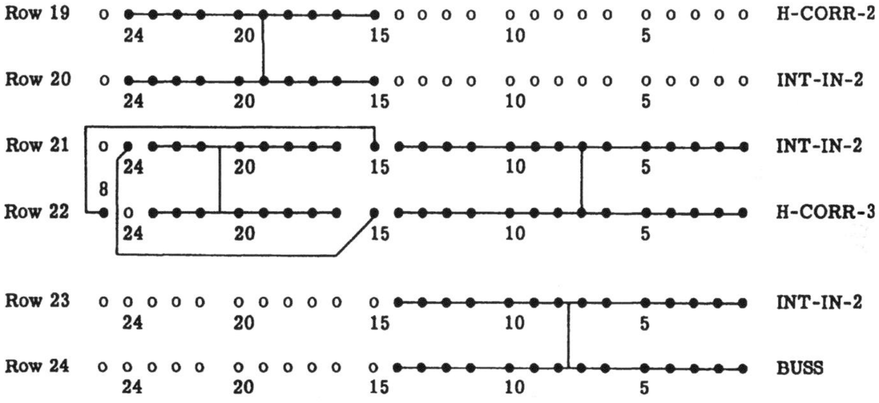

MP-DIV PLUGBOARD

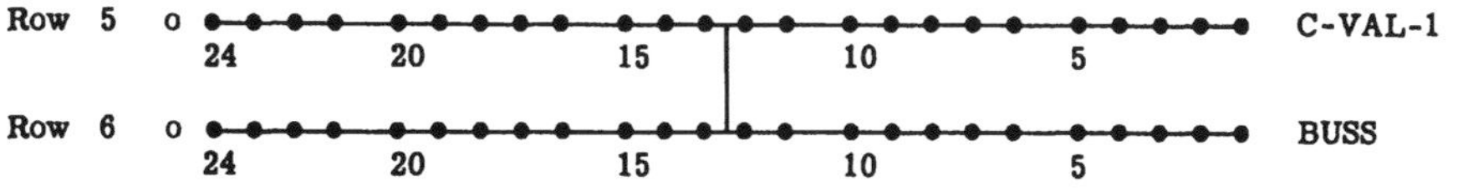

7. The operating decimal point lies between columns 15 and 16. In the functional tape, $\Delta a = 0.01$, highest order "h" = 13 and $|C_k| < 10^9$. The tape decimal point lies between columns 9 and 10. Plug interpolator II.

MP-DIV PLUGBOARD

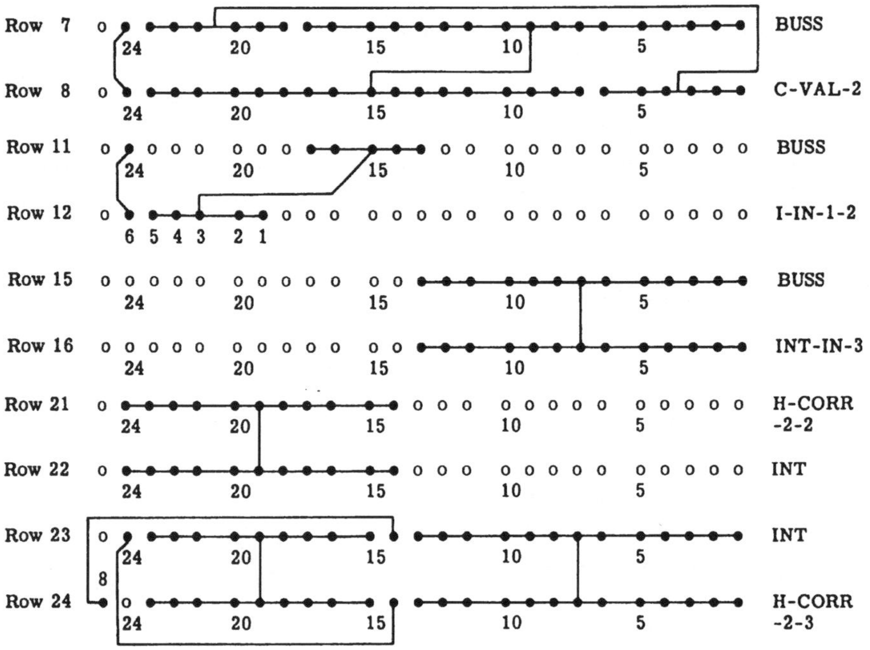

8. The operating decimal point lies between columns 15 and 16. In the functional tape, Δa = 0.001 and highest order "h" = 12. The tape decimal point lies between columns 15 and 16. Plug interpolator III.

MP-DIV PLUGBOARD

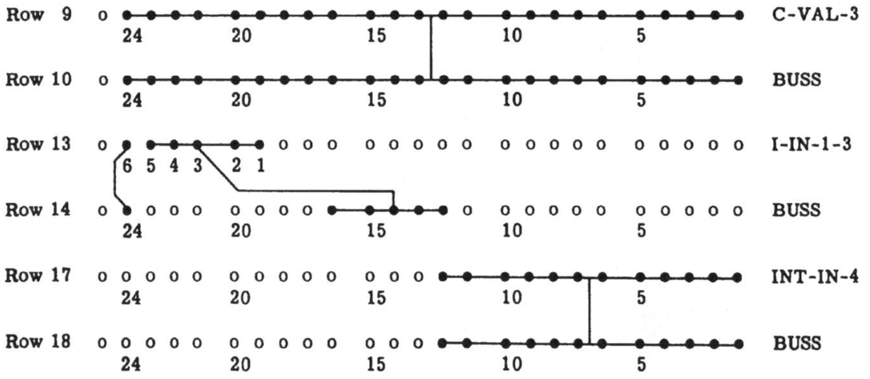

MP-DIV PLUGBOARD

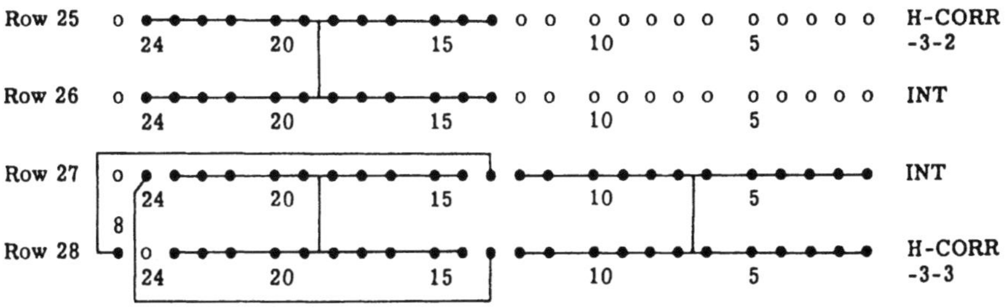

(17) For tape positioning, one half the number of arguments in the tape must be set in the push button switches labeled "Value tape set up 1/2 A values in tape" above the interpolator to be employed.

(18) The number of interpolational coefficients (including C_0) should be set in each of the dial switches above the interpolator, labeled "Set up number of C-values on each switch". In certain special cases, the dial switches need not be set alike. In order to position the tape, the right dial switch is set to the number of interpolational coefficients (including C_0) accompanying each argument in the tape. The left dial switch is set to the number of interpolational coefficients to be used in the interpolation computation.

CARD FEEDS

(1) The card feeds require plugging for the read-out from the card feed brushes into the buss. The card columns and corresponding card feed brushes and plughubs are numbered from left to right, whereas the buss plughubs or the calculator are numbered from right to left.

(2) If negative numbers are to be shifted to the left on reading into the calculator, they should be punched as complements on ten rather than on nine. If negative numbers are to be shifted to the right on reading into the calculator, auxiliary nines must be filled in to the left by plugging one brush plughub to more than one buss plughub. One brush plughub should not be plugged to more than nine buss plughubs.

(3) The card feed plugboard is located to the right of the sequence mechanism. The brush plughubs of card feed I lie in vertical row 8 and the corresponding buss plughubs in vertical row 5. The brush plughubs of card feed II lie in vertical row 4 and the corresponding buss plughubs in vertical row 1.

1. The operating decimal point lies between columns 15 and 16. Cards are to be fed from both feeds with decimal point between card columns 9 and 10. Plug the card feeds.

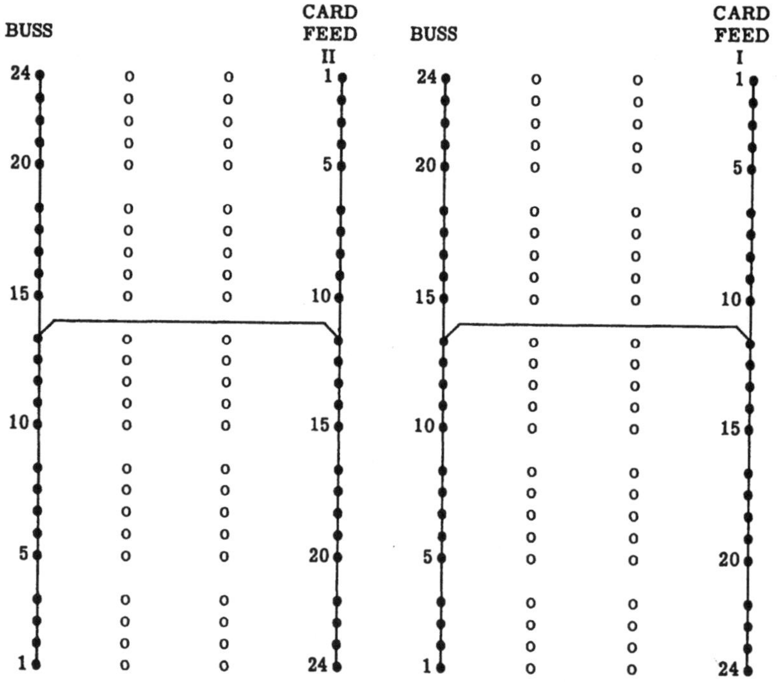

2. The operating decimal point lies between columns 15 and 16. Cards are to be fed from feed I with decimal point between card columns 15 and 16. Cards are to be fed from feed II with decimal point between card columns 3 and 4.

CARD FEEDS

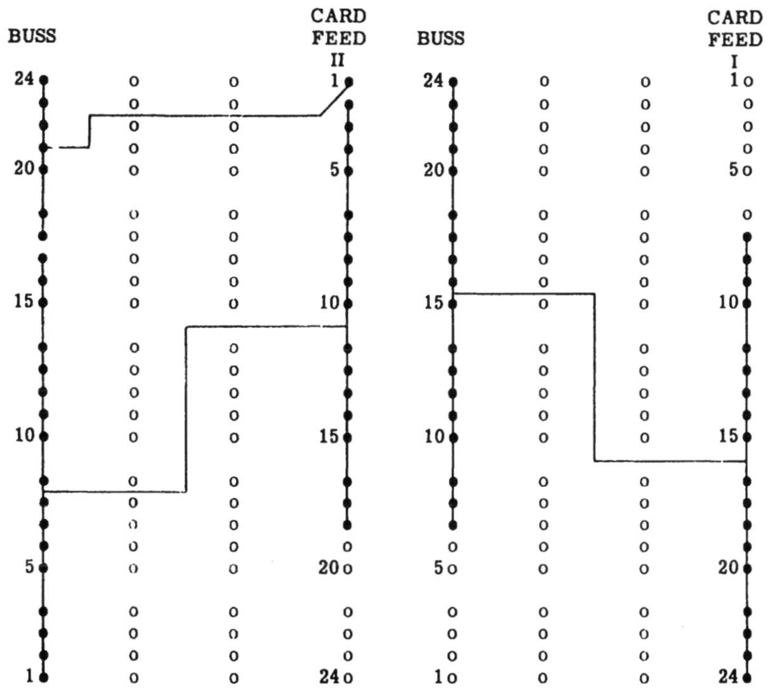

(4) The "Card Feed Reverse" switches are located to the left of the sequence mechanism. It should be noted that though these switches reverse the codes of the feeds they do not reverse the plugging.

CARD PUNCH

(1) The card punch requires plugging of the read-in from the punch counter to the punch magnets. The card columns are numbered from left to right, whereas the punch counter columns are numbered from right to left.

(2) To skip a card out, 24 card columns must be punched. If fewer than 24 columns are wired for punching, zeros in a master card in the duplicating rack will skip the card out.

(3) The plugboard for the card punch is located at the extreme right end of the machine, inside the cover. Only two sets of plughubs are used, labeled PUNCH MAGNETS and COMP MAG OR CTR TOT EXIT OR M S IN, the latter set being wired to the punch counter.

1. The operating decimal point lies between columns 15 and 16. Plug the punch to punch cards with decimal point between columns 9 and 10.

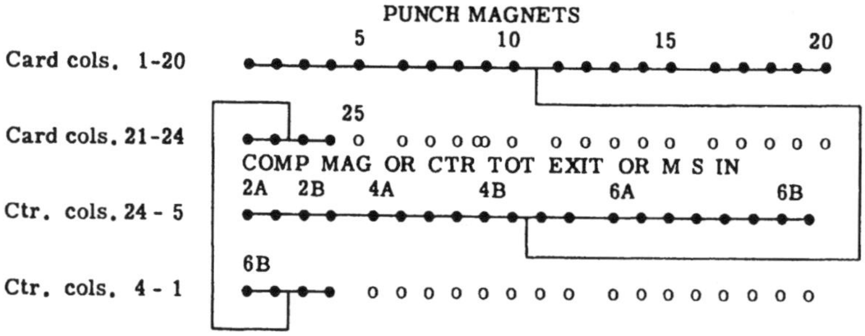

(4) Cards may be punched containing a function in the first columns of the cards and a serial number in the last columns of the card. After the function is punched, a duplicating card and skip bar control the punch.

2. The operating decimal point lies between columns 15 and 16. A function is to be punched in the first 24 card columns with decimal point between card columns 9 and 10. Serial numbers are to be punched in card columns 70, 73-76 and 79. Plug the punch.

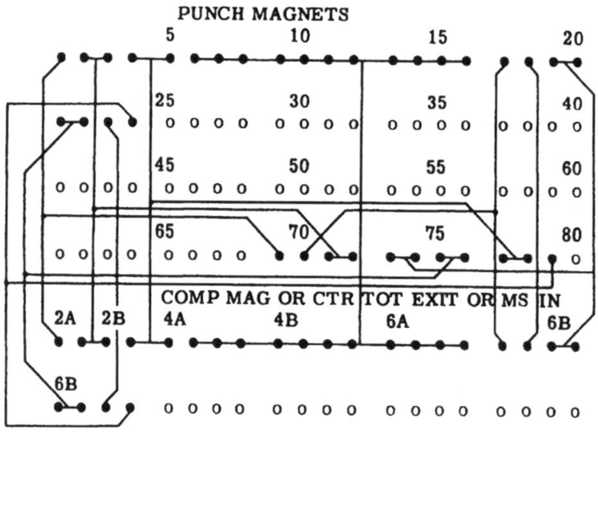

PRINTING

(1) The printing operation requires plugging for:

A. dropping off zeros to the left,
B. printing a minus sign,
C. the read-out of the print counter to the typewriter,
D. horizontal spacing of digits,
E. printing a decimal point,
F. dropping off zeros to the right,
G. tabulating and returning the carriage,
H. resetting print and print step counters,
I. vertical spacing,
J. adding a half-correction,
K. printing in half time.

(2) The plugging of each typewriter is complete and independent. The sequence of printing operations is controlled by a print step counter which advances at the rate of nine steps per second. The read-out of this counter is wired to 49 column selection plughubs, labeled COL-SEL-PRINT-1 and lying in rows 1, 2 and 3 of the functional plugboard for typewriter I, and COL-SEL-PRINT-2 lying in rows 8, 9 and 10 of the functional plugboard for typewriter II.

(3) In order to drop off zeros to the left, for typewriter I:

A. plughubs 24 and 25 of row 5 (RO-CONTROL-RELS) are connected,
B. plughub 25 of row 6 is plugged to the $n + 2$nd plughub of row 5, where the printed decimal point lies between columns n and $n + 1$ of the print counter.

In order to drop off zeros to the left, for typewriter II:

A. plughubs 24 and 25 of row 12 (RO-CONTROL-RELS) are connected,
B. plughub 25 of row 13 is plugged to the $n + 2$nd plughub of row 12, where the printed decimal point lies between columns n and $n + 1$ of the print counter.

No plughubs are available for dropping off zeros to the left if the printed decimal point lies between columns 22 and 23 or between columns 23 and 24. If for typewriter I the 25th plughub of row 6 is plugged to the 23rd plughub of row 5, or if for typewriter II the 25th plughub of row 13 is plugged to the 23rd plughub of row 12, then,

(a) if the printed decimal point lies between columns 22 and 23, decimal quantities will be printed with no zero preceding the decimal point;
(b) if the printed decimal point lies between columns 23 and 24, decimal quantities will be printed with no zero preceding the decimal point and if the digit following the decimal point should be a zero, a space will occur instead of a printed zero.

(4) In order to print the minus sign preceding a negative number, the plughub of the print counter read-out next above the plughub wired to print the highest significant digit must be plugged to a column selection plughub. Negative numbers may be printed as complements on nine by throwing the "Print Complement Switches" located to the right of the MP-DIV plugboard.

(5) The plughubs of the print counter read-out corresponding to the columns of the print counter containing the digits to be printed must be plugged to column selection plughubs. The print counter read-out plughubs are in row 4 for typewriter I and row 11 for typewriter II.

(6) If the digits of the quantity to be printed are to be spaced in horizontal groups, spaces must be plugged from plughubs 11-25 of row 3 for typewriter I, from plughubs 11-25 of row 10 for typewriter II. These spaces are plugged to the appropriate column selection plughubs between the connections from the print counter read-out plughubs.

(7) The decimal point is plugged from the 25th plughub of row 1 for typewriter I, of row 8 for typewriter II, to the column selection plughub lying between those two plughubs which are connected to the print counter read-out columns either side of the assumed decimal point.

(8) Zeros may be dropped off to the right of a quantity under control of the code 87 (called the "argument control") in the Out column of the line of coding initiating printing. One of the first two plughubs in row 18 is connected to the column selection plughub next after the plughub connected to the last digit to be printed.

(9) If only one vertical column of numbers is to be printed, a tab is plugged immediately after the last digit, five column selection plughubs are left blank and a second tab is plugged for the carriage return. This second tab is converted to a carriage return by adjusting the right hand margin stop. If more than one vertical column of numbers is to be printed, a tab is plugged immediately after the last digit of each quantity. The tab after the last quantity printed on any horizontal line is converted to a carriage return. Eight tab plughubs are provided for each typewriter. They are plughubs 21-24 of rows 1 and 2 for typewriter I, of rows 8 and 9 for typewriter II.

(10) The print step counter and print counter are reset simultaneously. Six column selection plughubs are left blank after the last tab and then the reset is plugged. The reset plughub is the 25th plughub of row 2 for typewriter I and of row 9 for typewriter II.

1. The operating decimal point lies between columns 15 and 16. Plug typewriter I to print quantities, which may be positive or negative, to 8 decimal places, grouped by threes to the right and left of the decimal point, argument control after 2 decimal places.

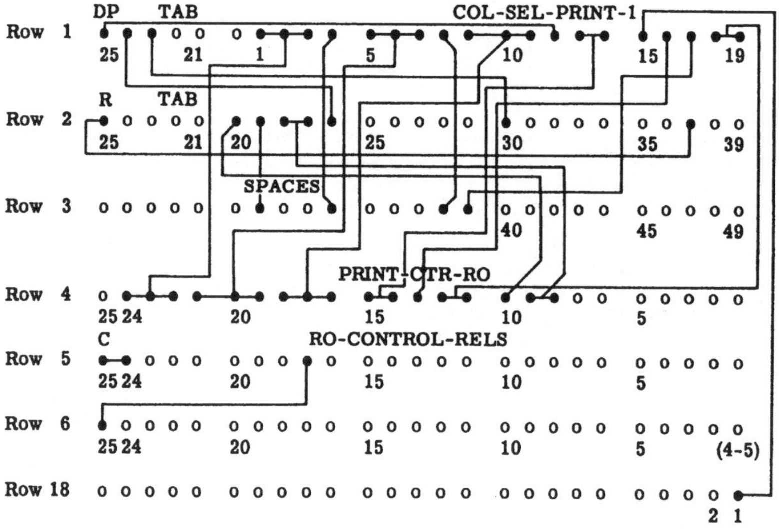

(4-5)

2. The operating decimal point lies between columns 21 and 22. Plug typewriter II to print quantities, which may be positive or negative, to 21 decimal places, digits in groups of 3, 5, 5, 5, 3 to the right of the decimal point.

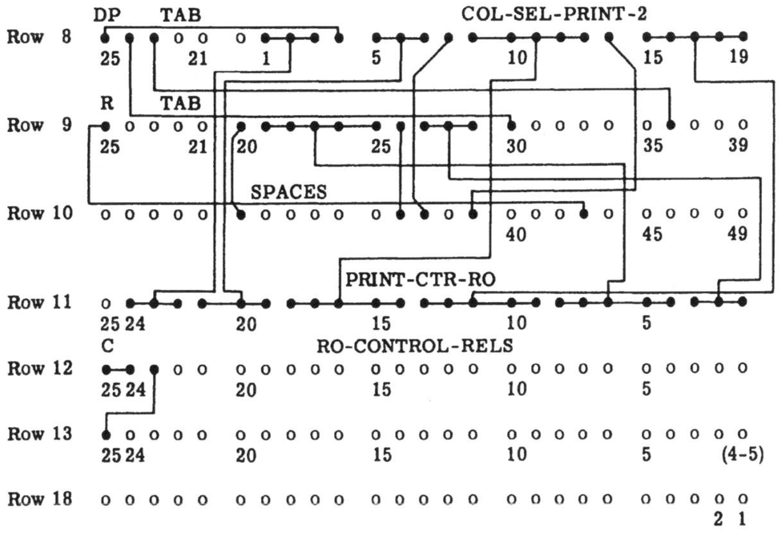

3. The operating decimal point lies between columns 15 and 16. Plug typewriter I to print all 23 digits of quantities, positive or negative, grouped by fives to the right and left of the decimal point, argument control after 2 decimal places.

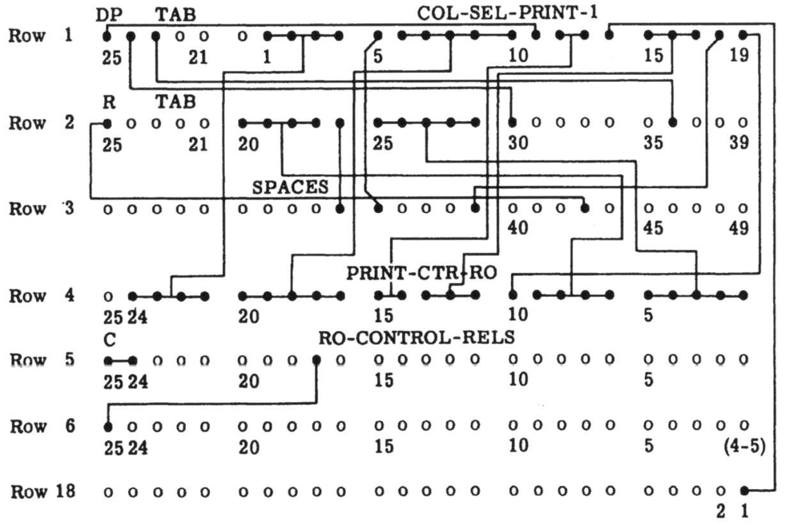

PLUGGING INSTRUCTIONS

(11) The first ten plughubs of rows 38 and 39 control the vertical grouping of quantities printed on typewriter I. The second set of ten plughubs on the same rows serve the same purpose for typewriter II. The vertical spacing of each typewriter is under control of the read-out of a line step counter (LS_1 and LS_2). These counters step every time a carriage return occurs. Various vertical groupings are possible but the pattern must repeat in groups of ten lines or less. At the end of the desired grouping, the line step counter must be reset. This reset is obtained by connecting plughub R (6 for typewriter I, 16 for typewriter II in row 39) to the line step counter read-out. When the step counter resets, a single line space is obtained. If an extra vertical space is desired, one of the extra space plughubs (1-5 for typewriter I, 11-15 for typewriter II in row 39) must be plugged to the step counter read-out.

4. Plug typewriter I for vertical groups alternately of 3 and 4 quantities. Plug typewriter II for vertical groups of 8 quantities.

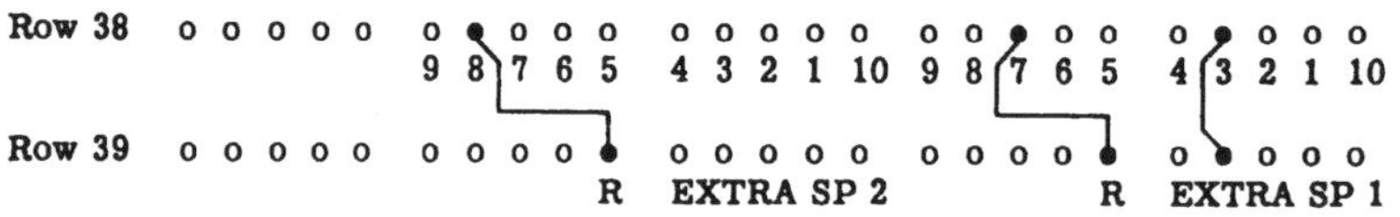

5. Plug typewriter I for vertical groups of 4 quantities. Plug typewriter II for vertical groups of 5 quantities.

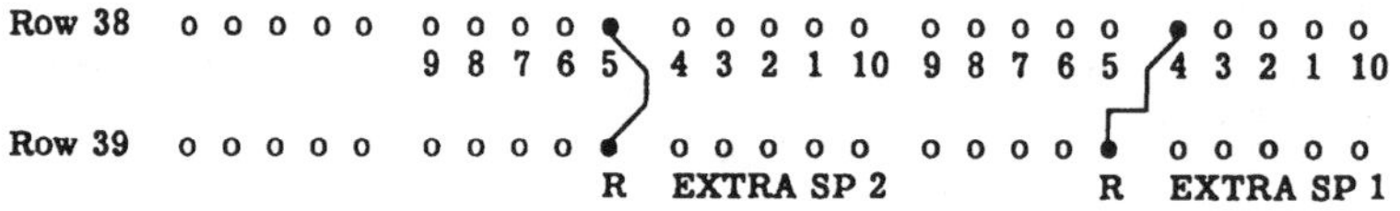

(12) The print counters may be plugged for a "half pick-up" which adds or subtracts five in the column to which it is plugged, according as the quantity in the print counter is positive or negative. Note that the typewriter reverse switches do not change over the half pick-up, which is not reversed but continues to add into the print counter for which it is coded and plugged. The half pick-up impulse plughubs lie in rows 6 and 13 for print counters I and II respectively, labeled IMPULSE 1/2 CORR. The impulse plughubs are plugged to rows 7 and 14 for print counters I and II respectively, labeled CTR.

6. The operating decimal point lies between columns 15 and 16. Plug print counter I for a half pick-up correcting the eighth decimal place.

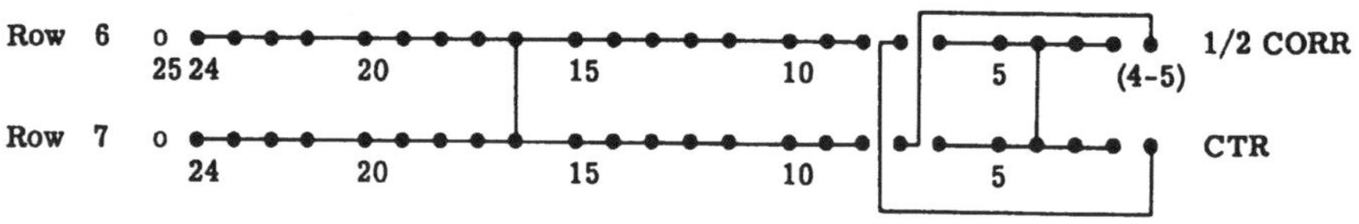

7. The operating decimal point lies between columns 19 and 20. Plug print counter II for a half pick-up correcting the tenth decimal place.

8. The operating decimal point lies between columns 15 and 16. Plug print counter and typewriter I to print on the same horizontal line:

   (a) an argument, zeros dropped off after 2 decimal places,
   (b) a positive or negative quantity to 10 decimal places, digits grouped by fives to the right and left of the decimal point, half pick-up correcting the tenth decimal place.

   Plug the line step counter for vertical groups of six lines.

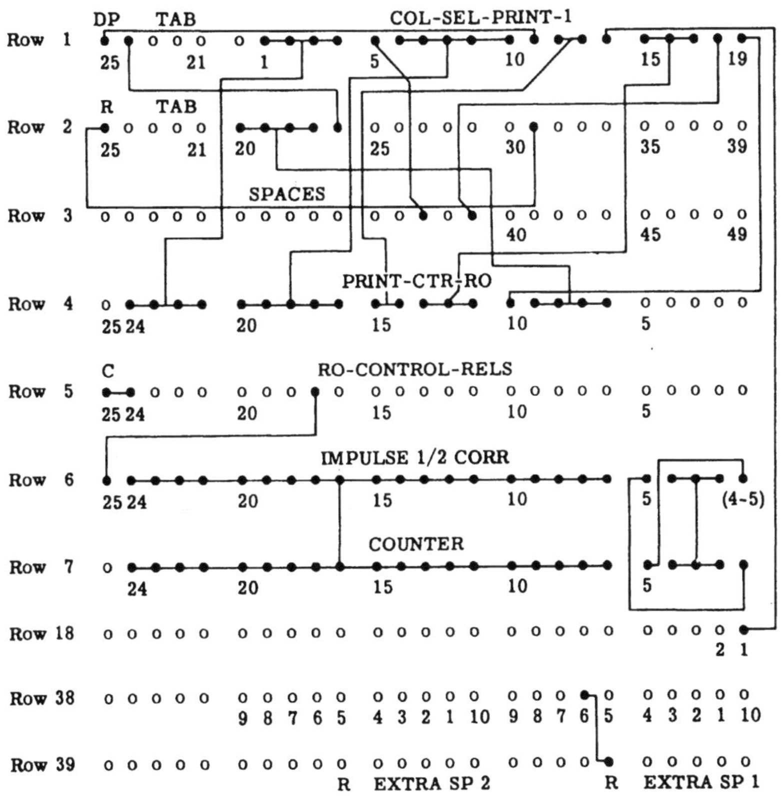

(13) If maximum reliability is required of the typewriters, they should be plugged to print in half time. In this case, a blank plughub is left between the column selection plughubs connected to successive digits unless there is already a space, a decimal point or an argument control plugged between them.

9. The operating decimal point lies between columns 15 and 16. Plug typewriter II to print in half time, positive or negative quantities, to 8 decimal places, digits grouped by threes to the right and left of the decimal point, argument control after 2 decimal places, half pick-up to correct the eighth decimal place. Plug the line step counter for vertical groups of five lines.

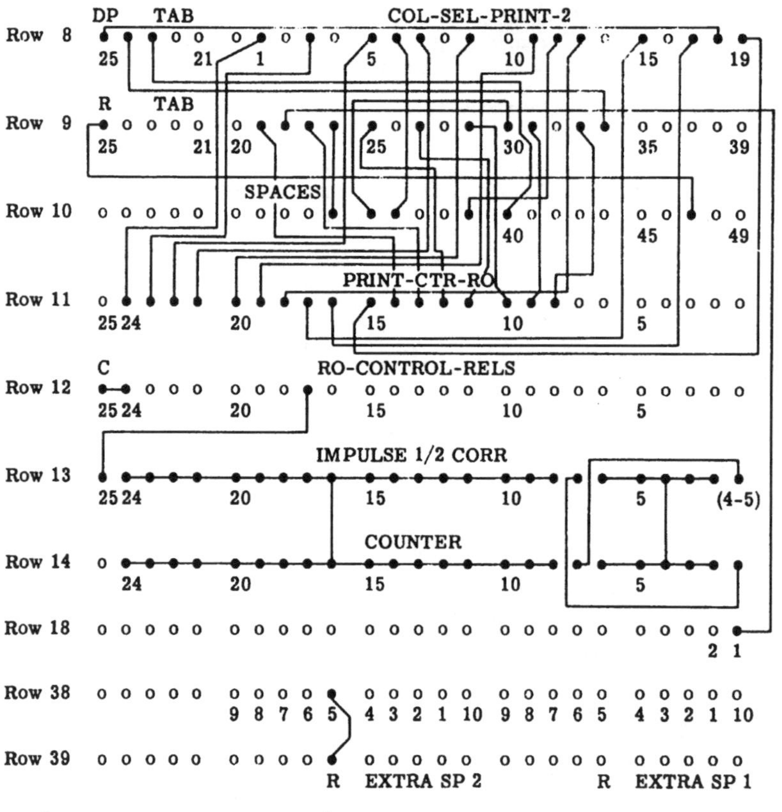

(14) The "Typewriter Reverse Switches" are located to the left of the sequence mechanism. It should be noted that, as stated in note (12), though these switches reverse the codes of the print counters and the codes initiating printing, they do not reverse either the plugging or the half pick-up coding.

SAMPLE PLUGGING

The plugging of the calculator is shown for operating decimal point between columns 15 and 16.

Division is plugged to provide 7, 14 or 22 digits in the PQ counter under control of Miscellaneous codes 643, 6431 and blank respectively.

Interpolator I is plugged for a functional tape in which $\Delta a = 0.1$, highest order "h" = 14 and the tape decimal point lies between columns 15 and 16.

Interpolator III is plugged for a functional tape in which $\Delta a = 0.01$, highest order "h" = 13 and the tape decimal point lies between columns 9 and 10.

Typewriter I is plugged for positive or negative quantities, all 23 columns of digits grouped by fives to the right and left of the decimal point, argument control after 2 decimal places. Line step counter 1 is plugged for vertical groups of six lines.

Typewriter II is plugged for positive or negative quantities, digits grouped by threes to the right and left of the decimal point, argument control after 2 decimal places, half pick-up to correct the eighth decimal place. Line step counter 2 is plugged for vertical groups of five lines.

The following switch settings must be made:

Divide N minus decimal switches = 07;
Log N value switches = 07;
Interpolator I, push button switches = 0051, dial switches = 3;
Interpolator III, push button switches = 0044, dial switches = 5.

Interpolator II reads a value tape and therefore requires no plugging. The card feed and card punch pluggings are assumed to be direct and are not shown.

MP-DIV PLUGBOARD

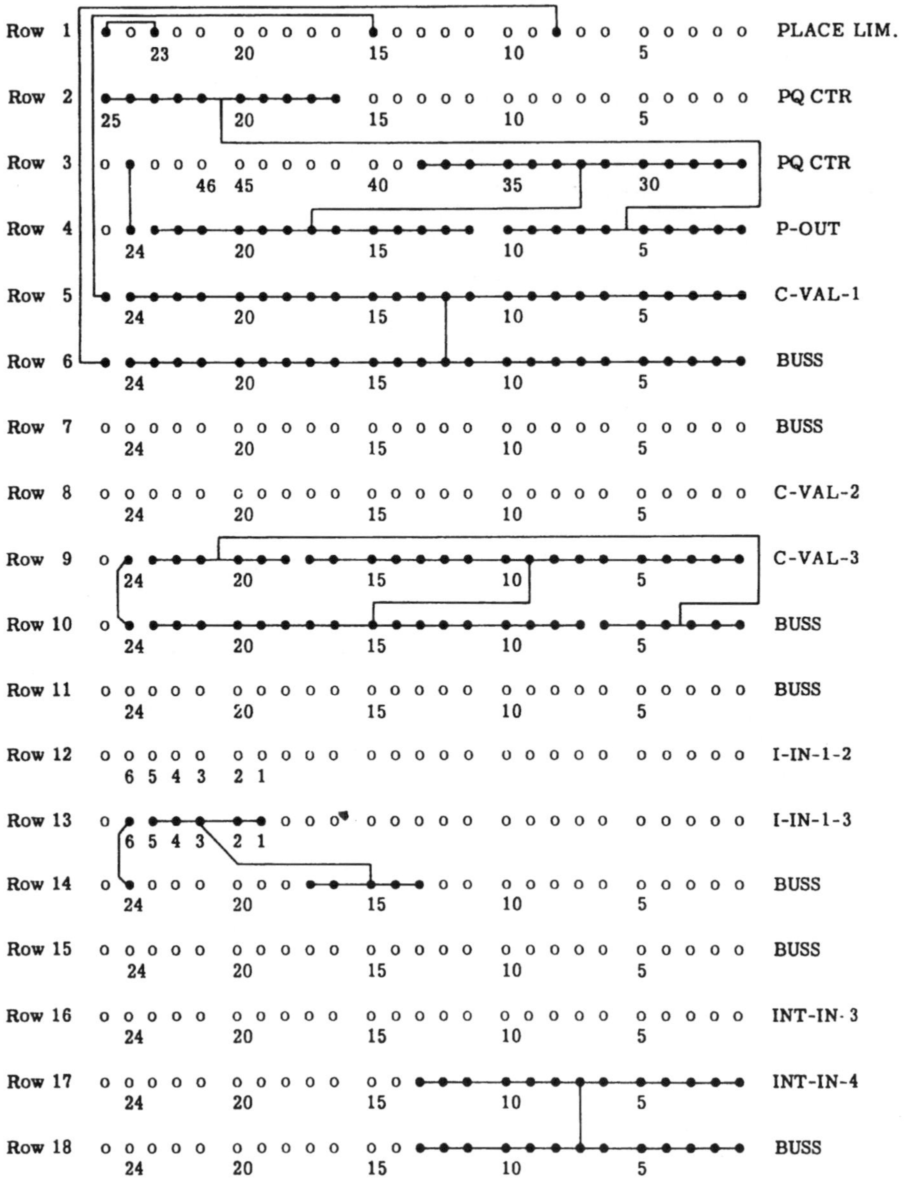

MP-DIV PLUGBOARD (continued)

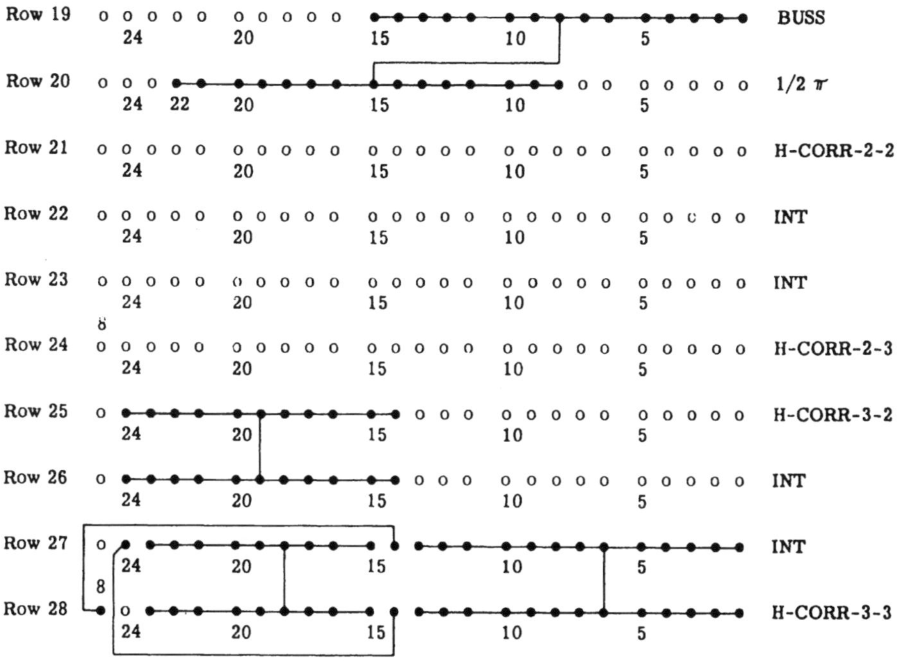

FUNCTIONAL PLUGBOARD

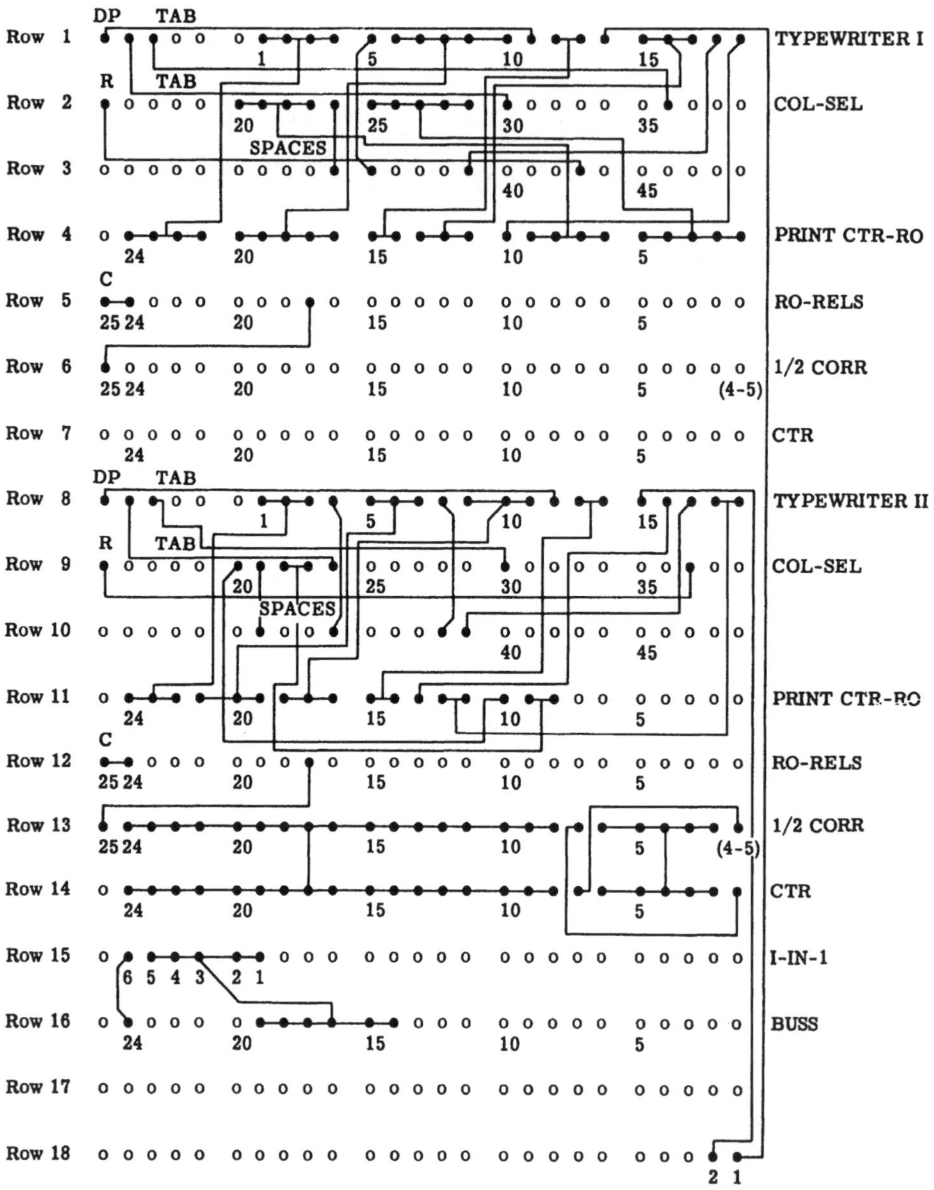

FUNCTIONAL PLUGBOARD (continued)

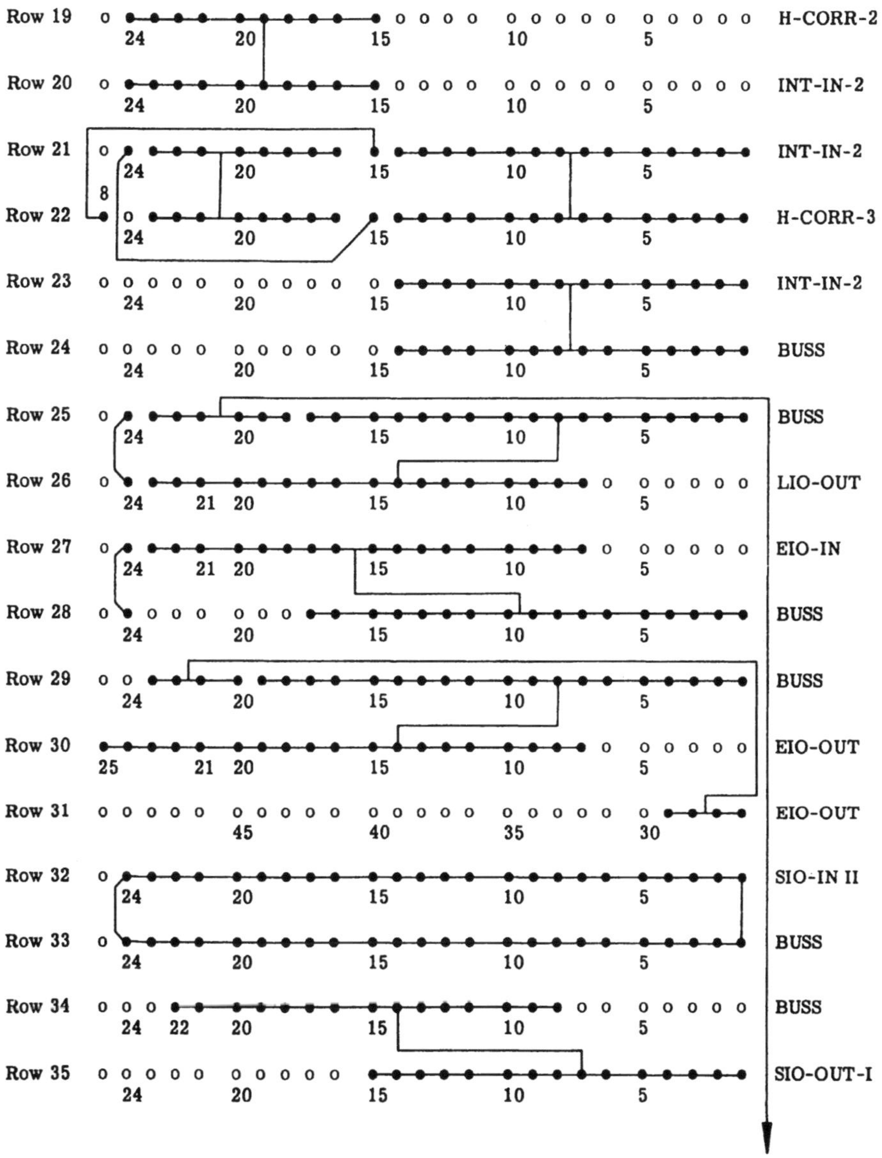

FUNCTIONAL PLUGBOARD (continued)

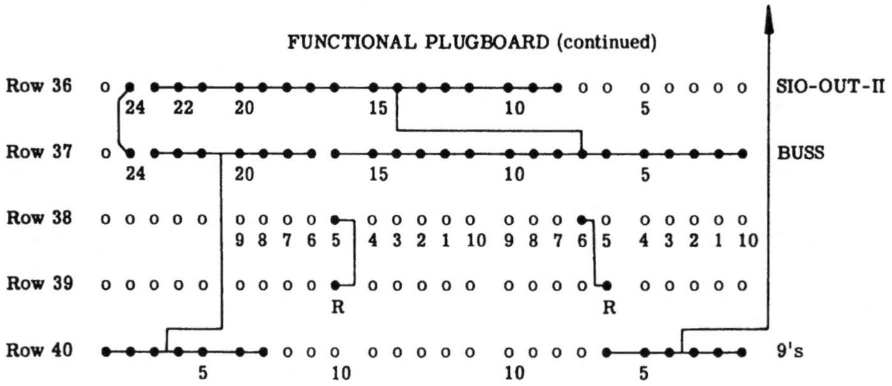

CHAPTER VI

SOLUTION OF EXAMPLES

In most cases there are several methods of adapting a problem for machine computation. After all methods of attack have been considered, one usually will show distinct advantages as regards speed and ease of operation and reliability of the checking procedures employed.

Since machine time is extremely valuable, the first consideration in planning a sequence tape is to reduce the computation time to a minimum consistent with the required accuracy. However, a fine balance must be maintained between computation time and the ensuing complexity of the coding. The conservation of one or two cycles of machine time will, for example, not be profitable if it means that the counters containing essential parts of a computation must be reset before the results are checked.

The second consideration in planning a computation is ease of operation. If switches must be altered or sequence tapes interchanged at relatively short intervals of time, these operations will constitute not only a loss of time but also a source of error.

Ease of rerunning a computation in the wake of an error and the possibility of computing for specific values of the independent variables must also be considered. Machine failures occur from time to time. The amount of time consumed in detecting the source of an error is usually dependent upon the complexity of the coding. The time required to resume operation after an error, which is dependent upon the number of manipulations the attendant must perform, should be reduced to a minimum in a well planned sequence tape. Specifically, no decisions or computations should be required on the part of the attendant. The operating instructions and the values printed or punched should provide all the information necessary for rerunning any part of the computation.

Finally, of paramount importance in the design of a sequence control tape are the checks on the computation. These must insure positive proof that the output values obtained are precisely those required and that they are correct to the desired accuracy. Four classes of errors must be taken into account: (1) errors inherent in the mathematical formulae; (2) errors produced by a repetition of the four fundamental operations of arithmetic; (3) errors introduced by manual operations; (4) errors due to mechanical or electrical failures within the calculator itself.

The errors inherent in the mathematical formulae must be evaluated during the preliminary analysis before the coding is begun. Decisions must be made as regards the number of terms of an infinite series to be retained, the number of times an iterative process must be applied and the order of interpolation required. These decisions are dependent upon the interval and increment of the independent variable and the accuracy desired in the computed results.

The loss of accuracy due to the repetition of the four basic arithmetical operations in a finite digital calculator must be subjected to a detailed analysis. For each operation, the maximum error must be assumed and the error of the final result computed. The simple expedient of using a certain number of extra computing columns will, in general, nullify errors from this source. Thus the choice of the operating decimal position will in part be dictated by the number of extra columns so allowed.

The two sources of human error mentioned in Chapter V, incorrect switch settings and incorrect plugging, are perhaps the most serious of all. If the mathematical nature of a problem permits a check of the final results, independent of the method of computation, the errors of the manual operations will be detected. If, however, the only checks which may be applied are those of an operational character; i.e., substantiating the fact that the desired sequence of operations has been correctly performed by the calculator, such errors as incorrect switch settings may not be detected. Hence meticulous precision on the operator's part and careful checking of all manual operations are essential.

Mechanical and electrical failures within the calculator itself are the final source of errors which must be checked. If a problem is properly coded, either operational or end result checks must be provided to detect such failures. In no case should the calculator be permitted to run more than twenty minutes without checks.

Although the probability is exceedingly small, a failure in the checking circuits of the machine may occur. To provide for the detection of such an event, all check quantities should be printed and kept under observation. If the check quantities are printed before the checking operation is performed, in case of failure, the magnitude and conformation of the error may provide a clue to its source. If possible, all quantities essential to the computation of the value being checked should be preserved in the calculator until the check is completed. These quantities may then be printed or punched and manual computation used to aid in tracing the source of the error. If the length of a computation is not too great, a rerun after a failure, with the tolerances set arbitrarily low so that the machine will stop even though the computation is correct, may provide correct values for comparison with those in error. Such a comparison will often lead directly to the particular source of difficulty.

Before the actual coding is begun, the storage counters should be allocated to the various parts of the computation. Then as the coding proceeds, a diagram should be prepared showing the lines of coding by which the counters are reset and the quantities they contain at every cycle of the computation.

A clear copy of the coding must be provided before an attempt is made to run a sequence tape on the calculator. The lines of perforations in the tape should be numbered to correspond to the lines of coding. In the coding sheets, colored indicators should call attention to all prints, interpolations and checks. All functional operations should be separated by horizontal rulings.

Before a sequence tape is run on the machine, a manual computation of a degenerate case, of the first point to be evaluated or of some arbitrary point, should be made. Comparison of the results of this manual computation with the results yielded by the tape will serve to check the coding and punching of the tape. The manual computation should parallel the operations dictated by the tape so that intermediate results may be compared if the final results fail to check.

Every sequence control tape must be accompanied by operating instructions. These instructions must be sufficiently complete to enable an experienced attendant to set up the problem and operate the calculator. All value and functional tapes and cards supplied with a problem must be thoroughly checked before a problem is ready to run. The only remaining source of input values, the switch settings, must be checked just before the machine is started. Directions for checking the switch settings must be given in the operating instructions. The quantities standing in the switches must be printed or punched for checking, either under control of a sequence tape or under manual control of the keyboard ordinarily used in the preparation of sequence tapes (see page 45, last paragraph). If blank tape is placed across the reading pins of the sequence mechanism, this keyboard may be connected to the calculator to transmit successive single lines of coding to the machine. Only an experienced attendant should attempt to use the keyboard, however, because of the rapid manipulations necessary in using automatic codes. The keyboard is most frequently used for printing and punching quantities when testing to locate a source of error.

SOLUTION OF EXAMPLES

It is often necessary to make preliminary computations and to set certain values in storage counters before a computation is begun. In such an event a starting tape is used. It is usually a short two-ended control tape and may well include printing quantities from the switches, checking plugging and resetting storage counters. If possible starting tapes should be used only at the beginning of a problem or to re-establish operation after failure to check. In general, they should not be used at the start of each individual run since too much time would be wasted in changing control tapes.

The operating instructions accompanying a sequence tape must include all of the following information.

(1) Switches.

All quantities to be set in switches must be listed. Both symbols and numerical values must be stated. All tolerances must be accompanied by a reference to the quantity to be checked.

(2) Tapes.

All value and functional tapes, together with a statement of the interpolator on which they are to be placed, must be listed. All tapes must be clearly labeled and starting lines indicated. On the sequence tape itself, the starting line and all rerun lines must be marked.

(3) Card Feeds.

The cards required by each feed must be identified by their serial numbers. The relationship of the serial numbers to the argument and function being computed must be clearly stated. In the instructions for reruns or any other special runs, further instructions for the replacement of cards must be given.

(4) Card Punch.

The quantities being punched and the printed values with which they may be compared must be identified. The composition of serial numbers in relation to the argument and function must be made clear. Instructions must be given for the labeling, filing and storing of all cards punched.

(5) Typewriters.

The mathematical symbols of the quantities printed and their relative positions must be stated. Sample headings of pages or rolls should be cited. It must also be stated whether or not the typewriter reverse switches may be used since these switches do not reverse the half pick-up coding.

(6) Storage Counters.

All manual resets of storage counters must be listed. In particular, if a counter is used to accumulate for each quantity or group of quantities printed, and stop the machine at the end of a page, this counter must be identified.

(7) Functional Counters.

All manual resets required must be listed.

(8) Checks.

All checks must be listed and the following information supplied for each check:

(a) quantity checked;

(b) amount of tolerance and switch from which it is derived;

(c) line of coding containing the check procedure;

(d) procedure in case of failure to check.

(9) Rerun Instructions.

In general, these will be of two types:

(a) rerun of the point on which the failure occurred;

(b) rerun of any other point.

Complete plugging instructions must also accompany every sequence control tape. These instructions must include all of the following information: (1) a statement of the position of the operating decimal point of the calculator and of the typewriter and punch decimal points, if these differ; (2) a list of the units of the calculator employed in the computation and diagrams of their plugging; (3) the switch settings for division, logarithms and interpolation must be listed if these functions are to be used; (4) for each typewriter, the horizontal grouping of the digits to be printed must be stated, the vertical grouping of the lines of the tabular values must be given, plugging diagrams for each typewriter must be provided.

If the logarithm, exponential, sine or interpolator units are to be used by a sequence tape, these units should be tested on known arguments before the tape itself is tested. Such known arguments must include, for the exponential and sine units, both positive and negative values. In the case of the sine unit, arguments from each of the four quadrants using both the sine and cosine series should be chosen. The reading pins of the interpolators should be tested by reading known values such as diagonal numbers.

If a sequence tape is of such general interest that it will be preserved in the tape library, its starting tape should be designed with care in order to check all switch settings, all plugging and all of the functional units employed, as well as to compute the initial values required by the main control tape. However, for problems to be run but once on the calculator, the starting tape should be as simple as is consistent with adequate provision for setting up the problem and rerunning in case of failures.

In the preparation of control tapes and operating instructions, a standard practice is necessary since the operation of large scale calculating machinery on a continuous basis is of necessity a group enterprise. The methods and techniques employed must be standardized in order that the required results may be obtained with a minimum of special instructions. The foregoing discussion covers the more important rules of coding developed in nearly two years of operation of the calculator. However, so brief a description cannot be expected to cover all the details involved. These will be illustrated by means of examples chosen for mathematical simplicity in order that the coding and checking may be the focal points of the discussion.

Example 1. It is required to evaluate the polynomial,

$$F(x) = x^4 + 3x^3 - 3x^2/4 - 22x + 3,$$

by successive multiplications, in the interval $5 \leq x \leq 10$, with $\Delta x = 0.01$. The values of $F(x)$ are to be punched in tabulating machine cards for use in further computation. Each card must be identified by a serial number consisting of the argument, x_n, punched with decimal point between card columns 75 and 76 (machine columns 5 and 6) and a one in the 80th card column (1 in 1st machine column). It is not required to print the values of $F(x)$. One value of $F(x)$ is to be computed during each revolution of the control tape. The tape is to be designed so that it may be rolled back and rerun without any additional manipulations. The starting tape is to be designed so that it may be used to re-establish the computation for any arbitrary value of the argument.

SOLUTION OF EXAMPLES

If F(x) is written in the form,

$$F(x) = (((x_n + 3)x_n - 3/4)x_n - 22)x_n + 3,$$

it should be clear that only three multiplications will be required to evaluate the given polynomial. In general a polynomial of nth degree will require not more than n multiplications. The constants will be supplied from switches. Since $F(x) < 2 \times 10^4$ in the interval under consideration, the standard position of the operating decimal point, between columns 15 and 16, may be assumed.

Switch Settings

No.	Code	Setting and Purpose
1	741	$\Delta x = 1$ in 14th machine column; increment of argument for computing
2	742	$\Delta x = 1$ in 4th machine column; increment of argument for punch card serial numbers
4	743	1 in 1st machine column; punch card code for F(x); zero check tolerance
5	7431	0.75
6	7432	22
7	74321	3
9	751	x_{n-1} = argument for computing; decimal point between columns 15 and 16; used in starting tape only
10	752	$x_{n-1} + 3$; decimal point between columns 15 and 16; used in starting tape only
11	7521	x_{n-1} = argument for punch card serial numbers; decimal point between columns 5 and 6; used in starting tape only

Since the argument is always ≥ 5, containing at least one non-zero digit, and is always used as the multiplier, four lines of coding may be interposed between the read-in of MP and the read-out of the product. The resets of the counters receiving the products, and the additions of the successive constants, are interposed in the multiplications.

<u>Starting Tape</u>

	Line	OUT	IN	MISC.
reset ctr. 1	1	1	1	7
x_{n-1} from sw. 9 to ctr. 1; argument for computing	2	751	1	7

	Line	OUT	IN	MISC.
reset ctr. 2	3	2	2	7
$x_{n-1} + 3$ from sw. 10 to ctr. 2	4	752	2	7
reset ctr. 64	5	7	7	7
x_{n-1} from sw. 11 to ctr. 64; argument for punch card serial number	6	7521	7	7

<u>Main Control Tape</u>

	Line	OUT	IN	MISC.
Δx from sw. 1 to ctr. 1; ctr. 1 = $x_{n-1} + \Delta x = x_n$; argument for computing	1	741	1	7
Δx from sw. 2 to ctr. 64; ctr. 64 = $x_{n-1} + \Delta x = x_n$; argument for punch card serial number	2	742	7	7
Δx from sw. 1 to ctr. 2; ctr. 2 = $x_{n-1} + \Delta x + 3 = x_n + 3$	3	741	2	7
$x_n + 3$ from ctr. 2 to MC — Rerun line	4	2	761	7
	5			7
	6			
x_n from ctr. 1 to MP	7	1		7
	8			7
	9			7
reset ctr. 3	10	21	21	7
-0.75 from sw. 5 to ctr. 3	11	7431	21	32
$(x_n + 3)x_n$ to ctr. 3; ctr. 3 = $(x_n + 3)x_n - 0.75$	12		21	7
$(x_n + 3)x_n - 0.75$ from ctr. 3 to MC	13	21	761	7
	14			7
	15			
x_n from ctr. 1 to MP	16	1		7
	17			7
	18			7
reset ctr. 4	19	3	3	7
-22 from sw. 6 to ctr. 4	20	7432	3	32
$((x_n + 3)x_n - 0.75)x_n$ to ctr. 4; ctr. 4 = $((x_n + 3)x_n - 0.75)x_n - 22$	21		3	7

	Line	OUT	IN	MISC.
$((x_n + 3)x_n - 0.75)x_n - 22$ from ctr. 4 to MP	22	3	761	7
	23			7
	24			
x_n from ctr. 1 to MP	25	1		7
	26			7
	27			7
reset ctr. 5	28	31	31	7
3 from sw. 7 to ctr. 5	29	74321	31	
$(((x_n + 3)x_n - 0.75)x_n - 22)x_n$ to ctr. 5; ctr. 5 = $F(x_n)$	30		31	7
$F(x_n)$ to punch ctr.	31	31	753	
initiate punching and wait until punching is completed	32			51
x_n from ctr. 64 to punch ctr. for serial number	33	7	753	
1 in 1st machine column to punch ctr.; code for $F(x)$	34	743	753	
initiate punching and continue operation	35			75
	36			87

Operating Instructions

(1) Set switches as listed. Punch the values set in the switches and compare the punched values with the list of switch settings.

(2) The quantities punched under control of the main tape are the values of $F(x_n)$. Each card is to be identified by a serial number consisting of the argument, x_n, punched in card columns 74-77 and a one, the code for $F(x)$, in card column 80. All cards punched are to be placed in the drawer provided for this purpose.

(3) Run starting tape.

(4) Run main control tape. If no failures occur, continue running until card for $x_n = 9.99$ has been punched, then press stop key.

(5) If a failure occurs during the computation for the argument, x_n, roll the tape back to line 4, marked "Rerun line", and repeat the computation for this value.

(6) If tests are made and counters disturbed, or if it is desired to compute for any arbitrary value of the argument, repeat the starting procedure with switches 9, 10 and 11 reset as listed.

(7) Since the maximum number of non-zero digits in any argument is three, the maximum time for any multiplication is ten cycles. Hence, the maximum time for each revolution of the control tape may be computed as follows:

accumulate arguments	3
three multiplications	30
punching of results	10
punching of serial number	3
	46 cycles = 13.8 seconds.

If further computations are added to this tape, it will be possible to interpose thirteen of these cycles reducing the computation time to 9.9 seconds.

(8) The first card punched under control of the main tape will be F(x) = 874.25 with the serial number 500001.

Plugging Instructions

(1) Plug the multiply unit for the standard position of the operating decimal point (see page 247).

(2) Plug the punch as shown in the diagram below.

PUNCH MAGNETS

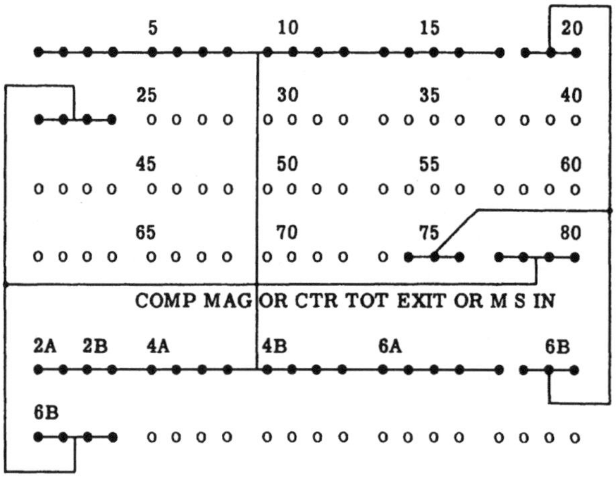

Example 2. It is required to evaluate the polynomial of example 1 using difference engine techniques.

Suppose five values of the function, F_{n-5}, F_{n-4}, F_{n-3}, F_{n-2}, F_{n-1}, to be available in punched cards. A starting tape will be designed to feed these five cards, and compute the differences associated with the argument x_{n-1}. Switch 8 will contain $\Delta^4 F$ = 0.000 000 24 and this quantity will be used to check the differences computed by the starting tape. Before beginning the computation with the calculator, F(4.95), F(4.96), F(4.97), F(4.98) and F(4.99) must be computed manually and punched in tabulating machine cards. Thereafter, F(x) must be punched in cards by the main control tape. Hence, in the event of a machine error, any five successive values of the function, known to be correct, may be used to re-establish the computation with the aid of the starting tape.

The main control tape is to be designed so that the value of the function and its differences computed in the m-1st revolution of the tape will be used in the mth revolution of the tape to compute the next succeeding value of the function and its differences. The standard decimal position will be used.

<u>Starting Tape</u>

reset ctr. 1

F_{n-5} to ctr. 1 from card feed I

reset ctr. 2

F_{n-4} to ctr. 2 from card feed I

reset ctr. 3

F_{n-3} to ctr. 3 from card feed I

reset ctr. 4

F_{n-2} to ctr. 4 from card feed I

reset ctr. 8

F_{n-1} to ctr. 8 from card feed I

reset ctr. 9

F_{n-1} from ctr. 8 to ctr. 9

$- F_{n-2}$ from ctr. 4 to ctr. 9; ctr. 9 $= \Delta F_{n-2}$

$- F_{n-3}$ from ctr. 3 to ctr. 4; ctr. 4 $= \Delta F_{n-3}$

$- F_{n-4}$ from ctr. 2 to ctr. 3; ctr. 3 $= \Delta F_{n-4}$

$- F_{n-5}$ from ctr. 1 to ctr. 2; ctr. 2 $= \Delta F_{n-5}$

reset ctr. 10

ΔF_{n-2} from ctr. 9 to ctr. 10

Line	OUT	IN	MISC.
1	1	1	7
2		1	7632
3	2	2	7
4		2	7632
5	21	21	7
6		21	7632
7	3	3	7
8		3	7632
9	4	4	7
10		4	7632
11	41	41	7
12	4	41	7
13	3	41	732
14	21	3	732
15	2	21	732
16	1	2	732
17	42	42	7
18	41	42	7

	Line	OUT	IN	MISC.
$-\Delta F_{n-3}$ from ctr. 4 to ctr. 10; ctr. 10 $= \Delta^2 F_{n-3}$	19	3	42	732
$-\Delta F_{n-4}$ from ctr. 3 to ctr. 4; ctr. 4 $= \Delta^2 F_{n-4}$	20	21	3	732
$-\Delta F_{n-5}$ from ctr. 2 to ctr. 3; ctr. 3 $= \Delta^2 F_{n-5}$	21	2	21	732
reset ctr. 11	22	421	421	7
$\Delta^2 F_{n-3}$ from ctr. 10 to ctr. 11	23	42	421	7
$-\Delta^2 F_{n-4}$ from ctr. 4 to ctr. 11; ctr. 11 $= \Delta^3 F_{n-4}$	24	3	421	732
$-\Delta^2 F_{n-5}$ from ctr. 3 to ctr. 4; ctr. 4 $= \Delta^3 F_{n-5}$	25	21	3	732
reset ctr. 12	26	43	43	7
$\Delta^3 F_{n-4}$ from ctr. 11 to ctr. 12	27	421	43	7
$-\Delta^3 F_{n-5}$ from ctr. 4 to ctr. 12; ctr. 12 $= \Delta^4 F_{n-5}$	28	3	43	732
reset comparison ctr. 5	29	31	31	7
$\Delta^4 F$ from sw. 8 to ctr. 5	30	75	31	7
$-\Delta^4 F_{n-5}$ from ctr. 12 to ctr. 5	31	43	31	732
reset check ctr. 72	32	74	74	7
zero check tolerance from sw. 4 to check ctr. 72	33	743	74	7
$\lvert \Delta^4 F - \Delta^4 F \rvert$ to check ctr. 72	34	31	74	71
check; reset check ctr. 72	35	74	74	64
reset ctr. 64	36	7	7	7
x_{n-1} from sw. 11 to ctr. 64; argument for punch card serial number	37	7521	7	7

Main Control Tape

	Line	OUT	IN	MISC.
reset working counters for differences computation	1	43	43	7
	2	431	431	7
	3	432	432	7
	4	4321	4321	7
transfer differences from storage to working counters F_{n-1} from ctr. 8 to ctr. 12	5	4	43	7
ΔF_{n-2} from ctr. 9 to ctr. 13	6	41	431	7

	Line	OUT	IN	MISC.
$\Delta^2 F_{n-3}$ from ctr. 10 to ctr. 14	7	42	432	7
$\Delta^3 F_{n-4}$ from ctr. 11 to ctr. 15	8	421	4321	7
$\Delta^4 F$ from sw. 8 to ctr. 15; ctr. 15 = $\Delta^3 F_{n-3}$	9	75	4321	7
$\Delta^3 F_{n-3}$ from ctr. 15 to ctr. 14; ctr. 14 = $\Delta^2 F_{n-2}$	10	4321	432	7
$\Delta^2 F_{n-2}$ from ctr. 14 to ctr. 13; ctr. 13 = ΔF_{n-1}	11	432	431	7
ΔF_{n-1} from ctr. 13 to ctr. 12; ctr. 12 = F_n	12	431	43	7
F_n from ctr. 12 to punch ctr.	13	43	753	7
reset ctr. 8; initiate punching; continue operation but complete punching before reading into punch ctr.	14	4	4	751
reset ctr. 9	15	41	41	7
reset ctr. 10	16	42	42	7
reset ctr. 11	17	421	421	7
Δx from sw. 2 to ctr. 64; ctr. 64 = $x_{n-1} + \Delta x = x_n$; argument for punch card serial number	18	742	7	
F_n from ctr. 12 to ctr. 8	19	43	4	7
ΔF_{n-1} from ctr. 13 to ctr. 9	20	431	41	7
$\Delta^2 F_{n-2}$ from ctr. 14 to ctr. 10	21	432	42	7
$\Delta^3 F_{n-3}$ from ctr. 15 to ctr. 11	22	4321	421	7
x_n from ctr. 64 to punch ctr. for serial number	23	7	753	
1 in 1st machine column to punch ctr.; code for F(x)	24	743	753	
initiate punching and continue operation	25			75
	26			87

Operating Instructions

(1) Set switches as listed on page 293, adding switch 8 = 0.000 000 24. Punch the values set in the switches and compare the punched values with the list of switch settings.

(2) The quantities punched under control of the main tape are the values of $F(x_n)$. Each card is to be identified by a serial number consisting of the argument, x_n, punched in card columns 74-77 and a one, the code for F(x), in card column 80. All cards punched are to be placed in the drawer provided for this purpose.

(3) Five cards, labeled "starting cards", must be placed in card feed I. These cards are identified by the serial numbers 495001, 496001, 497001, 498001 and 499001.

(4) Run starting tape. When cards run out, turn off card feed control switch and restart calculator. If the starting tape is completed correctly, the sequence mechanism will stop on a blank line of tape.

(5) If the check, on line 35 of the starting tape fails, the calculator will stop on line 36, reading (7, 7, 7). The starting cards must be refed and the starting tape rerun. If the check continues to fail, the counters used in the difference computation (ctrs. 1 through 15) and switch 8 must be tested.

(6) Run main control tape. If no failures occur, continue running until the card for $x_n = 9.99$ has been punched, then press the stop key.

(7) If it is necessary to rerun the computation, or to run it for an arbitrary value of the argument, x_n:

(a) five cards from those punched under control of the main tape must be placed in card feed I; these cards are identified by the arguments $x_{n-5}, x_{n-4}, x_{n-3}, x_{n-2}, x_{n-1}$, in that order, punched in card columns 74-77 and a one in card column 80;
(b) switch 11 must be set to x_{n-1};
(c) the starting procedure must be repeated and the computation continued under control of the main tape.

(8) The maximum time for each revolution of the main tape may be computed as follows:

computation of $F(x_n)$	12
punching $F(x_n)$	10
punching serial number	3
	25 cycles = 7.5 seconds.

(9) The first card punched under control of the main sequence tape will be $F(5.00) = 874.25$ with the serial number 500001.

Plugging Instructions

(1) Plug the card punch as in example 1 (see page 296).

(2) Plug card feed I direct (see page 272).

Example 3. It is required to design a single control tape incorporating the two methods of evaluating the polynomial, $F(x)$, defined in example 1. The two values of $F(x_n)$ independently computed in each revolution of the tape are to be compared providing an exact check on the computation. All other conditions of this example are the same as those of examples 1 and 2.

Starting Tape

Lines 1 through 35 will be lines 1 through 35 of the starting tape of example 2.

Lines 36 through 41 will be lines 1 through 6 of the starting tape of example 1.

Main Control Tape		Line	OUT	IN	MISC.
Δx to ctr. 1; ctr. 1 = $x_{n-1} + \Delta x = x_n$		1	741	1	7
Δx to ctr. 64; ctr. 64 = $x_{n-1} + \Delta x = x_n$		2	742	7	7
Δx to ctr. 2; ctr. 2 = $x_n + 3$		3	741	2	7
$x_n + 3$ to MC	Rerun line	4	2	761	7
		5	43	43	7
		6	431	431	
x_n to MP		7	1		7
		8	432	432	7
		9	4321	4321	7
		10	21	21	7
$-$ 0.75 to ctr. 3		11	7431	21	32
$(x_n + 3)x_n$ to ctr. 3		12		21	7
$(x_n + 3)x_n - 0.75$ to MC		13	21	761	7
F_{n-1} to ctr. 12		14	4	43	7
ΔF_{n-2} to ctr. 13		15	41	431	
x_n to MP		16	1		7
$\Delta^2 F_{n-3}$ to ctr. 14		17	42	432	7
$\Delta^3 F_{n-4}$ to ctr. 15		18	421	4321	7
		19	3	3	7
$-$ 22 to ctr. 4		20	7432	3	32
$((x_n + 3)x_n - 0.75)x_n$ to ctr. 4		21		3	7
$((x_n + 3)x_n - 0.75)x_n - 22$ to MC		22	3	761	7
$\Delta^4 F_{n-4}$ to ctr. 15; ctr. 15 = $\Delta^3 F_{n-3}$		23	75	4321	7
$\Delta^3 F_{n-3}$ to ctr. 14; ctr. 14 = $\Delta^2 F_{n-2}$		24	4321	432	
x_n to MP		25	1		7
$\Delta^2 F_{n-2}$ to ctr. 13; ctr. 13 = ΔF_{n-1}		26	432	431	7
ΔF_{n-1} to ctr. 12; ctr. 12 = F_n		27	431	43	7

	Line	OUT	IN	MISC.
	28	31	31	7
3 to ctr. 5	29	74321	31	
$(((x_n + 3)x_n - 0.75)x_n - 22)x_n$ to ctr. 5; ctr. 5 = F_n	30		31	7
F_n to punch ctr.	31	31	753	
	32	32	32	7
F_n by multiplication to ctr. 6	33	31	32	7
$- F_n$ by differences to ctr. 6	34	43	32	732
zero check tolerance to check ctr. 72	35	743	74	7
$\|F_n - F_n\|$ to check ctr. 72	36	32	74	71
check	37	74	74	64
initiate punching;continue operation, but complete punching before reading into punch ctr.	38	4	4	751
	39	41	41	7
	40	42	42	7
	41	421	421	7
F_n to ctr. 8	42	43	4	
ΔF_{n-1} to ctr. 9	43	431	41	7
$\Delta^2 F_{n-2}$ to ctr. 10	44	432	42	7
$\Delta^3 F_{n-3}$ to ctr. 11	45	4321	421	7
x_n for serial number to punch ctr.	46	7	753	
1 in 1st machine column to punch ctr.	47	743	753	
initiate punching and continue operation	48			75
	49			87

Operating Instructions

(1) Set switches as listed on page 293, adding switch 8 = 0.000 000 24. Punch the values set in the switches and compare the punched values with the list of switch settings.

(2) The quantities punched under control of the main tape are the values of $F(x_n)$. Each card is to be identified by a serial number consisting of the argument, x_n, punched in card columns 74-77

and a one, the code for F(x), in card column 80. All cards punched are to be placed in the drawer provided for this purpose.

(3) Five cards, labeled "starting cards", must be placed in card feed I. These cards are identified by the serial numbers 495001, 496001, 497001, 498001 and 499001.

(4) Run starting tape. When cards run out, turn off card feed control switch and restart calculator. If the starting tape is completed correctly, the sequence mechanism will stop on a blank line of tape.

(5) If the check, on line 35 of the starting tape fails, the calculator will stop on line 36, reading (7, 7, 7). The starting cards must be refed and the starting tape rerun. If the check continues to fail, the counters used in the difference computation (ctrs. 1 through 15) and switch 8 must be tested.

(6) Run main control tape. If no failures occur, continue running until the card for F(9.99) has been punched, then press the stop key.

(7) If the check on line 37 of the main tape fails, the tape must be rolled back to line 4, marked "Rerun line", and the computation repeated.

(8) If the check continues to fail, the computation should be re-established using the following procedure for x_n':

(a) five cards from those punched under control of the main tape must be placed in card feed I; these cards are identified by the arguments x_{n-5}, x_{n-4}, x_{n-3}, x_{n-2}, x_{n-1}, in that order, punched in card columns 74-77 and a one in card column 80;
(b) switches 9, 10 and 11 must be set to the values indicated in the list on page 293;
(c) the starting procedure must be repeated and the computation continued under control of the main tape.

(9) Repeated failure of the check under the roll back procedure of instruction (7) but correct operation under the procedure of instruction (8) probably indicates that the difference computation is the source of error.

(10) If it is desired to run the computation for any arbitrary value of the argument, the procedure of instruction (8) may be used.

(11) The maximum time for each revolution of the control tape may be computed as follows:

accumulate arguments	3
three multiplications	30
check procedure	6
punching F(x)	10
punching serial number	3
	52 cycles = 15.6 seconds.

(12) The first card punched under control of the main sequence tape will be F(5.00) = 874.25 with the serial number 500001.

Plugging Instructions

(1) Plug the multiply unit for the standard position of the operating decimal point (see page 247).

(2) Plug the card punch as in example 1 (see page 296).

(3) Plug card feed I direct (see page 272).

Example 4. It is required that the function,

$$U(x) = (x^2 - 1)^{-3/2},$$

be tabulated in the interval $5 \leq x \leq 10$, with $\Delta x = 0.01$, using an iterative process. It is further required that the values of $U(x)$ be in error by less than 5×10^{-10} and that the computation be completely checked. The values of $U(x)$ are to be punched in tabulating machine cards for use in further computation. Each card must be identified by a serial number consisting of the argument, x_n, punched with decimal point between card columns 75 and 76 (machine columns 5 and 6) and a two in card column 80 (2 in 1st machine column). It is not required to print the values of $U(x)$. One value of $U(x)$ is to be computed during each revolution of the control tape. The tape is to be designed so that it may be rolled back and rerun without any additional manipulations. The starting tape is to be designed so that it may be used to re-establish the computation for any arbitrary value of the argument.

The value of $U(x) = U(x_{n-1}) = U_{n-1}$ determined for the argument, x_{n-1}, will be used as the first approximation to $U(x_n) = U_n$. The value of U_n will be obtained by the iterative formula,

$$U_n = \frac{4U_{n-1}(N_n + N_{n-1})}{U_{n-1}^2(N_n + N_{n-1})^2 + 4N_n},$$

where $x_n = x_{n-1} + \Delta x$,

$N_{n-1} = (x_{n-1}^2 - 1)^3$,

$N_n = (x_n^2 - 1)^3$

and $U_n^2 = 1/N_n$.

The error after one application of the iterative formula is

$$e_1 = e_0^2 N_n^{3/2} /8,$$

where $e_0 = U_{n-1} - U_n$.

It can be shown that one application of the iterative formula will give an error in $U(x)$ of less than 2.7×10^{-11}, slightly better than the accuracy required.

The computation of x_n^2 will be checked by use of the identity,

SOLUTION OF EXAMPLES

$$\bar{x}_n^2 = x_{n-1}^2 + 2x_{n-1}\Delta x + \overline{\Delta x}^2 .$$

The computation of $N_n = (x_n^2 - 1)^3$ will be checked by comparing it with the value of

$$\bar{N}_n = ((x_n^2 - 3)x_n^2 + 3)x_n^2 - 1 .$$

The quantities U_nN_n and N_nU_n will be computed and compared with each other. Finally, the value of U_n will be checked by means of the identity,

$$U_n^2N_n = 1.$$

The operating decimal point will be assumed to lie between columns 15 and 16 and division will be plugged for 14 comparisons. The switch settings required by the starting tape and the main control tape are given in the following table.

Switch Settings

No.	Code	Setting and Purpose
1	741	$\Delta x = 1$ in 14th machine column; increment of argument for computing
2	742	$\Delta x = 1$ in 4th machine column; increment of argument for punch card serial numbers
4	743	1 in 1st machine column; zero check tolerance
7	74321	3
9	751	x_{n-1} = argument for computing; decimal point between columns 15 and 16; used in starting tape only
11	7521	x_{n-1} = argument for punch card serial numbers; decimal point between columns 5 and 6; used in starting tape only
12	753	$\overline{\Delta x}^2 = 1$ in 12th machine column
13	7531	2 in 1st machine column; code for U(x)
14	7532	$x_{n-2}\Delta x = x_{n-2}$ with decimal point between columns 13 and 14; used in starting tape only
15	75321	1
16	754	6 in 8th machine column; tolerance on check of U_n

<u>Starting Tape</u>

x_{n-1} to MC

Line	OUT	IN	MISC.
1	751	761	7
2	1	1	7

	Line	OUT	IN	MISC.
x_{n-1} to ctr. 1	3	751	1	
x_{n-1} to MP	4	751		7
	5	7	7	7
	6	52	52	7
- 1 to ctr. 18	7	75321	52	732
	8	5	5	
x^2_{n-1} to ctr. 16	9		5	7
x^2_{n-1} to ctr. 18; ctr. 18 = $x^2_{n-1} - 1$	10	5	52	7
$(x^2_{n-1} - 1)$ to MC	11	52	761	7
	12	74	74	7
x_{n-1} to ctr. 64	13	7521	7	
$(x^2_{n-1} - 1)$ to MP	14	52		7
	15	51	51	7
$x_{n-2}\Delta x$ to ctr. 17	16	7532	51	7
	17			7
	18	521	521	
$(x^2_{n-1} - 1)^2$ to ctr. 19	19		521	7
$(x^2_{n-1} - 1)^2$ to MC	20	521	761	7
	21			7
	22			
$(x^2_{n-1} - 1)$ to MP	23	52		7
	24			7
	25			7
	26	541	541	7
	27	53	53	
$(x^2_{n-1} - 1)^3$ to ctr. 20; ctr. 20 = N_{n-1}	28		53	7
U_{n-1} to ctr. 25 from card feed I	29		541	7632

	Line	OUT	IN	MISC.
U_{n-1} to MC	30	541	761	7
	31			7
	32			
N_{n-1} to MP	33	53		7
	34			7
	35			7
	36			7
	37	542	542	
$U_{n-1}N_{n-1}$ to ctr. 26	38		542	7

<u>Main</u> <u>Control</u> <u>Tape</u>

		Line	OUT	IN	MISC.
Δx to ctr. 1; ctr. 1 $= x_{n-1} + \Delta x = x_n$		1	741	1	7
Δx to ctr. 64; ctr. 64 $= x_{n-1} + \Delta x = x_n$		2	742	7	7
$\overline{\Delta x}^2$ to ctr. 17; ctr. 17 $= x_{n-2}\Delta x + \overline{\Delta x}^2 = x_{n-1}\Delta x$		3	753	51	7
x_n to MC	Rerun line	4	1	761	7
		5	3	3	7
x^2_{n-1} to ctr. 4		6	5	3	
x_n to MP		7	1		7
$x_{n-1}\Delta x$ to ctr. 4		8	51	3	7
		9	52	52	7
- 1 to ctr. 18		10	75321	52	732
		11	21	21	
x_n^2 to ctr. 3		12		21	7
x_n^2 to ctr. 18		13	21	52	7
$(x_n^2 - 1)$ to MC		14	52	761	7
$x_{n-1}\Delta x$ to ctr. 4		15	51	3	7
$\overline{\Delta x}^2$ to ctr. 4; ctr. 4 $= \bar{x}_n^2$		16	753	3	

	Line	OUT	IN	MISC.
$(x_n^2 - 1)$ to MP	17	52		7
	18	32	32	7
x_n^2 to ctr. 6	19	21	32	7
$-\bar{x}_n^2$ to ctr. 6	20	3	32	732
	21	521	521	
$(x_n^2 - 1)^2$ to ctr. 19	22		521	7
$(x_n^2 - 1)^2$ to MC	23	521	761	7
zero check tolerance to check ctr. 72	24	743	74	7
	25			
$(x_n^2 - 1)$ to MP	26	52		7
	27	531	531	7
- 3 to ctr. 21	28	74321	531	732
x_n^2 to ctr. 21	29	21	531	7
	30	53	53	
$(x_n^2 - 1)^3$ to ctr. 20; ctr. 20 = N_n	31		53	7
$(x_n^2 - 3)$ to MC	32	531	761	7
	33			7
	34	532	532	
x_n^2 to MP	35	21		7
3 to ctr. 22	36	74321	532	7
$-\left\lvert x_n^2 - \bar{x}_n^2 \right\rvert$ to check ctr. 72	37	32	74	71
check	38	74	74	64
	39		532	
$(x_n^2 - 3)x_n^2$ to ctr. 22	40		532	7
$(x_n^2 - 3)x_n^2 + 3$ to MC	41	532	761	7
	42			7
	43			

	Line	OUT	IN	MISC.
x_n^2 to MP	44	21		7
	45			7
	46			7
	47	5321	5321	7
- 1 to ctr. 23	48	75321	5321	32
$((x_n^2 - 3)x_n^2 + 3)x_n^2$ to ctr. 23; ctr. 23 = $\overline{N}_n$	49		5321	7
U_{n-1} to MC	50	541	761	7
	51	5421	5421	7
$U_{n-1}N_{n-1}$ to ctr. 27	52	542	5421	
N_n to MP	53	53		7
	54	3	3	7
N_n to ctr. 4	55	53	3	7
N_n to ctr. 4	56	53	3	7
N_n to ctr. 4	57	53	3	
$U_{n-1}N_n$ to ctr. 27	58		5421	7
$U_{n-1}(N_n + N_{n-1})$ to MC	59	5421	761	7
N_n to ctr. 4; ctr. 4 = $4N_n$	60	53	3	7
	61	31	31	
$U_{n-1}(N_n + N_{n-1})$ to MP	62	5421		7
$U_{n-1}(N_n + N_{n-1})$ to ctr. 5	63	5421	31	7
$U_{n-1}(N_n + N_{n-1})$ to ctr. 5	64	5421	31	7
$U_{n-1}(N_n + N_{n-1})$ to ctr. 5	65	5421	31	7
$U_{n-1}(N_n + N_{n-1})$ to ctr. 5; ctr. 5 = $4U_{n-1}(N_n + N_{n-1})$	66	5421	31	
$U_{n-1}^2(N_n + N_{n-1})^2$ to ctr. 4	67		3	7
$U_{n-1}^2(N_n + N_{n-1})^2 + 4N_n$ to DR	68	3	76	7
	69	321	321	7
	70			

	Line	OUT	IN	MISC.
$4U_{n-1}(N_n + N_{n-1})$ to DD	71	31		7
	72			7
	73			7
	74			7
	75			7
	76			7
	77			7
	78			7
	79	32	32	7
N_n to ctr. 6	80	53	32	7
$-\bar{N}_n$ to ctr. 6	81	5321	32	732
zero check tolerance to check ctr. 72	82	743	74	7
$-\lvert N_n - \bar{N}_n \rvert$ to check ctr. 72	83	32	74	71
check	84	74	74	64
	85		321	
U_n to ctr. 7	86		321	7
U_n to MC	87	321	761	7
	88			7
	89			
N_n to MP	90	53		7
	91			7
	92			7
	93			7
	94	43	43	
U_nN_n to ctr. 12	95		43	7
N_n to MC	96	53	761	7
	97			7

	Line	OUT	IN	MISC.
	98	432	432	
U_n to MP	99	321		7
- 1 to ctr. 14	100	75321	432	732
	101	32	32	7
U_nN_n to ctr. 6	102	43	32	7
	103	431	431	
N_nU_n to ctr. 13	104		431	7
U_n to MC	105	321	761	7
$-N_nU_n$ to ctr. 6	106	431	32	732
zero check tolerance to check ctr. 72	107	743	74	
U_nN_n to MP	108	43		7
	109			7
$-\lvert U_nN_n - N_nU_n \rvert$ to check ctr. 72	110	32	74	71
check	111	74	74	64
	112		432	
$U_n^2N_n$ to ctr. 14; ctr. 14 = $U_n^2N_n -1$	113		432	7
tolerance on U_n to check ctr. 72	114	754	74	7
$-\lvert U_n^2N_n - 1 \rvert$ to check ctr. 72	115	432	74	71
check	116	74	74	64
U_n to punch ctr.	117	321	753	
initiate punching	118	5	5	751
x_n^2 to ctr. 16	119	21	5	7
	120	541	541	7
U_n to ctr. 25	121	321	541	7
	122	542	542	7
U_nN_n to ctr. 26	123	43	542	
x_n for serial number to punch ctr.	124	7	753	

	Line	OUT	IN	MISC.
2 in 1st machine column to punch ctr.; code for U(x)	125	7531	753	
initiate punching and continue operation	126			75
	127			87

Operating Instructions

(1) Set switches as listed on page 305. Punch the values set in the switches and compare the punched values with the list of switch settings.

(2) The quantities punched under control of the main tape are the values of $U(x_n)$. Each card is identified by a serial number consisting of the argument, x_n, punched in card columns 74-77 and a two, the code for U(x), in card column 80. All cards punched are to be placed in the drawer provided for this purpose.

(3) One card labeled, "starting card", followed by a blank card, must be placed in card feed I. This card is identified by the serial number 499002.

(4) Run starting tape. When cards run out, turn off card feed control switch and restart calculator. When the starting tape is completed, the sequence mechanism will stop on a blank line of tape.

(5) Run main control tape. If no failures occur, continue running until the card for U(9.99) has been punched, then press stop key.

(6) If any of the checks in the main tape fail, the tape must be rolled back to line 4, marked "Rerun line", and the computation repeated.

(7) The following checks are included in the main control tape.

Lines	Quantity Checked	Tolerance
24, 37-38	$x_n^2 - \bar{x}_n^2$ from ctr. 6	1 in 1st machine column from sw. 4
82-84	$N_n - \bar{N}_n$ from ctr. 6	1 in 1st machine column from sw. 4
107, 110-111	$U_n N_n - N_n U_n$ from ctr. 6	1 in 1st machine column from sw. 4
114-116	$U_n^2 N_n - 1$ from ctr. 14	6 in 8th machine column from sw. 16

(8) If a check repeatedly fails, the quantities involved in the computation being checked should be punched in cards, and manual computations used to assist in tracing the source of error.

(9) If it is desired to run the computation for any arbitrary value of the argument, x_n, or to re-establish operation after tests have been made and counters disturbed, the following steps must be taken:

(a) a card from those punched under control of the main tape, followed by a blank card must be placed in card feed I; this card is identified by the argument, x_{n-1}, punched in card columns 74-77 and a two in card column 80; care must be taken to replace this card properly after it is used;

(b) switches 9, 11 and 14 must be set to the values indicated in the switch list on page 305;
(c) the starting procedure must be repeated and the computation continued under control of the main tape.

(10) The maximum time for each revolution of the control tape may be computed as follows:

accumulate arguments	3
additions	5
multiplication by x_n	10
4 multiplications by x_n^2 and $x_n^2 - 1$	48
2 multiplications by N_n	36
multiplication by U_n	15
multiplication by $U_{n-1}(N_n + N_{n-1})$	18
division to 14 comparisons	34
multiplication by U_nN_n	18
punching U(x)	10
punching serial number	3
	200 cycles = 60 seconds.

Plugging Instructions

(1) Plug the multiply unit for the standard position of the operating decimal point (see page 247).

(2) Plug the divide unit for 14 comparisons using the blank code as shown in the following diagram.

MP-DIV PLUGBOARD

```
        ┌───────────────────────────────────┐
Row 1   ● o o o o   o o o o o   o ● o o o   o o o o o   o o o o o
        25          20            15          10          5
```

Set divide switch to 07.

(3) Plug the card punch as in example 1 (see page 296).

(4) Plug card feed I direct (see page 272).

Example 5. The output cards containing F(x) and U(x) as obtained in examples 3 and 4 are to be fed to the calculator to form the function,

$$f(x) = F(x) \cdot U(x) .$$

It is required that a two column table be printed consisting of the argument, x_n, followed by the values of $f(x_n)$. The values of $f(x_n)$ are to be printed to six decimal places, the digits being grouped by threes to the right and left of the decimal point. The lines of the table are to be spaced in vertical groups of five lines. The quantities $F(x) \cdot U(x)$ and $U(x) \cdot F(x)$ are to be computed and compared with each other. The print counter read-out is to be checked. It will not be required to punch the values of f(x) in tabulating machine cards. This could be done, however, without loss of time.

Starting Tape

	Line	OUT	IN	MISC.
	1	1	1	7
x_{n-1} to ctr. 1	2	751	1	7

Main Control Tape

		Line	OUT	IN	MISC.
Δx to ctr. 1; ctr. 1 $= x_{n-1} + \Delta x = x_n$		1	741	1	
x_n to print ctr. I		2	1	7432	
initiate printing		3	87	752	76
		4	621	621	7
		5	63	63	7
F(x) to ctr. 35 from card feed I		6		621	7632
U(x) to ctr. 36 from card feed II		7		63	76321
F(x) to MC	Rerun line	8	621	761	7
		9	631	631	7
		10	632	632	
U(x) to MP		11	63		7
		12	6321	6321	7
		13	74	74	7
zero check tolerance to check ctr. 72		14	743	74	7
		15	64	64	
f(x) = F(x)U(x) to ctr. 37		16		631	
U(x) to MC		17	63	761	7
reset print ctr. I		18	842		7
		19			
F(x) to MP		20	621		7
f(x) to print ctr. I		21	631	7432	
f(x) from print ctr. I to ctr. 39		22	862	6321	7
- f(x) from ctr. 37 to ctr. 39		23	631	6321	732

	Line	OUT	IN	MISC.
f(x) to ctr. 40	24	631	64	7
$-\lvert f(x) - f(x) \rvert$ to check ctr. 72	25	6321	74	71
check of print ctr. I read-out	26	74	74	64
	27		632	
f(x) = U(x) F(x) to ctr. 38	28		632	7
zero check tolerance to check ctr. 72	29	743	74	7
- f(x) to ctr. 40	30	632	64	732
$-\lvert f(x) - f(x) \rvert$ to check ctr. 72	31	64	74	71
check multiplication	32	74	74	64
initiate printing	33		752	76
	34			87

Operating Instructions

(1) Set switches as listed. Punch the values set in the switches and compare the punched values with the list of switch settings.

Switch Settings

No.	Code	Setting and Purpose
1	741	$\Delta x = 1$ in 14th machine column; increment of argument for printing
4	743	1 in 1st machine column; zero check tolerance
9	751	x_{n-1} = argument for printing; decimal point between columns 15 and 16; used in starting tape only

(2) Card feed I must contain the cards for F(x), identified by the code 1 in the 80th card column. Card feed II must contain the cards for U(x), identified by the code 2 in the 80th card column. Care must be taken that the cards in each feed contain identical serial numbers in card columns 74-77. One card is fed from each feed during each revolution of the control tape. The first cards fed must contain the serial numbers 500001 and 500002 for card feeds I and II, respectively.

(3) Run starting tape. When the starting tape is completed, the sequence mechanism will stand on a blank line of tape.

(4) Start main control tape. The sequence mechanism will stop on line 2. Press start key and continue operation. If no failures occur, continue running until the argument 10.00 has been printed, then press stop key.

(5) If the check on line 26 fails, the print counter read-out should be tested. If the storage counters are not disturbed, the tape may then be rolled back to line 8 and the computation repeated.

(6) If the check on line 32 fails, the multiply unit should be tested. If the storage counters are not disturbed, the tape may then be rolled back to line 8 and the computation repeated.

(7) If storage counters have been disturbed by testing, the computation must be re-established using the following procedure for the argument, x_n:

(a) card feed I must contain the cards for F(x), (code 1 in the 80th card column), the first card containing the serial number x_n in card columns 74-77;
(b) card feed II must contain the cards for U(x), (code 2 in the 80th card column), the first card containing the serial number x_n in card columns 74-77;
(c) switch 9 must be set to x_{n-1}, the value indicated in the switch list;
(d) the starting procedure must be repeated and the computation continued under control of the main tape;
(e) the typewriter vertical spacing must be checked and properly reset.

(8) The maximum time for each revolution of the control tape may be computed as follows:

print argument	14
multiplication by U(x)	15
check f(x)	4
print f(x)	14
	47 cycles = 14.1 seconds.

Plugging Instructions

(1) Plug the multiply unit for the standard position of the operating decimal point (see page 247).

(2) Plug the card feeds direct (see page 272).

(3) Plug typewriter I as shown in the diagram below.

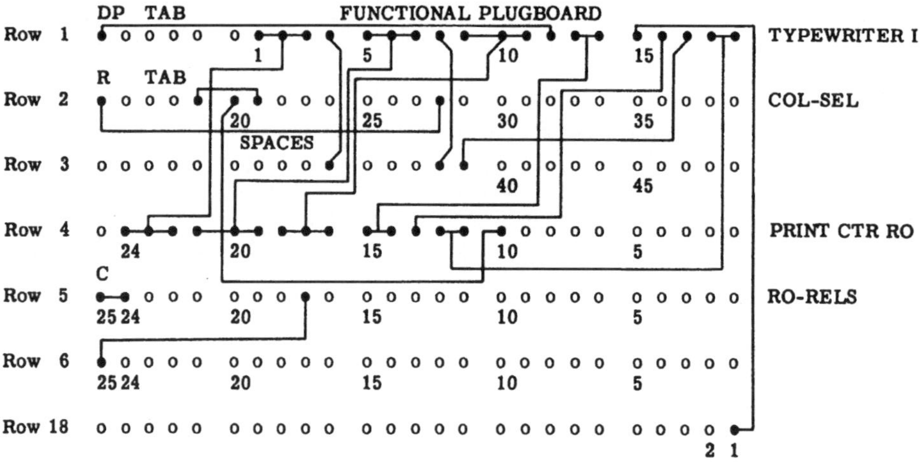

SOLUTION OF EXAMPLES

FUNCTIONAL PLUGBOARD

Row 38	o o o o o	o o o o o	o o o o o	o o o o •	o o o o o
		9 8 7 6 5	4 3 2 1 10	9 8 7 6 5	4 3 2 1 10
Row 39	o o o o o	o o o o o	o o o o o	o o o o •	o o o o o
		R		R	

Example 6. It is required that a single main control tape be designed to compute,

$$f(x) = F(x) \cdot U(x),$$

as defined in example 5. It is further required that the values of f(x) be in error by less than 5×10^{-11} and that the computation be completely checked. The values of f(x) are to be punched in tabulating machine cards for use in further computation. Each card must be identified by a serial number consisting of the argument, x_n, punched with decimal point between card columns 75 and 76 and a three in the 80th card column. It is not required to print the values of f(x). One value of f(x) is to be computed during each revolution of the control tape. The tape is to be designed so that it may be rolled back and rerun without any additional manipulations. The starting tape is to be designed so that it may be used to re-establish operation for any arbitrary value of the argument.

Since $F(x) < 2 \times 10^4$, U(x) must be in error by less than 2.5×10^{-15}, in order that f(x) be correct to the required accuracy. Two applications of the iterative process will be necessary to provide the desired accuracy in U(x).

In order to provide for rerunning and re-establishing the computation, it will be necessary to punch cards containing F(x) and U(x) during each revolution of the tape. Thus the main control tape will combine the tapes of examples 3, 4 and 5. The starting tape will combine the essential features of the starting tapes of these examples. The interweaving of the coding of these tapes is left as a problem for the reader.

The computation as performed by the three separate tapes would require:

computation of F(x)	15.6
computation of U(x) (including two iterations)	86.4
computation of f(x)	14.1
	116.1 seconds.

The computation as performed by a single control tape should not require more than 98 seconds.

Example 7. Let it be assumed that the function, $f(x)$ (defined in example 5), has been computed with an error of less than 4×10^{-10}, over the interval $4.99 \le x \le 10.02$, with $\Delta x = 0.01$, and punched in tabulating machine cards. The cards have been punched with serial numbers, equal to x_n with decimal point between card columns 22 and 23. It is now required to compute, check and print the values of the integral,

$$I(x) = \int_5^{x_n} f(x)dx,$$

over the interval $5 \le x \le 10$. It is further required that a two column table be printed consisting of the argument, x_n, followed by the values of $I(x_n)$. The lines of the table are to be spaced in vertical groups of five lines.

The approximate quadrature formulae,

$$\Delta I = \int_{x_{n-1}}^{x_n} f(x)dx = (-f_{n-1} + 8f_n + 5f_{n+1})\Delta x/12 + R,$$

$$\overline{\Delta I} = \int_{x_{n-1}}^{x_n} f(x)dx = (5f_n + 8f_{n+1} - f_{n+2})\Delta x/12 - R,$$

where

$$R = \overline{\Delta x}^4 f'''(\xi)/24,$$

in the interval $4.99 \le \xi \le 10.02$, may be used since for the given $f(x)$, $R < 6.66 \times 10^{-11}$. Hence the error in the integral $I(10)$ will be less than 3.4×10^{-8}. The values of $I(x)$ will be printed to eight decimal places, with a half-correction in the ninth place, making the tabular values in error by less than 4×10^{-8}. The digits will be grouped by fours to the right and left of the decimal point. Each revolution of the main control tape will compute and compare the quantities ΔI and $\overline{\Delta I}$. The values of ΔI will be used to accumulate the values of $I(x)$. The serial numbers of the cards supplying $f(x)$ will be checked. The print counter read-out and the half-correction will be checked before the tabular values are printed on typewriter II. Typewriter I will print the argument, the value of the integral and the difference, $\Delta I - \overline{\Delta I}$, before the checks are completed in order to provide information in case of machine failure. In order to provide for rerunning and re-establishing the computation, if necessary, the values of $I(x)$ will be punched in tabulating machine cards. The values set in the switches are listed under the operating instructions.

Starting Tape

	Line	OUT	IN	MISC.
	1	1	1	7
x_{n-1} to ctr. 1	2	751	1	7

	Line	OUT	IN	MISC.
	3	2	2	7321
$f_{n-1} + \bar{x}_{n-1}$ to ctr. 2 from card feed I	4		2	7632
$f_{n-1} + \bar{x}_{n-1}$ to SIO ctr.	5	2	874	7
	6	5	5	7
f_{n-1} to ctr. 16	7	874	5	7
	8	21	21	7
$\bar{x}_{n-1}$ to ctr. 3	9	84	21	7
	10	7	7	7
$\bar{x}_{n-1}$ to ctr. 64	11	7521	7	7
$- \underline{x}_{n-1}$ to ctr. 3	12	7	21	732
	13	74	74	7
zero check tolerance to check ctr. 72	14	743	74	7
$- \left\| \bar{x}_{n-1} + \underline{x}_{n-1} \right\|$ to check ctr. 72	15	21	74	71
check	16	74	74	64
	17	2	2	7321
$f_n + \bar{x}_n$ to ctr. 2 from card feed I	18		2	7632
$f_n + \bar{x}_n$ to SIO ctr.	19	2	874	7
	20	51	51	7
f_n to ctr. 17	21	874	51	7
	22	21	21	7
$\bar{x}_n$ to ctr. 3	23	84	21	7
$- \underline{x}_{n-1}$ to ctr. 3	24	7	21	732
- 1 in 1st machine column to ctr. 3	25	743	21	732
zero check tolerance to check ctr. 72	26	743	74	7
$- \left\| \bar{x}_n - \underline{x}_{n-1} - 1 \right\|$ to check ctr. 72	27	21	74	71
check	28	74	74	64
f_n to MC	29	51	761	7

	Line	OUT	IN	MISC.
	30	31	31	7
f_n to ctr. 5	31	51	31	
5 to MP	32	7541		7
f_n to ctr. 5; ctr. 5 = $2f_n$	33	51	31	7
f_n to ctr. 5; ctr. 5 = $3f_n$	34	51	31	7
f_n to ctr. 5; ctr. 5 = $4f_n$	35	51	31	7
	36	3	3	
$5f_n$ to ctr. 4	37		3	7
f_n to ctr. 5; ctr. 5 = $5f_n$	38	51	31	7
	39	32	32	7
$5f_n$ to ctr. 6	40	31	32	7
$- 5f_n$ to ctr. 6	41	3	32	732
zero check tolerance to check ctr. 72	42	743	74	7
$- \lvert 5f_n - 5f_n \rvert$ to check ctr. 72	43	32	74	71
check	44	74	74	64
	45	52	52	7
$5f_n$ to ctr. 18	46	3	52	7
f_n to MC	47	51	761	7
f_n to ctr. 5; ctr. 5 = $6f_n$	48	51	31	7
f_n to ctr. 5; ctr. 5 = $7f_n$	49	51	31	
8 to MP	50	7542		7
f_n to ctr. 5; ctr. 5 = $8f_n$	51	51	31	7
	52	32	32	7
$8f_n$ to ctr. 6	53	31	32	7
	54	3	3	
$8f_n$ to ctr. 4	55		3	7
$- 8f_n$ to ctr. 6	56	3	32	732

SOLUTION OF EXAMPLES

	Line	OUT	IN	MISC.
zero check tolerance to check ctr. 72	57	743	74	7
$-\lvert 8f_n - 8f_n \rvert$ to check ctr. 72	58	32	74	71
check	59	74	74	64
	60	521	521	7
$8f_n$ to ctr. 19	61	3	521	7
	62	2	2	7321
$f_{n+1} + \bar{x}_{n+1}$ to ctr. 2 from card feed I	63		2	7632
$f_{n+1} + \bar{x}_{n+1}$ to SIO counter	64	2	874	7
	65	53	53	7
f_{n+1} to ctr. 20	66	874	53	7
	67	21	21	7
$\bar{x}_{n+1}$ to ctr. 3	68	84	21	7
$-\underline{x}_{n-1}$ to ctr. 3	69	7	21	732
- 1 in 1st machine column to ctr. 3	70	743	21	732
- 1 in 1st machine column to ctr. 3	71	743	21	732
zero check tolerance to check ctr. 72	72	743	74	7
$-\lvert \bar{x}_{n+1} - \underline{x}_{n-1} - 1 - 1 \rvert$ to check ctr. 72	73	21	74	71
check	74	74	74	64
	75	2	2	7321
$I(x_{n-1}) + \bar{x}_{n-1}$ to ctr. 2 from card feed II	76		2	76321
$I(x_{n-1}) + \bar{x}_{n-1}$ to SIO counter	77	2	874	7
	78	531	531	7
$I(x_{n-1})$ to ctr. 21	79	874	531	7
	80	21	21	7
$\bar{x}_{n-1}$ to ctr. 3	81	84	21	7
$-\underline{x}_{n-1}$ to ctr. 3	82	7	21	732
zero check tolerance to check ctr. 72	83	743	74	7

		Line	OUT	IN	MISC.
$-\lvert \bar{x}_{n-1} - \underline{x}_{n-1} \rvert$ to check ctr. 72		84	21	74	71
check		85	74	74	64
		86	2	2	763
$-x_{n-1}$ to ctr. 2		87	1	2	732
$\underline{x}_{n-1}$ to LIO ctr.		88	7	765421	7
$\underline{x}_{n-1}$ to ctr. 2		89	831	2	7
zero check tolerance to check ctr. 72		90	743	74	7
$-\lvert -x_{n-1} + \underline{x}_{n-1} \rvert$ to check ctr. 72		91	2	74	71
check		92	74	74	64
		93			7

<u>Main</u> <u>Control</u> <u>Tape</u>

Δx to ctr. 1; ctr. 1 = $x_{n-1} + \Delta x = x_n$		1	741	1	7
x_n to print ctr. I		2	1	7432	
print with argument control		3	87	752	76
	Rerun line I	4	4321	4321	7
$f_{n+2} + \bar{x}_{n+2}$ to ctr. 15 from card feed I		5		4321	7632
f_{n+1} to MC	Rerun line II	6	53	761	7
		7	32	32	7
$-f_{n-1}$ to ctr. 6		8	5	32	32
5 to MP		9	7541		7
$8f_n$ to ctr. 6		10	521	32	7
		11	432	432	7
		12	321	321	7
		13	3	3	
$5f_{n+1}$ to ctr. 4		14		3	
x_n to print ctr. II		15	1	74321	

	Line	OUT	IN	MISC.
print with argument control	16	87	7521	7
f_{n+1} to MC	17	53	761	7
$5f_{n+1}$ to ctr. 6	18	3	32	7
$5f_n$ to ctr. 7	19	52	321	
8 to MP	20	7542		7321
$f_{n+2} + \bar{x}_{n+2}$ to SIO ctr.	21	4321	874	7
	22	21	21	7
f_{n+2} to ctr. 3	23	874	21	7
	24	31	31	
$8f_{n+1}$ to ctr. 5	25		31	7
- 1 in 1st machine column to ctr. 14	26	743	432	732
$(-f_{n-1} + 8f_n + 5f_{n+1})$ to MC	27	32	761	7
$8f_{n+1}$ to ctr. 7	28	31	321	7
$-f_{n+2}$ to ctr. 7	29	21	321	32
$\Delta x/12$ to MP	30	75421		7
- 1 in 1st machine column to ctr. 14	31	743	432	732
$\bar{x}_{n+2}$ to ctr. 14	32	84	432	7
Δx to ctr. 64; ctr. 64 $= \underline{x}_{n-1} + \Delta x = \underline{x}_n$	33	742	7	7
$-\underline{x}_n$ to ctr. 14	34	7	432	732
zero check tolerance to check ctr. 72	35	743	74	7
	36	421	421	7
$I(x_{n-1})$ to ctr. 11	37	531	421	7
	38	4	4	
$\Delta I(x_n)$ to ctr. 8	39		4	7
$\Delta I(x_n)$ to ctr. 11; ctr. 11 $= I(x_n)$	40	4	421	7
$I(x_n)$ to print ctr. I	41	421	7432	
	42		752	76

	Line	OUT	IN	MISC.
$(5f_n + 8f_{n+1} - f_{n+2})$ to MC	43	321	761	7
	44	41	41	7
	45	43	43	
$\Delta x/12$ to MP	46	75421		7
$I(x_{n-1})$ to ctr. 12	47	531	43	7
	48	431	431	7
$I(x_n)$ to ctr. 13	49	421	431	7
	50	42	42	7
$\Delta I(x_n)$ to ctr. 10	51	4	42	7
$-\left\lvert \bar{x}_{n+2} - \underline{x}_n - 1 - 1 \right\rvert$ to check ctr. 72	52	432	74	71
check	53	74	74	64
	54		41	
$\overline{\Delta I}$ to ctr. 9	55		41	7
$-\overline{\Delta I}$ to ctr. 10	56	41	42	32
$\Delta I - \overline{\Delta I}$ to print ctr. I	57	42	7432	
print	58		752	7
tolerance on ΔI to check ctr. 72	59	7543	74	7
$-\left\lvert \Delta I - \overline{\Delta I} \right\rvert$ to check ctr. 72	60	42	74	71
check	61	74	74	64
$\overline{\Delta I}$ to ctr. 12; ctr. 12 $= \overline{I(x_n)}$	62	41	43	7
	63	2	2	7
$I(x_n)$ to ctr. 2	64	421	2	7
$-\overline{I(x_n)}$ to ctr. 2	65	43	2	732
tolerance on ΔI to check ctr. 72	66	7543	74	7
$-\left\lvert I(x_n) - \overline{I(x_n)} \right\rvert$ to check ctr. 72	67	2	74	71
check	68	74	74	64
	69	5	5	7

	Line	OUT	IN	MISC.
f_n to ctr. 16	70	51	5	7
	71	51	51	7
f_{n+1} to ctr. 17	72	53	51	7
	73	52	52	7
$5f_{n+1}$ to ctr. 18	74	3	52	7
	75	521	521	7
$8f_{n+1}$ to ctr. 19	76	31	521	7
	77	53	53	7
f_{n+2} to ctr. 20	78	21	53	7
	79	531	531	7
$I(x_n)$ to ctr. 21	80	421	531	7
reset print ctr. II	81	8421		7
$I(x_n)$ to print ctr. II	82	421	74321	
half-correction to print ctr. II	83	75431	74321	
	84	2	2	7
$I(x_n)$ + half-correction to ctr. 2	85	8621	2	7
- half-correction to ctr. 2	86	75431	2	732
- $I(x_n)$ to ctr. 2	87	421	2	732
zero check tolerance to check ctr. 72	88	743	74	7
- $\lvert I(x_n)$ + half-correction - half-correction - $I(x_n) \rvert$ to check ctr. 72	89	2	74	71
check	90	74	74	64
print	91		7521	76
	92	21	21	7321
$I(x_n)$ to SIO ctr.	93	421	874	7
$\bar{x}_n$ to ctr. 3	94	7	21	7
$I(x_n)$ to ctr. 3	95	874	21	7
$I(x_n) + \bar{x}_n$ to punch ctr.	96	21	753	

	Line	OUT	IN	MISC.
punch	97			5
1 in 1st machine column to ctr. 71	98	743	7321	7
tolerance for end of page stop to check ctr. 72	99	7421	74	7
- number of lines to check ctr. 72	100	7321	74	71
check	101	74	74	64
	102			7
	103			87

Operating Instructions

(1) Set switches as listed in the following table. The operating decimal point lies between columns 16 and 17. Punch the values set in the switches and compare the punched values with the list of switch settings.

Switch Settings

No.	Code	Setting and Purpose
1	741	$\Delta x = 1$ in 15th machine column; increment of argument for printing
2	742	$\Delta x = 1$ in 1st machine column; increment of argument for punch card serial numbers
3	7421	5 in 2nd machine column
4	743	1 in 1st machine column; zero check tolerance
9	751	x_{n-1} = argument for printing; decimal point between columns 16 and 17; used in starting tape only
11	7521	x_{n-1} = argument for punch card serial numbers; decimal point between columns 2 and 3; used in starting tape only
17	7541	5
18	7542	8
19	75421	0.0008 3333 3333 = $\Delta x/12$
20	7543	tolerance on check of ΔI; 1 in 7th machine column, 4 in 6th machine column
21	75431	5 in 8th machine column; half-correction

(2) The "85-1 P.U." switch and the "SIO-OUT-2 Invert Control" switch must be in the off position before running any part of this computation, (see page 139).

(3) The values punched under control of the main tape are the values of $I(x_n)$. Each card is identified by a serial number, x_n, punched with decimal point between card columns 22 and 23. All cards punched are to be placed in the drawer provided for this purpose.

(4) Card feed I must contain the cards for f(x). When starting, the first card fed must contain the serial number 0499 in card columns 1-4. When rerunning for the argument, x_n, the first card fed must contain the serial number, x_{n-1}, in card columns 1-4. Three cards are fed under control of the starting tape, and one card during each revolution of the main tape. The card fed during the revolution of the control tape for x_n has the serial number x_{n+2}.

(5) Card feed II is used only when starting and rerunning. When starting the computation, card feed II must contain a starting card and a blank card. When rerunning for the argument, x_n, the card with serial number x_{n-1}, previously punched by the main control tape, followed by a blank card must be placed in card feed II. Care must be taken to replace this card properly after it is used.

(6) Run starting tape. When cards run out in card feed II, turn off card feed control switch and restart calculator. When the starting tape is completed correctly, the sequence mechanism will stop on a blank line of tape.

(7) The checks in the starting tape are listed in the following table.

Lines	Quantity Checked	Tolerance
14-16	serial number of 1st card from feed I	1 in 1st machine column from switch 4
26-28	serial number of 2nd card from feed I	1 in 1st machine column from switch 4
42-44	$5f_n$ computed by multiplication and by addition	1 in 1st machine column from switch 4
57-59	$8f_n$ computed by multiplication and by addition	1 in 1st machine column from switch 4
72-74	serial number of 3rd card from feed I	1 in 1st machine column from switch 4
83-85	serial number of card from feed II	1 in 1st machine column from switch 4
90-92	argument for printing	1 in 1st machine column from switch 4

(8) If the sequence mechanism stops on lines 17, 29, or 75 of the starting tape, the wrong cards have been fed from card feed I, and the starting tape should be rerun, with the cards corrected.

(9) If the sequence mechanism stops on line 86 of the starting tape, the wrong card has been fed from card feed II, and the starting tape should be rerun, with the cards corrected.

(10) If the sequence mechanism stops on line 45 or 60 of the starting tape, the failure is probably in the multiply unit or in counter 5. The starting tape must be rerun with the cards replaced in both feeds.

(11) If the sequence mechanism stops on the check on line 93 of the starting tape (blank, blank, 7), switches 9 and 11 and counters 1, 2, 64 and SIO should be tested since this check compares the argument for printing with the argument for the punch card serial numbers.

(12) Run main control tape until the "end of page stop" check stops the machine after 50 lines have been printed. Reset counter 71, start new page on typewriter II and space up typewriter I. If no failures occur, continue running until cards run out in card feed I, turn off card feed control switch, restart calculator and press stop key.

(13) The checks in the main control tape are listed in the following table.

Lines	Quantity Checked	Tolerance
35, 52-53	serial number of card feed I	1 in 1st machine column from switch 4
59-61	ΔI computed two ways	1 in 7th machine column, 4 in 6th machine column from switch 20
66-68	accumulation of I(x)	1 in 7th machine column, 4 in 6th machine column from switch 20
88-90	print counter II read-out and half-correction	1 in 1st machine column from switch 4

(14) If the sequence mechanism stops on line 54 of the main control tape, while computing for the argument, x_n, the wrong card has been fed from card feed I. The cards in card feed I must be checked and replaced, the card with serial number x_{n+2} being the first card fed. The main control tape must be rolled back to line 4, marked "Rerun line I", and the computation repeated. Typewriter I must be spaced up, and its vertical spacing checked as the computation proceeds.

(15) If the sequence mechanism stops on line 62 of the main control tape, the tape must be rolled back to line 6, marked "Rerun line II", and the computation repeated. Typewriter I must be spaced up, and its vertical spacing checked as the computation proceeds. Typewriter II must be turned off and kept off until after that line in the tape (line 30) at which the argument has finished printing. It must then be turned on in order to print the correct value of the function.

(16) If the sequence mechanism stops on line 69 of the main control tape, the addition of ΔI to I has failed, and the counters involved should be tested. If the quantities in the counters are not disturbed, the tape may be rolled back and rerun as in instruction (15).

(17) If the sequence mechanism stops on line 91 of the main control tape, either the print counter read-out or the half-correction has failed, and the counters involved should be tested. If the quantities in the counters are not disturbed, the tape may be rolled back and rerun as in instruction (15).

(18) If counters are disturbed in testing and it is necessary to re-establish the computation for the argument, x_n, the following procedure must be carried out:

(a) switches 9 and 11 must be set to x_{n-1} as indicated in the switch list on page 326;
(b) card feed I must contain the cards for f(x), the first card containing the serial number x_{n-1};
(c) card feed II must contain the card with serial number x_{n-1}, from among those previously punched by the main control tape, followed by a blank card; care must be taken to replace the functional card properly after it is used;
(d) run the starting tape; when the cards run out in card feed II turn off card feed control switch and restart calculator;

(e) run the main control tape starting on the "start line", and continue the computation;
(f) typewriter I must be spaced up and its spacing checked as the computation is continued;
(g) typewriter II must be turned off and kept off until just before the correct function is printed.

(19) The maximum time for one revolution of the main control tape may be computed as follows:

3 prints on typewriter I	48
2 prints on typewriter II	28
cycles not covered by printing	13
	88 cycles = 26.4 seconds.

Plugging Instructions

(1) The multiply unit must be plugged for operating decimal point between columns 16 and 17, with the plugging to the four lowest columns of the buss omitted as shown in the following diagram.

MP-DIV PLUGBOARD

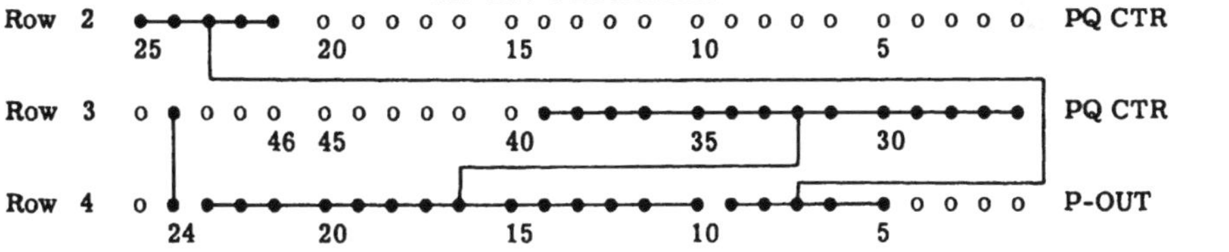

(2) The LIO counter must be plugged to read columns 1-4 of LIO to columns 15-18 of the buss as shown in the following diagram.

FUNCTIONAL PLUGBOARD

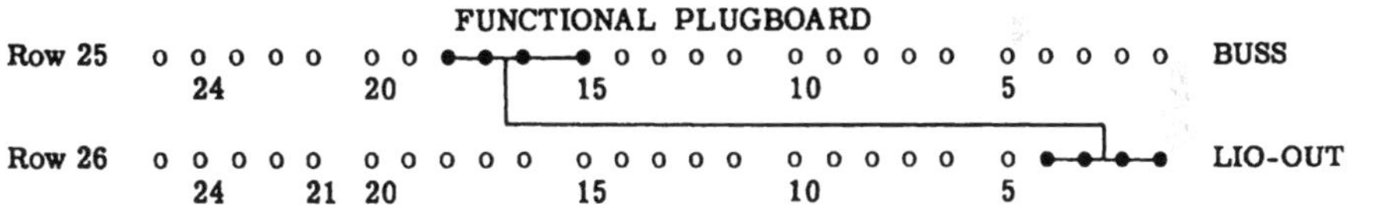

(3) The SIO counter must be plugged so that:

(a) SIO-OUT I reads columns 5-24 of SIO to columns 5-24 of the buss;
(b) SIO-OUT II reads columns 1-4 of SIO to columns 1-4 of the buss;

as shown in the following diagram.

FUNCTIONAL PLUGBOARD

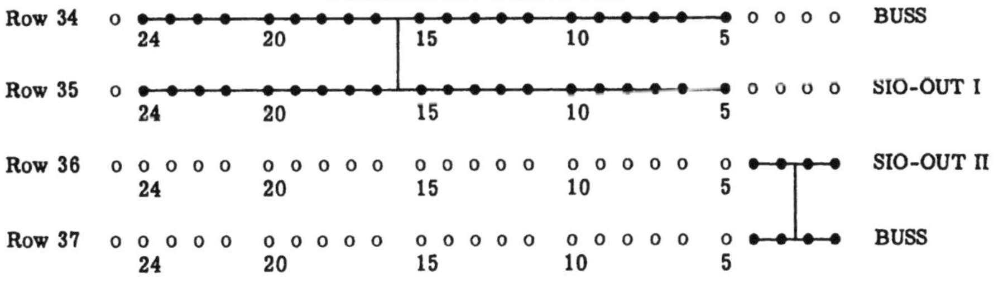

SOLUTION OF EXAMPLES

(4) The card feeds must be plugged direct (see page 272).

(5) The card punch must be plugged as shown in the following diagram.

PUNCH MAGNETS

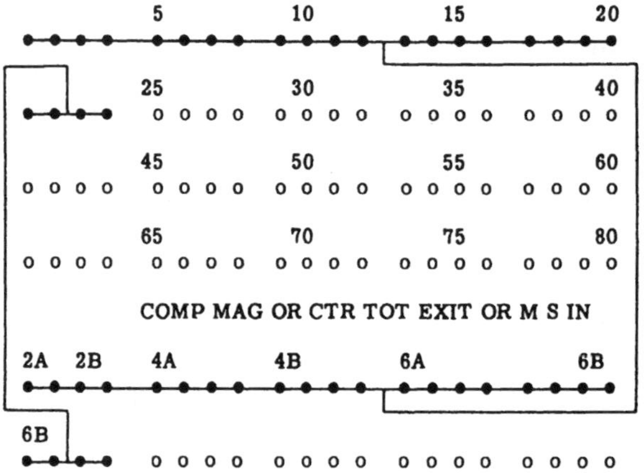

(6) Typewriter I must be plugged for positive or negative quantities, decimal point between columns 16 and 17, twelve digits to the right of the decimal point. The digits are to be grouped by fours to the right and left of the decimal point, argument control after two decimal places. Line step counter 1 is to be plugged for vertical groups of five lines. Typewriter II is to be plugged for positive or negative quantities, decimal point between columns 16 and 17, eight digits to the right of the decimal point. The digits are to be grouped by fours to the right and left of the decimal point, argument control after two decimal places. Line step counter 2 is to be plugged for vertical groups of five lines. The plugging for the typewriters is shown in the following diagram.

FUNCTIONAL PLUGBOARD

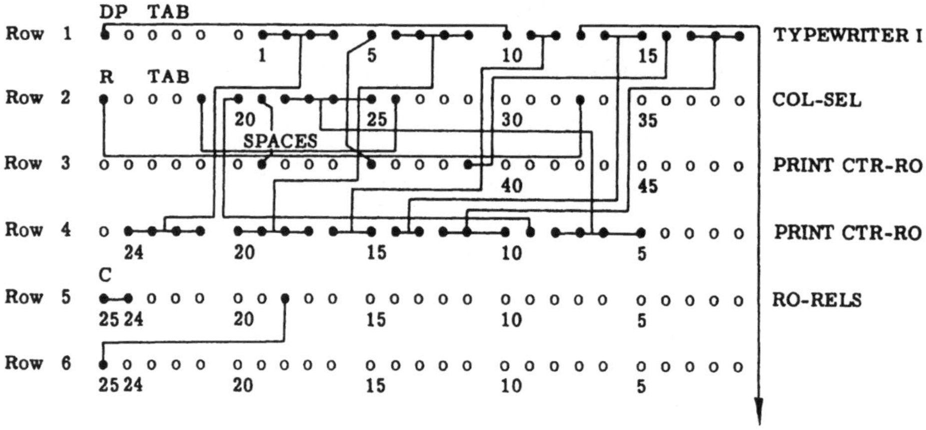

FUNCTIONAL PLUGBOARD

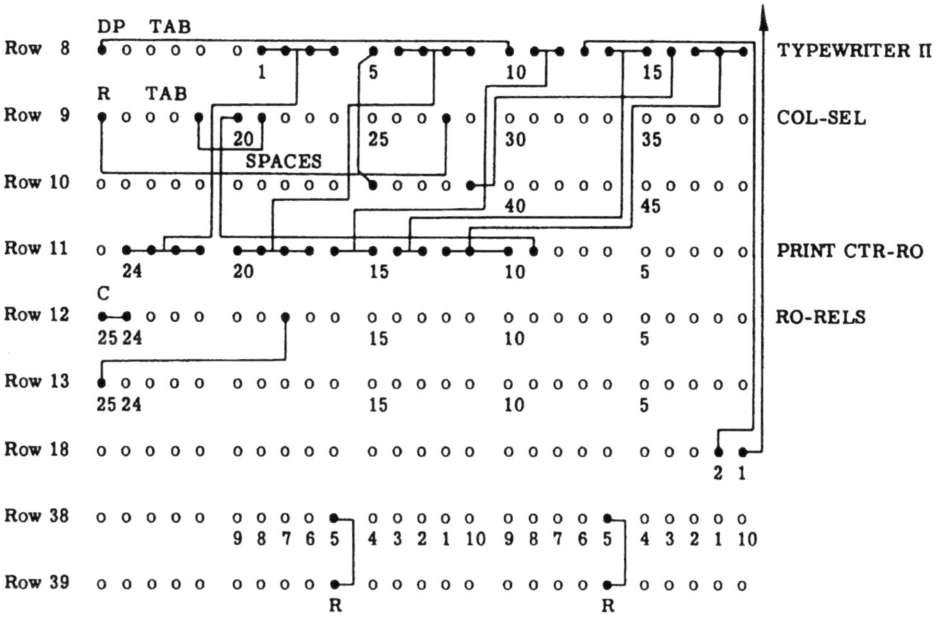

Example 8. It is to be noted that the starting and main control tapes of example 7 dictated only the sequence of operations to be performed. The actual numbers dealt with; i.e., arguments, functions, coefficients, tolerances, etc., were delivered to the machine from switches and punch cards. In some cases, these quantities were rearranged by plugging through which they passed on their way to and from the functional components of the calculator. Obviously, then, the tapes themselves are applicable to a whole class of problems of which example 7 is merely a special case. The reader is advised to arbitrarily formulate several problems similar to example 7 involving other integrands, and to devise the instructions necessary to the solution of the chosen problems on the calculator.

Example 9. It is required that a single main control tape be designed to tabulate the integral,

$$I(x) = \int_5^x f(x)dx,$$

as defined in example 7, where f(x) is the function defined in example 6. This requires the combination of the control tapes designed for examples 3, 4, 5 and 7. The interweaving of the coding of the tapes is left as an exercise for the reader. This computation as performed by a single control tape should not require more than 110 seconds per tabulated value of the integral.

Example 10. It is required that the series,

$$f(z) = a_0 + a_1 z + a_2 z^2 + a_3 z^3 + \dots + a_n z^n + R, \tag{1}$$

be evaluated in the complex plane. The real coefficients $a_0, a_1, a_2, a_3, \dots, a_n$ will be supplied from a value tape on interpolator I. The complex quantities will be stored with the real and imaginary parts in adjacent counters. Multiplication of a complex quantity by a real number requires two ordinary multiplications. The determination of an even power of a complex quantity requires three ordinary multiplications, while the determination of an odd power requires four. The following coding is designed to evaluate the first four terms of the series (1) for any point in the complex plane. The coding has been planned, however, as though the series had many terms and required the conservation of storage registers. The extension of the coding to care for terms involving powers of z greater than the third is left to the reader as an exercise. The coding given in this example represents a simplified version of the control tapes used to compute the modified Hankel functions of order one-third[1].

	Line	OUT	IN	MISC.
x or Δx from sw. 1 to ctr. 1	1	741	1	7
compute z^2	2	1	761	7
y or Δy from sw. 2 to ctr. 2	3	742	2	7
	4	21	21	
	5	2		7
	6	41	41	7
a_0 to ctr. 9 from interpolator I	7	85		753
	8		41	
	9		21	7
	10	1	761	7
	11	3	3	7

	Line	OUT	IN	MISC.
	12	4	4	
	13	1		7
a_1 to ctr. 8 from interpolator I	14	85		753
	15		4	7
	16	31	31	
	17		3	7
	18	2	761	732
	19	21	31	7
	20	21	31	
	21	2		7
	22	32	32	7
	23	321	321	7
	24	42	42	
	25		3	7
compute a_1z	26	4	761	
	27	1		
	28		41	7
	29	4	761	
	30	2		
	31		42	7
compute z^3	32	3	761	7
	33	21	21	7
	34	4	4	
	35	1		7
a_2 to ctr. 8 from interpolator I	36	85		753
	37		4	
	38		32	7

	Line	OUT	IN	MISC.
	39	31	761	32
	40	2		
	41		32	7
	42	3	761	
	43	2		
	44		321	7
	45	31	761	
	46	1		
	47		321	7
compute a_2z^2	48	4	761	
	49	3		
	50		41	7
	51	4	761	7
	52	4	4	
	53	31		7
a_3 to ctr. 8 from interpolator I	54	85		753
	55		4	
	56		42	7
compute a_3z^3	57	4	761	
	58	32		
	59		41	7
	60	4	761	7
	61	4	4	
	62	321		7
a_4 to ctr. 8 from interpolator I	63	85		753
	64		4	
	65		42	7

SOLUTION OF EXAMPLES

Example 11. It is suggested that the reader code the control tapes necessary for the computation and checking of a functional tape for $f(x) = \arcsin x$, $0 \le x \le 0.9$. The error in the interpolated values of $f(x)$ should be less than 6×10^{-11}. The following control tapes should be coded:

(a) starting and main control tapes to compute the interpolational coefficients;

(b) control tape to position the functional tape to the successive arguments and print the coefficients;

(c) control tape to interpolate on assigned values of the argument.

The control tape to compute the interpolational coefficients should use an iterative process for the computation of $(1 - x^2)^{-1/2}$. The iterative formulae and their codings are given on pages 176-179 and in example 4, pages 304-312. The number of interpolational coefficients required is discussed on pages 198-199. The coding of the control tapes necessary to check the functional tape is presented on pages 199-201.

Example 12. The Bessel function, J_0, has been computed for an increment of the argument equal to 0.01, and punched in tabulating machine cards. It is suggested that the reader code the control tapes necessary to subtabulate the function to tenths; i.e., for increment of the argument equal to 0.001. The tape must, of course, completely check the computation and verify the printed results. Such a tape, using the method described on pages 224-226, has been preserved in the tape library after being used to subtabulate the Bessel functions[2].

Example 13. It is suggested that the reader design a control tape for the solution of the system of linear algebraic equations,

$$a_{1,1}x_1 + a_{1,2}x_2 + \dots + a_{1,10}x_{10} = k_1$$
$$a_{2,1}x_1 + a_{2,2}x_2 + \dots + a_{2,10}x_{10} = k_2$$
$$\dots \quad \dots \quad \dots$$
$$a_{10,1}x_1 + a_{10,2}x_2 + \dots + a_{10,10}x_{10} = k_{10},$$

by the process of successive elimination. The elements of the given matrix must be manually punched in tabulating machine cards and stacked in two decks, one for the $a_{i,j}$, in the order $a_{1,1}, \dots, a_{1,10}, a_{2,1}, \dots, a_{2,10}, \dots, a_{10,1}, \dots, a_{10,10}$, and the other for the k_i, in the order $k_1, k_2, \dots, k_{10}$.

Assume the card decks containing the $a_{i,j}$ and the k_i to be placed in card feeds I and II respectively. A main control tape may then dictate the following operations:

(1) feed 10 cards from card feed I to any 10 storage counters;

(2) feed 1 card from card feed II to any other storage counter;

(3) take the reciprocal $a_{1,1}$;

(4) multiply $a_{1,2}, a_{1,3}, \ldots, a_{1,10}$ and k_1 by $1/a_{1,1}$;

(5) feed 10 cards from card feed I to any 10 storage counters not already in use;

(6) feed 1 card from card feed II to any storage counter not already in use;

(7) using the quantities read into storage counters in (5) and (6), repeat operations (3) and (4) for $a_{2,1}, a_{2,2}, \ldots, a_{2,10}$ and k_2;

(8) make the necessary subtractions;

(9) repeat these operations until the given system is reduced to the form

$$x_1 + b_{1,2}x_2 + b_{1,3}x_3 + \ldots + b_{1,10}x_{10} = h_1$$
$$x_2 + b_{2,3}x_3 + \ldots + b_{2,10}x_{10} = h_2$$
$$\ldots \ldots \ldots$$
$$x_{10} = h_{10}$$

where the $b_{i,j}$ and the h_i stand in 55 selected storage counters;

(10) the values of the x_j may then be obtained by substitution and printed or punched in tabulating machine cards for further computation.

For efficient operation, full advantage must be taken of the methods of interposition, and all operations must be checked. The computation and comparison of $\Sigma\, a_{i,j}/a_{i,1}$ and $(\Sigma\, a_{i,j})/a_{i,1}$ is one form of check procedure.

The required control tape includes 4964 lines of coding, produces and completely checks the values of x_j in approximately 55 minutes. The tape is one of the standard tapes preserved in the tape library.

Nearly two years have passed since the staff of the Computation Laboratory of Harvard University began operation with the Automatic Sequence Controlled Calculator as a project of the United States Navy. During this time, a great variety of problems has been solved finding application in nearly every branch of physics and engineering. The problems solved include:

(1) the tabulation of functions of a real variable defined by given equations;

(2) the subtabulation of empirical functions;

(3) the computation and tabulation of quantities defined by elaborate formulae and in terms of empirical variables;

(4) the tabulation of functions in the complex domain;

(5) the solution of systems of linear algebraic equations;

(6) statistical analysis;

(7) the determination of the zeros of functions;

(8) the evaluation of definite integrals;

(9) the solution of systems of ordinary differential equations;

(10) the solution of partial differential equations.

As previously mentioned, the examples given in this chapter have been chosen for their mathematical simplicity. However, the solutions of the problems listed in the foregoing tabulation have all been obtained by means of extensions of the techniques illustrated in the examples.

From time to time, the solution of these problems has required permanent changes in the wiring of the calculator, and the inclusion of new features, many of which have greatly improved its operation. Such improvements and alterations are still in progress of development. As a result, this book goes to press representing the standard procedure of the Computation Laboratory as of August 1945.

References

1. Annals of the Computation Laboratory of Harvard University, Volume II, Tables of the Modified Hankel Functions of Order One-Third and of Their Derivatives, Harvard University Press, Cambridge, Mass., 1945, xxxvi + 235 p.

2. Annals of the Computation Laboratory of Harvard University, Volume III, Bessel Functions of Orders Zero and One, to be published by the Harvard University Press in 1946.

   Annals of the Computation Laboratory of Harvard University, Volume IV, Bessel Functions of Orders Two and Three, to be published by the Harvard University Press in 1946.

BIBLIOGRAPHY
OF
NUMERICAL ANALYSIS

In practice, a computational problem is composed of three parts: the theoretical mathematical analysis; the construction of a numerical computational schedule suitable for the particular calculating machines to be used; the actual carrying out of the machine computation. In connection with the first two parts, it is necessary to consult widely scattered mathematical literature in an effort to find adequate methods to treat new types of problems of applied mathematics. These methods have to be further adapted to take full advantage of large scale calculating machinery.

In the preparation of this bibliography, full use has been made of available published bibliographies, particularly those contained in the report on numerical methods by H. Bateman, W. E. Milne and A. A. Bennett (see Ordinary Differential Equations). The bibliography is not intended to be exhaustive. It is composed principally of the references that have been found useful during the one and one-half years of operation of the Automatic Sequence Controlled Calculator.

In the bibliography, certain subjects that logically fall within the general field of numerical analysis have been omitted, for example, no mention is made of statistics. Such references as have been included, however, have been classified for ready reference. Some of the titles could be listed under several headings, and have been in the more important cases.

1. Historical Background of Automatic Calculating Machinery
2. Machine Methods in Arithmetic
3. General Numerical Methods
4. Linear Algebraic Equations, Determinants and Matrices
5. Least Squares Methods
6. Square Roots and Higher Roots of Numbers
7. The Location and Separation of the Zeros of a Polynomial
8. The Calculation of the Zeros of a Polynomial
    - A. Iterative Methods (Newton-Raphson, False Position, etc.)
    - B. Root-Squaring and Allied Methods
    - C. Miscellaneous Methods
9. The Zeros of Transcendental Equations
    - A. Iterative Methods (see also under 8A)
    - B. Miscellaneous Methods

1. HISTORICAL BACKGROUND OF AUTOMATIC CALCULATING MACHINERY

BABBAGE, C. On the Economy of Machinery and Manufactures. London, 1846.

BABBAGE, C. Passages from the Life of a Philosopher. London, 1864.

BAXANDALL, D. Catalogue of the Collections in the Science Museum, South Kensington. Mathematics I, Calculating Machines and Instruments. London, 1926.

CAJORI, F. A History of Mathematics. New York, 2nd ed. 1919.

CAJORI, F. History of the Logarithmic Slide Rule. New York, 1909.

CAJORI, F. William Oughtred. Chicago, 1916.

DYCK, W. Katalog mathematischer und mathematisch-physikalischer Modelle, Apparate und Instrumente. Munich, 1892.

GALLE, A. Mathematische Instrumente. Leipzig, 1912.

HORSBURGH, E. M. Calculating machines. A Dictionary of Applied Physics. Richard Glazebrook ed. London, 1923, vol. 3, p. 193-201.

HORSBURGH, E. M. Modern Instruments and Methods of Calculation. London, 1914.

JACOB, L. Le calcul mécanique. Paris, 1911.

D'OCAGNE, M. Le calcul simplifié. Paris,1905.

D'OCAGNE, M. Vue d'ensemble sur les machines à calculer. Paris, 1922.

POSSELT, E. A. The Jacquard Machine. Philadelphia, 189-?.

TURCK, J. A. V. Origin of Modern Calculating Machines. Chicago, 1921.

2. MACHINE METHODS IN ARITHMETIC

COMRIE, L. J. Mechanical computing. Appendix I, p. 462-473 of David Clark, Plane and Geodetic Surveying, vol. 2, 3rd ed., revised by James Glendenning. London, Constable, 1943.

COMRIE, L. J. Recent progress in scientific computing. Jour. Sci. Instr. 21, 129-135 (1944).

HARTKEMEIER, H. P. and MILLER, H. E. Obtaining differences from punched cards. Jour. Amer. Statist. Assoc. 37, 285-287 (1942).

KNUDSEN, L. F. A punched card technique to obtain coefficients of orthogonal polynomials. Jour. Amer. Statist. Assoc. 37, 496-506 (1942).

LANCASTER, O. E. Machine method for the extraction of cube root. Jour. Amer. Statist. Assoc. 37, 112-115 (1942).

McPHERSON, J. C. On mechanical tabulation of polynomials. Ann. Math. Statist. 12, 317-327 (1941).

McPHERSON, J. C. Mathematical operations with punched cards. Jour. Amer. Statist. Assoc. 37, 275-281 (1942).

SANDOMIRE, M. M. Accumulating cubes with punch cards. Jour. Amer. Statist. Assoc. 36, 507-514 (1941).

3. GENERAL NUMERICAL METHODS

BIERMANN, O. Vorlesungen über mathematischen Näherungsmethoden. Braunschweig, Vieweg, 1905, 226 p.

BRUNS, H. Grundlinien des wissenschaftlichen Rechnens. Leipzig, Teubner, 1903, 159 p.

CASSINIS, G. Calcoli numerici, grafici e meccanici. Pisa, Mariotti-Pacini, 1928, xix + 672 p.

CASSINA, U. Calcolo numerico con numerosi esempi e note storiche originali. Bologna, Zanichelli, 1928, xix + 453 p.

COURANT, R. Differential and Integral Calculus. (New revised edition) New York, Nordemann, 1940, vol. 1, chap. 7, p. 342-364.

HAYASHI, K. Tafeln für die Differenzenrechnung... Berlin, Springer, 1933, vi + 66 p.

LEHMER, D. H. On the value of the Napierian Base. Amer. Jour. Math. 48, 139-143 (1926).

LEHMER, D. N., BALLANTINE, J. P. and THOMPSON, D'A. W. On the multiplication of long decimals. Amer. Math. Month. 30, 67-69 (1923).

LINDOW, M. Numerische Infinitesimalrechnung. Berlin and Bonn, Dümmler, 1928, viii + 176 p.

LÜROTH, J. Vorlesungen uber numerisches Rechnen. Leipzig, Teubner, 1900, vi + 194 p.

MACCAFERRI, E. Calcolo numerico approssimato. Milan, Hoepli, 1919, 200 p.

MADER, K. Numerisches Rechnen. Handbuch der Physik, vol. 3. Berlin, Springer, 1928, p. 599-635.

BIBLIOGRAPHY

MAYER, J. E. Das Rechnen in der Technik und seine Hilfsmittel. Vol. 405 of Sammlung Göschen. Leipzig, Göschen, 1st ed. 1908; 2nd ed. 1913, 128 p.

MILNE-THOMPSON, L. M. Calculus of Finite Differences. London, Macmillan, 1933, xxiii + 558 p.

PESCI, G. ...Numeri decimali approssimati... Period. Mat.: (3) 1, 249-268; (3) 2, 1-21, 49-71 (1904).

RADAU, R. Étude sur les formules d'interpolation. Paris, Gauthier-Villars, 1891, 96 p.

RICE, H. L. Theory and Practice of Interpolation. Lynn, Nichols, 1899, 234 p.

RUNGE, C. and KÖNIG, H. Vorlesungen über Numerisches Rechnen. Berlin, Springer, 1924, viii + 371 p.

VON SANDEN, H. Praktische Analysis. Leipzig, Teubner, 2nd ed. 1923, xvi + 195 p.

VON SANDEN, H. Mathematisches Praktikum. I. Leipzig, Teubner, 1927, v + 122 p.

SCARBOROUGH, J. B. Numerical Mathematical Analysis. Baltimore, Johns Hopkins Press, 1930, xiv + 416 p.

SCHRUTKA, L. Zahlenrechnen. Leipzig, Teubner, 1923, 146 p.

SHEPPARD, W. F. Mensuration. Encyclopaedia Britannica. 14th ed. 1929, vol. 15, p. 253-257.

STEFFENSEN, J. F. Interpolation. Baltimore, Williams and Wilkins, 1927, ix + 248 p.

THIELE, T. N. Interpolationsrechnung. Leipzig, Teubner, 1909, 175 p.

UHLER, H. S. Multiplication of large numbers. Amer. Math. Month. 28, 447-448 (1921).

VAHLEN, T. Konstruktionen und Approximationen. Leipzig, Teubner, 1911, xii + 349 p.

WHITTAKER, E. T. and ROBINSON, G. The Calculus of Observations. A Treatise on Numerical Mathematics. London and Glasgow, Blackie, 3rd ed. 1940, xvi + 395 p.

WILLERS, F. A. Methoden der Praktischen Analysis. Berlin, de Gruyter, 1928, 344 p.

WORTHING, A. G. and GEFFNER, J. Treatment of Experimental Data. New York, Wiley, 1943, ix + 342 p.

XAVIER, A. Théorie des approximations numériques et du calcul abrégé. Paris, Gauthier-Villars, 1909.

ZORETTI, L. Exercices numériques et graphiques de mathématiques sur les leçons de mathématiques générales. Paris, Gauthier-Villars, 1914, xv + 124 p.

4. LINEAR ALGEBRAIC EQUATIONS, DETERMINANTS AND MATRICES.

AITKEN, A. C. Studies in practical mathematics. II. The evaluation of the latent roots and latent vectors of a matrix. Proc. Roy. Soc. Edin., Sect. A, 57, 269-304 (1936-1937).

BELLMAN, R. A note on determinants and Hadamard's inequality. Amer. Math. Month. 50, 550-551 (1943).

BINGHAM, M. D. A new method for obtaining the inverse matrix. Jour. Amer. Statist. Assoc. 36, 530-534 (1941).

BISSHOPP, K. E. The inverse of a stiffness matrix. Quart. Appl. Math. 3, 82-84 (1945).

BRAND, L. The method of moment distribution for the analysis of continuous structures. Bull. Amer. Math. Soc. 41, 901-906 (1935).

CHIÒ, F. Mémoire sur les fonctions connues sous le nom de résultantes ou de déterminants. Turin, 1853.

BIBLIOGRAPHY

COLLAR, A. R. On the reciprocation of certain matrices. Proc. Roy. Soc. Edin. 59, 195-206 (1939).

COLLATZ, L. Fehlerabschätzung für das Iterationsverfahren zur Auflösung linearer Gleichungssysteme. Zeit. Angew. Math. Mech. 22, 357-361 (1942).

COURANT, R. and HILBERT, D. Methoden der Mathematischen Physik. Vol. I. Berlin, Springer, 2nd ed. 1931, xiv + 469 p., chap. I.

CROSS, H. Analysis of continuous frames by distributing fixed-end moments. Paper No. 1793. Trans. Amer. Soc. Civil Engrs. 96, 1-10 (1932).

DRESDEN, A. On the iteration of linear homogeneous transformations. Bull. Amer. Math. Soc. 48, 577-579, 949 (1942).

DWYER, P. S. The evaluation of multiple and partial correlation coefficients from the factorial matrix. Psychometrika 5, 211-232 (1940).

DWYER, P. S. The solution of simultaneous equations. Psychometrika 6, 101-129 (1941).

DWYER, P. S. The evaluation of determinants. Psychometrika 6, 191-204 (1941).

DWYER, P. S. The evaluation of linear forms. Psychometrika 6, 355-365 (1941).

DWYER, P. S. The Doolittle technique. Ann. Math. Statist. 12, 449-458 (1941).

ERIKSSON, H. A. S. A technique for the approximate calculation of eigenvalues as zeros of a determinant. Application to the Li^+ -ion in the ground state. Arkiv för Mat. 30B, No. 6, 8 p. (1944).

ETHERINGTON, I. M. H. On errors in determinants. Proc. Edin. Math. Soc. (2) 3, 107-117 (1932).

FARNELL, A. B. Limits for the characteristic roots of a matrix. Bull. Amer. Math. Soc. 50, 789-794 (1944).

FRAZER, R. A., DUNCAN, W. J. and COLLAR, A. R. Elementary Matrices and some Applications to Dynamics and Differential Equations. Cambridge, Cambridge Univ. Press, 1938, p. 96-133.

FREEMAN, G. F. On the iterative solution of linear simultaneous equations. Phil. Mag. (7) 34, 409-416 (1943).

HADAMARD, J. Résolution d'une question relative aux déterminants. Bull. Sci. Math. (2) 17, 240-246 (1893).

HOEL, P. G. The errors involved in evaluating correlation determinants. Ann. Math. Statist. 11, 58-65 (1940).

HOEL, P. G. On methods of solving normal equations. Ann. Math. Statist. 12, 354-359 (1941).

HOPSTEIN, N. M. Solution of homogeneous linear equations by the iteration method. C. R. (Doklady) Acad. Sci. URSS (N.S.) 43, 372-375 (1944).

HORST, P. A non-graphical method for transforming an arbitrary factor matrix into a simple structure factor matrix. Psychometrika 6, 79-99 (1941).

HOTELLING, H. Simplified calculation of principal components. Psychometrika 1, 27-35 (1936).

HOTELLING, H. Some new methods in matrix calculation. Ann. Math. Statist. 14, 1-34 (1943).

HOTELLING, H. Further points on matrix calculation and simultaneous equations. Ann. Math. Statist. 14, 440-441 (1943).

IVANOV, V. On the convergence of the process of iteration in the solution of a system of linear algebraic equations. (Russian. English summary.). Bull. Acad. Sci. URSS Sér. Math.(Izvestia Akad. Nauk SSSR) 1939, 477-483 (1939).

BIBLIOGRAPHY

LEVY, S. Buckling of rectangular plates with built-in edges. Jour. Appl. Mech. 9, A171-A174 (1942).

LONSETH, A. T. Systems of linear equations with coefficients subject to error. Ann. Math. Statist. 13, 332-337 (1942).

LONSETH, A. T. On relative errors in systems of linear equations. Ann. Math. Statist. 15, 323-325 (1944).

MEHMKE, R. Über das Seidel'sche Verfahren, um lineare Gleichungen bei einer sehr grossen Anzahl der Unbekannten durch successive Annäherung aufzulösen. Math. Samml. Mosk. 16, 4 p. (1892).

MEHMKE, R. and NEKRASSOFF, P. A. Auflösung eines linearen Systems von Gleichungen durch successive Annäherung. Math. Samml. Mosk. 16, 23 p. (1892).

MEINEKE, H. Näherungsformel für die Berechnung von Strecken. Zeit. Angew. Math. Mech. 20, 359 (1940).

MILNE-THOMPSON, L. M. Determinant expansions. Math. Gaz. 25, 130-135 (1941).

MORRIS, J. and HEAD, J. W. Lagrangian frequency equations. An "escalator" method for numerical solution. Aircraft Engrg. 14, 312-314, 316 (1942).

OLDENBURGER, R. Convergence of Hardy Cross's balancing process. Jour. Appl. Mech. 7, A166-A170(1940).

PARKER, W. V. Limits to the characteristic roots of a matrix. Duke Math. Jour. 10, 479-482 (1943).

PIPES, L. A. The solution of a.c. circuit problems. Jour. Appl. Phys. 12, 685-691 (1941).

REIERSØL, O. A method for recurrent computation of all the principal minors of a determinant, and its application in confluence analysis. Ann. Math. Statist. 11, 193-198 (1940).

RICE, L. H. Some determinant expansions. Amer. Jour. Math. 42, 237-242 (1920).

RUNGE, C. and KÖNIG, H. Vorlesungen über numerisches Rechnen. Berlin, Springer, 1924, p. 183-188.

SAIBEL, E. A modified treatment of the iterative method. Jour. Franklin Inst. 235, 163-166 (1943).

SAIBEL, E. A rapid method of inversion of certain types of matrices. Jour. Franklin Inst. 237, 197-201 (1944).

SAMUELSON, P. A. A method of determining explicitly the coefficients of the characteristic equation. Ann. Math. Statist. 13, 424-429 (1942).

SATTERTHWAITE, F. E. Error control in matrix calculation. Ann. Math. Statist. 15, 373-387 (1944).

SCHMIDT, R. J. On the numerical solution of linear simultaneous equations by an iterative method. Phil. Mag. (7) 32, 369-383 (1941).

SCHULZ, G. Über die Lösung von Gleichungssystemen durch Iteration. Zeit. Angew. Math. Mech. 22, 234-235 (1942).

SEIDEL, L. Ueber ein Verfahren, die Gleichungen, auf welche die Methode der kleinsten Quadrate führt, sowie lineare Gleichungen überhaupt, durch successive Annäherung aufzulösen. Abh. Akad. München 11 (III), 81-108 (1874).

SEMENDIAEV, K. A. The determination of latent roots and invariant manifolds of matrices by means of iterations. (Russian. English summary.). Appl. Math. Mech. (Akad. Nauk SSSR. Prikl. Mat. Mech.) 7, 193-222 (1943).

SOUTHWELL, R. V. Stress calculations in frame-works by the method of systematic relaxation of constraints, I, II; III. Proc. Roy. Soc. Lond.: A151, 56-95; A153, 41-76 (1935).

SPOERL, C. A. A fundamental proposition in the solution of simultaneous linear equations. Trans. Actuar. Soc. Amer. 44, 276-288 (1943).

SPOERL, C. A. On solving simultaneous linear equations. Trans. Actuar. Soc. Amer. 45, 18-32. 67-69 (1944).

SYNGE, J. L. A geometrical interpretation of the relaxation method. Quart. Appl. Math. 2, 87-89 (1944).

TUCKER, L. R. The determination of successive principal components without computation of tables of residual correlation coefficients. Psychometrika 9, 149-153 (1944).

TUCKERMAN, L. B. On the mathematically significant figures in the solution of simultaneous linear equations. Ann. Math. Statist. 12, 307-316 (1941).

TURÁN, P. On extremal problems concerning determinants. (Hungarian. English summary.). Math. Naturwiss.Anz. Ungar. Akad. Wiss. 59, 95-105 (1940).

TURTON, F. J. On the solution of the numerical simultaneous equations arising in the analysis of redundant structures. Jour. Roy. Aeronaut. Soc. 49, 104-111(1945).

ULLMAN, J. The probability of convergence of an iterative process of inverting a matrix. Ann. Math. Statist. 15, 205-213 (1944).

WAYLAND, H. Expansion of determinantal equations into polynomial form. Quart. Appl. Math. 2, 277-306 (1945).

WHITTAKER, E. T. and ROBINSON, G. The Calculus of Observations. Glasgow, Blackie, 3rd ed. 1942,p. 71-77.

WHITTAKER, E. T. and WATSON, G. N. A course of Modern Analysis. Cambridge, Cambridge Univ. Press, Amer. ed. 1944, p. 212-213.

WRIGHT, L. T., Jr. The solution of simultaneous linear equations by an approximation method. Cornell Univ. Engrg. Exper. Station. Bull. No. 31, 1943, 6 p.

5. LEAST SQUARES

BANACHIEWICZ, T. An outline of the Cracovian algorithm of the method of least squares. Astr. Jour. 50, 38-41 (1942).

BERJMAN, E. A solution of the problem of least squares adjustment by Gauss polynomials. (Spanish). An. Soc. Ci. Argentina: 132, 34-48, 104-117, 212-217 (1941); 133, 208-215, 442-445 (1942).

BIRGE, R. T. and SHEA, J. D. A rapid method for calculating the least squares solution of a polynomial of any degree. Univ. of Calif. Publs. Math. 2, No. 5, 1927, p. 67-118.

BLEICK, W. E. A least squares accumulation theorem. Ann. Math. Statist. 11, 225-226 (1940).

DAVIS, H. T. Polynomial approximation by the method of least squares. Ann. Math. Statist. 4, 154-196 (1933).

DAVIS, H. T. and LATSHAW, V. V. Formulas for the fitting of polynomials by the method of least squares. Ann. of Math. (2) 31, 52-78 (1930).

DWYER, P. S. A matrix presentation of least squares and correlation theory with matrix justification of improved methods of solution. Ann. Math. Statist. 15, 82-89 (1944).

IDELSON, N. On the computation of weights of the unknowns in the method of least squares. (Russian. English summary.). Astr. Jour. Soviet Union 20, 11-13 (1943).

JACKSON, D. The Theory of Approximation. New York, Amer. Math. Soc. Colloq. Publs. vol. XI (Amer. Math. Soc.) 1930, viii + 178 p.

BIBLIOGRAPHY

KERAWALA, S. M. A rapid method for calculating the least squares solution of a polynomial of degree not exceeding the fifth. Indian Jour. Phys. 15, 241-276 (1941).

LEVENBERG, K. A method for the solution of certain non-linear problems in least squares. Quart. Appl. Math. 2, 164-168 (1944).

NAIR, K. R. and SHRIVASTAVA, M. P. On a simple method of curve fitting. Sankhyā 6, 121-132 (1942).

PLARR, G. Note sur une propriété commune aux séries dont le terme général dépend des fonctions X_n de Legendre, ou des cosinus et sinus des multiples de la variable. C. R. Acad. Sci. Paris 44, 984-986 (1857).

RÉMÈS, E. J. Sur les approximations par les moyennes d'ordre 2k et celles d'après le principe des moindres carrés. (Russian. French summary.). Rec. Math. (Mat. Sbornik) N.S. 9 (51) 437-450 (1941).

STONER, P. M. Fitting the exponential function and the Gomperts function by the method of least squares. Jour. Amer. Statist. Assoc. 36, 515-518 (1941).

6. SQUARE ROOTS AND HIGHER ROOTS OF NUMBERS

BOORMAN, J. M. Evolution simplified: Square root found by addition instead of division. Math. Mag. (publ. Artemas Martin) 1, 112-115 (1882-1884).

DEDERICK, L. S. A modified method for cube roots and fifth roots. Amer. Math. Month. 33, 469-472 (1926).

VON FEHRENTHEIL und GRUPPENBERG, L. R. Vereinfachte Quadratwurzelziehung mit der Rechenmaschine. Zeit. Instrumentenkunde 62, 227-230 (1942).

HOFMANN, J. E. Über ein "neues" Verfahren zur Annäherung von Quadratwurzeln und seine geschichtliche Bedeutung. Deutsche Math. 6, 453-461 (1942).

HUSSAIN, S. T. A method of extracting the nth root of a positive number. Math. Student 11, 12-15, (1943).

LANCASTER, O. E. Machine method for the extraction of cube root. Jour. Amer. Statist. Assoc. 37, 112-115 (1942).

LEHMER, D. H. On the use of the calculating machine for cube and fifth roots. Amer. Math. Month. 32, 377-379 (1925).

LOREY, W. Über ein Eulersches Verfahren zur Wurzelberechnung. Monatsh. Math. Phys. 48, 190-197 (1939).

MARTIN, A. Computation of the cube root of 2. Mess. of Math. 7, 50-51 (1878).

MARTIN, A. Extraction of square roots by series. Math. Mag. 1, 164-165, 172 (1882-1884).

PUTNAM, K. S. First-prize solution to problem of the best formula for $\sqrt[3]{x}$. To illustrate by $\sqrt[3]{2}$ to 100 decimals. Math. Visitor 2 (#2), 31 (1883).

WARD, G. W. Successive approximations to $\sqrt[n]{a}$. Math. Gaz. 17, 52-53, 127 (1933).

7. THE LOCATION AND SEPARATION OF THE ZEROS OF A POLYNOMIAL

ANGHELUTZA, T. Sur une limite des modules des zéros des polynomes. Acad. Roum. Bull. Sect. Sci. 21, 211-213 (1939).

BIBLIOGRAPHY

APARO, E. Di alcune avvertenze sulla risoluzione numerica delle equazioni algebriche. Univ. Roma e Ist. Naz. Alta Mat. Rend. Mat. e Appl. (5) 4, 125-147 (1943).

BIEBERBACH, L. Vorlesungen über Algebra. Leipzig and Berlin, Teubner, 1928, p. 171, 186.

BIEBERBACH, L. Lehrbuch der Funktionentheorie. Leipzig and Berlin, Teubner, 1930, vol.I, p. 190-192.

BUDAN, D. Nouvelle méthode pour la résolution des équations numériques... Paris, 2nd ed. 1822.

BURNSIDE, W. S. and PANTON, A. W. Theory of Equations. Dublin, Hodges and Figges, 8th ed. 1918, vol. I, chap. 10, 11.

CARACCIOLO, M. S. Delle equazioni a radici opposte. Boll. Mat. (4) 1, 33-38 (1940).

CAUCHY, A. L. Analyse algébrique. Note III. See Oeuvres complètes d'Augustin Cauchy, (2) vol. 3. Paris, Gauthier-Villars, 1897, p. 378-425.

CAUCHY, A. L. Exercices de mathématiques. See Oeuvres, (2) vol. 9. Paris, 1891, p. 109-132, 151-156.

COHN, A. Über die Anzahl der Wurzeln einer algebraischen Gleichung in einem Kreise. Math. Zeit. 14, 110-148 (1922).

CONKWRIGHT, N. B. An elementary proof of the Budan-Fourier theorem. Amer. Math. Month. 50, 603-605 (1943).

COPSON, E. T. An Introduction to the Theory of Functions of a Complex Variable. Oxford, Oxford Press, 1935, p. 119-121.

CORLISS, J. J. Upper limits to the real roots of an algebraic equation. Amer. Math. Month. 46, 334-338 (1939).

DELANGE, H. Sur la convergence des series de polynomes de la forme $\Sigma\, a_n P_n(z)$ et sur certaines suites de polynomes. Ann. Ecole Norm. Sup. 56, 173-275 (1939).

FEJÉR, L. Über die Wurzel vom kleinsten absoluten Betrage einer algebraischen Gleichung. Math. Ann. 65, 413-423 (1907-1908).

FOURIER, J. B. J. Analyse des équations déterminées. Paris, Didot, 1830, xxiv + 258 p.

FRAZER, R. A., DUNCAN, W. J. and COLLAR, A. R. Elementary Matrices and Some Applications to Dynamics and Differential Equations. Cambridge, Cambridge Univ. Press, 1938, p. 151-155.

FRICKE, R. Lehrbuch der Algebra. Braunschweig, Vieweg, 1924, vol. I part 2, chap. 3.

GENOCCHI, A. Démonstration d'un théorème de M. Sylvester. Nouv. Ann. Math. (2) 6, 6-20 (1867).

HERGLOTZ, G. Über die Wurzelanzahl algebraischer Gleichungen innerhalb und auf dem Einheitskreis. Math. Zeit. 19, 26-34 (1923).

HURWITZ, A. Ueber die Bedingungen, unter welchen eine Gleichung nur Wurzeln mit negativen reellen Theilen besitzt. Math. Ann. 46, 273-284 (1895).

KHARADSE, A. Eine Anwendung des Graceschen Faltungssatzes. (Russian. German summary.). Mitt. Georg. Abt. Akad. Wiss. USSR 1, 175-180 (1940).

KNESER, H. Zur Stetigkeit der Wurzeln einer algebraischen Gleichung. Math. Zeit. 48, 101-104 (1942).

KÖNIG, J. Ein allgemeiner Ausdruck für die ihrem absoluten Betrage nach kleinste Wurzel der Gleichung n-ten Grades. Math. Ann. 9, 530-540 (1875-1876).

KRONECKER, L. Über Systeme von Functionen mehrer Variablen. Ges. Werke, vol. I. Leipzig, Teubner, 1895, p. 177-226.

KRONECKER, L. Über die verschiedenen Sturm'schen Reihen und ihre gegenseitigen Beziehungen. Ges. Werke, vol. I. Leipzig, Teubner, 1895, p. 305-348.

BIBLIOGRAPHY

KRONECKER, L. Sur le théorème de Sturm. Ges. Werke vol. I. Leipzig, Teubner, 1895, p. 229-234.

KRONECKER, L. Über die Charakteristik von Functionen-Systemen. Ges. Werke vol. II. Leipzig, Teubner, 1897, p. 71-82.

LAGRANGE, J. L. De la résolution des équations numériques de tous les degrés. Paris, Duprat, 1798, vii + 268 p., chap. I, p. 4-20; Note iv, p. 124-135; Note viii, p. 165-180.

LIPKA, S. Über die Abzählung der reellen Wurzeln von algebraischen Gleichungen. Math. Zeit. 47, 343-351 (1941).

LIPKA, S. Über die Vorzeichenregeln von Budan-Fourier und Descartes. Jber. Deutsch. Math. Verein. 52, 204-217 (1942).

MADHAVA RAO, B. S. and SASTRY, B. S. On the limits for the roots of a polynomial equation. Jour. Mysore Univ. Sect. B. Vol. I, 5-8 (1940).

MARKOFF, A. On the determination of the number of roots of an algebraic equation, situated in a given domain. Rec. Math. (Mat. Sbornik) N. S. 7 (49), 3-6 (1940).

MAXIMOFF, I. On neighboring roots. C. R. (Doklady) Acad. Sci. URSS (N. S.) 37, 88-90 (1942).

MONTEL, P. Observation sur la communication précédente. C. R. Acad. Sci. Paris 210, 654-655 (1940).

MONTGOMERY, J. C. The roots of a polynomial and its derivative. Bull. Amer. Math. Soc. 47, 621-624 (1941).

NEWTON, I. Universal Arithmetick. (Translation and revision by Mr. Ralphson and Mr. Cunn of Arithmetica Universalis) London, 1728, iii + 271 p., p. 190-198, 204-208.

OBRESCHKOFF, N. Über algebraische Gleichungen, die nur Wurzeln mit negativen Realteilen besitzen. Math. Zeit. 45, 747-750 (1939).

OSTROWSKI, A. Sur la continuité relative des racines d'équations algébriques. C. R. Acad. Sci. Paris 209, 777-779 (1939).

PASCAL, E. Repertorium der höheren Mathematik. Vol. I (1). Leipzig, Teubner, 2nd ed. 1910, p. 349-352.

PERRON, O. Algebra. Berlin, de Gruyter, 2nd ed. 1927, vol. II, chap. I.

PHRAGMÉN, E. Sur une extension du théorème de Sturm. C. R. Acad. Sci. Paris 114, 205-208 (1892).

PUND, O. Algebra... Vol. 6 of Sammlung Schubert. Leipzig, Göschen, 1899, viii + 345 p., p. 243-267.

RUNGE, C. Gleichungen. Separation und Approximation der Wurzeln. Ency. Math. Wiss., Leipzig, Teubner, 1899, I B 3a sections 2-9, p. 407-432.

SERGESCU, P. Sur les limites de J. J. Bret. C. R. Acad. Sci. Paris 210, 652-654 (1940).

SERGESCU, P. Généralisations des limites de J. J. Bret. Acad. Roum. Bull. Sect. Sci. 22, 460-465 (1940).

SPECHT, W. Wurzelabschätzungen bei algebraischen Gleichungen. Jber. Deutsch. Math. Verein. 49, 179-190 (1940).

STERN, M. A. Über die Anwendung der Sturmschen Methode auf transcendente Gleichungen. Jour. Reine Angew. Math. 33, 363-365 (1846).

STURM, C. Mémoire sur la résolution des équations numériques. Par. Mém. Sav. (Etr.) 6, 271-318 (1835).

SYLVESTER, J. J. On an improved form of statement of a new rule for the separation of the roots of an algebraical equation, with a postscript containing a new theorem. Phil. Mag. (4) 31, 214-218 (1866).

VON SZ. NAGY, G. Über ganze Funktionen mit lauter reellen Nullstellen. Univ. Nac. Tucumán. Revista A. 1, 303-311 (1940).

TERRACINI, A. Some elementary remarks concerning the reality of the roots of an algebraic equation. (Spanish). Math. Notae 4, 137-144 (1944).

THOMAS, J. M. Sturm's theorem for multiple roots. Nat. Math. Mag. 15, 391-394 (1941).

THUE, A. Ein Fundamentaltheorem zur Bestimmung von Annäherungswerten aller Wurzeln gewisser ganzer Funktionen. Jour. Reine Angew. Math. 138, 96-108, (1910).

VIJAYARAGHAVAN, T. On a theorem of J. L. Walsh concerning the moduli of zeros of polynomials. Proc. Ind. Acad. Sci., Sect. A, 16, 83-86 (1942).

WARING, E. Meditationes algebraicae. Cambridge, 3rd ed. 1782, xliv + 403 p., p. 36-116.

WEBER, H. Lehrbuch der Algebra, Kleine Ausgabe. Braunschweig, Vieweg, 1912, chap. 6, p. 135-154.

WEISNER, L. Moduli of the roots of polynomials and power series. Amer. Math. Month. 48, 33-36 (1941).

WEISNER, L. Polynomials whose roots lie in a sector. Amer. Jour. Math. 64, 55-60 (1942).

WEISNER, L. Roots of certain classes of polynomials. Bull. Amer. Math. Soc. 48, 283-286 (1942).

8. THE CALCULATION OF THE ZEROS OF A POLYNOMIAL

A. Iterative Methods (Newton-Raphson, False Position, etc.)

BURNSIDE, W. S. and PANTON, A. W. Theory of Equations. Vol. 1. Dublin, Hodges and Figges, 8th ed., 1918, p. 225-248.

CASALE, F. Su di una equazione collegata a quella di Keplero. I, II. Rend. Ist. Lombardo 72, 333-346, 347-361 (1939).

DANDELIN, G. Recherches sur la résolution des équations numériques. Mém. Acad. Roy. Bruxelles 3, v + 71 p., (1826).

DARBOUX, J. G. Sur la méthode d'approximation de Newton. Nouv. Ann. Math. (2) 8, 17-27 (1869).

FABER, G. Über die Newtonsche Näherungsformel. Jour. Reine Angew. Math. 138, 1-21 (1910).

FABER, G. Über die Newtonsche Näherungsformel (Zweite Abhandlung). Jour. Reine Angew. Math. 146, 229-233 (1916).

FOURET, G. Sur la méthode d'approximation de Newton. Nouv. Ann. Math. (3) 9, 567-585 (1890).

FOURIER, J. B. J. Analyse des équations déterminées. Première partie. Paris, Didot, 1830, xxiv + 258 p., p. 157-223.

HEYMANN, W. Theorie der An-und Umläufe und Auflösung der Gleichungen vom vierten, fünften und sechsten Grade mittelst goniometrischer und hyperbolischer Functionen. Jour. Reine Angew. Math. 113, 267-302 (1894).

HEYMANN, W. Ueber die elementare Auflösung transcendenter Gleichungen. Zeit. Math. Naturwiss. Unterricht. 29, 1-15 (1898).

HEYMANN, W. Über Wurzelgruppen, welche durch Umläufe ausgeschnitten werden. Zeit. Math. Phys. 46, 265-297 (1901).

BIBLIOGRAPHY

HUBER, A. Über Konvergenz-und Divergenzintervalle des Newtonschen Verfahrens. Sitzber. Akad. Wiss. Wien. 134, 405-425 (1925).

ISENKRAHE, C. Ueber die Anwendung iterirter Functionen zur Darstellung der Wurzeln algebraischer und transcendenter Gleichungen. Math. Ann. 31, 309-317 (1888).

LAGRANGE, J. L. De la résolution des équations numériques de tous les degrés. Paris, 1798, chap. 3.

LAGUERRE, E. Sur l'approximation des fonctions circulaires au moyen des fonctions algébriques. Oeuvres de Laguerre, vol. 1. Paris, Gauthier-Villars, 1898, p. 104-107.

LEGENDRE, A. M. Supplément à l'essai sur la théorie des nombres, seconde (1808) édition. Paris, Courcier, 1816, p. 28-60.

LÉMERAY, E. M. Sur le calcul des racines des équations par approximations successives. Nouv. Ann. Math. (3) 17, 534-539 (1898).

LEVI, B. On the approximate solution of transcendental equations represented by Taylor series. (Spanish). Math. Notae 3, 1-40 (1943).

LÜROTH, J. Vorlesungen über numerisches Rechnen. Leipzig, Teubner, 1900, 194 p.

MEHMKE, R. Neue Methode beliebige numerische Gleichungen mit einer Unbekannten graphische aufzulösen. Ein Beitrag zum graphischen Rechnen. Civilingenieur (2) 35, 617-634 (1889).

MEHMKE, R. Praktische Methode zur Berechnung der reellen Wurzeln reeller algebraischer oder transcendenter numerischer Gleichungen mit einer Unbekannten. Zeit. Math. Phys. 36, 158-187 (1891).

NETTO, E. Ueber einen Algorithmus zur Auflösung numerischer algebraischer Gleichungen. Math. Ann. 29, 141-147 (1887).

NETTO, E. Vorlesungen über Algebra. I. Leipzig, Teubner, 1896, p. 281-290.

NETTO, E. Elementare Algebra. Akademische Vorlesungen für Studierende der ersten Semester. Articles 22, 45, 88. Leipzig, Teubner, 1904.

NEWTON, I. De analysi per aequationes numero terminorum infinitas: Cap. iv, Exempla per resolutionem aequationum. In vol. 1 of Isaaci Newtoni opera quae exstant omnia, Samuel Horsley, ed. London, J. Nichols, 1779, p. 268-270.

OSTROWSKI, A. Sur la convergence et l'estimation des erreurs dans quelques procédés de résolution des équations. Memorial volume dedicated to D. A. Grave. Moscow, 1940, p. 213-234.

PASCAL, E. Repertorium der höheren Mathematik. Vol. I (1). Leipzig, Teubner, 1910, p. 352-357.

PAWLEY, M. G. New criteria for accuracy in approximating real roots by the Newton-Raphson method. Nat. Math. Mag. 15, 111-120 (1940).

RAPHSON, J. Analysis aequationum universalis. London, 1690.

REHBOCK, F. Zur Konvergenz des Newtonschen Verfahrens für Gleichungssysteme. Zeit. Angew. Math. Mech. 22, 261-262 (1942).

RICHMOND, H. W. On certain formulae for numerical approximation. Jour.Lond.Math.Soc. 19, 31-38(1944).

RICHMOND, H. W. On the Newton-Raphson method of approximation. Edin. Math. Notes 34, 5-8 (1944).

ROSS, R. A method of solving algebraic equations. Nature: 78, 663-665 (1908); 79, 398-399 (1908).

RUNGE, C. Gleichungen. Separation und Approximation der Wurzeln. Ency. Math. Wiss., Leipzig, Teubner, 1899, I B 3a, p. 433-439, 446-448.

RUNGE, C. and KÖNIG, H. Vorlesungen über Numerisches Rechnen. Berlin, Springer, 1924, p. 152-157.

BIBLIOGRAPHY

SCARBOROUGH, J. B. Numerical Mathematical Analysis. Baltimore, Johns Hopkins Press, 1930, p. 178-195.

SCHEFFLER, H. Auflösung der algebraischen Gleichungen. Braunschweig, 1859. Quoted from Ency. Math. Wiss. Vol. 1, p. 446.

SCHROEDER, E. Über unendlich viele Algorithmen zur Auflösung der Gleichungen. Math. Ann. 2, 317-363 (1870).

SEIDEL, L. Über ein Verfahren, die Gleichungen, auf welche die Methode der Kleinsten Quadrate führt, sowie lineäre Gleichungen überhaupt, durch successive Annäherung aufzulösen. Abh. Akad. München 11, 81 (1874).

SMITH, D. E. History of Mathematics. Vol. 2: Special Topics of Elementary Mathematics. Boston, Ginn, 1925, p. 437-441.

TAUBER, A. Über die Newton'sche Näherungsmethode. Monatsh. Math. Phys. 6, 291-302 (1895).

WALLIS, J. De algebra tractatus... p. 1-482 of vol. 2 of Wallis' Opera Mathematica, Oxford, 1695, p. 381-398.

WAGNER, W. Bestimmung der Genauigkeit des Newton'schen Verfahrens. Berlin, (Latin, 1855; German, 1860). Quoted from Ency. Math. Wiss. Vol. 1, p. 434.

WARD, G. W. Successive approximations to $\sqrt[n]{a}$. Math. Gaz. 17, 52-53, 127 (1933).

WHITTAKER, E. T. and ROBINSON, G. The Calculus of Observations. Glasgow and London, Blackie, 1942, p. 94-95.

B. Root-Squaring and Allied Methods

BAIRSTOW, L. Applied Aerodynamics. New York, Longmans, 1920, p. 551-560.

BIEBERBACH, L. and BAUER, G. Vorlesungen über Algebra. Berlin, Teubner, 1928, p. 174-187.

BRODETSKY, S. and SMEAL, G. On Graeffe's method for complex roots of algebraic equations. Proc.Camb. Phil. Soc. 22, 83-87 (1924).

CARVALLO, M. E. Méthode pratique pour la résolution numérique complète des équations algébriques ou transcendantes. Paris, Nony, 1896, 32 p.

DANDELIN, G. Sur la résolution des équations numériques. Mém. Acad. Roy. Bruxelles 3, 48 (1826).

ENCKE, J. F. Allgemeine Auflösung der numerischen Gleichungen. Jour. Reine Angew. Math. 22,193-248 (1841).

GRÄFFE, C. H. Die Auflösung der höheren numerischen Gleichungen... Zürich, Schulthess, 1837, 34 p.

LEVI, D. On the approximate solution of transcendental equations represented by Taylor series. Math. Notae 3, 1-40 (1943).

OSTROWSKI, A. Recherches sur la méthode de Graeffe et les zéros des polynomes et des séries de Laurent. I-IV. Acta Math. 72, 99-257 (1940).

RUNGE, C. Gleichungen. Separation und Approximation der Wurzeln. Ency. Math. Wiss. Leipzig, Teubner, 1899, I B 3a, section 14, p. 440-446.

RUNGE, C. and KÖNIG, H. Vorlesungen über numerisches Rechnen. Berlin, Springer, 1924, p. 164-175.

RUNGE, C. Praxis der Gleichungen. Berlin, de Gruyter, 2nd ed. 1921, 172 p.

BIBLIOGRAPHY

SAN JUAN, R. Complements to Graeffe's method for the solution of algebraic equations. Revista Mat. Hisp.-Amer. (3) 1, 1-14 (1939).

SCARBOROUGH, J. B. Numerical Mathematical Analysis. Baltimore, Johns Hopkins Press, 1930, chap. X.

SEBASTIÃO e SILVA, J. Sur une méthode d'approximation semblable à celle de Graeffe. Portugaliae Math. 2, 271-279 (1941).

WHITTAKER, E. T. and ROBINSON, G. The Calculus of Observations. Glasgow, Blackie, 3rd ed. 1942,p. 106-119.

C. Miscellaneous Methods.

AITKEN, A. C. On Bernoulli's numerical solution of algebraic equations. Proc. Roy. Soc. Edin. 46, 289-305 (1926).

BERNOULLI, D. Observationes de seriebus quae formantur ex additione vel subtractione quaecunque terminorum se mutuo consequentum, ubi praesertim earundem insignis usus pro inveniendis radicum omnium aequationum algebraicarum ostenditur. Comment. Acad. Sci. Petropol. 3, 85-100 (1732).

COHN, F. Ueber die in recurrirender Weise gebildeten Grössen und ihren Zusammenhang mit den algebraischen Gleichungen. Math. Ann. 44, 473-538 (1894).

COLLATZ, L. Das Hornersche Schema bei komplexen Wurzeln algebraischer Gleichungen. Zeit. Angew. Math. Mech. 20, 235-236 (1940).

CORNOCK, A. F. and HUGHES, J. M. The evaluation of the complex roots of algebraic equations. Phil. Mag. (7) 34, 314-320 (1943).

EAGLE, A. Series for all the roots of a trinomial equation. Amer. Math. Month. 46, 422-425 (1939).

EICHLER, M. Zur numerischen Lösung von Gleichungen mit reellen Koeffizienten. Jour. Reine Angew. Math. 184, 124-128 (1942).

EULER, L. Introductio in analysin infinitorum. Lausanne, Bosquet, 1748, xvi + 320 p., chap. 17.

FOURIER, J. B. J. Analyse des équations déterminées. Paris, Didot, 1830, xxiv + 258 p., p. 68-86.

FRAZER, R. A., DUNCAN, W. J. and COLLAR, A. R. Elementary Matrices and Some Applications to Dynamics and Differential Equations. Cambridge, Cambridge Univ. Press, 1938, p. 148-151.

FÜRSTENAU. Darstellung der reellen Wurzeln algebraischer Gleichungen durch Determinanten der Coefficienten. Marburg, 1860. Quoted from Aitken, A. C., Proc. Roy. Soc. Edin. 46,1926, p. 303.

HITCHCOCK, F. L. Algebraic equations with complex coefficients. Jour. Math. Phys. (M.I.T.) 18,202-210 (1939).

HITCHCOCK, F. L. An improvement on the G.C.D. method for complex roots. Jour. Math. Phys. (M.I.T.) 23, 69-74 (1944).

HORNER, W. G. A new method of solving numerical equations of all orders, by continuous approximation. Phil. Trans. Roy. Soc. London 109 Part 2, 308-335 (1819); also Ladies Diary 135, 49-72 (1838).

HORNER, W. G. On the popular methods of approximation. Math. Repository, New Series, 4 Part 2, 131-136 (1819).

HORNER, W. G. Horae mathematicae. Math. Repository, New Series, 5 Part 2, 21-75 (1830).

JACOBI, C. J. G. Observatiunculae ad theoriam aequationum pertinentes. V. Quomodo regula Bernoulliana ad investigandas radices, quae maximam aut minimam sequuntur, extendi potest. Jour. Reine Angew. Math. 13, 349-353 (1835).

BIBLIOGRAPHY

KEMPNER, A. J. On the complex roots of algebraic equations. Bull. Amer. Math. Soc. 41, 809-843 (1935).

KÖNIG, J. Ueber eine Eigenschaft der Potenzreihen. Math. Ann. 23, 447-449 (1884).

KRAFFT, M. Über ein Eulersches Verfahren zur Wurzelberechnung. Monatsh. Math. Phys. 49, 312-315 (1941).

LAGRANGE, J. L. De la résolution des équations numériques de tous les degrés. Paris, Duprat, 1798 chap. 3.

LAGUERRE, E. Sur une méthode pour obtenir par approximation les racines d'une équation algébrique qui a toutes ses racines réelles. Oeuvres de Laguerre, vol. 1. Paris, Gauthier-Villars, 1898, p. 87-103.

LEWIS, A. J. The solution of algebraic equations by infinite series. Nat. Math. Mag. 10, 80-95 (1935).

LIN, SHIH-NGE. A method of successive approximations of evaluating the real and complex roots of cubic and higher-order equations. Jour. Math. Phys. (M.I.T.) 20, 231-242 (1941).

LIN, SHIH-NGE. A method for finding roots of algebraic equations. Jour. Math. Phys. (M.I.T.) 22, 60-77 (1943).

NAEGELSBACH, H. Studien zu Fürstenau's neuer Methode der Darstellung und Berechnung der Wurzeln algebraischer Gleichungen durch Determinanten der Coefficienten. Archiv Math. Phys.: 59, 147-192 (1876); 61, 19-85 (1877).

NIEWENGLOWSKI, B. Cours d'algèbre. Paris, Armand Colin, vol. 2, 7th ed. 1916, 570 p., p. 417-458.

PERRON, O. Algebra. Berlin, de Gruyter, vol. 2, 2nd ed. 1933, viii + 260 p., p. 47-56.

RUNGE, C. Gleichungen. Separation und Approximation der Wurzeln. Ency. Math. Wiss. Leipzig, Teubner, 1899, I B 3a, p. 439-440.

SHARP, H. S. A comparison of methods for evaluating the complex roots of quartic equations. Jour. Math. Phys. (M.I.T.) 20, 243-258 (1941).

STERN, M. A. Theorie der Kettenbrüche und ihre Anwendung. Jour. Reine Angew. Math. 11, 142-168, 277-306 (1834).

VINCENT, M. Note sur la résolution des équations numériques. Jour. Math. Pures Appl. 1, 341-372 (1836).

WEYL, H. Randbemerkungen zu Hauptproblemen der Mathematik. Math. Zeit. 20, 130-150, espec. 142-146 (1924).

WIENER, A. Die Berechnung der reellen Wurzeln der quartinomischen Gleichungen. Zeit. Math. Phys. 31, 65-87 (1886).

YOUNG, J. R. On the Theory and Solution of Algebraical Equations. London, Souter, 1st ed. 1835, xviii + 271 p.

9. THE ZEROS OF TRANSCENDENTAL EQUATIONS

A. Iterative Methods (see also under 8A)

BOURLET, C. Sur le problème de l'itération. Ann. Toulouse 12, C 1-12 (1898).

CAUCHY, A. L. Analyse algébrique. Note III. See Oeuvres complètes d'Augustin Cauchy, 2nd series, vol. 3. Paris, Gauthier-Villars, 1897, p. 381-386.

BIBLIOGRAPHY

DARY, M. Letter to Newton (August 1674). See Rigaud, S. P. and S. J., Correspondence of Scientific Men of the Seventeenth Century (Earl of Macclesfield Collection). Oxford, Oxford Univ. Press, 1841, vol. 2, 365-367.

DeMORGAN, A. Treatise on the Calculus of Functions. (Extracted from the Encyclopedia Metropolitana.) London, Baldwin and Cradock, 1836, 88 p.

DeMORGAN, A. Encyclopaedia Metropolitana. 1845, vol. 2, p. 305-389.

FOURIER, J. B. J. Théorie analytique de la chaleur. Paris, Didot, 1822, xxii + 639 p., p. 342-346.

FOURIER, J. B. J. Analyse des équations déterminées. Paris, Didot, 1830, xxiv + 258 p., p. 41.

FARKAS, J. Sur les fonctions itératives. Jour. Math. Pures Appl. 10, 101-108 (1884).

GERMANSKY, B. Notiz über die Lösung von Extremalaufgaben mittels Iteration. Zeit. Angew. Math. Mech. 14, 187 (1934).

GREGORY, J. Letter to Collins (April 1674). See Rigaud, S. P. and S. J., Correspondence of Scientific Men of the Seventeenth Century (Earl of Macclesfield Collection). Oxford, Oxford Univ. Press, 1841, vol. 2, p. 255-256.

HALL, N. A. The solution of the trinomial equation in infinite series by the method of iteration. Nat. Math. Mag. 15, 1-11 (1941).

HEYMANN, W. Über die elementare Auflösung transcendenter Gleichungen. Zeit. Math. Naturwiss. Unterricht 29, 1-15 (1898).

ISENKRAHE, C. Über die Anwendung iterirter Functionen zur Darstellung der Wurzeln algebraischer und transcendenter Gleichungen. Math. Ann. 31, 309-317 (1888).

ISENKRAHE, C. Das Verfahren der Functionswiederholung, seine geometrische Veranschaulichung und algebraische Anwendung. Wissenschaftliche Beilage zum Jahresbericht des Kgl.Kaiser-Wilhelm-Gymnasiums in Trier. 1897, viii + 113 p.

JULIA, G. Mémoire sur la convergence des séries formées avec les itérées successives d'une fraction rationelle. Acta Math. 56, 149-195 (1930).

KING, L. V. On the Direct Numerical Calculation of Elliptic Functions and Integrals. Cambridge, Cambridge Univ. Press, 1924, viii + 42 p.

KOENIGS, G. P. Recherches sur les substitutions uniformes. Bull. Sci. Math. (2) 7 (1), 340-357 (1883).

LEGENDRE, A. M. Supplément à l'essai sur la théorie des nombres, seconde (1808) édition. Paris, Courcier, 1816, p. 28-37.

LÉMERAY, E. M. Sur la convergence des substitutions uniformes. Nouv. Ann. Math.: (3) 16, 306-319 (1897); (3) 17, 75-80 (1898).

LÉMERAY, E. M. Sur quelques algorithmes et sur l'itération. Bull. Soc. Math. France 26, 10-15 (1898).

VON MISES, R. and POLLACZEK-GEIRINGER, H. Praktische Verfahren der Gleichungsauflösung. I. Zeit. Angew. Math. Mech. 9, 58-62 (1929).

MONTEL, P. L'Itération. Univ. Nac. La Plata Publ. Fac. Ci. Fisicomat. Revista (2) 3, 201-211 (1940).

NETTO, E. Vorlesungen über Algebra. Leipzig, Teubner, 1896, vol. 1, p. 300-323.

PELLET, A. Calcul des racines réelles d'une équation. C. R. Acad. Sci. Paris 133, 917-918, 1186-1187 (1901).

PERRIN, S. Sur la séparation et le calcul des racines réelles des équations. C. R. Acad. Sci. Paris 133, 1189-1191 (1901).

BIBLIOGRAPHY

PINCHERLE, S. Équations fonctionelles. Ency. Sci. Math. II 5 (1) 55-72 (1912).

RUNGE, C. and KÖNIG, H. Vorlesungen über Numerisches Rechnen. Berlin, Springer, 1924, p. 155-157.

SANCERY, L. De la méthode des substitutions successives pour le calcul des racines des équations. Nouv. Ann. Math. (2) 1, 305-312 (1862).

SCARBOROUGH, J. B. Numerical Mathematical Analysis. Baltimore, Johns Hopkins Press, 1930, p. 184-187, 191-195.

SCHROEDER, E. Ueber unendlich viele Algorithmen zur Auflösung der Gleichungen. Math.Ann. 2, 317-365 (1870).

SIEGEL, C. L. Iteration of analytic functions. Ann. of Math. (2) 43, 607-612 (1942).

SPOERL, C. A. Solving equations in the machine age. Record Amer. Inst. Actuar. 31, 129-149, 490-506 (1942).

VALIRON, G. Sur l'itération des fonctions holomorphes dans un demi-plan. Bull. Sci. Math. (2) 55, 105-128 (1931).

B. Miscellaneous Methods

AUGÉ, J. On the zeros of polynomials and Laurent series. (Spanish). Revista Mat. Hisp.-Amer. (4) 3, 176-185, 229-241 (1943).

BLEICK, W. E. Symmetric relations between the coefficients of reversed power series. Phil. Mag. (7) 33, 637-638 (1942).

BURKHARDT, H. Trigonometrische Reihen und Integrale bis etwa 1850: Darstellung der Wurzeln von Gleichungen durch Integrale. Ency. Math. Wiss., Leipzig, Teubner, 1915, II 1 (2) p. 1307-1311.

CAUCHY, A. L. Leçons sur le calcul différentiel. Note: sur la détermination approximative des racines... Oeuvres complètes d'Augustin Cauchy, (2) vol. 4. Paris, Gauthier-Villars, 1899, p. 573-609.

COHN, F. Ueber die in recurrirender Weise gebildeten Grössen und ihren Zusammenhang mit den algebraischen Gleichungen. Math. Ann. 44, 473-538 (1894).

CURRY, H. B. The method of steepest descent for non-linear minimization problems. Quart. Appl. Math. 2, 258-261 (1944).

DEHN, M. and HELLINGER, E. On James Gregory's Vera Quadratura. The James Gregory Tercentenary Memorial Volume. London, Bell, 1939, p. 468-478.

EULER, L. Introductio in analysin infinitorum, tomus primus. Lausanne, Bosquet, 1748, xvi + 320 p., section 355, p. 294-295.

EULER, L. De radicibis aequationis infinitae, $0 = 1 - xx/ n(n+1) + x^4/ n(n+1)(n+2)(n+3) - x^6/ n...(n+5) + ...$ etc. Nova Acta Acad. Sci. Petropol. 9, 19-40 (1791).

FUJIWARA, M. On the zero points of integral transcendental functions of finite genus. Jap. Jour. Math. 1, 27-28 (1924).

FUJIWARA, M. Über die Nullstellen der ganzen Funktionen vom Geschlecht Null und Eins. Tôhoku Math. Jour. 25, 27-35 (1925).

GERCEVANOFF, N. Quelques procédés de la résolution des équations fonctionelles linéaires par la méthode d'itération. C. R. (Doklady) Acad. Sci. URSS (N.S.) 39, 207-209 (1943).

BIBLIOGRAPHY

GOLOMB, M. Zeros and poles of functions defined by Taylor series. Bull. Amer. Math. Soc. 49, 581-592 (1943).

HILLMAN, A. P. and SALZER, H. E. Roots of sin z = z. Phil. Mag. (7) 34, 575 (1943).

HURWITZ, A. Über die Wurzeln einiger transcendenten Gleichungen. Mitt. Math. Ges. Hamburg 2, 25-31 (1890).

LEHMANN, A. Über die Inversion des Gaussschen Wahrscheinlichkeits-Integrals. Mitt. Verein Schweiz. Versich. Math. 38, 15-52 (1939).

LEVI, B. On the approximate solution of transcendental equations represented by Taylor series. (Spanish). Math. Notae 3, 1-40 (1943).

MEYER, F. Zur Auflösung der Gleichungen. Math. Ann. 33, 511-524 (1889).

PLUMMER, H. C. The numerical solution of a type of equation. Phil. Mag. (7) 32, 505-512 (1941).

POLYA, G. Über das Graeffesche Verfahren. Zeit. Math. Phys. 63, 275-290 (1914).

PONTRJAGIN, L. On zeros of some transcendental functions. (Russian. English summary.). Bull. Acad. Sci. URSS. Sér. Math. (Izvestia Akad. Nauk SSSR) 6, 115-134 (1942).

RUNGE, C. Entwicklung der Wurzeln einer algebraischen Gleichung in Summen von rationalen Functionen der Coefficienten. Acta Math. 6, 305-318 (1885).

SCHROEDER, E. Ueber unendlich viele Algorithmen zur Auflösung der Gleichungen. Math. Ann. 2, 317-365 (1870).

STERN, M. A. Ueber die Auflösung der transcendenten Gleichungen. Jour. Reine Angew. Math. 22, 1-62 (1841).

TCHEBOTARÖW, N. On the methods of Sturm and Fourier for transcendent functions. C. R. (Doklady) Acad. Sci. URSS (N.S.) 34, 2-4 (1942).

TCHEBOTARÖW, N. On a particular type of transcendent equations. C. R. (Doklady) Acad. Sci. URSS (N.S.) 34, 38-41 (1942).

TCHEBOTARÖW, N. On entire functions with real interlacing roots. C. R. (Doklady) Acad. Sci. URSS (N.S.) 35, 195-197 (1942).

WHITTAKER, E. T. A formula for the solution of algebraic or transcendental equations. Proc. Edin. Math. Soc. 36, 103-106 (1918).

WHITTAKER, E. T. and ROBINSON, G. The Calculus of Observations. Glasgow, Blackie, 3rd. ed. 1942, p. 120-123.

10. IMPLICIT FUNCTIONS

BIEBERBACH, L. Lehrbuch der Funktionentheorie, vol. I. Leipzig, Teubner, 3rd ed. 1930, p. 195-204.

COPSON, E. T. Introduction to the Theory of Functions of a Complex Variable. Oxford, Oxford Univ. Press, 1935, p. 121-125.

EAGLE, A. Series for all the roots of the equation $(z - a)^m = k(z - b)^n$. Amer. Math. Month. 46, 425-428 (1939).

EAGLE, A. Series for all the roots of a trinomial equation. Amer. Math. Month. 46, 422-425 (1939).

HURWITZ, A. and COURANT, R. Vorlesungen über Allgemeine Funktionentheorie und elliptische Funktionen. Berlin, Springer, 1929, xii + 534 p.

BIBLIOGRAPHY

LAGRANGE, J. L. Nouvelle méthode pour résoudre les équations litterales par le moyen des séries. Oeuvres de Lagrange, vol. 3. Paris, Gauthier-Villars, 1869, p. 1-73.

PFAFF, J. F. Disquisitiones analyticae maxime ad calculum integralem et doctrinam serierum pertinentes, vol. 1, sect. 2. Third paper: Tractatus de reversione serierum, sive de resolutione aequationum per series. Helmstedt, Fleckeisen, 1797, 350 p., p. 227-350.

PINCHERLE, S. Gli elementi della teoria delle funzioni analitiche. 1922, p. 239 ff; p. 213.

SCHLOEMILCH, O. Die allgemeine Umkehrung gegebener Funktionen. Halle, H. W. Schmidt, 1849, 56 p.

WHITTAKER, E. T. and WATSON, G. N. Modern Analysis. New York, Macmillan, Amer. ed. 1943, p. 128-133.

11. HARMONIC ANALYSIS

BERGER, E. R. Harmonische Analyse diskreter Zahlenreihen. Zeit. Angew. Math. Mech. 22, 269-272 (1942).

BRUNT, D. The Combination of Observations. Cambridge, Cambridge Univ. Press, 2nd ed. 1931, x + 239 p., chap. XI, p. 179-205.

CARSE, G. A. and SHEARER, G. A Course in Fourier's Analysis and Periodogram Analysis for the Mathematical Laboratory. Edin. Math. Tracts, No. 4. London, Bell, 1915, viii + 66 p.

CONRAD, V. Zur Berechnung höherer Glieder der Fourierschen Reihen. Meteorol. Zeit. 36, 160 (1919).

DALE, J. B. The resolution of a compound periodic function into simple periodic functions. Month. Notices Roy. Astr. Soc. 74, 628-648 (1914).

DANIELSON, G. C. and LANCZOS, C. Some improvements in practical Fourier analysis and their application to X-ray scattering from liquids. Jour. Franklin Inst. 233, 365-380, 435-452 (1942).

DIETSCH, G. and ROTZEIG, B. Eine neue Methode zur exakten Berechnung der Fourierkoeffizienten. Beiträge zur Geophysik (Gerlands Beiträge) 38, 276-281 (1933).

EAGLE, A. A practical Treatise on Fourier's Theorem and Harmonic Analysis: for Physicists and Engineers. London, Longmans Green, 1925, xiv + 178 p.

ESPLEY, D. C. Harmonic analysis by the method of central differences. Phil. Mag. (7) 28, 338-352 (1939).

FISCHER-HINNEN, J. Methode zur schnellen Bestimmung harmonischer Wellen. Elektrotech. Zeit. 22, 396-398 (1901).

LAGRANGE, J. L. Recherches sur la manière de former des tables des planètes d'après les seules observations. Oeuvres de Lagrange, vol. 6. Paris, Gauthier-Villars, 1873, p. 505-627.

LAGRANGE, J. L. Sur les interpolations. Oeuvres de Lagrange, vol. 7. Paris, 1877, p. 533-553.

LINCOLN, P. M. Wave form analysis. The Electric Jour. (Publ. by The Electric Club, Pittsburg, Pa.) 5, 386-392 (1908).

LIPKA, J. Graphical and Mechanical Computation. New York, Wiley, 1918, p. 170-208.

LOWAN, A. N. and LADERMAN, J. Table of Fourier coefficients. Jour. Math. Phys. (M.I.T.) 22, 136-147 (1943).

POLLAK, L. W. Rechentafeln zur Harmonischen Analyse. Leipzig, Barth, 1926, 22 p. text and 138 p. tables.

ROSS, M. A. S. Numerical Fourier analysis to twenty-nine harmonics. Nature 152, 302-303 (1943).

BIBLIOGRAPHY

RUNGE, C. Über die Zerlegung empirischgegebener periodischer Funktionen in Sinuswellen. Zeit. Math. Phys. 48, 443-456 (1903).

RUNGE, C. Über die Zerlegung einer empirischen Funktion in Sinuswellen. Zeit. Math. Phys. 52, 117-123 (1905).

RUNGE, C. and EMDE, F. Rechnungsformular zur Zerlegung einer empirisch gegebenen periodischen Funktion in Sinuswellen. Braunschweig, Vieweg, 1913.

RUSSELL, A. Practical harmonical analysis. Proc. Phys. Soc. Lond. 27, 149-170 (1915).

SCHLAEFKE, K. Zur harmonischen Analyse von Nockenkurven. Luftfahrtforschung 17, 87-88 (1940).

STUMPFF, K. Grundlagen und Methoden der Periodenforschung. Berlin, Springer, 1937, viii + 332 p.

STUMPFF, K. Tafeln und Aufgaben zur harmonischen Analyse und Periodogrammrechnung. Berlin, Springer, 1939, vii + 174 p.

TAYLOR, H. O. A mechanical process for constructing harmonic analysis schedules for waves having even and odd harmonics. Phys. Rev. (2) 6, 303-311 (1915).

THOMPSON, S. P. Note on a rapid approximate method of harmonic analysis. Proc. Phys. Soc. Lond. 19, 443-450 (1905).

THOMPSON, S. P. Nouvelle méthode d'analyse harmonique par la sommation algébrique d'ordonnées déterminées. C. R. Acad. Sci. Paris 153, 88-90 (1911).

THOMPSON, S. P. A new method of approximate harmonic analysis by selected ordinates. Proc. Phys. Soc. Lond. 23, 334-343 (1911).

TURNER, H. H. The facility of harmonic analysis. Jour. Brit. Astr. Assoc. 18, 250-254 (1908).

TURNER, H. H. Tables for facilitating the use of harmonic analysis. London, Humphrey Milford, 1913, 46 p.

ZECH, T. Harmonische Analyse mit Hilfe des Lochkartenverfahrens. Zeit. Angew. Math. Mech. 9, 425-427 (1929).

WHITTAKER, E. T. and ROBINSON, G. The Calculus of Observations. London, Blackie, 3rd ed. 1942, p. 260-284.

12. PERIODOGRAM ANALYSIS

ALTER, D. Application of Schuster's periodogram to long rainfall records, beginning 1748. Month. Weather Rev. 52, 479-487 (1924).

ALTER, D. An examination by means of Schuster's periodogram of rainfall data from long records in typical sections of the world. Month. Weather Rev. 54, 44-56 (1926).

ALTER, D. The criteria of reality in the periodogram. Month. Weather Rev. 54, 57-58 (1926).

ALTER, D. An extremely simple method of periodogram analysis. Proc. Nat. Acad.Sci. U.S.A. 19, 335-339 (1933).

BARTELS, J. Random fluctuations, persistence, and quasi-persistence in geophysical and cosmical periodicities. Terr. Magnetism 40, 1-60 (1935).

BERNSTEIN, F. Über die arithmetischer Ermittlung verborgener Periodizitäten. Zeit. Angew. Math. Mech. 7, 441-444 (1927).

BERNSTEIN, N. Analyse aperiodischer trigonometrischer Reihen. Zeit. Angew. Math. Mech. 7, 476-485 (1927).

BIBLIOGRAPHY

BROOKS, C. E. P. The difference-periodogram— a method for the rapid determination of short periodicities. Proc. Roy. Soc. Lond. A105, 346-359 (1924).

BRUNT, D. Periodicities in European Weather. Phil. Trans. Roy. Soc. Lond. A225, 247-302 (1925). See also An investigation of periodicities. Quart. Jour. Roy. Met. Soc. 53, 1-29 (1927).

BRUNT, D. The Combination of Observations. Cambridge, Cambridge Univ. Press, 2nd ed. 1931, x + 239 p., chap. XII, p. 206-231.

BRUNT, D. Harmonic analysis and the interpretation of the results of periodogram-investigations. Mem. Roy. Met. Soc. 2, No. 15, 48-68 (1928).

CARSE, G. A. and SHEARER, G. A Course in Fourier's Analysis and Periodogram Analysis for the Mathematical Laboratory, Edin. Math. Tracts No. 4. London, Bell, 1915, viii + 66 p.

CONRAD, V. Der Expektanzbegriff von Arthur Schuster. Meteorol. Zeit. 59, 299-306, 389-390 (1924).

GIBB, D. The periodogram analysis of the variations of SS Cygni. Month. Notices Roy. Astr. Soc. 74, 678-686 (1914).

HIRAYAMA, S. Note on the method to find the period of a periodic function from equidistant observations. Proc. Tokyo Math. Phys. Soc. (2) 7, 268-274 (1916).

HOLTZHEY-LINDAU, R. Eine Ausgleichungsbetrachtung. Zeit. Angew. Met. 48, 83-91 (1931).

KELLER, L. Die Periodographie als Statistisches Problem. Beitr. Physik frei Atmosph. 19, 173-187 (1932).

KELLEY, T. L. The evidence for periodicity in short time series. Jour. Amer. Statist. Assoc. 38, 319-326 (1943).

KRASSOWSKI, J. Analyse, au moyen de la méthode de M. Schuster, des périodes de la variation de la latitude. Bull. Internat. Acad. Sci. Cracovie, Cl. Sci. Math. Nat. 1909, 543-548 (1909).

LABROUSTE, H. Analyse des courbes résultant de la superposition de sinusoïdes. C. R. Acad. Sci. Paris 184, 259-261 (1927).

VON LAUE, M. Ein Satz der Wahrscheinlichkeitsrechnung und seine Anwendung auf die Strahlungstheorie. Ann. der Phys. (4) 47, 853-878 (1915).

McNISH, A. G. Principles of statistical analysis occasionally overlooked. Jour. Franklin Inst. 215 697-703 (1933).

MÜNZNER, H. Günstigste Bestimmung der Umkehrung der Laplace-Transformierten zur Auffindung Verborgener Periodizitäten. Dissertation, Göttingen, 1932, 45 p.

REINSBERG, C. Beiträge zur Theorie der Aufsuchung versteckter Periodizitäten. Astr. Nachr. 248, 421-438 (1933).

REINSBERG, C. Zur Theorie der Exponentialperiodogramme. Astr. Nachr. 252, 336-346 (1934).

RIETZ, H. L. and BAUR, F. Handbuch der Mathematischen Statistik. Leipzig, Teubner, 1930, vi + 285 p.

RUSSELL, A. Practical harmonical analysis. Proc. Phys. Soc. Lond. 27, 149-168 (1915).

SAVUR, S. R. A simplified method for calculating periodicities. Proc. Ind. Assoc. Sci. 6, 527-541 (1931).

SCHUSTER, A. On lunar and solar periodicities of earthquakes. Proc.Roy.Soc.Lond. 61, 455-465 (1897).

SCHUSTER, A. The investigation of hidden periodicities. Terr. Magnetism 3, 13-41 (1898).

SCHUSTER, A. The periodogram of magnetic declination as obtained from the records of the Greenwich Observatory during the years 1871-1895. Trans. Camb. Phil. Soc. 18, 107-135 (1900).

BIBLIOGRAPHY

SCHUSTER, A. The periodogram and its optical analogy. Proc. Roy. Soc. Lond. A77, 136-140 (1906).

SCHUSTER, A. On the periodicities of sun spots. Phil. Trans. Roy. Soc. Lond. A206, 69-100 (1906).

STERNE, T. E. and CAMPBELL, L. Properties of the light-curve of $\zeta\zeta$ - Cygni. Ann. Harvard Coll. Obs. 90, No. 6, 189-206 (1934).

STUMPFF, K. Tafeln und Aufgaben zur harmonischen Analyse und Periodogrammrechnung. Berlin, Springer, 1939, vii + 174 p.

STUMPFF, K. Grundlagen und Methoden der Periodenforschung. Berlin, Springer, 1937, vii + 332 p.

TURNER, H. H. Tables for Facilitating the Use of Harmonic Analysis. Oxford, Oxford Univ. Press, 1913, 46 p.

TURNER, H. H. On double lines in periodograms. Proc. 5 Internat. Math. Congr. vol. 2. Cambridge, Cambridge Univ. Press, 1913, p. 177-181.

WALKER, G. T. On periodicity. Quart. Jour. Roy. Met. Soc. 51, 337-346 (1925).

WALKER, G. T. On periodicity and its existence in European weather. Mem. Roy. Met. Soc. 1, No. 9, 119-126 (1927).

WALKER, G. T. On periodicity iii. Criteria for reality. Mem. Roy. Met. Soc. 3, No. 25, 97-101(1930).

WALKER, G. T. On periodicity in series of related terms. Proc. Roy. Soc. Lond. A131, 518-532 (1931).

WORTHING, A. G. and GEFFNER, J. Treatment of Experimental Data. New York, Wiley, 1943, iv + 342 p.

13. FINITE DIFFERENCES

ABRAMOWITZ, M. Note on the computation of the differences of the Si(x), Ci(x), Ei(x) and -Ei(-x) functions. Bull. Amer. Math. Soc. 46, 332-333 (1940).

ADAMS, C. R. Bibliography, supplementary to Nörlund's bibliography on the calculus of finite differences and difference equations. Bull. Amer. Math. Soc. 37, 383-400 (1931).

ANDOYER, H. Calcul des différences et interpolation. Vol. I, part 21 in 1(4) fasc. 1 of Ency. des Sci. Math., 1906, p. 47-160.

BENNETT, H. F. Computation of polynomial functions by summation of finite differences. Jour. Opt. Soc. Amer. 33, 519-526 (1943).

BEZOUT, E. Théorie générale des équations algébriques. Paris, P. D. Pierres, 1779, xxviii + 471 p. p. 1-19.

BLEICH, F. and MELAN, E. Die gewöhnlichen und partiellen Differenzengleichungen der Baustatik. Berlin, Springer, 1927. Chap. 1, p. 1-34.

BOOLE, G. A Treatise on the Calculus of Finite Differences. London, Macmillan, 3rd ed. J. F. Moulton 1880. Reprinted New York, Stechert, 1931, xii + 336 p.

BOSSUT, C. Différence. Encyclopédie méthodique, mathématiques. Paris, 1, 512-520 (1789).

BRIGGS, H. Trigonometria Britannica: sive De doctrina triangulorum libri duo. Gouda, Rammasenius, 1633, 110 p., liber primus, cap. xii, p. 35-40.

BURN, J. and BROWN, E. H. Elements of Finite Differences... London, Layton, 2nd ed. 1915, 289 p., p. 1-73.

CARMICHAEL, R. A Treatise on the Calculus of Operations: Designed to facilitate the processes of the Differential and Integral Calculus and the Calculus of Finite Differences. London, Longmans, 1855, xii + 170 p., p. 137-152.

BIBLIOGRAPHY

CASORATI, F. Il calcolo delle differenze finite interpretato ed accresciuto di nuovi teoremi a sussidio principalmente delle odierne ricerche basate sulla variabilità complessa. Ann.Mat. Pura Appl. (2) 10, 10-43 (1880-1882).

COTES, R. Canonotechnica sive Constructio tabularum per differentias. See Opera Miscellanea Rogeri Cotes. Cambridge, 1722, 125 p., p. 35-71 (Publ. with but paged separately from Harmonia mensurarum.).

DeMORGAN, A. The Differential and Integral Calculus. London, Baldwin, 1842, xx + 849 p., p. 77-85, 253-266.

DZIOBEK, O. Vorlesungen über Differential-und Integralrechnung. Leipzig, Teubner, 1910, x + 648 p.

EMERSON, W. The Method of Increments. London, J. Nourse, 1763, viii + 147 p.

ENCKE, J. F. Ueber mechanische Quadratur. See Gesammelte mathematische und astronomische Abhandlungen von J. F. Encke, vol. 1. Berlin, Dümmler, 1888, 211 p., p. 21-60.

EULER, L. Institutiones calculi differentialis. St. Petersbourg (Leningrad), 1755, xxiv + 880 p.

FORSYTH, C. H. An Introduction to the Mathematical Analysis of Statistics. New York, Wiley, 1924, vii + 241 p., chap. 2, p. 12-32.

GAU, E. P. Calculs numériques et graphiques. (Coll. Armand Colin, No. 60) Paris, Colin, 1925, 206 p.

GIBB, D. A Course in Interpolation and Numerical Integration for the Mathematical Laboratory. Edin. Math. Tracts No. 2. London, Bell, 1915, viii + 90 p.

GRANT, J. D. Notes on the Calculus of Finite Differences. Ann Arbor, Edwards Bros., 1926, 94 p. mimeo.

HANSEN, P. A. Relationen einestheils zwischen Summen und Differenzen und anderntheils zwischen Integralen und Differentialen. Abh. Ges. Wiss. Leipzig 7, 506-583 (1865).

HERSCHEL, J. F. W. A Collection of Examples of the Applications of the Calculus of Finite Differences. Cambridge, Deighton, 1820, v + 171 p.

HYMERS, J. A Treatise on Differential Equations and on the Calculus of Finite Differences. London, Longmans, 2nd ed. 1858, viii + 318 p., second treatise, 139 p.

JARRET, T. An Essay on Algebraic Development... and in the Calculus of Finite Differences. Cambridge, Deighton, 1831, iv + 192 p., p. 40-65.

JOLLEY, L. B. W. Summation of Series. London, Chapman and Hall, 1925, xi + 232 p.

JORDAN, C. Statistique Mathématique. Paris, Gauthier-Villars, 1927, xvii + 344 p.

JORDAN, C. Calculus of Finite Differences. Budapest, Eggenberger Book Shop, 1939, xxi + 654 p.

KOWALEWSKI, G. Interpolation und genäherte Quadratur. Leipzig, Teubner, 1932, vi + 146 p.

LACROIX, S. F. Traité du Calcul Différentiel et du Calcul Intégral. Troisième Partie. Des Différences et des Séries. Paris, Courcier, 2nd ed. 1819, xxiv + 776 p.

LACROIX, S. F. Traité Elémentaire de Calcul Différentiel et de Calcul Intégral, vol.2.Paris, Mallet-Bachelier, 6th ed. 1862, viii + 491 p., p. 1-104.

DE LAGNY,T. F. Méthodes nouvelles pour former et résoudre toutes les équations. Hist.Acad.Sci. Paris 1705, 277-300 (1705).

DE LAGNY,T. F. Traité des progressions arithmétiques de tous les degrés. Hist. Acad. Sci. Paris 1722, 264-320 (1722).

LAGRANGE, J. L. Sur une nouvelle espèce de calcul relatif à la différentiation et à l'intégration. Oeuvres de Lagrange, vol. 3. Paris, Gauthier-Villars, 1869, p. 439-476.

BIBLIOGRAPHY

LAPLACE, P. S. Théorie analytique des probabilités, 3rd ed., book 1. Oeuvres complètes de Laplace, vol. 7. Paris, Gauthier-Villars, 1886, p. 7-180.

LAPLACE, P. S. Mémoire sur la usage du calcul aux différences partielles dans la théorie des suites. Oeuvres, vol. 9, 1893, p. 311-335. See also Mémoire sur les suites. Oeuvres, vol. 10, 1894, p. 1-89.

LAURENT, H. Traité d'Analyse, vol. 1. Paris, Gauthier-Villars, 1885, xi + 392 p., p. 97-118.

LEGENDRE, A. M. Exercices de calcul intégral, vol. 2. Paris, Courcier, 1817, xx + 544 p., p.72-96, 131-136.

LEGENDRE, A. M. Traité des fonctions elliptiques et des intégrales Eulériennes. Vol.2.Paris, Huzard Courcier, 1826, viii + 596 p., p. 1-120.

LEHMER, D. H. On the maxima and minima of Bernoulli polynomials. Amer. Math. Month. 47, 533-538 (1940).

LIDSTONE, G. J. Notes on interpolation. Jour. Inst. Actuar. 71, 68-95 (1941).

LOWAN, A. N. On the computation of the second differences of the Si(x), Ei(x) and Ci(x) functions. Bull. Amer. Math. Soc. 45, 583-588 (1939).

MARKOFF, A. A. Differenzenrechnung. Leipzig, Teubner, 1896, v + 194 p.

MIKELADZE, S. Über dividierte Differenzen mit wiederholten Argumentwerten. Trav. Inst. Math. Tbilissi (Trudy Tbiliss. Mat. Inst.) 9, 49-60 (1941).

DE MOIVRE, A. De fractionibus algebraicis radicalitate immunibis ad fractiones simplicores reducendis deque summandis terminis quarumdam serierum aequallo intervallo a se distantibus. Phil. Trans. Roy. Soc. Lond. 32, 162-178 (1722-1723).

DE MOIVRE, A. Miscellanea analytica de seriebus ed quadratis. London, Tonson and Watts, 1730.

DE MONTMORT, P. R. De seriebus infinitis tractatus. Phil. Trans. Roy. Soc. Lond. 30, 633-675 (1717-1719).

MOUTON, G. Observationes diametrorum Solis et Lunae... Book III, chap. 3: De nonnullis numerorum proprietabus. Lyon, Liberal, 1670, p. 268-395.

NEWTON, I. Methodus differentialis. In vol. 1 of Isaaci Newtoni Opera... Samuel Horsley,ed.London, J. Nichols, 1779, p. 521-528.

NICOLE, F. Traité du calcul des différences finies. Hist. Acad. Sci. Paris: 1717, 7-21; 1723, 20-37, 181-198; 1724, 138-158.

NÖRLUND, N. E. Vorlesungen über Differenzenrechnung. Berlin, Springer, 1924, ix + 551 p.

NÖRLUND, N. E. Sur la "Somme" d'une fonction. Mém. des Sci. Math., Fasc. 24, Paris, Gauthier-Villars, 1927, 54 p.

PASCAL, E. Calcolo delle variazioni e calcolo delle differenze finite. Part 3 of Lezioni de calcolo infinitesimale. Milan, Hoepli, 1897, xii + 330 p., p. 207-330.

PERL, E. Untersuchungen über Differenzenkoefficienten erster und zweiter Art...(Koenigsberg Diss.). Leipzig, Hoffman, 1911, 126 p.

PINCHERLE, S. and AMALDI, U. Le operazioni distributive e le loro applicazioni all' analisi. Bologna, Zanichelli, 1901, xii + 490 p.

DE PRONY, G. C. Cours d'analyse appliquée à la mécanique. Jour. École Polytech. Paris: 1 (1), 107-119; 1 (2), 1-23; 1 (3), 209-273; 1 (4), 459-569 (1796-1797).

RICHARDSON, L. F. The deffered approach to the limit I. Single lattice. Phil. Trans. Roy. Soc. Lond. A226, 299-349 (1927).

RUSSELL, W. H. L. On the calculus of finite differences. Mess. of Math. (2) 11, 33-36 (1881-1882).

SALZER, H. E. Table of coefficients for differences in terms of derivatives. Jour. Math. Phys. (M.I.T.) 23, 210-212 (1944).

SCHLÖMILCH, O. Theorie der Differenzen und Summen. Halle, Schmidt, 1848, v + 241 p.

SCHWEINS, F. Theorie der Differenzen und Differentiale. Heidelberg, 1825, vi + 666 p., p. 1-113.

SELIWANOFF, D. Lehrbuch der Differenzenrechnung. Vol. 13 of Teubners Sammlung von Lehrbüchern. Leipzig, Teubner, 1904, vi + 92 p.

STEFFENSEN, J. F. Note on divided differences. Danske Vid. Selsk. Math.-Fys. Medd., 17,No. 3, 12 p., 1939.

STIRLING, J. Methodus differentialis Newtoniana illustrata. Phil. Trans. Roy. Soc. Lond.30, 1050-1070 (1717-1719).

STIRLING, J. Methodus differentialis: sive Tractatus de summatione et interpolatione serierum infinitarum. London, Whiston and White, 1754, iv + 154 p.

STUDNICKA, F. J. Beiträge zum Operationscalcul. Sitzber. böhm. Ges. Prag 1871, 39-43 (1871).

STURM, C. Cours d'Analyse, vol. 2. Paris, Mallet-Bachelier, 1859, p. 231-257.

TAYLOR, B. Methodus incrementorum directa ed inversa. London, Innys, 1717, vi + 119 p.

TAYLOR, B. De seriebus infinitis tractatus. Appendix, quâ methodo diversâ eadem materia tractatur. Phil. Trans. Roy. Soc. Lond. 30, 676-689 (1717-1719).

TIMERDING, H. E. Differenzenrechnung. Chap. 9, vol . 1 (1) of Pascal's Repertorium der höheren Analyse. Leipzig, Teubner, 2nd ed. 1910.

LE VERRIER, U. J. Recherches astronomiques. Ann. de l'Observ. Paris, 1, 122-128, 151-154 (1855).

14. DIFFERENCE EQUATIONS

BIRKHOFF, G. D. Note on linear difference and differential equations. Proc. Nat. Acad. Sci. U.S.A. 27,65-67 (1941).

BLEICH, F. and MELAN, E. Die gewöhnlichen und partiellen Differenzengleichungen der Baustatik. Berlin, Springer, 1927, vii + 350 p.

BÖHMER, P. E. Differenzengleichungen und Bestimmte Integrale. Leipzig, Koehler, 1939, vi + 148 p.

CHARLES, J. A. C. Intégral (Calcul intégral des équations en différences finies). Ency. Meth., Math. Vol. 2, p. 221-225. Paris, 1789.

COURNOT, M. Traité élémentaire de la théorie des fonctions et du calcul infinitésimal,vol.2.Paris, Hachette, 2nd ed. 1857, 533 p., p. 431-480.

FUNK, P. Die linearen Differenzengleichungen und ihre Anwendung in der Theorie der Baukonstruktionen. Berlin, Springer, 1920, 84 p.

GERONIMUS, J. Sur quelques équations aux différences finies et les systèmes correspondants des polynomes orthogonaux. C. R. (Doklady) Acad. Sci. URSS (N.S.) 29, 536-538 (1940).

HEYMANN, W. Studien über die Transformation und Integration der Differential- und Differenzengleichungen. Leipzig, Teubner, 1891, x + 436 p.

ISAACS, R. P. A finite difference function theory. Univ. Nac. Tucumán. Revista A. 2, 177-201 (1941).

BIBLIOGRAPHY

JORDAN, C. Calculus of Finite Differences. Budapest, 1939. (See sect. 13, Jordan, C.).

LANCASTER, O. E. Sequences defined by non-linear algebraic difference equations. Ann. of Math. (2) 42, 251-280 (1941).

LAURENT, P. M. Traité d'analyse. Paris, Gauthier-Villars, 1890, vol. 6. (Calcul intégral. Équations différentielles partielles, iv + 339 p.).

NÖRLUND, N. E. Vorlesungen über Differenzenrechnung. Berlin, Springer, 1924, ix + 551 p.

OLTRAMARE, G. Calcul de généralisation. Paris, Hermann, 1899, viii + 191 p.

PASCAL, E. Repertorium der höheren Mathematik. Art. by Guldberg, vol. I_2, p. 555-560.

RACLIS, R. Solution principale de l'équation linéaire aux différences finies. Acta Math.55, 277-394 (1930).

SPOERL, C. A. A fundamental proposition in the solution of simultaneous linear equations. Trans. Actuar. Soc. Amer. 44, 276-288 (1943).

SPOERL, C. A. Difference-equation interpolation. Trans. Actuar. Soc. Amer. 44, 289-325 (1943).

WEINNOLDT, E. H. F. Über Funktionen welche gewisse Differenzengleichungen n. Ordnung Genüge leisten (Diss., Kiel). Kiel, Lipsius and Tischer, 1885, 41 p.

15. DIRECT INTERPOLATION

A. Functions of a Single Variable

ABASON, E. Sur l'approximation minimum d'ordre n sur un ensemble de n + 2 points. Bull. Sci. Ec. Polyt. Timişoara 3, 64-67 (1930).

ABASON, E. Sur la condition pour que n + 2 points soient situés sur une parabole du n-ième degré. Bull. Soc. Sci. Cluj 5, 188-190 (1931).

AITKEN, A. C. On a generalisation of formulae for polynomial interpolation. Jour. Inst. Actuar. 61, 107-112 (1930).

AITKEN, A. C. On interpolation by iteration of proportional parts, without the use of differences. Proc. Edin. Math. Soc. (2) 3, 56-76 (1932).

AMPÈRE, A. M. Essai sur un nouveau mode d'exposition des principes du calcul différentiel, du calcul aux différences et de l'interpolation des suites considerées comme dérivant d'une source commune. Ann. Math. (Gergonne) 16, 329-349 (1825-26).

ANDOYER, H. Calcul des différences et interpolation. Vol. I, part 21 in 1 (4), Fasc. 1 of Ency. des Sci. Math., 1906, p. 47-160.

ARBOGAST, L. F. A. Du calcul des dérivations. Strasbourg, Levrault, 1800, xxii + 404 p., p. 375-404.

BAUSCHINGER, J. Interpolation. Part I D 3 of Ency. der Math. Wiss., I(2). Leipzig, Teubner, 1901, p. 799-820.

BAUSCHINGER, J. Tafeln zur theoretischen Astronomie. Leipzig, Engelmann, 1901, iv + 148 p.

BELARDINELLI, G. Il problema dell'interpolazione. Rend. Sem. Mat. Fis. Milano 3, 13-28 (1930).

BENNETT, A. A. The interpolational polynomial. Chap. 1 of Numerical Integration of Differential Equations. (Report of Committee on Numerical Integration). Bull. Nat. Res. Council, No. 92, p. 11-50 (1933).

BIBLIOGRAPHY

BIERMANN, O. Vorlesungen über mathematische Näherungsmethoden. Braunschweig, Vieweg, 1905, ix + 227p., p. 92-169.

BLANCH, G. and RHODES, I. Seven-point Lagrangian integration formulas. Jour. Math. Phys. (M.I.T.) 22, 204-207 (1943).

BOOLE, G. A Treatise on the Calculus of Finite Differences. London, Macmillan, 1860, iv + 248 p.

BOYER, J. Osculatory interpolation in practice. Record Amer. Inst. Actuar.: 31, 337-350(1942); 32, 83-96 (1943).

BRAUNSCHMIDT, O. Über Interpolation. Jour. Reine Angew. Math. 185, 14-55 (1943).

CAJORI, F. A History of Mathematical Notations. Vol. 2. Chicago, Open Court, 1929, xviii + 367 p., p. 42-43, 263-267.

CAMP, K. Actuarial note: practical interpolation methods with second-order curves. Trans. Actuar. Soc. Amer. 40, 426-439 (1939).

CAUCHY, A. L. Cours d'analyse de l'école royale polytechnique. I partie, analyse algébrique. Note V. Sur la formule de Lagrange relative à l'interpolation. Oeuvres complètes d'Augustin Cauchy, 2nd series, vol. 3. Paris, Gauthier-Villars, 1897, p. 429-433.

CAUCHY, A. L. Sur les fonctions interpolaires. Oeuvres complètes d'Augustin Cauchy, 1st series, vol. 5. Paris, Gauthier-Villars, 1885, p. 409-424.

CHARLES, J. A. C. Interpolation (mathématiques et physique). Ency. Meth., Math. Vol. 2, p. 233-237, Paris, 1789.

CLAUSEN, T. Über mechanische Quadraturen. Jour. Reine Angew. Math. 6, 287-289 (1830).

COMRIE, L. J. Interpolation and Allied Tables. Reprint from the Nautical Almanac for 1937. London, H. M. Stationery Office, 1936, 45 p.

CROUT, P. D. A method for deriving formulas of interpolation. Jour. Math. Phys. (M.I.T.)8, 18-55, 119-128 (1929).

DAVIS, H. T. Tables of the Higher Mathematical Functions, vol. 1. Bloomington, Indiana, Principia Press, 1933, xiii + 377 p., p. 65-100.

DeMORGAN, A. The Differential and Integral Calculus. London, Baldwin and Cradock, 1842, Chap. 18, p. 542-560.

DIESTEL, F. Beiträge zu der Interpolationsrechnung. (Göttingen Diss.). Göttingen, Vandenhoeck and Ruprecht, 1890, 47 p.

ECHOLS, W. H. On some forms of Lagrange's interpolation formula. Ann. of Math. (1) 8, 22-24 (1893).

EGGER, H. Praktische Interpolation. Zeit. Angew. Math. Mech. 22, 362-364 (1942).

ENCKE, J. F. Über Interpolation. Gesammelte mathematische und astronomische Abhandlungen von J. F. Encke, vol. 1. Berlin, Dümmler, 1888, p. 1-20.

ERDÖS, P. and TURÁN, P. On interpolation. Ann. of Math. (2): 38, 142-155 (1937); 39, 703-724 (1938); 41, 510-533 (1940).

EVERETT, J. D. On the algebra of difference tables. Quart. Jour. Pure Appl. Math. 31, 357-376 (1900).

EVERETT, J. D. On interpolation formulae. Quart. Jour. Pure Appl. Math. 32, 306-313 (1901).

FAVARD, J. Sur l'interpolation. Bull. Soc. Math. France 67, 102-113 (1939).

FAVARD, J. Sur l'interpolation. Jour. Math. Pures Appl. (9) 19, 281-306 (1940).

BIBLIOGRAPHY

FEJÉR, L. Über Interpolation. Nachr. Ges. Wiss. Göttingen p. 66-91 (1916).

FEJÉR, L. Über Interpolation und konforme Abbildung. Nachr. Ges. Wiss. Göttingen p. 319-331 (1918).

FEJÉR, L. Über Weierstrasssche Approximation, besonders durch Hermitesche Interpolation. Math. Ann. 102, 707-725 (1929).

FEJÉR, L. Lagrangesche Interpolation und die zugehörigen konjugierten Punkte. Math. Ann. 106, 1-55 (1932).

FEKETE, M. Über Interpolation. Zeit. Angew. Math. Mech. 6, 410-413 (1926).

FELLER, W. On A. C. Aitken's method of interpolation. Quart. Appl. Math. 1, 86-87 (1943).

FISHER, R. A. and WISHART, J. On the distribution of error of an interpolated value and on the construction of tables. Proc. Camb. Phil. Soc. 23, 912-921 (1927).

FORSYTH, C. H. An Introduction to the Mathematical Analysis of Statistics. New York, Wiley, 1924. Chap. 3, p. 33-55.

FRASER, D. C. Newton's interpolation formulas. Jour. Inst. Actuar.:51, 77-106, 211-232 (1919); 52, 117-135 (1921).

FRASER, D. C. Newton's Interpolation Formulas. London, Layton, 1927, iv + 95 p.

GIBB, D. A Course in Interpolation and Numerical Integration. Edin. Math. Tracts. No. 2. London, Bell, 1915, viii + 90 p.

GLOVER, J. W. Interpolation, summation and graduation. Chap. 3 of Handbook of Mathematical Statistics. Boston, Houghton-Mifflin, 1924, p. 34-61.

GONTCHAROFF, M. Sur quelques séries d'interpolation généralisant celles de Newton et de Stirling. (Russian. French summary.). Uchenye Zapiski Moskov. Gos. Univ. Mat. 30, 17-48 (1939).

GREVILLE, T. N. E. A generalization of Waring's formula. Ann. Math. Statist. 15, 218-219 (1944).

GRÜNWALD, G. On a convergence theorem for the Lagrange interpolation polynomials. Bull. Amer. Math. Soc. 47, 271-275 (1941).

GRÜNWALD, G. Note on interpolation. Bull. Amer. Math. Soc. 47, 257-260 (1941).

HADAMARD, J. Cours d'analyse, vol. I. Paris, Hermann, 1925, p. 132-151.

HEINHOLD, J. Zur Interpolation bei ungleichen Tafelabständen. Zeit. Angew. Math. Mech. 22, 235-238 (1942).

HENDERSON, R. and SHEPPARD, H. N. Graduation of Mortality and Other Tables. Actuarial Studies No. 4. New York, Actuarial Soc. of Amer., 1919, v + 82 p.

HERMITE, C. Sur la formule d'interpolation de Lagrange. Jour. Reine Angew. Math. 84, 70-79 (1878).

ISSERLIS, L. Note on Chebysheff's interpolation formula. Biometrika 19, 87-93 (1927).

JACKSON, D. The Theory of Approximation. Amer. Math. Soc. Colloquium Publs., vol. 11. New York, Amer. Math. Soc., 1930, viii + 178 p.

JACKSON, D. Fourier Series and Orthogonal Polynomials. Carus Monograph Series, No. 6. Oberlin, Ohio, Math. Assoc. Amer., 1941, xii + 234 p.

JOFFE, S. A. Interpolation formulae and central-difference notation. Trans. Actuar. Soc. Amer. 18, 72-98 (1917).

JORDAN, C. Cours d'analyse de l'école polytechnique, vol. 2. Paris, Gauthier-Villars, 3rd ed. 1913, 705 p., p. 125-132.

JORDAN, C. Statistique mathématique. Paris, Gauthier-Villars, 1927, xvii + 344 p.

KAMENETZKY, I. M. Sur l'interpolation au moyen des dérivées et les procédés d'interpolation correspondants. I, II. C. R. (Doklady) Acad. Sci. URSS (N.S.): 25, 356-358 (1939); 26, 217-219 (1940).

KING, G. Institute of Actuaries' Text Book of the Principles of Interest, Life Annuities, and Assurances, and their Practical Application. Part II. Life Contingencies. London, Layton, 2nd ed. 1902, xxxi + 569 p., p. 420-457.

KOWALEWSKI, A. Newton, Cotes, Gauss, Jacobi. Vier grundlegende Abhandlungen über Interpolation und genährte Quadratur. Leipzig, Veit, 1917, vi + 104 p.

KOWALEWSKI, G. Interpolation und genäherte Quadratur. Leipzig, Teubner, 1932, v + 146 p.

LAGRANGE, J. L. Sur une méthode particulière d'approximation et interpolation. Oeuvres de Lagrange, vol. 5. Paris, Gauthier-Villars, 1870, p. 517-531.

LAGRANGE, J. L. Sur les interpolations. Oeuvres, vol. 7, 1877, p. 533-553.

LAGRANGE, J. L. Mémoire sur la méthode d'interpolation. Oeuvres, vol. 5, 1870, p. 661-684.

LAURENT, P. M. H. Traité d'analyse, vol. 3. Paris, Gauthier-Villars, 1888, 511 p., p. 418-497.

LEVER, E. H. On obtaining the values of life annuities at isolated rates of interest. Jour. Inst. Actuar. 52, 171-179 (1921).

LIDSTONE, G. J. Notes on Everett's interpolation formula. Proc. Edin. Math. Soc. 40, 21-26 (1921-1922).

LIDSTONE, G. J. Notes on interpolation. Jour. Inst. Actuar. 71, 68-95 (1941).

LINDOW, M. Numerische Infinitesimalrechnung. Berlin, Dümmler, 1928, viii + 176 p.

DE LOSADA Y PUGA, C. The interpolation formula of Stirling deduced from Taylor's series. (Spanish). Revista Univ. Catolica Peru 7, 177-186 (1939).

LOSINSKY, S. Sur le procédé d'interpolation de Fejér. C. R. (Doklady) Acad. Sci. URSS (N.S.) 24, 318-321 (1939).

LOWAN, A. N. and SALZER, H. E. Formulas for complex interpolation. Quart. Appl. Math. 2, 272-274 (1944).

MAENNCHEN, P. Über ein Interpolationsverfahren des jugendlichen Gauss. Jber. Deutsch Math. Verein 28, 80-84 (1919).

MARKOFF, A. A. Differenzenrechnung. Leipzig, Teubner, 1896, v + 194 p.

MAZZONI, P. Su un metodo d'interpolazione. Boll. Un. Mat. Ital. 8, 29-39 (1929).

MAZZONI, P. Alcune applicazioni dei polinomi di Tchebychev. Boll. Un. Mat. Ital. 8, 246-248 (1929).

MAZZONI, P. Sul metodo d'interpolazione di Tchebychev. Boll. Un. Mat. Ital. 9, 132-141 (1930).

McCLINTOCK, E. A new general method of interpolation. Amer. Jour. Math. 2, 307-314 (1879).

MIRAKYAN, G. Approximation des fonctions continues au moyen de polynômes de la forme $e^{-nx}\sum_{k=0}^{m} x^k C_{k,n}$. C. R. (Doklady) Acad. Sci. URSS (N.S.) 31, 201-205 (1941).

MONTEL, P. Leçons sur les séries de polynomes à une variable complexe. Coll. Borel, Paris, Gauthier-Villars, 1910.

NEWTON, I. Methodus differentialis. In vol. 1 of Isaaci Newtoni opera quae exstant omnia, Samuel Horsley, ed. London, 1779, p. 521-528.

BIBLIOGRAPHY

NIELSEN, N. Traité élémentaire des nombres de Bernoulli. Paris, Gauthier-Villars, 1923, x + 398 p.

NÖRLUND, N. E. Vorlesungen über Differenzenrechnung. Berlin, Springer, 1924, ix + 551 p.

NÖRLUND, N. E. Leçons sur les séries d'interpolation. Coll. Borel, Paris, Gauthier-Villars, 1926, vii + 236 p.

OGURA, K. Sur la théorie de l'interpolation. C. R. Congr. Intern. Math. Strasbourg, 1920, p. 316-322, Toulouse, Edouard Privat, 1921.

PEANO, G. Residuo in formula de quadratura Cavalieri-Simpson. L'Ens. Math. 18, 124-129 (1916).

PEARSON, K. Tracts for Computers, No. 2. On the Construction of Tables and on Interpolation. Part I, Uni-variate Tables. Cambridge, Cambridge Univ. Press, 1920, 70 p.

PIPES, L. A. The method of symmetrical components applied to harmonic analysis. Phil. Mag. (7) 29, 66-74 (1940).

QUADE, W. Abschätzungen zur trigonometrischen Interpolation. Deutsche Math. 5, 482-512 (1941).

RADAU, R. Études sur les formules d'interpolation. Paris, Gauthier-Villars, 1891, 96 p.

RICE, H. L. The Theory and Practice of Interpolation. Lynn (Mass.), Nichols, 1899, 234 p.

RUTLEDGE, G. The explicit determination of Cotes' coefficients for polynomial area. Jour. Math. Phys. (M.I.T.) 1, 78-85 (1922).

RUTLEDGE, G. The polynomial determined by 2n + 1 points. Jour. Math. Phys. (M.I.T.) 2,47-62(1923).

RUTLEDGE, G. Limiting values of Lagrangean coefficients. Jour. Math. Phys. (M.I.T.) 8, 13-17 (1929).

SAMUELSON, P. A. A simple method of interpolation. Proc. Nat. Acad. Sci. U.S.A. 29, 397-401 (1943).

SHEPPARD, W. F. Interpolation. Encyclopaedia Britannica 11th ed., 14, 706-710 (1910).

SHEPPARD, W. F. Mathematics for the study of frequency statistics. Math. Gaz. 15, 232-249 (1930).

SHOHAT, J. Application of orthogonal Tchebycheff polynomials to Lagrangean interpolation and to the general theory of polynomials. Ann. Mat. Pura Appl. 18, 201-238 (1939).

SPOERL, C. A. Difference-equation interpolation. Trans. Actuar. Soc. Amer.: 44, 289-325 (1943); 45, 70-82 (1944).

STEFFENSEN, J. F. Interpolation. Baltimore, Williams and Wilkins, 1927.

STOCK, J. S. A method of graphic interpolation. Jour. Amer. Statist. Assoc. 34, 709-713 (1939).

TAYLOR, B. Methodus incrementorum directa et inversa. London, Innys, 1717, 118 p.

THIELE, T. N. Interpolationsrechnung. Leipzig, Teubner, 1909, xii + 175 p.

VERNOTTE, P. Sur la représentation d'une fonction expérimentale par une fraction rationnelle. C. R. Acad. Sci. Paris 213, 433-435 (1941).

WEBSTER, M. S. Note on certain Lagrange interpolation polynomials. Bull. Amer. Math. Soc. 45, 870-873 (1939).

WHITTAKER, E. T. and ROBINSON, G. The Calculus of Observations. Glasgow, Blackie, 3rd ed. 1942, chaps. 1, 2 and 3, also p. 369-371.

WILLERS, F. A. Benutzung projektiver Skalen zur Unterteilung von Skalen anderer Funktionen. Zeit. Angew. Math. Mech. 20, 291-292 (1940).

BIBLIOGRAPHY

B. Functions of Several Variables

BIERMANN, O. Über näherungsweise Cubaturen. Monatsh. Math. Phys. 14, 211-225 (1903).

BROWN, E. H. and BURN, J. Elements of Finite Differences. London, Layton, 1915, 289 p., p. 45-61.

ELDERTON, W. P. Some notes on interpolation in n-dimension space. Biometrika 6, 94-103 (1908).

KRONECKER, L. Über einige Interpolationsformeln für ganze Functionen mehrerer Variablen (1869). Ges. Werke, Vol. I. Leipzig, Teubner, 1895, p. 135-141.

LAGRANGE, J. L. Sur une nouvelle espèce de calcul relatif à la différentiation et à l'intégration des quantités variables. Oeuvres de Lagrange, vol. 3. Paris, Gauthier-Villars, 1869, p. 441-476.

LAL, D. N. and DASGUPTA, P. N. Interpolation polynomials in two and more variables. Bull. Calcutta Math. Soc. 32, 7-14 (1940).

LAMBERT, J. H. Beyträge zum Gebrauche der Mathematik und deren Anwendung. Theil III. Anmerkungen über das Einschalten. Berlin, Buchandlung der Realschule, 1772, p. 66-104.

NARUMI, S. Some formula in the theory of interpolation of many independent variables. Tôhoku Math. Jour. 18, 309-321 (1920).

PEARSON, K. On the Construction of Tables and on Interpolation. Part II. Bi-variate Tables. Tracts for Computers, No. III. Cambridge, Cambridge Univ. Press, 1920, 54 p.

ROURE, H. Sur une généralisation de la série de Lagrange, avec applications à l'astronomie. C. R. Acad. Sci. Paris 216, 332-353 (1943).

WHITTAKER, E.T. and ROBINSON, G. The Calculus of Observations. London, Blackie, 3rd ed. 1942, p. 371-374.

16. INVERSE INTERPOLATION, TABULATION AND SUBTABULATION

AITKEN, A. C. On interpolation by iteration of proportional parts, without the use of differences. Proc. Edin. Math. Soc. (2) 3, 56-76 (1932).

COMRIE, L. J. On the construction of tables by interpolation. Month. Not. Roy. Astr. Soc. 88, 506-523 (1928).

COMRIE, L. J. Inverse interpolation. Nautical Almanac, 1937. London, H. M. Stationery Office, 1936, p. 934-939.

PEANO, G. Interpolazione nelle tavole numeriche. Atti Accad. Sci. Torino 53, 693-716 (1917).

PEARSON, K. Tracts for Computers, No. II. On the Construction of Tables and on Interpolation. Part I. Uni-variate Tables. London, Cambridge Univ. Press, 1920, 70 p.

SALZER, H. E. A new formula for inverse interpolation. Bull. Amer. Math. Soc. 50, 513-516 (1944).

VAN ORSTRAND, C. E. Inverse interpolation by means of a reversed series. Phil. Mag. (6) 15, 628-638 (1908).

WHITTAKER, E. T. and ROBINSON, G. The Calculus of Observations. London, Blackie, 3rd ed. 1942, p. 53-57, 60-61, 96-98.

17. INTERPOLATION TABLES

COMRIE, L. J. Tables for interpolation to tenths and fifths by the end-figure process. Nautical Almanac, 1931. London, H. M. Stationery Office, 1929, p. 828-859.

BIBLIOGRAPHY

COMRIE, L. J. Interpolation and Allied Tables. Reprint from Nautical Almanac for 1937, London, H. M. Stationery Office, 1936, 45 p.

COMRIE, L. J. and HARTLEY, H. O. Table of Lagrangian coefficients for harmonic interpolation in certain tables of percentage points. Biometrika 32, 183-186 (1941).

DAVIS, H. T. Tables of the Higher Mathematical Functions, vol. 1. Bloomington, Indiana, Principia Press, 1933, xiii + 377 p., p. 101-176.

GLOVER, J. W. Tables of Applied Mathematics in Finance, Insurance, Statistics. Ann Arbor, George Wahr, 1930, xiii + 678 p., p. 414-433.

HENDERSON, R. and SHEPPARD, H. N. Graduation of Mortality and Other Tables. Actuarial Studies No. 4. New York, Actuar. Soc. of Amer., 1919, vi + 82 p.

HUNTINGTON, E. V. Tables of Lagrangean coefficients for interpolating without differences. Proc. Amer. Acad. Arts Sci. 63, 421-437 (1929).

LAMPE, E. Zur mechanischen Quadratur. Jber. Deutsch. Math. Verein 25, 325-332 (1917).

LITTLE, A. S. A Table of Interpolation Multipliers. London, Rutledge, 1927.

LOWAN, A. N. and SALZER, H. E. Coefficients for interpolation within a square grid in the complex plane. Jour. Math. Phys. (M.I.T.) 23, 156-166 (1944).

MATH. TABLES PROJECT (W.P.A.). Tables of Lagrangian Interpolation Coefficients. New York, Columbia Univ. Press, 1944, xxxvi + 392 p.

RUTLEDGE, G. Explicit determination of Cotes' coefficients for polynomial area. Jour. Math. Phys. (M.I.T.) 1, 78-85 (1922).

RUTLEDGE, G. The polynomial determined by 2n + 1 points. Jour. Math. Phys. (M.I.T.) 2, 47-62 (1922).

RUTLEDGE, G. Fundamental table for Lagrangean coefficients. Jour. Math. Phys. (M.I.T.) 8, 1-12(1929).

RUTLEDGE, G. and CROUT, P. D. Tables and methods of extending tables for interpolation without differences. Mass. Inst. of Tech. Publs. (Dept. of Math.) Ser. 2, No. 176, July, 1930, p. 166-180.

SALZER, H. E. Table of coefficients for inverse interpolation with central differences. Jour. Math. Phys. (M.I.T.) 22, 210-224 (1943).

SALZER, H. E. Table of coefficients for inverse interpolation with advancing differences. Jour. Math. Phys. (M.I.T.) 23, 75-102 (1944).

THOMPSON, A. J. Table of Coefficients of Everett's Central-Difference Interpolation Formula. Tracts for Computers, No. 5. Cambridge, Cambridge Univ. Press, 2nd ed. 1943, viii + 32 p.

18. ASYMPTOTIC EXPANSIONS

BARNES, E. W. The asymptotic expansion of integral functions defined by Taylor's series. Phil. Trans. Roy. Soc. Lond. 206A, 249-297 (1906).

BARNES, E. W. The asymptotic expansion of integral functions defined by generalised hypergeometric series. Proc. Lond. Math. Soc. (2) 5, 59-116 (1907).

BARNES, E. W. A new development of the theory of the hypergeometric functions. Proc. Lond. Math. Soc. (2) 6, 141-177 (1908).

BIBLIOGRAPHY

BOLZA, O. Ueber die linearen Relationen zwischen den zu verschiedenen singulären Punkten gehörigen Fundamentalsystemen von Integralen der Riemann'schen Differentialgleichung. Math. Ann. 42, 526-536 (1893).

BOREL, É. Leçons sur les séries divergentes. Coll. de Monographies sur la Théorie des Fonctions. Paris, Gauthier-Villars, 2nd ed. 1928, 260 p.

FORD, W. B. Studies on Divergent Series and Summability. Mich. Sci. Series vol. II. New York, Macmillan, 1916, xi + 194 p.

FORD, W. B. On the behavior of integral functions in distant portions of the plane. Bull. Amer. Math. Soc. 34, 91-106 (1928).

FORD, W. B. The Asymptotic Developments of Functions defined by Maclaurin Series. Univ. of Mich. Studies, Scientific Series vol. XI. Ann Arbor, Univ. of Mich. Press, 1936, viii + 143 p.

HAAR, A. Über asymptotische Entwicklungen von Funktionen. Math. Ann. 96, 69-107 (1927).

JACOBSTHAL, W. Asymptotische Darstellungen von Lösungen linearer Differentialgleichungen. Math. Ann. 56, 129-154 (1902).

JEFFREYS, H. On certain approximate solutions of linear differential equations of the second order. On certain approximate solutions of Mathieu's equation. On the modified Mathieu's equation. Proc. Lond. Math. Soc. 23, 428-454 (1924).

KNOPP, K. Theory and Application of Infinite Series. (Translation of 2nd German ed., by R.C. Young.). London, Blackie, 1928, xii + 571 p., p. 520-563.

LANGER, R. E. The asymptotic solutions of ordinary linear differential equations of the second order with special reference to the Stokes phenomenon. Bull. Amer. Math. Soc. 40, 545-582 (1934).

LENSE, J. Reihenentwicklungen in der mathematischen Physik. Berlin, de Gruyter, 1933, 178 p., p. 145-162.

LEROY, E. Sur les séries divergentes et les fonctions définies par un développement de Taylor. Ann. Toulouse 2, 317-430 (1900).

LITTLEWOOD, J. E. On the asymptotic approximation to integral functions of zero order. Proc. Lond. Math. Soc. (2) 5, 361-410 (1907).

POINCARÉ, H. Les méthodes nouvelles de la mécanique céleste, vol. 2. Paris, Gauthier-Villars, 1893, viii + 479 p.

PUGACHOV, V. S. Evaluation of error of asymptotic representations of integrals of linear differential equations containing a parameter. (Russian. English summary.). Appl. Math. Mech. (Akad. Nauk SSSR. Prikl. Mat. Mech.) 6, 203-208 (1942).

WATSON, G. N. A Treatise on the Theory of Bessel Functions. Cambridge and New York, Cambridge Univ. Press (Macmillan), 2nd ed. 1944, vi + 804 p., p. 194-270.

WHITTAKER, E. T. and WATSON, G. N. Modern Analysis. Cambridge, Cambridge Univ. Press, 1944, 608 p., chap. VIII, p. 150-159.

WIRTINGER, W. Einige Anwendungen der Euler-Maclaurinsche Summenformel, insbesondere auf eine Aufgabe von Abel. Acta Math. 26, 255-271 (1902).

WRIGHT, E. M. The asymptotic expansion of the generalized hypergeometric function. Proc. Lond. Math. Soc. (2) 46, 389-408 (1940).

WRIGHT, E. M. The asymptotic expansion of integral functions defined by Taylor's series. Phil. Trans. Roy. Soc. Lond. 238A, 423-451 (1940).

BIBLIOGRAPHY

19. NUMERICAL DIFFERENTIATION AND HIGHER DERIVATIVES

BABINI, J. On the application of finite differences to the successive derivation of composite functions. (Spanish). Revista Union Mat. Argentina 8, 160-164 (1942).

BICKLEY, W. G. Formulae for numerical differentiation. Math. Gaz. 25, 19-27 (1941).

BICKLEY, W. G. and MILLER, J. C. P. Numerical differentiation near the limits of a difference table. Phil. Mag. (7) 33, 1-14 (1942).

BRUNS, H. Grundlinien des wissenschaftlichen Rechnens. Leipzig, Teubner, 1903, vii + 159 p., p. 62-67.

CRANK, J., HARTREE, D. R., INGHAM, J. and SLOANE, R. W. Distribution of potential in cylindrical thermionic valves. Proc. Phys. Soc. Lond. 51, 952-971 (1939).

GAUNT, A. The deferred approach to the limit. II. Interpenetrating lattices. Phil. Trans. Roy. Soc. Lond. A226, 350-361 (1927).

HANSEN, P. A. Relationen einestheils zwischen Summen und Differenzen und anderntheils zwischen Integralen und Differentialen. Abh. Math. Phys. Klasse König. Sächs. Ges. Wiss. Leipzig 7, 507-583 (1865).

LINDOW, M. Numerische Infinitesimalrechnung. Berlin, Dümmler, 1928, viii + 176 p., chap. 2.

LOWAN, A., SALZER, H. E. and HILLMAN, A. A table of coefficients for numerical differentiation. Bull. Amer. Math. Soc. 48, 920-924 (1942).

MARKOFF, A. A. Differenzenrechnung. Leipzig, Teubner, 1896, vi + 194 p., p. 20-27.

VON OPPOLZER, T. Lehrbuch zur Bahnbestimmung der Kometen und Planeten. Vol. 2. Leipzig, Engelmann, 1880, p. 16-31.

SALZER, H. E. Coefficients for numerical differentiation with central differences. Jour. Math. Phys. (M.I.T.) 22, 115-135 (1943).

SAUER, R. and PÖSCH, H. Rechnerische Differentiation von Kurven. Zeit. Verein. Deutsch. Ing. 85 195-197 (1941).

SCHWATT, I. J. An Introduction to the Operations with Series. Philadelphia, Univ. of Penn.Press, 1924, vii + 287 p.

WHITTAKER, E. T. and ROBINSON, G. The Calculus of Observations. Glasgow, Blackie, 1942, p. 62-70.

20. NUMERICAL INTEGRATION OF DEFINITE INTEGRALS

A. Functions of a Single Variable

ABASON, E. Asupra unor formule pentru calculul cu aproximati al ariilor. Gaz. Mat. 36, 41-45 (1930).

ABASON, E. Sur la moyenne des fonctions paraboliques. Bull.Sci. Ec. Polyt. Timişoara 3, 235-243(1930).

ACHYESER, N. I. and KREIN, M. C. On some quadrature formulas of P. Tschebyscheff and A. Markoff. (Russian). Memorial volume dedicated to D. A. Grave. Moscow, 1940, p. 15-28.

AUBERT, P. and PAPELIER, G. Exercices de calcul numérique, vol. 2. Paris, Vuibert, 1920, 246 p., p. 135-159.

BACKMAN, G. Methodik der theoretischen Wiedergabe beobachteter Wachstumsserien. Lunds Univ. Års-skrift 35, No. 8, 20 p., 1939.

BIBLIOGRAPHY

BENNETT, A. A. The interpolational polynomial. Chap. 1 of: Numerical Integration of Differential Equations. (Report of Committee on Numerical Integration). Bull. Nat. Res. Council, No. 92, Nov. (1933), p. 11-50.

BERKELEY, E. C. Summation as a function of any terms. Record Amer. Inst. Actuar. 29, 314-348 (1940).

BICKLEY, W. G. Formulae for numerical integration. Math. Gaz. 23, 352-359 (1939).

BERTRAND, J. Traité de calcul différentiel et de calcul intégral. Vol. 2. Calcul intégral. Intégrales définies et indéfinies. Paris, Gauthier-Villars, 1870, p. 331-352.

BIERMANN, O. Zur näherungsweisen Quadratur und Cubatur. Monatsh. Math. Phys. 14, 226-242 (1903).

BOUNITZKY, E. Remarque sur la formule d'Euler-Maclaurin. Casopis pest. mat. a fys. (Prague) 57, 95-102 (1928).

BRUNS, H. Grundlinien des wissenschaftlichen Rechnens. Leipzig, Teubner, 1903, vii + 159 p., p. 68-113.

CASSINA, U. Formole sommatorie e di quadratura ad ordinate estreme. Rend. Ist. Lombardo 72, 225-274 (1939).

CASSINA, U. Formole sommatorie e di quadratura con l'ordinata media. Atti Accad.Sci. Torino 74, 300-325 (1939).

CASSINA, U. Estensione del teorema di Rolle al calcolo delle differenze ed applicationi. Rend. Ist. Lombardo 72, 323-332 (1939).

CLAUSEN, T. Über mechanische Quadraturen. Jour. Reine Angew. Math. 6, 287-289 (1830).

CROUT, P. D. A method for deriving formulas for the approximate calculation of integrals. Jour. Math. Phys. (M.I.T.): 7, 126-159 (1928); 8, 119-128 (1929).

CROUT, P. D. An application of the invariant area properties of algebraic polynomials to the derivation of formulas for mechanical integration. Jour. Math. Phys. (M.I.T.) 8, 200-215(1929).

CROUT, P. D. The approximation of functions and integrals by a linear combination of functions. Jour. Math. Phys. (M.I.T.) 9, 278-314 (1930).

CZUBER, E. Vorlesungen über Differential- und Integralrechnung, vol. 2. Leipzig, Teubner, 3rd ed. 1913, p. 256-268.

DANIELL, P. J. Remainders in interpolation and quadrature formulae. Math. Gaz. 24, 238-244 (1940).

DUFTON, A. F. A new method for approximate evaluation of definite integrals between finite limits. Nature 105, 355, 455-456 (1920).

ENCKE, J. F. Ueber mechanische Quadratur. Gesammelte mathematische und astronomische Abhandlungen von J. F. Encke, vol. 1. Berlin, Dümmler, 1888, p. 21-60.

ENCKE, J. F. Ueber eine andere Methode, zu den Formeln der mechanischen Quadratur zu gelangen. Ges. Abh., vol. 1, p. 61-99 (1888).

ENCKE, J. F. Ueber die Cotes'eschen Integrations-Factoren. Ges. Abh., vol. 1. p. 100-124 (1888).

FRANK, P. and VON MISES, R. Die Differential-und Integralgleichungen der Mechanik und Physik. Vol. 1. Braunschweig, Vieweg, 1930, p. 34-36, 289-292, 394-397, 467-469.

GAU, E. P. Calculs numériques et graphiques. Collection Armand Colin, No. 60. Paris, Colin, 1925, vi + 206 p., p. 107-120.

GERONIMUS, J. On Gauss' and Tchebycheff's quadrature formulas. Bull. Amer. Math. Soc. 50, 217-221, (1944).

BIBLIOGRAPHY

GIBB, D. A Course in Interpolation and Numerical Integration. Edin. Math. Tracts, No. 2.London, Bell, 1915, p. 63-90.

GIRAUD, G. Sur une méthode pour calculer les intégrales. Bull. Sci. Math. (2) 48, 233-245 (1924).

GIRAUD, G. Sur le calcul numérique des intégrales définies. Bull. Sci. Math. (2) 48, 397-412 (1924).

GROAT, B. F. Mean value of the ordinate of the locus of the rational integral algebraic function of degree n expressed as a weighted mean of n + 1 ordinates... Amer. Math. Month. 38, 212-219 (1931).

GUERONIMUS, J. L. Sur l'erreur des quadratures mécaniques de Gauss. Bull. Cl. Sci. Phys. Math. Kieff 4, 57-66 (1929).

GUERONIMUS, J. L. On some quadrature-formulae. Bull. Acad. Sci. URSS (Math. Phys.) (7) 3, 399-408 (1930).

HARROLD, O. G. On the expansion of the remainder in the open-type Newton-Cotes quadrature formula. Amer. Jour. Math. 59, 275-289 (1937).

HEINE, E. Handbuch der Kugelfunctionen. Vol. 2. Berlin, Reimer, 2nd ed. 1881, p. 1-31.

IGLISCH, R. Bemerkung über die Trapezregel: Zusatz. Zeit. Angew. Math. Mech. 10, 616-618 (1930).

IRWIN, J. O. On Quadrature and Cubature, or on Methods of Determining Approximately Single and Double Integrals. Tracts for Computers, No. 10. London, Cambridge Univ. Press, 1923.

KLÜGEL, G. S. Mathematisches Wörterbuch. Vol. 4. Leipzig, Schwickert, 1823, p. 123-165.

KOWALEWSKI, A. Newton, Cotes, Gauss, Jacobi. Vier grundlegende Abhandlungen über Interpolation und genäherte Quadratur. Leipzig, 1917, vi + 104 p.

KOWALEWSKI, G. Bemerkung über die Trapezregel. Zeit. Angew. Math. Mech. 10, 615-616 (1930).

KOWALEWSKI, G. Interpolation und genäherte Quadratur. Leipzig and Berlin, Teubner, 1932, v + 146 p.

LADEN, H. N. Fundamental polynomials of Lagrange interpolation and coefficients of mechanical quadrature. Duke Math. Jour. 10, 145-151 (1943).

LENSE, J. Reihenentwicklungen in der mathematischen Physik. Berlin, de Gruyter, 1933, p. 107-113.

LINDOW, M. Numerische Infinitesimalrechnung. Berlin, Dümmler, 1928, viii + 176 p.,chap. 3.

LOSINSKY, S. Über mechanische Quadraturen. (Russian. German summary.). Bull. Acad. Sci. URSS Sér. Math. (Izvestia Akad. Nauk SSSR) 4, 113-126 (1940).

LOWAN, A. N. and SALZER, H. E. Table of coefficients in numerical integration formulae. Jour. Math. Phys. (M.I.T.) 22, 49-50 (1943).

LOWAN, A. N., DAVIDS, N. and LEVENSON, A. Errata to "Table of the zeros of the Legendre polynomials of order 1-16 and the weight coefficients for Gauss' mechanical quadrature formula". Bull. Amer. Math. Soc. 49, 939 (1943).

MAJID, M. A. and CHAPMAN, S. Approximate formulae for functions expressed as definite integrals. Phil. Mag. (7) 33, 115-130 (1942).

MARKOFF, A. A. Differenzenrechnung. Leipzig, Teubner, 1896, chap. 5, 9, 10.

MERRIFIELD, C. W. Report on the present state of knowledge of the application of quadratures and interpolation to actual data. Brit. Assoc. Rep. for 1880, p. 321-378.

MIKELADZE, S. E. Untersuchungen über Formeln der mechanischen Quadratur. (Russian. German summary.). Trav. Inst. Math. Tbilissi 2, 43-107 (1937).

MIKELADZE, S. E. Quadrature formulas using differences (Russian. Georgian summary.). Bull. Acad. Sci. Georgian SSR 3, 1001-1003 (1942).

BIBLIOGRAPHY

MIKELADZE, S. E. On formulas for mechanical cubatures, containing partial derivatives of the integrand. Bull. Acad. Sci. Georgian SSR 4, 297-300 (1943).

VON MISES, R. Einfache Quadraturformel. Zeit. Angew. Math. Mech. 1, 73-74 (1921).

DE MONTESSUS, R. and D'ADHÉMAR, R. Calcul numérique. Paris, Doin, 1911, 248 p., p. 139-237.

MOORS, B. P. Valeur approximative d'une intégrale définie. Paris, Gauthier-Villars, 1905, vii + 195 p. and tables.

VON OPPOLZER, T. Lehrbuch zur Bahnbestimmung der Kometen und Planeten, vol.2. Leipzig, Engelmann, 1880, vii + 635 p., p. 32-68.

PICONE, M. Lezioni di analisi infinitesimale. Catania, Circ. Mat. de Catania, 1923, vol. 1, part 2, chap. 5, sec. 2, p. 564-602.

POLYA, G. Über die Konvergenz von Quadraturverfahren. Math. Zeit. 37, 264-286 (1933).

RADAU, R. Étude sur les formules d'approximation qui servent à calculer la valeur numérique d'une intégral définie. Jour. Math. Pures et Appl. (3) 6, 283-336 (1880).

RÉMÈS, E. J. Sur certaines classes de fonctionelles linéaires dans les espaces C_p et sur les termes complémentaires des formules d'analyse approximative. (Ukrainian. Russian and French summary.). Acad. Sci. RSS Ukraine. Rec. Trav. (Zbirnik Prace) Inst. Math., p. 47-82, 1940.

RÉMÈS, E. J. Sur les termes complémentaires de certaines formules d'analyse approximative. C. R. (Doklady) Acad. Sci. URSS (N.S.) 26, 129-133 (1940).

SALZER, H. E. Coefficients for numerical integration with central differences. Phil. Mag. (7) 35, 262-264 (1944).

SCHELLBACH, C. H. Ueber mechanische Quadratur. (Programm, Berlin.). Berlin, Mayer and Miller, 1884.

SHOHAT, J. Sur les quadratures mécaniques et sur les zéros des polynomes de Tchebycheff dans un intervalle infini. C. R. Acad. Sci. Paris 185, 597-598 (1927).

SHOHAT, J. and TAMARKIN, J. D. The Problem of Moments. Amer. Math. Soc. Mathematical Surveys, vol. II. New York, Amer. Math. Soc., 1943, xiv + 140 p., chap. 4.

STEFFENSEN, J. F. On the remainder term of certain formulas of mechanical quadrature. Skand. Aktuarietidskrift 4, 201-209 (1921).

STEFFENSEN, J. F. On a class of quadrature formulas. Proc. Intern. Math. Congr. Toronto, 1924, vol. 2. Toronto, Toronto Univ. Press, 1928, p. 837-844.

STEKLOV, V. Sur l'approximation des fonctions à l'aide des polynomes de Tchébychef et sur les quadratures. Bull. Acad. Impériale Sci. (Izvestia Imperatorskoi Akademii Nauk.) (6) 11, 187-218, 535-566, 687-718 (1917).

STEKLOV, V. Remarques sur les quadratures. Bull. Acad. Sci. Russ. (Izvestia Rossiiskoi Akademii Nauk.) (6) 12, 99-118 (1918).

STEKLOV, V. Quelques remarques complémentaires sur les quadratures. Bull.Acad. Sci. Russ. (Izvestia Rossiiskoi Akademii Nauk.) (6) 12, 587-614 (1918).

STEKLOV, V. Sur les quadratures. Bull. Acad. Sci. Russ. (Izvestia Rossiiskoi Akademii Nauk.) (6): 12, 1859-1890 (1918); 13, 65-96 (1919).

STRÁNSKÝ, J. Bemerkung zum oberen Artikel. Aktuárské Vědy 1, 61-62 (1930). See Tauber, A.

TAUBER, A. Ueber ein Problem der Näherungsrechnung und die Makeham'schen Rentenwerte. Aktuárské Vědy 1, 49-61 (1930).

THIELE, T. N. Interpolationsrechnung. Leipzig, Teubner, 1909, xii + 175 p., p. 21-28.

USPENSKY, J. V. On the convergence of quadrature formulas related to an infinite interval. Trans. Amer. Math. Soc. 30, 542-559 (1928).

BIBLIOGRAPHY

VAHLEN, T. Konstruktionen und Approximationen. Leipzig, Teubner, 1911, xii + 347 p., p. 206-214.

VERITY, E. R. Mathematics for Technical Students. London, Longmans, 1924, p. 419-433.

WALTHER, A. Zur numerischen Integration. Skand. Aktuarietidskrift 8, 148-162 (1925).

WALTHER, A. Bemerkungen über das Tschebyscheffsche Verfahren zur numerischen Integration. Skand. Aktuarietidskrift 13, 168-192 (1930).

WILLERS, F. A. Numerische Integration. Berlin, de Gruyter, 1923.

WINSTON, C. On mechanical quadrature formulae involving the classical orthogonal polynomials. Ann. of Math. (2) 35, 658-677 (1934).

WOLFF, C. E. Note on numerical integration. Proc. Edin. Math. Soc. (2) 1, 139-148 (1928).

B. Functions of Several Variables

AITKEN, A. C. and FREWIN, G. L. The numerical evaluation of double integrals. Proc. Edin. Math. Soc. 42, 2-13 (1923-1924).

ARTMELADZE, N. Über Formeln der mechanischen Kubaturen. (Russian. German summary.). Trav. Inst. Math. Tbilissi (Trudy Tbiliss. Mat. Inst.) 7, 147-160 (1940).

BIERMANN, O. Über näherungsweise Cubaturen. Monatsh. Math. Phys. 14, 211-225 (1903).

BIERMANN, O. Zur näherungsweisen Quadratur und Cubatur. Monatsh. Math. Phys. 14, 226-242 (1903).

BURNSIDE, W. An approximate quadrature formula. Mess. of Math. (2) 37, 166-167 (1907-1908).

DAS GUPTA, P. N. On an interpolation formula connected with a definite integral in n-variables. Bull. Calcutta Math. Soc. 33, 41-44 (1941).

SADOWSKY, M. A formula for approximate computation of a triple integral. Amer. Math. Month. 47, 539-543 (1940).

SHEPPARD, W. F. Central-difference formulae. Proc. Lond. Math. Soc. 31, 449-488 (1899).

SHEPPARD, W. F. Some quadrature-formulae. Proc. Lond. Math. Soc. 32, 258-277 (1900).

WHITTAKER, E. T. and ROBINSON, G. The Calculus of Observations. Glasgow, Blackie, 1942, p. 374-375.

21. ORDINARY DIFFERENTIAL EQUATIONS

D'ADHÉMAR, R. La balistique extérieure. Mém. Sci. Math. fasc. 65, 1934, 54 p.

ANDOYER, H. Sur la méthode de Gauss pour le calcul des perturbations séculaires. C. R. Acad. Sci. Paris 152, 418-420 (1918).

D'ASCIA, M. Saggio del metodo dei minimi quadrati per l'integrazione numerica delle equazioni differenziali lineari. Rend. Accad. dei Lincei Roma (6) 11, 450-457 (1930).

BABAKOV, I. M. Zur Berechnung der höheren Eigenfrequenzen der Drehschwingungen von reduzierter Welle. (Russian. German summary.). Jour. Appl. Math. Mech. (Akad. Nauk SSSR.Zhurnal Prikl. Mat. Mech.) 5, 109-124 (1941).

BABINI, J. Sobre la integración aproximada de las ecuaciones diferenciales de segundo orden. Atti Congr. Intern. Bologna 1928, vol. 3. Bologna, Zanichelli, 1930, p. 103-107.

BIBLIOGRAPHY

BALLANTINE, J. P. A numerical method of solving differential equations with a remainder. (Abstract). Bull. Amer. Math. Soc. 32, 195-196 (1926).

BASHFORTH, F. and ADAMS, J. C. An Attempt to Test the Theories of Capillary Action... with an Explanation of the Method of Integration Employed... Cambridge, Cambridge Univ.Press, 1883, 80 p. + 59 p. tables, p. 15-62.

BATEMAN, H. Differential Equations. London, Longmans Green and Co., Longmans Modern Math. Series, 1918, chap. 11, p. 287-295.

BENDIXON, I. Sur le calcul des intégrales d'un système d'équations différentielles par des approximations successives. Stockh. Akad. Förh. 50, 599-612 (1893).

BENDIXON, I. Sur les courbes définies par des équations différentielles. Acta Math. 24, 1-88 (1900).

BENNETT, A. A. Introduction to Ballistics. Washington, D. C., Govt. Printing Office, 1921.

BENNETT, A. A. Tables for Interior Ballistics. Washington, D. C., 1923.

BENNETT, A. A., MILNE, W. E. and BATEMAN, H. Numerical Integration of Differential Equations. Bull. Nat. Res. Council No. 92, 1933, p. 51-87.

BICKLEY, W. G. A simple method for the numerical solution of differential equations. Phil. Mag. (7) 13, 1006-1114 (1932).

BICKLEY, W. G. Formulae for numerical differentiation. Math. Gaz. 25, 19-27 (1941).

BIEBERBACH, L. Über neuere Lehrbücher der praktischen Analysis. Zeit. Angew. Math. Mech. 1, 61-67 (1921).

BIEBERBACH, L. Theorie der Differentialgleichungen. Berlin, Springer, 3rd ed. 1930, chap. 2, p. 27-55.

BLISS, G. A. Functions of lines in ballistics. Trans. Amer. Math. Soc. 21,93-106 (1920).

BLISS, G. A. Mathematics for Exterior Ballistics. New York, John Wiley, 1944, vii + 128 p.

BÖDEWADT, U. T. Von den freien Schwingungen eines Kreiselpendels bei endlichen Ausschlägen. Zeit. Angew. Math. Mech. 20, 218-234 (1940).

BOUFFARD, J. Balistique extérieure. Nouvelle méthode de calcul et d'étude de la trajectoire d'un projectile. Paris, Hermann et Cie, Actual. Sci. Ind., No. 907, 1942, 78 p.

BRISTOW, L. Expansion theory associated with linear differential equations and their regular singular points. Trans. Amer. Math. Soc. 33, 455-474 (1931).

BRUN, V. Über die Durchführung der Eulerschen Differentiation bei Lösung der Differentialgleichung $y' = f(x,y)$. 8 Skand. Math. Kongr. Stockholm 1934, (1935) p. 80-88.

BRUNS, E. H. Über eine Differentialgleichung der Störungstheorie. Astr. Nachr. No. 2533, No. 2553, 1883.

BÜCKNER, H. Über eine Näherungslösung der gewöhnlichen linearen Differentialgleichung 1. Ordnung. Zeit. Angew. Math. Mech. 22, 143-152 (1942).

BURRAU, C. Recherches numériques concernant des solutions périodiques d'un cas spécial du problème des trois corps. Astr. Nachr. No. 3230: 135, 233-240 (1894); No. 3251: 136, 161-174 (1894).

BUSCHE, E. Zur Integration der ballistischen Hauptgleichung. Deutsche Math. 6, 97-99 (1941).

CALLANDREAU, O. Sur une équation différentielle de la théorie des perturbations et remarques relatives aux Nos. 2389 et 2435 des Astr. Nachr. Astr. Nachr. No. 2547 (1881).

CAQUÉ, J. Méthode nouvelle pour l'intégration des équations différentielles linéaires ne contenant qu'une variable indépendante. Jour. Math. Pures Appl. (2) 9, 185-222 (1864).

BIBLIOGRAPHY

CAUCHY, A. L. Méthode simple et générale pour la détermination numérique des coefficients que renferme le développement de la fonction perturbatrice. Oeuvres complètes d'Augustin Cauchy, 1st ser., vol. 5. Paris, Gauthier-Villars, 1885, p. 288-310.

CHADAJA, F. G. On the problem of numerical integration of ordinary differential equations. (Russian. Georgian summary.). Bull. Acad. Sci. Georgian SSR 2, 601-608 (1941).

CHADAJA, F. G. On the error in the numerical integration of ordinary differential equations by the method of finite differences. (Russian. Georgian summary.). Trav. Inst. Math. Tbilissi 11, 97-108 (1942).

CHARBONNIER, P. Traité de balistique extérieure, vol. 2. Paris, Gauthier-Villars, 1927, 797 p., p. 691-786.

CHERRY, T. M. Integrals of systems of ordinary differential equations. Proc. Camb. Phil. Soc. 22, 273-281 (1924).

CLEMENTE, P. Maggiorazione dell'errore nel calcolo col metodo dei minimi quadrati della soluzione periodica di una equazione differenziale, lineare, ordinaria, del secondo ordine. Rendiconti Accad. dei Lincei Roma (6) 17, 262-264 (1933).

COLLATZ, L. Eine Verallgemeinerung des Differenzenverfahrens für Differentialgleichungen. Zeit. Angew. Math. Mech. 14, 350-351 (1934).

COLLATZ, L. Konvergenzbeweis und Fehlerabschätzung für das Differenzenverfahren bei Eigenwertproblemen gewöhnlicher Differentialgleichungen zweiter und vierter Ordnung. Deutsche Math. 2, 189-215 (1937).

COLLATZ, L. Schranken für den ersten Eigenwert bei gewöhnlichen Differentialgleichungen zweiter Ordnung. Ing. Arch. 8, 325-331 (1937).

COLLATZ, L. Genäherte Berechnung von Eigenwerten. Zeit. Angew. Math. Mech. 19, 224-249, 297-318 (1939).

COLLATZ, L. Natürliche Schrittweite bei numerischer Integration von Differentialgleichungssystemen. Zeit. Angew. Math. Mech. 22, 216-225 (1942).

COLLATZ, L. and ZURMÜHL, R. Beiträge zu den Interpolationsverfahren der numerischen Integration von Differentialgleichungen 1. und 2. Ordnung. Zeit. Angew. Math. Mech. 22, 42-55 (1942).

COLLATZ, L. and ZURMÜHL, R. Zur Genauigkeit verschiedener Integrationsverfahren bei gewöhnlichen Differentialgleichungen. Ing. Arch. 13, 34-36 (1942).

CORIOLIS, G. Mémoire sur le degré d'approximation... Jour. Math. Pures Appl. 2, 229-244 (1837).

COTTON, E. Sur l'intégration approchée des équations différentielles. Bull. Soc. Math. France 36, 225-246 (1908).

COTTON, E. Sur l'intégration approchée des équations différentielles. Acta Math. 31, 107-126 (1908).

COTTON, E. Approximations successives et équations différentielles. Paris, Gauthier-Villars, Mém. Sci. Math. fasc. 28, 1928, 47 p.

DARWIN, G. H. Periodic orbits. Acta Math. 21, 99-242, espec. 118 ff. (1897).

DEDERICK, L. S. The mathematics of exterior ballistics computations. Amer. Math. Month. 47, 628-634 (1940).

DUFFING, G. Zur numerischen Integration gewöhnlicher Differentialgleichungen. Forschungsarbeiten auf dem Gebiete des Ingenieurwesens 224, 29-50 (1920).

EULER, L. Institutionum calculi integralis, vol. 1. St. Petersbourg (Leningrad), 1768, 542 p., p. 493-508.

FALKNER, V. M. A method of numerical solution of differential equations. Phil. Mag. (7)21, 624-640 (1936).

BIBLIOGRAPHY

FANTA, W. Über die angenäherte Auflösung von gewöhnlichen Differentialgleichungen und Anwendung auf Probleme der Mechanik. (Berlin Diss.). Vienna, Carl Gerold's Sohn, 1931, 40 p.

FEINSTEIN, L. and SCHWARZSCHILD, M. Automatic integration of linear second-order differential equations by means of punched card machines. Rev. Sci. Instr. 12, 405-408 (1941).

FORD, L. R. The numerical integration of differential equations (abstract). Bull. Amer. Math. Soc. 30, 215 (1924).

FORSYTH, A. R. Treatise on Differential Equations. London, Macmillan, 6th ed. 1929, p. 53-56.

FOWLER, R. H., GALLOP, E. G., LOCK, C. N. and RICHMOND, H. W. The aerodynamics of a spinning shell. Phil. Trans. Roy. Soc. Lond. A221, 295-387 (1920).

FRAZER, R. A., JONES, W. P. and SKAN, S. W. Note on approximations to functions and to solutions of differential equations. Phil. Mag. (7) 25, 740-746 (1938).

FUBINI, G. An elementary observation of the equations of external ballistics. (Spanish). Math. Notae 2, 3-10 (1942).

FUNK, P. Ueber Duffings Methode zur numerischen Integration von gewöhnlichen Differentialgleichungen. Zeit. Angew. Math. Mech. 7, 410-411 (1927).

GAJAS, M. La comparaison des intégrales successives de M. Picard avec l'intégral cherchée. Bull. Sci. Math. (2) 58, 236-240 (1934).

GARCÍA, G. Mouvement des projectiles autour de son centre de gravité. Sur le mouvement gyroscopique; mouvement pendulaire des projectiles; dérivation. Revista Ci. Lima 42, 541-685 (1940).

GAU, E. Sur un théorème de M. É. Picard. Bull. Soc. Math. France 43, 62-69 (1915).

GEBELEIN, H. Zur praktischen Lösung gewöhnlicher Differentialgleichungen mittels schrittweiser Annäherung. Zeit. Angew. Math. Mech. 13, 385-386 (1933).

GOLAB, S. Un théorème de la théorie des équations différentielles approchées. Mathematica (Cluj) 16, 61-65 (1940).

GOURSAT, É. Cours d'analyse mathématique, vol. 2. Paris, Gauthier-Villars, 5th ed. 1933, 685 p., p. 384-402.

GRAMMEL, R. Ein Beitrag zur Lösung des Dreikörperproblems. Astronomical Papers dedicated to Elis Strömgren. Copenhagen, Einar Munksgaard, 1940, p. 40-50.

GROENEVELD, J. Numerische Integration der Hauptgleichung der äusseren Ballistik. Zeit. Angew. Math. Mech. 7, 150-151 (1927).

GRONWALL, T. H. Qualitative properties of the ballistic trajectory. Ann. of Math. (2)22, 44-65(1920).

HADAMARD, J. Cours d'analyse, vol. 2. Paris, Hermann, 1930,721 p., p. 297-313.

HARTREE, D. R. Ballistic calculations. Nature 106, 152-154 (1921).

HARTREE, D. R. On an equation occurring in Falkner and Skan's approximate treatment of the equations of the boundary layer. Proc. Camb. Phil. Soc. 33, 223-239 (1937).

HERMANN, E. E. Exterior Ballistics, 1935. Annapolis, U. S. Naval Inst., reprint 1940, viii + 305 p.

HILL, G. W. Researches in the lunar theory. Amer. Jour. Math. 1, 5-26, 129-147, 245-260 (1878).

HIRSCHFELD, H. O. A generalization of Picard's method of successive approximation. Proc. Camb. Phil. Soc. 32, 86-95 (1936).

HORNSTEIN, M. Einige Bemerkungen über lineare Differenzengleichungen zweiter Ordnung und über Kettenbrüche. Rec. Math. (Mat. Sbornik) N.S. 5 (47), 269-288 (1939).

BIBLIOGRAPHY

HORT, W. Die Differentialgleichungen des Ingenieurs. Berlin, Springer, 2nd ed. 1925, xii + 700 p., p. 216-325.

IGLISCH, R. Zur praktischen Behandlung von Randwertaufgaben gewöhnlicher linearer Differentialgleichungen mit nicht konstanten Koeffizienten. Zeit. Angew. Math. Mech. 14, 51-58 (1934).

INCE, E. L. Ordinary Differential Equations. London, Longmans, 1927, p. 540-547.

INFELD, L. On a new treatment of some eigenvalue problems. Phys. Rev. (2) 59, 737-747 (1941).

JACKSON, D. The method of numerical integration in exterior ballistics. War Department document No. 984. Washington, D. C., Govt. Printing Office, 1921, 43 p.

KANTOROVITCH, L. The method of successive approximations for functional equations. Acta Math. 71, 63-97 (1939).

KELLER, E. G. Beat theory of non-linear circuits. Jour. Franklin Inst. 228, 319-337 (1939).

KLOSE, A. Zur Integration der ballistischen Gleichung. Deutsche Math. 2, 473-479 (1937).

KNOBLOCH, H. Zur Interpolation von Kurvenscharen. Zeit. Angew. Math. Mech. 22, 364-366 (1942).

KORMES, M. A note on the integration of linear second-order differential equations by means of punched cards. Rev. Sci. Instr. 14, 118 (1943).

KORN, A. Über eine Methode der sukzessiven Näherungen zur Lösung linearer gewöhnlicher und partieller Differentialgleichungen. Sitzber. Berl. Math. Ges. 15, 115-119 (1916).

KRAWTCHOUK, M. Sur la méthode de N. Kryloff pour l'intégration approchée des équations de la physique mathématique. C. R. Acad. Sci. Paris 183, 474-476 (1926).

KRAWTCHOUK, M. On a method of N. Kryloff for the integration of ordinary differential equations. (Ukrainian). Mém. Acad. Sci. Kiev (2) 5, 12-33 (1927).

KRAWTCHOUK, M. Sur l'intégration approchée des équations différentielles linéaires. Atti Congr. Intern. Bologna 1928, vol. 3, Bologna, Zanichelli, 1930, p. 109-115.

KRAWTCHOUK, M. Sur les derivées des intégrales approchées de certaines équations différentielles. Rend. Circ. Mat. Palermo 54, 194-198 (1930).

KRYLOFF, N. Les méthodes de solution approchée des problèmes de la physique mathématique. Mém.Sci. Math., fasc. 49. Paris, Gauthier-Villars, 1931, 70 p.

KRYLOFF, N. Sur la solution approchée des problèmes de la physique mathématique et de la science d'ingénieur. Bull. Acad. Sci. URSS Leningrad (Izvestia Akad. Nauk SSSR) (7) 1930, 1089-1114 (1930). Reprint Revista Mat. Hisp. Amer. (2) 6, 213-238 (1931).

KRYLOFF, N. and BOGOLIUBOFF, N. Upon some new results in the domain of non-linear mechanics. Proc. Indian Acad. Sci. A 3, 523-526 (1936).

KRYLOFF, N. and BOGOLIUBOFF, N. Introduction to Non-Linear Mechanics. (Tr. Lefschetz, S.). Annals of Mathematics Studies, No. 11. Princeton, N. J., Princeton Univ. Press, 1943.

KUTTA, W. Beitrag zur näherungsweisen Integration totaler Differentialgleichungen. Zeit. Math. Phys. 46, 435-453 (1901).

LAGRANGE, J. L. Essai sur le problème des trois corps. Oeuvres de Lagrange, vol. 6. Paris, Gauthier-Villars, 1873, p. 227-331.

LAHAYE, E. Une méthode nouvelle d'intégration de certains groupes d'équations différentielles. C. R. Acad. Sci. Paris 185, 172-173 (1927).

LAHAYE, E. Les itérations intégrales convergentes. Application aux équations différentielles. du premier ordre algébriques en y et dy/dx. Acad. Roy. Belgique, Cl. Sci. Mém. Coll. 18, No. 5, 1939, 65 p.

LAHAYE, E. Les itérations intégrales convergentes et leur application aux équations différentielles du premier ordre, algébriques en y et y'. C. R. Acad. Sci. Paris 210, 621-624 (1940).

LAHAYE, E. Sur la résolution des équations dz/dx = r(x,z)(r rationnel en z) par des itérations intégrales et différentielles convergentes. Jour. Math. Pures Appl. (9) 22, 1-23 (1943).

LANCZOS, C. A new approximation method in solving linear differential equations with non-oscillating coefficients. (Abstract). Bull. Amer. Math. Soc. 41, 183-184 (1935).

LANCZOS, C. A new approximation method in solving linear differential equations with rational coefficients. (Abstract). Bull. Amer. Math. Soc. 42, 30 (1936).

LAURITZEN, S. Nogle Bemaerkninger om Diffrentialligningen dy/dx = f(x,y). Mat. Tidsskr. B, København 1937, 104-108 (1937).

LEGENDRE, A. M. Dissertation sur la question de balistique proposée par l'Académie Royale des Sciences et Belles-Lettres de Prusse pour le prix de 1782. Berlin, G. J. Decker,1782, 68p.

LEVY, H. The numerical solution of a certain class of differential equations. Proc. Lond. Math. Soc. (2) 24, 459-470 (1926).

LEVY, H. A numerical study of differential equations. Jour. Lond. Math. Soc. 7, 305-318 (1932).

LEVY, H. and BAGGOTT, E. A. Numerical Studies in Differential Equations, vol. 1. London, Watts, 1934, viii + 238 p.

LIAPOUNOFF, A. M. Sur une série dans la théorie des équations différentielles linéaires de second ordre à coefficients périodiques. Mém. Acad. St. Pétersbourg (8) 13, No. 2, 70 p. (1902).

LINDELÖF, E. Sur l'application des méthodes d'approximations successives à l'étude des intégrales réelles des équations différentielles. Jour.Math. Pures Appl.(4) 10, 117-128 (1894).

LINDELÖF, E. Remarques sur l'intégration numérique des équations différentielles ordinaires. Acta Soc. Sci. Fennicae A(2) 2, No. 13, 21 p. (1938).

LINDSTEDT, A. Beitrag zur Integration der Differentialgleichungen der Störungstheorie. Mem. Acad. St. Petersbourg (7) 31, No. 4, 20 p. (1883).

LIOUVILLE, J. Sur le developpement des fonctions ou parties de fonctions en series dont les divers termes sont assujettis a satisfaire a une meme equation differentielle du second ordre contenant une parametre variable. Jour. Math. Pures Appl. 2, 16-22 (1837).

LIOUVILLE, J. Sur la théorie des équations différentielles linéaires et sur les développements des fonctions en séries. Jour. Math. Pures Appl. 3, 561-614 (1838).

LIPSCHITZ, R. Sur la possibilité d'intégrer complètement un système donné d'équations différentielles. Bull. Sci. Math. 10, 149-159 (1876).

LIPSCHITZ, R. Lehrbuch der Analysis, vol. 2. Bonn, Cohen, 1880, xiv + 734 p., p. 500-512.

MADELUNG, E. Über eine Methode zur schnellen numerischen Lösung von Differentialgleichungen zweiter Ordnung. Zeit. Phys. 67, 516-518 (1931).

MADER, K. Mathematische Hilfsmittel in der Physik. (Vol. III of Handbuch der Physik). Berlin, Springer, 1928, chap. 15, p. 631-635.

MARCHANT METHODS. Starting values for Milne-method integration of ordinary differential equations of first order, or of second order when first derivatives are absent. The method of Taylor's series. MM-261, Oct. 1943, 4 p. Marchant Calc. Mach. Co., Oakland, Calif.

MARCHANT METHODS. Starting value for Milne-method integration of ordinary differential equations of the first order. The method of Milne. MM-260, Jan., 1944, 11 p.

BIBLIOGRAPHY

MARCHANT METHODS. Milne method of step-by-step double integration of second order differential equations in which first derivatives are absent. MM-216A, Jan., 1943, 6 p.

MARCHANT METHODS. Milne method of step-by-step integration of ordinary differential equations when starting values are known. MM-216, June, 1942, 10 p.

MASSERA, J. F. Formulae for finite differences with applications to the approximate integration of differential equations of the first order. (Spanish). Publ. Inst. Mat. Univ. Nac. Litoral 4, 99-166 (1943).

McEWEN, W. H. Problems of closest approximation connected with the solution of linear differential equations. Trans. Amer. Math. Soc. 33, 979-997 (1931).

McEWEN, W. H. On the approximate solution of linear differential equations with boundary conditions. Bull. Amer. Math. Soc. 38, 887-894 (1932).

MIKELADZE, S. Über die Integration von Differentialgleichungen mit Hilfe der Differenzenmethode. (Russian. German summary.). Bull. Acad. Sci. URSS Sér. Math. (Izvestia Akad. Nauk SSSR) 1939, 627-642 (1939).

MIKELADZE, S. Verallgemeinerung der Methode der numerischen Integration von Differentialgleichungen mit Hilfe der Formeln der mechanischen Quadratur. (Russian. German summary.). Trav. Inst. Math. Tbilissi (Trudy Tbiliss. Mat. Inst.) 7, 47-63 (1940).

MIKELADZE, S. On the approximate integration of linear differential equations with discontinuous coefficients. (Russian.). Bull. Acad. Sci. Georgian SSR 3, 633-639 (1942).

MIKELADZE, S. New formulas for the numerical integration of differential equations. (Russian.). Bull. Acad. Sci. Georgian SSR 4, 215-218 (1943).

MILNE, W. E. Numerical integration of ordinary differential equations. Amer. Math. Month. 33, 455-460 (1926).

MILNE, W. E. On the numerical solution of a boundary value problem. Amer. Math. Month. 38, 14-17 (1931).

MILNE, W. E. On the numerical integration of certain differential equations of the second order. Amer. Math. Month. 40, 322-327 (1933).

MILNE, W. E. The numerical integration of $y'' + g(x)y = f(x)$. Amer. Math. Month. 49, 96-98 (1942).

MIRANDA, C. Teoremi e metodi per l'integrazione numerica della equazione differenziale di Fermi. Memorie Reale Accad. d'Italia 5, 285-322 (1934).

VON MISES, R. Zur numerischen Integration von Differentialgleichungen. Zeit. Angew. Math. Mech. 10, 81-92 (1930).

MOIGNO, F. N. M. Leçons de calcul différentiel et de calcul intégral, vol. 2. Paris, Bachelier, 1844, xlviii + 783 p., p. 385-434, 513-534.

DE MONTESSUS, R. and D'ADHÉMAR, R. Calcul numérique. Paris, Doin, 1911, 249 p., p. 139-237.

MOULTON, F. R. Periodic Orbits. Washington, D. C., Carnegie Institution, 1920, xiii + 524 p.

MOULTON, F. R. Numerical solution of differential equations. Chap. X of Smithsonian mathematical formulae and tables of elliptic functions. (Edited Adams, E. P. and Hippisley, R. L.). Smithsonian Miscellaneous Collections 74, No. 1, 220-242 (1922).

MOULTON, F. R. Differential Equations. New York, Macmillan, 1930, p. 179-231.

MOULTON, F. R. New Methods in Exterior Ballistics. Chicago, Univ. Chicago Press, 1926.

MÜLLER, M. Ueber die Eindeutigkeit der Integrale eines Systems gewöhnlicher Differentialgleichungen und die Konvergenz einer Gattung von Verfahren zur Approximation dieser Integrale. Sitzber. Heidelberg, 1927 (9 Abh.), 38 p.

BIBLIOGRAPHY

MÜLLER, M. Über das Fundamentaltheorem in der Theorie der gewöhnlichen Differentialgleichungen. Math. Zeit. 26, 619-645 (1927).

MÜLLER, M. Über den Konvergenzbereich des Verfahrens der schrittweisen Näherungen bei gewöhnlicher Differentialgleichungen. Math. Zeit. 41, 163-175 (1936).

MÜLLER, M. Über die Existenz periodischer Lösungen bei gewissen Systemen gewöhnlicher Differentialgeleichungen erster Ordnung. Math. Zeit. 48, 128-135 (1942).

NAGUMO, M. Über das Verfahren der sukzessiven Approximationen zur Integration gewöhnlicher Differentialgleichung und die Eindeutigkeit ihrer Integrale. Jap. Jour. Math.7, 143-160 (1930).

NAGUMO, M. Über das Verhalten der Integrale von $\lambda y'' + f(x,y,y', \lambda) = 0$ für $\lambda \rightarrow 0$. Proc. Phys.-Math. Soc. Japan 21, 529-534 (1939).

NASTA, M. Contributo al calcolo delle velocità critiche degli alberi motori. Rend. Accad. dei Lincei Roma (6) 12, 209-216 (1930).

NIEMYTZKI, V. Intégration qualitative approximative du système d'équations $dx/dt = Q(x,y)$, $dy/dt = P(x,y)$. C. R. (Doklady) Acad. Sci. URSS (N. S.) 38, 62-65 (1943).

NOETHER, F. Über analytische Berechnung der Geschosspendelungen. Gött. Nachr. 1919, 373-391.

NOWAKOWSKI, A. Zur numerischen Integration gewöhnlicher Differentialgleichungen mit der Rechenmaschine. Zeit. Angew. Math. Mech. 13, 299-322 (1933).

NUMEROV, B. Note on the numerical integration of $d^2x/dt^2 = f(x,t)$. Astr. Nachr. 230, 359-364 (1927).

NYSTRÖM, E. J. Über die numerische Integration von Differentialgleichungen. Acta Soc. Sci. Fennicae 50, No. 13, 56 p. (1925).

OKAMURA, H. Sur l'approximation successive et l'unicité de la solution de $dy/dx = f(x,y)$. Memoirs Coll. Sci. Kyoto Imperial Univ. 14, 85-96 (1931).

PAINLEVÉ, P. Sur le calcul des intégrales d'un système différentiel par la méthode de Cauchy-Lipschitz. Bull. Soc. Math. France 27, 149-152 (1899).

PAINLEVÉ, P. Gewöhnliche Differentialgleichungen; Existenz der Lösungen. Ency. Math. Wiss., vol. II 1, 1; article II A 4a. Leipzig, Teubner, 1900, p. 189-229.

PEANO, G. Intégration par séries des équations différentielles linéaires. Math. Ann. 32, 450-456 (1888).

PÉRÈS, J. Sur la méthode des fonctions majorantes et la méthode des approximations successives. Bull. Sci. Math. (2) 39, 179-181 (1915).

PETROVITCH, M. Intégration qualitative des équations différentielles. Mém. Sci. Math. fasc.48. Paris, Gauthier-Villars, 1931, 58 p.

PIAGGIO, H. T. H. An Elementary Treatise on Differential Equations and Their Applications. London, Bell, 2nd ed. 1928, p. 94-108, 224-228.

PIAGGIO, H. T. H. On the numerical integration of differential equations. Phil. Mag. (6) 37, 596-600 (1919).

PICARD, É. Mémoire sur la théorie des équations aux dérivées partielles et la méthode des approximations successives. Jour. Math. Pures Appl. (4) 6, 145-210, 231 (1890).

PICARD, É. Sur l'application des méthodes d'approximations successives à l'étude de certaines équations différentielles ordinaires. Jour. Math. Pures Appl. (4) 9, 217-271 (1893).

PICARD, É. Traité d'analyse. Paris, Gauthier-Villars: vol. 2, 3rd ed. 1926, p. 368-394; vol.3, 3rd ed. 1928, p. 88-99.

BIBLIOGRAPHY

PICONE, M. Sul metodo delle minime potenze ponderate e sul metodo di Ritz per il calcolo approssimato nei problemi della fisica-matematica. Rend. Circ. Mat. Palermo 52, 225-253 (1928).

PICONE, M. Maggiorazione dell'errore d'approssimazione nel metodo d'integrazione Cauchy-Lipschitz dei sistemi di equazioni differenziali ordinarie. Rend. Accad. Lincei Roma (6) 15, 859-864 (1932).

POINCARÉ, H. Les méthodes nouvelles de la mécanique céleste, vol. 1. Paris, Gauthier-Villars, 1892, 385 p.

POMEY, L. Sur le théorème d'existence, etc. C. R. Acad. Sci. Paris 180,569-571, 725-727, 1093-1096, 2006-2008 (1925).

POPOFF, K. Ueber eine Eigenschaft der ballistischen Kurve und ihre Anwendung auf die Integration der Bewegungsgleichungen. Zeit. Angew. Math. Mech. 1, 96-106 (1921).

POPOFF, K. Les méthodes d'intégration de Poincare et le problème générale de la balistique exterieure. Paris, Gauthier-Villars, 1925, 76 p.

PORTER, M. B. On the roots of functions connected by a linear recurrent relation of the second order. Ann. of Math. (2) 3, 55-70 (1902).

PUGACHEV, V. S. Notes on exterior ballistics of projectiles and bombs. (Russian. English summary.). Appl. Math. Mech. (Akad. Nauk SSSR. Prikl. Mat. Mech.) 6, 347-368 (1942).

PUGACHEV, V. S. Approximate method of solving the non-linear problem of a rotating projectile. (Russian. English summary.). Appl. Math. Mech. (Akad. Nauk SSSR. Prikl. Mat. Mech.) 7, 313-324 (1943).

RANKIN, A. W. On the average-slope method of solving differential equations. Amer. Math. Month. 45, 461-462 (1938).

RATZERDORFER, J. Determination of the buckling load of struts with successive approximation. Jour. Roy. Aeronaut. Soc. 47, 103-105 (1943).

REMES, E. Some approximate formulae for the numerical integration of differential equations. Phil. Mag. (7) 5, 392-400 (1928).

RICHARDSON, L. F. How to solve differential equations approximately by arithmetic. Math. Gaz. 12, 415-421 (1925).

RIEBESELL,P. Über die Integration der ballistischen Hauptgleichung bei Andwendung des Sommerfeldschen Luftwiderstandsgesetzes. Arch. Math. Phys. (3) 25, 103-108 (1916).

ROOT, R. E. The Mathematics of Engineering. Baltimore, Williams and Wilkins, 1927, p. 514-528.

RUNGE, C. Ueber die numerische Auflösung von Differentialgleichungen. Math. Ann. 46, 167-178 (1895).

RUNGE, C. and WILLERS, F. A. Numerische und graphische Quadratur und Integration gewöhnlicher und partieller Differentialgleichungen. Ency. Math. Wiss., vol. II 3, 1; article II C2.Leipzig, Teubner, 1915, p. 47-176.

VON SANDEN, H. Zur Berechnung des kleinsten Eigenwerts von $y'' + \lambda p(x)y = 0$. Zeit. Angew. Math. Mech. 21, 381-382 (1941).

SAUER, R. Über Interpolation von Kurvenscharen mit Anwendung auf die Berechnung von Geschossflugbahnen. Zeit. Angew. Math. Mech. 20, 280-284 (1940).

SAUER, R. and PÖSCH, H. Anwendungen des Adamsschen Integrationsverfahrens in der Ballistik. Ing. Arch. 12, 158-168 (1941).

SCARBOROUGH, J. B. Numerical Mathematical Analysis. Baltimore, Johns Hopkins Press, 1930, p. 218-283.

SCHEFFÉ, H. Linear differential equations with two-term recurrence formulas. Jour. Math. Phys. (M. I.T.) 21, 240-249 (1942).

BIBLIOGRAPHY

SCHELKUNOFF, S. A. Solution of linear and slightly nonlinear differential equations. Quart. Appl. Math. 3, 348-355 (1946).

SCHULZ, G. Interpolationsverfahren zur numerischen Integration gewöhnlicher Differentialgleichungen. Zeit. Angew. Math. Mech. 12, 44-59 (1932).

SCHULZ, G. Fehlerabschätzung für das Störmersche Integrationsverfahren. Zeit. Angew. Math. Mech. 14, 224-234 (1934).

SEVERINI, C. Sull'integrazione approssimata delle equazioni differenziali ordinarie. Bologna, Zanichelli, 1899, 27 p.

SHOHAT, J. A new analytical method for solving van der Pol's and certain related types of non-linear differential equations, homogeneous and non-homogeneous. Jour.Appl. Phys. 14, 40-48 (1943).

SHOHAT, J. On van der Pol's and non-linear differential equations. Jour. Appl. Phys. 15, 568-574 (1944).

SOUTHWELL, R. V. On the natural frequencies of vibrating systems. Proc. Roy. Soc. Lond. 174A, 433-457 (1940).

STANGE, K. Zur Berechnung einer Flugbahnschar nach dem Athenschen Verfahren. Zeit. Angew. Math. Mech. 20, 350-357 (1940).

STEFFENSEN, J. F. On the degree of rigour required in numerical integrations. 5 Kongr.Skand. Math. in Helsingfors, p. 125-130, 1922.

STEKLOFF, W. Sur les problèmes de représentations des fonctions à l'aide de polynomes, du calcul approché des intégrales définies, du développement des fonctions en séries infinies suivant les polynomes et de l'interpolation, considerées au point de vue des idées de Tchébycheff. Proc. Intern. Math. Congr. Toronto, 1924, vol. 1, 1928, p. 631-640.

STOHLER, K. Eine Vereinfachung bei der numerischen Integration gewöhnlicher Differentialgleichungen. Zeit. Angew. Math. Mech. 23, 120-122 (1943).

STÖRMER, C. Sur les trajectoires des corpuscules electrisés dans l'espace sous l'action du magnétisme terrestre avec application aux aurores boréales. Arch. Sci. Phys. Nat. Genève (4) 24, 5-18, 113-158, 221-247 (1907).

STÖRMER, C. Resultats des calculs numériques des trajectoires des corpuscules électriques dans le champ d'un aimant élémentaire. Videnskapsselskapets Skrifter, Kristiania 1913: 1, No.4, 74 p.; 2, No. 10, 58 p.; 2, No. 14, 64 p. (1913).

STÖRMER, C. Méthode d'intégration numérique des équations différentielles ordinaires. C. R. Congr. Intern. Math. Strasbourg 1920. Toulouse, Privat, 1921, p. 243-257.

STRUTT, M. J. O. Der charakteristische Exponent der Hillschen Differentialgleichung. Math. Ann. 101, 559-569 (1929).

SUBBOTIN, M. F. Numerical integration of differential equations. (Russian. French summary.). Bull. Univ. Tashkent 16, 273-286 (1927).

TA LI. Über die allgemeine lineare Differentialgleichung. Comment. Math. Helv. 12, 1-19 (1939-1940).

TAMARKINE, J. D. Sur la méthode de C. Störmer pour l'intégration approchée des équations différentielles ordinaires. Math. Zeit. 16, 214-219 (1923).

TAMBS LYCHE, R. Solution explicite de l'équation différentielle générale du premier ordre. Avhandl. 25-Årsjubileet Tekniske Høiskole Trondheim, 1935, p. 765-786. Reprint Det Kgl.Norske Videnskabers Selskabs Skrifter, Trondheim 1935, (2), No. 35, 24 p. (1935).

TOLLMIEN, W. Über die Fehlerabschätzung beim Adamsschen Verfahren zur Integration gewöhnlicher Differentialgleichungen. Zeit. Angew. Math. Mech. 18, 83-90 (1938).

TSCHAPPAT, W. H. Ballistics. Encyclopaedia Britannica, New Volumes 30, 386-394 (1922).

BIBLIOGRAPHY

TURTON, F. J. The errors in the numerical solution of differential equations. Phil. Mag. (7) 28, 359-363 (1939).

TURTON, F. J. Two notes on the numerical solution of differential equations. Phil. Mag. (7) 28, 381-384 (1939).

VAHLEN, T. Beiträge zur Ballistik. Arch. Math. Phys. (3): 25, 209-231 (1916); 26, 119-125 (1917).

VIETORIS, L. Über die Integration gewöhnlicher Differentialgleichungen durch Iteration. Monatsh. Math. Phys.:39, 15-50 (1932); 41, 384-391 (1934).

WAR DEPARTMENT, UNITED STATES OF AMERICA. A Course in Exterior Ballistics. War Dept. document No. 1051. Washington, D. C., Govt. Printing Office, 1921, 127 P.

WEBSTER, A. G. On the Springfield rifle and the Leduc formula. Proc. Nat. Acad. Sci. U.S.A. 6, 289 (1920).

WEINEL, E. Eine Erweiterung des Grammelschen Verfahrens zur Berechnung von Eigenwerten und Eigenfunktionen. Ing. Arch. 10, 283-291 (1939).

WEYL, H. Concerning the differential equations of some boundary-layer problems. Proc. Nat. Acad. Sci. U.S.A.: 27, 578-583 (1941); 28, 100-102 (1942).

WEYL, H. On the differential equations of the simplest boundary-layer problems. Ann. of Math. (2) 43, 381-407 (1942).

WHITEHEAD, A. N. Graphical solution for high-angle fire. Proc. Roy. Soc. Lond. A94, 301-307 (1917-1918).

WIENER, O. Die streckenweise Berechnung der Geschossflugbahnen. Abh. Ges. Wiss. Leipzig 36, No. 1, 66 p., (1918).

WILLERS, F. A. Methoden der praktischen Analysis. Berlin, de Gruyter, 1928, 344 p., p. 305-334.

ZAREMBA, S. K. Remarques sur l'intégration approchée des équations différentielles. Bull. Intern. Acad. Polon. Sci. Lett., Cl. Sci. Math. Nat. A 1936, 528-535 (1937).

ZECH, T. Anschauliches zur Picarditeration der Differentialgleichungen. Zeit. Angew. Math. Mech. 17, 341-352 (1937).

ZECH, T. Zum Abklingen nichtlinearer Schwingungen. Ing. Arch. 13, 21-33 (1942).

ZURMÜHL, R. Zur numerischen Integration gewöhnlicher Differentialgleichungen zweiter und höherer Ordnung. Untersuchungen zu den Verfahren von Blaess und Runge-Kutta-Nyström. Zeit. Angew. Math. Mech. 20, 104-116 (1940).

22. PARTIAL DIFFERENTIAL EQUATIONS

ALLEN, D. N., SOUTHWELL, R. V. and VAISEY, G. Relaxation methods applied to engineering problems. XI. Problems governed by the "quasi-plane-potential equation". Proc. Roy. Soc. Lond. 183A, 258-283 (1945).

ARTEMIEFF, N. Die Anwendung des Störungsverfahrens zur Berechnung der Eigenwerte bei Deformation des Randes. Rec. Math. Moscou (Mat. Sbornik) 39, No. 3, 52-66 (1932).

BATEMAN, H. Partial Differential Equations. Cambridge, Cambridge Univ. Press, 1932, xii + 522 p., p. 76, 144-152.

BENNETT, A. A., MILNE, W. E. and BATEMAN, H. Numerical integration of differential equations. Report of committee on numerical integration. Bull. Nat. Res. Council, No. 92. Washington, D. C., Nat. Acad. Sci., 1933, chap. 4.

BIBLIOGRAPHY

BERGMANN, S. Über die Entwicklung der harmonischen Funktionen der Ebene und des Raumes nach Orthogonalfunktionen. Math. Ann. 86, 238-271 (1922).

BERGMANN, S. Ein Näherungsverfahren zur Lösung gewisser partieller, linearer Differentialgleichungen. Zeit. Angew. Math. Mech. 11, 323-330 (1931).

BERGMANN, S. Zur Theorie der Funktionen, die eine lineare partielle Differentialgleichung befriedigen I. C. R. (Doklady) Acad. Sci. URSS. (N.S.) 15, 227-230 (1937).

BERGMAN, S. The approximation of functions satisfying a linear partial differential equation. Duke Math. Jour. 6, 537-561 (1940).

BICKLEY, W. G. Experiments in approximating to solutions of a partial differential equation. Phil. Mag. (7) 32, 50-66 (1941).

BIEZENO, C. B. and GRAMMEL, R. Technische Dynamik. Berlin, Springer, 1939 (Reprint, Ann Arbor, Edwards, 1944) p. 135-180.

BINDER, L. Über Wärmeübergang auf ruhige oder bewegte Lufte sowie Lüftung und Kühlung elektrischer Maschinen. Halle, Knapp, 1911, v + 112 p., p. 20-26.

BIRKHOFF, G. E. Circular plates of variable thickness. Phil Mag. (6) 43, 953-962 (1922).

BLAISDELL, B. E. The physical properties of fluid interfaces of large radius of curvature. Jour. Math. Phys. (M.I.T.) 19, 186-245 (1940).

BOUKIDIS, N. A. and RUGGIERO, R. J. An iterative method for determining dynamic deflections and frequencies. Jour. Aeronaut. Sci. 11, 319-328 (1944).

BOUSSINESQ, J. Sur le calcul de plus en plus approché des vitesses bien continues de régime uniforme par des polynomes, dans un tube prismatique à section carrée. C. R. Acad. Sci. Paris 158, 1743-1749 (1914).

BREMEKAMP, H. Quelques applications de la méthode des approximations successives. Proc. Akad. Wet. Amsterdam 41, 291-300 (1938).

BRILLOUIN, M. La méthode des moindres carrés et les équations aux dérivées partielles de la physique mathématique. Ann. de Phys. 6, 137-233 (1916).

BROUWER, F. Wellenmechanische Eigenwertprobleme und Integration durch Reihen. Ann. der Phys. 84, 915-929 (1927).

CARMICHAEL, R. D. Boundary value and expansion problems. Amer. Jour. Math.: 43, 69-101, 232-270 (1921); 44, 129-152 (1922).

CHRISTOPHERSON, D. G. A new mathematical method for the solution of film lubrication problems. Jour. Proc. Inst. Mech. Engrs. 146, 126-135 (1942).

CHRISTOPHERSON, D. G. and SOUTHWELL, R. V. Relaxation methods applied to engineering problems. III. Problems involving two independent variables. Proc. Roy. Soc. Lond. 168A, 317-350 (1938).

COLLATZ, L. Bemerkungen zur Fehlerabschätzung für das Differenzenverfahren bei partiellen Differentialgleichungen. Zeit. Angew. Math. Mech. 13, 56-57 (1933).

COLLATZ, L. Das Differenzenverfahren mit höherer Approximation für lineare Differentialgleichungen. Schr. Math. Sem. Inst. Angew. Math. Univ. Berlin 3, 1-34 (1935).

COLLATZ, L. Über das Differenzenverfahren bei Anfangswertproblemen partieller Differentialgleichungen. Zeit. Angew. Math. Mech. 16, 239-247 (1936).

COURANT, R. Über die Methode des Dirichletschen Prinzipes. Math. Ann. 72, 517-550 (1912).

COURANT, R. Über die Eigenwerte bei den Differentialgleichungen der mathematischen Physik. Math. Zeit. 7, 1-57 (1920).

BIBLIOGRAPHY

COURANT, R. Über ein konvergenzerzeugendes Prinzip in der Variationsrechnung. Gött. Nachr. 1922, 144-150.

COURANT, R. Über die Theorie der linearen partiellen Differenzengleichungen. Gött.Nachr. 1925,98-109.

COURANT, R. Bemerkungen zur Frage der numerischen Auflösung von Randwertproblemen, die aus der Variationsrechnung entspringen. Gött. Nachr. 1925, 122-127.

COURANT, R. Über Randwertaufgaben bei partiellen Differenzengleichungen. Zeit. Angew. Math. Mech. 6, 322-325 (1926).

COURANT, R. Über direkte Methoden der Variationsrechnung und über verwandte Fragen. Math. Ann. 97, 711-736 (1927).

COURANT, R. Advanced Methods in Applied Mathematics. New York, New York Univ. Lectures, 1941, (mimeo), p. 66-76.

COURANT, R., FRIEDRICHS, K. and LEWY, H. Über die partiellen Differenzengleichungen der mathematischen Physik. Math. Ann. 100, 32-74 (1928).

DANIELL, P. J. Orthogonal potentials. Phil. Mag. (7) 2, 247-258 (1926).

DRACH, J. Sur les valeurs moyennes partielles et leur application aux problèmes de physique mathématique. C. R. Acad. Sci. Paris 192, 1327-1331 (1931).

DUNCAN, W. J. Galerkin's method in mechanics and differential equations. Gt. Brit.Aeronaut. Research Comm. Reports and Mem. No. 1798, 33 p. (1937).

DUNCAN, W. J. Principles of Galerkin's method. Gt. Brit. Aeronaut. Research Comm. Reports and Mem. No. 1848, 24 p. (1938).

DUSINBERRE, G. M. Numerical methods for transient heat-flow. Trans. Amer. Soc. Mech.Engrs. 67, 703-709 (1945).

EMMONS, H. W. The numerical solution of partial differential equations. Quart. Appl. Math. 2, 173-195 (1944).

EMMONS, H. W. The numerical solution of heat-conduction problems. Trans. Amer. Soc. Mech. Engrs. 65, 607-615 (1943).

FOWLER, C. M. Analysis of numerical solutions of transient heat-flow problems. Quart. Appl. Math. 3, 361-376 (1946).

FOX, L. Solution by relaxation methods of plane potential problems with mixed boundary conditions. Quart. Appl. Math. 2, 251-257 (1944).

FRANK, P. and VON MISES, R. Die Differential- und Integralgleichungen der Mechanik und Physik, vol. 1. Braunschweig, Vieweg, 2nd ed. 1930, xxiii + 916 p., p. 734-737.

FRAZER, R. A., JONES, W. P. and SKAN, S. W. Approximations to functions and to the solutions of differential equations. Gt. Brit. Aeronaut. Research Comm. Reports and Mem. No. 1799, 33 p. (1937).

FRIEDRICHS, K. O. and STOKER, J. J. Buckling of the circular plate beyond the critical thrust. Jour. Appl. Mech. 9, A7-A14 (1942).

FROCHT, M. M. and LEVEN, M. M. A rational approach to the numerical solution of Laplace's equation. Jour. Appl. Phys. 12, 596-604 (1941).

GANDY, R. W. G. and SOUTHWELL, R. V. Relaxation methods applied to engineering problems. V. Conformal transformation of a region in plane space. Phil. Trans.Roy. Soc. Lond. 238A, 453-475 (1940).

GERMAY, R. H. Intégration, par approximations successives, les équations aux dérivées partielles. C. R. Acad. Sci. Paris 178, 685-688 (1924).

BIBLIOGRAPHY

GERMAY, R. H. Sur l'intégration par approximations successives des systèmes d'équations aux dérivées partielles du premier ordre de forme résolue. C. R. Acad. Sci. Paris 179, 1580-1583 (1924).

GERSCHGORIN, S. Fehlerabschätzung für das Differenzenverfahren zur Lösung partieller Differentialgleichungen. Zeit. Angew. Math. Mech. 10, 373-382 (1930).

GOLDMANN, E. Anwendung der Ritzschen Methode auf die Theorie der Transversalschwingungen frei schwingender Platten von rechteckiger, rhombischer, dreieckiger und elliptischer Begrenzung (Inaug. -Diss. Breslau.). Breslau, Fleischmann, 1918, 67 p.

GOLDSBOROUGH, G. R. The tides in oceans on a rotating globe. Proc. Roy. Soc. Lond. 117A, 692-718 (1928).

GOLDSBOROUGH, G. R. Note on the method of Ritz for the solution of problems in elasticity. Phil. Mag. (7) 7, 332-337 (1929).

GRAMMEL, R. Ein neues Verfahren zur Lösung technischer Eigenwertprobleme. Ing. Arch. 10, 35-46 (1939).

HADAMARD, J. Mémoire sur le problème d'analyse relatif à l'équilibre des plaques élastiques incastrées. Paris, Mém. Sav. Étrang. (2) 33, No. 14, 128 p. (1908).

HAUSEN, H. Näherungsverfahren zur Berechnung des Wärmeaustausches in Regeneratoren. Zeit. Angew. Math. Mech. 11, 105-114 (1931).

HENCKY, H. Die Berechnung dünner rechteckiger Platten mit verschwindender Biegungsteifigkeit. Zeit. Angew. Math. Mech. 1, 81-89, 423-424 (1921).

HENCKY, H. Die numerische Bearbeitung von partiellen Differentialgleichungen in der Technik. Zeit. Angew. Math. Mech. 2, 58-66 (1922).

HENCKY, H. Eine wichtige Vereinfachung der Methode von Ritz zur angenäherten Behandlung von Variationsproblemen. Zeit. Angew. Math. Mech. 7, 80-81 (1927).

HILBERT, D. Über das Dirichletsche Prinzip. Math. Ann. 59, 161-186 (1904); Jour. Reine Angew. Math. 129, 63-67 (1905).

HRENNIKOFF, A. Solution of problems of elasticity by the framework method. Jour. Appl. Mech. 8, A169-A175 (1941).

JAMES, H. M. Some applications of the Rayleigh-Ritz method to the theory of the structure of matter. Bull. Amer. Math. Soc. 47, 869-884 (1941).

JEFFCOTT, H. H. On the vibration of beams under the action of moving loads. Phil. Mag. (7) 8, 66-97 (1929).

KANTOROVIC, L. Sur une méthode de résolution approchée d'équations différentielles aux dérivées partielles. (Russian and French.). C. R. (Doklady) Acad. Sci. URSS (N.S.) 2, 532-536(1934).

KAISER, R. Rechnerische und experimentelle Ermittlung der Durchbiegungen und Spannungen von quadratischen Platten bei freien Auflagerung an den Rändern, gleichmässig verteilter Last und grossen Ausbiegungen. Zeit. Angew. Math. Mech. 16, 73-98 (1936).

VON KÁRMÁN, T. The engineer grapples with non-linear problems. Bull. Amer. Math. Soc. 46, 615-683 (1940).

KARAS, K. Die Eigenschwingungen inhomogener Saiten. Sitzber. Akad. Wiss. Wien 145 (IIa), 797-816 (1936).

KELLNER, G. W. Die Ionisierungsspannung des Heliums nach der Schrödingerschen Theorie. Zeit. Phys. 44, 91-109 (1927).

KIESSLING, F. Eine Methode zur approximativen Berechnung einseitig eingespannter Druckstäbe mit veränderlichen Querschnitt. Zeit. Angew. Math. Mech. 10, 594-599 (1930).

BIBLIOGRAPHY

KIMBALL, G. E. and SHORTLEY, G. H. The numerical solution of Schrödinger's equation. Phys. Rev. (2) 45, 815-820 (1934).

KNOTT, C. G. Comparison of Mr. Crawford's measurements of the deflection of a clamped square plate with Ritz's solution. Proc. Roy. Soc. Edin. 32, 390-392 (1912).

KOCH, J. J. Bestimmung höherer kritischer Drehzahlen schnell laufender Wellen.Proc.Intern.Congr. Appl. Mech. Zürich, 1926. Zürich, Füssli,1927, p. 213-218.

KORMES, M. Numerical solution of the boundary value problem for the potential equation by means of punched cards. Rev. Sci. Instr. 14, 248-250 (1943).

KORMES, J. P. and KORMES, M. Numerical solution of initial value problems by means of punched-card machines. Rev. Sci. Instr. 16, 7-9 (1945).

KORN, A. Ueber eine Methode der successive Näherungen zur Lösung linearer gewöhnlicher und partieller Differentialgleichungen. Sitzber. Berl. Math. Ges.: 15, 115-119 (1916); 16, 51-55 (1917).

KOVNER, S. S. On the technique of numerical integration of differential equations with partial derivatives. C. R. (Doklady) Acad. Sci. URSS (N. S.) 37, 20-23 (1942).

KRON, G. Numerical solution of ordinary and partial differential equations by means of equivalent circuits. Jour. Appl. Phys. 16, 172-186 (1945).

KRYLOFF, N. Sur les généralisations de la méthode de Walther Ritz. C. R. Acad. Sci. Paris 164, 853-856 (1917).

KRYLOFF, N. Sur quelques recherches récentes dans le domaine de la solution approchée des problèmes de la physique mathématique. Atti Congr. Intern. Mat. Bologna 1928, vol. 5. Bologna, Zanichelli, 1931, p. 257-273.

KRYLOFF, N. and BOGOLIUBOFF, N. On Rayleigh's principle in the theory of differential equations of mathematical physics and on Euler's method in the calculus of variations. Ann. of Math. (2) 29, 255-275 (1928).

LAHAYE, E. Sur l'application de la méthode des approximations successives à la résolution des équations aux derivées partielles linéaires du second ordre. Bull. Acad. Roy. Belg., Cl. Sci. (5) 27, 537-551 (1941).

LAPAURI, I. D. On numerical integration of differential equations of hyperbolic type. (Georgian. Russian summary.). Trav.Inst.Math. Tbilissi (Trudy Tbiliss. Mat. Inst.) 10, 93-109 (1941).

LEMKE, A. Experimentelle Untersuchungen zur W. Ritzschen Theorie der Transversalschwingungen quadratischer Platten. Ann. der Phys. (4) 86, 717-750 (1928).

LEWY, H. Über einen Ansatz zur numerischen Lösung von Randwertproblemen. Gött. Nachr. 1925, 118-121.

LEWY, H. Über die Methode der Differenzengleichungen zur Lösung von Variations- und Randwertproblemen. Math. Ann. 98, 107-124 (1927).

LIEBMANN, H. Die angenäherte Ermittlung harmonischer Funktionen und konformer Abbildungen (nach Ideen von Boltzmann und Jacobi). Sitzber. Akad. Wiss. München 1918, 385-416.

LOVE, A. E. H. The application of the method of W. Ritz to the theory of the tides. Proc. Intern. Congr. Math. Cambridge 1912, vol. 2. Cambridge, Cambridge Univ. Press, 1913, p. 202-208.

LUCKERT, H. J. Über die Integration der Differentialgleichungen einer Gleitschicht in zäher Flüssigkeit. Schr. Math. Sem. Inst. Math., Univ. Berlin 1, 245-274 (1933).

MACDONALD, J. K. L. Successive approximations by the Rayleigh-Ritz variation method. Phys. Rev. (2) 43, 830-833 (1933).

MACDONALD, J. K. L. On the modified Ritz variation method. Phys. Rev. (2) 46, 828 (1934).

BIBLIOGRAPHY

MACI, G. Sulla integrazione approssimata delle equazioni differentiali a derivate parziali. Boll. Mat. (Firenze) 32, 1-3 (1936).

MAIER, E. Biegeschwingungen von spannungslos verwundenen Stäben, insbesondere von Luftschraubenblättern. Ing. Arch. 11, 73-98 (1940).

MEYER ZUR CAPELLEN, W. Methode zur angenäherten Lösung von Eigenwertproblemen mit Anwendungen auf Schwingungsprobleme. Ann. der Phys. (5) 8, 297-352 (1931).

MIKELADZE, S. E. Über die numerische Lösung der Differentialgleichung $\frac{\partial^2 u}{\partial x^2} + \frac{\partial^2 u}{\partial y^2} + \frac{\partial^2 u}{\partial z^2} = \phi(x,y,z)$. C. R. (Doklady) Acad. Sci. URSS, (N.S.) 14, 177-179 (1937).

MIKELADZE, S. E. Über numerische Integration der Laplaceschen und Poissonschen Gleichungen. C. R. (Doklady) Acad. Sci. URSS, (N.S.) 14, 181-182 (1937).

MIKELADZE, S. E. Über die numerische Lösung der Differentialgleichungen von Laplace und Poisson. (Russian. German summary.). Bull. Acad. Sci. URSS, Sér. Math. (Izvestia Akad. Nauk SSSR) 1938, 271-292 (1938).

MIKELADZE, S. E. Über die Lösung von Randwertproblemen mit der Differenzenmethode. C. R. (Doklady) Acad. Sci. URSS,(N.S.) 28, 400-402 (1940).

MIKELADZE, S. E. On the question of numerical integration of partial differential equations by means of nets. (Russian). Mitt. Georg. Abt. Akad. Wiss. USSR 1, 249-254 (1940).

MIKELADZE, S. E. Numerische Integration der Gleichungen vom elliptischen und parabolischen Typus. (Russian. German summary.). Bull. Acad. Sci. URSS, Sér. Math. (Izvestia Akad. Nauk SSSR) 5, 57-74 (1941).

MILNE, W. E. On the numerical solution of a boundary problem.Amer. Math. Month. 38, 14-17 (1931).

MINORSKY, N. Control problems. Jour. Franklin Inst. 232, 451-487, 519-551 (1941).

VON MISES, R. and POLLACZEK-GEIRINGER, H. Praktische Verfahren der Gleichungsauflösung. Zeit. Angew. Math. Mech. 9, 152-164 (1929).

MORGANS, W. R. On the solution of second order differential equations satisfying boundary conditions. Phil. Mag. (7) 32, 483-488 (1941).

MORROW, J. On the lateral vibration of bars of uniform and varying sectional area. Phil. Mag.(6) 10, 113-125 (1905).

MORROW, J. On the lateral vibration of loaded and unloaded bars. Phil. Mag. (6) 11, 354-374 (1906).

MORROW, J. On the lateral vibration of bars subjected to forces in the direction of their axis. Phil. Mag. (6) 12, 233-243 (1906).

MORROW, J. On the lateral deflection and vibration of "clamped-directed" bars. Phil. Mag. (6) 18, 452-465 (1909).

MOSKOVITZ, D. The numerical solution of Laplace's and Poisson's equations. Quart. Appl. Math. 2, 148-163 (1944).

NEWING, R. A. On the variation calculation of eigenvalues. Phil. Mag. (7) 24, 114-127 (1937).

NEWING, S. T. Determination of the shearing stresses in axially symmetrical shafts under torsion by finite difference methods. Phil. Mag. (7) 32, 33-49 (1941).

PANOW, D. Über die angenäherte numerische Lösung des Problems der Wärmeleitung. Zeit. Angew. Math. Mech. 12, 185-188 (1932).

PASCHOUD, M. Application de la méthode de Walther Ritz au problème du régime uniforme dans un tube à section carrée. C. R. Acad. Sci. Paris 159, 158-160 (1914).

BIBLIOGRAPHY

PASTERNAK, P. Vereinfachte Berechnung der Biegebeanspruchung in dünnwandigen, kreisrunden Behältern. Proc. Intern. Congr. Appl. Mech. Zürich, 1926. Zürich, Füssli, 1927, p. 427-433.

PELLEW, A. and SOUTHWELL, R. V. Relaxation methods applied to engineering problems. VI. The natural frequencies of systems having restricted freedom. Proc.Roy.Soc. Lond. 175A, 262-290 (1940).

PFEIFFER, F. Zur numerischen Integration hyperbolischer partieller Differentialgleichungen zweiter Ordnung. Zeit. Angew. Math. Mech. 18, 233-236 (1938).

PHILLIPS, H. B. and WIENER, N. Nets and the Dirichlet problem. Jour. Math. Phys. (M.I.T.)2, 105-124 (1923).

PICARD, É. Mémoire sur la théorie des équations aux dérivées partielles et la méthode des approximations successives. Jour. Math. Pures Appl. (4) 6, 145-210, 231 (1890).

PLANCHEREL, M. Sur la méthode d'intégration de Ritz. Bull. Sci. Math. (2): 47, 376-383, 397-412 (1923); 48, 12-48, 58-80, 93-109 (1924).

POLHAUSEN, B. E. Berechnung der Eigenschwingungen statisch bestimmter Fachwerke. Zeit. Angew. Math. Mech. 1, 28-42 (1921).

PRASAD, G. The numerical solution of partial differential equations. Phil. Mag. (7) 9, 1074-1081 (1930).

LORD RAYLEIGH. On the calculation of the frequency of vibration of a system in its gravest mode with an example from hydrodynamics. Phil. Mag. (5) 47, 566-572 (1899).

LORD RAYLEIGH. On the calculation of Chladni's figures for a square plate. Phil. Mag. (6) 22, 225-229 (1911).

RICHARDSON, L. F. The approximate arithmetical solution by finite differences of physical problems involving differential equations with an application to the stresses in a masonry dam.Phil. Trans.Roy. Soc. Lond. 210A, 307-357 (1910).

RICHARDSON, L. F. How to solve differential equations approximately by arithmetic. Math.Gaz. 12,415-421 (1925).

RICHARDSON, R. G. D. A new method in boundary problems from differential equations. Trans.Amer.Math. Soc. 18, 489-518 (1917).

RITZ, W. Über eine neue Methode zur Lösung gewisser Variationsprobleme der mathematischen Physik. Jour.Reine Angew. Math. 135, 1-61 (1908), or Gesammelte Werke,Paris, Gauthier-Villars.1911, p. 192-250.

RITZ, W. Über eine neue Methode zur Lösung gewisser Randwertaufgaben. Gött. Nachr. 1908, p. 236-248, or Ges. Werke, 1911, p. 251-264.

RITZ, W. Theorie der Transversalschwingungen einer quadratischen Platte mit freien Rändern. Ann. der Phys. (4) 28, 737-786 (1909), or Ges. Werke, 1911, p. 265-316.

ROSENBLATT, A. Sur l'application de la méthode des approximations successives de M. Picard à l'étude de certaines équations non linéaires du quatrième ordre. Bull. Sci. Math. (2) 58, 117-136, 151-168 (1934).

ROSENBLATT, A. Sur les équations biharmoniques non linéaires à deux variables indépendantes.Bull. Sci. Math. (2) 58, 248-264 (1934).

LE ROUX, J. Sur le problème de Dirichlet. Jour. Math. Pures Appl. (6) 10, 189-230 (1914).

RUNGE, C. and WILLERS, F. A. Numerische und graphische Quadratur und Integration gewöhnlicher und partieller Differentialgleichungen. Ency. Math. Wiss. Leipzig, Teubner, 1915, vol. II(3) 2, article II C2, p. 47-176.

SHERWOOD, T. K. and REED, C. E. Applied Mathematics in Chemical Engineering. New York, McGraw-Hill, 1938, xi + 403 p., p. 241-255.

BIBLIOGRAPHY

SHORTLEY, G. H. and WELLER, R. The numerical solution of Laplace's equation. Jour. Appl. Phys. 9, 334-348 (1938).

SHORTLEY, G. H. and WELLER, R. Calculation of stresses within the boundary of photoelastic models. Jour. Appl. Mech. 61, A71-A78 (1939).

SHORTLEY, G. H., WELLER, R. and FRIED, B. Numerical solution of Laplace's and Poisson's equations with applications to photoelasticity and torsion. Ohio State Univ. Studies, Engrg. Series, vol. 11, No. 5. Engrg. Exp. Station, Bull. No. 107. Columbus, Ohio, 1940, iii + 51 p.

SIDDIQI, M. R. Boundary Problems in Non-linear Partial Differential Equations. Lucknow Univ. Studies, No. 11. Allahabad, India, Allahabad Law Journal Press, 1939, xiv + 136 p.

SOKOLNIKOFF, I. S. On a solution of Laplace's equation with an application to the torsion problem for a polygon with reentrant angles. Trans. Amer. Math. Soc. 33, 719-732 (1931).

SOUTHWELL, R. V. Relaxation Methods in Engineering Science. A Treatise on Approximate Computation. Oxford Engrg. Sci. Ser., New York, Oxford Univ. Press, 1940, vii + 252 p., chap. VII, VIII.

SOUTHWELL, R. V. New pathways in aeronautical theory. Fifth Wright Brothers Lecture. Jour. Aeronaut. Sci. 9, 77-89 (1942).

SOUTHWELL, R. V. and VAISEY, G. Relaxation methods applied to engineering problems. VIII. Plane-potential problems involving specified normal gradients. Proc. Roy. Soc. Lond. 182A, 129-151 (1943).

TAMARKIN, J. D. and FELLER, W. Partial Differential Equations. (Mimeo.) Providence, Brown Univ., 1941, chap. V, p. 160-196.

TEMPLE, G. The general theory of relaxation methods applied to linear systems. Proc. Roy. Soc. Lond. 169A, 476-500 (1939).

THOM, A. The flow past circular cylinders at low speeds. Proc. Roy. Soc. Lond. 141A, 651-669 (1933).

THORNE, C. J. and ATANASOFF, J. V. A functional method for the solution of thin plate problems applied to a square, clamped plate with a central point load. Iowa State Coll. Jour. Sci. 14, 333-343 (1940).

TIMOSHENKO, S. A membrane analogy to flexure. Proc. Lond. Math. Soc. (2) 20, 398-407 (1921).

TIMOSHENKO, S. The approximate solution of two-dimensional problems in elasticity. Phil. Mag. (6) 47, 1095-1104 (1924).

TIMOSHENKO, S. Theory of Plates and Shells. New York, McGraw-Hill, 1940, xii + 492 p., p. 180-187.

TREFFTZ, E. Ein Gegenstück zum Ritz'schen Verfahren. Proc. Intern. Congr. Appl. Mech. Zürich, 1926. Zürich, Füssli, 1927, p. 131-137.

TREFFTZ, E. Konvergenz und Fehlerabschätzung beim Ritzschen Verfahren. Math. Ann. 100, 503-521 (1928).

TREFFTZ, E. Über Fehlerabschätzung bei Berechnung von Eigenwerten. Math. Ann. 108, 595-604 (1933).

TREFFTZ, E. Die Bestimmung der Knicklast gedrückter, rechteckiger Platten. Zeit. Angew. Math. Mech. 15, 339-344 (1935).

VASILESCO, F. Sur une méthode de M. Riabouchinsky ayant pour but de résoudre le problème de Dirichlet, en vue du calcul du potentiel des vitesses. C. R. Acad. Sci. Paris 193, 1162-1164 (1931).

VAZSONYI, A. A numerical method in the theory of vibrating bodies. Jour. Appl. Phys. 15, 598-606 (1944).

BIBLIOGRAPHY

VERNOTTE, P. Méthode très générale pour étudier le début des perturbations régies par les équations aux derivées partielles de la physique mathématique. Application à la chaleur et à l'hydrodynamique. C. R. Acad. Sci. Paris 210, 42-44 (1940).

VOIGT, W. Die Grundschwingungen kreisförmiger Klangplatten aus Kristallen. Gött.Nachr. 1915,345-391.

WASCHAKIDZE, D. Über die numerische Lösung der biharmonischen Gleichung. (Russian. German summary.). Trav. Inst. Math. Tbilissi (Trudy Tbiliss. Mat. Inst.) 9, 61-73 (1941).

WEINSTEIN, D. H. Modified Ritz method. Proc. Nat. Acad. Sci. U.S.A. 20, 529-532 (1934).

WEINSTEIN, A. On a minimal problem in the theory of elasticity. Jour. Lond. Math. Soc. 10, 184-192 (1935).

WEINSTEIN, A. Les vibrations et le calcul des variations. Portugaliae Math. 2, 36-55 (1941).

WELLER, R., SHORTLEY, G. H. and FRIED, B. The solution of torsion problems by numerical integration of Poisson's equation. Jour. Appl. Phys. 11, 283-290 (1940).

WOLF, F. Über die angenäherte numerische Berechnung harmonischer und biharmonischer Funktionen. Zeit. Angew. Math. Mech. 6, 118-150 (1926).

23. INTEGRAL EQUATIONS

BAIRSTOW, L. and BERRY, A. Two dimensional solutions of Poisson's and Laplace's equations. Proc. Roy. Soc. Lond. 95A, 457-475 (1919).

BATEMAN, H. Report on the history and present state of the theory of integral equations. British Assoc. Rep. 1910, p. 345-424.

BATEMAN, H. On the numerical solution of linear integral equations. Proc. Roy. Soc. Lond. 100A, 441-448 (1922).

BLOCK, H. Sur la solution de certaines équations fonctionnelles. Arkiv för Mat. 3, No. 22,18 p., (1907).

BLUMENTHAL, O. Über die Knickung eines Balkens durch Längskräfte. Zeit.Angew. Math. Mech. 17, 232-244 (1937).

BÔCHER, M. An Introduction to the Study of Integral Equations. Cambridge Math. Tracts No. 10, London, Cambridge Univ. Press, 2nd ed. 1914, reprint 1926, 70 p., p. 13-19, 24-37.

BOGGIO, T. Integrazione dell'equazione funzionale che regge la caduta di una sfera in un liquido viscoso. Rend. Accad. dei Lincei Roma (5) 16-2, 613-620, 730-737 (1907).

COLLATZ, L. Vergleich der Integralgleichungsmethode von Bucerius mit dem Ritzschen Verfahren zur genäherten Lösung von Differentialgleichungen. Astr. Nachr. 271, 116-120 (1941).

COLLET, A. Sur les solutions approchées de certaines équations intégrales non linéaires. Ann.Toulouse (3) 4, 199-249 (1912).

CROUT, P. D. An application of polynomial approximation to the solution of integral equations arising in physical problems. Jour. Math. Phys. (M.I.T.) 19, 34-92 (1940).

DAVIS, H. T. A Survey of Methods for the Inversion of Integrals of the Volterra Type. Indiana Univ. Studies, 14, No. 76-77, 72 p. (1927).

VAN DEN DUNGEN, F. H. Les équations intégrales à plusieurs paramètres et la technique des vibrations. Proc. Intern. Congr. Appl. Mech. Zürich 1926. Zürich, Füssli, 1927, p. 113-118.

ENSKOG, D. Kinetische Theorie der Vorgänge in mässig verdünnten Gasen. (Diss. Uppsala). Uppsala, Almquist and Wiksells, 160 p., 1917.

BIBLIOGRAPHY

ENSKOG, D. Die numerische Berechnung der Vorgänge in mässig verdünnten Gasen. Arkiv för Mat. 16, No. 16, 60 p., 1921.

ENSKOG, D. Eine allgemeine Methode zur Auflösung von linearen Integralgleichungen. Math. Zeit. 24, 670-685 (1926).

FRANK, P. and VON MISES, R. Die Differential- und Integralgleichungen der Mechanik und Physik, vol. 1. Braunschweig, Vieweg, 2nd ed. 1930, p. 555-562.

FREDHOLM, I. Sur une nouvelle méthode pour la résolution du problème de Dirichlet. Öfversigt af Kongl. Svenska Vetenskaps Akademiens Förhandlingar 57, 39-46 (1900).

FREDHOLM, I. Sur une classe d'équations fonctionnelles. C. R. Acad. Sci. Paris 134, 1561-1564 (1902).

FREDHOLM, I. Sur une classe de transformations rationnelles. C. R. Acad. Sci. Paris 134, 219-222 (1902).

FREDHOLM, I. Sur une classe d'équations fonctionnelles. Acta Math. 27, 365-390 (1903).

GORGIDZE, A. I. and RUCHADZE, A. K. On a numerical solution of integral equations of the plane problem of the theory of elasticity. (Russian.). Mitt. Georg. Abt. Akad. Wiss. USSR 1, 255-258 (1940).

GYLLENBERG, W. Über eine graphische Lösung einer Integralgleichung. Astr. Nachr. 269, 52-53 (1939).

HAVELOCK, T. H. The solution of an integral equation occurring in certain problems of viscous fluid motion. Phil. Mag. (6) 42, 620-628 (1921).

HECKE, E. Über die Integralgleichung der Kinetischen Gastheorie. Math. Zeit. 12, 274-286 (1922).

HELLINGER, E. and TOEPLITZ, O. Integralgleichungen und Gleichungen mit unendlichvielen Unbekannten. Ency. Math. Wiss. vol. 2 (3), article II C13, 1335-1597 (1927).

HILBERT, D. Grundzüge einer allgemeinen Theorie der linearen Integralgleichungen. Gött. Nachr. 1904, 49-91, 213-259.

HILDEBRAND, F. B. The approximate solution of singular integral equations arising in engineering practice. Proc. Amer. Acad. Arts Sci. 74, 287-295 (1941).

HILDEBRAND, F. B. and CROUT, P. D. A least square procedure for solving integral equations by polynomial approximation. Jour. Math. Phys. (M.I.T.) 20, 310-335 (1941).

HILL, G. W. On the part of the motion of the lunar perigee which is a function of the mean motions of the sun and moon. Acta. Math. 8, 1-36 (1886).

HITCHCOCK, F. L. A method for the numerical solution of integral equations. Jour. Math. Phys. (M.I.T.) 1, 88-104 (1922).

HORT, W. Die Differentialgleichungen des Ingenieurs. Berlin, Springer, 2nd ed. 1925, xii + 700 p., p. 639-667.

HOWLAND, R. C. J. Application of an integral equation to the whirling speeds of shafts. Phil. Mag. (7) 3, 513-528 (1927).

INGRAM, W. H. On the integral equations of continuous dynamical systems. Phil. Mag. (7) 30, 16-38 (1940).

KIESSLING, F. Eine Methode zur Approximativen Berechnung einseitig eingespanneter Druckstäbe mit veränderlichem Querschnitt. Zeit. Angew. Math. Mech. 10, 594-599 (1930).

KNOTT, C. G. The propagation of earthquake waves through the earth and connected problems. Proc. Roy. Soc. Edin. 39, 157-208 (1919).

KÖNIG, M. Über ein neues Verfahren zur Ermittlung von Schwingungsperioden von Turbinenscheiben. Proc. Intern. Congr. Appl. Mech. Zürich 1926. Zürich, Füssli, 1927, p. 173-177.

BIBLIOGRAPHY

KORN, A. Über freie und erzwungene Schwingungen. Leipzig, Teubner, 1910, v + 136 p., p. 50-136.

KORN, A. Über die Anwendung der Methode der sukzessiven Näherungen zur Lösung von linearen Integralgleichungen mit unsymmetrischen Kernen. Arch. Math. Phys. (3): 25, 148-173 (1917); 27, 97-120 (1918).

KOSTITZIN, V. A. Applications des équations intégrales. (Applications statistiques). Mém. Sci.Math. fasc. 69, 48 p. (1935).

MAGNUSSON, P. C. A numerical method of solving integral equations in two independent variables. Jour. Math. Phys. (M.I.T.) 21, 250-263 (1942).

MEYER ZUR CAPELLEN, W. Kleine Änderungen des Kerns einer symmetrischen homogenen, linearen Integralgleichung. Zeit. Angew. Math. Mech. 13, 323-324 (1933).

MICHE, R. Le calcul pratique de problèmes élastiques à deux dimensions par la méthode des équations intégrales. Proc. Intern. Congr. Appl. Mech. Zürich 1926. Zürich, Füssli, 1927, 126-130.

MIKELADZE, S. E. De la résolution numérique des équations intégrales. (Russian. French summary.). Bull. Acad. Sci. URSS (Izvestia Akad. Nauk SSSR) (7) 1, 255-300 (1935).

MÜNTZ, C. Solution directe de l'équation séculaire et de quelques problèmes analogues transcendantes. C. R. Acad. Sci. Paris 156, 43-46 (1913).

NYSTRÖM, E. J. Über die praktische Auflösung von linearen gleichungen mit Anwendungen auf Randwertaufgaben der Potentialtheorie. Soc. Sci. Fennica Comment. Phys.-Math. 4, No. 15, 52 p. (1928).

NYSTRÖM, E. J. Über die praktische Auflösung von Integralgleichungen. Soc. Sci. Fennica Comment. Phys.-Math. 5, No. 5, 22 p. (1929).

NYSTRÖM, E. J. Über die praktische Auflösung von Integralgleichungen mit Anwendungen auf Randwertaufgaben. Acta Math. 54, 185-204 (1930).

OBERG, E. N. The approximate solutions of integral equations (abstract). Bull. Amer. Math. Soc.39, 513 (1933).

PEKERIS, C. L. A pathological case in the numerical solution of integral equations. Proc. Nat. Acad. Sci. U.S.A. 26, 433-437 (1940).

PICARD, É. Sur une équation fonctionnelle. C. R. Acad. Sci. Paris 139, 245-248 (1904).

PRAGER, W. Die Druckverteilung an Körpern in ebener Potentialstromung. Phys. Zeit. 29, 865-869 (1928).

PRASAD, G. On the numerical solution of integral equations. Proc.Edin. Math. Soc. 42, 46-59 (1924).

PRASAD, G. On the numerical solution of integral equations. Proc. Intern. Congr.Math. Toronto 1924, vol. 1. Toronto, Univ. of Toronto Press, 1928, p. 683.

REIZ, A. On the numerical solution of certain types of integral equations. Arkiv för Mat. 29 A, No. 29, 21 p. (1943).

SCHMIDT, E. Zur Theorie der linearen und nichtlinearen Integralgleichungen. Math. Ann.: 63, 433-476 (1907); 64, 161-174 (1907).

SCHROEDER, K. Über die Prandtlsche Integro-Differentialgleichung der Tragflügeltheorie. Abh. Preuss. Akad. Wiss. Math.-Nat. Kl. 1939, No. 16, 35 p.

SCHWERIN, E. Über die Transversalschwingungen von Stäben veränderlichen Querschnitts. Proc. Intern. Congr. Appl. Mech. Zürich 1926. Zürich, Füssli, 1927, p. 138-145.

SERINI, R. Teoria del condensatore electrico a piatti circolari. Rend. Accad. dei Lincei Roma (5) 29-2, 34-37, 257-261 (1920).

BIBLIOGRAPHY

TEOFILATO, P. Risoluzione grafica e numerica approssimata di un equazione integrale. Atti della Pontificia Accad. Romana dei Nuovi Lincei 76, 36-45 (1922-1923).

TRICOMI, F. Sulla risoluzione numerica delle equazioni integrali di Fredholm. Rend. Accad. dei Lincei Roma (5) 33-1, 483-486 (1924).

TRICOMI, F. Ancora sulla risoluzione numerica delle equazioni integrali di Fredholm. Rend. Accad. dei Lincei Roma (5) 33-2, 26-30 (1924).

VITERBI, A. Sulla risoluzione approssimata delle equazioni integrali di Volterra e sulla applicazione di questa allo studio analitico delle curve. Rend. Ist. Lombardo (2) 45, 1027-1060 (1912).

WHITTAKER, E. T. On the numerical solution of integral-equations. Proc. Roy. Soc. Lond. 94A,367-383 (1918).

WHITTAKER, E. T. and ROBINSON, G. The Calculus of Observations. Glasgow, Blackie, 3rd ed. 1942, p. 376-381.

WIARDA, G. Integralgleichungen, unter besondere Berücksichtigung der Anwendungen. Leipzig, Teubner, Sammlung Math.-phys. Lehrbücher, 1930, 183 p.

ABBREVIATIONS

Abh. Akad. München: Abhandlungen der Gesellschaft Bayerischen Akademie der Wissenschaften. Mathematisch-naturwissenschaftliche Abteilung.

Abh. Ges. Wiss. Leipzig: Abhandlungen der mathematisch-physischen Klasse der Sächsischen Akademie der Wissenschaften.

Acad. Roum. Bull. Sect. Sci.: Académie Roumaine Bulletin de la section scientifique. Bucharest.

Acad. Roy. Belgique Cl. Sci. Mém Coll.: Académie Royale de Belgique. Classe des Sciences. Mémoires collections en 4° et 8°.

Acad Sci. RSS Ukraine Rec. Trav. (Zbirnik Prace) Inst. Math.: Académie des Sciences de l'Ukraine. Institut mathématique, Recuillis Travaux. (Akademiia Nauk URSR. Institut Matematiki Zbirnik Prace).

Acta Math.: Acta Mathematica. Uppsala.

Acta Soc. Sci. Fennicae: Acta Societatis Scientiarum Fennicae. A: Opera Physico-mathematica. Helsingfors (Helsinki).

Acta Univ. Szeged Sect. Sci. Math: Acta Litterarum ac Scientiarum Regiae Universitatis Hungaricae Francisco-Iosephinae. Sectio Scientiarum Mathematicarum. Szeged.

Aircraft Engrg.: Aircraft Engineering. London.

Amer. Jour. Math.: American Journal of Mathematics. Baltimore.

Amer. Math. Month: The American Mathematical Monthly. The Official Journal of the Mathematical Association of America.

Ann. de Gergonne: Annales de Mathématiques Pures et Appliquées. Recueil Periodique, Redigé et Publiée par J. D. Gergonne.

Ann. de l'Observ.: Annales de l'Observatoire de Paris.

Ann. de Phys.: Annales de Physique. Paris.

Ann. der Phys.: Annalen der Physik. Leipzig.

Ann. Ecole Norm. Sup.: Annales Scientifiques de l'Ecole Normale Superieure. Paris.

Ann. Harvard Coll. Obs. Annals of the Astronomical Observatory of Harvard College.

Ann. Math. Statist.: The Annals of Mathematical Statistics. The Official Journal of the Institute of Mathematical Statistics. Baltimore.

Ann. Mat. Pura Appl.: Annali di Matematica Pura ed Applicata. Bologna.

Ann. of Math.: Annals of Mathematics. Princeton.

Ann. Sci. Univ. Jassy: Annales Scientifiques de l'Université de Jassy.

Ann. Toulouse: Annales de la Faculté des Sciences de l'Université de Toulouse pour les Sciences Mathématiques et les Sciences Physiques.

An. Soc. Sci. Argentina: Anales de la Sociedad Científica Argentina, Adoptados para sus Publicaciones por la Academia Nacional de Ciencias Exactas, Físicas y Naturales. Buenos Aires.

Appl. Math. Mech. (Akad. Nauk SSSR Prikl. Mat. Mech.): Applied Mathematics and Mechanics (Prikladnaia Matematika i Mekhanika).

Arch. Math. Phys.: Archiv der Mathematik und Physik mit besonderer Rücksicht auf die Bedürfnisse der Lehrer an höheren Unterrichtsanstalten. Gegründet 1841 durch J. A. Grunert.

Arch. Sci. Phys. Nat. Genève: Bibliothèque Universelle. Archives des Sciences Physiques et Naturelles. Geneva.

ABBREVIATIONS

Arkiv för Mat.: Arkiv för Matematik, astronomi och fysik. Utgivet av K. Svenska Vetenskapsakademien. Stockholm.

Astr. Jour.: Astrophysical Journal. An International Review of Spectroscopy and Astronomical Physics. University of Chicago Press.

Astr. Jour. Soviet Union: Astronomical Journal of the Soviet Union (Akademiia Nauk SSSR. Astronomiceskii Zhurnal.). Moscow.

Astr. Nachr.: Astronomische Nachrichten. Kiel.

Atti Accad. Sci. Torino: Atti della Reale Accademia della Scienze di Torino. I: Classe di Scienze, Fisiche, Matematiche e naturali.

Beiträge zur Geophys.: Beiträge zur angewandten Geophysik. (Started as Gerlands Beiträge zur Geophysik). Leipzig.

Beitr. Physik frei. Atmosph.: Beiträge zur Physik der freien Atmosphäre. Zeitschrift für die Erforschung der höheren Luftschichten und der Strömungserscheinungen in der Atmosphäre. Leipzig.

Ber. Verh. Saechs. Akad. Wissen. Leipzig: Berichte über die Verhandlungen der Sächsischen Akademie der Wissenschaften zu Leipzig. Mathematisch-physische Klasse.

Boll. Mat.: Il Bolletino di Matematica. Giornale Scientifico-didattico per l'Incremento degli Studi Matematici nelle Scuole Medie... Florence.

Boll. Un. Mat. Ital.: Bolletino della Unione Matematica Italiana. Bologna.

Brit. Assoc. Rep.: British Association for the Advancement of Science. Report of the Annual Meeting. London.

Bull. Acad. Sci. URSS Sér. Math. (Izvestia Akad. Nauk SSSR): Bulletin de l'Académie des Sciences de l'URSS. Classe des Sciences mathématiques et naturelles.

Bull. Internat. Acad. Sci. Cracovie, Cl. Sci. Math. Nat.: Bulletin International de l'Académie des Sciences de Cracovie. Classe des Sciences Mathématiques et Naturelles. Polska Akademja Umiejetnosci. Cracow.

Bull. Intern. Acad. Polon. Sci. Lett., Cl. Sci. Math. Nat.: Bulletin International de l'Académie Polonaise des Sciences et des Lettres. Classes des Science Mathématiques et Naturelles. Série A: Sciences Mathématiques. Polska Akademja Umiejetnosci. Cracow.

Bull. Amer. Math. Soc.: Bulletin of the American Mathematical Society.

Bull. Calcutta Math. Soc.: Bulletin of the Calcutta Mathematical Society.

Bull. Cl. Sci.-Phys. Math. Kieff: Bulletin de la Classe des Sciences Physiques et Mathématiques. (Ukrainska Akademiia Nauk. Zapiski Fizicno-matematicnogo Viddilu.). Kiev.

Bull. Math. Phys. Ecole Polyt. Bucharest: Bulletin de Mathématiques et de Physiques Pures et Appliquées de l'Ecole Polytechnique Roi Carol II, Bucarest.

Bull. Nat. Res. Council: Bulletin of the National Research Council. Washington, D. C.

Bull. Sci. Ec. Timişoara: Bulletin Scientifique de l'Ecole Polytechnique de Timişoara. Timişoara, Roumania.

Bull. Sci. Math.: Bulletin des Sciences Mathématiques. (Started as Bulletin des Sciences Mathématiques et Astronomiques.). Paris.

Bull. Soc. Math. France: Bulletin de la Société Mathématique de France Publié par les Secrétaires. Paris.

ABBREVIATIONS

Bull. Soc. Sci. Cluj: Bulletin de la Société des Sciences de Cluj. (Buletinul Societății de Ştințe din Cluj.).

Bull. Univ. Tashkent: Bulletin de l'Université de l'Asie Centrale. (Biulletini Sredne-Aziatskogo Gosudarstvennogo Universiteta.). Tashkent.

Casopis pest. mat. a fys.: Casopis pro Péstováni Matematiky a Fysiky v Praze. Prague.

Comment. Acad. Sci. Petropol.: Commentarii Academiae Scientiarum Imperialis Petropolitanae.

Comment. Math. Helv.: Commentarii Mathematici Helvetici. Editi Societate Mathematica Helvetica. Zurich.

C. R. Acad. Sci. Paris: Comptes Rendus Hebdomaires des Séances de l'Académie des Sciences par MM. les Secrétaires Perpetuéls. Paris.

Danske Vid. Selsk. Math.-Fys. Medd.: Det Kgl. Danske Videnskabernes Selskab. Matematisk-fysiske Meddelser. Copenhagen.

Deutsche Math.: Deutsche Mathematik. Im Auftrage der Deutschen Forschungsgemeinschaft.

Duke Math. Jour.: Duke Mathematical Journal. Durham, N. C.

Edin. Math. Tracts: Edinburgh Mathematical Tracts.

Electrotech. Zeit.: Elektrotechnische Zeitschrift. Organ des Elektrotechnischen Vereins seit 1880 und des Verbandes Deutscher Elektrotechniker seit 1894.

L'Ens. Math.: L'Enseignement Mathématique. Organ Officiel de la Commission Internationale de l'Enseignement Mathématique. Paris and Geneva.

Ergebnisse der Math.: Ergebnisse der Mathematik und ihrer Grenzgebiete. Berlin.

Gaz. Mat.: Gazeta Matematica Apare Odată pe Lună. Bucharest.

Gött. Nachr.: Nachrichten von der Gessellschaft der Wissenschaften zu Göttingen. Mathematisch-Physikalische Klasse.

Greenwich Observations: Observations made at the Royal Observatory, Greenwich in the year ____, in Astronomy, Magnetism, and Meteorology.

Indian Jour. Phys.: Indian Journal of Physics and Proceedings of the Indian Association for the Cultivation of Science.

Ing.-Arch.: Ingenieur-Archiv. Berlin.

Jap. Jour. Math.: Japanese Journal of Mathematics. Tokyo.

Jber. Deutsch. Math. Verein.: Jahresbericht der Deutschen Mathematiker-Vereinigung. Leipzig.

Jour. Aeronaut. Sci.: Journal of the Aeronautical Sciences. Easton, Penn.

Jour. Amer. Statist. Assoc.: Journal of the American Statistical Association. Washington, D. C.

Jour. Appl. Mech.: Journal of Applied Mechanics. Publ. as Supplement to Trans. Amer. Soc.Mech.Engrs.

Jour. Appl. Phys.: Journal of Applied Physics. American Institute of Physics. New York.

Jour. Brit. Astr. Assoc.: Journal of the British Astronomical Association.

Jour. Exp. Teor. Phys.: Zhurnal Eksperimental'noi i Teoreticeskoi Fisiki. Akademiia Nauk SSSR Leningrad.

Jour. Ecole Polytech. Paris: Journal de l'École Polytechnique Publié par le Conseil d'Instruction de cet Etablissement. Paris.

ABBREVIATIONS

Jour. Franklin Inst.: Journal of the Franklin Institute devoted to Science and the Mechanic Arts. Philadelphia.

Jour. Inst. Actuar.: Journal of the Institue of Actuaries. London.

Jour. Lond. Math. Soc.: The Journal of the London Mathematical Society.

Jour. Math. Phys. (M.I.T.): Journal of Mathematics and Physics. Massachusetts Institute of Technology.

Jour. Math. Pures Appl.: Journal de Mathematiques Pures et Appliquées. Paris.

Jour. Mysore Univ. Sect. B: The Half-yearly Journal of the Mysore University. New Series.Section B-Science.

Jour. Opt. Soc. Amer.: Journal of the Optical Society of America. American Institute of Physics. New York.

Jour. Reine. Angew. Math.: Journal für die Reine und Angewandte Mathematik. Berlin.

Jour. Roy. Aeronaut. Soc.: The Journal of the Royal Aeronautical Society with which is incorporated The Institution of Aeronautical Engineers. A Monthly Illustrated Magazine Devoted to All Subjects Connected with the Navigation of Air. London.

Jour. Sci. Instr.: Journal of Scientific Instruments. A Publication Dealing with their Principles, Construction and Use and the Applications of Physics in Industry. Produced by the Institute of Physics with the Cooperation of the National Physical Laboratory. Cambridge, Eng.

Lunds Univ. Årsskrift: Acta Universitatis Lundensis. Nova Series. Lunds Universitets Årsskrift. Ny Földjd. Andra Avdelningen. Medicin Samt Matematiska och naturvetenskapliga Ämnen.

Mass. Inst. of Tech. Publs. (Math.): Publications from the Massachusetts Institute of Technology. Contribution from the Department of Mathematics.

Math. Ann.: Mathematische Annalen. Berlin.

Mathematica (Cluj): Mathematica, Publicatie a Seminarului de Matematici al Universitatii, Cluj.

Math. Gaz.: The Mathematical Gazette. London.

Math. Mag.: The Mathematical Magazine. A Journal of Elementary Mathematics. Washington, D. C.

Math. Naturwiss. Anz. Ungar. Akad. Wiss.: Mathematischer und naturwissenschaftlicher Anzeiger der Ungarischen Akademie der Wissenschaften. Budapest.

Math. Notae: Mathematicae Notae. Boletin del Instituto de Matematica. Universidad Nacional del Litoral. Facultad de Ciencias Matematicas. Rosario, Argentina.

Math. Repository: New Series of the Mathematical Repository. By Thomas Leybourn of the Royal Military College. London.

Math. Student: The Mathematics Student. A Quarterly Dedicated to the Service of Students and Teachers in India. Published by the Indian Mathematical Society. Madras.

Math. Visitor: The Mathematical Visitor. Erie, Penn.

Math. Zeit.: Mathematische Zeitschrift. Berlin.

Mat. Tidsskr. B: Matematisk Tidsskrift B, Udgivet af Matematisk Forening i København.

Mém. Acad. Roy. Bruxelles: Mémoires de l'Académie Impériale et Royale des Sciences et Belles-Lettres de Bruxelles.

Mém. Acad. St. Petersbourg: Mémoires de l'Académie Impériale des Sciences de St. Pétersbourg. (Zapiski Imperatorskoi Akademii Nauk.).

Mem. Coll. Sci. Kyoto Imperial Univ.: Memoirs of the College of Science. Kyoto Imperial University. Series A.

ABBREVIATIONS

Mém. Acad. Sci. Kiev: Académie des Sciences d'Ukraine Mémoires de la Classe des Sciences Mathématiques et Physiques (Trudy Fizichno-Mathematichnii Viddil) or Mémoires de la classe des Sciences Naturelles et Techniques (Trudy Prirodnichno-Tekhnichnii Viddil).

Mem. Roy. Met. Soc.: Memoirs of the Royal Meteorological Society. London.

Memorie Reale Accad. d'Italia: Reale Accademia d'Italia. Memorie della Classe di Scienze Fisiche, Matematiche, e Naturali. Rome.

Mém. Sci. Math.: Mémorial des Sciences Mathématiques. Paris.

Mém. Soc. Royale Sci. Liège: Mémoires de la Société Royale des Sciences de Liège.

Mess. of Math.: The Messenger of Mathematics. Cambridge.

Meteorol. Zeit.: Meteorologische Zeitschrift. Im Auftrage der Deutschen Meteorologischen Gesellschaft, München.

Mitt. Georg. Abt. Akad. Wiss.: Akademiia Nauk SSSR (Leningrad). Mitteilungen der Georgischen Abteilung der Akademie der Wissenschaften der USSR. (Gruzinskii Filial. Soobscenija...).

Mitt. Math. Ges. Hamburg: Mitteilungen der Mathematischen Gesellschaft in Hamburg.

Mitt. Verein. Schweiz. Versich. Math.: Mitteilungen der Vereinigung Schweizerischer Versicherungsmathematiker. (Bulletin de l'Association des Actuaires Suisses.). Bern.

Monatsh. Math. Phys.: Monatshefte für Mathematik und Physik.

Month. Not. Roy. Astr. Soc.: Monthly Notices of the Royal Astronomical Society, Containing Papers, Abstracts of Papers and Reports of the Proceedings of the Society. London.

Month. Weather Rev.: Monthly Weather Review. U. S. Weather Bureau. Washington, D. C.

Nat. Math. Mag.: National Mathematics Magazine. (Formerly Mathematics News Letters.). Baton Rouge, La.

Nouv. Ann. Math.: Nouvelles Annales de Mathématiques.Journal des Candidats aux Écoles Spéciales, à la Licence et à l'Agregation. Paris.

Nova Acta Acad. Sci. Petropol.: Nova Acta Academiae Scientiarum Imperialis Petropolitanae.

Par. Mém. Sav. (Etr.): Mémoires Présentés par Divers Savants à l'Académie des Sciences de l'Institut de France. (Mémoires des Savants Etrangers.). Paris.

Period. Mat.: Periodico di Mathematiche. Storia, Didattica, Filosofia. Bologna.

Phil. Mag.: The London, Edinburgh and Dublin Philosophical Magazine and Journal of Science.London.

Phil. Trans. Roy. Soc. Lond: Philosophical Transactions of the Royal Society of London. (Series A. Mathematical and Physical Sciences.).

Phys. Rev.: The Physical Review. A Journal of Experimental and Theoretical Physics... American Physical Society. New York.

Portugaliae Math.: Portugaliae Mathematica. Lisbon.

Proc. Amer. Acad. Arts Sci: Proceedings of the American Academy of Arts and Sciences. Boston.

Proc. Akad. Wet. Amsterdam: K. Akademie van Wetenschappen, Amsterdam. Proceedings of the Section of Sciences.

Proc. Camb. Phil. Soc.: Proceedings of the Cambridge Philosophical Society.

Proc. Edin. Math. Soc.: Proceedings of the Edinburgh Mathematical Society.

ABBREVIATIONS

Proc. Ind. Acad. Sci.: Proceedings of the Indian Academy of Sciences. Section A. Hebbal, Bangalore, India.

Proc. Ind. Assoc. Sci.: Proceedings of the Indian Association for the Cultivation of Science. Calcutta.

Proc. Lond. Math. Soc.: Proceedings of the London Mathematical Society.

Proc. Nat. Acad. Sci. U.S.A.: Proceedings of the National Academy of Sciences of the United States of America. Washington, D. C.

Proc. Phys.-Math. Soc. Japan: Proceedings of the Physico-Mathematical Society of Japan. Faculty of Science, Tokyo Imperial University.

Proc. Phys. Soc. Lond.: Proceedings of the Physical Society. London.

Proc. Roy. Soc. Edin.: Proceedings of the Royal Society of Edinburgh. (Section A. Mathematical and Physical Sciences.).

Proc. Roy. Soc. Lond.: Proceedings of the Royal Society of London. Series A. Mathematical and Physical Sciences.

Proc. Tokyo Math.-Phys. Soc.: Proceedings of the Tokyo Mathematico-Physical Society.

Publ. Inst. Mat. Univ. Nac. Litoral: Publicaciones del Instituto de Matematica. Facultad de Ciencias Matematicas etc., de la Universidad National del Litoral.

Quart. Appl. Math.: Quarterly of Applied Mathematics. Providence, R. I.

Quart. Jour. Math.: The Quarterly Journal of Pure and Applied Mathematics. London. Superseded by The Quarterly Journal of Mathematics, Oxford Series. Oxford.

Quart. Jour. Roy. Met. Soc.: Quarterly Journal of the Royal Meteorological Society. London.

Rec. Math. (Mat. Sbornik): Académie des Sciences de l'URSS. Recueil Mathématique (Akademiia Nauk SSSR. Matematiceskii Sbornik.). Moscow.

Record Amer. Inst. Actuar.: The Record. American Institute of Actuaries. Chicago.

Rend. Accad. dei Lincei Roma: Atti della Reale Accademia Nazionale dei Lincei. Rendiconti. Classe di Scienze, Fisiche, Matematiche e Naturali. Rome.

Rend. Circ. Mat. Palermo: Rendiconti del Circolo Matematico di Palermo.

Rend. Ist. Lombardo: Reale Istituto Lombardo di Scienze e Lettere. Rendiconti. Milan.

Rend. Sem. Math. Fis. Milano: Rendiconti del Seminario Matematico e Fisico di Milano.

Revista Ci. Lima: Revista de Ciencias. Organo de la Facultad de Ciencias de la Universidad Nacional Mayor de San Marcos. Lima, Peru.

Revista Mat. Hisp.-Amer.: Revista Matematica Hispano-America. Publicada bajo los Auspicions de la Sociedad Matemática Española y del Laboratorio-Seminario Matematico. Madrid.

Revista Union Mat. Argentina: Revista Unión Matemática Argentina. Buenos Aires.

Revista Univ. Catolica Peru: Revista de la Universidad Católica del Peru. Lima.

Rev. Sci. Instr.: The Review of Scientific Instruments. American Institute of Physics. New York.

Sankyā: Sankyā, The Indian Journal of Statistics. Calcutta.

Schr. Math. Sem. Inst. Angew. Math. Univ. Berlin: Schriften des mathematischen Seminars und des Instituts für angewandte Mathematik an der Universität Berlin.

ABBREVIATIONS

Sitzber. Akad. Wiss. München: Akademie der Wissenschaften, München. Sitzungsberichte der mathematisch-naturiwissenschaftlichen Abteilung. Munich.

Sitzber. Akad. Wiss. Wien: Kaiserliche Akademie der Wissenschaften, Wien. Sitzungsberichte der mathematisch-naturwissenschaftlichen Klasse. Vienna.

Sitzber. Berl. Math. Ges.: Sitzungsberichte der Berliner Mathematischen Gesellschaft. (Published as a supplement to Archiv der Mathematik und Physik, third series.).

Sitzber. böhm. Ges. Prag: Sitzungsberichte der Königlichen Böhmischen Gesellschaft der Wissenschaften. Prague.

Sitzber. Heidelberg: Sitzungsberichte der Heidelbergen Akademie der Wissenschaften. Mathematisch-naturwissenschaftliche Klasse.

Skand. Aktuarietidskr.: Skandinavisk Aktuarietidskrift. Utgiven av den Danske Aktuarforening, Finlands Aktuarforening, den Norske Aktuarforening och Svenska Aktuarforeningen. Uppsala.

Soc. Sci. Fennica. Comment. Phys-Math.: Societatis Scientiarum Fennica. Commentationes Physico-Mathematicae. Helsingfors (Helsinki.).

Stockh. Akad. Förh.: Öfversigt af Kongl. Vetenskaps-Akademiens Förhandlingar. Stockholm.

Terr. Magnetism: Terrestrial Magnetism and Atmospheric Electricity. An International Quarterly Journal. Baltimore, etc.

Tôhoku Math. Jour.: The Tôhoku Mathematical Journal. The Tôhoku Imperial University, Sendai.

Trans. Actuar. Soc. Amer.: Actuarial Society of America. Transactions. New York.

Trans. Amer. Math. Soc.: Transactions of the American Mathematical Society. New York.

Trans. Amer. Soc. Civil Engrs.: Transactions of the American Society of Civil Engineers. New York.

Trans. Amer. Soc. Mech. Engrs.: American Society of Mechanical Engineers. Transactions.

Trans. Camb. Phil. Soc.: Transactions of the Cambridge Philosophical Society. Cambridge, Eng.

Trav. Inst. Math. Tbilissi (Trudy Tbiliss. Mat. Inst.): Akademiia Nauk SSSR Leningrad. Gruzinski filial. Matematischeskii Institut, Trudy.

Uchenye Zapiski Moscov. Univ. Mat.: Uchenye Zapiski Moscovskogo Gosudarstvennogo Universiteta. Moscow.

Univ.Nac. la Plata Publ. Fac. Ci. Fisicomat. Revista: Universidad Nacional de la Plata.Publicaciones de la Faculdad de Ciencias Físicomatematicas. Contributión al Estudio de las Ciencias Físicas y Matemáticas. Serie Técnica. La Plata, Argentina.

Univ. Nac. Tucumán Revista: Universidad Nacional de Tucumán. Revista. Serie A, Matematicas y Fisica Teorica. Tucumán, Argentina.

Zeit Angew. Math. Mech.: Zeitschrift für angewandte Mathematik und Mechanik. Ingenieurwissenschaftliche Forschungsarbeiten. Berlin.

Zeit. Angew. Met.: Zeitschrift fur angewandte Meteorologie-Das Wetter. Mit Unterstützung des Reichsamts für Wetterdienst.

Zeit. Instrumentenkunde: Zeitschrift für Instrumentenkunde. Organ für Mitteilungen aus dem gesamten Gebiete der wissenschaftlichen Technik. Berlin.

Zeit. Math. Naturwiss. Unterricht: Zeitschrift fur mathematische und naturwissenschaftliche Unterricht aller Schulgattungen. Leipzig.

Zeit. Math. Phys.: Zeitschrift fur Mathematik und Physik... Organ fur angewandte Mathematik. Leipzig.

ABBREVIATIONS

Zeit. Phys.: Zeitschrift für Physik. Herausgegeben unter Mitwirkung der Deutschen physikalischen Gesellschaft. Berlin.

Zeit. Verein. Deutsch. Ing.: Zeitschrift des Vereines Deutscher Ingenieure. Berlin.

INTRODUCTION TO THE APPENDICES

Chapter III discussed the operations of the various electrical components of the calculator. In that discussion, the circuits were, for the sake of clarity, considerably abbreviated. Elements not necessary to the understanding of the principle of operation of any section of the machine were omitted. Where circuits are duplicated, either exactly or with minor modifications, usually only one of the duplicated circuits was discussed. It is the purpose of these appendices to present, so far as possible, the circuits as they actually occur, rather than their simplified forms heretofore employed.

These appendices are given on the pages indicated in the following table.

INTRODUCTION TO THE APPENDICES

Appendix I lists in tabular form the A, B and C relays energized by the reading of the various sequence codes. Appendices II, III, IV and V indicate cycle by cycle the subsequent operations which take place as a result of the pick up of these relays. In each of the appendices II, III, IV and V, the following form is employed.

(a) The order in which the various relays are energized is stated in words.

(b) A timing diagram indicating that portion of the cycle during which each relay is energized is given. The period of time during which each relay is energized through its pick up circuit is shown by a heavy bar covering the appropriate portion of the cycle. The period of time during which the relay is energized through its hold circuit is indicated by an outline bar.

(c) A circuit diagram is presented, showing graphically the pick up and hold circuits of each relay. All relay points are shown in their normal (unenergized) positions.

Appendices VI, VII and VIII list the various relays, cams and fuses employed, together with the purposes of each. Thus appendices I through V will enable the reader to trace an operation of the calculator through the network of electric circuits involved, while appendices VI through VIII will be useful in determining the purpose of a particular relay, cam or fuse.

From its inception to its completion, the circuits of the calculator have undergone a process of constant evolution. In fact, changes are at the present time still being made. This is quite understandable, in view of the fact that the Automatic Sequence Controlled Calculator is the first general purpose calculator to be successfully completed and put into operation. This series of changes has, however, necessarily led to certain inconsistencies in the nomenclature of the various electrical components of the calculator. To begin with, most of the electrical elements are designated by two separate names: first, a colloquial name brought about by common usage, such as "Q-control relay", "X's right relay", "DD-carry control relay", etc.; second, a specific numerical designation which is the outgrowth of the originally logical system of numbering the various parts of the calculator. It is this latter designation that will be discussed here.

(1) Relay Coil Designations

1. Except for a relatively few heavy duty relays, all relays in the calculator are of a standard type, of which six varieties are employed; namely:

4 point single coil	4 point double coil
6 point single coil	6 point double coil
12 point single coil	12 point double coil .

2. When a double coil relay is used, one coil serves for pick up, the other for hold.

3. The coils of these relays are designated according to their use in the calculator by a combination of letters and numbers, usually consisting of a group of letters followed by three groups of numbers. Each group is separated from the others by dashes, and the right hand group is enclosed in parentheses: thus:

Seq-29-1-(12), B-3-1,2,3-(12).

4. The letter or group of letters on the left indicates the "section" of the machine in which the relay is used. Sectional prefixes are given in the following tabulation.

Seq	Sequence Relay
Sw1, Sw2, ..., Sw60	Switch Relay
A	Code Selection Relay (Out Relay)
B	Code Selection Relay (In Relay)
C	Code Selection Relay (Miscellaneous Relay)
SC1, SC2, ..., SC72	Storage Counter Relay
Check	Check Counter Relay
Choice	Choice Counter Relay
Sp64, Sp65, Sp68, Sp69	Special Purpose Relay
CI	Carry Interlock Relay
(none)	MP-DIV or Functional Relay

In several places in the appendices, the relays associated with switch A are referred to by the prefix SwA, and the relays associated with storage counter A by the prefix SCA.

5. An exception to this system of literal prefixes is the prefix HD. In general this denotes a heavy duty relay, and thus refers to the type relay employed, not to its place in the circuits of the calculator. The single relay HD-3-1-(4) wc is, however, a wire contact rather than a heavy duty relay, a fact denoted by the suffix wc. This is the only relay prefixed with HD that is not of the heavy duty type.

6. When it is required that more than 12 points operate simultaneously, a number of relays of 4, 6 or 12 points each are wired in parallel as a "bank". Reading from left to right, the three groups of numbers in the relay designation denote respectively the number of the bank, the numbers of the relays in the bank, and the number of points on each of these relays; thus:

(a) Seq-29-1-(12) denotes Sequence Relay Bank 29, one twelve point relay;

(b) B-3-1,2,3-(12) denotes Code Selection In, Bank 3, relays 1, 2 and 3, each of twelve points.

7. As indicated in the tabulation of sectional prefixes, relays without literal prefix are either MP-DIV or Functional relays. The banks of MP-DIV relays are numbered 1 through 104. The banks of functional relays are numbered from 100 consecutively upward. Thus there are

two completely independent banks of relays for each of the bank numbers 100, 101, 102, 103 and 104.

8. When relays of varying numbers of points are employed in the same bank, any one of several alternate designations may be used.

(a) Several lines may be employed.

Sw8-1,2-(12)
Sw8-3-(4) denotes Switch Bank 8, relays 1 and 2 each of 12 points and relay 3 of 4 points.

(b) If the relays of the different varieties occur periodically within the bank, several of the numbers 4, 6 and 12 may be placed in the parentheses in the order in which the corresponding relays recur; thus:

5-1,...,27-(12,12,4)

could be written in place of

5-1,2,4,5,7,8,10,11,13,14,16,17,19,20,22,23,25,26-(12)
5-3,6,9,12,15,18,21,24,27-(4).

(c) Even though there is no periodicity in their recurrence, the relays of varying numbers of points are sometimes written on one line; thus:

33-47,...,70-(4,6 or 12).

This is a non-specific designation, since it does not give information as to which of the 24 relays have 4, 6 and 12 points respectively. In order to give a specific designation in this case, it is necessary that several lines be used.

9. There is one and only one instance of a bank in which the individual relays are not numbered consecutively. This is bank 29 of the MP-DIV panel. This bank has in addition to the 36 relays, 29-1,...,36-(12,12,6), a single 4 point relay designated as 29-9(2)-(4), which operates with relay 29-9-(6).

(2) Relay Point Designations

1. In the interest of simplicity, the relay coils and their associated points are separated in the following circuit diagrams. The designation of any relay point consists of a group of letters followed by three groups of numbers, the groups being separated by dashes; thus:

C-1-11-11, Seq-32-1-2.

2. The letter or group of letters and the two groups of numbers on the left refer respectively to the section, bank and individual relay in question. The number on the right denotes the particular point of that relay. The letters NC or NO are often suffixed to the point designation to denote normally closed or normally open respectively; thus:

(a) C-1-11-11NC denotes the normally closed side of the 11th point of the 11th relay of the 1st bank of the Miscellaneous relays of the code selection cascade;

(b) Seq-32-1-2 denotes the 2nd point of the 1st relay of the 32nd bank of the sequence relays.

(3) Further Abbreviations

1. When only one relay is used in a bank, the number "one" of that relay will frequently be omitted. Thus the relay Seq-31-1-(4) would be abbreviated to Seq-31-(4). The designation of the third point of this relay would be shortened from Seq-31-1-3 to Seq-31-3.

2. There are several instances of only one bank in a section of the calculator, and only one

relay in that bank. In these cases, both bank numbers and relay numbers may be omitted. Thus the relay Check-1-1-(4) is written Check-(4) and Choice-1-1-(6) is written Choice-(6). Similarly, the 4th point of the check relay is written Check-4 and the third point of the choice relay, Choice-3.

(4) Cam Designations

1. As explained in Chapter III, the timing of the various operations of the machine is controlled by cam contacts. Three series of these cam contacts are used. They are distinguished on the following diagrams and lists by the prefixed letters:

   (a) CC denotes computing cam contacts (used principally for timing the operations of the MP-DIV unit);

   (b) FC denotes functional cam contacts (used for timing the sequence and functional units);

   (c) SC denotes storage cam contacts (used for timing impulses through the storage counters and switches).

2. The number following this pair of letters denotes a particular cam of the series. The numbers in parentheses give the timing of the cam; thus:

   (a) SC-11 (12-0) denotes storage cam contact number 11, makes at 12 time, breaks at 0 time;

   (b) CC-39 (1/3 15 - 12) denotes computing cam contact number 39, makes 1/3 before 15 time, breaks at 12 time.

3. Certain of the CC cams operate 16 times per cycle. In these cases, the letter L is used to denote each one of the 16 subdivisions of the cycle in turn; thus:

   (a) CC-23 (1/16 L - L 1/2) denotes cam contact number 23, makes 1/16 before line, breaks 1/2 after line; i.e.,

Makes	Breaks
1/16 9	9 1/2
1/16 8	8 1/2
......	......
1/16 0	0 1/2
......	......
1/16 16	16 1/2.

4. Closely associated cams are given the same group number, but distinguished from each other by a letter following that number; thus:

   (a) CC-24B (L 1/4 - L 7/8) denotes B cam contact of group 24, makes 1/4 after line, breaks 7/8 after line.

(5) Designations of Other Electrical Elements

1. Counter Wheels

   (a) The coils are clearly labeled counter magnet or Ctr. Mag.

   (b) The spots or "read-outs" are numbered 0, 1, ..., 9 and labeled collectively ctr. R.O.

   (c) Nines and tens carry contacts are labeled with a 9 and a 10 respectively.

2. Counter Registers

   Names of registers are clearly given on the diagrams. The elements belonging to specific component counter wheels are labeled col. 1, col. 2, ..., col. 24.

3. Fuses

Fuses are prefixed either with the letter F, or the letters MP, according as to whether they are mounted on the functional panel or on the MP-DIV panel. Each series is numbered consecutively from one upward.

4. Binding Posts

Binding posts are divided into series each prefixed by VBP, SBP, FBP, BBP, VTP, ABP or SWBP. Each series is numbered consecutively.

(6) Cycle Designations

1. Various functional operations extend over several cycles of the calculator. The multiple cycle operations considered here are:

   M Multiply
   D Divide
   NR Normalizing Register

   Thus a relay would be said to operate in cycle D-6 if it were energized during the 6th cycle of the division sequence of operations.

(7) Miscellaneous Symbols

1. Several special designations occur in Appendix VI. The letters S and D suffixed to the relay designations denote respectively single coil and double coil. The numbers in the column headed "Row" refer to the physical rows of relays in the MP-DIV panel.

SEQUENCE CODES

The following table lists the cascade of relays which are involved in the reading of any given sequence code. The codes are tabulated according to the sequence column, A, B or C, in which they are read. The first column of the table states the given code; the second, the functional cam which provides the impulse; the third, the open points through which the impulse travels; the fourth, the normally closed points through which the impulse travels; the fifth, the unit controlled by the sequence code.

OUT CODES- A RELAYS

Code	FC	Open	NC	Controls	Code	FC	Open	NC	Controls
1	92	1-1-1	8-1-1 7-1-1 6-1-1 5-1-1 4-1-1 3-1-1 2-1-1	Storage Counter #1- OUT	32	92	3-1-1 2-1-2	8-1-1 7-1-1 6-1-1 5-1-1 4-1-1 1-1-4	Storage Counter #6- OUT
2	92	2-1-1	8-1-1 7-1-1 6-1-1 5-1-1 4-1-1 3-1-1 1-1-2	Storage Counter #2- OUT	321	92	3-1-1 2-1-2 1-1-4	8-1-1 7-1-1 6-1-1 5-1-1 4-1-1	Storage Counter #7- OUT
21	92	2-1-1 1-1-2	8-1-1 7-1-1 6-1-1 5-1-1 4-1-1 3-1-1	Storage Counter #3- OUT	4	92	4-1-1	8-1-1 7-1-1 6-1-1 5-1-1 3-1-2 2-1-3 1-1-5	Storage Counter #8- OUT
3	92	3-1-1	8-1-1 7-1-1 6-1-1 5-1-1 4-1-1 2-1-2 1-1-3	Storage Counter #4- OUT	41	92	4-1-1 1-1-5	8-1-1 7-1-1 6-1-1 5-1-1 3-1-2 2-1-3	Storage Counter #9- OUT
31	92	3-1-1 1-1-3	8-1-1 7-1-1 6-1-1 5-1-1 4-1-1 2-1-2	Storage Counter #5- OUT	42	92	4-1-1 2-1-3	8-1-1 7-1-1 6-1-1 5-1-1 3-1-2 1-1-6	Storage Counter #10- OUT
					421	92	4-1-1 2-1-3 1-1-6	8-1-1 7-1-1 6-1-1	

<u>OUT</u> <u>CODES</u>- <u>A</u> <u>RELAYS</u> -continued-

Code	FC	Open	NC	Controls
421 cont.			5-1-1 3-1-2	Storage Counter #11- OUT
43	92	4-1-1 3-1-2	8-1-1 7-1-1 6-1-1 5-1-1 2-1-4 1-1-7	Storage Counter #12- OUT
431	92	4-1-1 3-1-2 1-1-7	8-1-1 7-1-1 6-1-1 5-1-1 2-1-4	Storage Counter #13- OUT
432	92	4-1-1 3-1-2 2-1-4	8-1-1 7-1-1 6-1-1 5-1-1 1-1-8	Storage Counter #14- OUT
4321	92	4-1-1 3-1-2 2-1-4 1-1-8	8-1-1 7-1-1 6-1-1 5-1-1	Storage Counter #15- OUT
5	92	5-1-1	8-1-1 7-1-1 6-1-1 4-1-2 3-1-3 2-1-5 1-1-9	Storage Counter #16- OUT
51	92	5-1-1 1-1-9	8-1-1 7-1-1 6-1-1 4-1-2 3-1-3 2-1-5	Storage Counter #17- OUT
52	92	5-1-1 2-1-5	8-1-1 7-1-1 6-1-1	
52 cont.			4-1-2 3-1-3 1-1-10	Storage Counter #18- OUT
521	92	5-1-1 2-1-5 1-1-10	8-1-1 7-1-1 6-1-1 4-1-2 3-1-3	Storage Counter #19- OUT
53	92	5-1-1 3-1-3	8-1-1 7-1-1 6-1-1 4-1-2 2-1-6 1-1-11	Storage Counter #20- OUT
531	92	5-1-1 3-1-3 1-1-11	8-1-1 7-1-1 6-1-1 4-1-2 2-1-6	Storage Counter #21- OUT
532	92	5-1-1 3-1-3 2-1-6	8-1-1 7-1-1 6-1-1 4-1-2 1-1-12	Storage Counter #22- OUT
5321	92	5-1-1 3-1-3 2-1-6 1-1-12	8-1-1 7-1-1 6-1-1 4-1-2	Storage Counter #23- OUT
54	92	5-1-1 4-1-2	8-1-1 7-1-1 6-1-1 3-1-4 2-1-7 1-2-1	Storage Counter #24- OUT
541	92	5-1-1 4-1-2 1-2-1	8-1-1 7-1-1 6-1-1 3-1-4 2-1-7	Storage Counter #25- OUT

OUT CODES- A RELAYS -continued-

Code	FC	Oper.	NC	Controls
542	92	5-1-1 4-1-2 2-1-7	8-1-1 7-1-1 6-1-1 3-1-4 1-2-2	Storage Counter #26- OUT
5421	92	5-1-1 4-1-2 2-1-7 1-2-2	8-1-1 7-1-1 6-1-1 3-1-4	Storage Counter #27- OUT
543	92	5-1-1 4-1-2 3-1-4	8-1-1 7-1-1 6-1-1 2-1-8 1-2-3	Storage Counter #28- OUT
5431	92	5-1-1 4-1-2 3-1-4 1-2-3	8-1-1 7-1-1 6-1-1 2-1-8	Storage Counter #29- OUT
5432	92	5-1-1 4-1-2 3-1-4 2-1-8	8-1-1 7-1-1 6-1-1 1-2-4	Storage Counter #30- OUT
54321	92	5-1-1 4-1-2 3-1-4 2-1-8 1-2-4	8-1-1 7-1-1 6-1-1	Storage Counter #31- OUT
6	92	6-1-1	8-1-1 7-1-1 5-1-2 4-1-3 3-1-5 2-1-9 1-2-5	Storage Counter #32- OUT
61	92	6-1-1 1-2-5	8-1-1 7-1-1 5-1-2 4-1-3	

Code	FC	Open	NC	Controls
61 cont.			3-1-5 2-1-9	Storage Counter #33- OUT
62	92	6-1-1 2-1-9	8-1-1 7-1-1 5-1-2 4-1-3 3-1-5 1-2-6	Storage Counter #34- OUT
621	92	6-1-1 2-1-9 1-2-6	8-1-1 7-1-1 5-1-2 4-1-3 3-1-5	Storage Counter #35- OUT
63	92	6-1-1 3-1-5	8-1-1 7-1-1 5-1-2 4-1-3 2-1-10 1-2-7	Storage Counter #36- OUT
631	92	6-1-1 3-1-5 1-2-7	8-1-1 7-1-1 5-1-2 4-1-3 2-1-10	Storage Counter #37- OUT
632	92	6-1-1 3-1-5 2-1-10	8-1-1 7-1-1 5-1-2 4-1-3 1-2-8	Storage Counter #38- OUT
6321	92	6-1-1 3-1-5 2-1-10 1-2-8	8-1-1 7-1-1 5-1-2 4-1-3	Storage Counter #39- OUT
64	92	6-1-1 4-1-3	8-1-1 7-1-1 5-1-2 3-1-6	

OUT CODES- A RELAYS -continued-

Code	FC	Open	NC	Controls
64 cont.	92		2-1-11 1-2-9	Storage Counter #40- OUT
641	92	6-1-1 4-1-3 1-2-9	8-1-1 7-1-1 5-1-2 3-1-6 2-1-11	Storage Counter #41- OUT
642	92	6-1-1 4-1-3 2-1-11	8-1-1 7-1-1 5-1-2 3-1-6 1-2-10	Storage Counter #42- OUT
6421	92	6-1-1 4-1-3 2-1-11 1-2-10	8-1-1 7-1-1 5-1-2 3-1-6	Storage Counter #43- OUT
643	92	6-1-1 4-1-3 3-1-6	8-1-1 7-1-1 5-1-2 2-1-12 1-2-11	Storage Counter #44- OUT
6431	92	6-1-1 4-1-3 3-1-6 1-2-11	8-1-1 7-1-1 5-1-2 2-1-12	Storage Counter #45- OUT
6432	92	6-1-1 4-1-3 3-1-6 2-1-12	8-1-1 7-1-1 5-1-2 1-2-12	Storage Counter #46- OUT
64321	92	6-1-1 4-1-3 3-1-6 2-1-12 1-2-12	8-1-1 7-1-1 5-1-2	Storage Counter #47- OUT
65	92	6-1-1 5-1-2	8-1-1 7-1-1 4-1-4	

Code	FC	Open	NC	Controls
65 cont.			3-1-7 2-2-1 1-3-1	Storage Counter #48- OUT
651	92	6-1-1 5-1-2 1-3-1	8-1-1 7-1-1 4-1-4 3-1-7 2-2-1	Storage Counter #49- OUT
652	92	6-1-1 5-1-2 2-2-1	8-1-1 7-1-1 4-1-4 3-1-7 1-3-2	Storage Counter #50- OUT
6521	92	6-1-1 5-1-2 2-2-1 1-3-2	8-1-1 7-1-1 4-1-4 3-1-7	Storage Counter #51- OUT
653	92	6-1-1 5-1-2 3-1-7	8-1-1 7-1-1 4-1-4 2-2-2 1-3-3	Storage Counter #52- OUT
6531	92	6-1-1 5-1-2 3-1-7 1-3-3	8-1-1 7-1-1 4-1-4 2-2-2	Storage Counter #53- OUT
6532	92	6-1-1 5-1-2 3-1-7 2-2-2	8-1-1 7-1-1 4-1-4 1-3-4	Storage Counter #54- OUT
65321	92	6-1-1 5-1-2 3-1-7 2-2-2 1-3-4	8-1-1 7-1-1 4-1-4	Storage Counter #55- OUT
654	92	6-1-1 5-1-2	8-1-1 7-1-1	

OUT CODES- A RELAYS -continued-

Code	FC	Open	NC	Controls
654 cont.		4-1-4	3-1-8 2-2-3 1-3-5	Storage Counter #56- OUT
6541	92	6-1-1 5-1-2 4-1-4 1-3-5	8-1-1 7-1-1 3-1-8 2-2-3	Storage Counter #57- OUT
6542	92	6-1-1 5-1-2 4-1-4 2-2-3	8-1-1 7-1-1 3-1-8 1-3-6	Storage Counter #58- OUT
65421	92	6-1-1 5-1-2 4-1-4 2-2-3 1-3-6	8-1-1 7-1-1 3-1-8	Storage Counter #59- OUT
6543	92	6-1-1 5-1-2 4-1-4 3-1-8	8-1-1 7-1-1 2-2-4 1-3-7	Storage Counter #60- OUT
65431	92	6-1-1 5-1-2 4-1-4 3-1-8 1-3-7	8-1-1 7-1-1 2-2-4	Storage Counter #61- OUT
65432	92	6-1-1 5-1-2 4-1-4 3-1-8 2-2-4	8-1-1 7-1-1 1-3-8	Storage Counter #62- OUT
654321	92	6-1-1 5-1-2 4-1-4 3-1-8 2-2-4 1-3-8	8-1-1 7-1-1	Storage Counter #63- OUT
7	92	7-1-1	8-1-1	

Code	FC	Open	NC	Controls
7 cont.			6-1-2 5-1-3 4-1-5 3-1-9 2-2-5 1-3-9	Storage Counter #64- OUT
71	92	7-1-1 1-3-9	8-1-1 6-1-2 5-1-3 4-1-5 3-1-9 2-2-5	Storage Counter #65- OUT
72	92	7-1-1 2-2-5	8-1-1 6-1-2 5-1-3 4-1-5 3-1-9 1-3-10	Storage Counter #66- OUT
721	92	7-1-1 2-2-5 1-3-10	8-1-1 6-1-2 5-1-3 4-1-5 3-1-9	Storage Counter #67- OUT
73	92	7-1-1 3-1-9	8-1-1 6-1-2 5-1-3 4-1-5 2-2-6 1-3-11	Storage Counter #68- OUT
731	92	7-1-1 3-1-9 1-3-11	8-1-1 6-1-2 5-1-3 4-1-5 2-2-6	Storage Counter #69- OUT
732	92	7-1-1 3-1-9 2-2-6	8-1-1 6-1-2 5-1-3 4-1-5 1-3-12	Storage Counter #70- OUT

OUT CODES- A RELAYS -continued-

Code	FC	Open	NC	Controls
7321	92	7-1-1 3-1-9 2-2-6 1-3-12	8-1-1 6-1-2 5-1-3 4-1-5	Storage Counter #71- OUT
74	92	7-1-1 4-1-5	8-1-1 6-1-2 5-1-3 3-1-10 2-2-7 1-4-1	Storage Counter #72- OUT
741	92	7-1-1 4-1-5 1-4-1	8-1-1 6-1-2 5-1-3 3-1-10 2-2-7	Switch #1- OUT
742	92	7-1-1 4-1-5 2-2-7	8-1-1 6-1-2 5-1-3 3-1-10 1-4-2	Switch #2- OUT
7421	92	7-1-1 4-1-5 2-2-7 1-4-2	8-1-1 6-1-2 5-1-3 3-1-10	Switch #3- OUT
743	92	7-1-1 4-1-5 3-1-10	8-1-1 6-1-2 5-1-3 2-2-8 1-4-3	Switch #4- OUT
7431	92	7-1-1 4-1-5 3-1-10 1-4-3	8-1-1 6-1-2 5-1-3 2-2-8	Switch #5- OUT
7432	92	7-1-1 4-1-5 3-1-10 2-2-8	8-1-1 6-1-2 5-1-3 1-4-4	Switch #6- OUT

Code	FC	Open	NC	Controls
74321	92	7-1-1 4-1-5 3-1-10 2-2-8 1-4-4	8-1-1 6-1-2 5-1-3	Switch #7- OUT
75	92	7-1-1 5-1-3	8-1-1 6-1-2 4-1-6 3-1-11 2-2-9 1-4-5	Switch #8- OUT
751	92	7-1-1 5-1-3 1-4-5	8-1-1 6-1-2 4-1-6 3-1-11 2-2-9	Switch #9- OUT
752	92	7-1-1 5-1-3 2-2-9	8-1-1 6-1-2 4-1-6 3-1-11 1-4-6	Switch #10- OUT
7521	92	7-1-1 5-1-3 2-2-9 1-4-6	8-1-1 6-1-2 4-1-6 3-1-11	Switch #11- OUT
753	92	7-1-1 5-1-3 3-1-11	8-1-1 6-1-2 4-1-6 2-2-10 1-4-7	Switch #12- OUT
7531	92	7-1-1 5-1-3 3-1-11 1-4-7	8-1-1 6-1-2 4-1-6 2-2-10	Switch #13- OUT
7532	92	7-1-1 5-1-3 3-1-11 2-2-10	8-1-1 6-1-2 4-1-6 1-4-8	Switch #14- OUT

OUT CODES- A RELAYS -continued-

Code	FC	Open	NC	Controls
75321	92	7-1-1 5-1-3 3-1-11 2-2-10 1-4-8	8-1-1 6-1-2 4-1-6	Switch #15- OUT
754	92	7-1-1 5-1-3 4-1-6	8-1-1 6-1-2 3-1-12 2-2-11 1-4-9	Switch #16- OUT
7541	92	7-1-1 5-1-3 4-1-6 1-4-9	8-1-1 6-1-2 3-1-12 2-2-11	Switch #17- OUT
7542	92	7-1-1 5-1-3 4-1-6 2-2-11	8-1-1 6-1-2 3-1-12 1-4-10	Switch #18- OUT
75421	92	7-1-1 5-1-3 4-1-6 2-2-11 1-4-10	8-1-1 6-1-2 3-1-12	Switch #19- OUT
7543	92	7-1-1 5-1-3 4-1-6 3-1-12	8-1-1 6-1-2 2-2-12 1-4-11	Switch #20- OUT
75431	92	7-1-1 5-1-3 4-1-6 3-1-12 1-4-11	8-1-1 6-1-2 2-2-12 1-4-11	Switch #21- OUT
75432	92	7-1-1 5-1-3 4-1-6 3-1-12 2-2-12	8-1-1 6-1-2 1-4-12	Switch #22- OUT

Code	FC	Open	NC	Controls
754321	92	7-1-1 5-1-3 4-1-6 3-1-12 2-2-12 1-4-12	8-1-1 6-1-2	Switch #23- OUT
76	92	7-1-1 6-1-2	8-1-1 5-1-4 4-1-7 3-2-1 2-3-1 1-5-1	Switch #24- OUT
761	92	7-1-1 6-1-2 1-5-1	8-1-1 5-1-4 4-1-7 3-2-1 2-3-1	Switch #25- OUT
762	92	7-1-1 6-1-2 2-3-1	8-1-1 5-1-4 4-1-7 3-2-1 1-5-2	Switch #26- OUT
7621	92	7-1-1 6-1-2 2-3-1 1-5-2	8-1-1 5-1-4 4-1-7 3-2-1	Switch #27- OUT
763	92	7-1-1 6-1-2 3-2-1	8-1-1 5-1-4 4-1-7 2-3-2 1-5-3	Switch #28- OUT
7631	92	7-1-1 6-1-2 3-2-1 1-5-3	8-1-1 5-1-4 4-1-7 2-3-2	Switch #29- OUT
7632	92	7-1-1 6-1-2	8-1-1 5-1-4	

OUT CODES- A RELAYS -continued-

Code	FC	Open	NC	Controls
7632 cont.		3-2-1 2-3-2	4-1-7 1-5-4	Switch #30- OUT
76321	92	7-1-1 6-1-2 3-2-1 2-3-2 1-5-4	8-1-1 5-1-4 4-1-7	Switch #31- OUT
764	92	7-1-1 6-1-2 4-1-7	8-1-1 5-1-4 3-2-2 2-3-3 1-5-5	Switch #32- OUT
7641	92	7-1-1 6-1-2 4-1-7 1-5-5	8-1-1 5-1-4 3-2-2 2-3-3	Switch #33- OUT
7642	92	7-1-1 6-1-2 4-1-7 2-3-3	8-1-1 5-1-4 3-2-2 1-5-6	Switch #34- OUT
76421	92	7-1-1 6-1-2 4-1-7 2-3-3 1-5-6	8-1-1 5-1-4 3-2-2	Switch #35- OUT
7643	92	7-1-1 6-1-2 4-1-7 3-2-2	8-1-1 5-1-4 2-3-4 1-5-7	Switch #36- OUT
76431	92	7-1-1 6-1-2 4-1-7 3-2-2 1-5-7	8-1-1 5-1-4 2-3-4	Switch #37- OUT
76432	92	7-1-1 6-1-2 4-1-7	8-1-1 5-1-4 1-5-8	

Code	FC	Open	NC	Controls
76432 cont.	92	3-2-2 2-3-4		Switch #38- OUT
764321	92	7-1-1 6-1-2 4-1-7 3-2-2 2-3-4 1-5-8	8-1-1 5-1-4	Switch #39- OUT
765	92	7-1-1 6-1-2 5-1-4	8-1-1 4-1-8 3-2-3 2-3-5 1-5-9	Switch #40- OUT
7651	92	7-1-1 6-1-2 5-1-4 1-5-9	8-1-1 4-1-8 3-2-3 2-3-5	Switch #41- OUT
7652	92	7-1-1 6-1-2 5-1-4 2-3-5	8-1-1 4-1-8 3-2-3 1-5-10	Switch #42- OUT
76521	92	7-1-1 6-1-2 5-1-4 2-3-5 1-5-10	8-1-1 4-1-8 3-2-3	Switch #43- OUT
7653	92	7-1-1 6-1-2 5-1-4 3-2-3	8-1-1 4-1-8 2-3-6 1-5-11	Switch #44- OUT
76531	92	7-1-1 6-1-2 5-1-4 3-2-3 1-5-11	8-1-1 4-1-8 2-3-6	Switch #45- OUT
76532	92	7-1-1 6-1-2	8-1-1 4-1-8	

OUT CODES- A RELAYS -continued-

Code	FC	Open	NC	Controls
76532 cont.		5-1-4 3-2-3 2-3-6	1-5-12	Switch #46- OUT
765321	92	7-1-1 6-1-2 5-1-4 3-2-3 2-3-6 1-5-12	8-1-1 4-1-8	Switch #47- OUT
7654	92	7-1-1 6-1-2 5-1-4 4-1-8	8-1-1 3-2-4 2-3-7 1-6-1	Switch #48- OUT
76541	92	7-1-1 6-1-2 5-1-4 4-1-8 1-6-1	8-1-1 3-2-4 2-3-7	Switch #49- OUT
76542	92	7-1-1 6-1-2 5-1-4 4-1-8 2-3-7	8-1-1 3-2-4 1-6-2	Switch #50- OUT
765421	92	7-1-1 6-1-2 5-1-4 4-1-8 2-3-7 1-6-2	8-1-1 3-2-4	Switch #51- OUT
76543	92	7-1-1 6-1-2 5-1-4 4-1-8 3-2-4	8-1-1 2-3-8 1-6-3	Switch #52- OUT
765431	92	7-1-1 6-1-2 5-1-4 4-1-8	8-1-1 2-3-8	
765431 cont.		3-2-4 1-6-3		Switch #53- OUT
765432	92	7-1-1 6-1-2 5-1-4 4-1-8 3-2-4 2-3-8	8-1-1 1-6-4	Switch #54- OUT
7654321	92	7-1-1 6-1-2 5-1-4 4-1-8 3-2-4 2-3-8 1-6-4	8-1-1	Switch #55- OUT
8	92	8-1-1	7-1-2 6-1-3 5-1-5 4-1-9 3-2-5 2-3-9 1-6-5	Switch #56- OUT
81	92	8-1-1 1-6-5	7-1-2 6-1-3 5-1-5 4-1-9 3-2-5 2-3-9	Switch #57- OUT
82	92	8-1-1 2-3-9	7-1-2 6-1-3 5-1-5 4-1-9 3-2-5 1-6-6	Switch #58- OUT
821	92	8-1-1 2-3-9 1-6-6	7-1-2 6-1-3 5-1-5 4-1-9 3-2-5	Switch #59- OUT

OUT CODES- A RELAYS -continued-

Code	FC	Open	NC	Controls
83	92	8-1-1 3-2-5	7-1-2 6-1-3 5-1-5 4-1-9 2-3-10 1-6-7	Switch #60- OUT
831	92	8-1-1 3-2-5 1-6-7	7-1-2 6-1-3 5-1-5 4-1-9 2-3-10	LIO- OUT (plugged)
832	92	8-1-1 3-2-5 2-3-10	7-1-2 6-1-3 5-1-5 4-1-9 1-6-8	EIO- OUT
8321	92	8-1-1 3-2-5 2-3-10 1-6-8	7-1-2 6-1-3 5-1-5 4-1-9	Normalizing Register- OUT
84	92	8-1-1 4-1-9	7-1-2 6-1-3 5-1-5 3-2-6 2-3-11 1-6-9	SIO- OUT #2 (plugged)
841	92	8-1-1 4-1-9 1-6-9	7-1-2 6-1-3 5-1-5 3-2-6 2-3-11	"h" Correction to Intermediate Ctr.
842	92	8-1-1 4-1-9 2-3-11	7-1-2 6-1-3 5-1-5 3-2-6 1-6-10	Print Counter #1- Reset
8421	92	8-1-1 4-1-9	7-1-2 6-1-3	

Code	FC	Open	NC	Controls
8421 cont.		2-3-11 1-6-10	5-1-5 3-2-6	Print Counter #2- Reset
843	92	8-1-1 4-1-9 3-2-6	7-1-2 6-1-3 5-1-5 2-3-12 1-6-11	Punch Counter- Reset
8431	92	8-1-1 4-1-9 3-2-6 1-6-11	7-1-2 6-1-3 5-1-5 2-3-12	IVS- OUT
85	92	8-1-1 5-1-5	7-1-2 6-1-3 4-1-10 3-2-7 2-4-1 1-7-1	Interpolator #1- Read Tape
851	92	8-1-1 5-1-5 1-7-1	7-1-2 6-1-3 4-1-10 3-2-7 2-4-1	Interpolator #2- Read Tape
852	92	8-1-1 5-1-5 2-4-1	7-1-2 6-1-3 4-1-10 3-2-7 1-7-2	Interpolator #3- Read Tape
853	92	8-1-1 5-1-5 3-2-7	7-1-2 6-1-3 4-1-10 2-4-2 1-7-3	MIO Counter- Cols.13-24 to Buss Cols. 13-24
8531	92	8-1-1 5-1-5 3-2-7 1-7-3	7-1-2 6-1-3 4-1-10 2-4-2	MIO Counter- Cols.13-24 to Buss Cols.1-12

OUT CODES- A RELAYS -continued-

Code	FC	Open	NC	Controls	Code	FC	Open	NC	Controls
86	92	8-1-1 6-1-3	7-1-2 5-1-6 4-1-11 3-2-9 2-4-5 1-7-9	PQ Counter- Cols.1-23 Product-Out	8731 cont.		3-3-1 1-9-3	4-2-1 2-5-2	Typewriter #1- OFF
862	92	8-1-1 6-1-3 2-4-5	7-1-2 5-1-6 4-1-11 3-2-9 1-7-10	Print Counter #1- OUT	8732	92	8-1-1 7-1-2 3-3-1 2-5-2	6-1-4 5-1-7 4-2-1 1-9-4	Typewriter #2- OFF
8621	92	8-1-1 6-1-3 2-4-5 1-7-10	7-1-2 5-1-6 4-1-11 3-2-9	Print Counter #2- OUT	874	92	8-1-1 7-1-2 4-2-1	6-1-4 5-1-7 3-3-2 2-5-3 1-9-5	SIO- OUT #1 (plugged)
863	92	8-1-1 6-1-3 3-2-9	7-1-2 5-1-6 4-1-11 2-4-6 1-7-11	Punch Counter- OUT	8741	92	8-1-1 7-1-2 4-2-1 1-9-5	6-1-4 5-1-7 3-3-2 2-5-3	SIO- OUT #3 (direct)
87	92	8-1-1 7-1-2	6-1-4 5-1-7 4-2-1 3-3-1 2-5-1 1-9-1	Argument Control					
871	92	8-1-1 7-1-2 1-9-1	6-1-4 5-1-7 4-2-1 3-3-1 2-5-1	Typewriter #1- ON					
872	92	8-1-1 7-1-2 2-5-1	6-1-4 5-1-7 4-2-1 3-3-1 1-9-2	Typewriter #2- ON					
8731	92	8-1-1 7-1-2	6-1-4 5-1-7						

IN CODES- B RELAYS

Code	FC	Open	NC	Controls
1	93	1-1-1	8-1-1 7-1-1 6-1-1 5-1-1 4-1-1 3-1-1 2-1-1	Storage Counter #1- IN
2	93	2-1-1	8-1-1 7-1-1 6-1-1 5-1-1 4-1-1 3-1-1 1-1-2	Storage Counter #2- IN
21	93	2-1-1 1-1-2	8-1-1 7-1-1 6-1-1 5-1-1 4-1-1 3-1-1	Storage Counter #3- IN
3	93	3-1-1	8-1-1 7-1-1 6-1-1 5-1-1 4-1-1 2-1-2 1-1-3	Storage Counter #4- IN
31	93	3-1-1 1-1-3	8-1-1 7-1-1 6-1-1 5-1-1 4-1-1 2-1-2	Storage Counter #5- IN
32	93	3-1-1 2-1-2	8-1-1 7-1-1 6-1-1 5-1-1 4-1-1 1-1-4	Storage Counter #6- IN
321	93	3-1-1	8-1-1	
321 cont.		2-1-2 1-1-4	7-1-1 6-1-1 5-1-1 4-1-1	Storage Counter #7- IN
4	93	4-1-1	8-1-1 7-1-1 6-1-1 5-1-1 3-1-2 2-1-3 1-1-5	Storage Counter #8- IN
41	93	4-1-1 1-1-5	8-1-1 7-1-1 6-1-1 5-1-1 3-1-2 2-1-3	Storage Counter #9- IN
42	93	4-1-1 2-1-3	8-1-1 7-1-1 6-1-1 5-1-1 3-1-2 1-1-6	Storage Counter #10- IN
421	93	4-1-1 2-1-3 1-1-6	8-1-1 7-1-1 6-1-1 5-1-1 3-1-2	Storage Counter #11- IN
43	93	4-1-1 3-1-2	8-1-1 7-1-1 6-1-1 5-1-1 2-1-4 1-1-7	Storage Counter #12- IN
431	93	4-1-1 3-1-2 1-1-7	8-1-1 7-1-1 6-1-1 5-1-1 2-1-4	Storage Counter #13- IN

IN CODES- B RELAYS -continued-

Code	FC	Open	NC	Controls
432	93	4-1-1 3-1-2 2-1-4	8-1-1 7-1-1 6-1-1 5-1-1 1-1-8	Storage Counter #14- IN
4321	93	4-1-1 3-1-2 2-1-4 1-1-8	8-1-1 7-1-1 6-1-1 5-1-1	Storage Counter #15- IN
5	93	5-1-1	8-1-1 7-1-1 6-1-1 4-1-2 3-1-3 2-1-5 1-1-9	Storage Counter #16- IN
51	93	5-1-1 1-1-9	8-1-1 7-1-1 6-1-1 4-1-2 3-1-3 2-1-5	Storage Counter #17- IN
52	93	5-1-1 2-1-5	8-1-1 7-1-1 6-1-1 4-1-2 3-1-3 1-1-10	Storage Counter #18- IN
521	93	5-1-1 2-1-5 1-1-10	8-1-1 7-1-1 6-1-1 4-1-2 3-1-3	Storage Counter #19- IN
53	93	5-1-1 3-1-3	8-1-1 7-1-1 6-1-1 4-1-2 2-1-6 1-1-11	Storage Counter #20- IN

Code	FC	Open	NC	Controls
531	93	5-1-1 3-1-3 1-1-11	8-1-1 7-1-1 6-1-1 4-1-2 2-1-6	Storage Counter #21- IN
532	93	5-1-1 3-1-3 2-1-6	8-1-1 7-1-1 6-1-1 4-1-2 1-1-12	Storage Counter #22- IN
5321	93	5-1-1 3-1-3 2-1-6 1-1-12	8-1-1 7-1-1 6-1-1 4-1-2	Storage Counter #23- In
54	93	5-1-1 4-1-2	8-1-1 7-1-1 6-1-1 3-1-4 2-1-7 1-2-1	Storage Counter #24- In
541	93	5-1-1 4-1-2 1-2-1	8-1-1 7-1-1 6-1-1 3-1-4 2-1-7	Storage Counter #25- IN
542	93	5-1-1 4-1-2 2-1-7	8-1-1 7-1-1 6-1-1 3-1-4 1-2-2	Storage Counter #26- IN
5421	93	5-1-1 4-1-2 2-1-7 1-2-2	8-1-1 7-1-1 6-1-1 3-1-4	Storage Counter #27- IN
543	93	5-1-1 4-1-2 3-1-4	8-1-1 7-1-1 6-1-1 2-1-8 1-2-3	Storage Counter #28- IN

IN CODES- B RELAYS -continued-

Code	FC	Open	NC	Controls
5431	93	5-1-1 4-1-2 3-1-4 1-2-3	8-1-1 7-1-1 6-1-1 2-1-8	Storage Counter #29- IN
5432	93	5-1-1 4-1-2 3-1-4 2-1-8	8-1-1 7-1-1 6-1-1 1-2-4	Storage Counter #30- IN
54321	93	5-1-1 4-1-2 3-1-4 2-1-8 1-2-4	8-1-1 7-1-1 6-1-1	Storage Counter #31- IN
6	93	6-1-1	8-1-1 7-1-1 5-1-2 4-1-3 3-1-5 2-1-9 1-2-5	Storage Counter #32- IN
61	93	6-1-1 1-2-5	8-1-1 7-1-1 5-1-2 4-1-3 3-1-5 2-1-9	Storage Counter #33- IN
62	93	6-1-1 2-1-9	8-1-1 7-1-1 5-1-2 4-1-3 3-1-5 1-2-6	Storage Counter #34- IN
621	93	6-1-1 2-1-9 1-2-6	8-1-1 7-1-1 5-1-2 4-1-3 3-1-5	Storage Counter #35- IN
63	93	6-1-1 3-1-5	8-1-1 7-1-1	

Code	FC	Open	NC	Controls
63 cont.			5-1-2 4-1-3 2-1-10 1-2-7	Storage Counter #36- IN
631	93	6-1-1 3-1-5 1-2-7	8-1-1 7-1-1 5-1-2 4-1-3 2-1-10	Storage Counter #37- IN
632	93	6-1-1 3-1-5 2-1-10	8-1-1 7-1-1 5-1-2 4-1-3 1-2-8	Storage Counter #38- IN
6321	93	6-1-1 3-1-5 2-1-10 1-2-8	8-1-1 7-1-1 5-1-2 4-1-3	Storage Counter #39- IN
64	93	6-1-1 4-1-3	8-1-1 7-1-1 5-1-2 3-1-6 2-1-11 1-2-9	Storage Counter #40- IN
641	93	6-1-1 4-1-3 1-2-9	8-1-1 7-1-1 5-1-2 3-1-6 2-1-11	Storage Counter #41- IN
642	93	6-1-1 4-1-3 2-1-11	8-1-1 7-1-1 5-1-2 3-1-6 1-2-10	Storage Counter #42- IN
6421	93	6-1-1 4-1-3 2-1-11 1-2-10	8-1-1 7-1-1 5-1-2 3-1-6	Storage Counter #43- IN

<u>IN CODES</u>- <u>B RELAYS</u> -continued-

Code	FC	Open	NC	Controls	Code	FC	Open	NC	Controls
643	93	6-1-1 4-1-3 3-1-6	8-1-1 7-1-1 5-1-2 2-1-12 1-2-11	Storage Counter #44- IN	653	93	6-1-1 5-1-2 3-1-7	8-1-1 7-1-1 4-1-4 2-2-2 1-3-3	Storage Counter #52- IN
6431	93	6-1-1 4-1-3 3-1-6 1-2-11	8-1-1 7-1-1 5-1-2 2-1-12	Storage Counter #45- IN	6531	93	6-1-1 5-1-2 3-1-7 1-3-3	8-1-1 7-1-1 4-1-4 2-2-2	Storage Counter #53- IN
6432	93	6-1-1 4-1-3 3-1-6 2-1-12	8-1-1 7-1-1 5-1-2 1-2-12	Storage Counter #46- IN	6532	93	6-1-1 5-1-2 3-1-7 2-2-2	8-1-1 7-1-1 4-1-4 1-3-4	Storage Counter #54- IN
64321	93	6-1-1 4-1-3 3-1-6 2-1-12 1-2-12	8-1-1 7-1-1 5-1-2	Storage Counter #47- IN	65321	93	6-1-1 5-1-2 3-1-7 2-2-2 1-3-4	8-1-1 7-1-1 4-1-4	Storage Counter #55- IN
65	93	6-1-1 5-1-2	8-1-1 7-1-1 4-1-4 3-1-7 2-2-1 1-3-1	Storage Counter #48- IN	654	93	6-1-1 5-1-2 4-1-4	8-1-1 7-1-1 3-1-8 2-2-3 1-3-5	Storage Counter #56- IN
651	93	6-1-1 5-1-2 1-3-1	8-1-1 7-1-1 4-1-4 3-1-7 2-2-1	Storage Counter #49- IN	6541	93	6-1-1 5-1-2 4-1-4 1-3-5	8-1-1 7-1-1 3-1-8 2-2-3	Storage Counter #57- IN
652	93	6-1-1 5-1-2 2-2-1	8-1-1 7-1-1 4-1-4 3-1-7 1-3-2	Storage Counter #50- IN	6542	93	6-1-1 5-1-2 4-1-4 2-2-3	8-1-1 7-1-1 3-1-8 1-3-6	Storage Counter #58- IN
6521	93	6-1-1 5-1-2 2-2-1 1-3-2	8-1-1 7-1-1 4-1-4 3-1-7	Storage Counter #51- IN	65421	93	6-1-1 5-1-2 4-1-4 2-2-3 1-3-6	8-1-1 7-1-1 3-1-8	Storage Counter #59- IN

IN CODES- B RELAYS -continued-

Code	FC	Open	NC	Controls
6543	93	6-1-1 5-1-2 4-1-4 3-1-8	8-1-1 7-1-1 2-2-4 1-3-7	Storage Counter #60- IN
65431	93	6-1-1 5-1-2 4-1-4 3-1-8 1-3-7	8-1-1 7-1-1 2-2-4	Storage Counter #61- IN
65432	93	6-1-1 5-1-2 4-1-4 3-1-8 2-2-4	8-1-1 7-1-1 1-3-8	Storage Counter #62- IN
654321	93	6-1-1 5-1-2 4-1-4 3-1-8 2-2-4 1-3-8	8-1-1 7-1-1	Storage Counter #63- IN
7	93	7-1-1	8-1-1 6-1-2 5-1-3 4-1-5 3-1-9 2-2-5 1-3-9	Storage Counter #64- IN
71	93	7-1-1 1-3-9	8-1-1 6-1-2 5-1-3 4-1-5 3-1-9 2-2-5	Storage Counter #65- IN
72	93	7-1-1 2-2-5	8-1-1 6-1-2 5-1-3 4-1-5 3-1-9 1-3-10	Storage Counter #66- IN

Code	FC	Open	NC	Controls
721	93	7-1-1 2-2-5 1-3-10	8-1-1 6-1-2 5-1-3 4-1-5 3-1-9	Storage Counter #67- IN
73	93	7-1-1 3-1-9	8-1-1 6-1-2 5-1-3 4-1-5 2-2-6 1-3-11	Storage Counter #68- IN
731	93	7-1-1 3-1-9 1-3-11	8-1-1 6-1-2 5-1-3 4-1-5 2-2-6	Storage Counter #69- IN
732	93	7-1-1 3-1-9 2-2-6	8-1-1 6-1-2 5-1-3 4-1-5 1-3-12	Storage Counter #70- IN
7321	93	7-1-1 3-1-9 2-2-6 1-3-12	8-1-1 6-1-2 5-1-3 4-1-5	Storage Counter #71- IN
74	93	7-1-1 4-1-5	8-1-1 6-1-2 5-1-3 3-1-10 2-2-7 1-4-1	Storage Counter #72- IN
741	93	7-1-1 4-1-5 1-4-1	8-1-1 6-1-2 5-1-3 3-1-10 2-2-7	EIO- IN
7432	93	7-1-1 4-1-5	8-1-1 6-1-2	

IN CODES- B RELAYS -continued-

Code	FC	Open	NC	Controls
7432 cont.		3-1-10 2-2-8	5-1-3 1-4-4	Print Counter #1- IN
74321	93	7-1-1 4-1-5 3-1-10 2-2-8 1-4-4	8-1-1 6-1-2 5-1-3	Print Counter #2- IN
752	93	7-1-1 5-1-3 2-2-9	8-1-1 6-1-2 4-1-6 3-1-11 1-4-6	Typewriter #1- Initiate Printing
7521	93	7-1-1 5-1-3 2-2-9 1-4-6	8-1-1 6-1-2 4-1-6 3-1-11	Typewriter #2- Initiate Printing
753	93	7-1-1 5-1-3 3-1-11	8-1-1 6-1-2 4-1-6 2-2-10 1-4-7	Punch Counter- IN
76	95	7-1-3 6-1-5	8-1-2 5-1-4 4-1-7 3-2-1 2-3-1 1-5-1	Divide
761	95	7-1-3 6-1-5 1-5-1	8-1-2 5-1-4 4-1-7 3-2-1 2-3-1	Multiply
762	95	7-1-3 6-1-5 2-3-1	8-1-2 5-1-4 4-1-7 3-2-1 1-5-2	Logarithm

Code	FC	Open	NC	Controls
7621	95	7-1-3 6-1-5 2-3-1 1-5-2	8-1-2 5-1-4 4-1-7 3-2-1	Exponential
763	95	7-1-3 6-1-5 3-2-1	8-1-2 5-1-4 4-1-7 2-3-2 1-5-3	Interpolate
7631	95	7-1-3 6-1-5 3-2-1 1-5-3	8-1-2 5-1-4 4-1-7 2-3-2	Sine
7654	95	7-1-3 6-1-5 5-1-4 4-1-8	8-1-2 3-2-4 2-3-7 1-6-1	Select Interpolator #1
76541	95	7-1-3 6-1-5 5-1-4 4-1-8 1-6-1	8-1-2 3-2-4 2-3-7	Select Interpolator #2
76542	95	7-1-3 6-1-5 5-1-4 4-1-8 2-3-7	8-1-2 3-2-4 1-6-2	Select Interpolator #3
765421	95	7-1-3 6-1-5 5-1-4 4-1-8 2-3-7 1-6-2	8-1-2 3-2-4	LIO- IN
76543	95	7-1-3 6-1-5 5-1-4 4-1-8 3-2-4	8-1-2 2-3-8 1-6-3	Print Counter #1- Half Pick-up

IN RELAYS- B RELAYS - continued-

Code	FC	Open	NC	Controls	Code	FC	Open	NC	Controls
765431	95	7-1-3 6-1-5 5-1-4 4-1-8 3-2-4 1-6-3	8-1-2 2-3-8	Print Counter #2- Half Pick-up	874	93	8-1-1 7-1-2 4-2-1	6-1-4 5-1-7 3-3-2 2-5-3 1-9-5	SIO- IN #1 (direct)
8321	93	8-1-1 3-2-5 2-3-10 1-6-8	7-1-2 6-1-3 5-1-5 4-1-9	Normalizing Register- IN	8741	93	8-1-1 7-1-2 4-2-1 1-9-5	6-1-4 5-1-7 3-3-2 2-5-3	SIO- IN #2 (plugged)
853	93	8-1-1 5-1-5 3-2-7	7-1-2 6-1-3 4-1-10 2-4-2 1-7-3	MIO Counter- IN Buss Cols.13-24 to MIO Cols.13-24					
8531	93	8-1-1 5-1-5 3-2-7 1-7-3	7-1-2 6-1-3 4-1-10 2-4-2	MIO Counter- IN Buss Cols.1-12 to MIO Cols.13-24					
87	93	8-1-1 7-1-2	6-1-4 5-1-7 4-2-1 3-3-1 2-5-1 1-9-1	Storage Counter #64- Special IN					
871	93	8-1-1 7-1-2 1-9-1	6-1-4 5-1-7 4-2-1 3-3-1 2-5-1	Storage Counter #65- Special IN					
873	93	8-1-1 7-1-2 3-3-1	6-1-4 5-1-7 4-2-1 2-5-2 1-9-3	Storage Counter #68- Special IN					
8731	93	8-1-1 7-1-2 3-3-1 1-9-3	6-1-4 5-1-7 4-2-1 2-5-2	Storage Counter #69- Special IN					

MISCELLANEOUS CODES- C RELAYS

Code	FC	Open	NC	Controls
1	94	1-1-1	6-1-1 5-1-1 4-1-1 3-1-1 2-1-1	Storage Counter- Read-Out Negative Absolute Value
2	94	2-1-1	6-1-1 5-1-1 4-1-1 3-1-1 1-1-2	Storage Counter- Read-Out Positive Absolute Value
21	94	2-1-1 1-1-2	6-1-1 5-1-1 4-1-1 3-1-1	Switch- Invert
3	94	3-1-1	6-1-1 5-1-1 4-1-1 2-1-2 1-1-3	Intermediate Counter- Reset
31	94	3-1-1 1-1-3	6-1-1 5-1-1 4-1-1 2-1-2	EIO- Reset
32	94	3-1-1 2-1-2	6-1-1 5-1-1 4-1-1 1-1-4	Storage Counter and Switch- Invert
321	94	3-1-1 2-1-2 1-1-4	6-1-1 5-1-1 4-1-1	SIO- Reset
432	94	4-1-1 3-1-2 2-1-4	6-1-1 5-1-1 1-1-8	Read-Out Under Control of Counter #70
5	94	5-1-1	6-1-1 4-1-2 3-1-3 2-1-5 1-1-9	Initiate Punching

Code	FC	Open	NC	Controls
51	94	5-1-1 1-1-9	6-1-1 4-1-2 3-1-3 2-1-5	Initiate and Complete Punching
53	94	5-1-1 3-1-3	6-1-1 4-1-2 2-1-6 1-1-11	Interpolator #1- Step Ahead
531	94	5-1-1 3-1-3 1-1-11	6-1-1 4-1-2 2-1-6	Interpolator #2- Step Ahead
532	94	5-1-1 3-1-3 2-1-6	6-1-1 4-1-2 1-1-12	Interpolator #3- Step Ahead
54	94	5-1-1 4-1-2	6-1-1 3-1-4 2-1-7 1-2-1	Interpolator #1- Step Back
541	94	5-1-1 4-1-2 1-2-1	6-1-1 3-1-4 2-1-7	Interpolator #2- Step Back
542	94	5-1-1 4-1-2 2-1-7	6-1-1 3-1-4 1-2-2	Interpolator #3- Step Back
6	96	6-1-2	5-1-2 4-1-3 3-1-5 2-1-9 1-2-5	Print and Complete Printing
61	96	6-1-2 1-2-5	5-1-2 4-1-3 3-1-5 2-1-9	Interpolation- Drop out Tape Selection Relays
62	96	6-1-2 2-1-9	5-1-2 4-1-3 3-1-5 1-2-6	Pick up Interpolation- Sequence Control Relay

MISCELLANEOUS CODES- C RELAYS -continued-

Code	FC	Open	NC	Controls	Code	FC	Open	NC	Controls
63	96	6-1-2 3-1-5	5-1-2 4-1-3 2-1-10 1-2-7	LIO- Reset	87	106	8-1-1 7-1-2		Stop- with Stop Key
632	96	6-1-2 3-1-5 2-1-10	5-1-2 4-1-3 1-2-8	Card Feed #1- OUT					
6321	96	6-1-2 3-1-5 2-1-10 1-2-8	5-1-2 4-1-3	Card Feed #2- OUT					
64	96	6-1-2 4-1-3	5-1-2 3-1-6 2-1-11 1-2-9	Automatic Check					
641	96	6-1-2 4-1-3 1-2-9	5-1-2 3-1-6 2-1-11	Interpolator- Position					
643	96	6-1-2 4-1-3 3-1-6	5-1-2 2-1-12 1-2-11	Division- Place Limitation					
6431	96	6-1-2 4-1-3 3-1-6 1-2-11	5-1-2 2-1-12	Division- Place Limitation					
6432	96	6-1-2 4-1-3 3-1-6 2-1-12	5-1-2 1-2-12	Division- Place Limitation					
64321	96	6-1-2 4-1-3 3-1-6 2-1-12 1-2-12	5-1-2	Division- Place Limitation					
7	107 106	7-1-1 7-1-3		Repeat Stop- with Emergency Switch and Stop Key					

SEQUENCING - START, STOP, REPEAT

The start key is depressed and the start relay energized. Through the start relay, the read control relay, the start interlock relay and the clutch magnet are energized. The sequence mechanism reads the line of coding (A, B, 7). The corresponding sequence relays including C-7 and thus the repeat relay are picked up. The pick up of the start interlock relay will open the circuit through the start key to the start relay, preventing the flow of current to the start relay in the event that the start key is held down. If the repeat relay is energized, the start relay will pick up. If the emergency switch is on and the stop key depressed, the energized sequence relay C-7 will permit the stop control relay to pick up. The pick up of stop control opens the circuit to the read control relay and the clutch magnet. The stop control relay may also be picked up through the stop key and points of sequence relays C-8 and C-7.

Magnet	9 Cycle 0 9 Cycle 1 9
Seq-33-1 Start Seq-31-1 Read Control Clutch Magnet Seq-28-1 Start Interlock Seq-C-7-1 Seq-27-1 Repeat Seq-32-1 Stop Control	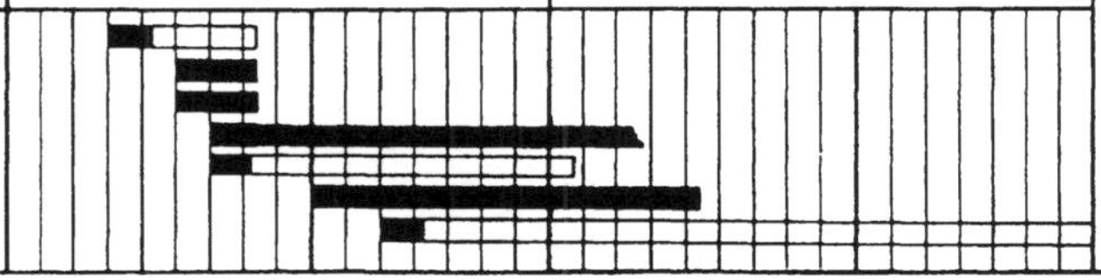

Pick Up Circuit	Magnet	Hold Circuit
Start Key or Seq-27-1-1 VBP-276 FC-103 (6-5 1/3) VBP-277 Seq-27-1-2 Seq-28-1-1 NC	Seq-33-1-(4) Start	FC-108 (6-2 1/2) VBP-278 Seq-33-1-4
FC-105 (4-2 1/2) Sequence Cut-off Switch Card Feed #1 Sw. Card Feed #2 Sw. BBP-64 Seq-33-1-1 Seq-32-1-1,2 NC	Seq-31-1-(4) Read Control and Clutch Magnet	
Seq-27-1-1 or Start Key VBP-276 FC-104 (3-2 1/2) VBP-279 Seq-33-1-3	Seq-28-1-(4) Start Interlock	Seq-27-1-1 or Start Key VBP-276 Seq-28-1-4

Circuit Diagram

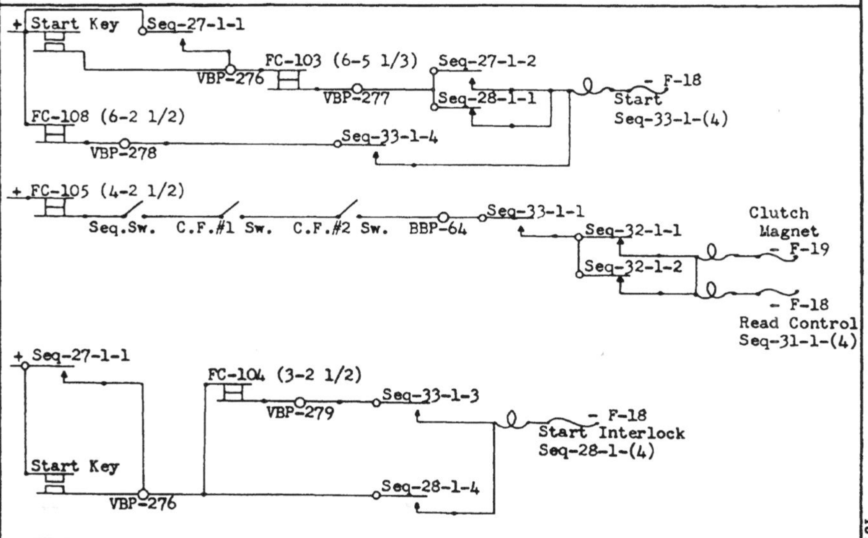

SEQUENCING - START, STOP, REPEAT -continued-

Pick Up Circuit	Magnet	Hold Circuit	Circuit Diagram
FC-101 (3-2 1/3) VBP-100 Seq-31-1,2,3,4 Reading Pins	C-7-1-(4)	FC-102 (4-9 3/4) VBP-225 C-7-1-4	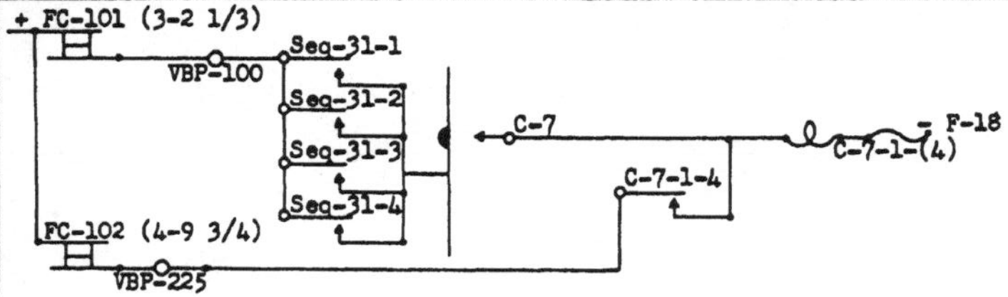
FC-107 (0-5 1/4) VBP-280 C-7-1-1	Seq-27-1-(4) Repeat	FC-107 (0-5 1/4) VBP-280 Seq-27-1-4	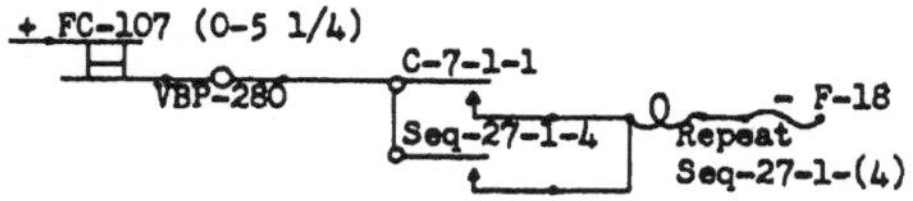
Stop Key VBP-281 FC-106 (12-13 1/3) VBP-282 C-7-1-3 Emergency Sw.	Seq-32-1-(4) Stop Control	Stop Key VBP-281 Seq-32-1-4	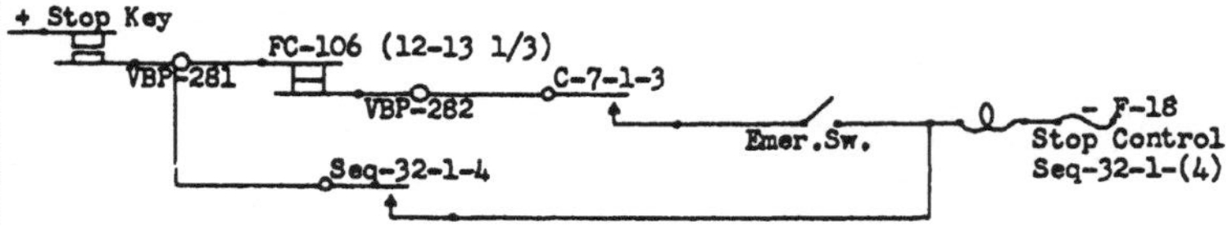
FC-101 (3-2 1/3) VBP-100 Seq-31-1,2,3,4 Reading Pins	C-8-1-(4) C-7-1-(4)	FC-102 (4-9 3/4) VBP-225 C-8-1-4 C-7-1-4	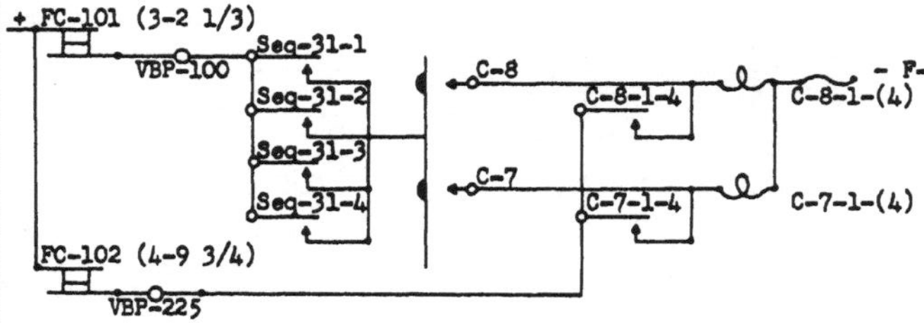
Stop Key VBP-281 FC-106 (12-13 1/3) VBP-282 C-7-1-2 C-8-1-1	Seq-32-1-(4) Stop Control	Stop Key VBP-281 Seq-32-1-4	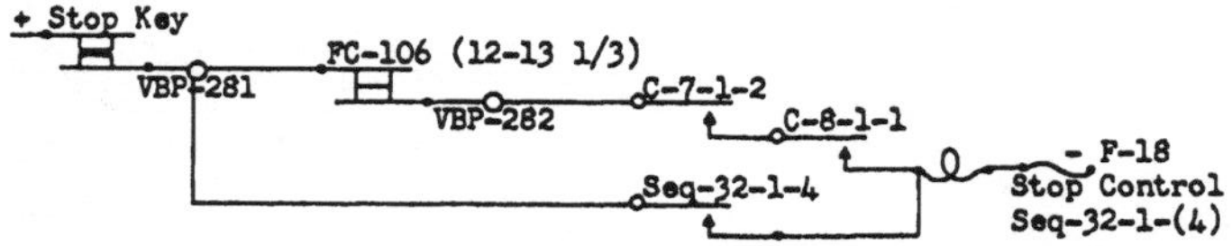

SEQUENCING - AUTOMATICS

As mentioned on page 15, the code Miscellaneous 7 which controls the repeat relay may be replaced by certain automatic continue operation codes. The circuits controlled by these automatic codes are presented in the following table, except for the circuit operated by the check code, Miscellaneous 64, which is included in the automatic check counter circuits. Each of these circuits may replace the circuit through the start relay to pick up the read control relay and the clutch magnet. For all automatic codes, the cam contact FC-105 provides the impulse which travels through the card feed control circuits, as shown in the card feed circuit, to BBP-64. The alternate circuits employed by the automatic codes of the different components of the machine are shown between BBP-64 and FBP-98. All of the circuits are completed from FBP-98 to the read control relay and the clutch magnet as shown in the last diagram of this group.

Pick Up Circuit	Magnet	Hold Circuit	Circuit Diagram
BBP-64 12-1,2-3 or BBP-110 44-5-1 BBP-111 FBP-133 216-1-2 NC and 55-3-2 NC 78-2-8 NC 81-2-9 NC BBP-52 FBP-99 201-1-2 NC FBP-98			MULTIPLY-DIVIDE UNIT 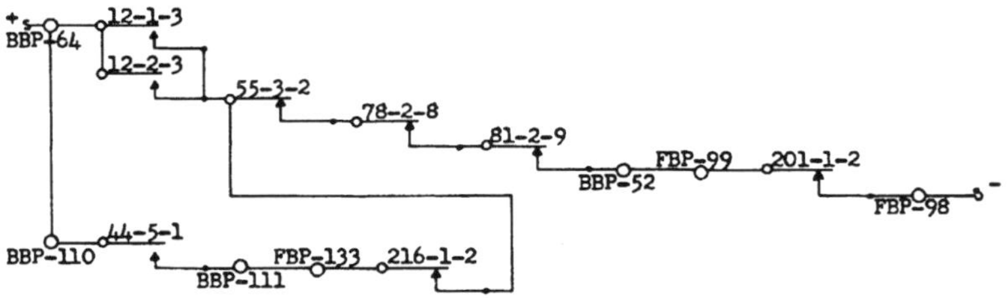
BBP-64 79-1-7 48-1-7 BBP-54 or BBP-110 and 165-1-8 290-1-2 NC or 162-1-7 130-1-2 NC 176-1-2 NC or 254-3-1 255-3-1 256-1-2 257-1-2 and FBP-98			INTERPOLATION UNIT 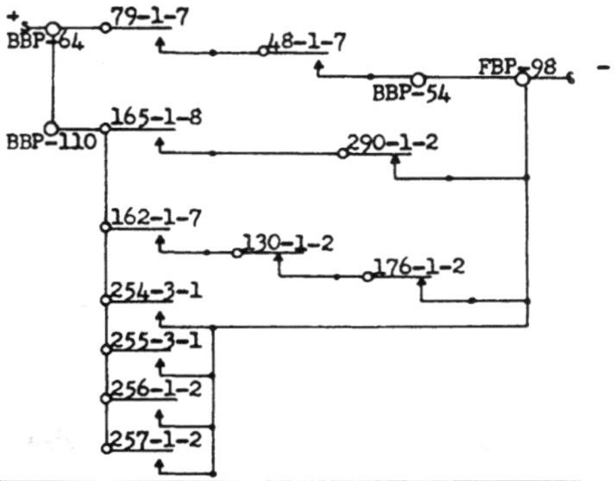

SEQUENCE - AUTOMATIC -continued-

<table>
<tr><th>Pick Up Circuit</th><th>Magnet</th><th>Hold Circuit</th><th>Circuit Diagram</th></tr>
<tr><td>BBP-64
11-1-5
34-3-8(not used)
BBP-54
or
BBP-110
FBP-135
207-1-1
and
FBP-98</td><td></td><td></td><td>LOG UNIT
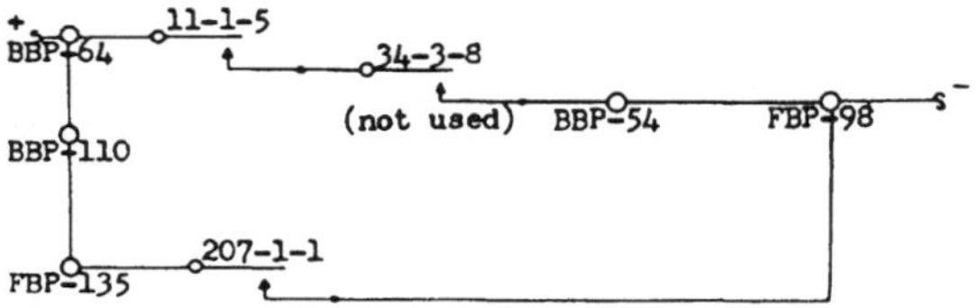
</td></tr>
<tr><td>BBP-64
12-1,2-3
or
BBP-110
44-5-1
BBP-111
FBP-133
216-1-2 NC
or
FBP-135
266-3-1
217-3-1
216-1-3
and
55-3-2 NC
78-2-8 NC
81-2-9 NC
BBP-52
FBP-99
201-1-2 NC
or ....
216-1-2
225-1-3 NC
FBP-181
BBP-53 ....
or
224-3-1
and
FBP-98</td><td></td><td></td><td>EXPONENTIAL UNIT
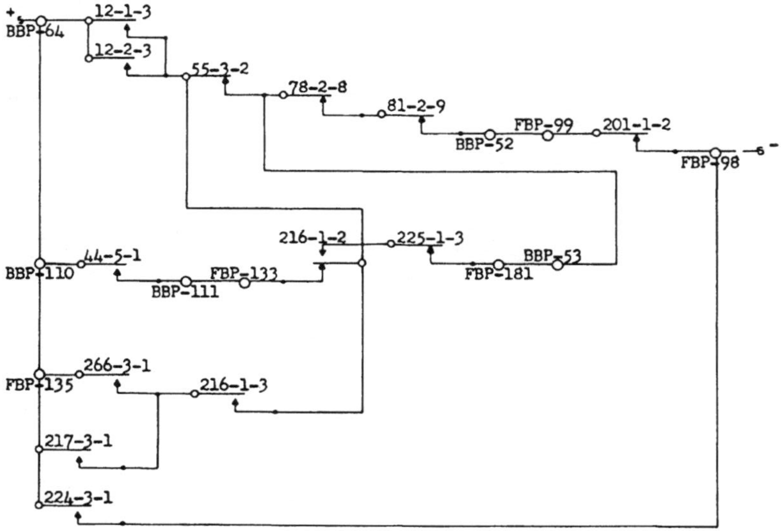
</td></tr>
</table>

SEQUENCING - AUTOMATICS -continued-

Pick Up Circuit	Magnet	Hold Circuit	Circuit Diagram
BBP-64 81-3-1 NC 230-3-3 FBP-98			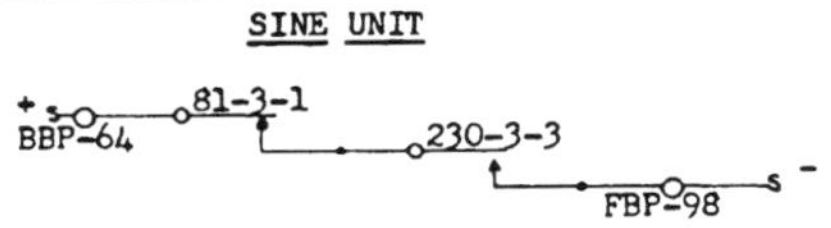
BBP-64 BBP-110 FBP-135 113-3-2 112-1-3 103-3-1 102-3-12 143-3-2 142-1-3 133-3-1 132-3-12 100-1-2 FBP-98			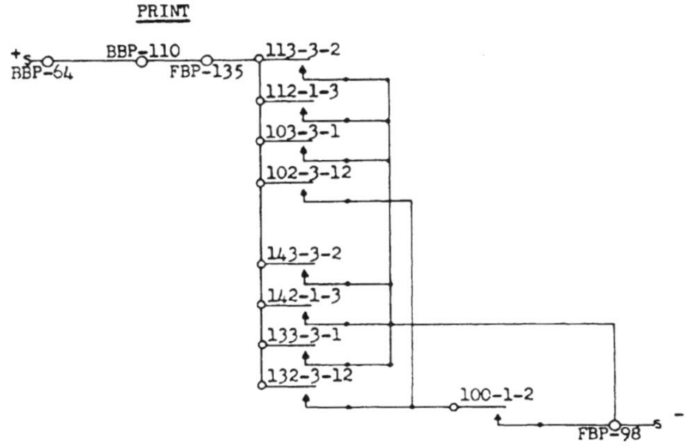
BBP-64 BBP-110 FBP-135 246-3-2 248-1-11 or Card Indicator- 1,2 NC 245-3-2 and FBP-98			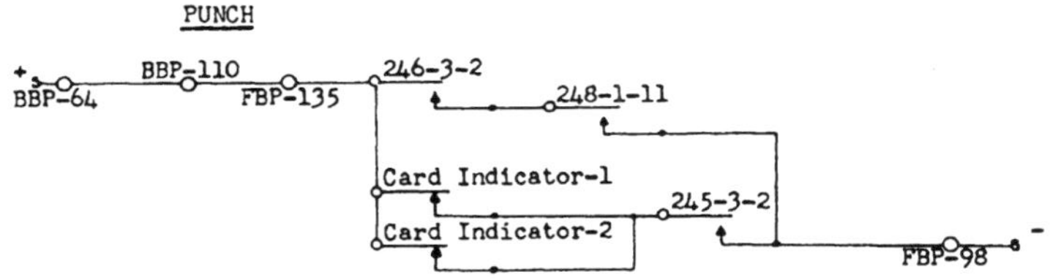

SEQUENCING - AUTOMATICS -continued-

Pick Up Circuit	Magnet	Hold Circuit	Circuit Diagram
FC-105 (4-2 1/2) Sequence Cut-off Switch Seq-25-1-1,2 Seq-26-1-1,2 Card Feed #1 Sw. Card Feed #2 Sw. BBP-64			CARD FEED 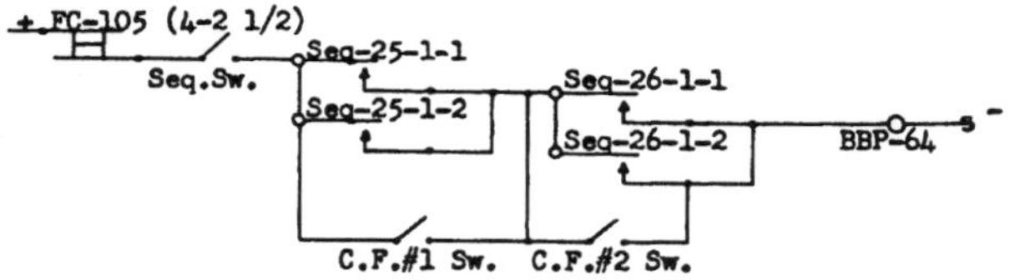
FBP-98 Seq-32-1-1 NC Seq-32-1-2 NC	Seq-31-1-(4) Read Control and Clutch Magnet		(Completion of Preceding Circuits) 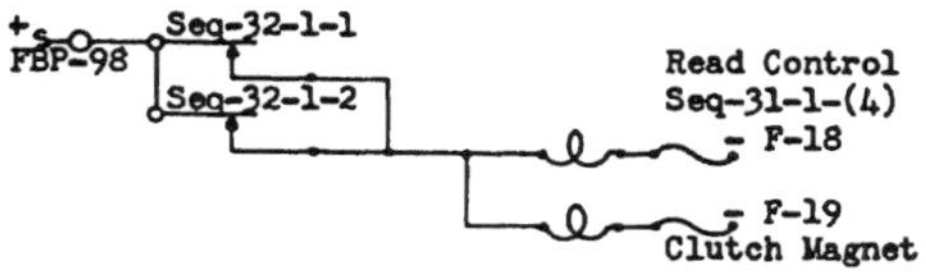

SWITCHES

CYCLE 0. Assuming it is desired to read out of switch 8, code 75, into storage counter 5, code 31, the sequence mechanism reads the line of coding (75, 31, blank). The sequence relays are picked up. The switch 8 out and storage counter 5 in relays are energized. If the code 32 is used in the Miscellaneous column, the storage counter invert relay is picked up. If the code 21 is used in the Miscellaneous column, the switch invert relay and the IVS invert relay are picked up. If the code 8431 in the Out column is read, the independent variable switch (IVS) out relays are energized.
CYCLE 1. The storage counter magnets are energized. The carry circuits, which are presented under storage counters, are closed and the carry impulse completes the entry.

Magnet
Seq-A-7-1
Seq-A-5-1
Seq-B-3-1,2,3
Seq-B-1-1,..,11
SC5-4,5,6 Str Ctr In
Sw8-1,2,3 Switch Out
Str Ctr Magnets
Seq-C-2-1,..,6
Seq-C-1-1,..,11
Switch Invert
Seq-A-8-1
Seq-A-4-1,2
Seq-A-3-1,2,3
Seq-A-1-1,..,11
Seq-30-1,2,3 IVS Out
Seq-29-1 IVS Invert

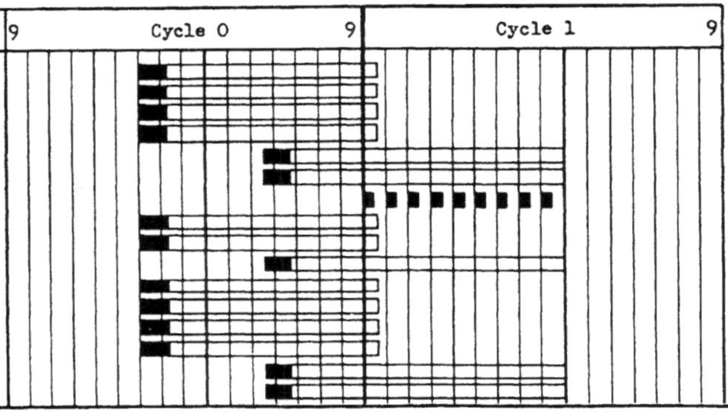

Pick Up Circuit	Magnet	Hold Circuit	Circuit Diagram
FC-101 (3-2 1/3) VBP-100 Seq-31-1,2,3,4 Reading Pins	A-7-1-(4) A-5-1-(12) B-3-1,2,3-(12) B-1-1,..,11-(12)	FC-102 (4-9 3/4) VBP-225 A-7-1-4 A-5-1-11 B-3-3-11 B-1-11-11	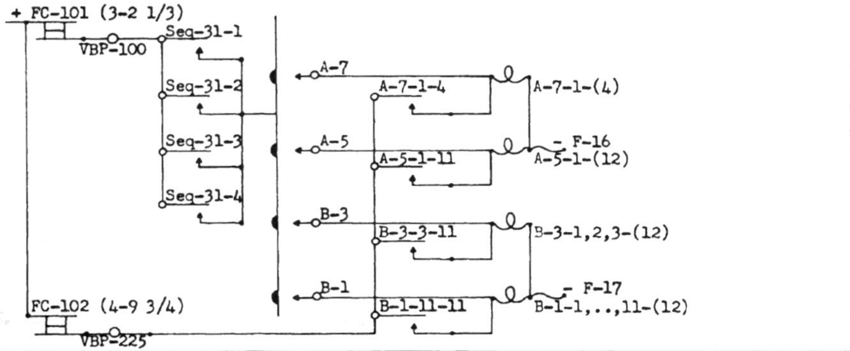

SWITCHES -continued-

Pick Up Circuit	Magnet	Hold Circuit
FC-92 (12 1/2-13 2/3) VBP-150 A-8-1-1 NC A-7-1-1 A-6-1-2 NC A-5-1-3 A-4-1-6 NC A-3-1-11 NC A-2-2-9 NC A-1-4-5 NC SwBP-2-8	Sw8-1,2-(12) Sw8-3-(4)	SC-11 (12-0) SBP-1-2 SwBP-3-28 Sw8-3-4
SC-1,..,9 Str Ctr Reset NC Str Counter Invert NC SBP-3-1,..,9 SwBP-1-1,..,9 Switch Invert NC SwBP-1-11,..,20 Switch RO Sw8-1,2 Sw Out Buss SC5-4,5 Str Ctr In	Str Counter Magnets	
FC-101 (3-2 1/3) VBP-100 Seq-31-1,2,3,4 Reading Pins	C-2-1,..,5-(12) C-2-6-(6) C-1-1,..,11-(12)	FC-102 (4-9 3/4) VBP-225 C-2-6-6 C-1-11-11

Circuit Diagram

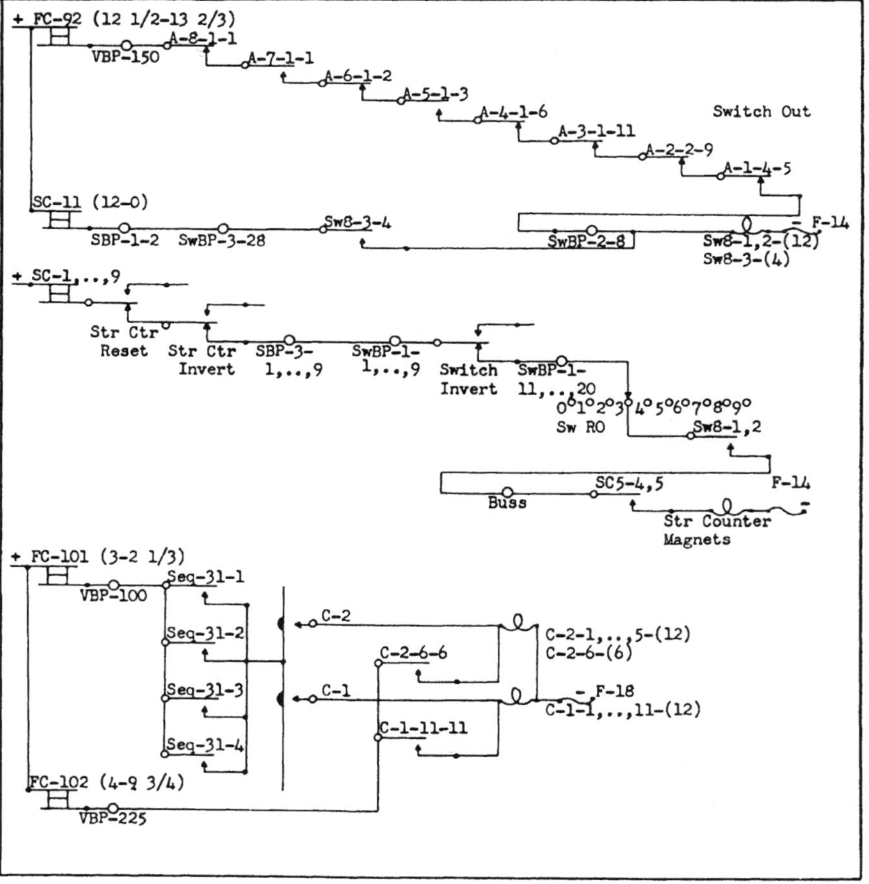

SWITCHES -continued-

Pick Up Circuit	Magnet	Hold Circuit	Circuit Diagram
SC-1,..,9 Str Ctr Reset NC Str Counter Invert NC SBP-3-1,..,9 and SBP-6-10 SwBP-1-1,..,9 Switch Invert NC SwBP-1-11,..,20	Switch Common and RO		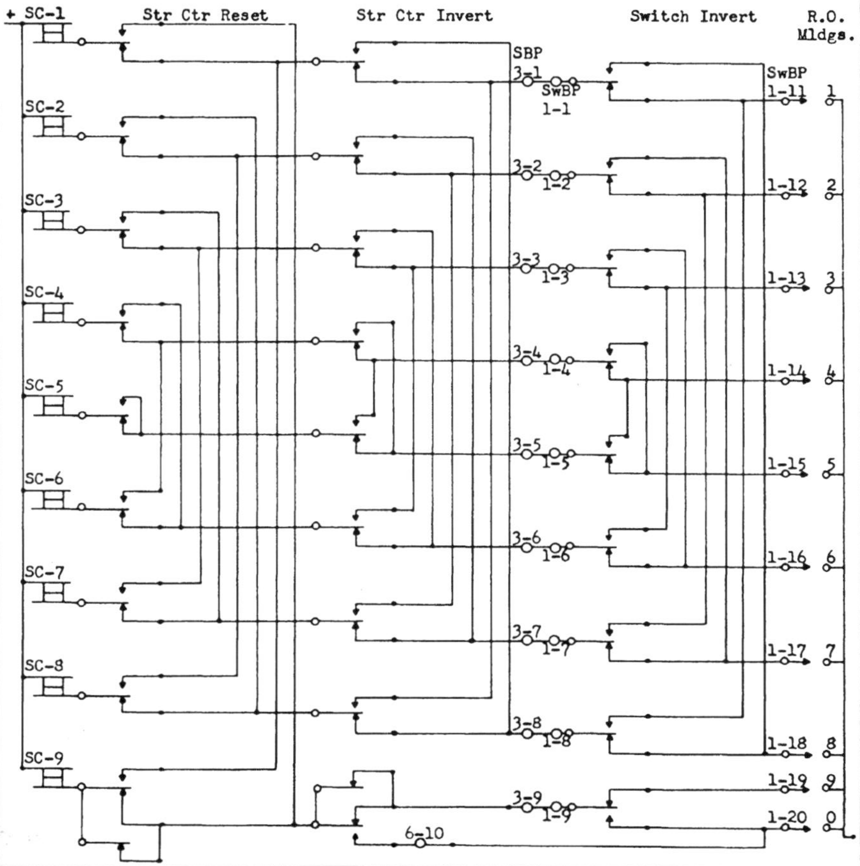

SWITCHES -continued-

Pick Up Circuit	Magnet	Hold Circuit	Circuit Diagram
FC-94 (12 1/2-13 2/3) VBP-148 C-6-1-1 NC C-5-1-1 NC C-4-1-1 NC C-3-1-1 NC C-2-1-1 C-1-1-2 SBP-1-9 SwBP-3-26	Switch Invert	SC-11 (12-0) SBP-1-2 SwBP-3-28 Sw Invert-11	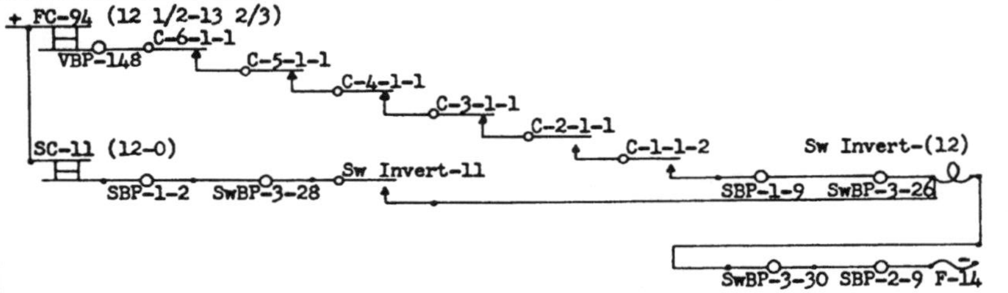
FC-92 (12 1/2-13 2/3) VBP-150 A-8-1-1 A-7-1-2 NC A-6-1-3 NC A-5-1-5 NC A-4-1-9 A-3-2-6 A-2-3-12 NC A-1-6-11	Seq-30-1,2-(12) Seq-30-3-(4) IVS-OUT	FC-97 (12-0) VBP-173 Seq-30-3-4	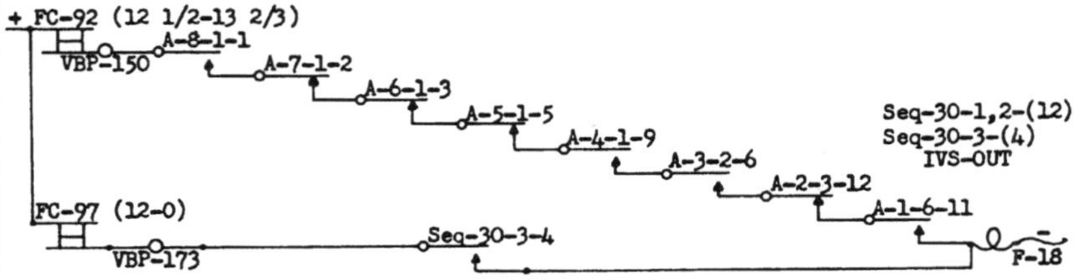
FC-1,..,9 FBP-33,..,49 VBP-267,..,275 Seq-29-1 NC IVS RO Seq-30-1,2 Buss SC5-4,5	Str Counter Magnets		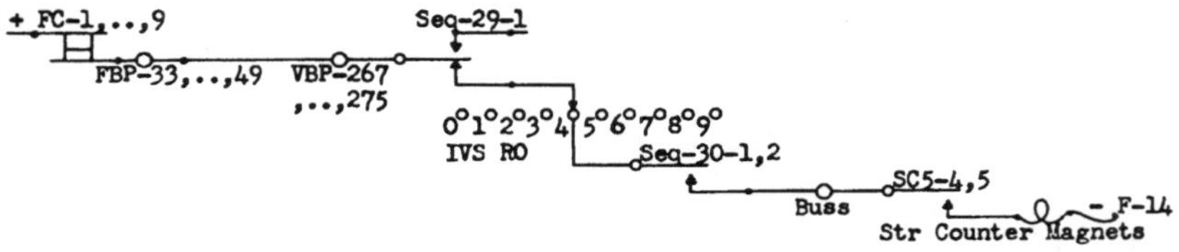
FC-94 (12 1/2-13 2/3) VBP-148 C-6-1-1 NC C-5-1-1 NC C-4-1-1 NC C-3-1-1 NC C-2-1-1 C-1-1-2	Seq-29-1-(12) IVS Invert	FC-97 (12-0) VBP-173 Seq-29-1-12	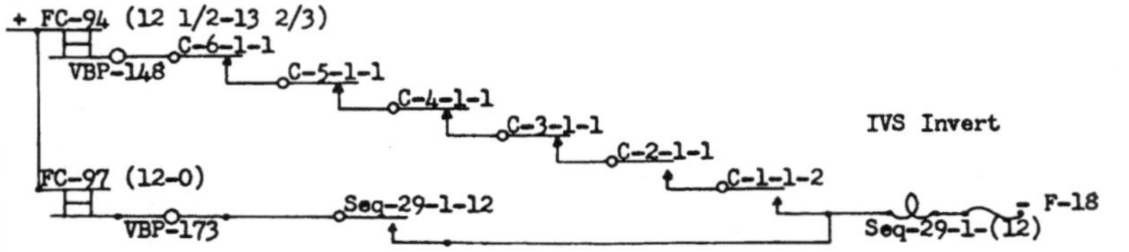

STORAGE COUNTERS

CYCLE 0. Assuming that is is desired to read out of storage counter 3, code 21, into storage counter 1, code 1, the sequence mechanism reads the line of coding (21, 1, blank). The sequence relays are picked up. The storage counter 3 out and storage counter 1 in relays are energized. If the code 1 in the Miscellaneous column is read, an additional circuit is closed, if a 0 stands in the 24th column of counter 3, picking up the storage counter invert relay and thus causing the negative absolute value to be read out. If the code 2 in the Miscellaneous column is read, an additional circuit is closed, if a 9 stands in the 24th column of counter 3, picking up the storage counter invert relay and thus causing the positive absolute value to be read out. Assuming that it is desired to reset counter 1, the sequence mechanism reads the line of coding (1, 1, blank). The storage counter 1 out and in relays and the storage counter reset relays are picked up. The energizing of the storage counter reset relay opens the circuit to the carry control relay.
CYCLE 1. The storage counter magnets are energized. The storage counter carry control, carry and 24th column carry relays are picked up. The carry impulse completes the storage counter entry.

Magnet

Seq-A-2-1,..,6
Seq-A-1-1,..,11
Seq-B-1-1,..,11
SC3-1,2,3 Storage Counter Out
SC1-4,5,6 Storage Counter In
Storage Counter Magnets
SC1-9 Storage Counter Carry Control
SC1-7,8 Storage Counter Carry
SC1-10,11 24th Column Carry
SC3-10,11 24th Column Carry
Storage Counter Invert
Str Ctr Invert (- Absolute Value)
Str Ctr Invert (+ Absolute Value)
Storage Counter Reset

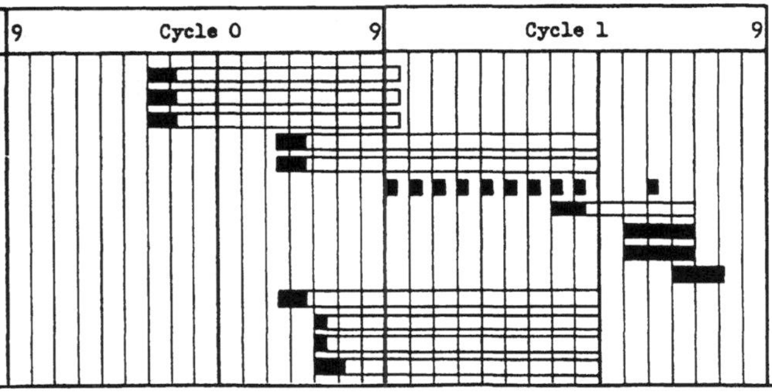

Pick Up Circuit	Magnet	Hold Circuit
FC-101 (3-2 1/3) VBP-100 Seq-31-1,2,3,4 Reading Pins	A-2-1,..,5-(12) A-2-6-(6) A-1-1,..,11-(12) B-1-1,..,11-(12)	FC-102 (4-9 3/4) VBP-225 A-2-6-6 A-1-11-11 B-1-11-11

Circuit Diagram

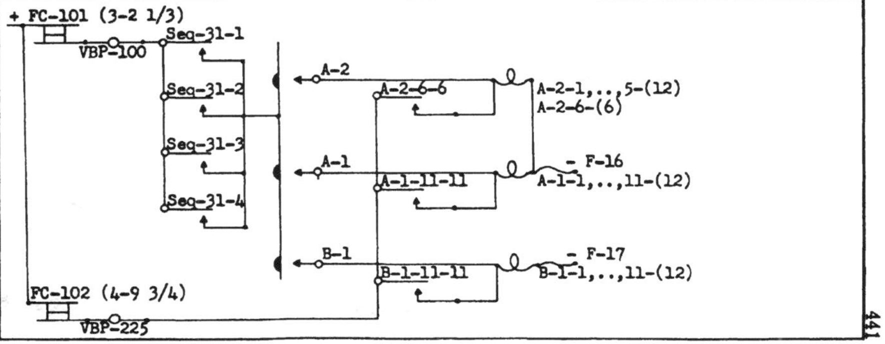

STORAGE COUNTERS -continued-

Pick Up Circuit	Magnet	Hold Circuit	Circuit Diagram
FC-92 (12 1/2-13 2/3) VBP-150 A-8-1-1 NC A-7-1-1 NC A-6-1-1 NC A-5-1-1 NC A-4-1-1 NC A-3-1-1 NC A-2-1-1 A-1-1-2 SBP-10-3	Storage Ctr Out SC3-1,2-(12) SC3-3-(4)	SC-11 (12-0) SBP-1-2 SC3-3-4	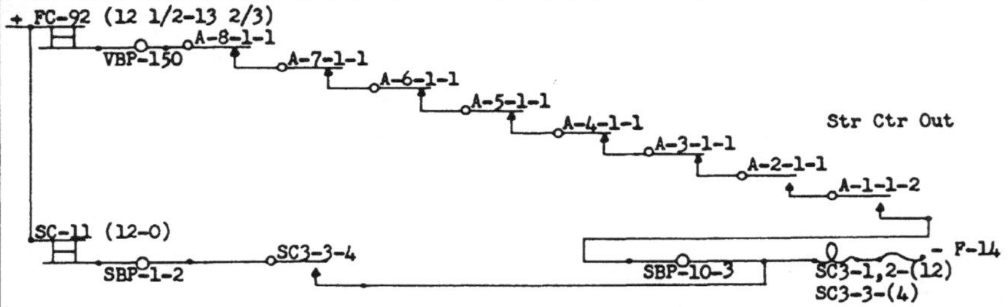
FC-93 (12 1/2-13 2/3) VBP-149 B-8-1-1 NC B-7-1-1 NC B-6-1-1 NC B-5-1-1 NC B-4-1-1 NC B-3-1-1 NC B-2-1-1 NC B-1-1-1 SBP-8-1	Storage Ctr In SC1-4,5-(12) SC1-6-(4)	SC-11 (12-0) SBP-1-2 SC1-6-4	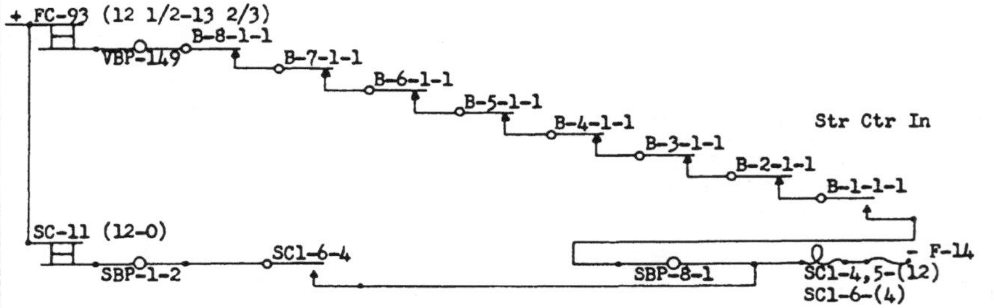
SC-1,..,9 Str Ctr Reset NC Str Counter Invert NC SBP Rows 3,..,7 Str Ctr RO SC3-1,2 Str Ctr Out Buss SC1-4,5 Str Ctr In	Storage Ctr Magnets		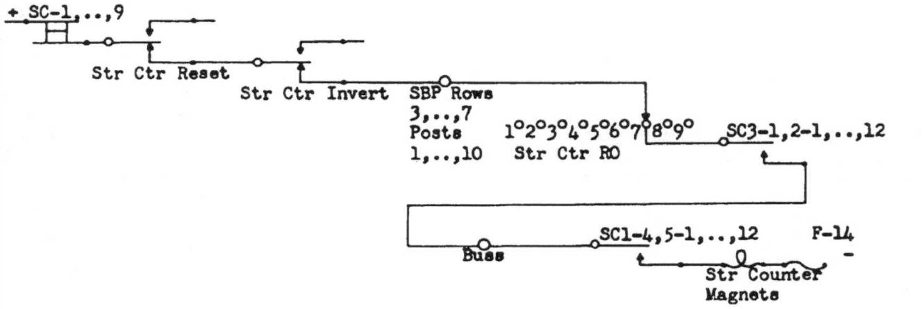

STORAGE COUNTERS -continued-

Pick Up Circuit	Magnet	Hold Circuit	Circuit Diagram
SC-1,..,9 Str Ctr Reset NC Str Counter Invert NC SBP Rows 3,..,7	Str Counter RO Moldings		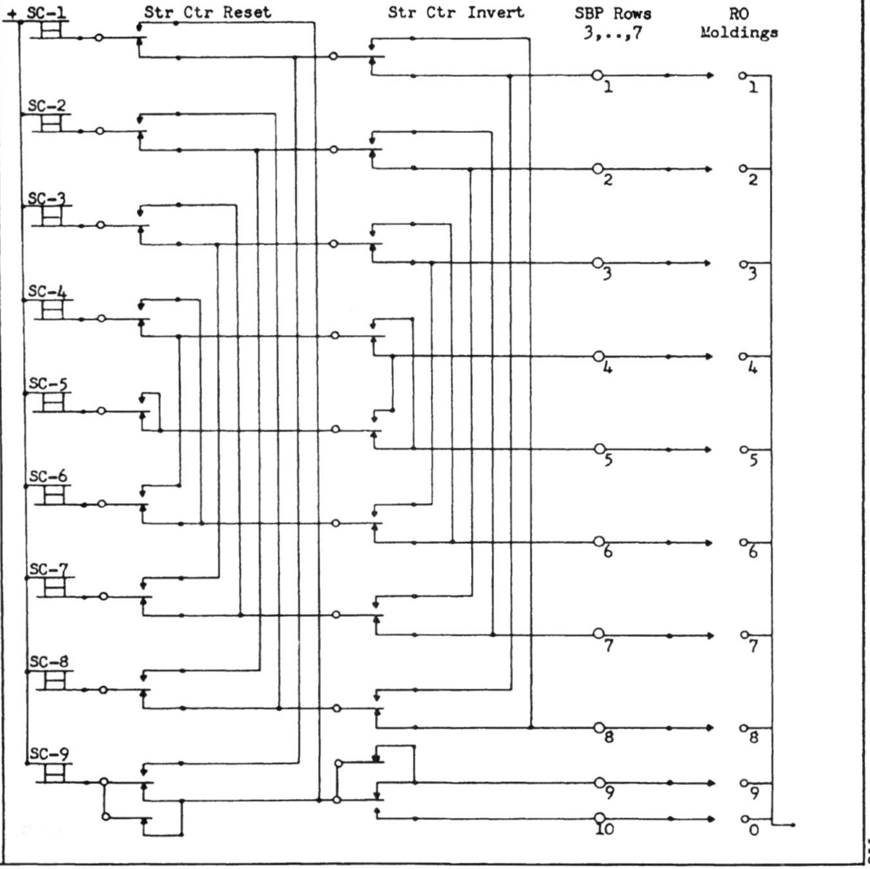

STORAGE COUNTERS -continued-

Pick Up Circuit	Magnet	Hold Circuit	Circuit Diagram
SC-13 (2-1 1/2) Reset-10 NC SBP-1-4 SC1-6-1	Str Ctr Carry Control SC1-9-(4)	SC-14 (2-14 1/16) SBP-1-5 SC1-9-4	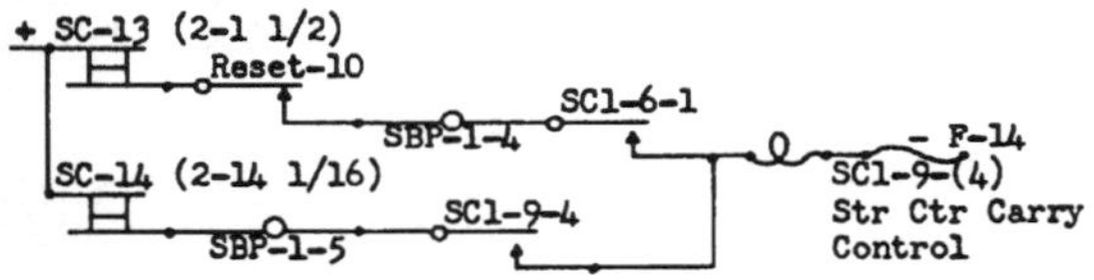
SC-12 (11-14) SBP-1-3 SC1-9-1	Str Ctr Carry SC1-7,8-(12)		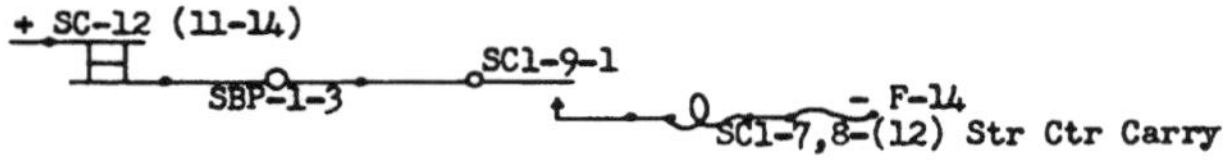
SC-12 (11-14) SBP-1-3 SC1-9-2 9 or 10 Contact	24th Col Carry SC1-11-(4) or SC1-10-(4)		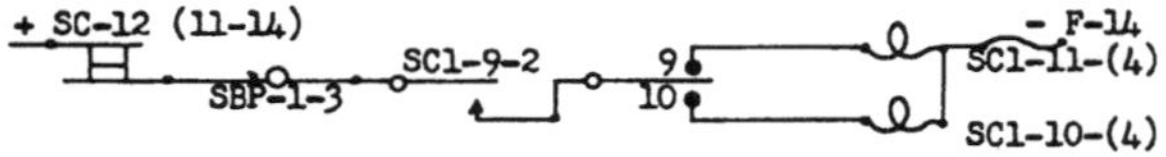
SC-15 (13-15 1/3) SBP-1-6 SC3-3-1 9 or 10 Contact	24th Col Carry SC3-11-(4) or SC3-10-(4)		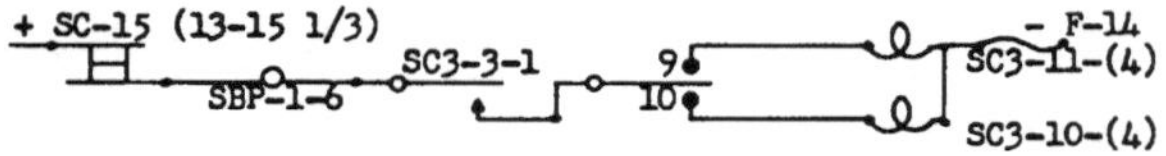
FC-94 (12 1/2-13 2/3) VBP-148 C-6-1-1 NC C-5-1-1 NC C-4-1-1 NC C-3-1-1 C-2-1-2 C-1-1-4 NC SBP-1-12	Str Ctr Invert- (12)	SC-11 (12-0) Invert-12	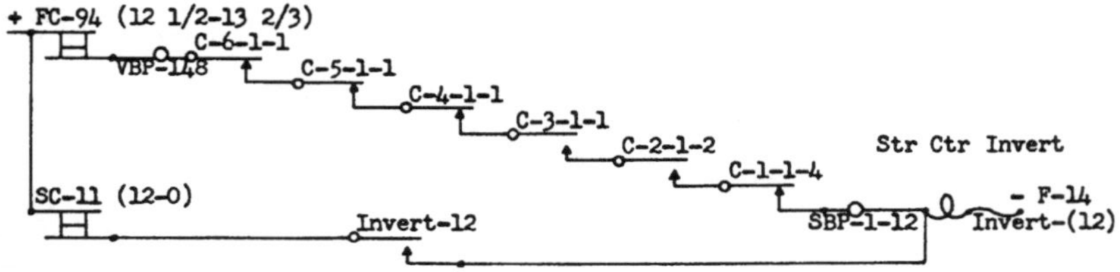
FC-100 (13-15 1/4) Seq-10-1-1 SC-17(14-14 1/2) SBP-1-10 SC3-11-2 NC SC3-3-3 SBP-1-12	Invert (Minus Absolute RO)- (12)	SC-11 (12-0) Invert-12	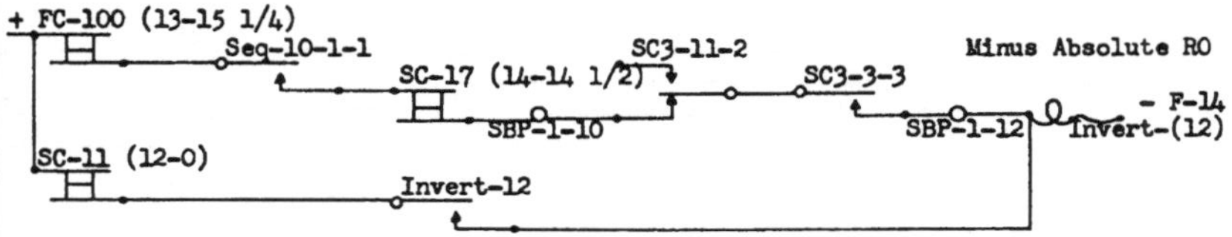

STORAGE COUNTERS -continued-

<table>
<tr><th>Pick Up Circuit</th><th>Magnet</th><th>Hold Circuit</th><th>Circuit Diagram</th></tr>
<tr><td>FC-100
(13-15 1/4)
Seq-11-1-1
SC-18(14-14 1/2)
SBP-1-11
SC3-11-2
SC3-3-3
SBP-1-12</td><td>Invert (Plus Absolute RO)-(12)</td><td>SC-11 (12-0)
Invert-12</td><td>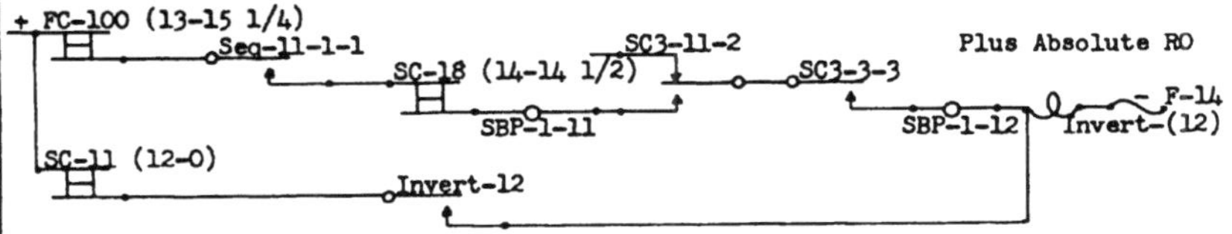
</td></tr>
<tr><td>SC-16
(14-15 1/3)
SBP-1-7
SC1-6-2
SC1-3-2
SBP-2-12</td><td>Str Counter Reset-(12)</td><td>SC-11 (12-0)
Reset-12</td><td>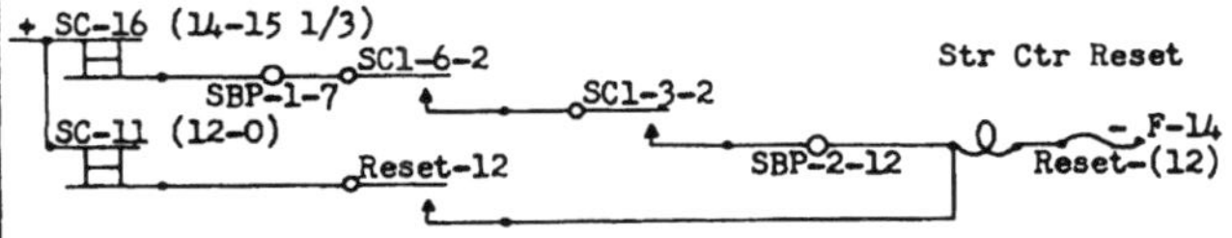
</td></tr>
<tr><td>SC-10
(12-12 1/2)
SBP-1-1
Str Ctr Carry Contacts
SC1-7,8-1,..,12
SC1-11,10-1</td><td>Str Counter Magnets</td><td></td><td>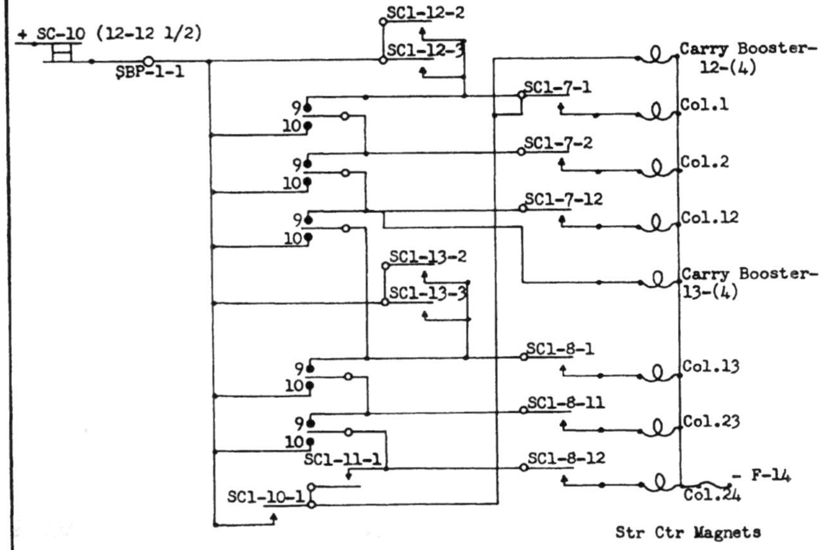
</td></tr>
</table>

HIGH ACCURACY

CYCLE 0. Assuming that it is desired to read from register R into storage counter 68, code 73, with the ganged carry control, the sequence mechanism reads the line of coding (R, 873, blank). The sequence relays are picked up. The storage counter 68 in relay and the special storage counter 68 in relay are picked up.

CYCLE 1. Through the special storage counter 68 in relay, the carry interlock relay, ganging the carry circuits of counter 68 and 69, is picked up.

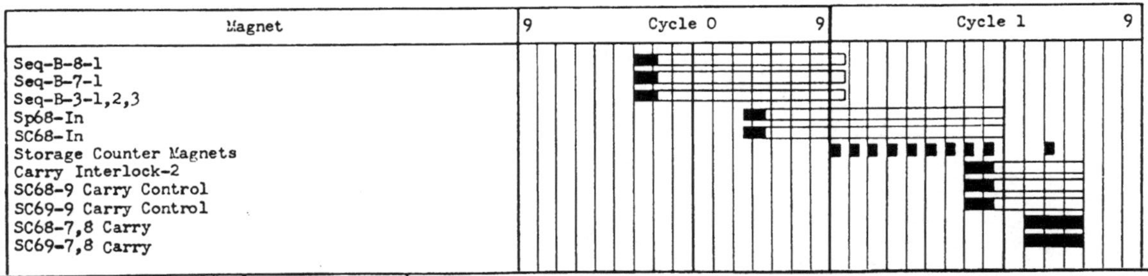

Pick Up Circuit	Magnet	Hold Circuit
FC-101 (3-2 1/3) VBP-100 Seq-31-1,2,3,4 Reading Pins	B-8-1-(4) B-7-1-(4) B-3-1,2,3-(12)	FC-102 (4-9 3/4) VBP-225 B-8-1-4 B-7-1-4 B-3-3-11

Circuit Diagram

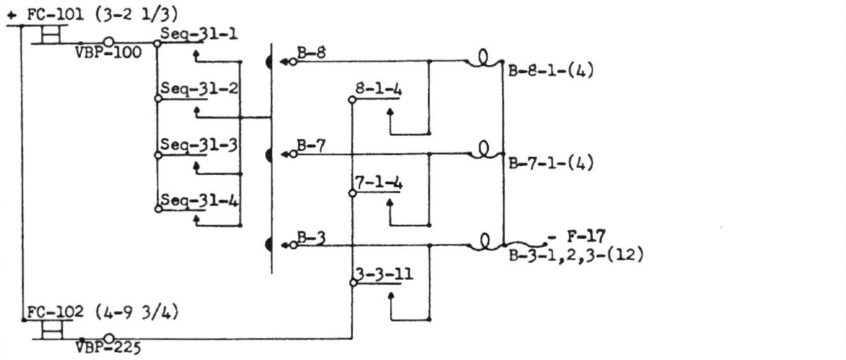

HIGH ACCURACY -continued-

Pick Up Circuit	Magnet	Hold Circuit	Circuit Diagram
FC-93 (12 1/2-13 2/3) VBP-149 B-8-1-1 B-7-1-2 B-6-1-4 NC B-5-1-7 NC B-4-2-1 NC B-3-3-1 B-2-5-2 NC B-1-9-3 NC	Sp68-IN-(4)	SC-11 (12-0) SBP-2-2 and SC68-6-4 Sp68-1 or Sp68-4	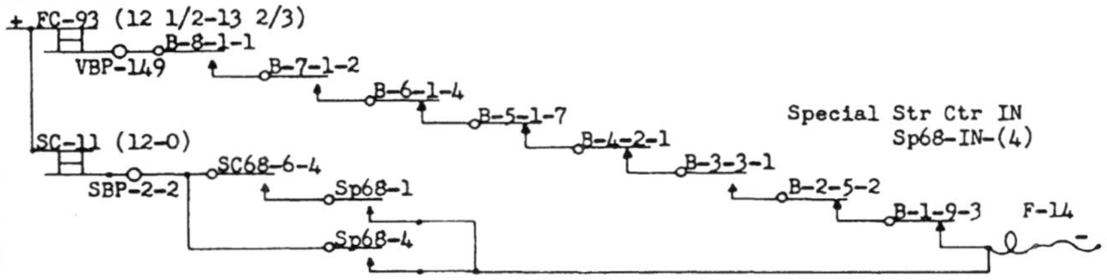
FC-93 (12 1/2-13 2/3) VBP-149 B-8-1-1 B-7-1-2 B-6-1-4 NC B-5-1-7 NC B-4-2-1 NC B-3-3-1 B-2-5-2 NC B-1-9-3 NC Sp68-1	SC68-4,5-(12) SC68-6-(4)	SC-11 (12-0) SBP-2-2 SC68-6-4	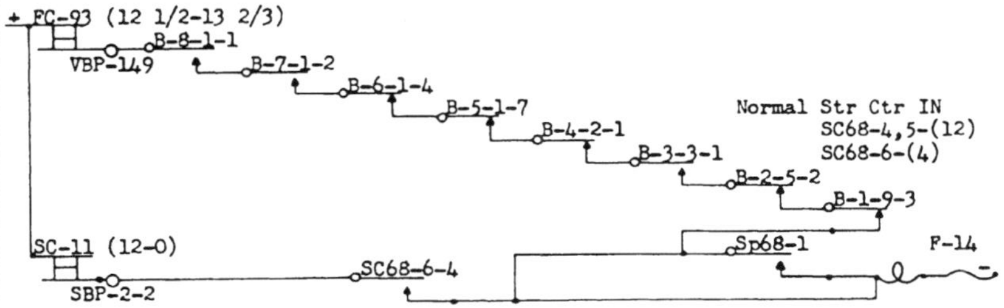
SC-13 (2-1 1/2) Reset-10 NC SBP-2-4 Sp68-3 Sp69-3	Carry Interlock- 2-(6)	SC-14 (2-14 1/16) SBP-2-5 CI-2-6	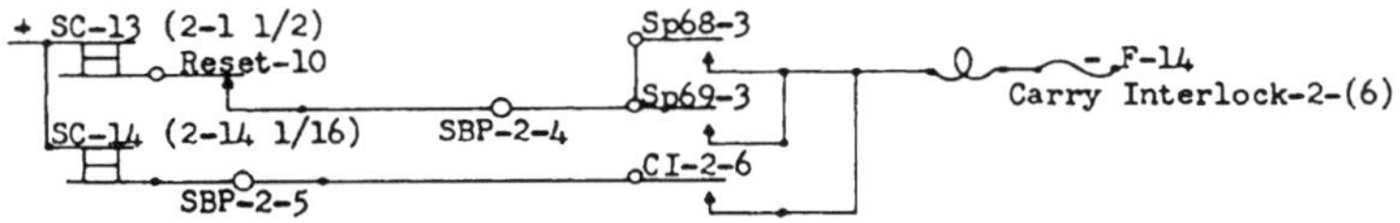
SC-13 (2-1 1/2) Reset-10 NC SBP-2-4 SC68-6-1	Carry Control SC68-9-(4)	SC-14 (2-14 1/16) SBP-2-5 SC68-9-4	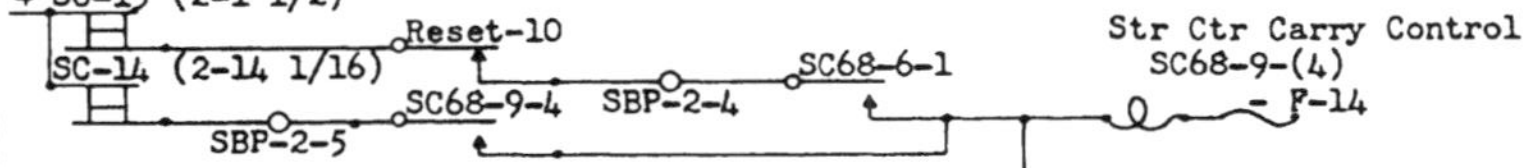
SC-13 (2-1 1/2) Reset-10 NC SBP-2-4 SC69-6-1	Carry Control SC69-9-(4)	SC-14 (2-14 1/16) SBP-2-5 SC69-9-4	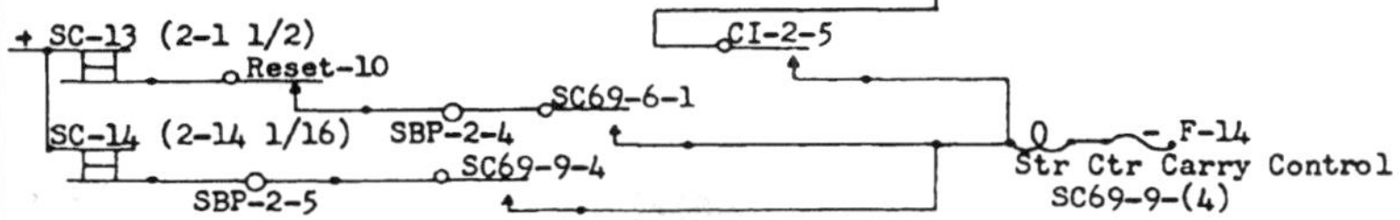

HIGH ACCURACY -continued-

Pick Up Circuit	Magnet	Hold Circuit	Circuit Diagram
SC-10 (12-12 1/2) SBP-2-1 Str Ctr Carry Contacts SC68-7-1,..,12 SC69-8-1,..,12 SC68-11,10-1 SC69-7-1,..,12 SC69-8-1,..,12 SC69-11,10-1	Counter Magnets Ctrs 68 and 69		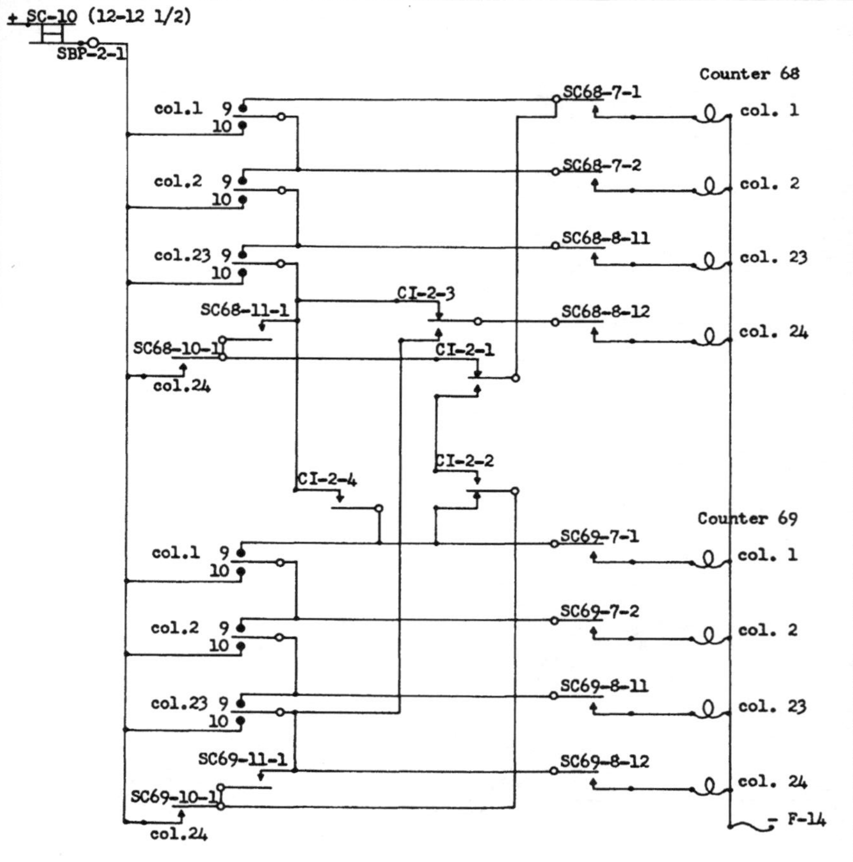

CHOICE COUNTER

CYCLE 0. **The sequence mechanism reads the Miscellaneous code 432 and picks up the corresponding sequence relays. The choice relay of counter 70 is picked up. Through the choice relay the storage counter 70 24th column carry relay is picked up. If there is a 9 standing in the 24th column of counter 70, the energized choice relay completes a circuit to pick up the storage counter invert relay.**

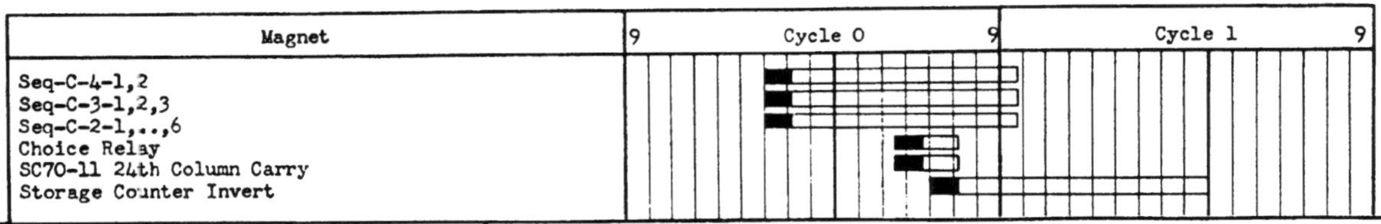

Pick Up Circuit	Magnet	Hold Circuit	Circuit Diagram
FC-101 (3-2 1/3) VBP-100 Seq-31-1,2,3,4 Reading Pins	C-4-1-(12) C-4-2-(6) C-3-1,2,3-(12) C-2-1,..,5-(12) C-2-6-(6)	FC-102 (4-9 3/4) VBP-225 C-4-2-6 C-3-3-11 C-2-6-6	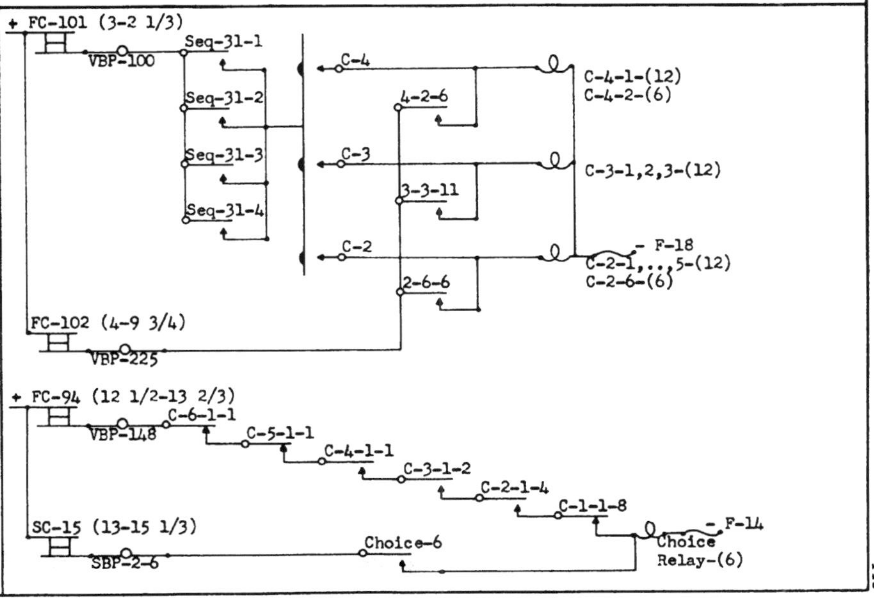
FC-94 (12 1/2-13 2/3) VBP-148 C-6-1-1 NC C-5-1-1 NC C-4-1-1 C-3-1-2 C-2-1-4 C-1-1-8 NC	Choice Relay-(6)	SC-15 (13-15 1/3) SBP-2-6 Choice-6	

CHOICE COUNTER -continued-

Pick Up Circuit	Magnet	Hold Circuit	Circuit Diagram
FC-94 (12 1/2-13 2/3) VBP-148 C-6-1-1 NC C-5-1-1 NC C-4-1-1 C-3-1-2 C-2-1-4 C-1-1-8 NC Choice-6 Choice-1 9 Contact	24th Column Carry SC70-11-(4)	SC-15 (13-15 1/3) SBP-2-6 Choice-1	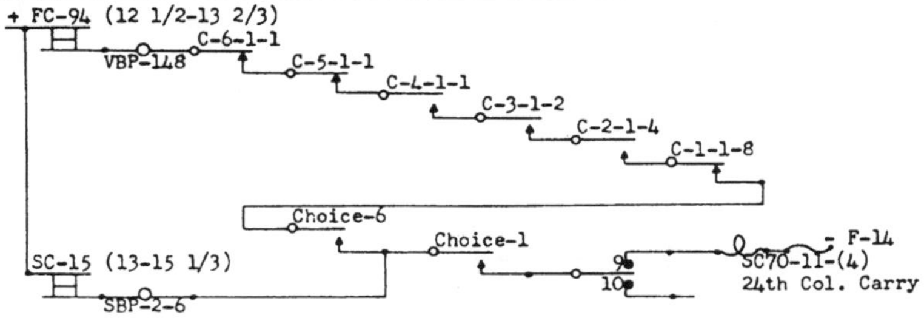
SC-16 (14-15 1/3) SBP-2-7 SC70-11-3 Choice-2 SBP-1-12	Str Counter Invert-(12)	SC-11 (12-0) Invert-12	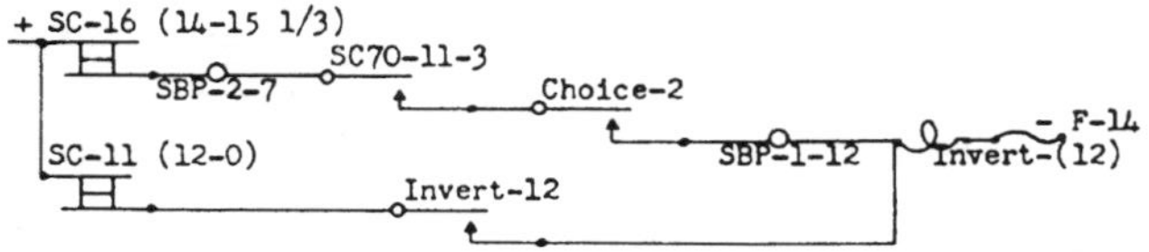

MIO COUNTER (Normal)

If the code Out 7321 or In 7321 is read by the sequence mechanism, the normal storage counter 71 out control or the normal storage counter 71 in control relay is energized. These in turn control the pick up of the normal storage counter 71 out and normal storage counter 71 in relays respectively.

MIO COUNTER (Special)

CYCLE 0. Assuming that columns 13-24 of the MIO counter are to be read to columns 13-24 of register R, the sequence mechanism reads the line of coding (853, R, blank). The sequence relays are energized. The special out (direct) relay is energized and through it the normal storage counter out relays 2 and 3 are picked up. Assuming that columns 13-24 of the MIO counter are to be read to columns 1-12 of register R, the sequence mechanism reads the line of coding (8531, R, blank). Through the corresponding sequence relays, the special out (shifted) relay is energized and in turn the normal storage counter out relay 3 is picked up.

Assuming that columns 13-24 of register R are to be read into columns 13-24 of the MIO counter, the sequence mechanism reads the line of coding (R, 853, blank). The sequence relays are energized. The special in (direct) relay is energized and through it the normal storage counter in relays 5 and 6 are picked up. Assuming that columns 1-12 of register R are to be read to columns 13-24 of the MIO counter, the sequence mechanism reads the line of coding (R, 8531, blank). Through the corresponding sequence relays, the special in (shifted) relay is energized and in turn the normal storage counter in relay 6 is picked up.

CYCLE 1. If reading into the MIO counter, the carry control, carry, 24th column carry and carry back control relays are energized. The energized carry back control relay opens the carry circuit from column 12 to column 13 and closes an end around carry circuit from column 24 to column 13. The carry impulse may then complete the MIO counter entry.

MIO COUNTER -continued-

Magnet	Cycle 0 / Cycle 1
Sequence relays SC71-14 Normal Str Ctr Out Control SC71-1,2,3 Normal Str Ctr Out SC71-16 Normal Str Ctr In Control SC71-4,5,6 Normal Str Ctr In SC71-15 Special Out (direct) SC71-18-1,2 Special Out (shifted) SC71-17 Special In (direct) SC71-19-1,2 Special In (shifted) SC71-20 Carry Back Control Storage Counter Magnets	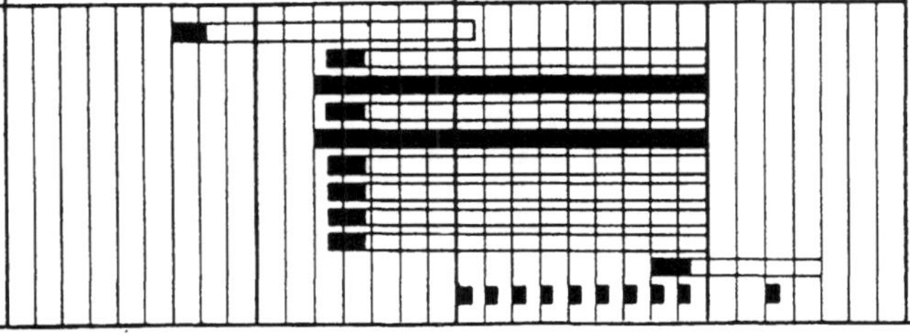

Pick Up Circuit	Magnet	Hold Circuit
FC-92 (12 1/2-13 2/3) VBP-150 A-8-1-1 NC A-7-1-1 A-6-1-2 NC A-5-1-3 NC A-4-1-5 NC A-3-1-9 A-2-2-6 A-1-3-12	Normal Str Ctr Out Control SC71-14-(6)	SC-11 (12-0) SBP-2-2 SC71-14-6
SC-11 (12-0) SBP-2-2 SC71-14-1	Normal Str Ctr Out SC71-1-(12)	
SC-11 (12-0) SBP-2-2 SC71-14-2 SC71-15-1	Normal Str Ctr Out SC71-2-(12)	
SC-11 (12-0) SBP-2-2 SC71-14-3 SC71-15-2 SC71-18-2-1	Normal Str Ctr Out SC71-3-(4)	

Circuit Diagram

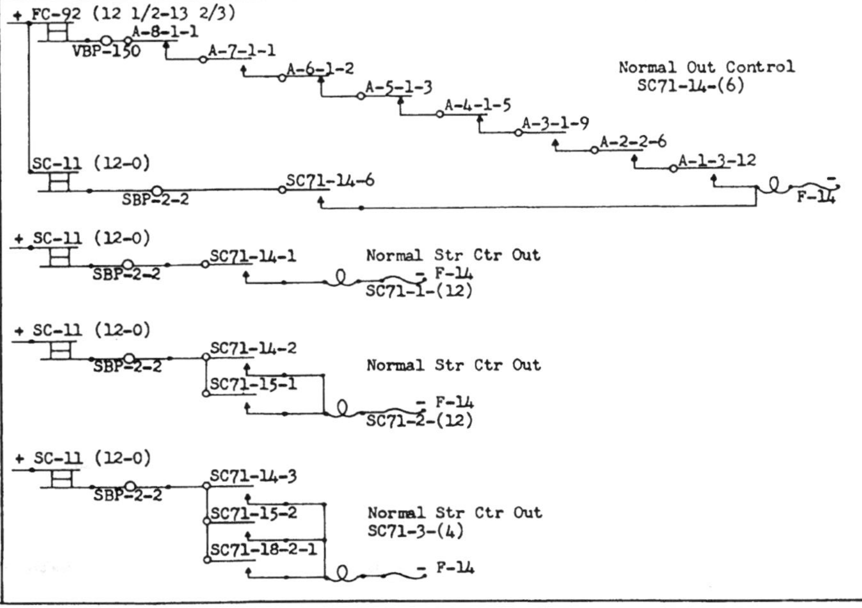

MIO COUNTER -continued-

Pick Up Circuit	Magnet	Hold Circuit	Circuit Diagram
FC-93 (12 1/2-13 2/3) VBP-149 B-8-1-1 NC B-7-1-1 B-6-1-2 NC B-5-1-3 NC B-4-1-5 NC B-3-1-9 B-2-2-6 B-1-3-12	Normal Str Ctr In Control SC71-16-(6)	SC-11 (12-0) SBP-2-2 SC71-16-6	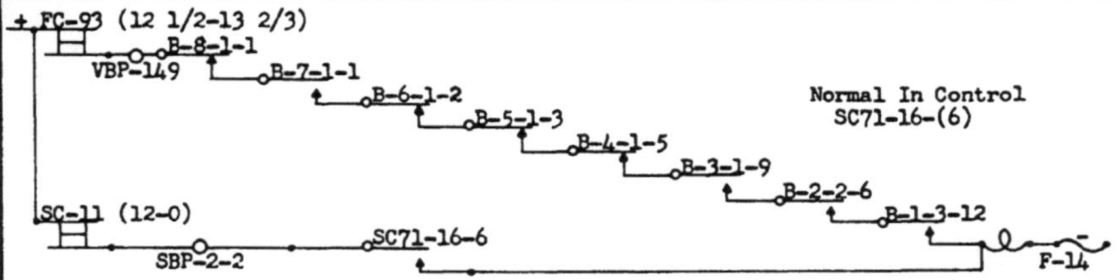
SC-11 (12-0) SBP-2-2 SC71-16-1	Normal Str Ctr In SC71-4-(12)		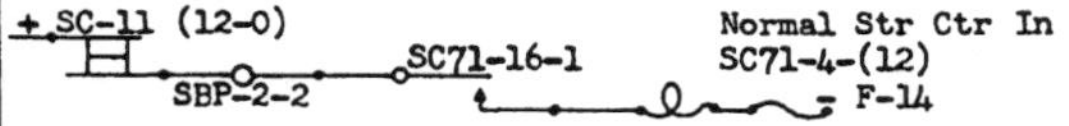
SC-11 (12-0) SBP-2-2 SC71-16-2 SC71-17-1	Normal Str Ctr In SC71-5-(12)		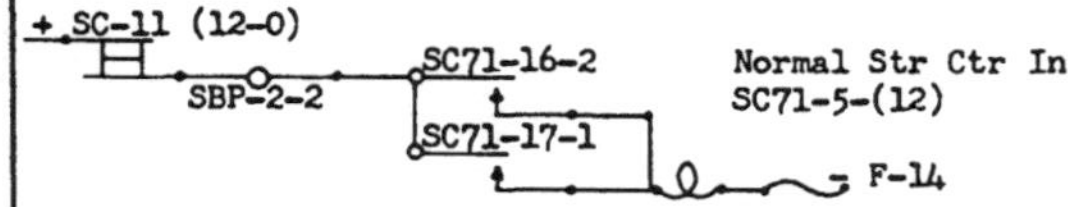
SC-11 (12-0) SBP-2-2 SC71-16-3 SC71-17-2 SC71-19-2-1	Normal Str Ctr In SC71-6-(4)		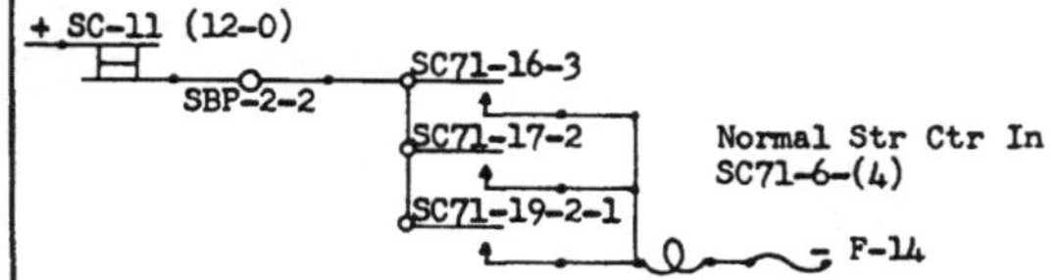
FC-92 (12 1/2-13 2/3) VBP-150 A-8-1-1 A-7-1-2 NC A-6-1-3 NC A-5-1-5 A-4-1-10 NC A-3-2-7 A-2-4-2 NC A-1-7-3 NC	Special Out (direct-cols. 13-24 to cols. 13-24) SC71-15-(6)	SC-11 (12-0) SBP-2-2 SC71-15-6	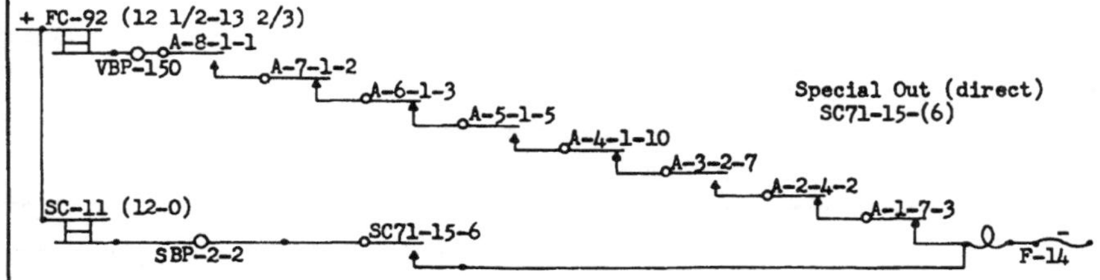

MIO COUNTER -continued-

Pick Up Circuit	Magnet	Hold Circuit
FC-92 (12 1/2-13 2/3) VBP-150 A-8-1-1 A-7-1-2 NC A-6-1-3 NC A-5-1-5 A-4-1-10 NC A-3-2-7 A-2-4-2 NC A-1-7-3	Special Out (shifted-cols. 13-24 to cols. 1-12) SC71-18-1-(12) SC71-18-2-(6)	SC-11 (12-0) SBP-2-2 SC71-18-2-6
FC-93 (12 1/2-13 2/3) VBP-149 B-8-1-1 B-7-1-2 NC B-6-1-3 NC B-5-1-5 B-4-1-10 NC B-3-2-7 B-2-4-2 NC B-1-7-3 NC	Special In (direct-cols. 13-24 to cols. 13-24) SC71-17-(6)	SC-11 (12-0) SBP-2-2 SC71-17-6
FC-93 (12 1/2-13 2/3) VBP-149 B-8-1-1 B-7-1-2 NC B-6-1-3 NC B-5-1-5 B-4-1-10 NC B-3-2-7 B-2-4-2 NC B-1-7-3	Special In (shifted-cols. 1-12 to cols. 13-24) SC71-19-1-(12) SC71-19-2-(6)	SC-11 (12-0) SBP-2-2 SC71-19-2-6
SC-13 (2-1 1/2) Reset-10 NC SBP-2-4 SC71-17-3 SC71-19-2-2	Carry Back Control SC71-20-(6)	SC-14 (2-14 1/16) SBP-2-5 SC71-20-6

Circuit Diagram

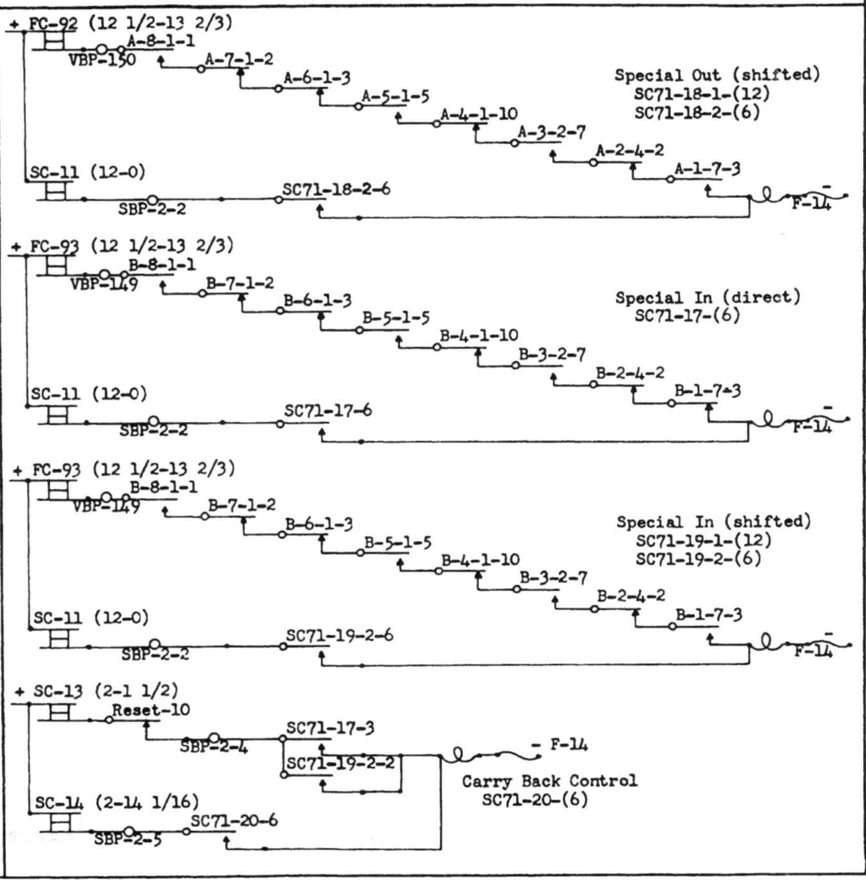

MIO COUNTER -continued-

Pick Up Circuit	Magnet	Hold Circuit	Circuit Diagram
SC-10 (12-12 1/2) SBP-2-1 Str Ctr Carry Contacts SC71-7,8-1,..,12 SC71-11,10-1 SC71-20-1	Str Counter Magnets		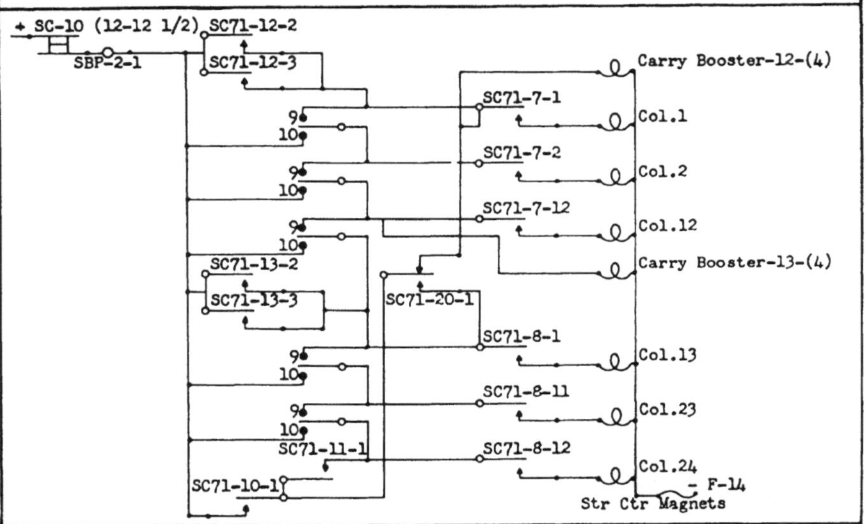

AUTOMATIC CHECK COUNTER

CYCLE 0. Assuming that a positive tolerance is stored in switch R, the sequence mechanism reads the line of coding (R, 74, 7), and steps to the next line. The corresponding sequence relays and through them the switch R out and storage counter 72 in relays are energized.

CYCLE 1. The tolerance is read from switch R into storage counter 72. Assuming that the quantity to be checked lies in storage counter A, the sequence mechanism reads the line of coding (A, 74, 71), and steps to the next line. The corresponding sequence relays and through them the storage counter A out relay, the storage counter 72 in relay and, if necessary to provide the negative absolute value, the storage counter invert relay are energized.

CYCLE 2. The negative absolute value of the quantity standing in counter A is read into counter 72. The normal carry circuits are closed and the carry impulse completes the entry. The sequence mechanism reads the line of coding (blank, blank, 64),and steps to the next line. The corresponding sequence relays are energized and through them the check control relay is picked up. If the absolute value of the quantity read in from counter A is less than the tolerance, the 24th column tens carry contact is made and the check relay is picked up.

CYCLE 3. The energized check relay closes a circuit shunted across the start relay points to pick up the read control relay and the clutch magnet. Thus the calculator continues in operation only if the check relay is picked up.

AUTOMATIC CHECK COUNTER -continued-

Magnet
Seq-C-6-1 Seq-C-4-1,2 Seq-8-1 Check Control SC72-9 Str Ctr Carry Control SC72-10 24th Column Carry Check Relay Seq-31-1 Read Control and Clutch Magnet

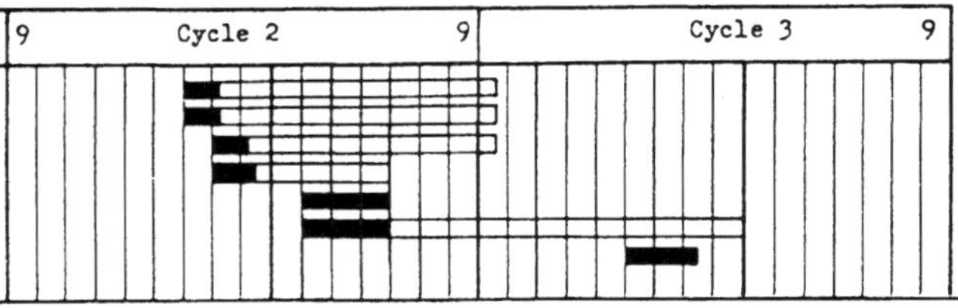

Pick Up Circuit	Magnet	Hold Circuit
FC-101 (3-2 1/3) VBP-100 Seq-31-1,2,3,4 Reading Pins	C-6-1-(6) C-4-1-(12) C-4-2-(6)	FC-102 (4-9 3/4) VBP-225 C-6-1-6 C-4-2-6
FC-96 (2-1 1/3) VBP-172 C-6-1-2 C-5-1-2 NC C-4-1-3 C-3-1-6 NC C-2-1-11 NC C-1-2-9 NC	Check Control Seq-8-1-(4)	FC-102 (4-9 3/4) VBP-225 Seq-8-1-3
SC-12 (11-14) SBP-2-3 SC72-9-2 10 Contact	Str Ctr 24th Col. Carry SC72-10-(4)	
SC-12 (11-14) SBP-2-3 SC72-10-2 Seq-8-1-1,2	Check Relay-(4)	SC-11 (12-0) SBP-2-2 Check-4

Circuit Diagram

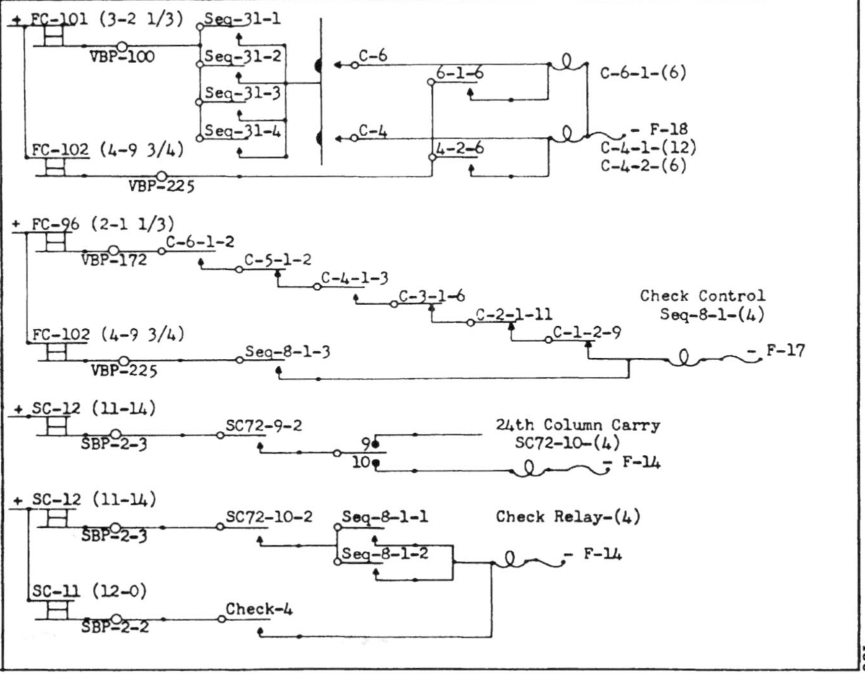

AUTOMATIC CHECK COUNTER -continued-

Pick Up Circuit	Magnet	Hold Circuit	Circuit Diagram
FC-105 (4-2 1/2) Sequence Cut-off Switch Card Feed #1 Sw. Card Feed #2 Sw. BBP-64 Check-1 BBP-54 FBP-98 Seq-32-1-1,2 NC	Control Relay Seq-31-(4)		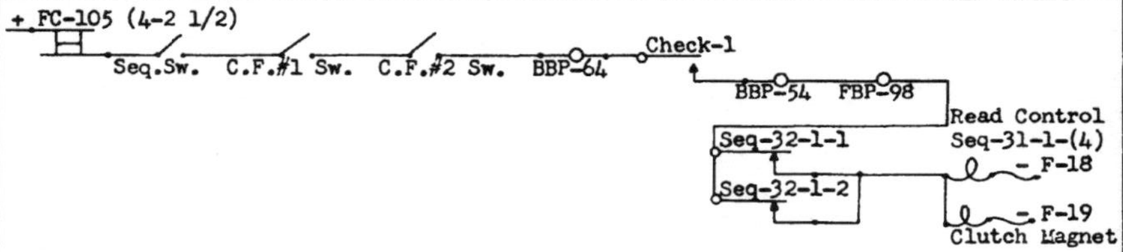

MULTIPLICATION CYCLE O

To start multiplication, assuming the MC to lie in counter 8, code 4, the sequence mechanism reads the line of coding (4, 761, blank). The sequence relays are picked up. The multiply #1 and #2 relays are picked up. The sequence counter is advanced to read-out position 1. The storage counter out and intermediate counter in relays are picked up. The DD-PQ reset relays are picked up.

Magnet
Seq-27 Repeat
Seq-33 Start
Seq-31 Control
Seq-A-4-1,2
Seq-B-7-1
Seq-B-6-1
Seq-B-1-1,..,11
41 Multiply #1
38 Multiply #2
Sequence Counter Magnet
SC8-1,2,3 Storage Counter Out
50 Intermediate In
58 DD-PQ Reset
HD-6 DD-PQ Reset

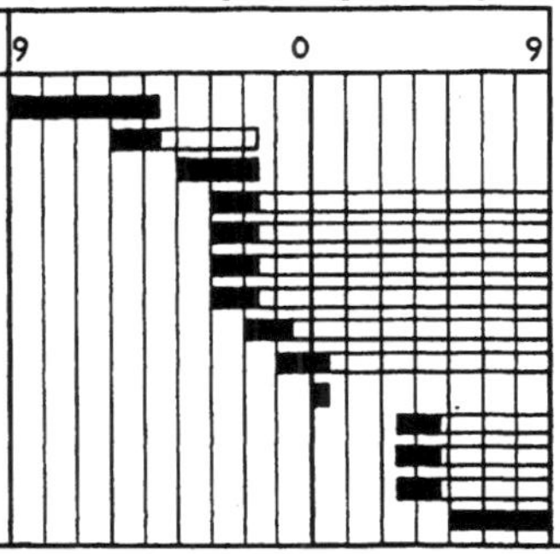

Pick Up Circuit	Magnet	Hold Circuit
Seq-27-1 VBP-276 FC-103 (6-5 1/2) VBP-277 Seq-27-2	Start Seq-33-(4)	FC-108 (6-2 1/2) VBP-278 Seq-33-4
FC-105 (4-2 1/2) Sequence Cut-off Switch Card Feed #1 Sw. Card Feed #2 Sw. BBP-64 Seq-33-1 Seq-32-1,2 NC	Control Seq-31-(4)	
FC-101 (3-2 1/2) VBP-100 Seq-31-1,..,4 Reading Pins	Sequence A-4-1-(12) A-4-2-(6) B-7-1-(4) B-6-1-(4) B-1-1,..,11-(12)	FC-102 (4-9 3/4) VBP-225 A-4-2-6 B-7-1-4 B-6-1-4 B-1-11-11

Circuit Diagram

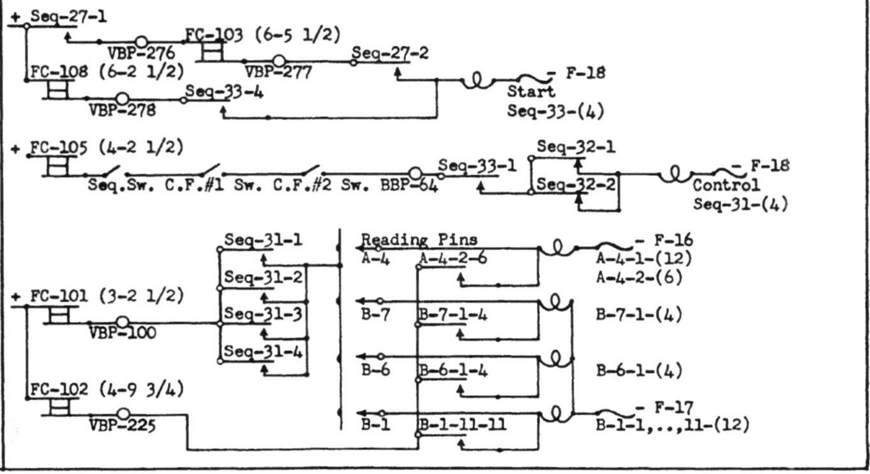

MULTIPLICATION CYCLE 0 -continued-

Pick Up Circuit	Magnet	Hold Circuit	Circuit Diagram
FC-95 (2-1 1/3) VBP-171 B-8-1-2 NC B-7-1-3 B-6-1-5 B-5-1-4 NC B-4-1-7 NC B-3-2-1 NC B-2-3-1 NC B-1-5-1	Multiply #1 41-1,2-(12)	48-1-1 NC or CC-52 (1/3 3-16) and 41-2-11	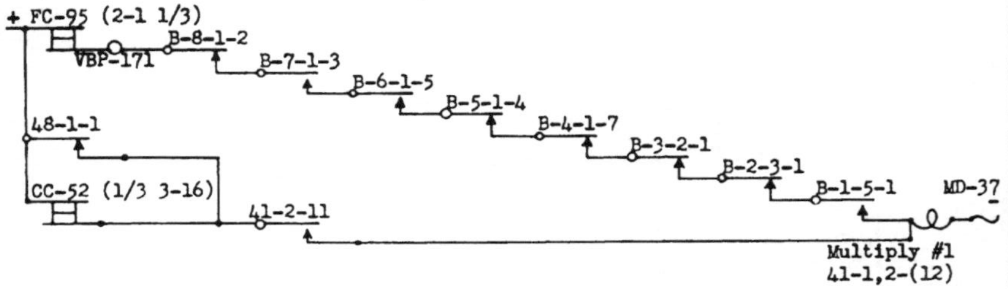
CC-49 (1-0 1/3) 41-2-5	Multiply #2 38-1,2,3-(12)	48-1-1 NC or CC-52 (1/3 3-16) and 38-3-11	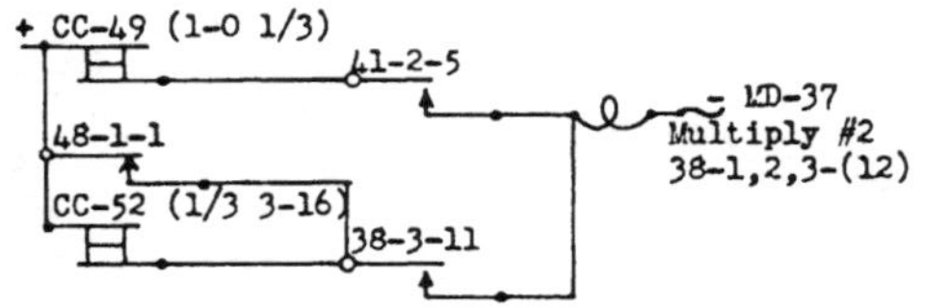
CC-10 (0-0 1/2) 38-3-3 14-1-3 NC 84-1-1 NC	Sequence Counter Magnet		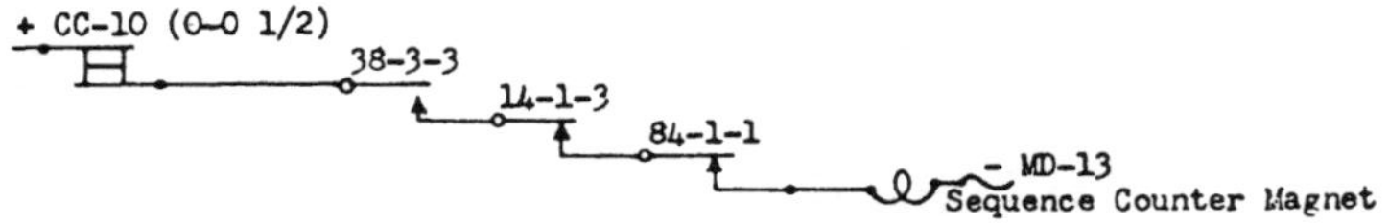
FC-92 (12 1/2-13 2/3) VBP-150 A-8-1-1 NC A-7-1-1 NC A-6-1-1 NC A-5-1-1 NC A-4-1-1 A-3-1-2 NC A-2-1-3 NC A-1-1-5 NC	Storage Counter #8 Out SC8-1,2-(12) SC8-3-(4)	SC-11 (12-0) SC8-3-4	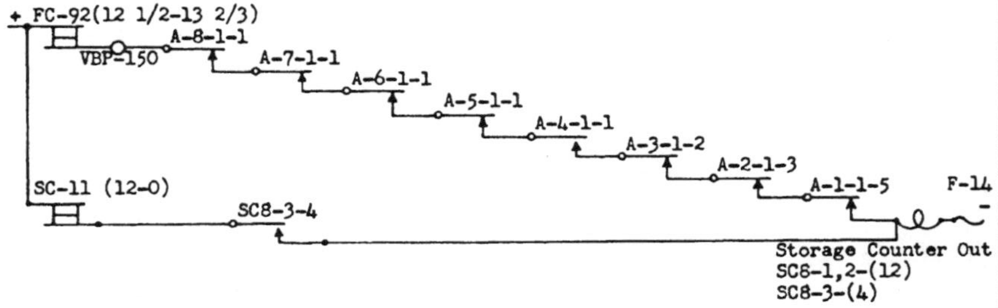

MULTIPLICATION CYCLE 0 -continued-

Pick Up Circuit	Magnet	Hold Circuit	Circuit Diagram
14-1-4 NC CC-55 (12 1/2-13 2/3) Seq Ctr RO B-1 41-1-1	Intermediate In 50-1,2,3-(12)	CC-43 (12-0) ABP-31-32-33 50-3-11	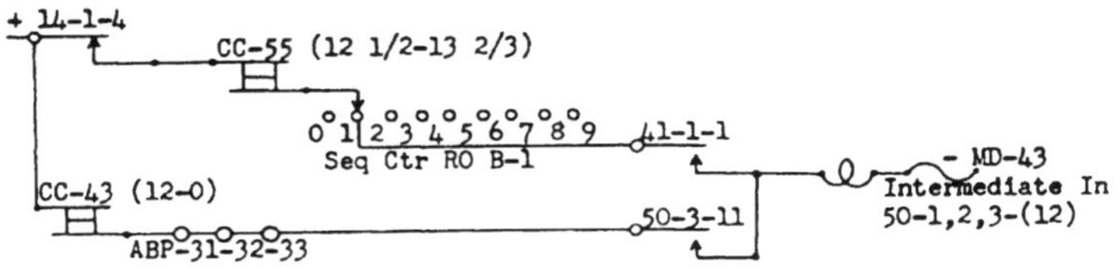
14-1-4 NC CC-57 (12 1/2-13 2/3) Seq Ctr RO D-1 41-1-2	DD-PQ Reset 58-1,..,8-(12)	CC-43 (12-0) ABP-31-32-33 58-8-12 58-4-11,12	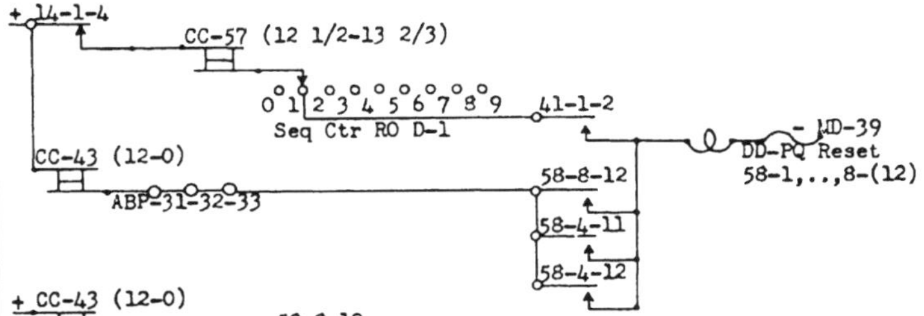
CC-43 (12-0) ABP-31-32-33 58-8-12 58-4-11,12 CC-62 (14-0)	DD-PQ Reset HD-6-(12)		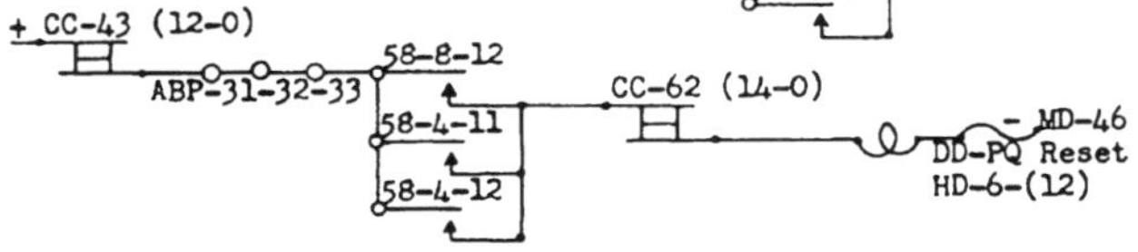

CYCLE 1

The MC is read from storage to the intermediate counter. The intermediate counter carry control and carry relays are picked up and the carry impulse completes the entry into the intermediate counter. The entry of a nine into the 24th column of the intermediate counter (a negative MC) picks up the intermediate 24th column read-out control relay. The DD and PQ counters reset. The sequence counter is advanced to read-out position 2. In preparation for the next cycle, the intermediate invert control and intermediate invert relays are picked up if MC is negative. The "no shift" relays and MC-DR in relays are picked up in order to read the MC from the intermediate counter to the MC-DR counters (1-2), (3-6), (5), (7) and (9). The entry control relays on MC-DR (1-2) and (3-6) prevent the multiple molding counters from short circuiting the number impulses when the counters are in motion.

MULTIPLICATION CYCLE 1 -continued-

Magnet
41 Multiply #1
38 Multiply #2
SC8-1,2,3 Storage Counter Out
50 Intermediate In
Intermediate Counter Magnets
23 Intermediate Carry Control
53 Intermediate Carry
89 Intermediate 24th column RO Control
58 DD-PQ Reset
HD-6 DD-PQ Reset
PQ Counter Magnets
DD Counter Magnets
Sequence Counter Magnet
94 Intermediate Invert Control
HD-1 Intermediate Invert
43 MC-DR In
36 Shift
91 MC-DR Entry Control (1-2)
92 MC-DR Entry Control (3-6)

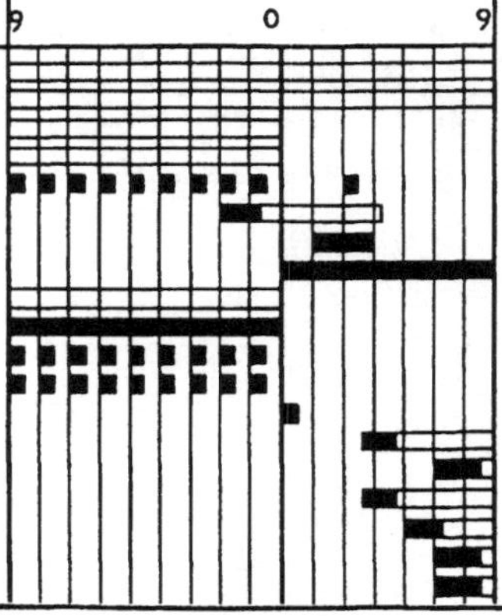

Pick Up Circuit	Magnet	Hold Circuit
SC-1,..,9 Str Ctr Reset NC Storage Ctr Invert NC Str Ctr BP Str Ctr RO SC8-1-1,.., SC8-2-12 BBP-65,..,88 50-1-1,.., 50-2-12	Intermediate Counter Magnets	
CC-44 (2-1 1/3) 50-3-1	Intermediate Carry Control 23-1-(4)	CC-46 (2-13 1/3) ABP-35 23-1-4
CC-45 (1/16 11-13) 23-1-1	Intermediate Carry 53-1,2-(12)	

Circuit Diagram

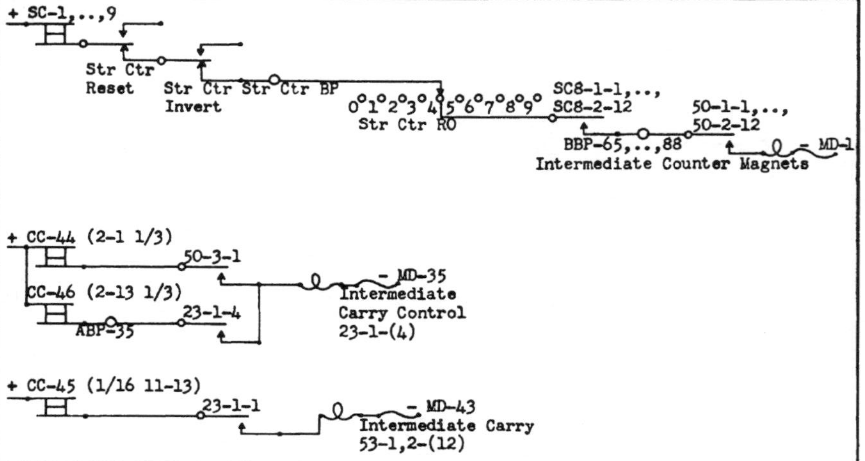

MULTIPLICATION CYCLE 1 -continued-

Pick Up Circuit	Magnet	Hold Circuit	Circuit Diagram
CC-12 (12-12 1/2) Intermediate Counter Carry Contacts 53-1,2-12 Carry Booster 12-2,3 Carry Booster 13-2,3	Intermediate Counter Magnets		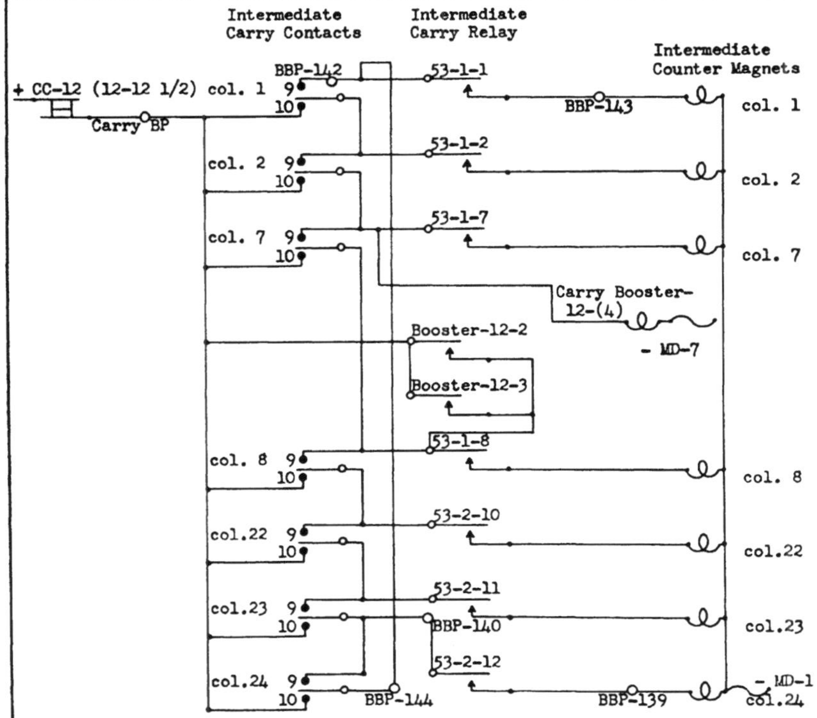 Carry Booster-13 lies between columns 18 and 19.
24th col 3rd mldg 9 spot Intermediate Counter	Intermediate 24th col RO Control 89-1-(4)		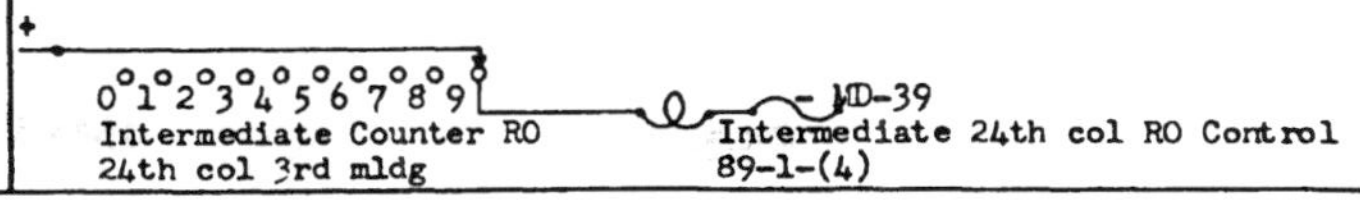

MULTIPLICATION CYCLE 1 -continued-

Pick Up Circuit	Magnet	Hold Circuit	Circuit Diagram
CC-1,..,9 HD-6-1,..,9 58-1-1,..., 58-4-10	PQ Counter Magnets		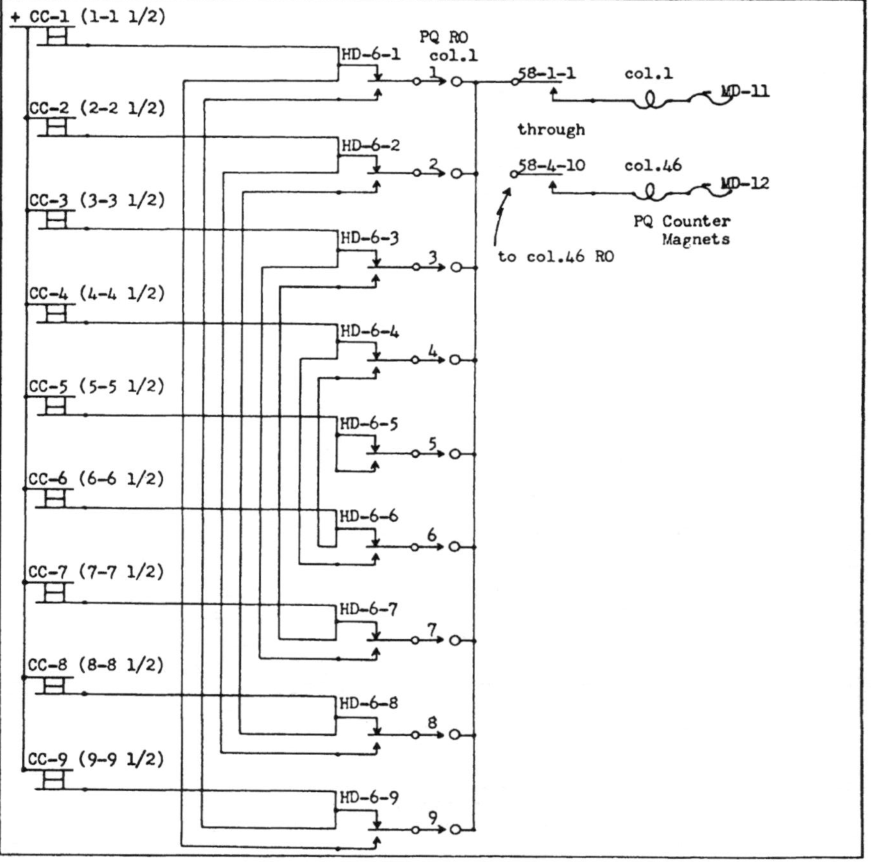

MULTIPLICATION CYCLE 1 -continued-

Pick Up Circuit	Magnet	Hold Circuit	Circuit Diagram
CC-1,..,9 HD-6-1,..,9 58-5-1,.., 58-8-9	DD Counter Magnets		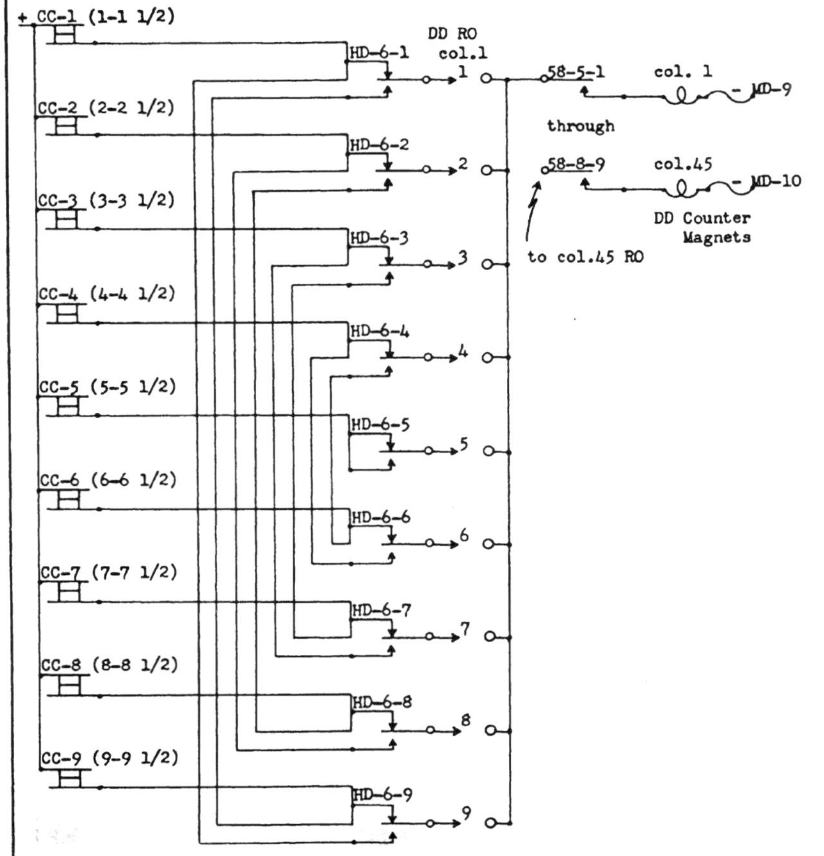

MULTIPLICATION CYCLE 1 -continued-

Pick Up Circuit	Magnet	Hold Circuit	Circuit Diagram
CC-10 (0-0 1/2) 38-3-3 14-1-3 NC 84-1-1 NC	Sequence Counter Magnet		
14-1-4 NC CC-57 (12 1/2-13 2/3) Seq Ctr RO D-2	Intermediate Invert Control 94-1-(4)	CC-43 (12-0) ABP-31-32-33 94-1-4	
CC-69 (15-16 1/3) 94-1-1,2 9 in 24th col Intermediate Counter	Intermediate Invert HD-1-(12)	CC-43 (12-0) ABP-31-32-33 HD-1-12	
14-1-4 NC CC-56 (12 1/2-13 2/3) Seq Ctr RO C-2 41-1-3	MC-DR In 43-1,..,10-(12) 43-11,12-(4)	CC-43 (12-0) ABP-31-32-33 43-10-12 43-12-3,4	
CC-33 (14-15 1/3) 43-2-12 35-45-1 NC 35-46-1 NC	Shift (No Shift) 36-37, 38-(12) 36-39-(4)	CC-43 (12-0) ABP-31 36-39-2	

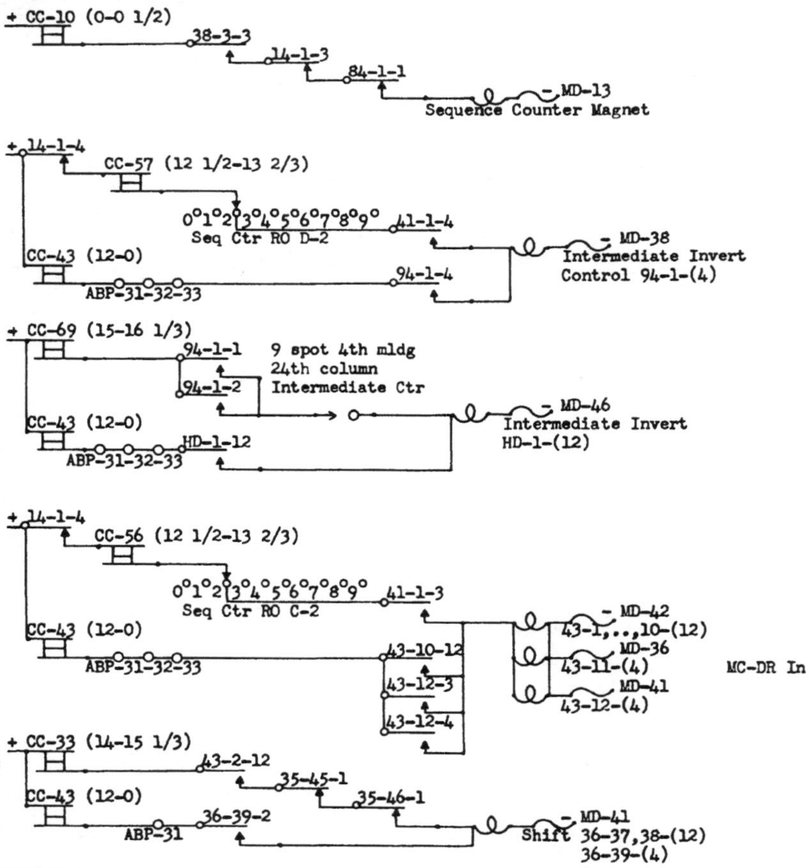

MULTIPLICATION CYCLE 1 -continued-

Pick Up Circuit	Magnet	Hold Circuit	Circuit Diagram
CC-76 (15-16 1/2) 43-12-1	MC-DR Entry Control (1-2) 91-1,2,3-(12)	CC-77 (16-0) 91-3-12	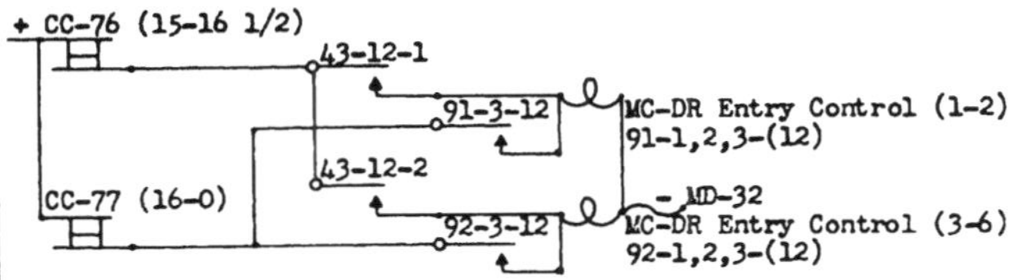
43-12-2	MC-DR Entry Control (3-6) 92-1,2,3-(12)	92-3-12	

CYCLE 2

The sign control relays are picked up if the intermediate 24th column read-out control relay is up. The positive absolute value of the MC reads from the intermediate counter to MC-DR counters (1-2), (3-6), (5),(7) and (9). The sequence counter advances to read-out position 3. In preparation for the next cycle, the intermediate reset, first build-up, first and second build-up and the entry control relays for MC-DR (3-6) and (4-8) are picked up.

Magnet
41 Multiply #1
38 Multiply #2
89 Intermediate 24th col RO Control
70 Sign Control #1
71 Sign Control #2
94 Intermediate Invert Control
HD-1 Intermediate Invert
43 MC-DR In
36 Shift
91 MC-DR Entry Control (1-2)
MC-DR Counter Magnets (1-2)
92 MC-DR Entry Control (3-6)
MC-DR Counter Magnets (3-6)
MC-DR Counter Magnets (5)
MC-DR Counter Magnets (7)
MC-DR Counter Magnets (9)
Sequence Counter Magnet
52 Intermediate Reset
HD-4 Intermediate Reset
44 First Build Up
45 First and Second Build Up
92 MC-DR Entry Control (3-6)
93 MC-DR Entry Control (4-8)

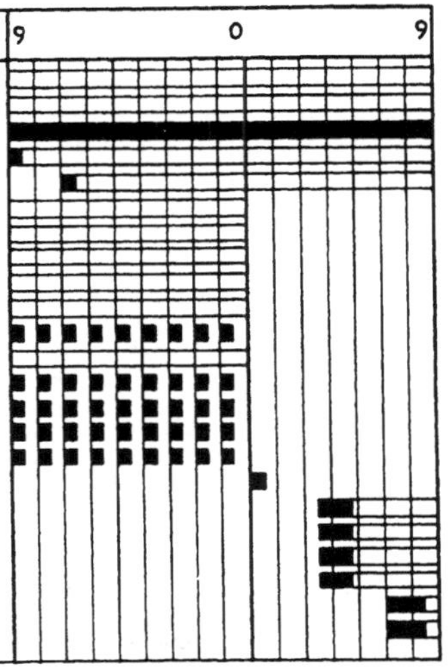

MULTIPLICATION CYCLE 2 -continued-

Pick Up Circuit	Magnet	Hold Circuit	Circuit Diagram
CC-9 (9-9 1/2) 43-6-12 or 39-3-2 or 57-3-2 and 89-1-1	Sign Control #1 70-1-(4)	CC-75 (11-8) BBP-145 or BBP-60 52-3-6 NC and 70-1-4	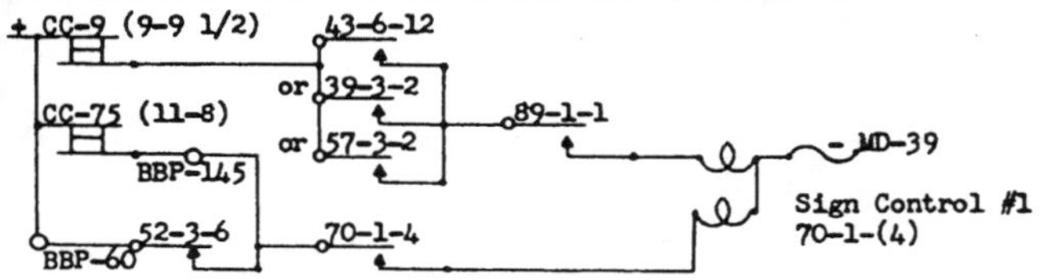
CC-7 (7-7 1/2) 43-11-4 70-1-2	Sign Control #2 71-1-(4)	CC-74 (13 1/2-16) or 47-13-1 NC and 71-1-4	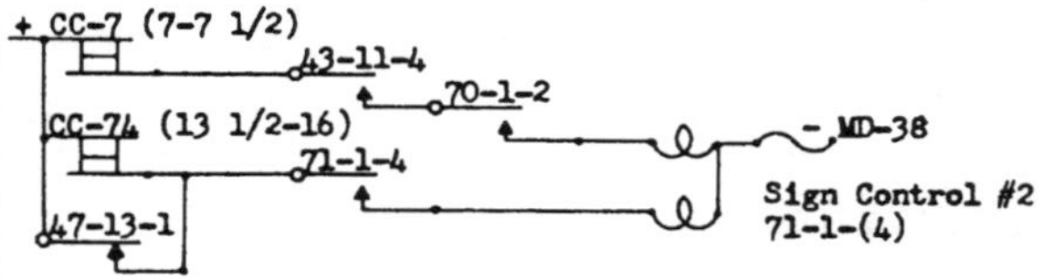
CC-1,..,9 HD-1-1,..,10 NC if MC was > 0 HD-1-1,..,10 NO if MC was < 0 HD-4-1,..,9 NC Intermediate RO 36-37-1,.., 36-38-12	Counter Magnets		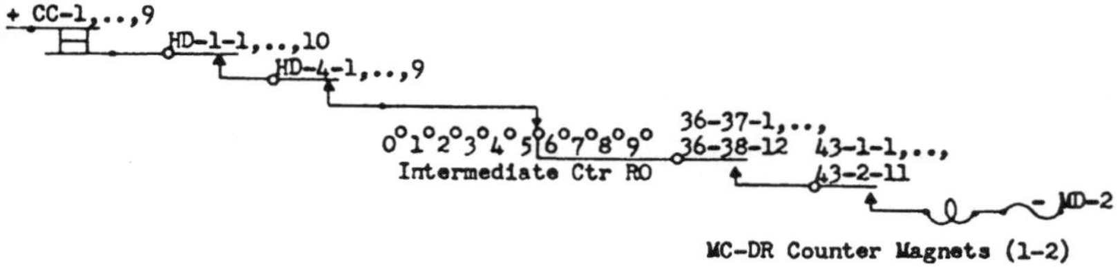
43-1-1,.., 43-2-11	MC-DR (1-2)		
43-3-1,.., 43-4-11	MC-DR (3-6)		
43-5-1,.., 43-6-11	MC-DR (5)		
43-7-1,.., 43-8-11	MC-DR (7)		
43-9-1,.., 43-10-11	MC-DR (9)		
CC-10 (0-0 1/2) 38-3-3 14-1-3 NC 84-1-1 NC	Sequence Counter Magnet		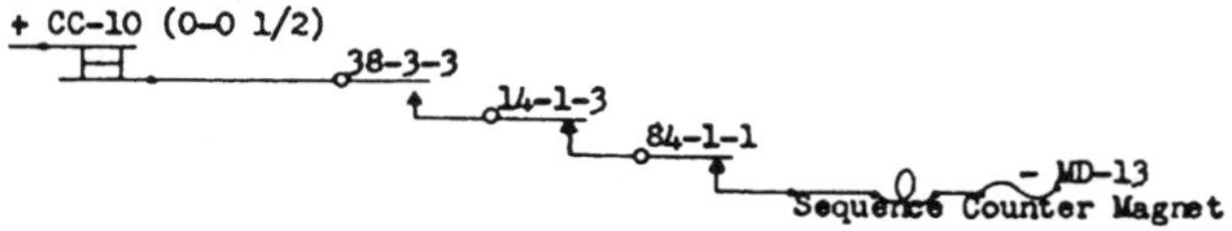

MULTIPLICATION CYCLE 2 -continued-

Pick Up Circuit	Magnet	Hold Circuit	Circuit Diagram
14-1-4 NC CC-57 (12 1/2-13 2/3) Seq Ctr RO D-3 41-1-7	Intermediate Reset 52-1,2,3-(12)	CC-43 (12-0) ABP-31-32-33 52-3-11	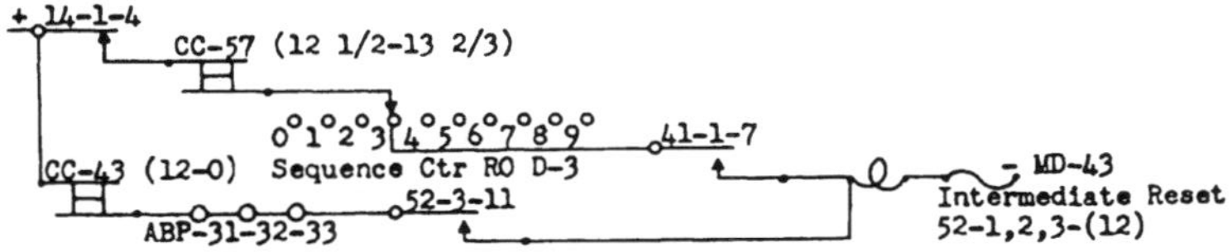
14-1-4 NC CC-57 (12 1/2-13 2/3) Seq Ctr RO D-3 41-1-7 CC-61 (12-0)	Intermediate Reset HD-4-(12)	CC-43 (12-0) ABP-31-32-33 52-3-11 CC-61 (12-0)	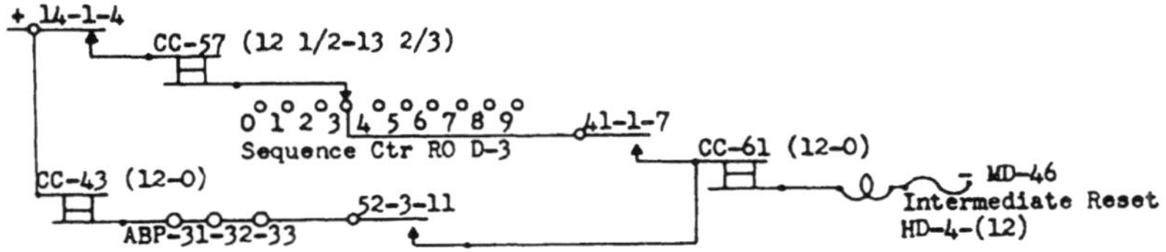
14-1-4 NC CC-55 (12 1/2-13 2/3) Seq Ctr RO B-3 41-1-5	First Build Up 44-1,..,5-(12)	CC-43 (12-0) ABP-31-32-33 44-5-11	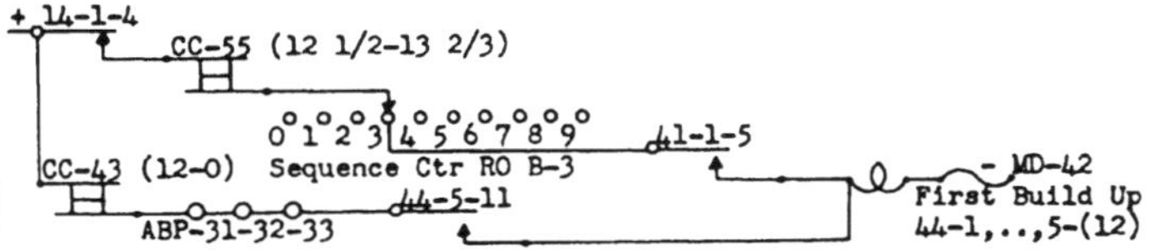
14-1-4 NC CC-56 (12 1/2-13 2/3) Seq Ctr RO C-3 41-1-6	First and Second Build Up 45-1,..,5-(12)	CC-43 (12-0) ABP-31-32-33 45-5-11	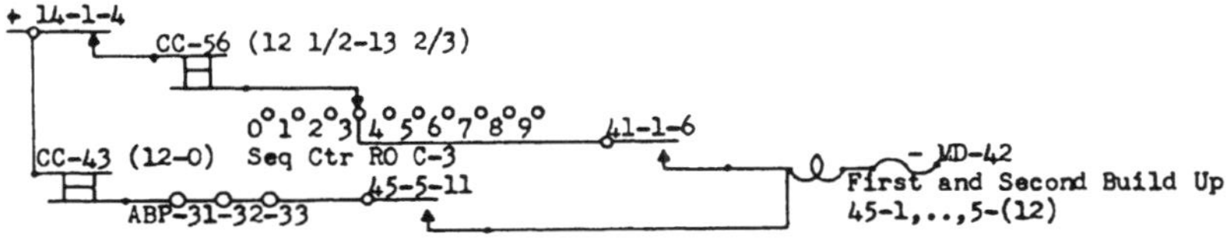
CC-76 (15-16 1/2) 44-5-8 45-5-2	MC-DR Entry Control (3-6) 92-1,2,3-(12) MC-DR Entry Control (4-8) 93-1,2,3-(12)	CC-77 (16-0) 92-3-12 93-3-12	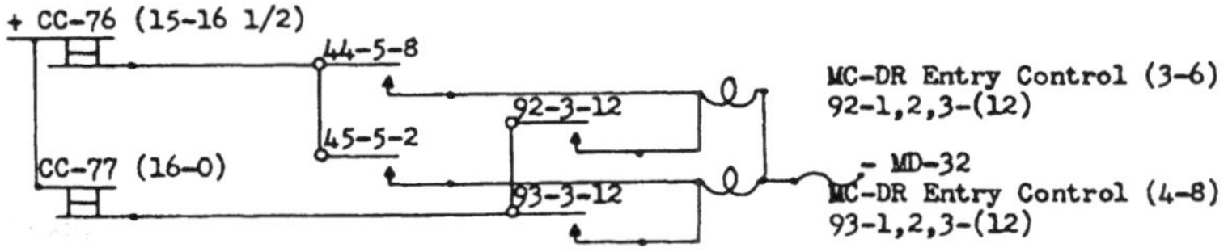

MULTIPLICATION CYCLE 3

The intermediate counter resets. Sign Control #1 drops out. If a nine stood in the 24th column of the intermediate counter a nine is read to the 47th column of the PQ counter. The first build up takes place; i.e., twice the MC is read from the doubling moldings of MC-DR (1-2) to MC-DR (3-6), (4-8), (5) and (9). The MC-DR carry control and carry relays are picked up and the carry impulse completes the first build up. Assuming the MP to lie in storage counter 20, code 53, the sequence mechanism reads the line of coding (53, blank, blank), and the sequence relays are picked up. The storage counter out and intermediate in relays are picked up in order to read the MP to the intermediate counter. The sequence counter is advanced to read-out position 4. In preparation for the next cycle, the first and second build up, second build up and the entry control relays for MC-DR (4-8) are picked up.

Magnet
41 Multiply #1
38 Multiply #2
52 Intermediate Reset
HD-4 Intermediate Reset
Intermediate Counter Magnets
70 Sign Control #1
71 Sign Control #2
PQ 47th column Counter Magnet
44 First Build Up
92 MC-DR Entry Control (3-6)
MC-DR Counter Magnets (3-6)
45 First and Second Build Ups
93 MC-DR Entry Control (4-8)
MC-DR Counter Magnets (4-8)
MC-DR Counter Magnets (5)
MC-DR Counter Magnets (9)
26 MC-DR Carry Control
49 MC-DR Carry
Seq-31 Control
Seq-A-5-1
Seq-A-3-1,2,3
SC20-1,2,3 Storage Counter Out
Sequence Counter Magnet
50 Intermediate In
45 First and Second Build Ups
46 Second Build Up
93 MC-DR Entry Control (4-8)

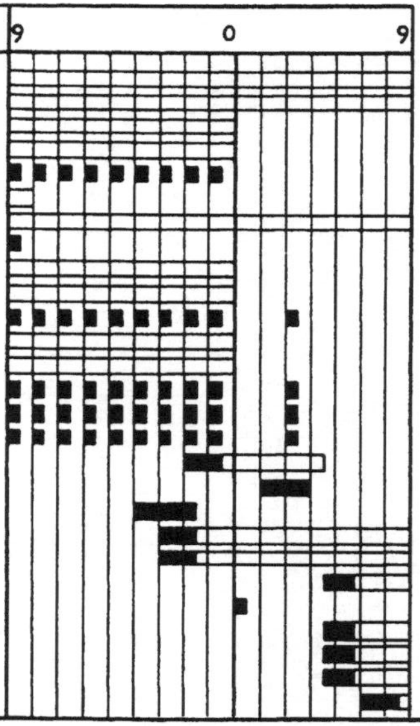

Pick Up Circuit	Magnet	Hold Circuit	Circuit Diagram
CC-9 (9-9 1/2) 82-1-9 NC 52-3-7 70-1-1	PQ 47th column Counter Magnet		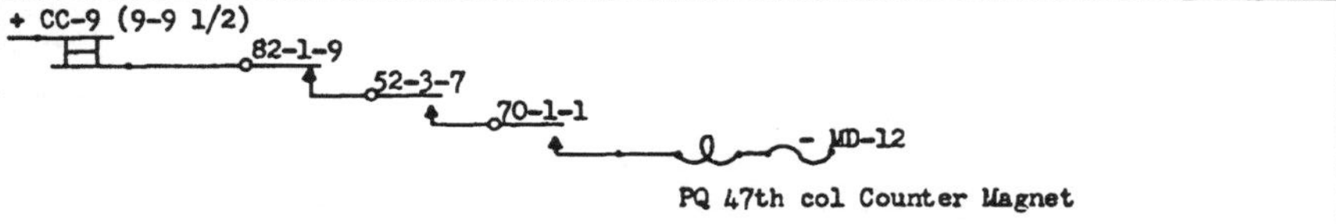

MULTIPLICATION CYCLE 3 -continued-

Pick Up Circuit	Magnet	Hold Circuit	Circuit Diagram
CC-1,..,9 HD-6-1,..,9 52-1-1,.., 52-2-11 and 52-3-5	Intermediate Counter Magnets		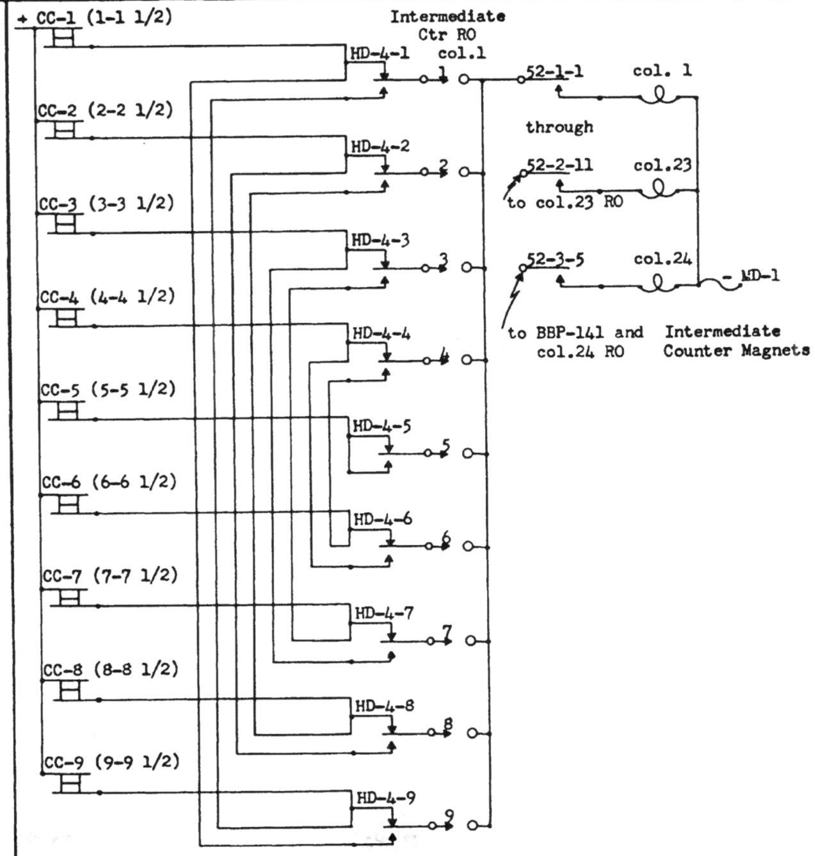

MULTIPLICATION CYCLE 3 -continued-

Pick Up Circuit	Magnet	Hold Circuit	Circuit Diagram
MC-DR Doubling Read-out 91-3-1 on columns 1-6 91-3-2 on columns 7-12 etc.			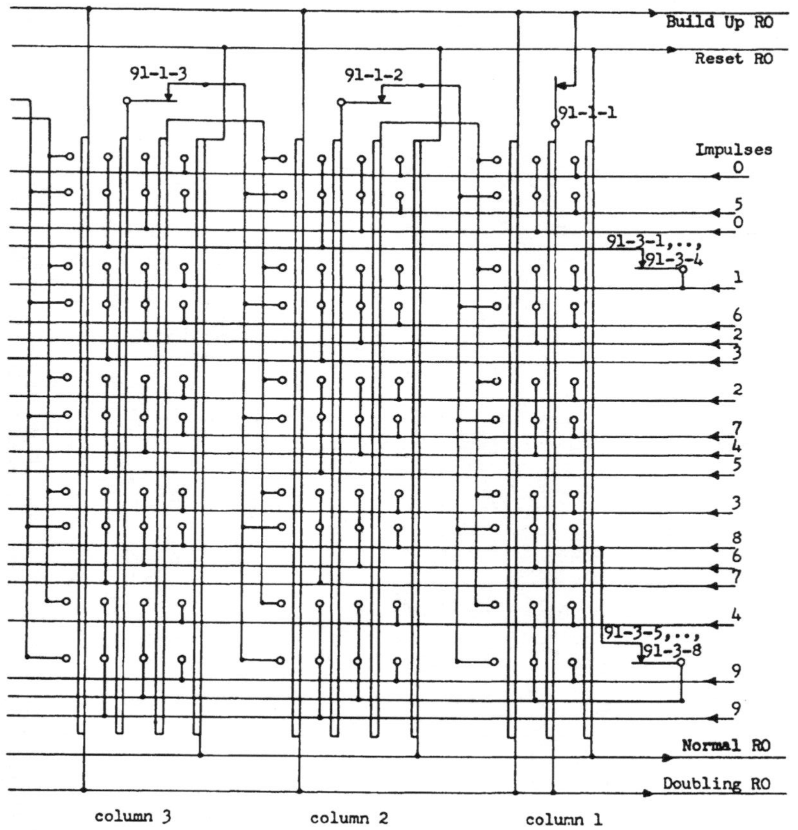

MULTIPLICATION CYCLE 3 -continued-

Pick Up Circuit	Magnet	Hold Circuit	Circuit Diagram
CC-1,..,9 HD-2-1,..,10 NC HD-5-1,..,9 NC MC-DR (1-2) Doubling RO 44-1-1,.., 44-2-12 44-3-1,.., 44-4-12 45-1-1,.., 45-2-12 45-3-1,.., 45-4-12	MC-DR Counter Magnets (3-6) MC-DR Counter Magnets (9) MC-DR Counter Magnets (4-8) MC-DR Counter Magnets (5)		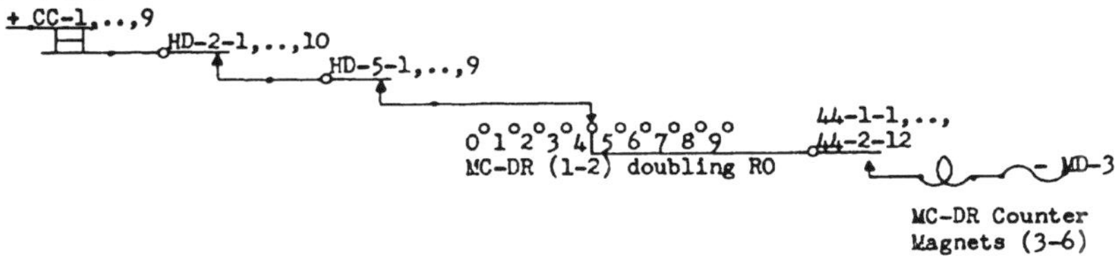
CC-44 (2-1 1/3) 45-5-1	MC-DR Carry Control 26-1-(4)	CC-46 (2-13 1/2) ABP-35 26-1-4	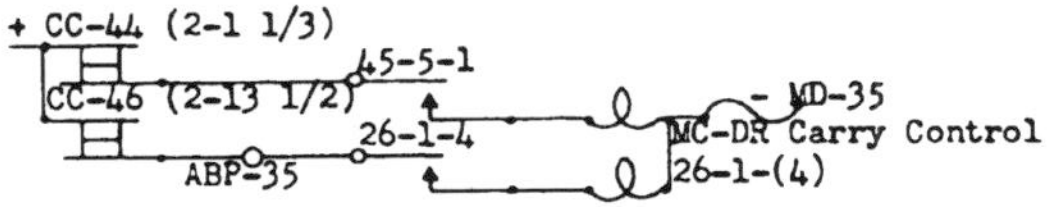
CC-45 (1/16 11-13) 26-1-1	MC-DR Carry 49-1,..,10-(12)		
CC-12 (12-12 1/2) Carry BP Carry Transfer Contacts 49-1,..,10-12 MC-DR (3-6) Carry Booster-1 MC-DR (4-8) Carry Booster-2 MC-DR (5) Carry Booster-3 MC-DR (7) Carry Booster-4 MC-DR (9) Carry Booster-5	MC-DR Counter Magnets		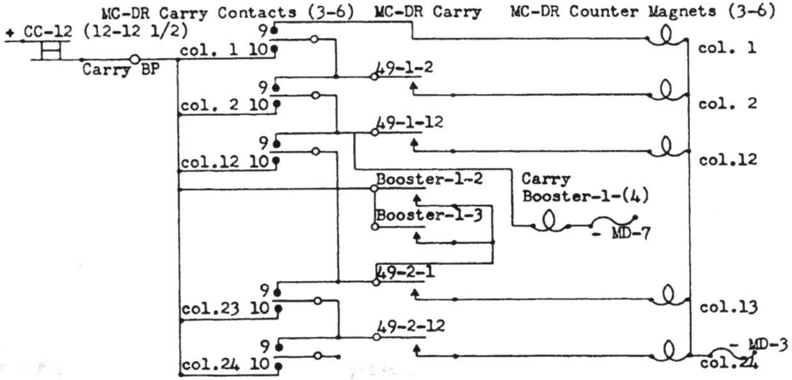

MULTIPLICATION CYCLE 3 -continued-

Pick Up Circuit	Magnet	Hold Circuit	Circuit Diagram
FC-105 (4-2 1/2) Sequence Cut-off Switch Card Feed #1 Sw. Card Feed #2 Sw. BBP-64,110 44-5-1 BBP-111 FBP-133 216-1-2 NC 55-3-2 NC 78-2-8 NC 81-1-9 NC BBP-52 FBP-99 201-1-2 NC FBP-98 Seq-32-1,2 NC	Control Relay Seq-31-(4) Clutch Magnet		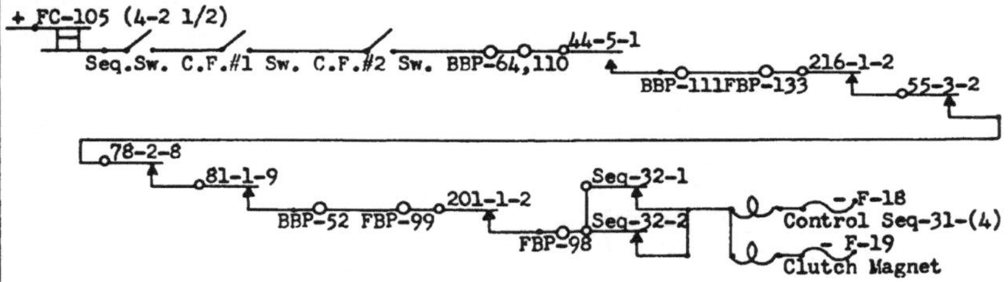
FC-101 (3-2 1/2) VBP-100 Seq-31-1,..,4 Reading Pins	A-5-1-(12) A-3-1,2,3-(12)	FC-102 (4-9 3/4) VBP-225 A-5-1-11 A-3-3-11	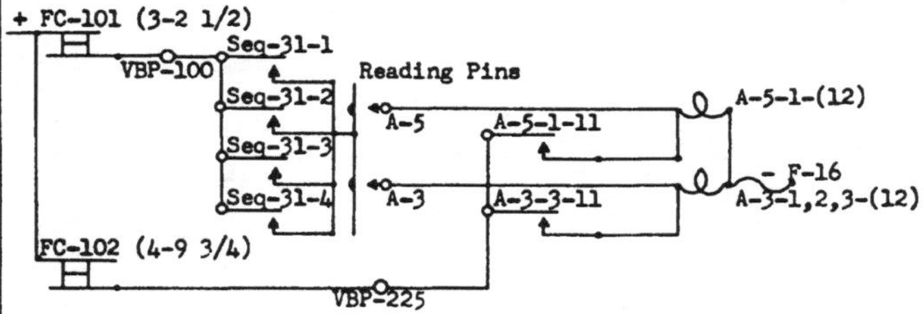
FC-92 (12 1/2-13 2/3) VBP-150 A-8-1-1 NC A-7-1-1 NC A-6-1-1 NC A-5-1-1 A-4-1-2 NC A-3-1-3 A-2-1-6 NC A-1-1-11 NC	Storage Counter #20 Out SC20-1,2 -(12) SC20-3-(4)	SC-11 (12-0) SC20-3-4	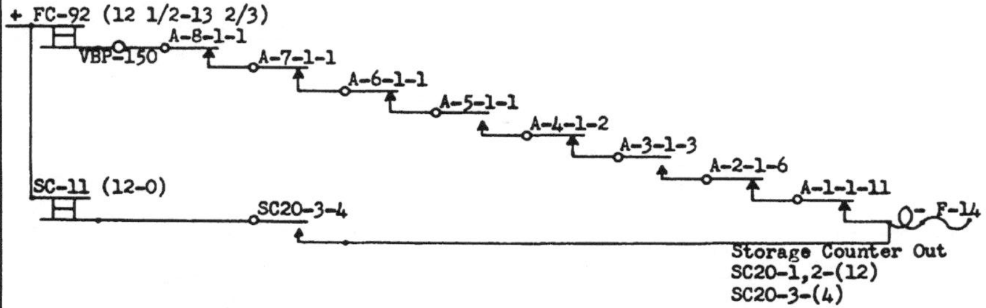

MULTIPLICATION CYCLE 3 -continued-

Pick Up Circuit	Magnet	Hold Circuit	Circuit Diagram
CC-10 (0-0 1/2) 38-3-3 14-1-3 NC 84-1-1 NC	Sequence Counter Magnet		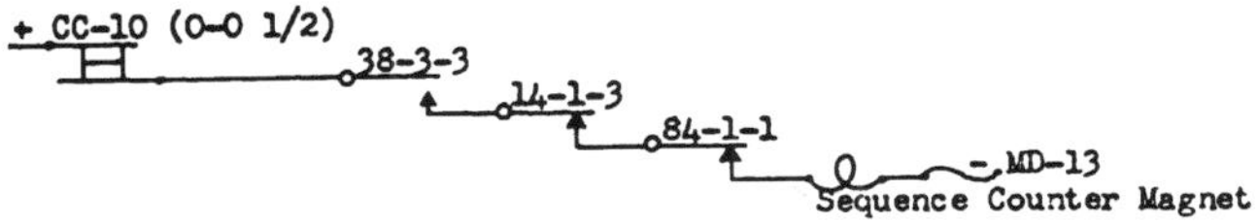
14-1-4 NC CC-55 (12 1/2-13 2/3) Seq Ctr RO B-4 41-1-8	Intermediate In 50-1,2,3-(12)	CC-43 (12-0) ABP-31-32-33 50-3-11	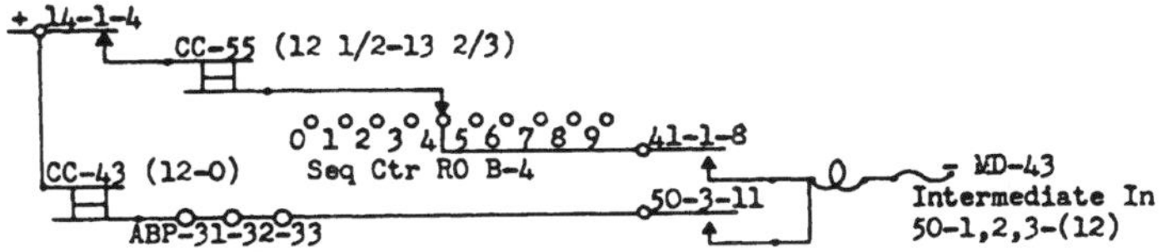
14-1-4 NC CC-56 (12 1/2-13 2/3) Seq Ctr RO C-4 41-1-9	First and Second Build Up 45-1,..,5-(12)	CC-43 (12-0) ABP-31-32-33 45-5-11	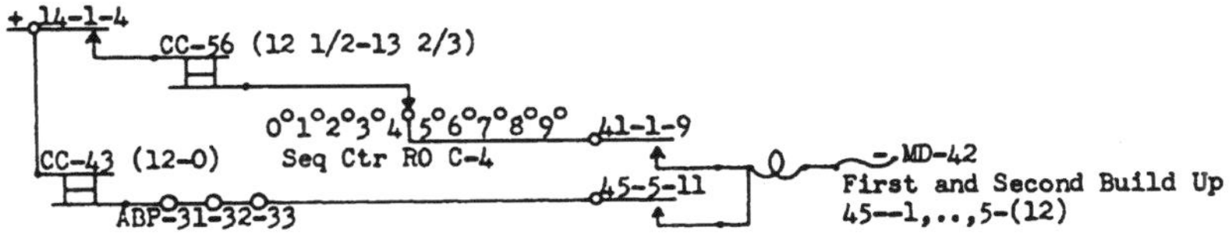
14-1-4 NC CC-57 (12 1/2-13 2/3) 41-1-10	Second Build Up 46-1,..,5-(12)	CC-43 (12-0) ABP-31-32-33 46-5-11	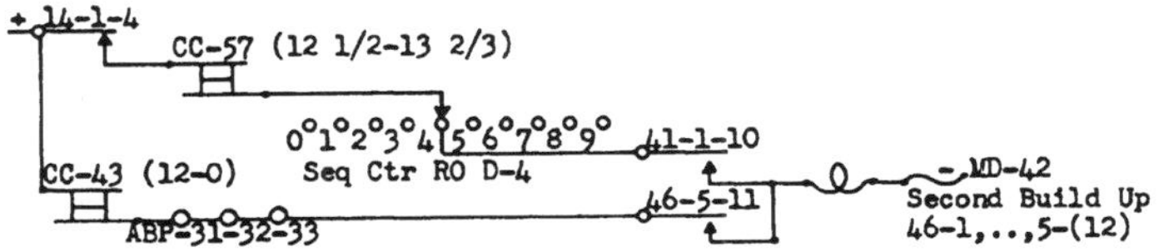
CC-76 (15-16 1/2) 45-5-2	MC-DR Entry Control (4-8) 93-1,2,3-(12)	CC-77 (16-0) 93-3-12	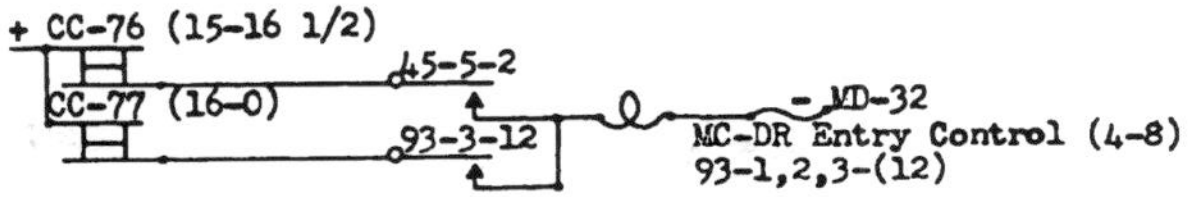

MULTIPLICATION CYCLE 4

The MP is read from storage to the intermediate counter as in cycle 1. The intermediate carry control and intermediate carry relays are picked up and the carry impulse completes the entry into the intermediate counter as in cycle 1. The entry of a nine into the 24th column of the intermediate counter (a negative MP) picks up the intermediate 24th column read-out control relay as in cycle 1. The second build up takes place; i.e., twice the MC is read from the doubling moldings of MC-DR (1-2) to MC-DR (4-8) and (5); six times the MC is read from the doubling moldings of MC-DR (3-6) to MC-DR (7) and (9). The MC-DR carry control and carry relays are picked up and the carry impulse completes the second build up as in cycle 3. The sequence counter is advanced to read-out position 5. In preparation for the next cycle the intermediate invert control and intermediate invert relays are picked up if MP is negative. The MP in relay is picked up.

Magnet
41 Multiply #1
38 Multiply #2
SC20-1,2,3 Storage Counter Out
50 Intermediate In
Intermediate Counter Magnets
23 Intermediate Carry Control
53 Intermediate Carry
89 Intermediate 24th column RO Control
71 Sign Control #2
45 First and Second Build Up
93 MC-DR Entry Control (4-8)
MC-DR Counter Magnets (4-8)
MC-DR Counter Magnets (5)
46 Second Build Up
MC-DR Counter Magnets (7)
MC-DR Counter Magnets (9)
26 MC-DR Carry Control
49 MC-DR Carry
Sequence Counter Magnet
94 Intermediate Invert Control
HD-1 Intermediate Invert
39 MP In

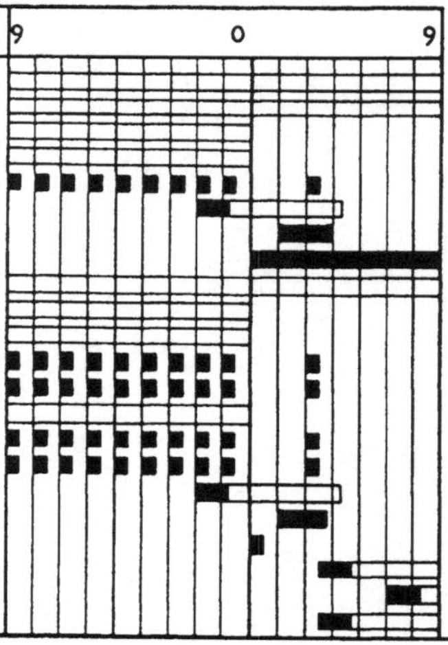

Pick Up Circuit	Magnet	Hold Circuit	Circuit Diagram
CC-1,..,9 HD-2-1,..,10NC HD-5-1,..,9 NC MC-DR (1-2) doubling RO			
45-1-1,.., 45-2-12	MC-DR Counter Magnets (4-8)		
45-3-1,.., 45-4-12	MC-DR Counter Magnets (5)		
46-1-1,.., 46-2-12	MC-DR Counter Magnets (7)		
46-3-1,.., 46-4-12	MC-DR Counter Magnets (9)		

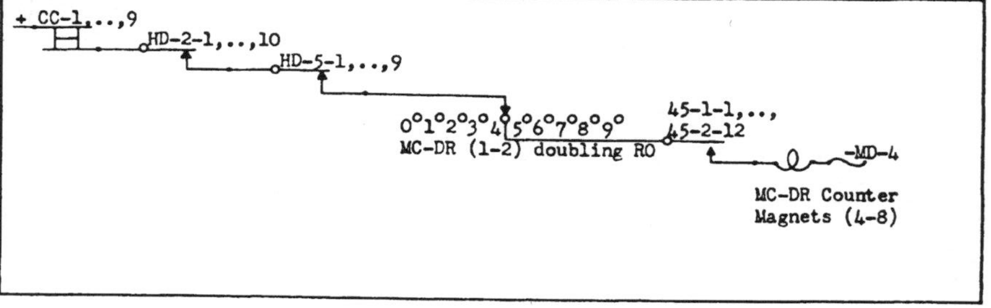

MULTIPLICATION CYCLE 4 -continued-

Pick Up Circuit	Magnet	Hold Circuit	Circuit Diagram
CC-10 (0-0 1/2) 38-3-3 14-1-3 NC 84-1-1 NC	Sequence Counter Magnet		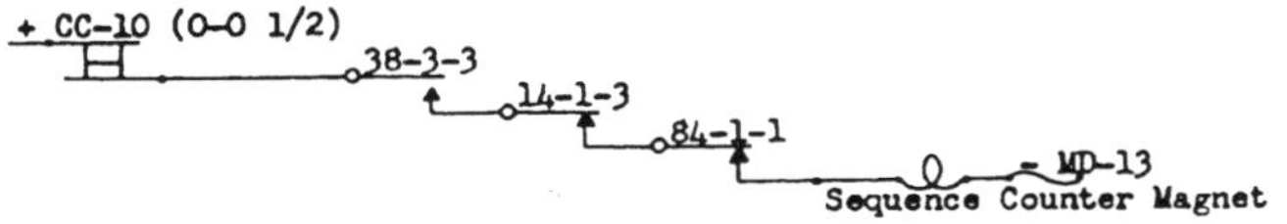
14-1-4 NC CC-57 (12 1/2-13 2/3) Seq Ctr RO D-5 41-1-12	Intermediate Invert Control 94-1-(4)	CC-43 (12-0) ABP-31-32-33 94-1-4	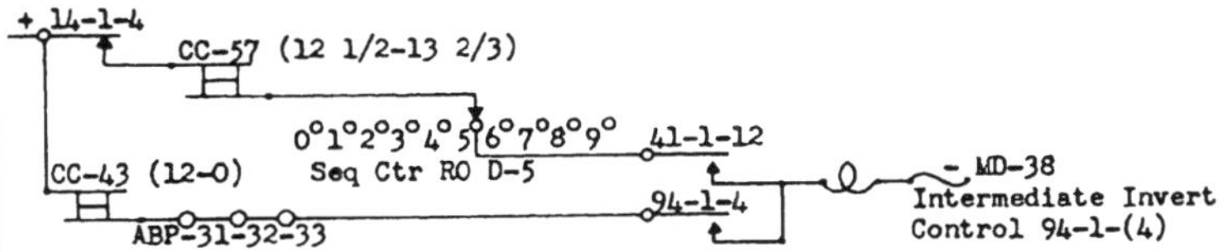
CC-69 (15-16 1/3) 94-1-1,2 9 in 24th col Intermediate Counter	Intermediate Invert HD-1-(12)	CC-43 (12-0) ABP-31-32-33 HD-1-12	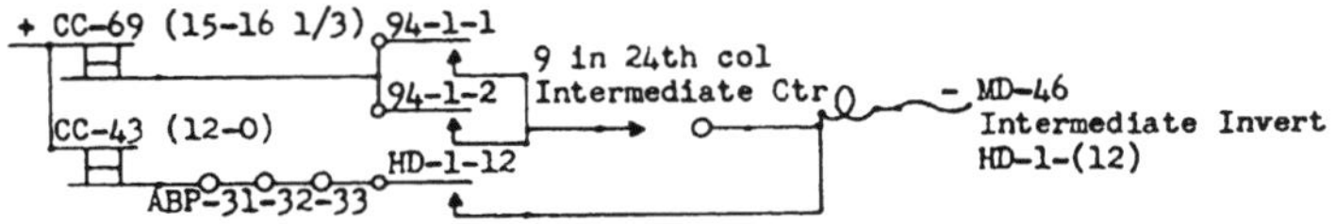
14-1-4 NC CC-55 (12 1/2-13 2/3) Seq Ctr RO C-5 41-1-11	MP In 39-1,2,3-(12)	CC-43 (12-0) ABP-31-32-33 39-3-11	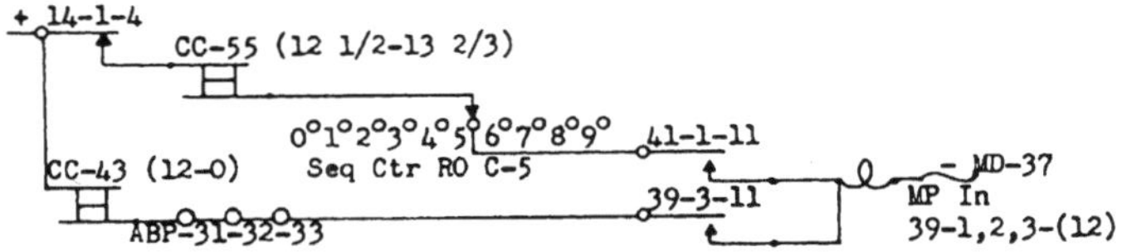

CYCLE 5

Sign Control #1 is picked up if the intermediate 24th column read-out control relay is up as in cycle 2. The positive absolute value of the MP reads from the intermediate counter to the MP counter and simultaneously the MP cycle control pick up relays, which are wired in parallel with the MP counter magnets, are energized. The MP cycle control hold relays are set up by their pick up coils. The MP-DIV control relay is picked up. The sequence counter is advanced to read-out position 6. The intermediate reset relay is picked up. The cycle counter is advanced to read-out position 1. The MP-DIV control hold relay is picked up preventing the sequence counter from advancing when CC-10 makes and further, preventing the passage of impulses from CC-55, 56 and 57 through the sequence counter read-out. The column shift left and right relays are picked up. Impulses through the column shift left and right relays and the 2nd read-out molding of the MP counter energize the required times left and right relays. If MP is zero, the C2, D2 and DD-PQ transfer #1 relays are picked up in place of the column shift relays as in cycle 8 (5 + n).

MULTIPLICATION CYCLE 5 -continued-

Magnet	9 0 9
41 Multiply #1 38 Multiply #2 89 Intermediate 24th column RO Control 70 Sign Control #1 71 Sign Control #2 94 Intermediate Invert Control HD-1 Intermediate Invert 39 MP In MP Counter Magnets 37 MP Cycle Control 13 MP-DIV Control Pick Up Sequence Counter Magnet 52 Intermediate Reset HD-4 Intermediate Reset Cycle Counter Magnet 14 MP-DIV Control Hold 21 Column Shift Left 29 Column Shift Right 4 Times Left 5 Times Right	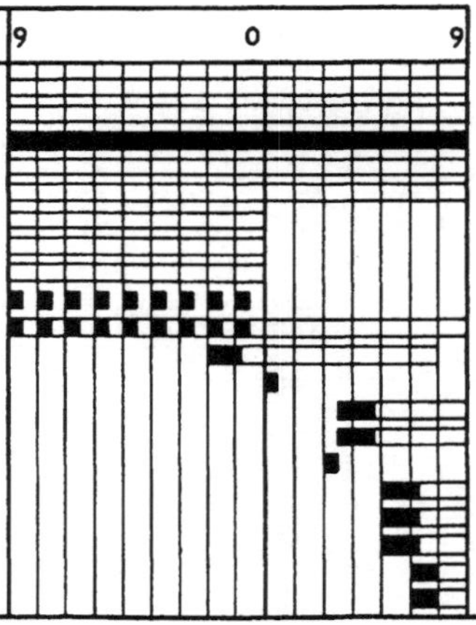

Pick Up Circuit	Magnet	Hold Circuit	Circuit Diagram
CC-1,..,9 HD-1-1,..,10 NC HD-4-1,..,9 NC Intermediate Counter RO 39-1-1,.., 39-2-11 40-2-1 NC,.., 40-3-11 NC	MP Counter Magnets MP Cycle Control Pick Up MP Cycle Control Hold 37-1,..,26-(4, 6 or 12)	CC-41 (12-15) ABP-34 or BBP-133 30-1-1,2,8,9 NC 31-1-1,2,8,9 NC and 37-2-3 37-4-3 37-5,..,10-12 37-11,12-6 37-13,14-4 37-16-3 37-17,..,22-12 37-23,24-6 37-25,26-4	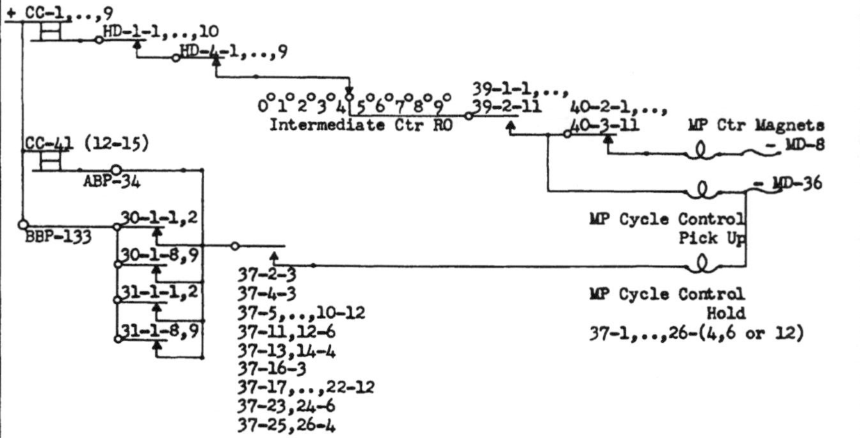

MULTIPLICATION CYCLE 5 -continued-

Pick Up Circuit	Magnet	Hold Circuit	Circuit Diagram
CC-26 (2-1 1/3) 39-2-12	MP-DIV Control Pick Up 13-1-(6)	CC-47 (3 1/2-16) 13-1-6	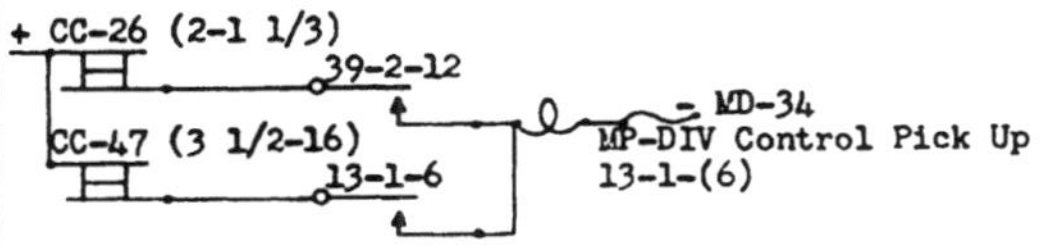
CC-10 (0-0 1/2) 38-3-3 14-1-3 NC 84-1-1 NC	Sequence Counter Magnet		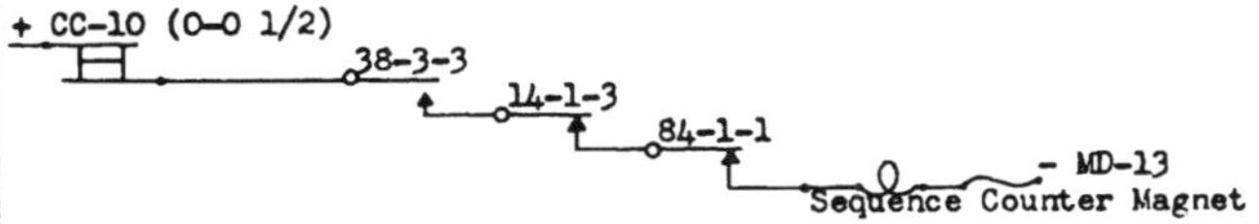
14-1-4 NC CC-57 (12 1/2-13 2/3) Seq Ctr RO D-6 41-2-1	Intermediate Reset 52-1,2,3-(12)	CC-43 (12-0) ABP-31-32-33 52-3-11	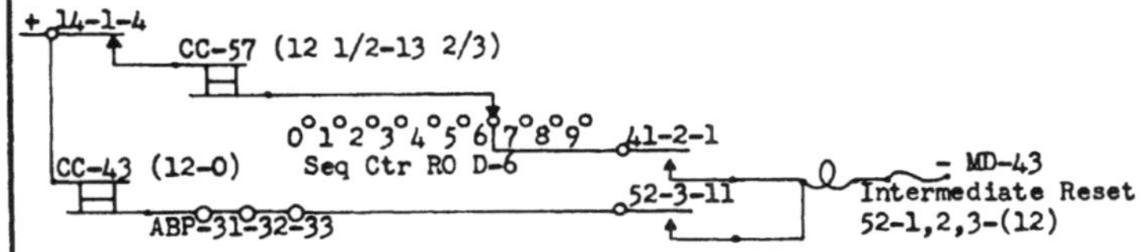
14-1-4 NC CC-57 (12 1/2-13 2/3) Seq Ctr RO D-6 41-2-1 CC-61 (12-0)	Intermediate Reset HD-4-(12)	CC-43 (12-0) ABP-31-32-33 52-3-11	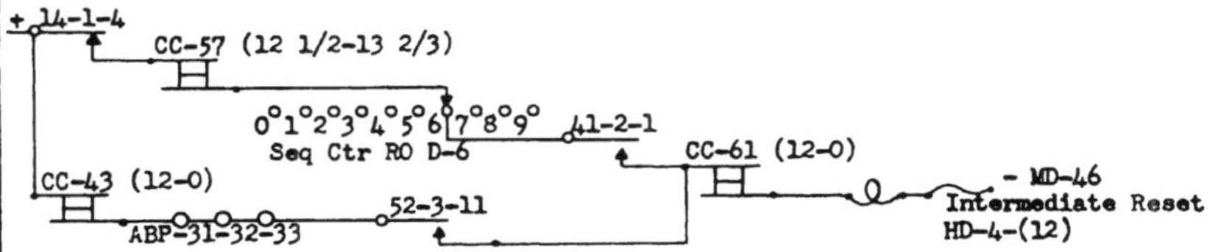
CC-80 (1/16 12-9) 7-1,..,9-2 NC 13-1-1 CC-54 (12-12 1/2)	Cycle Counter Magnet		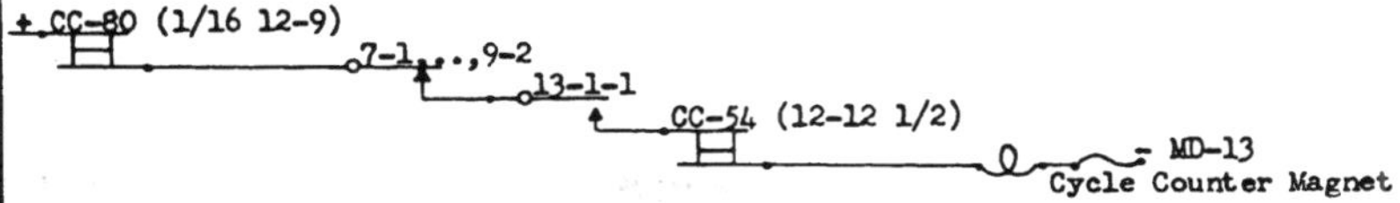

MULTIPLICATION CYCLE 5 -continued-

Pick Up Circuit	Magnet	Hold Circuit	Circuit Diagram
69-2-1,2 NC 13-1-3 CC-58 (14-15 1/3) 13-1-2	MP-DIV Control Hold 14-1-(12)	12-1,2-2 NC or CC-32 (8 1/2-2) and 14-1-11	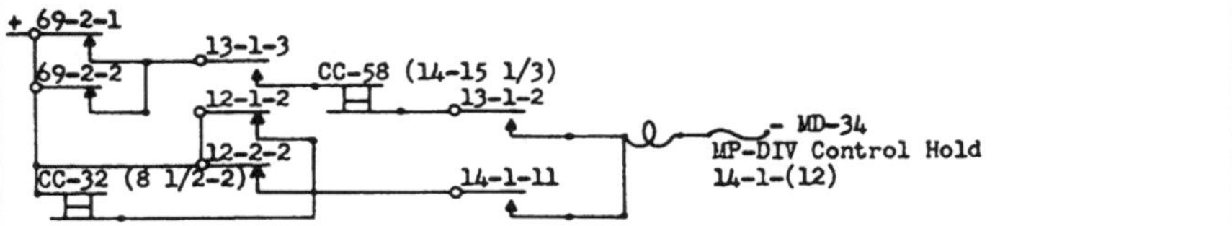
69-2-1,2 NC 13-1-3 CC-58 (14-15 1/3) 19-1-1 NC 18-1-1 NC Cycle Ctr RO A-1 38-1-1,.., 38-2-1 37-1-1,.., 37-14-2	Column Shift Right 29-1,..,36- (12,12,6)	CC-36 (12-0) ABP-27 29-3n-6	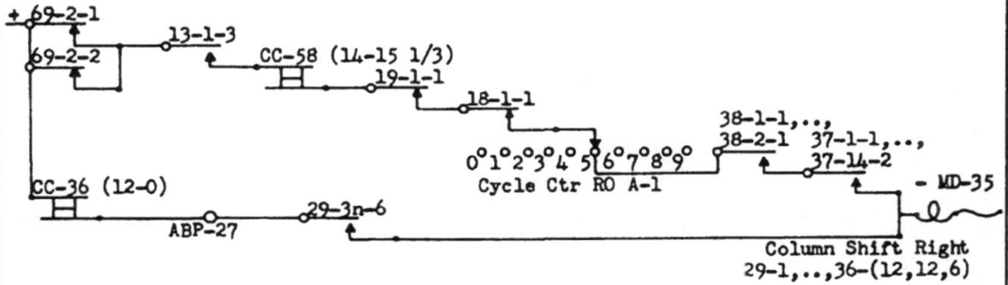
69-2-1,2 NC 14-1-1 CC-59 (14-15 1/3) 38-3-6 18-1-2 NC Cycle Ctr RO C-1 38-2-2,.., 38-3-1 37-15-1,.., 37-26-2	Column Shift Left 21-1,..,33- (12,12,6)	CC-36 (12-0) ABP-27 21-3n-6	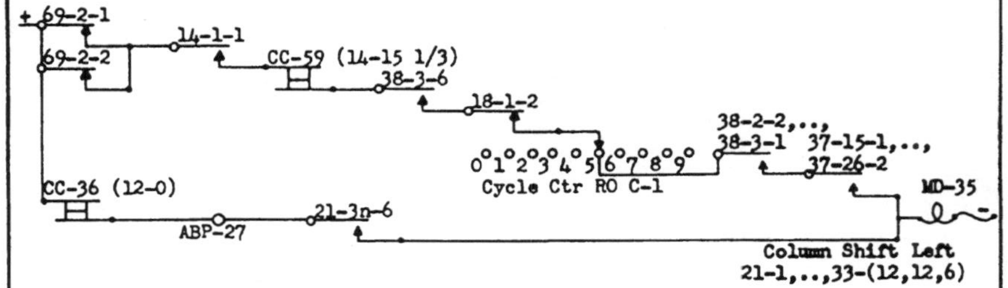
CC-78 (15-16) 29-3n-5 MP Ctr RO 2nd mldg (odd column)	Times Right 5-1,..,27- (12,12,4)	CC-36 (12-0) ABP-27 5-3n-4	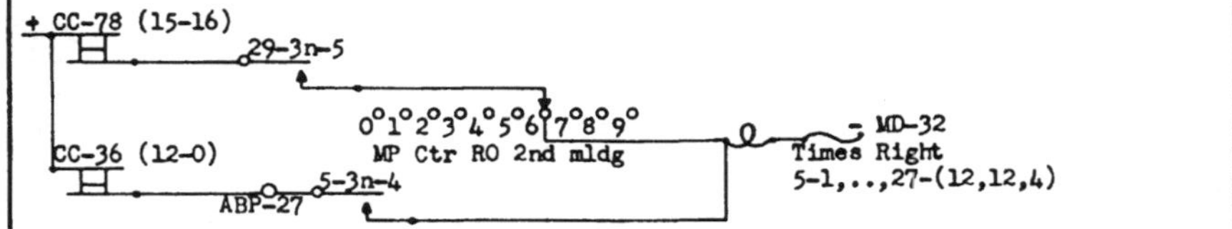

MULTIPLICATION CYCLE 5 -continued-

Pick Up Circuit	Magnet	Hold Circuit	Circuit Diagram
CC-78 (15-16) 21-3n-5 MP Ctr RO 2nd mldg (even column)	Times Left 4-1,..,27- (12,12,4)	CC-36 (12-0) ABP-27 4-3n-4	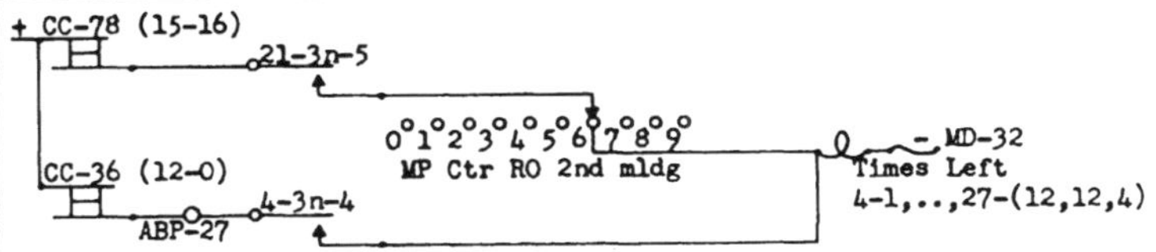

CYCLE 6

The intermediate counter resets as in cycle 3. Sign Control #1 drops out. If a nine stood in the 24th column of the intermediate counter a nine is read into the 47th column of the PQ counter as in cycle 3. The MC multiple selected by the times right relay is added into the PQ counter. The PQ carry control and PQ carry relays are picked up and the carry impulse completes the entry into the PQ counter. The MC multiple selected by the times left relay is added into the DD counter. The DD carry control and the DD carry relays are picked up and the carry impulse completes the entry into the DD counter. The cycle counter is advanced. As in cycle 5 the column shift left and right and times left and right relays are picked up. The MC multiples continue to be added in this manner in each successive cycle. When the cycle counter reaches read-out position 9, the E relay is picked up. If MP was zero, this cycle (6) combines with cycle (6 + n). The first DD-PQ transfer takes place and the relays terminating the multiplication process are picked up as in cycle (6 + n). Here n indicates the number of non-zero digits in the odd or even columns of the MP whichever is the greater.

Magnet	9 0 9
41 Multiply #1	
38 Multiply #2	
70 Sign Control #1	
71 Sign Control #2	
PQ 47th column Counter Magnet	
52 Intermediate Reset	
HD-4 Intermediate Reset	
Intermediate Counter Magnets	
37 MP Cycle Control	
14 MP-DIV Control	
21 Column Shift Left	
29 Column Shift Right	
4 Times Left	
5 Times Right	
PQ Counter Magnets	
24 PQ Carry Control	
62 PQ Carry	
DD Counter Magnets	
27 DD Carry Control	
61 DD Carry	
Cycle Counter Magnet	
17 E	

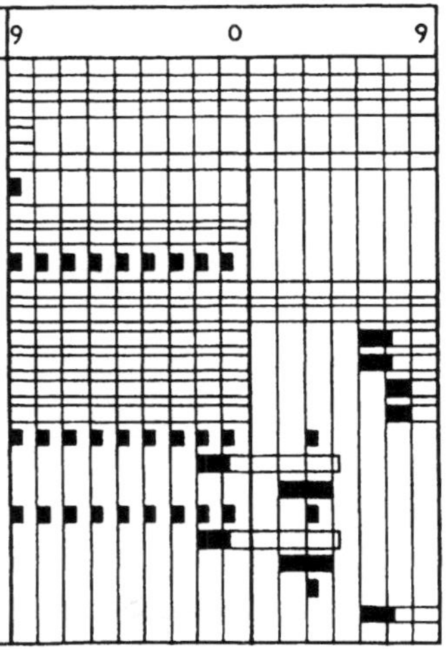

MULTIPLICATION CYCLE 6 -continued-

Pick Up Circuit	Magnet	Hold Circuit	Circuit Diagram
CC-1,..,9 HD-2-1,..,10 NC HD-5-1,..,9 NC MC-DR RO 5-1-1,..,5-26-12 3-19-1 NC,.., 3-20-12 NC 29-1-1,.., 29-36-12 56-3-1 NC,.., 56-6-9 NC	PQ Counter Magnets		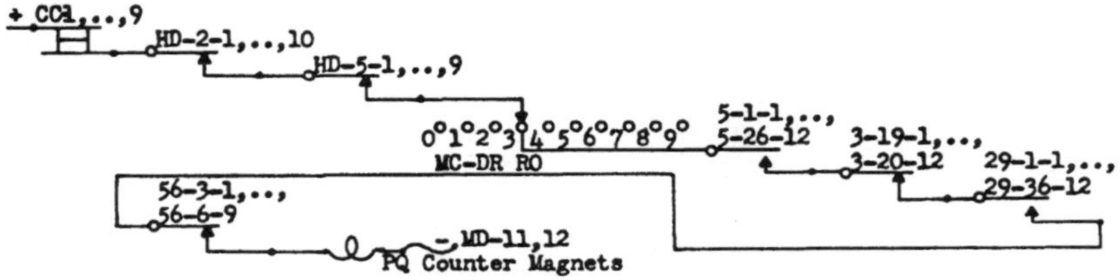
CC-44 (2-1 1/3) 5-3n-1 38-3-7	PQ Carry Control 24-1-(4)	CC-46 (2-13 1/3) ABP-35 24-1-4	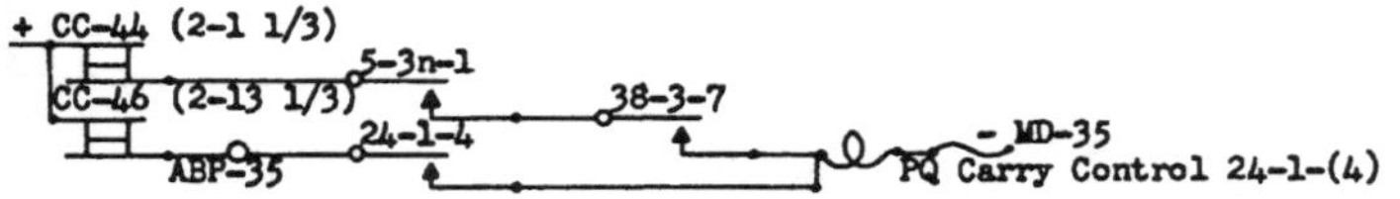
CC-45 (1/16 11-13) 24-1-1	PQ Carry 62-1,..,4-(12)		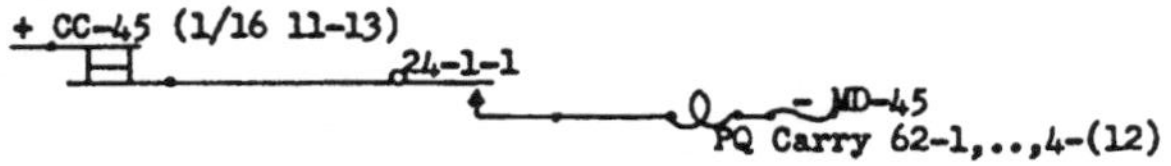
CC-1,..,9 HD-2-1,..,10 NC HD-5-1,..,9 NC MC-DR RO 4-1-1,..,4-26-12 56-1-1 NC,.., 56-2-12 NC 21-1-1,.., 21-36-12 3-21-1 NC,.., 3-24-9 NC	DD Counter Magnets		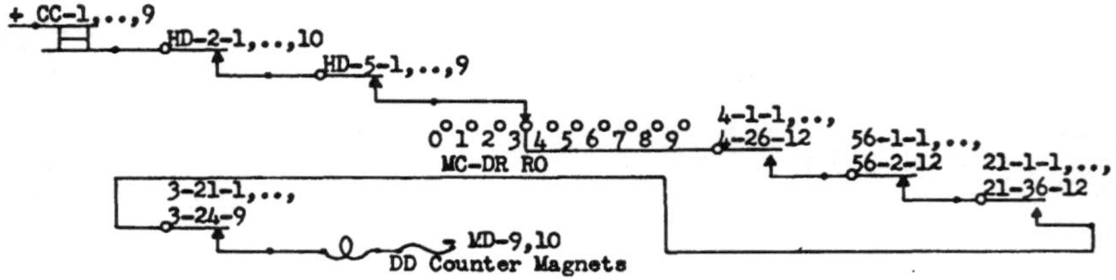
CC-44(2-1 1/3) 4-3n-1 38-3-8	DD Carry Control 27-1-(4)	CC-46(2-13 1/3) ABP-35 27-1-4	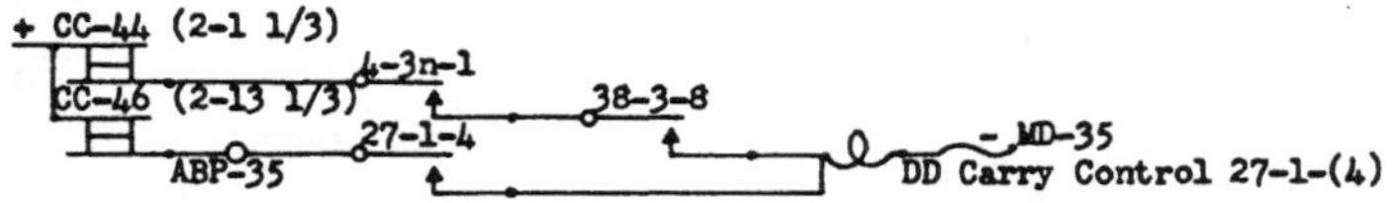
CC-45 (1/16 11-13) 27-1-1	DD Carry 61-1,..,4-(12)		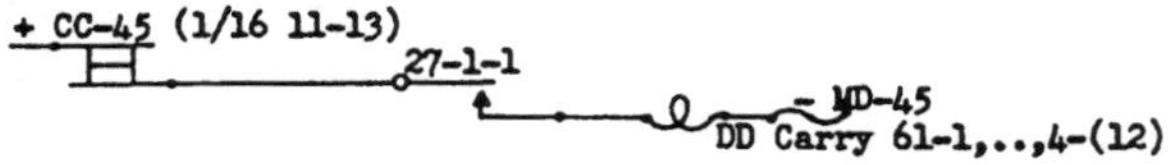

MULTIPLICATION CYCLE 6 -continued-

Pick Up Circuit	Magnet	Hold Circuit	Circuit Diagram
CC-12 (12-12 1/2) Carry BP PQ Counter Carry Contacts 62-1-1,.., 62-4-9 Carry Booster- 9-2,3 Carry Booster- 10-2,3 Carry Booster- 11-2,3	PQ Counter Magnets		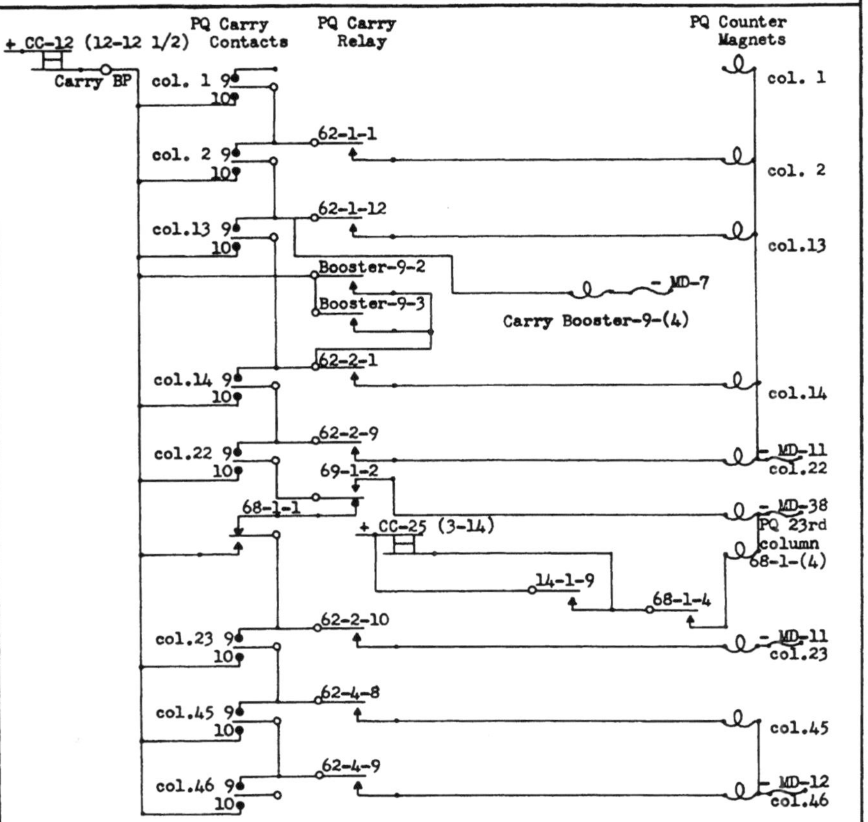 Carry Booster-10 lies between columns 24 and 25. Carry Booster-11 lies between columns 36 and 37.

MULTIPLICATION CYCLE 6 -continued-

Pick Up Circuit	Magnet	Hold Circuit	
CC-12 (12-12 1/2) Carry BP DD Counter Carry Contacts 61-1-1,.., 61-4-9 60-2,..,23-2 NC Carry Booster- 6-2,3 Carry Booster- 7-2,3 Carry Booster- 8-2,3	DD Counter Magnets		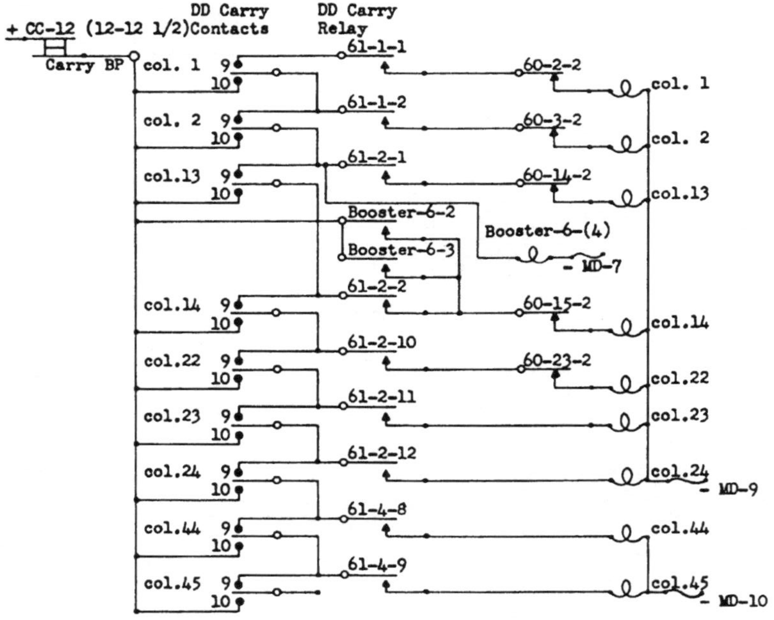 Carry Booster-7 lies between columns 24 and 25. Carry Booster-8 lies between columns 36 and 37.
CC-80 (1/16 12-9) 7-1,..,9-2 NC 14-1-5 CC-54 (12-12 1/2)	Cycle Counter Magnet		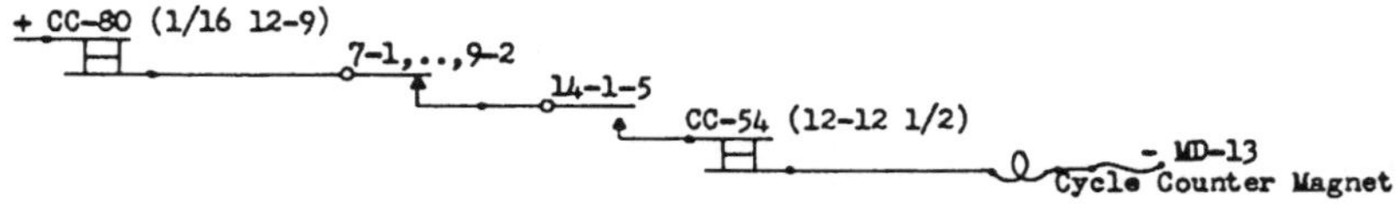

MULTIPLICATION CYCLE 6 -continued-

Pick Up Circuit	Magnet	Hold Circuit	Circuit Diagram
69-2-1,2 NC 14-1-1 CC-58 (14-15 1/3) 19-1-1 NC 18-1-1 NC Cycle Counter Carry Contact	E Relay 17-1-(4)	CC-36 (12-0) ABP-27 17-1-4	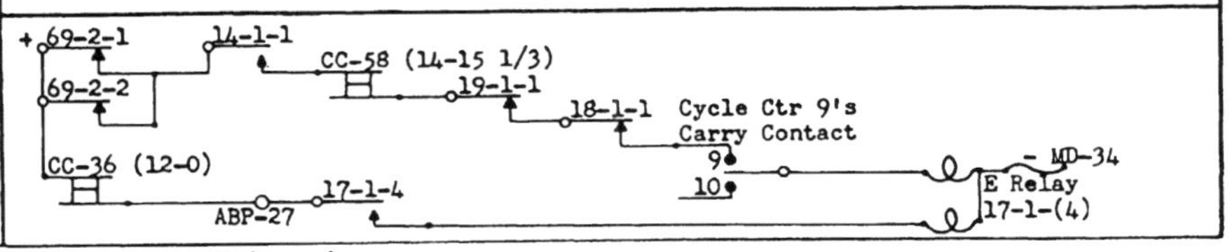

CYCLE 7 (4 + n)

The selected multiples are added into PQ and DD. The appropriate column shift left and right and times left and right relays are picked up. If the E relay was picked up in the previous cycle, the F relay is now picked up altering the read-outs of the cycle counter to read-outs B and D. The cycle counter is advanced as in the previous cycle.

Magnet	9 0 9
41 Multiply #1 38 Multiply #2 71 Sign Control #2 37 MP Cycle Control 14 MP-DIV Control 21 Column Shift Left 29 Column Shift Right 4 Times Left 5 Times Right PQ Counter Magnets 24 PQ Carry Control 62 PQ Carry DD Counter Magnets 27 DD Carry Control 61 DD Carry 17 E 18 F Cycle Counter Magnet	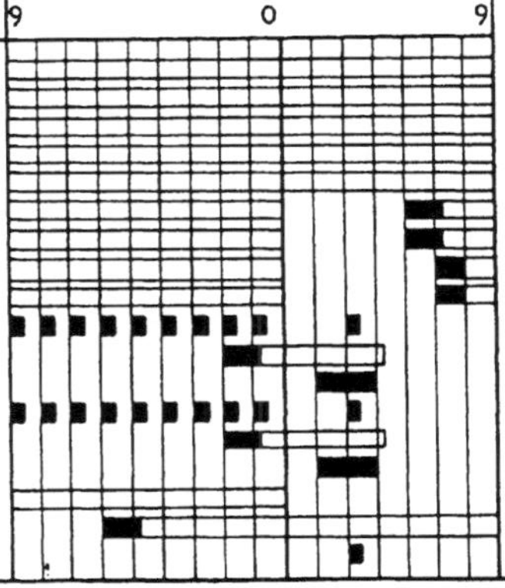

Pick Up Circuit	Magnet	Hold Circuit	Circuit Diagram
69-2-1,2 NC 14-1-1 CC-79 (6-5 1/2) 38-3-5 17-1-1	F Relay 18-1-(4)	12-1,2-2 NC or CC-32 (8 1/2-2) and 18-1-4	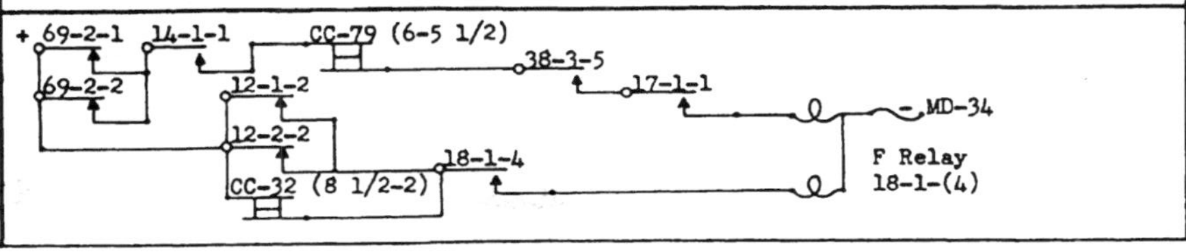

MULTIPLICATION CYCLE 8 (5 + n)

The successive multiples of MC are added to DD and PQ. The cycle counter is advanced. When all the significant figures in MP have been used, the C2, D2 and DD-PQ transfer #1 relays are energized.

Magnet
41 Multiply #1
38 Multiply #2
71 Sign Control #2
37 MP Cycle Control
14 MP-DIV Control
18 F
21 Column Shift Left
29 Column Shift Right
4 Times Left
5 Times Right
PQ Counter Magnets
24 PQ Carry Control
62 PQ Carry
DD Counter Magnets
27 DD Carry Control
61 DD Carry
Cycle Counter Magnet
66 C2
67 D2
74 DD-PQ Transfer #1

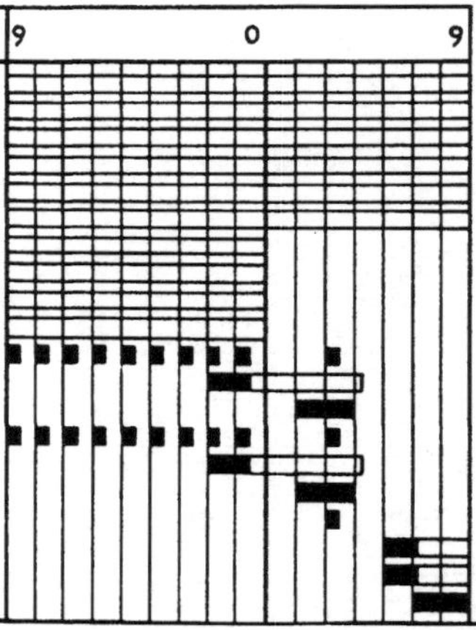

Pick Up Circuit	Magnet	Hold Circuit	Circuit Diagram
69-2-1,2 NC 14-1-1 CC-59 (14-15 1/3) 38-3-6 18-1-2 NC Cycle Ctr RO 38-2-2,..,38-3-1 37-26-2 NC 30-1-10 NC	C2 66-1-(4)	69-1-3 NC or CC-30 (1/16 3-1) and 66-1-4	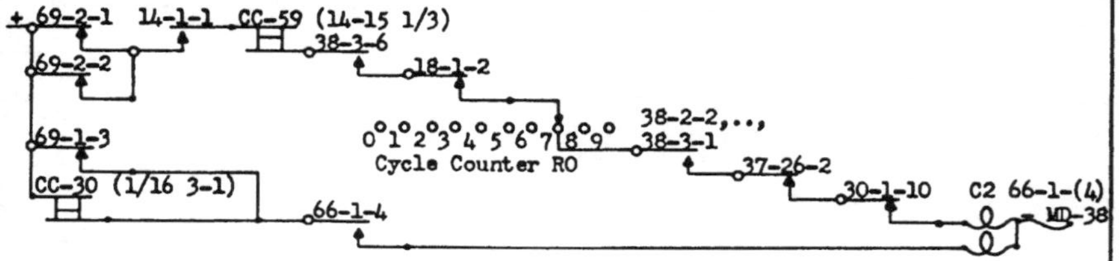
69-2-1,2 NC 14-1-1 CC-58 (14-15 1/3) 19-1-1 NC 18-1-1 NC Cycle Ctr RO 38-1-1,..,38-2-1 37-14-2 NC 31-1-10 NC	D2 67-1-(4)	69-1-3 NC or CC-30 (1/16 3-1) and 67-1-4	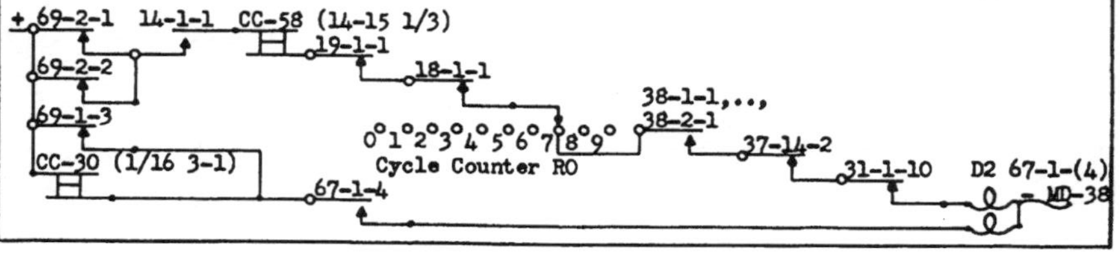

Pick Up Circuit	Magnet	Hold Circuit	Circuit Diagram
CC-40 (1/16 15-9) 66-1-1 67-1-1	DD-PQ Transfer #1 74-1,2-(12) 74-3-(4)	CC-43 (12-0) ABP-31-32-33 74-3-4	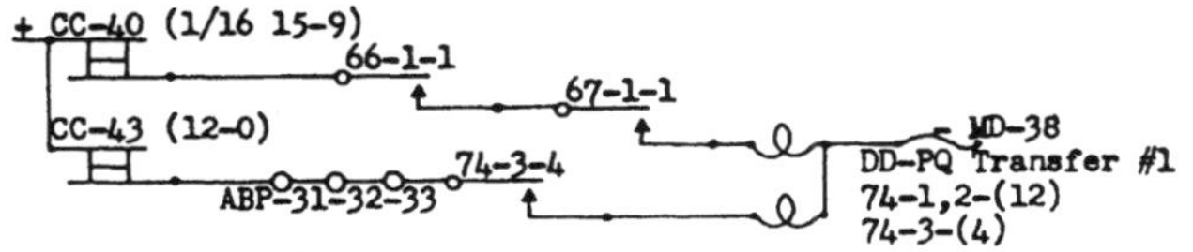

CYCLE 9 (6 + n)

The first DD-PQ transfer takes place. Columns 1-22 of DD are added to columns 1-22 of PQ. The usual carry circuits are set up in the PQ counter. The CD control relay picks up which permits the C and D relays to be energized. Picking up C and D drops out the MP cycle control hold relays. The cycle counter is advanced. The energized C and D relays permit DD-PQ transfer #2, MP reset and MC-DR reset to be picked up. The MC-DR entry control relays are picked up. The pick up of MC-DR reset drops out sign control #2. If MP was zero, this cycle combines with cycle 6.

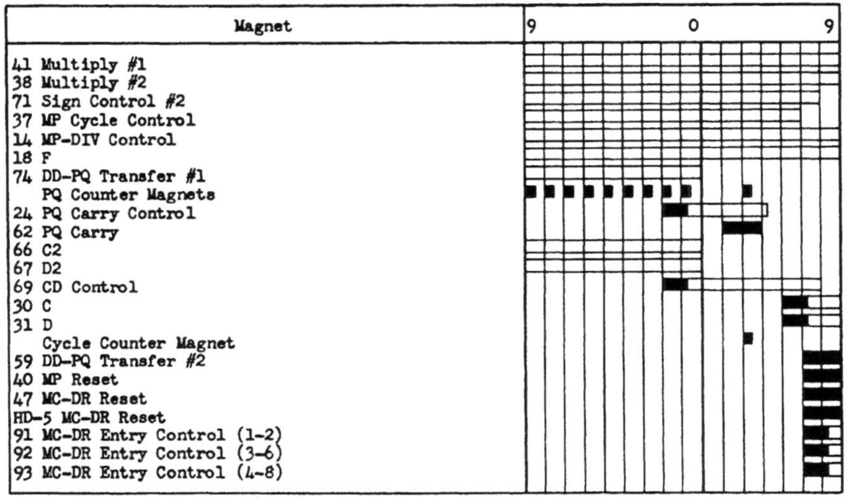

MULTIPLICATION CYCLE 9 (6 + n) -continued-

Pick Up Circuit	Magnet	Hold Circuit	Circuit Diagram
CC-1,..,9 HD-3-1,..,10 NC HD-6-1,..,9 NC DD Counter RO 74-1-1,.., 74-2-10	PQ Counter Magnets		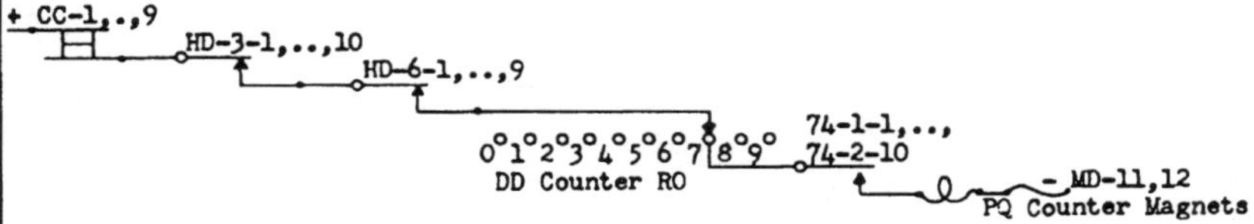
CC-44 (2-1 1/3) 74-3-1	PQ Carry Control 24-1-(4)	CC-46 (2-13 1/2) ABP-35 24-1-4	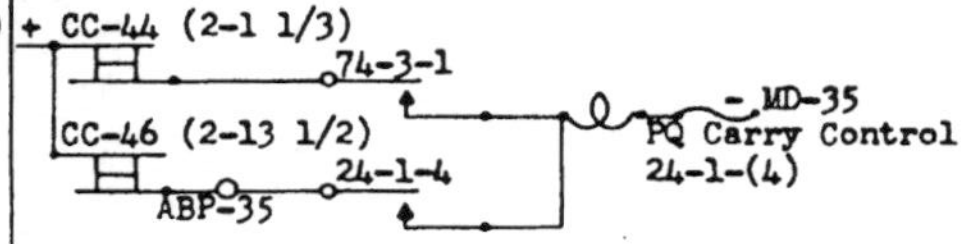
CC-26 (2-1 1/3) 74-2-11	CD Control 69-1,2-(4)	CC-47 (3 1/2-16) 69-1-4	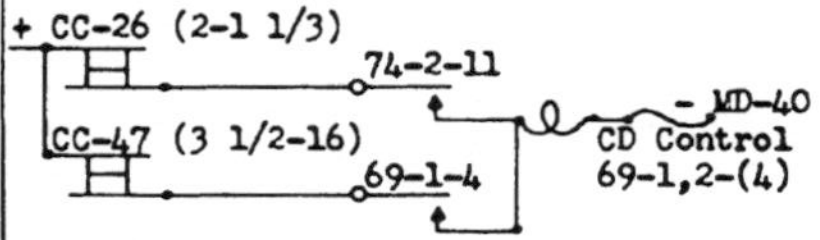
CC-33 (14-15 1/3) 69-1-1	C Relay 30-1-(12) D Relay 31-1-(12)	CC-38 (11 1/2-9) 30-1-11 31-1-11	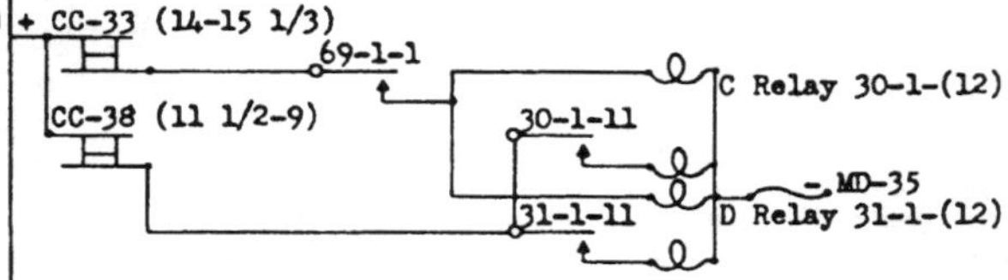
CC-40 (1/16 15-9) 30-1-3 31-1-3	DD-PQ Transfer #2 59-1,2-(12) 59-3-(6)	CC-43 (12-0) ABP-31-32-33 59-3-6	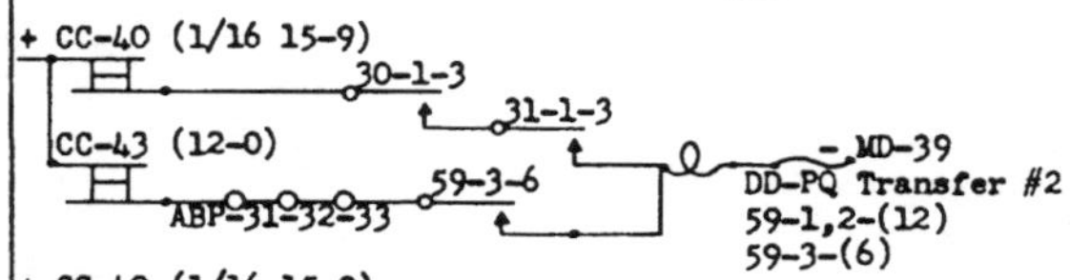
CC-40 (1/16 15-9) 30-1-3 31-1-3	MP Reset 40-1,2,3-(12)	CC-43 (12-0) ABP-31-32-33 40-3-12	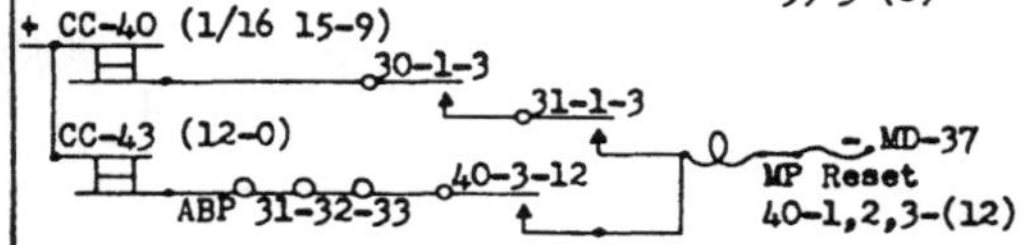

MULTIPLICATION CYCLE 9 (6 + n) -continued-

Pick Up Circuit	Magnet	Hold Circuit	Circuit Diagram
CC-40 (1/16 15-9) 30-1-3 31-1-3 41-2-4	MC-DR Reset 47-1,..,13-(12)	CC-43 (12-0) ABP-31-32-33 47-13-10,11,12	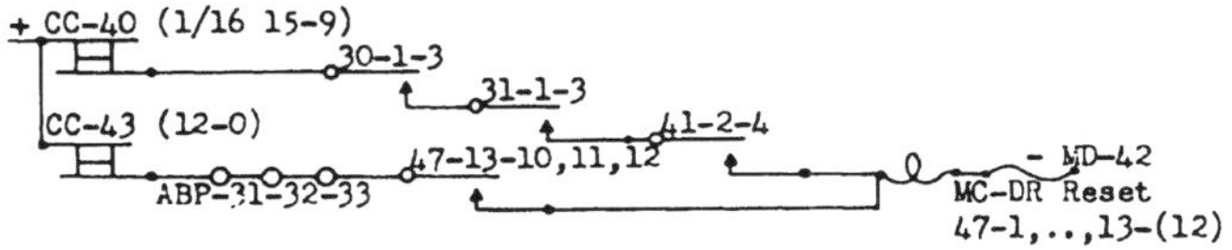
CC-40 (1/16 15-9) 30-1-3 31-1-3 41-2-4 CC-63 (12-0)	MC-DR Reset HD-5-(12)	CC-43 (12-0) ABP-31-32-33 47-13-10,11,12 CC-63 (12-0)	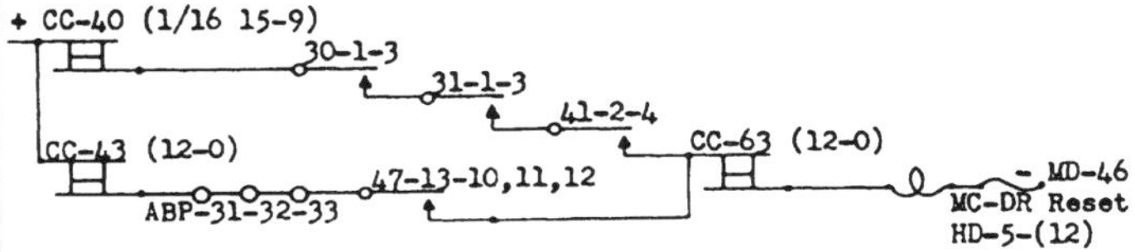
CC-76 (15-16 1/3) 47-13-2	MC-DR Entry Control (1-2) 91-1,2,3-(12)	CC-77 (16-0) 91-3-12	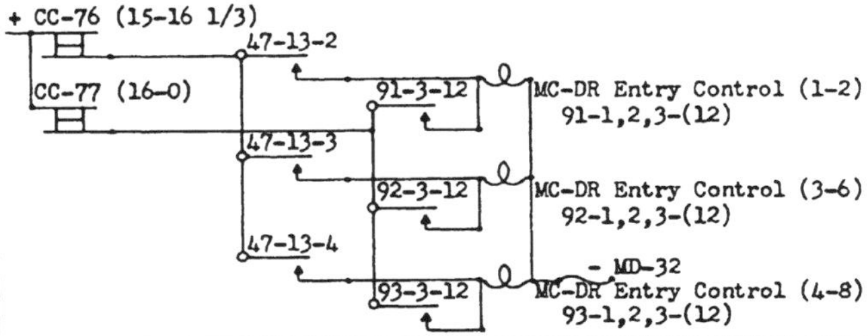
47-13-3	MC-DR Entry Control (3-6) 92-1,2,3-(12)	92-3-12	
47-13-4	MC-DR Entry Control (4-8) 93-1,2,3-(12)	93-3-12	

CYCLE 10 (7 + n)

The second DD to PQ transfer, adding columns 23-45 of DD to columns 23-45 of PQ takes place. The usual carry circuits are set up in the PQ counter. The MC-DR, MP and cycle counters reset. The A relay is picked up, and the B relay also if PQ 47th column nines carry contact is closed. Energizing of the A relay will cause the MP-DIV control relay to drop out and prevent further advance of the cycle counter. The sequence counter advances to read-out position 7. In preparation for the next cycle, the product out and sequence counter reset relays are picked up. If the B relay is energized, the PQ invert relay is picked up. Assuming the product is to be delivered to storage counter 40, code 64, the sequence mechanism reads the line of coding (blank, 64, 7). The sequence relays are picked up. The repeat relay and the storage counter in relays are energized.

MULTIPLICATION CYCLE 10 (7 + n) -continued-

Magnet
41 Multiply #1
38 Multiply #2
59 DD-PQ Transfer #2
PQ Counter Magnets
24 PQ Carry Control
62 PQ Carry
47 MC-DR Reset
HD-5 MC-DR Reset
91 MC-DR Entry Control (1-2)
MC-DR Counter Magnets (1-2)
92 MC-DR Entry Control (3-6)
MC-DR Counter Magnets (3-6)
93 MC-DR Entry Control (4-8)
MC-DR Counter Magnets (4-8)
MC-DR Counter Magnets (5)
MC-DR Counter Magnets (7)
MC-DR Counter Magnets (9)
40 MP Reset
MP Counter Magnets
14 MP-DIV Control
Cycle Counter Magnet
18 F
12 A
16 B
Sequence Counter Magnet
34 Product Out
48 Sequence Counter Reset
HD-3 DD-PQ Invert
Seq-31 Control
Seq-B-6-1
Seq-B-4-1,2
Seq-C-7-1
Seq-27 Repeat
SC40-4,5,6 Storage Counter In

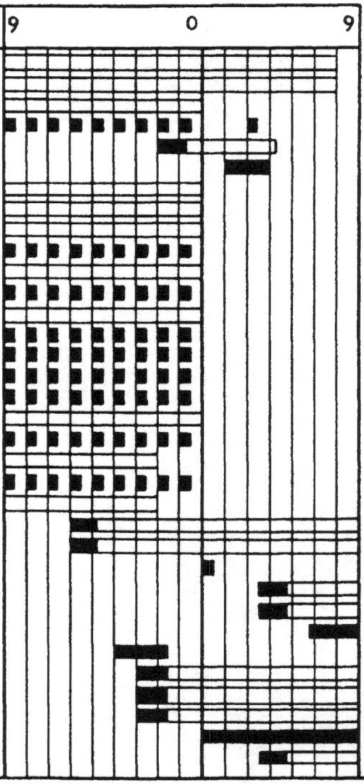

Pick Up Circuit	Magnet	Hold Circuit	Circuit Diagram
CC-1,..,9 HD-3-1,..,10 NC HD-6-1,..,9 NC DD Counter RO 59-1-1,.., 59-2-11	PQ Counter Magnets		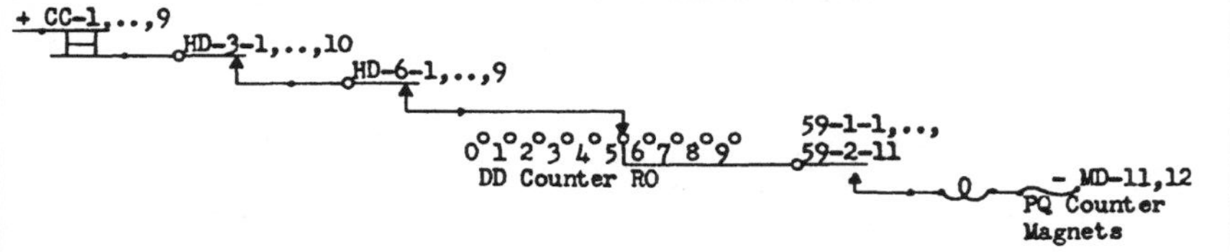

MULTIPLICATION CYCLE 10 (7 + n) -continued-

Pick Up Circuit	Magnet	Hold Circuit	Circuit Diagram
CC-44 (2-1 1/3) 59-3-1	PQ Carry Control 24-1-(4)	CC-46 (2-13 1/3) ABP-35 24-1-4	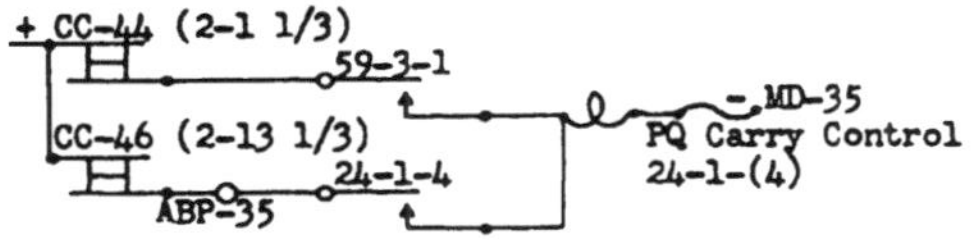
CC-1,..,9 HD-5-1,..,9 MC-DR RO 47-1-1,.., 47-12-12	MC-DR Counter Magnets		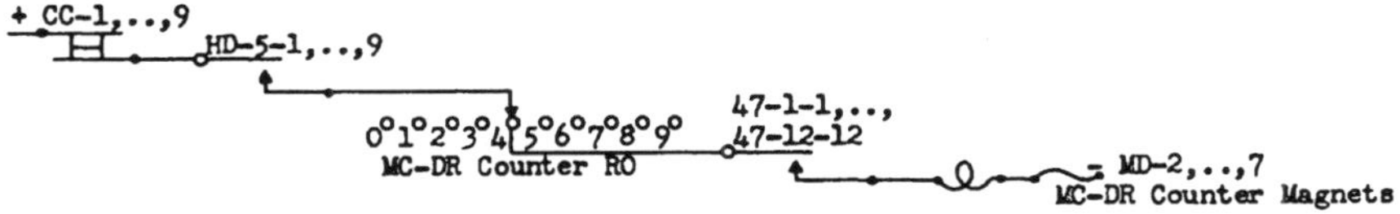
CC-1,..,9 40-1-1,..,9 MP Counter RO 40-2-1,.., 40-3-11	MP Counter Magnets		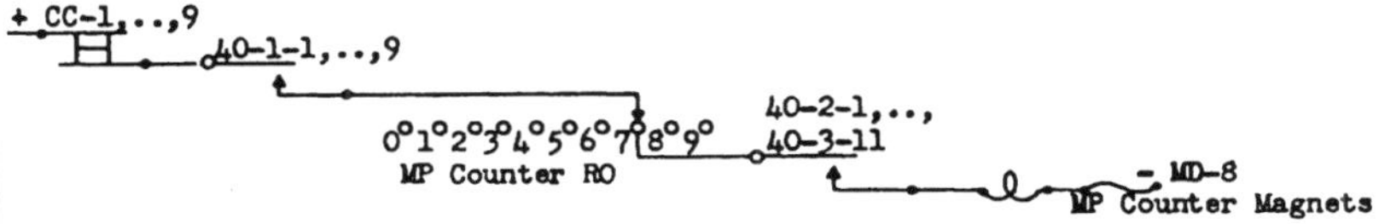
CC-1,..,9 Cycle Counter RO 59-3-3 or 47-2-12	Cycle Counter Magnet		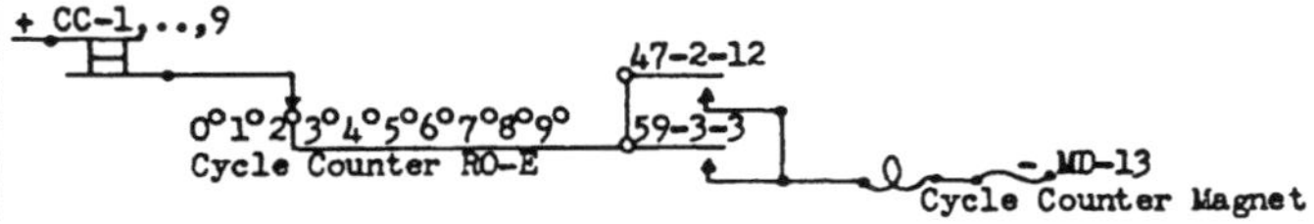
69-2-1,2 NC 14-1-1 CC-60 (6-5 1/3) 59-3-2	A Relay 12-1,2-(4)	CC-29 (6-8) 12-1-4	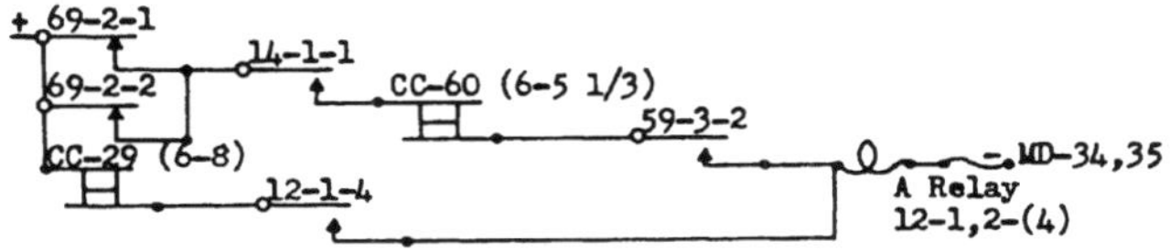
69-2-1,2 NC 14-1-1 CC-60 (6-5 1/3) 59-3-2 PQ 47th column 9's carry contact	B Relay 16-1-(4)	CC-29 (6-8) 16-1-4	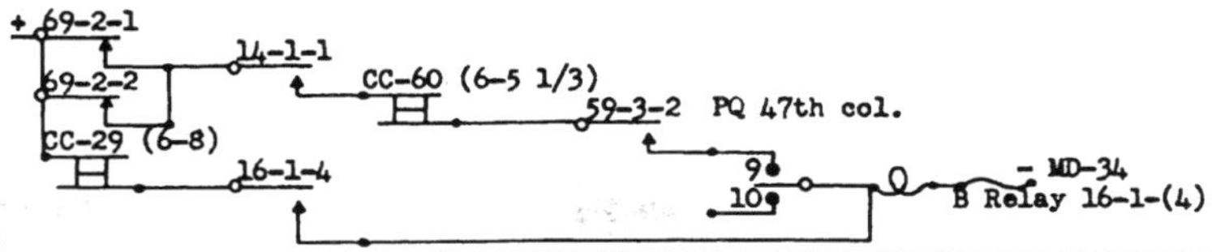

MULTIPLICATION CYCLE 10 (7 + n) -continued-

Pick Up Circuit	Magnet	Hold Circuit	Circuit Diagram
CC-10 (0-0 1/2) 38-3-3 14-1-3 NC 84-1-1 NC	Sequence Counter Magnet		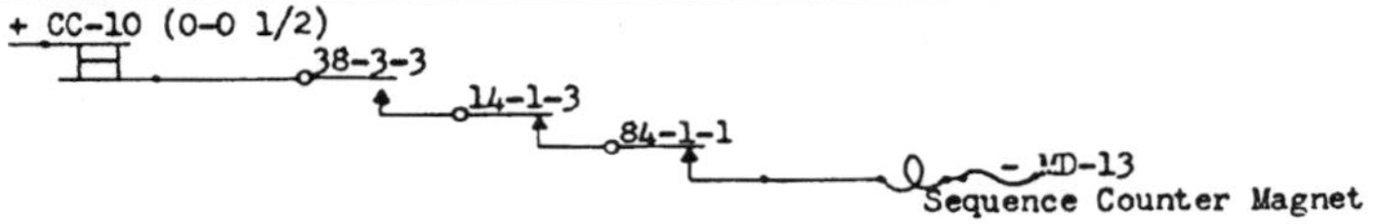
14-1-4 NC CC-57 (12 1/2-13 2/3) Seq Ctr RO D-7 41-2-3 and 41-2-6	Product Out 34-3-(12) 34-1,2-(12) 34-4-(4)	CC-43 (12-0) ABP-31-32-33 34-3-12 CC-43 (12-0) ABP-31-32-33 34-4-4	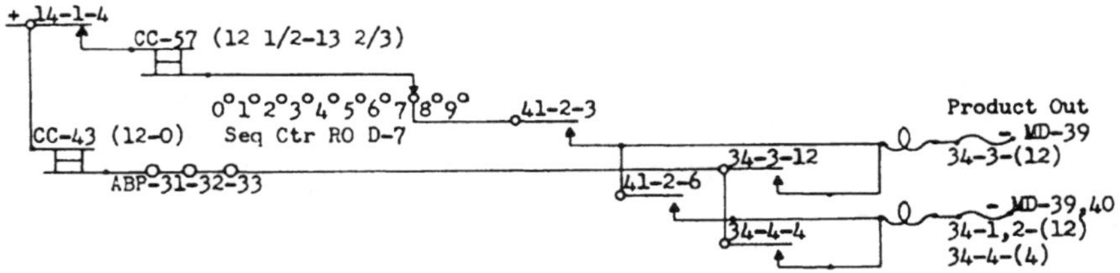
14-1-4 NC CC-55 (12 1/2-13 2/3) Seq Ctr RO B-7 41-2-2	Sequence Counter Reset 48-1-(12)	CC-43 (12-0) ABP-31-32-33 48-1-6	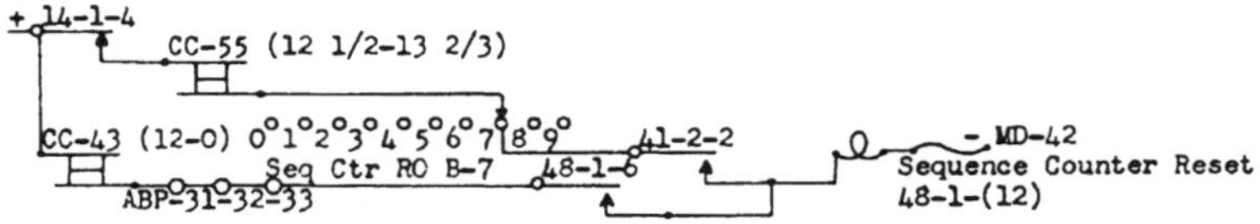
CC-40 (1/16 15-9) 229-3-2 NC 16-1-1	DD-PQ Invert HD-3-(12) and HD-3-(4)wc	CC-43 (12-0) ABP-31-32-33 HD-3-12	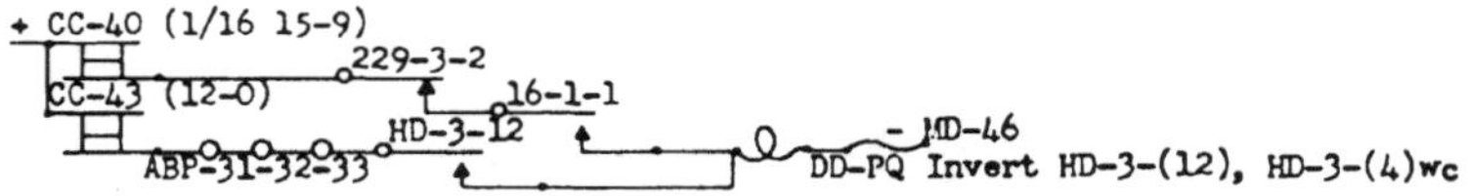
FC-105 (4-2 1/2) Seq Cut-off Sw. Card Feed #1 Sw. Card Feed #2 Sw. BBP-64 12-1,2-3 55-3-2 NC 78-2-8 NC 81-2-9 NC BBP-52, FBP-99 201-1-2 NC FBP-98 Seq-32-1,2 NC	Control Seq-31-(4) Clutch Magnet		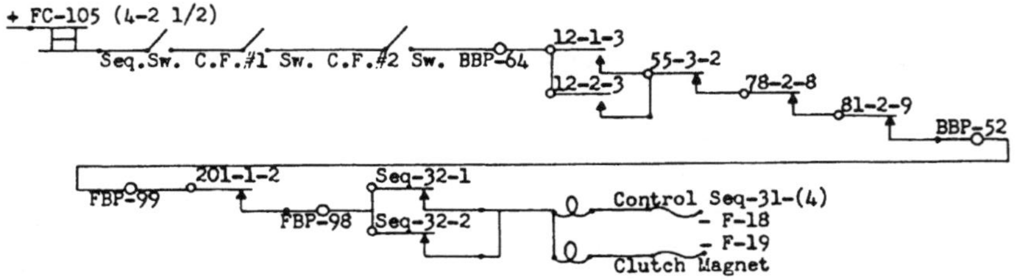

MULTIPLICATION CYCLE 10 (7 + n) -continued-

Pick Up Circuit	Magnet	Hold Circuit	Circuit Diagram
FC-101 (3-2 1/2) VBP-100 Seq-31-1,..,4 Reading Pins	B-6-1-(6) B-4-1-(12) B-4-2-(6) C-7-1-(4)	FC-102 (4-9 3/4) VBP-225 B-6-1-6 B-4-2-6 C-7-1-4	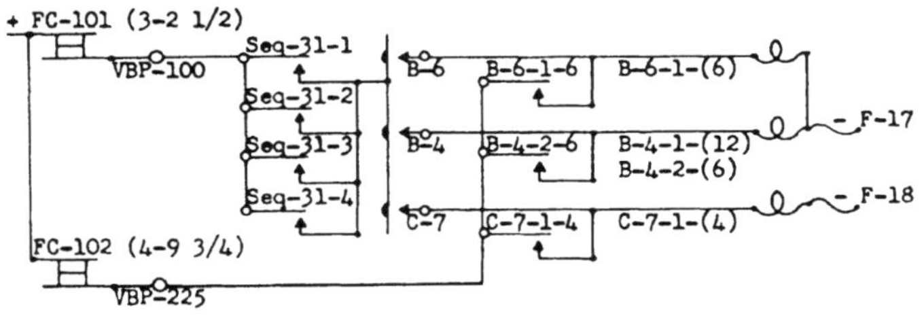
FC-107 (0-5 1/4) VBP-280 C-7-1-1	Repeat Relay Seq-27-(4)	FC-107 (0-5 1/4) VBP-280 Seq-27-4	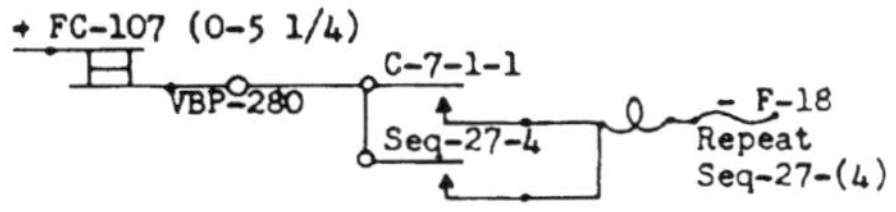
FC-93 (12 1/2-13 2/3) VBP-149 B-8-1-1 NC B-7-1-1 NC B-6-1-1 B-5-1-2 NC B-4-1-3 B-3-1-6 NC B-2-1-11 NC B-1-2-9 NC	Storage Counter #40 In SC40-4,5-(12) SC40-6-(4)	SC-11 (12-0) SC40-6-4	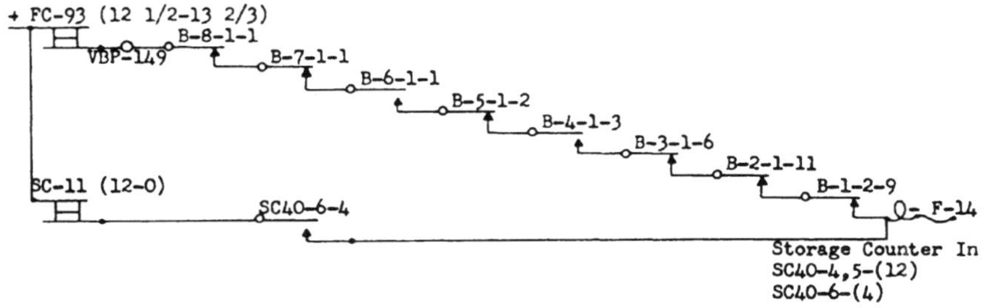

CYCLE 11 (8 + n)

The product is read from the PQ counter to storage. The storage counter carry is completed. The sequence counter and the 47th column of PQ counter are reset. The repeat relay permits the energizing of the start relay. The calculator continues in operation.

MULTIPLICATION CYCLE 11 (8 + n) -continued-

Magnet	9 0 9
34 Product Out HD-3 DD-PQ Invert SC40-4,5,6 Storage Counter In Storage Counter Magnet SC40-9 Storage Counter Carry Control SC40-7,8 Storage Counter Carry 12 A 16 B 48 Sequence Counter Reset Sequence Counter Magnet PQ 47th column Counter Magnet Seq-27 Repeat Seq-33 Start Seq-31 Control Seq Relays	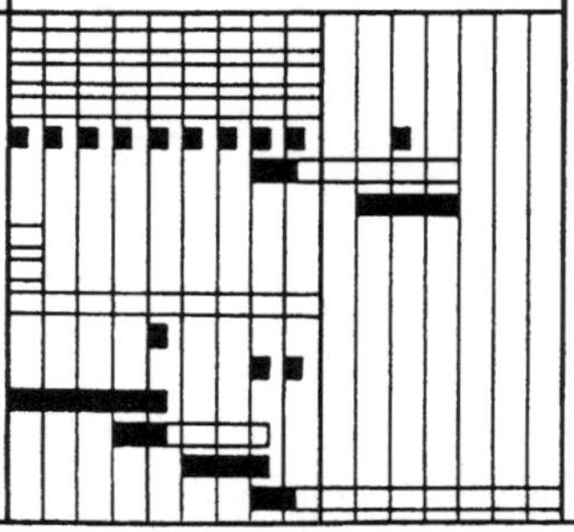

Pick Up Circuit	Magnet	Hold Circuit	Circuit Diagram
CC-1,..,9 HD-3-1,..,9 NC HD-3-10 HD-6-1,..,9 NC PQ Counter RO Plug Wires 34-1-1,.., 34-2-11 Buss SC40-4,5-(12)	Storage Counter Magnet (cols. 1-23)		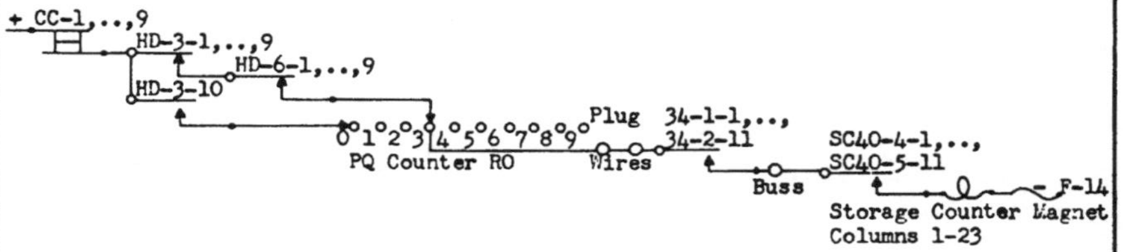
CC-5 (5-5 1/2) Seq Ctr RO BBP-43 78-2-10 NC 83-1-4 NC 80-1-1 NC BBP-44 FBP-176 238-1-2 NC FBP-177 BBP-45 82-1-4 NC 42-2-5 NC 55-2-9 NC 15-1-1 NC 48-1-2	Sequence Counter Magnet		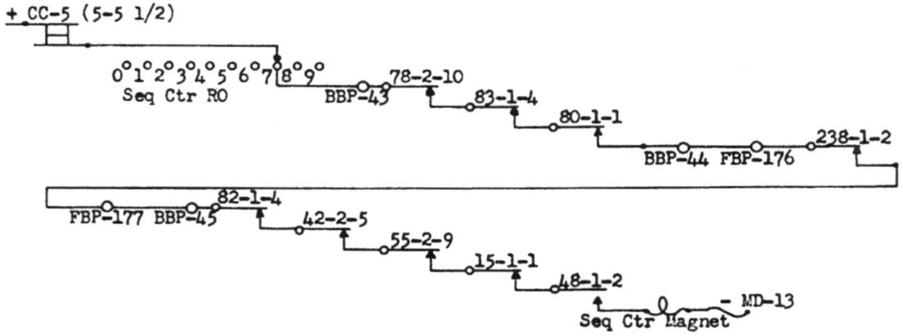

MULTIPLICATION CYCLE 11 (8 + n) -continued-

Pick Up Circuit	Magnet	Hold Circuit	Circuit Diagram
CC-9 (9-9 1/2) HD-3-10 Col.46 zero Col.47 zero or 8 HD-3-11 Col.47 9 spot Plug Wires 34-2-12 Buss SC40-5-12	Read 9 from 47th col. of PQ to 24th col. of storage counter		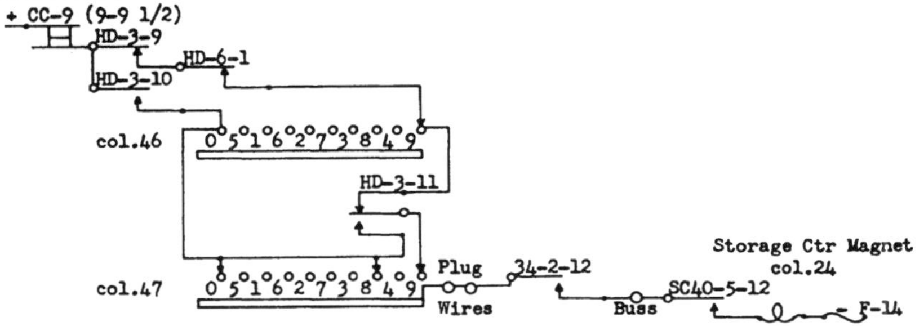
CC-2 (2-2 1/2) 71-1-3 NC CC-1 (1-1 1/2) 71-1-2 NC PQ 47th column RO 34-3-9	PQ 47th column Counter Magnet		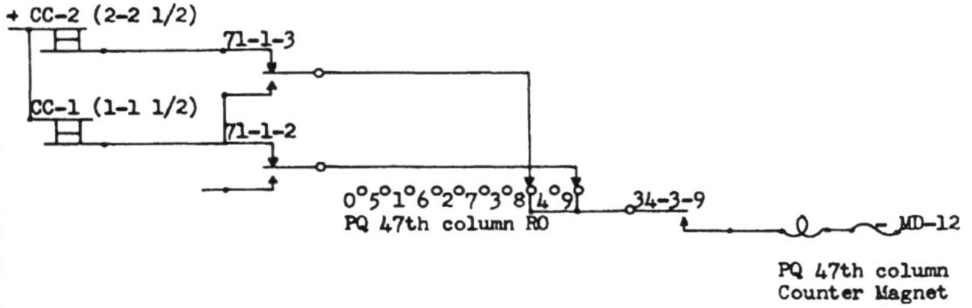
Seq-27-1 VBP-276 FC-103 (6-5 1/2) VBP-277 Seq-27-2	Start Seq-33-(4)	FC-108 (6-2 1/2) VBP-278 Seq-33-4	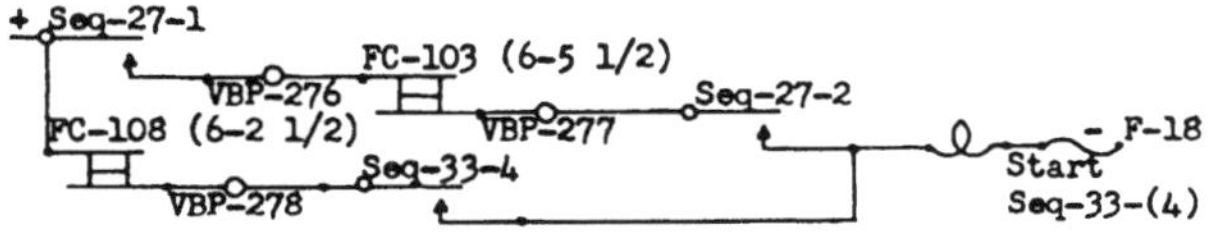
FC-105 (4-2 1/2) Sequence Cut-off Switch Card Feed #1 Sw. Card Feed #2 Sw. BBP-64 Seq-33-1 Seq-32-1,2 NC	Control Seq-31-(4)		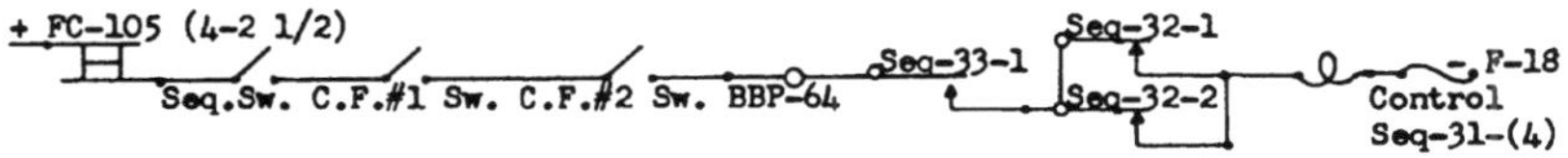

READ-OUT of PQ LOW-ORDER COLUMNS

CYCLE 11 (8 + n). Assuming that the low order columns of the product are to be delivered to storage counter 3, code 21, the sequence mechanism reads the line of coding (86, 21, 7). The sequence relays are picked up. The special PQ out relay, the repeat relay and the storage counter in relay are energized. If the B relay is energized, the special sign relay and the DD-PQ invert relay are picked up.

CYCLE 12 (9 + n). The storage counter magnets are energized and the storage counter carry circuits completed. The repeat relay permits the energizing of the start relay. The calculator continues in operation.

Magnet	9 Cycle 11 9	Cycle 12 9
Sequence Relays		
100-1 Special Sign		
99-1,2,3 Special PQ Out		
HD-3, HD-3 wc DD-PQ Invert		
Storage Counter Magnets		

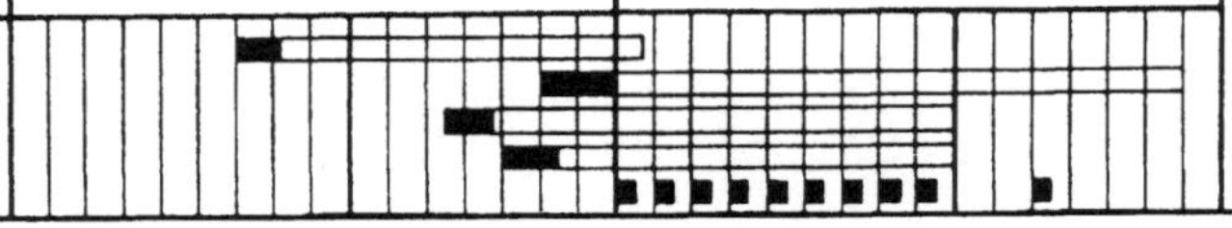

Pick Up Circuit	Magnet	Hold Circuit
FC-92 (12 1/2-13 2/3) VBP-150 A-8-1-1 A-7-1-2 NC A-6-1-3 A-5-1-6 NC A-4-1-11 NC A-3-2-9 NC A-2-4-5 NC A-1-7-9 NC	99-1,2-(12) 99-3-(4) Special PQ Out (col.1-23)	CC-43 (12-0) ABP-31-32-33 99-3-4
CC-40 (1/16 15-9) 229-3-2 NC 16-1-1	100-1-(4) Special Sign	CC-47(3 1/2-16) 100-1-4
CC-33 (14-15 1/3) 99-3-1,2 100-1-1,2	HD-3-(12) HD-3-(4) wc DD-PQ Invert	CC-43 (12-0) ABP-31-32-33 HD-3-12
CC-9 (9-9 1/2) HD-3-1 wc 99-2-12 Buss SC3-5-12	Str Ctr Magnet 24th col.	

Circuit Diagram

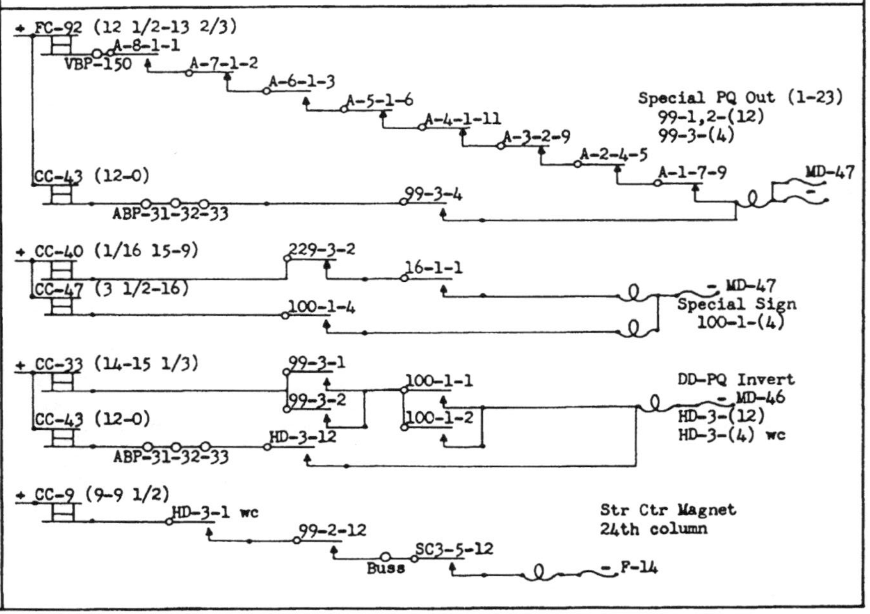

READ-OUT of PQ LOW-ORDER COLUMNS -continued-

Pick Up Circuit	Magnet	Hold Circuit	
CC-1,..,9 HD-3-1,..,10 NC HD-6-1,..,9 NC PQ Ctr RO (1-23) 99-1-1,.., 99-2-11 SC3-4-1,.., SC3-5-11	Str Ctr Magnets cols.1-23		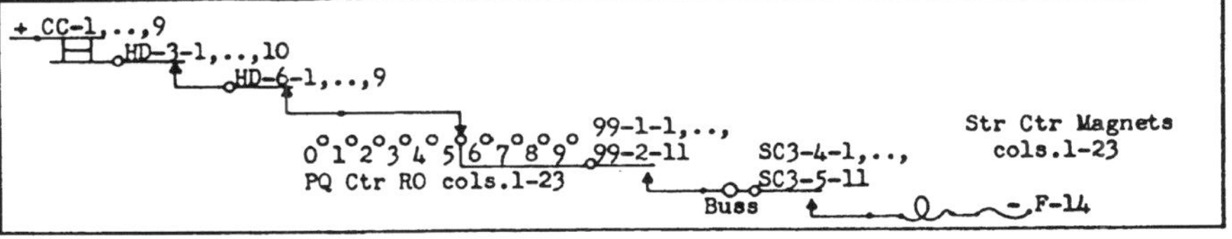

NORMALIZING REGISTER

The function of the normalizing register is discussed on pages 23-4. The special coding required for its operation is given on pages 159-61. This coding assumes that: (1) the quantity to be normalized lies in storage counter A; (2) the constant K lies in switch SC; (3) storage counters B, C, D and E are reset.

CYCLE 0. The sequence mechanism reads the line of coding (A, 761, 7), and steps to the next line. The sequence, storage counter and multiply circuits are completed as in multiplication cycle 0.

CYCLE 1. The operations of multiplication cycle 1 are carried out. The sequence mechanism reads the line of coding (SC, B, 7), and steps to the next line. The sequence, switch SC out and storage counter B in relays are energized.

CYCLE 2. The operations of multiplication cycle 2 are carried out. The quantity in switch SC is read into storage counter B. The sequence mechanism reads the line of coding (A, 8321, blank), and steps to the next line. The sequence and normalizing register read-in relays are energized.

CYCLE 3. The operations of multiplication cycle 3 are carried out. The digit sensing and shift positioning relays are picked up. The sequence mechanism reads the line of coding (blank, E, 7), and steps to the next line. The sequence and storage counter E in relays are energized.

Magnet	9 Cycle 2 9	9 Cycle 3 9
Sequence Relays 101-1,2 Normalizing Register Read-in 102-1,..,23 Digit Sensing 103-1,..,23 Shift Positioning	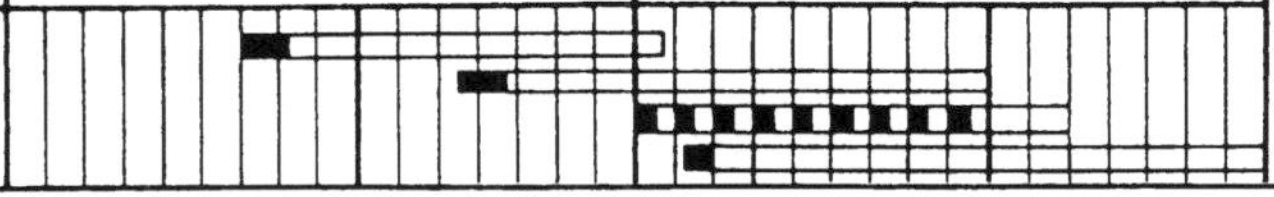	

Pick Up Circuit	Magnet	Hold Circuit	Circuit Diagram
FC-93 (12 1/2-13 2/3) VBP-149 B-8-1-1 B-7-1-2 NC B-6-1-3 NC B-5-1-5 NC B-4-1-9 NC B-3-2-5 B-2-3-10 B-1-6-8	101-1,2-(12) Norm. Reg. Read-in	CC-43 (12-0) ABP-31-32-33 101-2-12	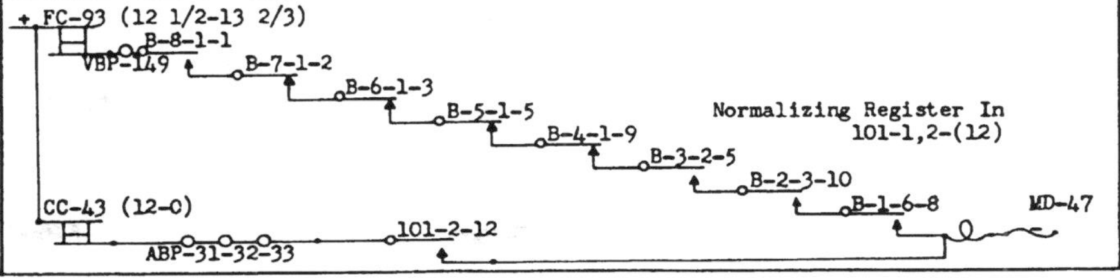

NORMALIZING REGISTER -continued-

Pick Up Circuit	Magnet	Hold Circuit	Circuit Diagram
SC-1,..,9 Str Ctr Reset NC Str Counter Invert-NC Str Ctr BP Str Ctr RO col.n SCA-1-1,.., SCA-2-11 Buss 101-1-1,.., 101-2-11 CC-37 (11-1/4 12) 102-23,..,1-1	102-1,..,23-(4) Digit Sensing 103-23,..,1-(4)	CC-35 (9-12) ABP-21 102-n-4 48-1-1 NC or CC-52(1/3 3-16) and 103-23,..,1-4	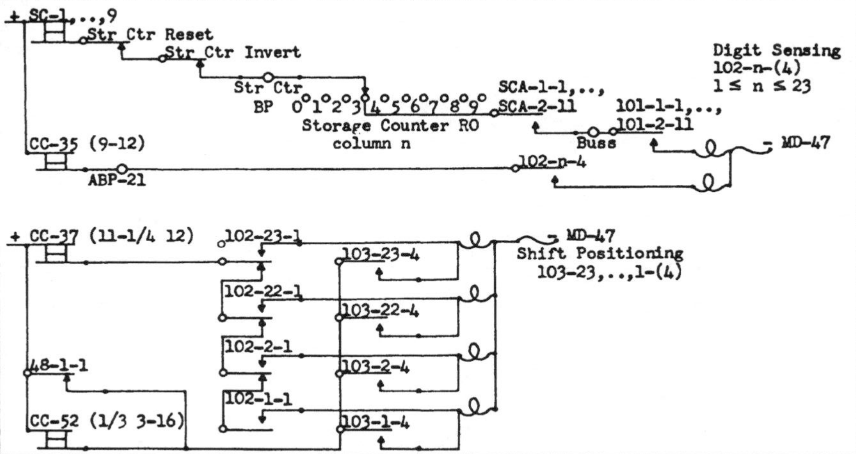

CYCLE 4. The power of ten selected by the digit sensing and shift positioning relays is read into the intermediate counter and into storage counter E. The operations of multiplication cycle 4 are carried out. The sequence mechanism reads the line of coding (8321, C, 7), and steps to the next line. The normalizing register read-out relay and storage counter C in relay are energized.

CYCLE 5. The operations of multiplication cycle 5 are completed. The amount of shift is read into storage counter C.

Magnet	9 Cycle 4 9 Cycle 5 9
103-1,..,23 Shift Positioning Intermediate Counter Magnet 104-1 Normalizing Register Read-Out Storage Counter Magnets	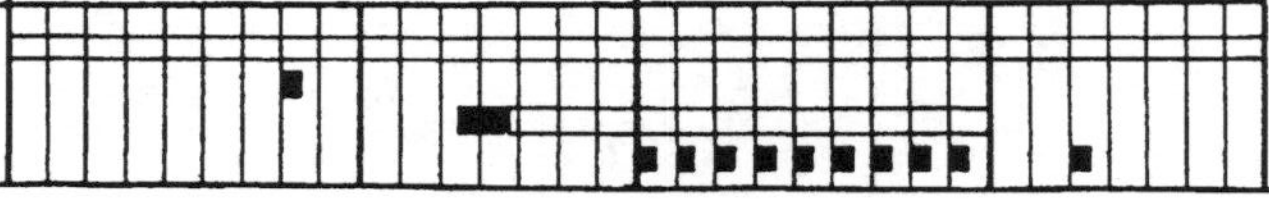

Pick Up Circuit	Magnet	Hold Circuit	Circuit Diagram
CC-1 (1-1 1/2) 46-5-2 103-(n)-1 Buss 50-1-1,.,50-2-12	Intermediate Ctr Magnet col.(24-n)		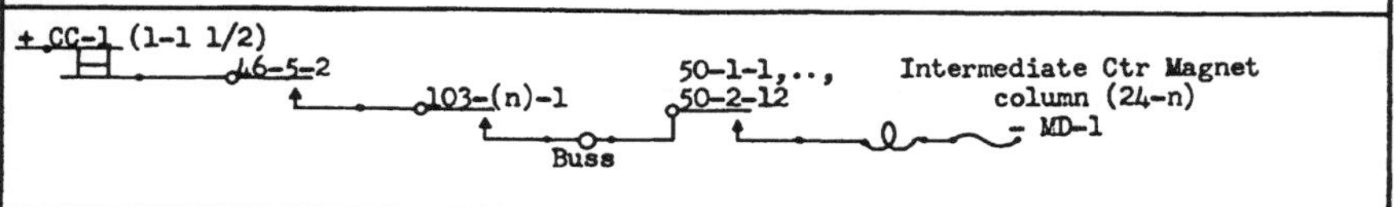

NORMALIZING REGISTER -continued-

Pick Up Circuit	Magnet	Hold Circuit	Circuit Diagram
FC-92 (12 1/2-13 2/3) VBP-150 A-8-1-1 A-7-1-2 NC A-6-1-3 NC A-5-1-5 NC A-4-1-9 NC A-3-2-5 A-2-3-10 A-1-6-8	104-1-(4) Norm. Reg. Read-out	CC-43 (12-0) ABP-31-32-33 104-1-4	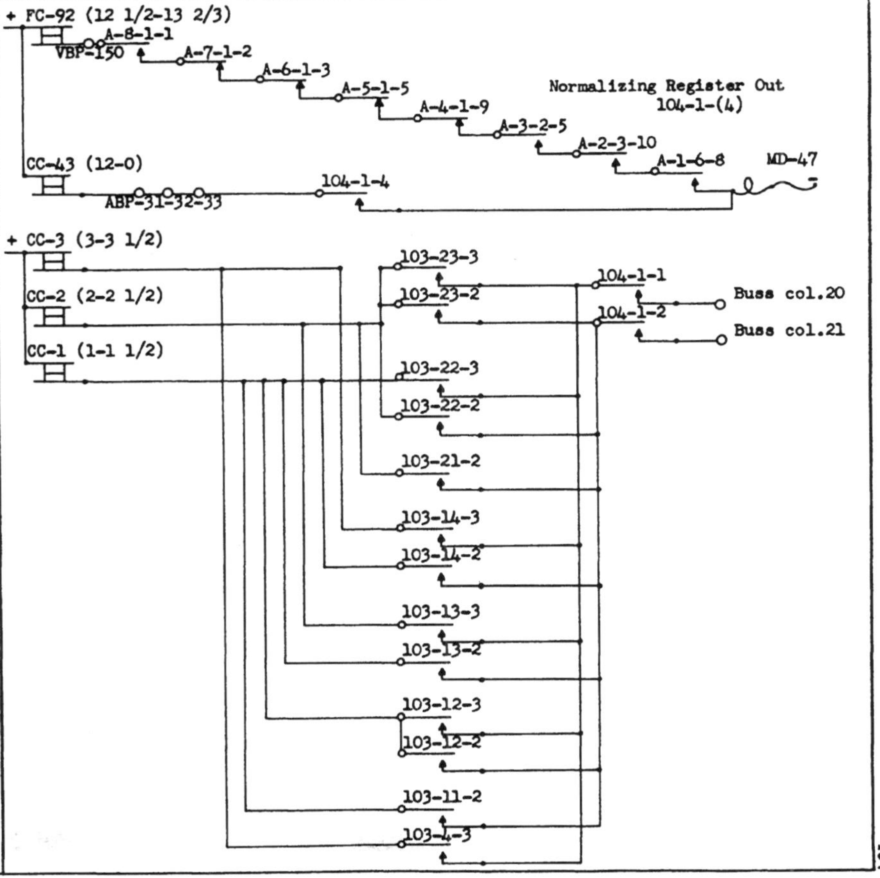
CC-1,..,9 103-n-2 or 3 104-1-1 or 2	Buss cols.20 and 21		

NORMALIZING REGISTER -continued-

CYCLE 6. The operations of multiplication cycles 6 and 8 (5 + n) are carried out.

CYCLE 7. The operations of multiplication cycle 9 (6 + n) are carried out. The sequence mechanism reads the line of coding (C, B, 32), and steps to the next line. The sequence relays, storage counter C out relay, storage counter B in relay and the storage counter invert relay are picked up.

CYCLE 8. The operations of multiplication cycle 10 (7 + n) are carried out. The nines complement of the amount of shift is read from storage counter C to storage counter B completing the computation of the exponent. The sequence mechanism reads the line of coding (blank, blank, 7), and steps to the next line. The sequence relays are picked up.

CYCLE 9. Except for the pick up of the storage counter in relay, the operations of multiplication cycle 11 (8 + n) are carried out. The sequence mechanism reads the line of coding (86, D, 7), and steps to the next line. The sequence relays, the special PQ out relay and the storage counter D in relay are energized.

CYCLE 10. The normalized quantity is read into storage counter D with its highest significant digit in the 23rd column. The repeat relay permits the pick up of the start relay. The calculator continues in operation.

DIVISION CYCLE 0

To start division, assuming the DR to lie in counter 8, code 4, the sequence mechanism reads the line of coding (4, 76, blank). As in multiplication cycle 0, the sequence relays are picked up. The divide relay is picked up. The sequence counter advances to read-out position 1. The storage counter out relays are picked up as in multiplication cycle 0. The intermediate in and DD-PQ reset relays are picked up. The heavy duty DD-PQ reset relay is energized as in multiplication cycle 0.

Magnet	9 0 9
Seq-27 Repeat Seq-33 Start Seq-31 Control Seq-A-4-1,2 Seq-B-7-1 Seq-B-6-1 56 Divide Sequence Counter Magnet SC8-1,2,3 Storage Counter Out 50 Intermediate In 58 DD-PQ Reset HD-6 DD-PQ Reset	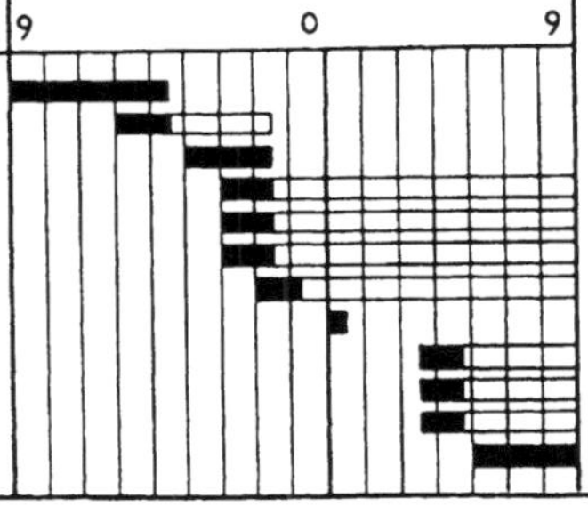

Pick Up Circuit	Magnet	Hold Circuit	Circuit Diagram
FC-95 (2-1 1/3) VBP-171 B-8-1-2 NC B-7-1-3 B-6-1-5 B-5-1-4 NC B-4-1-7 NC B-3-2-1 NC B-2-3-1 NC B-1-5-1 NC BBP-103	Divide 56-1,..,13-(12)	48-1-1 NC or CC-52 (1/3 3-16) and CC-53 (11-16) or BBP-91 FBP-140 199-1-1 NC FBP-197 BBP-132 and 56-13-11	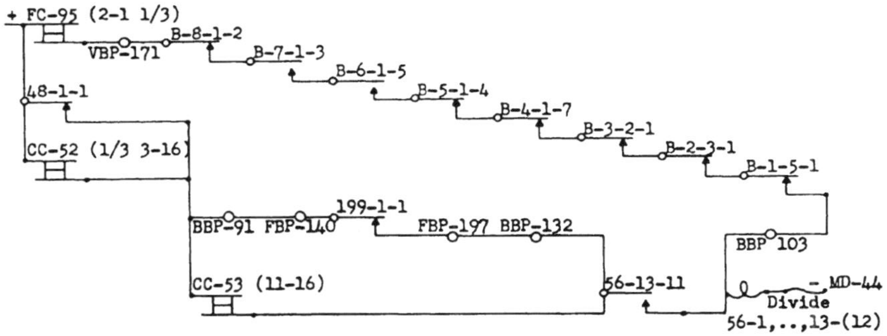
CC-10 (0-0 1/2) 56-13-1 14-1-3 NC 84-1-1 NC	Sequence Counter Magnet		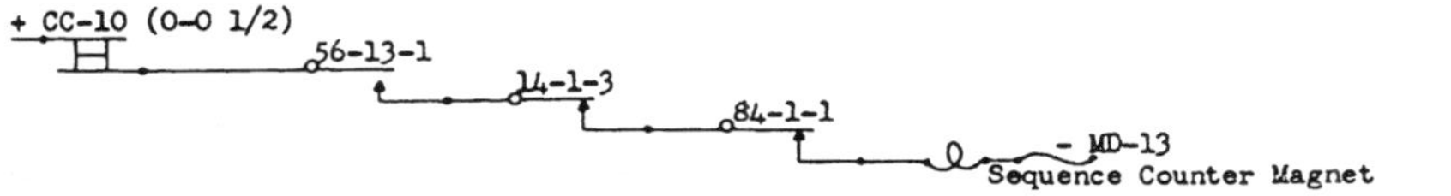

DIVISION CYCLE 0 -continued-

Pick Up Circuit	Magnet	Hold Circuit	Circuit Diagram
14-1-4 NC CC-55 (12 1/2-13 2/3) Seq Ctr RO B-1 56-11-1	Intermediate In 50-1,2,3-(12)	CC-43 (12-0) ABP-31-32-33 50-3-11	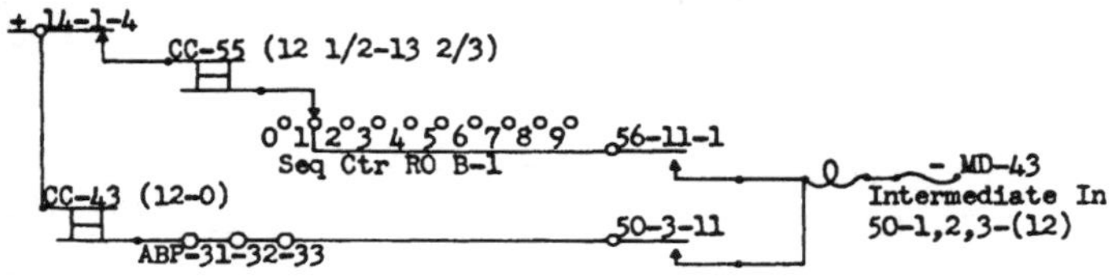
14-1-4 NC CC-57 (12 1/2-13 2/3) Seq Ctr RO D-1 56-11-2	DD-PQ Reset 58-1,..,8-(12)	CC-43 (12-0) ABP-31-32-33 58-8-12 58-4-11,12	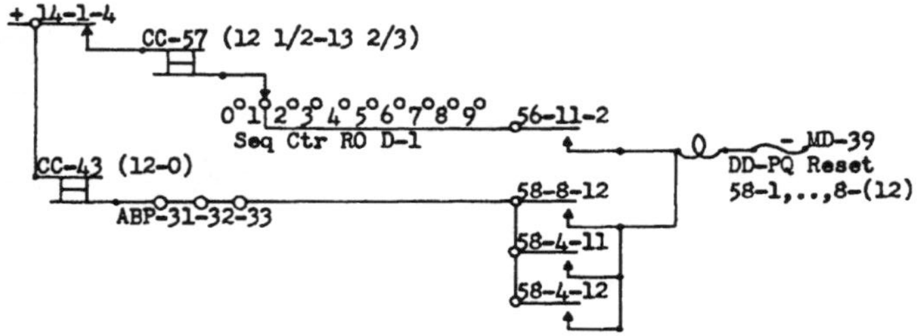
CC-43 (12-0) 58-8-12 58-4-11,12 CC-62 (14-0)	DD-PQ Reset HD-6-(12)		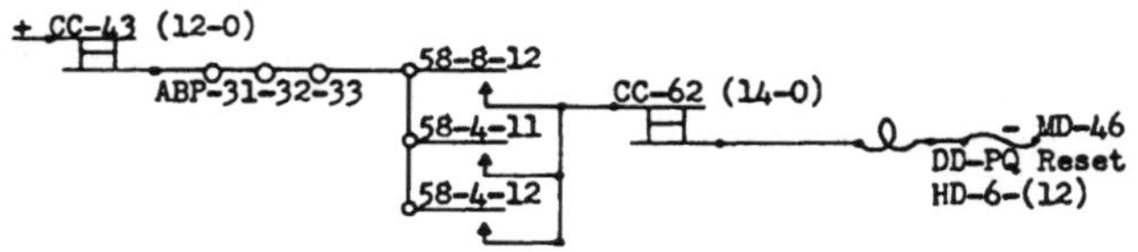

DIVISION CYCLE 1

The DR is read from storage to the intermediate counter. The entry of a nine into the 24th column of the intermediate counter (a negative DR) picks up the intermediate 24th column read-out control relay. The DD, PQ and Q-shift counters reset. The sequence counter is advanced to read-out position 2. In preparation for the next cycle the intermediate invert control and intermediate invert relays are picked up if DR is negative. The shift pick up, shift and MC-DR in relays are picked up in order to read the DR from the intermediate counter to the MC-DR counters with its first significant digit in the 23rd column of MC-DR (1-2). The entry control relays on MC-DR (1-2) and (3-6) are energised as in multiplication cycle 1.

DIVISION CYCLE 1 -continued-

Magnet	9 0 9
56 Divide SC8-1,2,3 Storage Counter Out 50 Intermediate In Intermediate Counter Magnets 89 Intermediate 24th column RO Control 58 DD-PQ Reset HD-6 DD-PQ Reset PQ Counter Magnets DD Counter Magnets Q-Shift Counter Magnets Sequence Counter Magnet 22 Q-Shift Invert 94 Intermediate Invert Control HD-1 Intermediate Invert 35 Shift Pick Up 36 Shift 43 MC-DR In 91 MC-DR Entry Control (1-2) 92 MC-DR Entry Control (3-6)	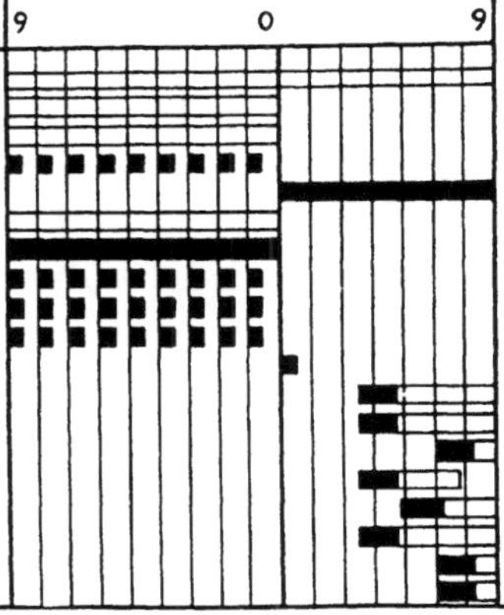

Pick Up Circuit	Magnet	Hold Circuit	Circuit Diagram
CC-1,..,9 HD-6-1,..,9 Q-Shift RO 58-8-10,11 14-1-4 NC CC-55 (12 1/2-13 2/3) Seq Ctr RO B-2 56-11-3 Intermediate Ctr 24th column 2nd mldg 0 to 2nd mldgs 0's or 24th column 2nd mldg 9 to 3rd mldgs 9's	Q-Shift Ctr Magnets Shift Pick Up 35-1,..,46-(4)	 CC-42 (12-1/3 16) 35-1,..,46-4	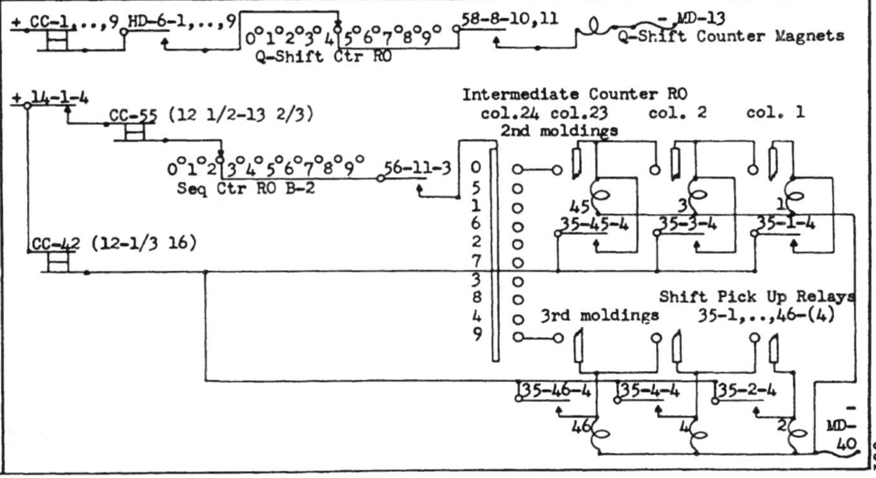

<u>DIVISION CYCLE 1</u> -continued-

Pick Up Circuit	Magnet	Hold Circuit	Circuit Diagram
14-1-4 NC CC-56 (12 1/2-13 2/3) Seq Ctr RO C-2 56-11-4	MC-DR In 43-1,..,10-(12) 43-11,12-(4)	CC-43 (12-0) ABP-31-32-33 43-10-12 43-12-3,4	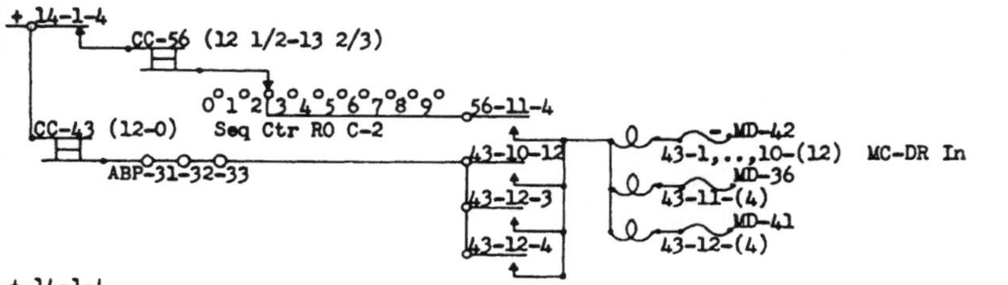
14-1-4 NC CC-56 (12 1/2-13 2/3) Seq Ctr RO C-2 56-11-5	Q-Shift Invert 22-1-(12)	CC-43 (12-0) ABP-31-32-33 22-1-11	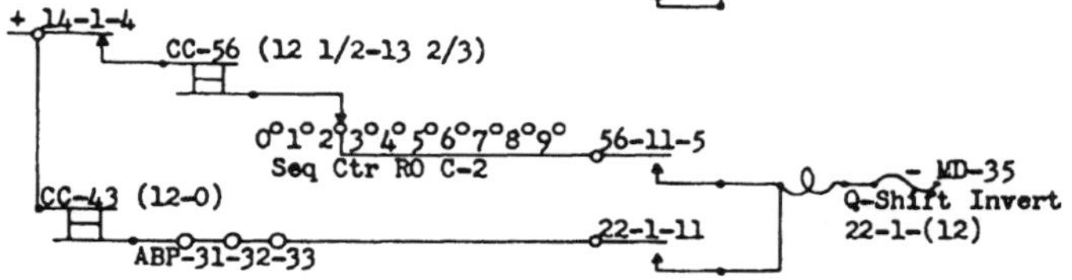
14-1-4 NC CC-57 (12 1/2-13 2/3) Seq Ctr RO D-2 56-11-6	Intermediate Invert Control 94-1-(4)	CC-43 (12-0) ABP-31-32-33 94-1-4	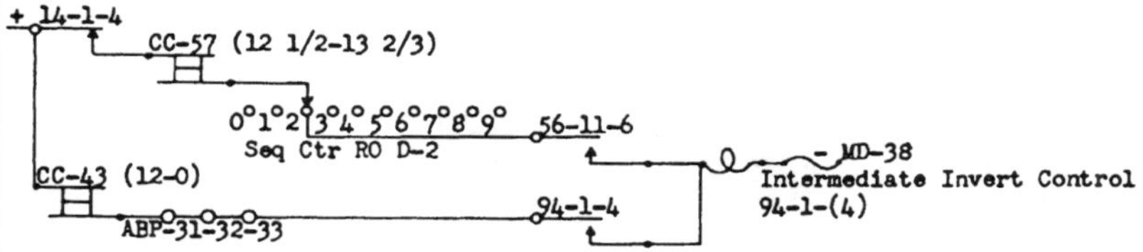
CC-33 (14-15 1/3) 43-2-12 35-(2n+1)-1 35-(2n-1)-1 NC 35-(2n)-1 NC	Shift 36-1,..,39- (4,6 or 12)	CC-43 (12-0) ABP-31 36-1-4,.., 36-39-2	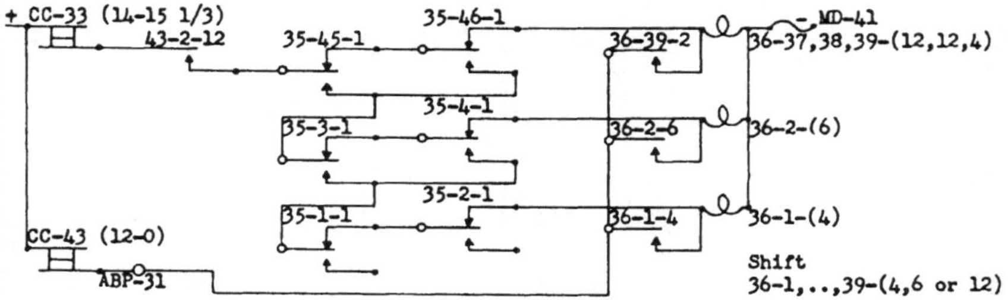

DIVISION CYCLE 2

The sign control relays are picked up if the intermediate 24th column read-out control relay is up as in multiplication cycle 2. The positive absolute value of DR reads from the intermediate counter to MC-DR counters (1-2), (3-6), (5), (7) and (9). The positive absolute value of DR is read through the shift relay so that its first significant digit lies in column 23 of MC-DR (1-2). The complement on nine of the number of columns the DR is shifted left on reading into MC-DR (1-2) is read into the Q-shift counter. At carry time an elusive one is read into the Q-shift counter. The sequence counter advances to read-out position 3. In preparation for the next cycle, the intermediate reset, the first build-up and the first and second build-up relays are picked up. The entry control relays for MC-DR(3-6) and (4-8) are energized as in multiplication cycle 2.

Magnet
56 Divide
89 Intermediate 24th column RO Control
70 Sign Control #1
71 Sign Control #2
94 Intermediate Invert Control
HD-1 Intermediate Invert
43 MC-DR In
36 Shift
91 MC-DR Entry Control (1-2)
MC-DR Counter Magnets (1-2)
92 MC-DR Entry Control (3-6)
MC-DR Counter Magnets (3-6)
MC-DR Counter Magnets (5)
MC-DR Counter Magnets (7)
MC-DR Counter Magnets (9)
22 Q-Shift Invert
87 Q-Shift "Elusive One" Control
88 Q-Shift "Elusive One"
Q-Shift Counter Magnets
Sequence Counter Magnet
44 First Build Up
45 First and Second Build Up
52 Intermediate Reset
HD-4 Intermediate Reset
92 MC-DR Entry Control (3-6)
93 MC-DR Entry Control (4-8)

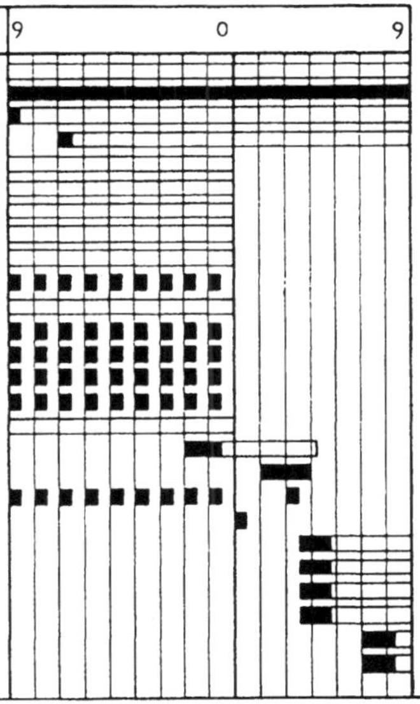

Pick Up Circuit	Magnet	Hold Circuit	Circuit Diagram
CC-10 (0-0 1/2) 56-13-1 14-1-3 NC 84-1-1 NC	Sequence Counter Magnet		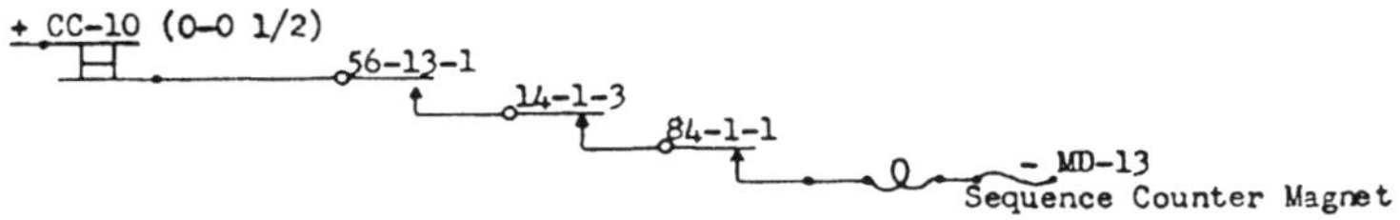

DIVISION CYCLE 2 -continued-

Pick Up Circuit	Magnet	Hold Circuit	Circuit Diagram
CC-12 (12-12 1/2) Carry BP Q-Shift Ctr Carry Contact 88-1-1,2 28-1-1 NC	Q-Shift Ctr Magnets		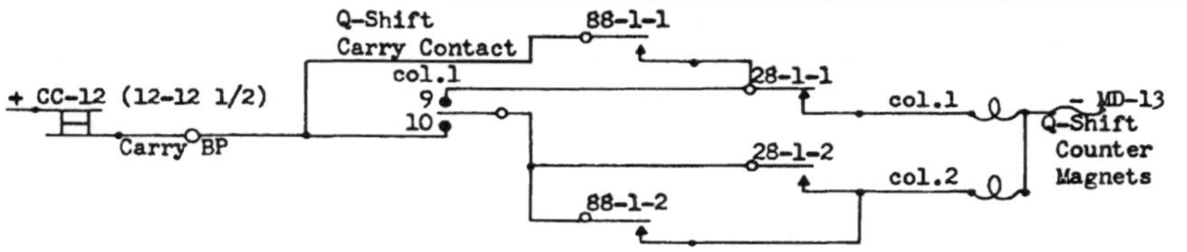
14-1-4 NC CC-55 (12 1/2-13 2/3) Seq Ctr RO B-3 56-11-7	First Build Up 44-1,..,5-(12)	CC-43 (12-0) ABP-31-32-33 44-5-11	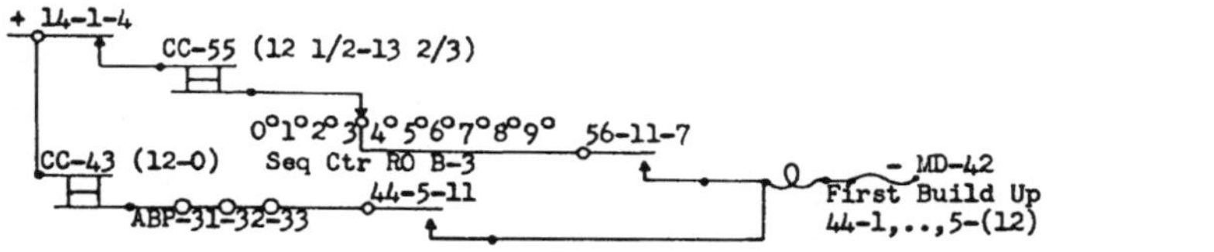
14-1-4 NC CC-56 (12 1/2-13 2/3) Seq Ctr RO C-3 56-11-8	First and Second Build Up 45-1,..,5-(12)	CC-43 (12-0) ABP-31-32-33 45-5-11	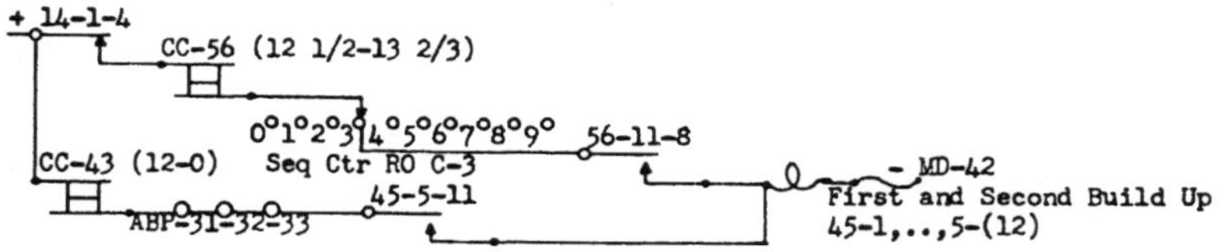
14-1-4 NC CC-57 (12 1/2-13 2/3) Seq Ctr RO D-3 56-11-9	Intermediate Reset 52-1,2,3-(12)	CC-43 (12-0) ABP-31-32-33 52-3-11	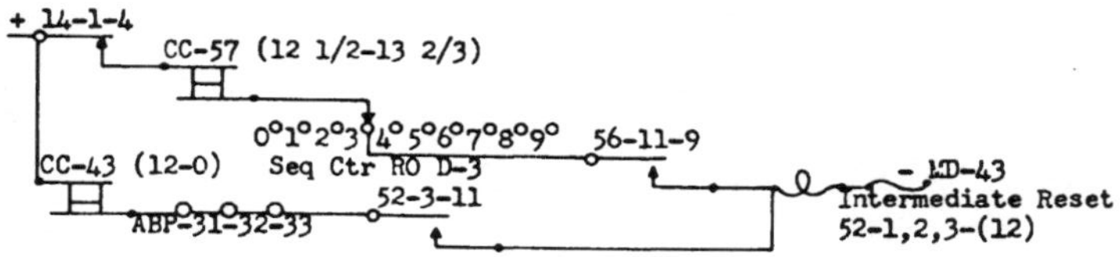
14-1-4 NC CC-57 (12 1/2-13 2/3) Seq Ctr RO D-3 56-11-9 CC-61 (12-0)	Intermediate Reset HD-4-(12)	CC-43 (12-0) ABP-31-32-33 52-3-11 CC-61 (12-0)	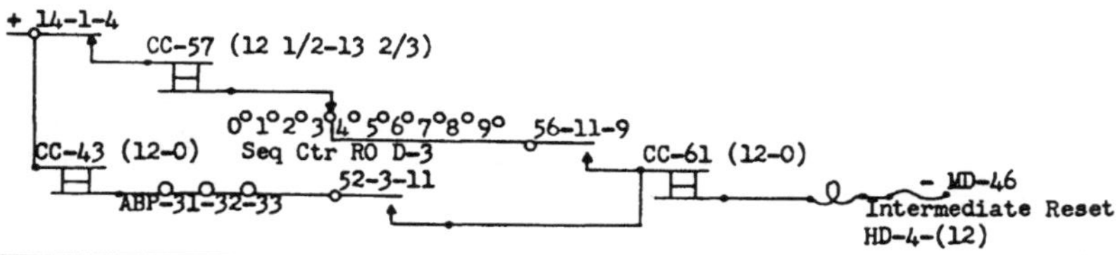

DIVISION CYCLE 2 -continued-

Pick Up Circuit	Magnet	Hold Circuit	Circuit Diagram
CC-1,..,9 HD-1-1,..,10 NC if DR was > 0 HD-1-1,..,10 NO if DR was < 0 HD-4-1,..,9 NC Intermediate RO 36-1-1 or 36-2-1,2 or,.., 36-37-1,.., 36-38-11	Counter Magnets		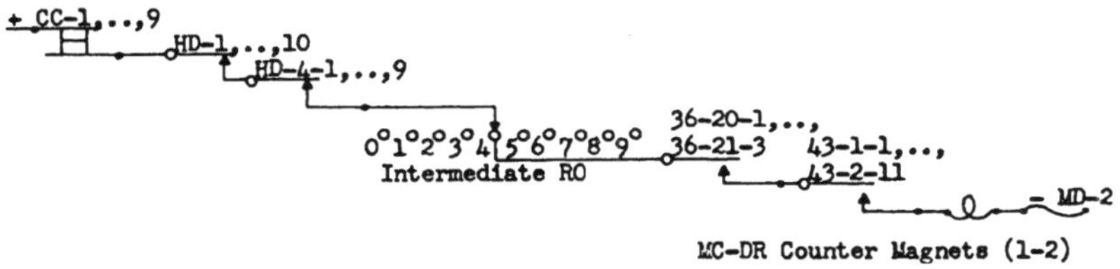
43-1-1,.., 43-2-11	MC-DR (1-2)		
43-3-1,.., 43-4-11	MC-DR (3-6)		
43-5-1,.., 43-6-11	MC-DR (5)		
43-7-1,.., 43-8-11	MC-DR (7)		
43-9-1,.., 43-10-11	MC-DR (9)		
CC-1,..,9 22-1-1,..,10 36-1-2,3 or,.., 36-35-11,12	Q-Shift Ctr Magnets		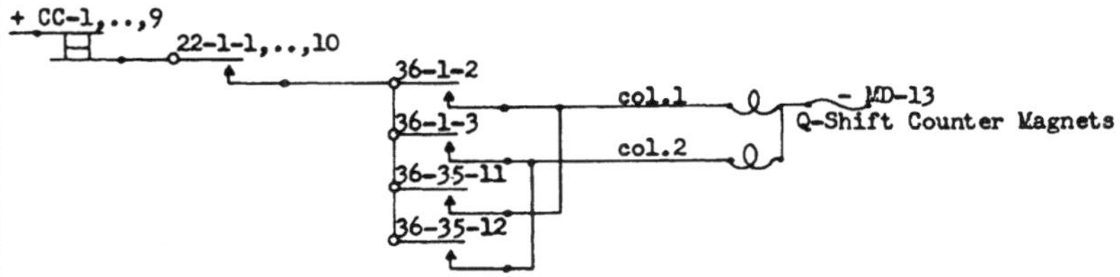
CC-44 (2-1 1/3) 43-4-12 36-39-1 NC	Q-Shift "Elusive One" Control 87-1-(4)	CC-46 (2-13 1/3) ABP-35 87-1-4	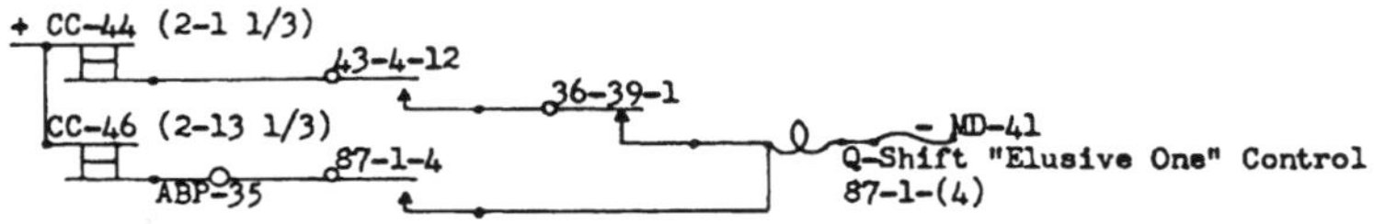
CC-45 (1/16 11-13) 87-1-1	Q-Shift "Elusive One" 88-1-(4)		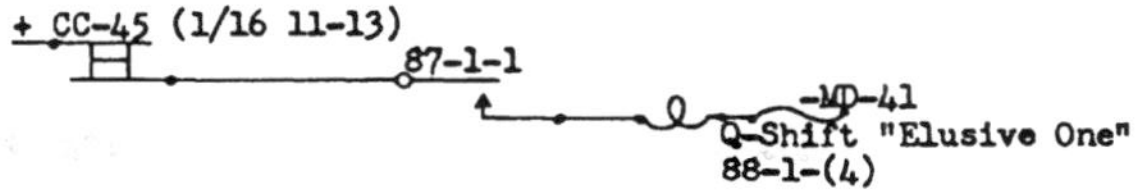

DIVISION CYCLE 3

As in multiplication cycle 3, the intermediate counter resets. If a nine stood in the 24th column of the intermediate counter, a nine is read to the 47th column of the PQ counter as in multiplication cycle 3. The first build up takes place; i.e., twice the DR is read from the doubling moldings of MC-DR (1-2) to MC-DR (3-6), (4-8), (5) and (9). The MC-DR carry control and carry relays are picked up and the carry impulse completes the first build up. Assuming the DD to lie in storage counter 20, code 53, the sequence mechanism reads the line of coding (53, blank, blank). The sequence relays and the storage counter out relays are picked up as in multiplication cycle 3. The sequence counter is advanced to read-out position 4. In preparation for the next cycle the intermediate in, first and second build up, second build up and add-22 relays are energized. The entry control relays for MC-DR (4-8) are picked up as in multiplication cycle 3.

Magnet

56 Divide
52 Intermediate Reset
HD-4 Intermediate Reset
Intermediate Counter Magnets
70 Sign Control #1
71 Sign Control #2
PQ 47th column Counter Magnet
44 First Build Up
92 MC-DR Entry Control (3-6)
MC-DR Counter Magnets (3-6)
45 First and Second Build Up
MC-DR Entry Control (4-8)
MC-DR Counter Magnets (4-8)
MC-DR Counter Magnets (5)
MC-DR Counter Magnets (9)
26 MC-DR Carry Control
49 MC-DR Carry
Seq-31 Control
Seq-A-5-1
Seq-A-3-1,2,3
SC20-1,2,3 Storage Counter Out
Sequence Counter Magnet
50 Intermediate In
45 First and Second Build Up
46 Second Build Up
93 MC-DR Entry Control (4-8)
32 Add 22

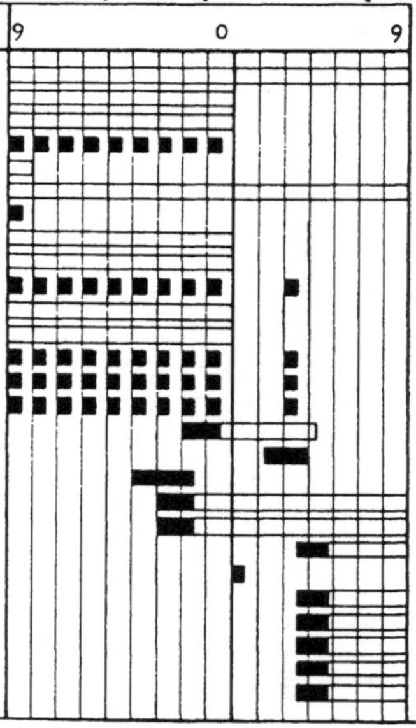

Pick Up Circuit	Magnet	Hold Circuit	Circuit Diagram
CC-10 (0-0 1/2) 56-13-1 14-1-3 NC 84-1-1 NC	Sequence Counter Magnet		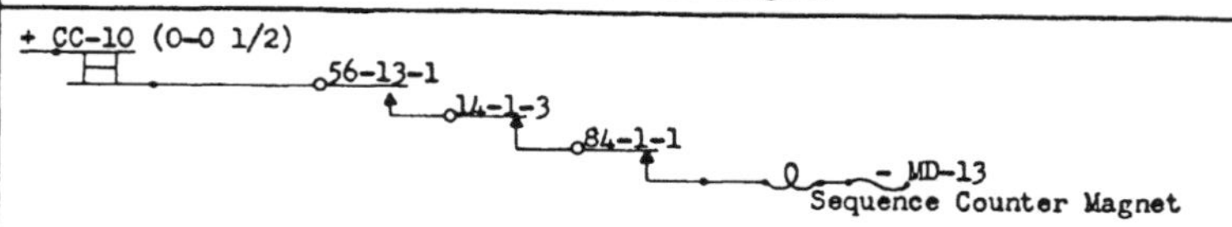

DIVISION CYCLE 3 -continued-

Pick Up Circuit	Magnet	Hold Circuit	Circuit Diagram
14-1-4 NC CC-55 (12 1/2-13 2/3) Seq Ctr RO B-4 56-11-10	Intermediate In 50-1,2,3-(12)	CC-43 (12-0) ABP-31-32-33 50-3-11	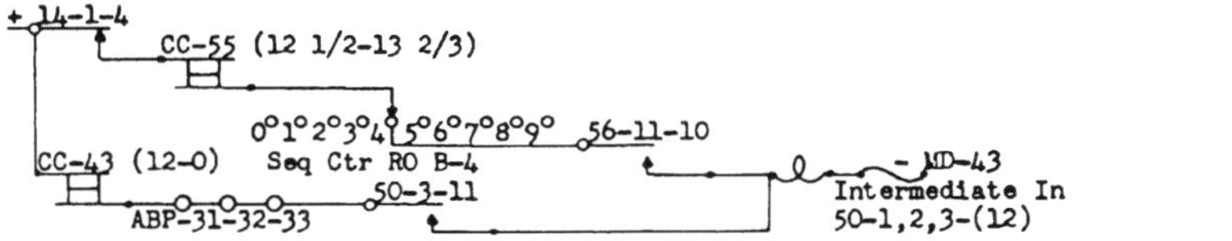
14-1-4 NC CC-56 (12 1/2-13 2/3) Seq Ctr RO C-4 56-11-11	First and Second Build Up 45-1,..,5-(12)	CC-43 (12-0) ABP-31-32-33 45-5-11	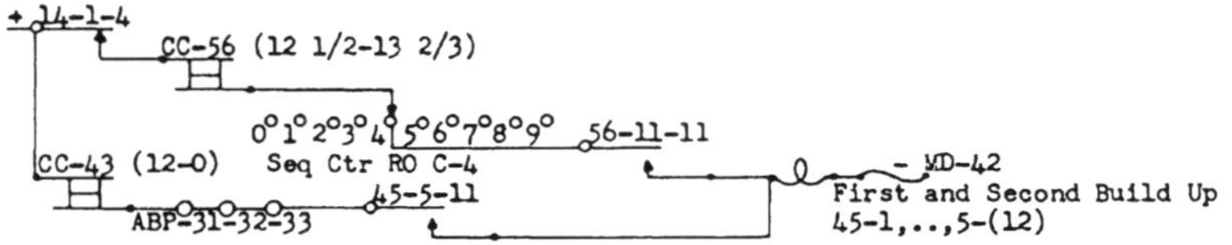
14-1-4 NC CC-57 (12 1/2-13 2/3) Seq Ctr RO D-4 56-11-12	Second Build Up 46-1,..,5-(12)	CC-43 (12-0) ABP-31-32-33 46-5-11	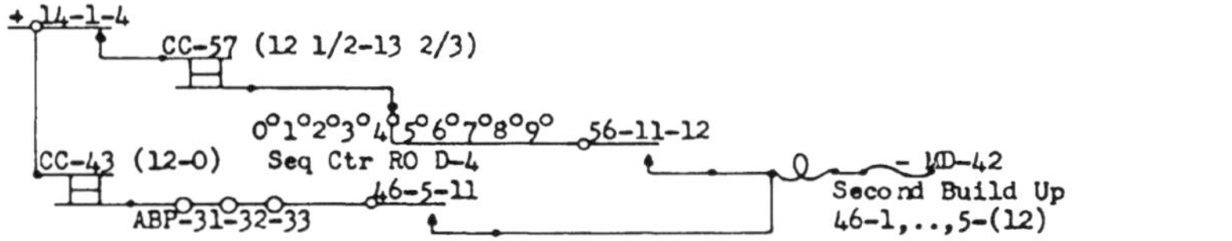
14-1-4 NC CC-57 (12 1/2-13 2/3) Seq Ctr RO D-4 56-12-1	Add-22 32-1-(4)	CC-43 (12-0) ABP-31-32-33 32-1-4	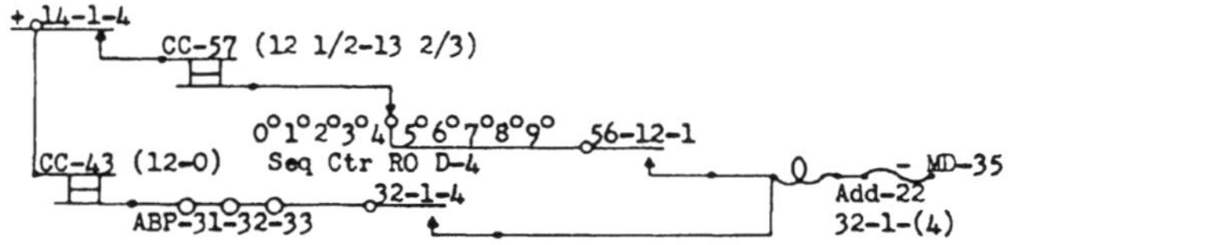

DIVISION CYCLE 4

The DD is read from storage to the intermediate counter as in cycle 1. The entry of a nine into the 24th column of the intermediate counter (a negative DD) picks up the intermediate 24th column read-out control relay as in cycle 1. The second build up takes place as in multiplication cycle 4; i.e., twice the DR is read from the doubling moldings of MC-DR (1-2) to MC-DR (4-8) and (5); six times the DR is read from the doubling moldings of MC-DR (3-6) to MC-DR (7) and (9). The MC-DR carry control and carry relays are picked up and the carry impulse completes the second build up as in multiplication cycle 3. From two dial switches, 22-N (where the operating decimal point lies between columns N and N + 1) is added into the Q-shift counter. The Q-shift carry control and carry relays are picked up and the carry impulse completes the entry. The sequence counter is advanced to read-out position 5. In preparation for the next cycle, the intermediate

DIVISION CYCLE 4 -continued-

invert control and intermediate invert relays (as in multiplication cycle 4) are picked up if DD is negative. The shift pick up, shift and DD in relays are picked up in order to read DD from the intermediate counter to the DD counter with its first significant digit in the 45th column of DD.

Magnet

56 Divide
SC20-1,2,3 Storage Counter Out
50 Intermediate In
Intermediate Counter Magnets
89 Intermediate 24th column RO Control
71 Sign Control #2
45 First and Second Build Up
93 MC-DR Entry Control (4-8)
MC-DR Counter Magnets (4-8)
MC-DR Counter Magnets (5)
46 Second Build Up
MC-DR Counter Magnets (7)
MC-DR Counter Magnets (9)
26 MC-DR Carry Control
49 MC-DR Carry
32 Add-22
Q-Shift Counter Magnets
25 Q-Shift Carry Control
28 Q-Shift Carry
Sequence Counter Magnet
94 Intermediate Invert Control
HD-1 Intermediate Invert
35 Shift Pick Up
57 DD In
36 Shift

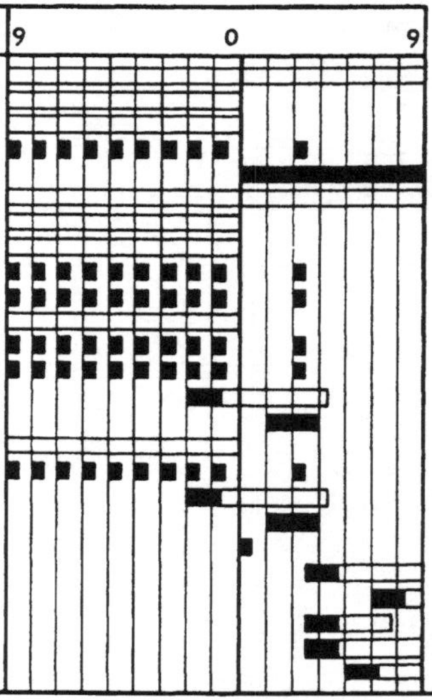

Pick Up Circuit	Magnet	Hold Circuit	Circuit Diagram
CC-1,..,9 Add-22 Switches 86-1-1,2 NC 32-1-1,2	Q-Shift Ctr Magnets		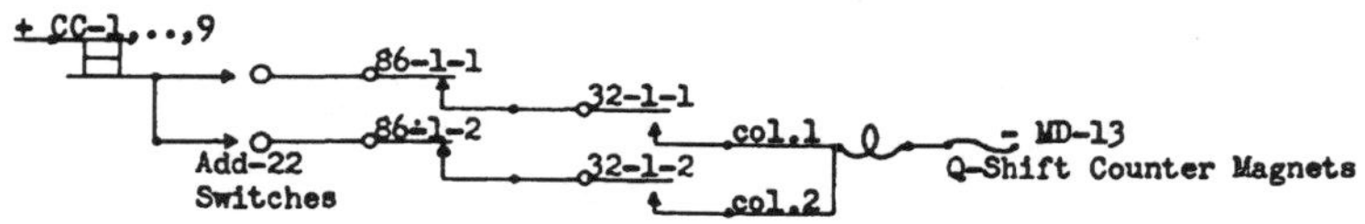
CC-44 (2-1 1/3) 32-1-3	Q-Shift Carry Control 25-1-(4)	CC-46 (2-13 1/3) ABP-35 25-1-4	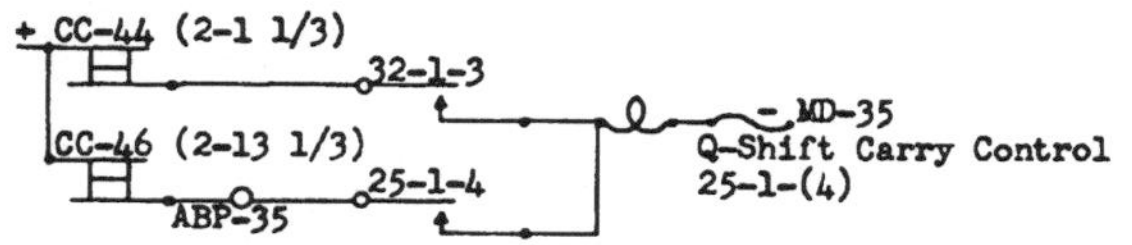

DIVISION CYCLE 4 -continued-

Pick Up Circuit	Magnet	Hold Circuit	Circuit Diagram
CC-45 (1/16 11-13) 25-1-1	Q-Shift Carry 28-1-(4)		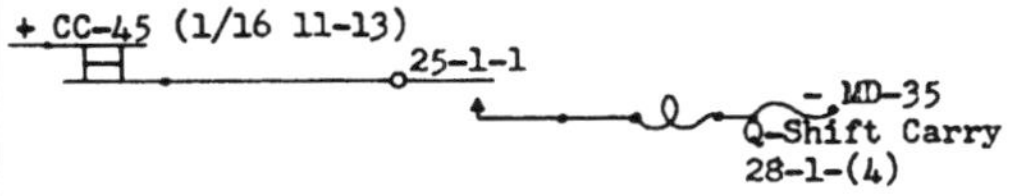
14-1-4 NC CC-57 (12 1/2-13 2/3) Seq Ctr RO D-5 56-12-4	Intermediate Invert Control 94-1-(4)	CC-43 (12-0) ABP-31-32-33 94-1-4	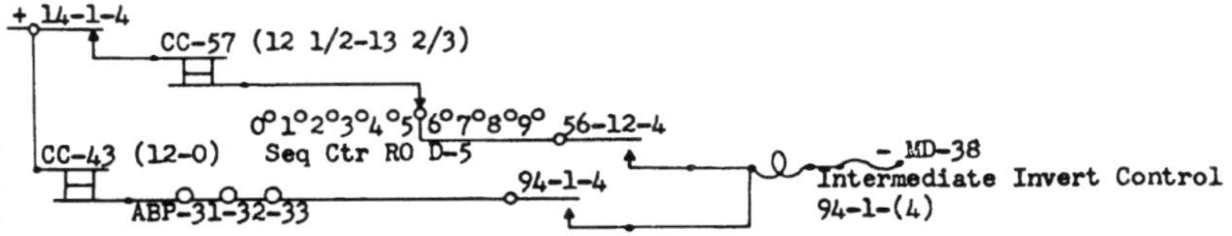
14-1-4 NC CC-55 (12 1/2-13 2/3) Seq Ctr RO B-5 56-12-2 Intermediate Counter 24th column 2nd mldg 0 to 2nd mldgs 0's 24th column 2nd mldg 9 to 3rd mldgs 9's	Shift Pick Up 35-1,..,46-(4)	CC-42 (12-1/3 16) 35-1,..,46-4	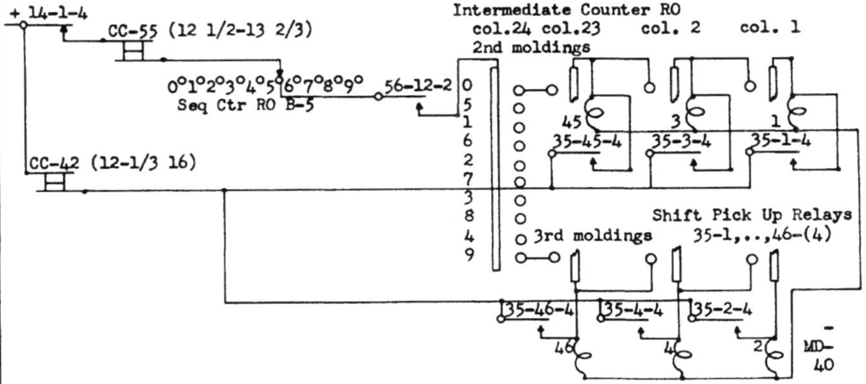
14-1-4 NC CC-56 (12 1/2-13 2/3) Seq Ctr RO C-5 56-12-3	DD In 57-1,2,3-(12)	CC-43 (12-0) ABP-31-32-33 57-3-11	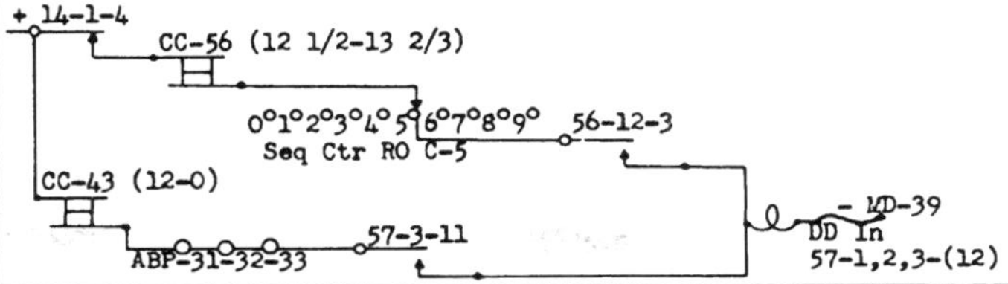

DIVISION CYCLE 4 -continued-

Pick Up Circuit	Magnet	Hold Circuit	Circuit Diagram
CC-33 (14-15 1/3) 57-2-12 35-(2n+1)-1 35-(2n-1)-1 NC 35-(2n)-1 NC	Shift 36-1,..,39- (4, 6 or 12)	CC-43 (12-0) ABP-31 36-1-4,.., 36-39-2	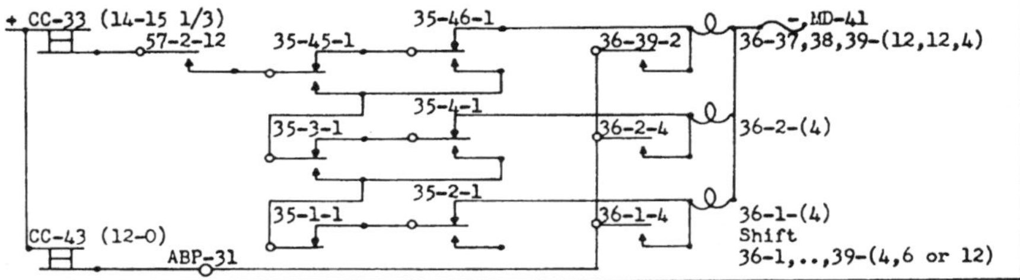

DIVISION CYCLE 5

Sign control #1 is picked up if the intermediate 24th column read-out control relay is up as in multiplication cycle 2. The positive absolute value of the DD reads from the intermediate counter to the DD counter. The value of DD is read through the shift relay so that its first significant digit reads into column 45 of the DD counter. The amount of the DD shift left is read into the Q-shift counter. The Q-shift carry circuits are as in cycle 4. The sequence counter is advanced to read-out position 6. The intermediate reset relay is picked up. The MP-DIV control pick up is energized. The cycle counter is advanced to read-out position 1. The MP-DIV control hold relay is picked up preventing the sequence counter from advancing when CC-10 makes and further, preventing the passage of impulses from CC-55, 56 and 57 through the sequence counter read-out. The compare control, compare in and column shift right relays are picked up.

Magnet	9 0 9
56 Divide 89 Intermediate 24th column RO Control 70 Sign Control #1 71 Sign Control #2 94 Intermediate Invert Control HD-1 Intermediate Invert 36 Shift 57 DD In DD Counter Magnets Q-Shift Counter Magnets 25 Q-Shift Carry Control 28 Q-Shift Carry Sequence Counter Magnet 52 Intermediate Reset HD-4 Intermediate Reset 13 MP-DIV Control Pick Up Cycle Counter Magnet 8 Compare Control 14 MP-DIV Control Hold 3 Compare In 29 Column Shift Right	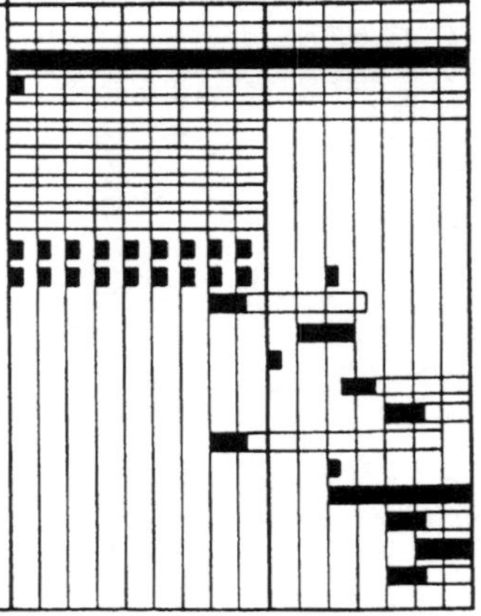

DIVISION CYCLE 5 -continued-

Pick Up Circuit	Magnet	Hold Circuit	Circuit Diagram
CC-1,..,9 HD-1-1,..,10 NC if DD was > 0 HD-1-1,..,10 NO if DD was < 0 HD-4-1,..,9 NC Intermediate RO 36-1-1,.., 36-38-11 57-1-1,.., 57-2-11	DD Counter Magnets		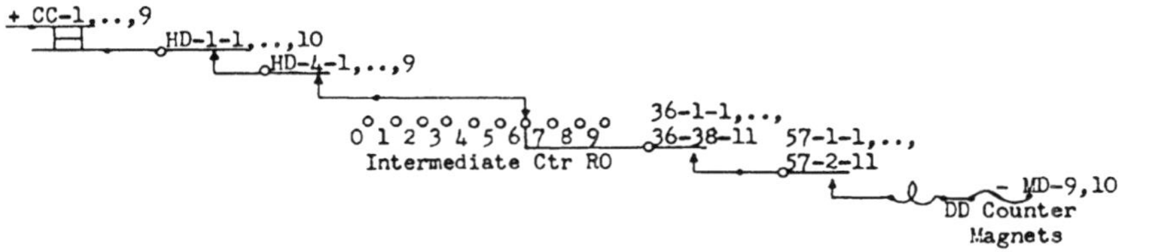
CC-1,..,9 22-1-1,..,10 NC 36-1-2,3 or,.., 36-35-11,12 (see Relay List)	Q-Shift Counter Magnets		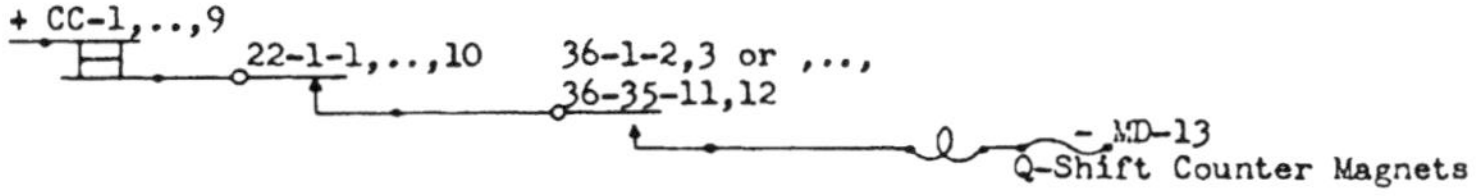
CC-44 (2-1 1/3) 57-3-1	Q-Shift Carry Control 25-1-(4)	CC-46 (2-13 1/3) ABP-35 25-1-4	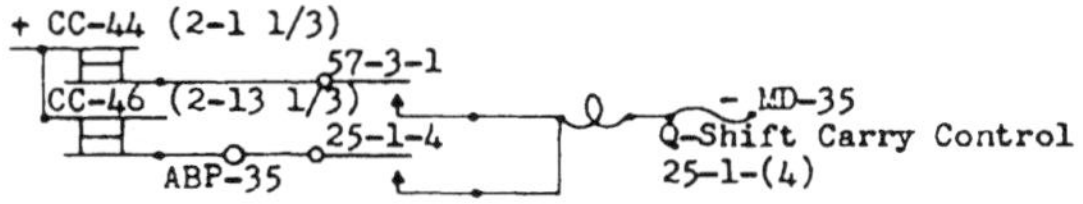
CC-45 (1/16 11-13) 25-1-1	Q-Shift Carry 28-1-(4)		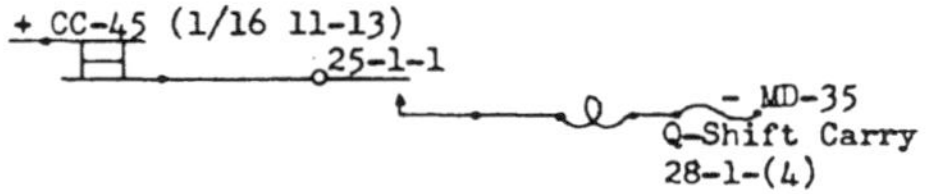
14-1-4 NC CC-57 (12 1/2-13 2/3) Seq Ctr RO D-6 56-12-5	Intermediate Reset 52-1,2,3-(12)	CC-43 (12-0) ABP-31-32-33 52-3-11	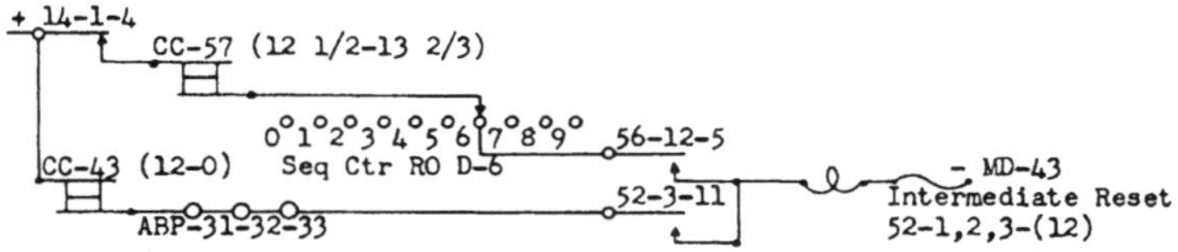
CC-26 (2-1 1/3) 57-3-4	MP-DIV Control Pick Up 13-1-(6)	CC-47 (3 1/2-16) 13-1-6	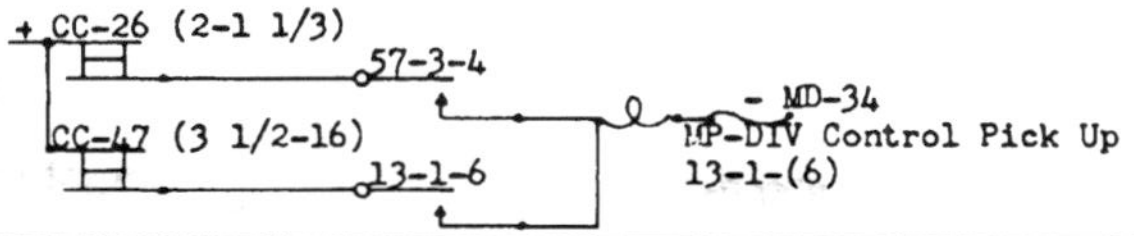

DIVISION CYCLE 5 -continued-

Pick Up Circuit	Magnet	Hold Circuit	Circuit Diagram
CC-80 (1/16 12-9) 7-1,..,9-2 NC 13-1-1 CC-54 (12-12 1/2)	Cycle Counter Magnet		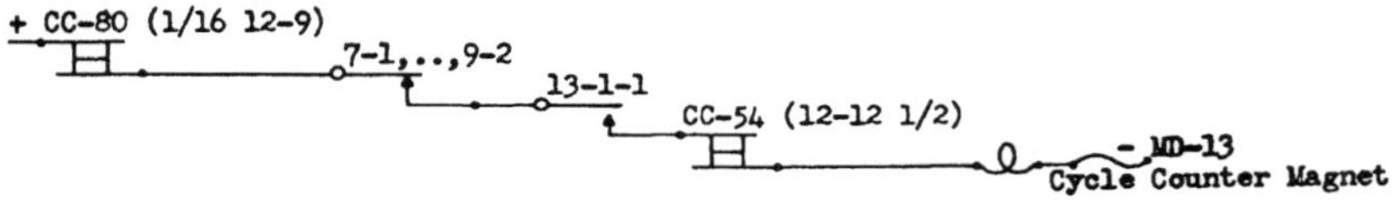
CC-80 (1/16 12-9) 7-1,..,9-2 NC 13-1-1	Compare Control 8-1-(4)		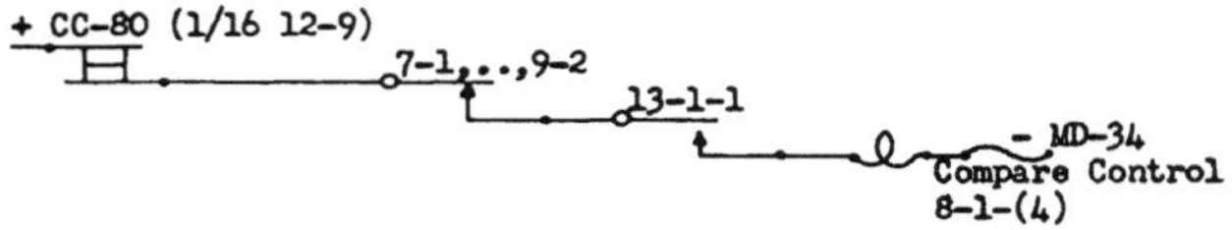
69-2-1,2 NC 13-1-3 CC-58 (14-15 1/3) 13-1-2	MP-DIV Control Hold 14-1-(12)	12-1,2-2 NC or CC-32 (8 1/2-2) and 14-1-11	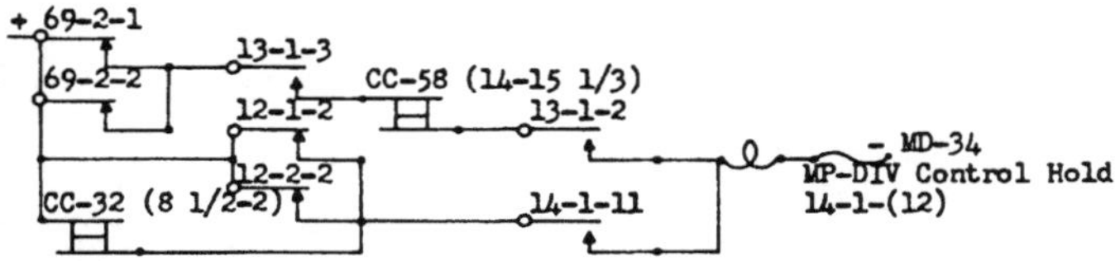
CC-40 (1/16 15-9) 13-1-4 56-13-2 8-1-3,4	Compare In 3-1,..,24-(12) 3-25-(4)	CC-39 (1/3 15-12) 3-24-11 3-25-1,2	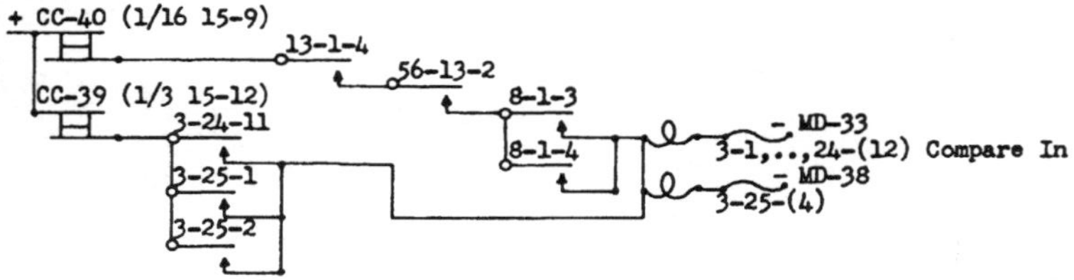
69-2-1,2 NC 13-1-3 CC-58 (14-15 1/3) 19-1-1 NC 18-1-1 NC Cycle Ctr RO A-1 56-9-1,.., 56-10-11	Column Shift Right 29-34,35,36- (12,12,6)	CC-36 (12-0) ABP-27 29-36-6	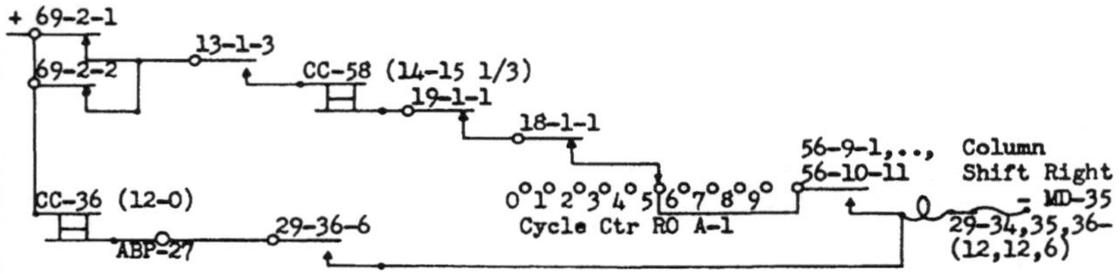

DIVISION CYCLE 6

The intermediate counter resets as in cycle 3. Sign control #1 drops out. If a nine stood in the 24th column of the intermediate counter a nine is read into the 47th column of the PQ counter as in multiplication cycle 3. The DD and DR read into the DD and DR compare relays. The comparison is made and the appropriate over-under relays picked up. The over-under relay permits the appropriate Q control relay to be energized which picks up the proper times right relay. The column shift right and MC-DR invert relays are picked up in order to subtract the DR multiple during the next cycle.

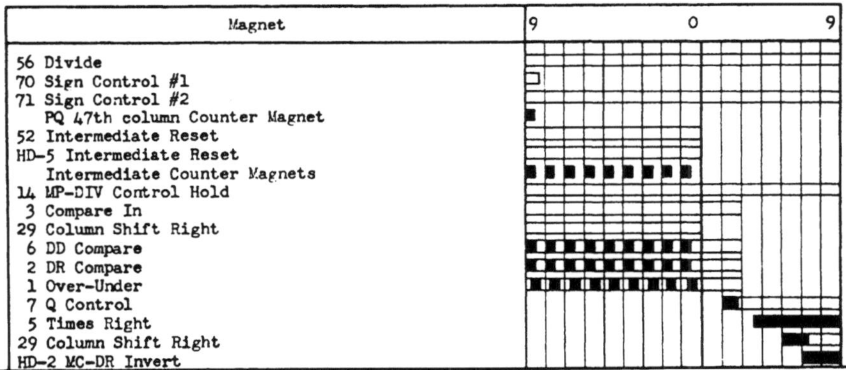

Pick Up Circuit	Magnet	Hold Circuit	Circuit Diagram
CC-1,..,9 HD-3-1,..,10 NC HD-6-1,..,9 NC DD RO 3-21-1,.., 3-24-9 56-3-1,.., 56-6-9 29-34-1,.., 29-35-11 3-19-1,.., 3-20-11	DD Compare 6-1,..,24-(12)	CC-28 (9-12) ABP-24 6-1,..,24-12	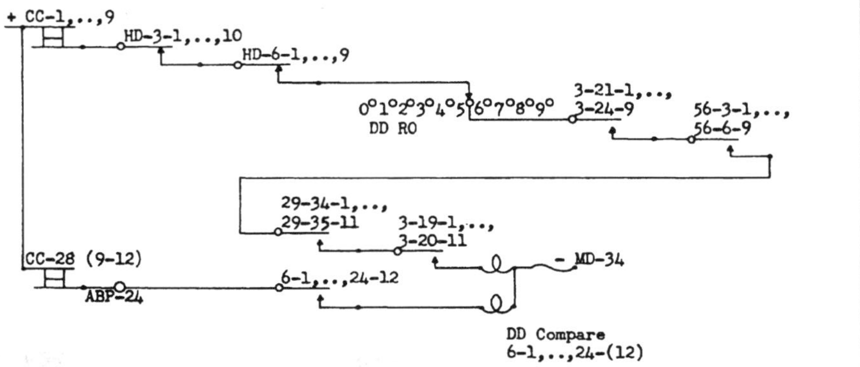

DIVISION CYCLE 6 -continued-

Pick Up Circuit	Magnet	Hold Circuit	Circuit Diagram
CC-1,..,9 HD-2-1,...,10 NC HD-5-1,...,9NC MC-DR RO 3-1-1,.., 3-18-12	DR Compare 2-1,..,216-(4)	CC-27 (9-12) ABP-23 2-1,..,120-4 CC-28 (9-12) ABP-24 2-121,..,216-4	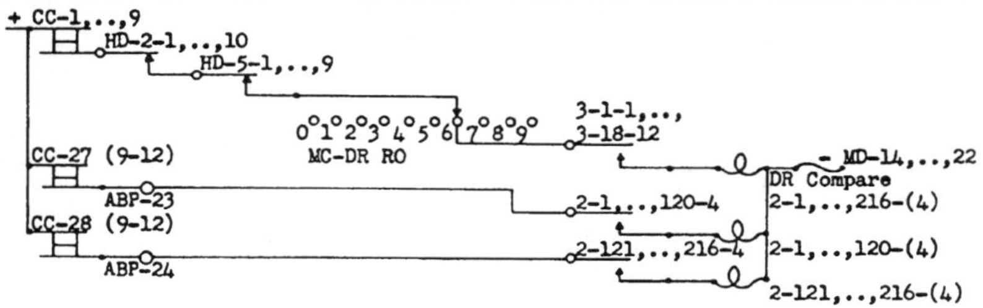
CC-24 A,B,C,D ABP-25,26 6-1,..,24- 1,..,9 2-1,..,216-1 NC 2-1,..,216-2	Over-Under 1-1,..,423-(4)	CC-34 (9-12) ABP-20 1-1,..,235-3 CC-35 (9-12) ABP-21 1-236,..,423-3	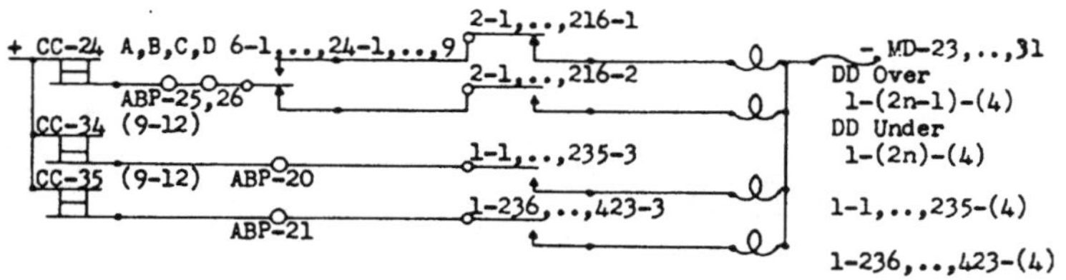
CC-37 (11-1/4 12) 3-24-10,12 1-1,..,432-1	Q Control 7-1,..,9-(4)	CC-38 (11 1/2-9) 7-1-3	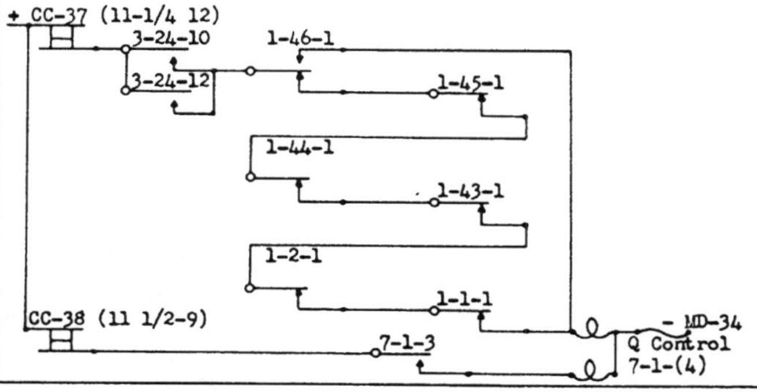

DIVISION CYCLE 6 -continued-

Pick Up Circuit	Magnet	Hold Circuit	Circuit Diagram
CC-31 (12 1/2-9) 7-1,..,9-1	Times Right 5-1,..,27- (12,12,4)	CC-36 (12-0) ABP-27 5-3n-4	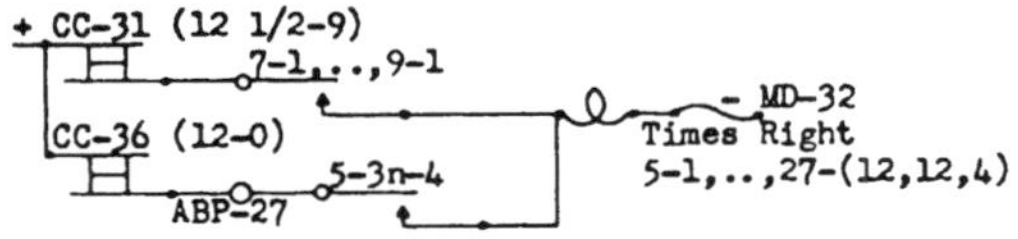
69-2-1,2 NC 14-1-1 CC-58 (14-15 1/3) 19-1-1 NC 18-1-1 NC Cycle Ctr RO A-1 56-9-1,.., 56-10-11	Column Shift Right 29-34,35,36- (12,12,6)	CC-36 (12-0) ABP-27 29-36-6	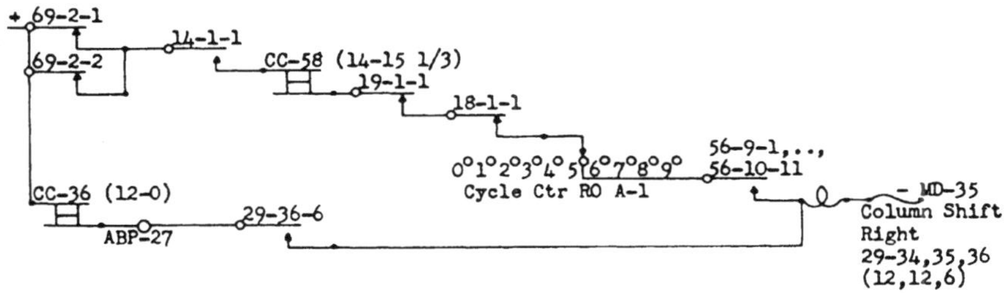
CC-40 (1/16 15-9) 14-1-2 56-13-2 8-1-3,4 NC	MC-DR Invert HD-2-(12)	CC-39 (1/3 15-12) HD-2-(12)	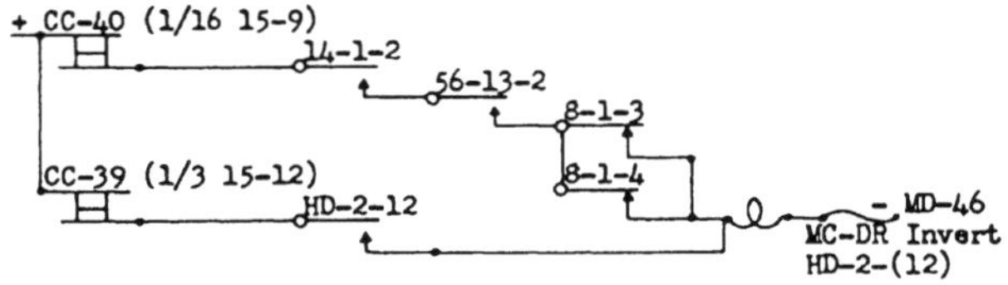

DIVISION CYCLE 7

The selected DR multiple is subtracted from DD (the elusive one substitutes for the end around carry). The first digit of the quotient is added into PQ. The cycle counter is advanced. The compare control, compare in and column shift left relays are picked up.

DIVISION CYCLE 7 -continued-

Magnet	9 0 9
56 Divide 71 Sign Control #2 14 MP-DIV Control Hold HD-2 MC-DR Invert 5 Times Right 29 Column Shift Right DD Counter Magnets 27 DD Carry Control 61 DD Carry 60 Elusive One PQ Counter Magnets 8 Compare Control Cycle Counter Magnet 3 Compare In 21 Column Shift Left	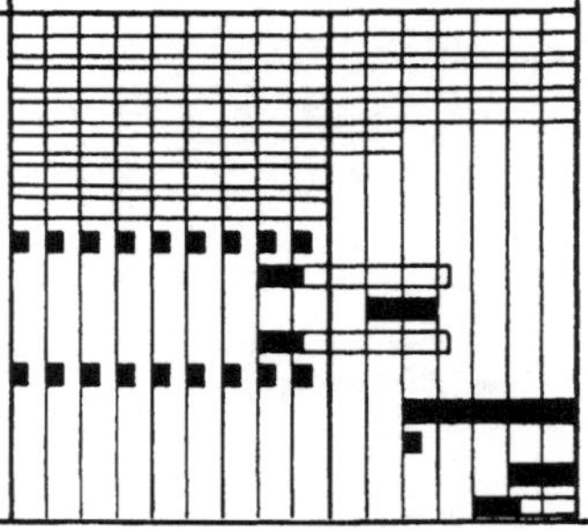

Pick Up Circuit	Magnet	Hold Circuit	Circuit Diagram
CC-1,..,9 HD-2-1,..,10 HD-5-1,..,9 NC MC-DR RO 5-n-1,.., 5-2n-12 3-19-1 NC,.., 3-20-12 NC 29-34-1,.., 29-35-12 56-3-1,.., 56-6-9 3-21-1 NC,.., 3-24-9 NC	DD Counter Magnets		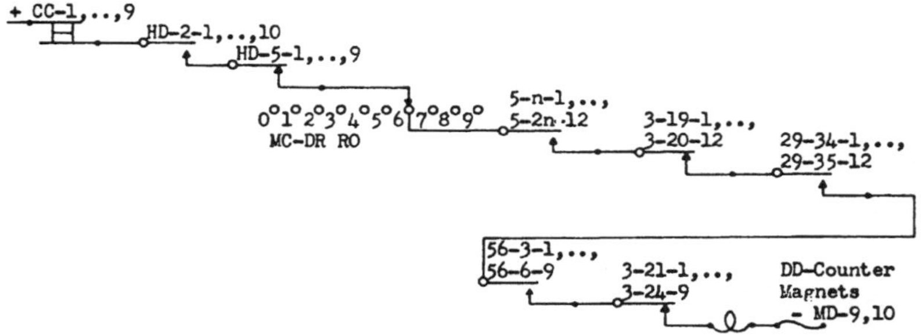
CC-44 (2-1 1/3) 5-3n-1 56-13-4	DD Carry Control 27-1-(4)	CC-46 (2-13 1/3) ABP-35 27-1-4	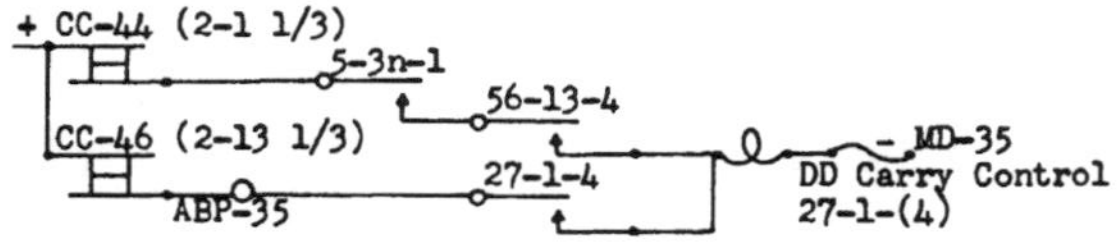
CC-45 (1/16 11-13) 27-1-1	DD Carry 61-1,..,4-(12)		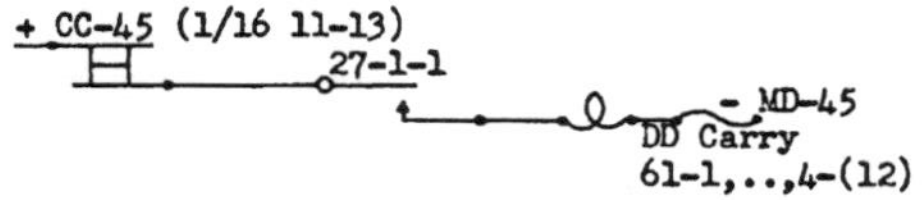

DIVISION CYCLE 7 -continued-

Pick Up Circuit	Magnet	Hold Circuit	Circuit Diagram
CC-44 (2-1 1/3) 5-3n-1 56-13-3 29-3n-1 or 21-3n-1	Elusive One 60-1,..,23-(4)	CC-46 (2-13 1/3) ABP-35 60-1,..,23-4	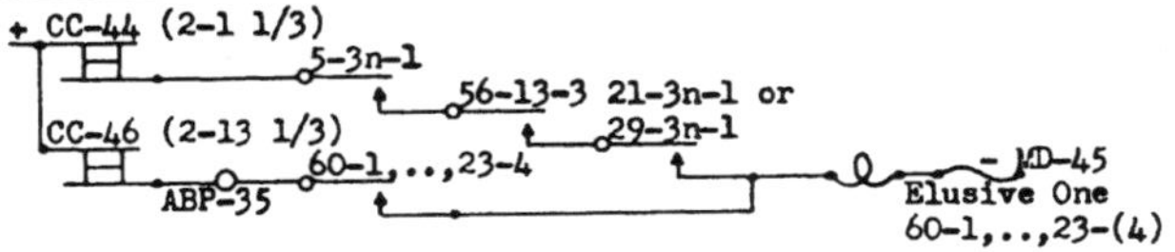
CC-12 (12-12 1/2) Carry BP DD Carry Contacts 61-1-1,.., 61-4-9 60-1-1 60-2-1,2,.., 60-23-1,2	DD Counter Magnets		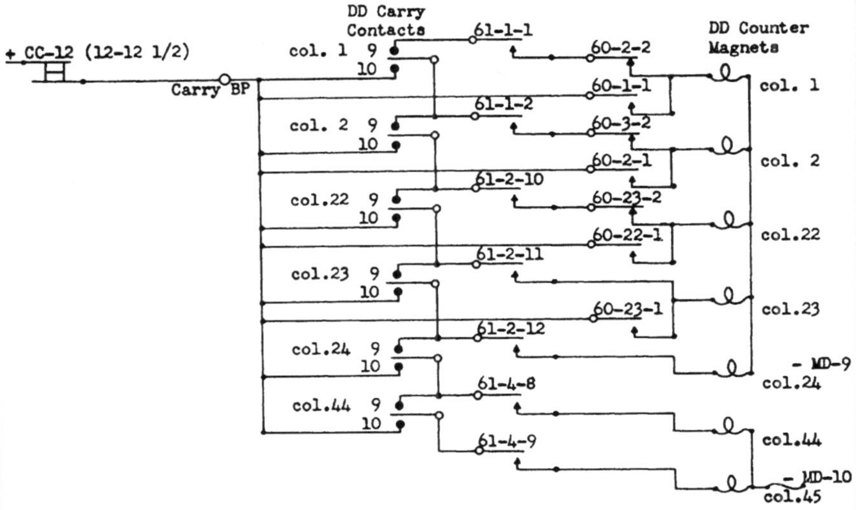
CC-1,..,9 5-3n-2 21-3n-2 or 29-3n-2 56-7-1,.., 56-8-11	PQ Counter Magnets		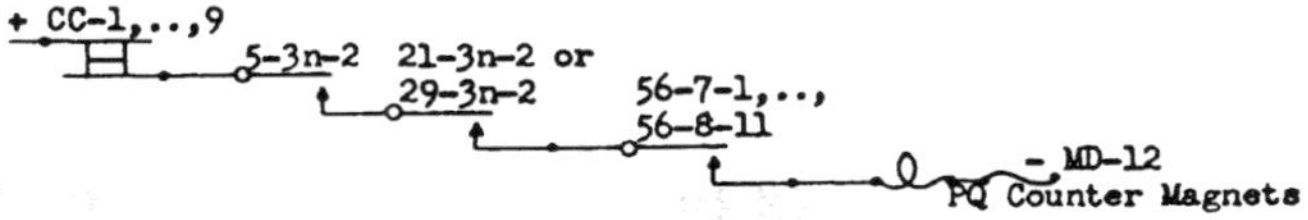

DIVISION CYCLE 7 -continued-

Pick Up Circuit	Magnet	Hold Circuit	Circuit Diagram
CC-80 (1/16 12-9) 7-1,..,9-2 NC 14-1-5	Compare Control 8-1-(4)		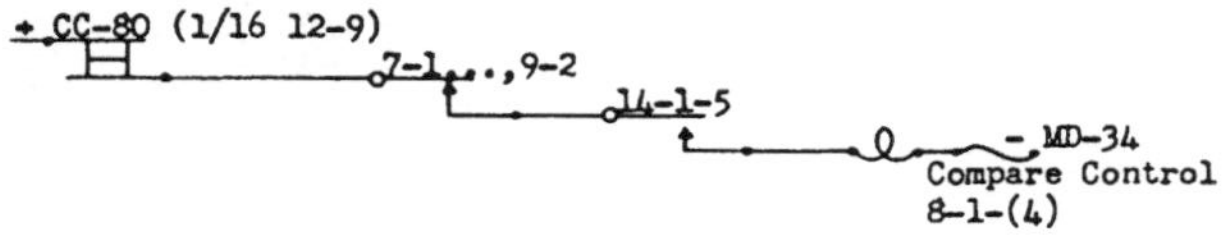
CC-40 (1/16 15-9) 14-1-2 56-13-2 8-1-3,4	Compare In 3-1,..,24-(12) 3-25-(4)	CC-39 (1/3 15-12) 3-24-11 3-25-1,2	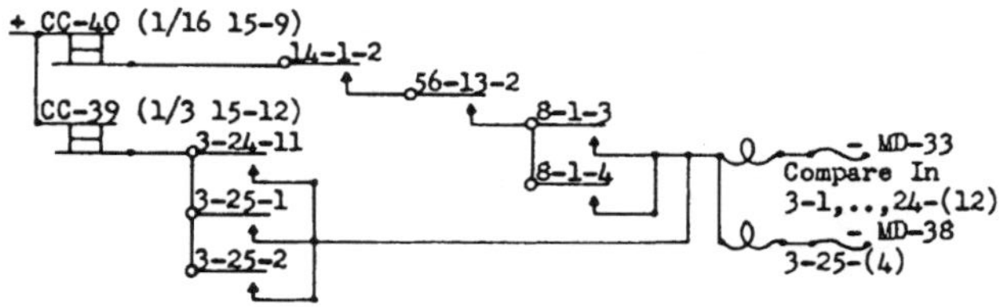
69-2-1,2 NC 14-1-1 CC-58 (14-15 1/3) 19-1-1 NC 18-1-1 NC Cycle Ctr RO A-2 56-9-1,.., 56-10-12	Column Shift Left 21-31,32,33- (12,12,6)	CC-36 (12-0) ABP-27 21-33-6	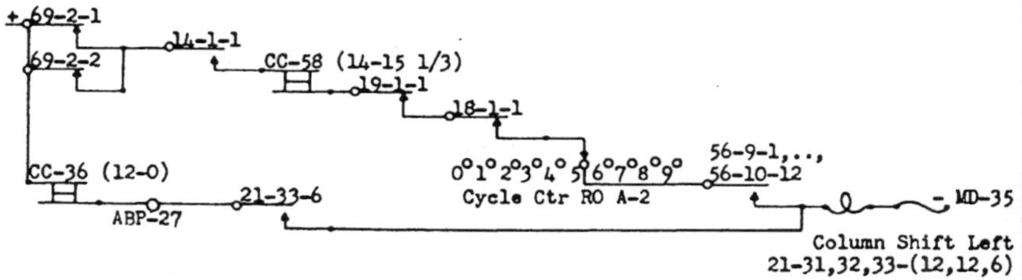

DIVISION CYCLE 8

This cycle duplicates the compare operations of cycle 6. During the latter part of the cycle, column shift left and times right relays are picked up in preparation for the next cycle.

DIVISION CYCLE 8 -continued-

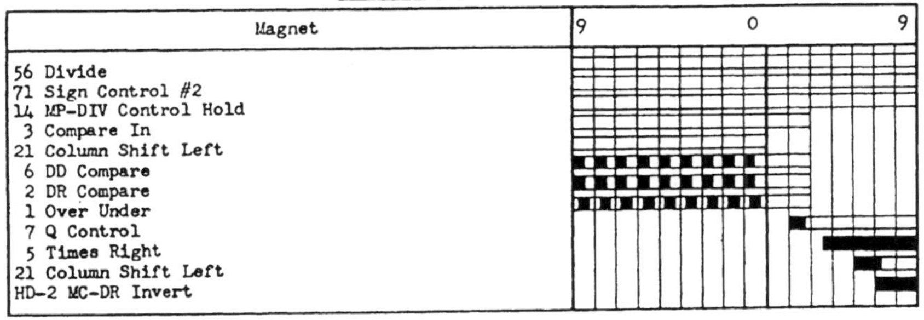

DIVISION CYCLE 9

This cycle duplicates the subtract operations of cycle 7 and the entry into the PQ counter, except for the interchange of right and left on the column shift relays.

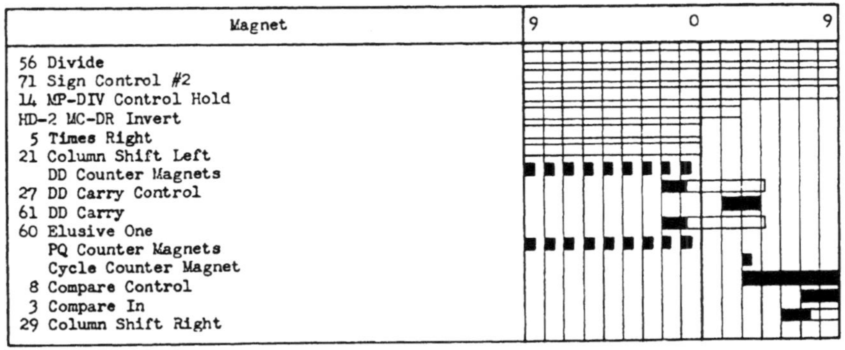

DIVISION CYCLE 10

The alternate compare and subtract cycles continue as in cycles 8 and 9. When the cycle counter reaches read-out position 9, the E relay is picked up.

DIVISION CYCLE 10 -continued-

Magnet	9 0 9
56 Divide 71 Sign Control #2 14 MP-DIV Control Hold 3 Compare In 29 Column Shift Right 6 DD Compare 2 DR Compare 1 Over-Under 7 Q-Control 5 Times Right 29 Column Shift Right HD-2 MC-DR Invert 17 E	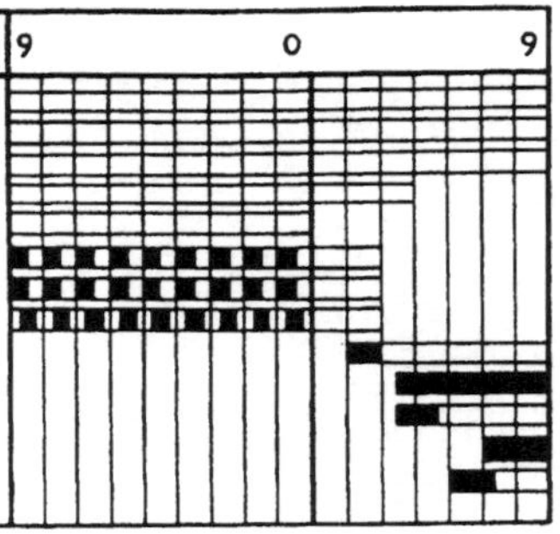

Pick Up Circuit	Magnet	Hold Circuit	Circuit Diagram
69-2-1,2 NC 14-1-1 CC-58 (14-15 1/3) 19-1-1 NC 18-1-1 NC Cycle Ctr 9's Carry Contact	E Relay 17-1-(4)	CC-36 (12-0) ABP-27 17-1-4	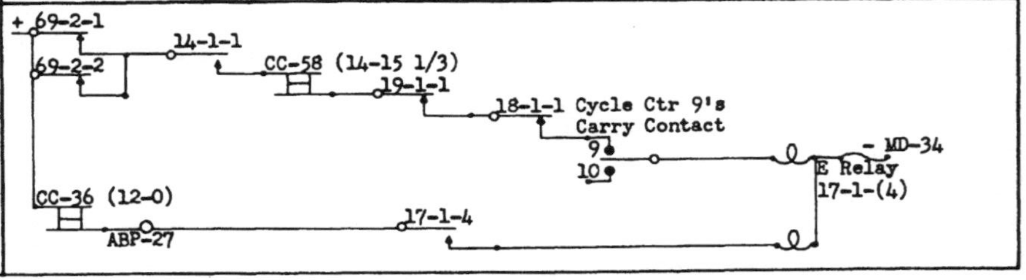

DIVISION CYCLE 11

This is a normal subtract cycle. If the E relay was picked up on the previous cycle, the F relay is now energized, whether or not the previous cycle was a "no-go", by means of the E relay and the F control relay. If the division has proceeded as far as the column shift right relay 29-7,8,9-(12,12,6), shifting the DR to subtract from columns 4-27 of DD, the G relay is picked up altering the read-out molding of the cycle counter to molding C, since this counter has reached read-out position 19.

DIVISION CYCLE 11 -continued-

Magnet	9 0 9
56 Divide 71 Sign Control #2 14 MP-DIV Control Hold HD-2 MC-DR Invert 5 Times Right 29 Column Shift Right DD Counter Magnets 27 DD Carry Control 61 DD Carry 60 Elusive One PQ Counter Magnets 64 F Control 65 G Control 17 E 18 F 19 G 8 Compare Control Cycle Counter Magnet 3 Compare In 21 Column Shift Left	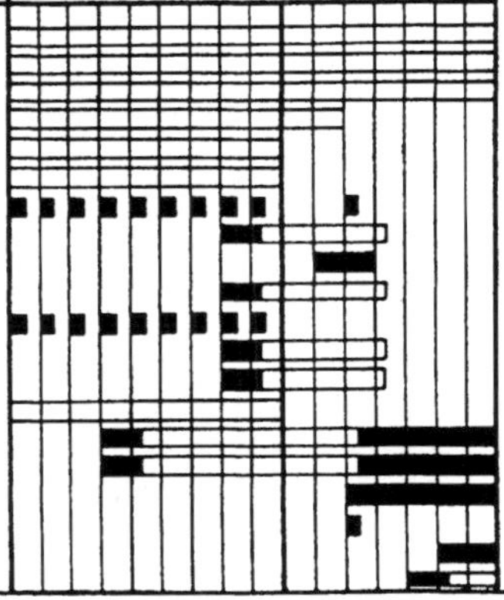

Pick Up Circuit	Magnet	Hold Circuit	Circuit Diagram
CC-44 (2-1 1/3) 17-1-2	F Control 64-1-(4)	CC-46 (2-13 1/3) ABP-35 64-1-4	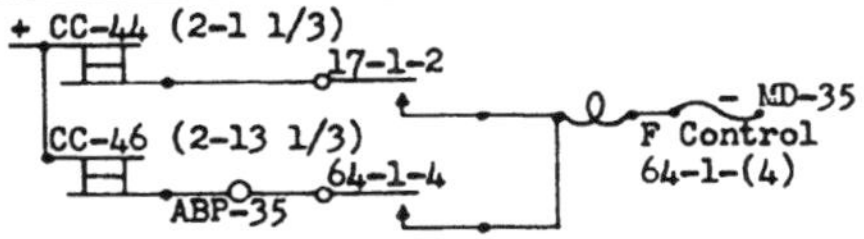
CC-44 (2-1 1/3) 29-9(2)-1	G Control 65-1-(4)	CC-46 (2-13 1/3) ABP-35 65-1-4	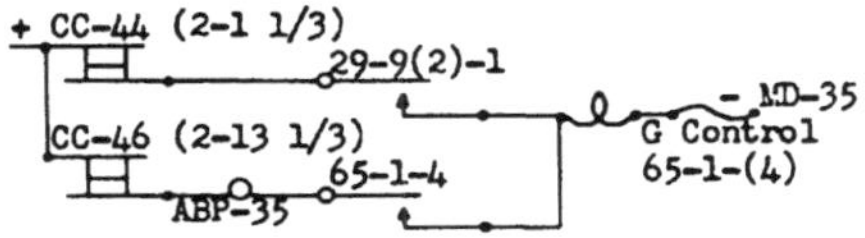
69-2-1,2 NC 14-1-1 CC-79 (6-5 1/3) HD-2-11 17-1-1 or CC-31 (12 1/2-9) 8-1-1 63-1-1 64-1-1	F Relay 18-1-(4)	12-1,2-2 NC or CC-32 (8 1/2-2) and 18-1-4	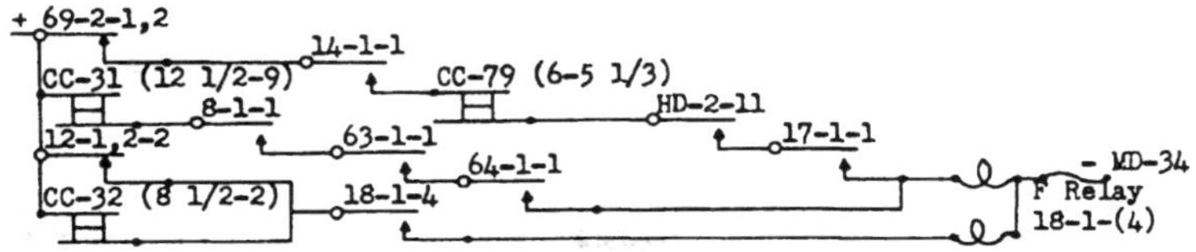

DIVISION CYCLE 11 -continued-

Pick Up Circuit	Magnet	Hold Circuit	Circuit Diagram
69-2-1,2 NC 14-1-1 CC-60 (6-5 1/3) HD-2-11 56-13-6 29-9-4 or CC-31 (12 1/2-9) 8-1-1 63-1-1 65-1-1	G Relay 19-1-(4)	12-1,2-2 NC or CC-32 (8 1/2-2) and 19-1-4	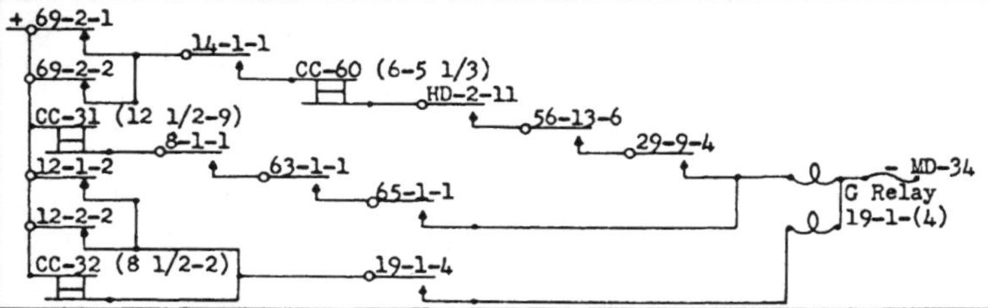

DIVISION CYCLE 12

This cycle, a compare cycle, shows the pick up of the "no-go" relay if the remainder standing in DD is less than all DR multiples for a particular columnar position. Since the Q control relay is not picked up, the cycle counter is advanced and the cycle terminates by picking up the relays preliminary to another compare cycle.

Magnet	9 0 9
56 Divide 71 Sign Control #2 14 MP-DIV Control Hold 3 Compare In 21 Column Shift Left 6 DD Compare 2 DR Compare 63 No-Go 18 F 19 G Cycle Counter Magnet 8 Compare Control 3 Compare In 29 Column Shift Right	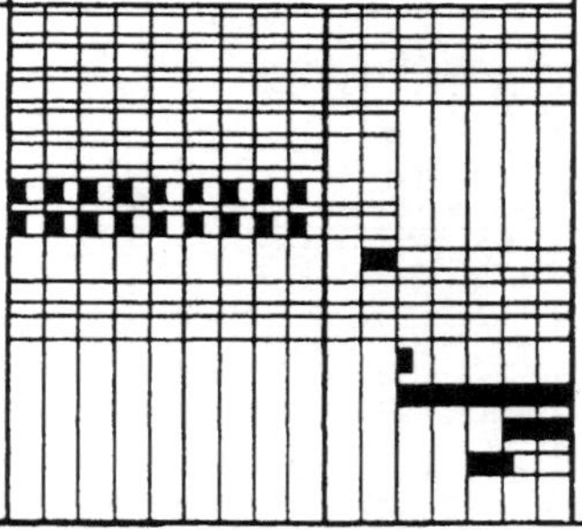

Pick Up Circuit	Magnet	Hold Circuit	Circuit Diagram
CC-37 (11-1/4 12) 3-24-10,12	No-Go 63-1-(4)	CC-38 (11 1/2-9) 63-1-4	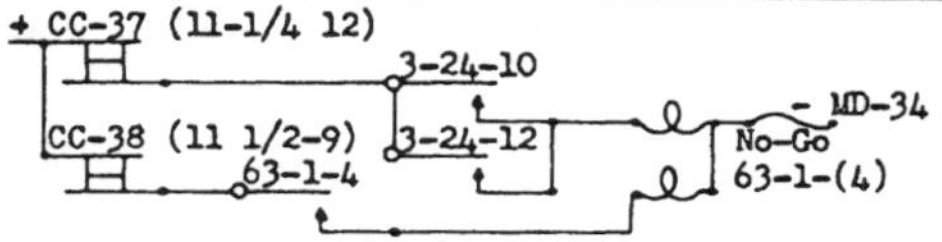

DIVISION CYCLE 13

In this cycle division has been carried sufficiently far to arrive at the place limitation plugging and energize the "9" relay preliminary to terminating the division. It is a compare cycle similar to all other compare cycles.

Magnet
56 Divide
71 Sign Control #2
14 MP-DIV Control Hold
18 F
19 G
3 Compare In
29 Column Shift Right
6 DD Compare
2 DR Compare
1 Over-Under
7 Q-Control
5 Times Right
29 Column Shift Right
HD-2 MC-DR Invert
9 "9"

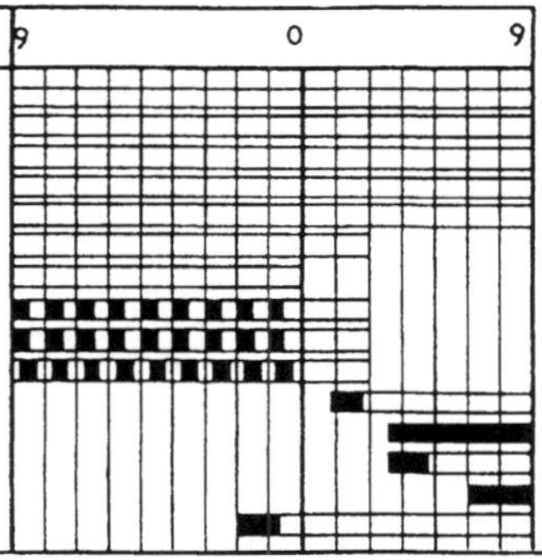

Pick Up Circuit	Magnet	Hold Circuit	Circuit Diagram
CC-44 (2-1 1/3) 56-13-5 29-3n-3 or 21-3n-3 Plug Wire	"9" Relay 9-1-(4)	CC-48 (2-4) 9-1-4	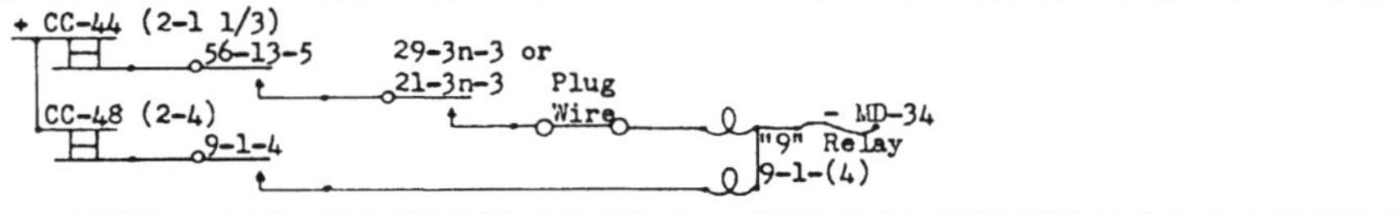

DIVISION CYCLE 14

The subtraction from DD and the entry of the digit of the quotient into the PQ counter are completed as in all subtract cycles. The "9" relay permits the energizing of the A relay and the B relay also if the 47th column of PQ stands at 9. The energized A relay permits the sequence mechanism to read setting up the sequence relays and in turn the storage counter in and repeat relays. Energizing of the A relay will cause the MP-DIV control relay to drop out. This prevents further advance of the cycle counter and permits the sequence counter to advance to read-out position 7. In preparation for the next cycle, under control of the sequence counter, the sequence counter reset, the MC-DR reset, the Q-shift and the H relays are picked up. If the B relay is energized (a nine in the 47th column of PQ) the DD-PQ invert relay is picked up. The MC-DR entry control (1-2), (3-6) and (4-8) relays are picked up under control of the MC-DR reset relay as in multiplication cycle 9.

DIVISION CYCLE 14 -continued-

Magnet
56 Divide
71 Sign control #2
14 MP-DIV Control Hold
18 F
19 G
HD-2 MC-DR Invert
5 Times Right
29 Column Shift Right
DD Counter Magnets
27 DD Carry Control
61 DD Carry
60 Elusive One
PQ Counter Magnets
9 "9"
12 A
16 B
Seq-31 Control
Seq-B-6-1
Seq-B-4-1,2
Seq-C-7-1
Seq-27 Repeat
Sequence Counter Magnet
SC40-4,5,6 Storage Counter In
48 Sequence Counter Reset
47 MC-DR Reset
HD-5 MC-DR Reset
91 MC-DR Entry Control (1-2)
92 MC-DR Entry Control (3-6)
93 MC-DR Entry Control (4-8)
33 Q Shift
20 H
HD-3 DD-PQ Invert

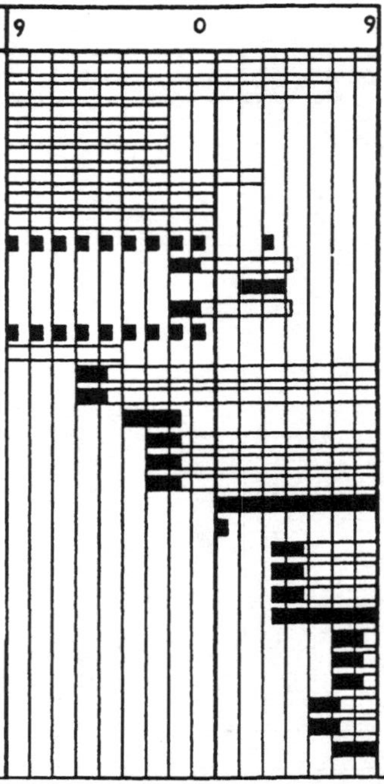

Pick Up Circuit	Magnet	Hold Circuit	Circuit Diagram
69-2-1,2 NC 14-1-1 CC-60 (6-5 1/3) 9-1-1	A Relay 12-1,2-(4)	CC-29 (6-8) 12-1-4	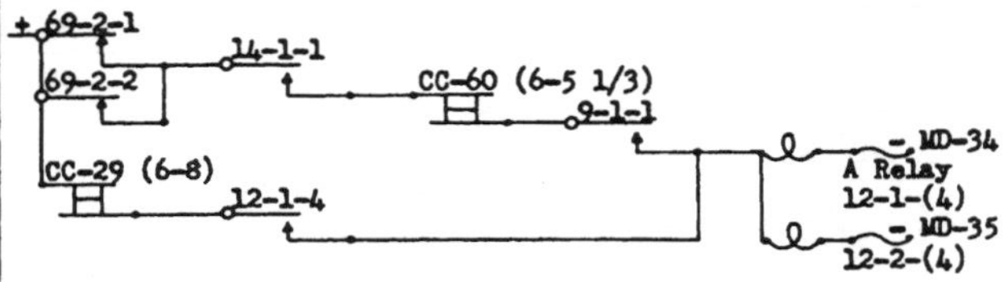

Pick Up Circuit	Magnet	Hold Circuit	Circuit Diagram
69-2-1,2 NC 14-1-1 CC-60 (6-5 1/3) 9-1-1 PQ 47th column 9's Carry Contact	B Relay 16-1-(4)	CC-29 (6-8) 16-1-4	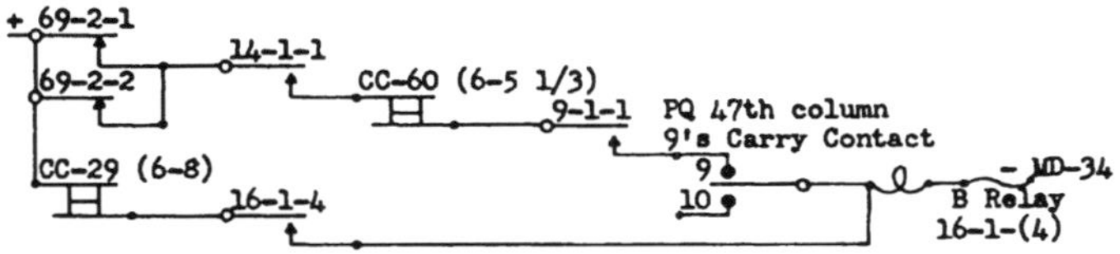
14-1-4 NC CC-55 (12 1/2-13 2/3) Seq Ctr RO B-7 56-12-6	Sequence Counter Reset 48-1-(12)	CC-43 (12-0) ABP-31-32-33 48-1-6	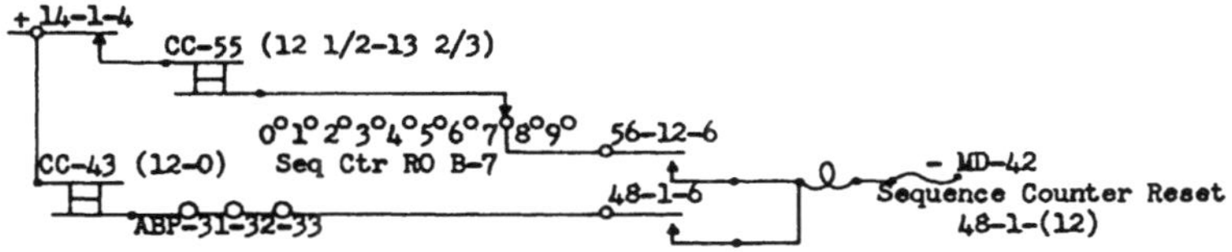
14-1-4 NC CC-56 (12 1/2-13 2/3) Seq Ctr RO C-7 56-12-7	MC-DR Reset 47-1,..,13-(12)	CC-43 (12-0) ABP-31-32-33 47-13-10,11,12	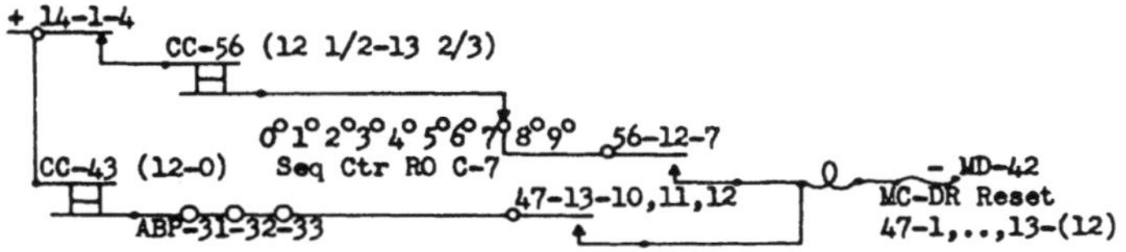
14-1-4 NC CC-56 (12 1/2-13 2/3) Seq Ctr RO C-7 56-12-7 CC-63 (12-0)	MC-DR Reset HD-5-(12)	CC-43 (12-0) ABP-31-32-33 47-13-10,11,12 CC-63 (12-0)	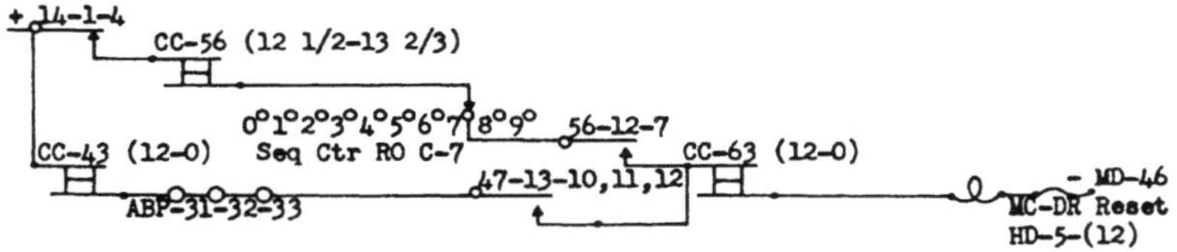
CC-33 (14-15 1/3) 48-1-8 56-13-9 Q-Shift Ctr RO	Q-Shift 33-1,..,80- (4,6 or 12)	CC-43 (12-0) ABP-31 33-2n-12	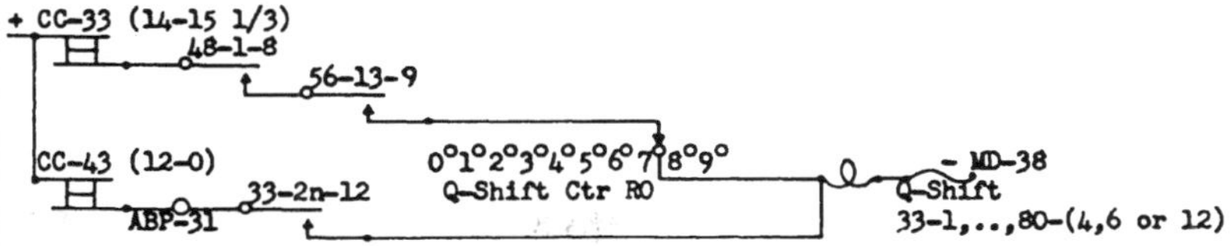

DIVISION CYCLE 14 -continued-

Pick Up Circuit	Magnet	Hold Circuit	Circuit Diagram
CC-33 (14-15 1/3) 48-1-8 56-13-8	H Relay 20-1-(4)	CC-43 (12-0) 20-1-4	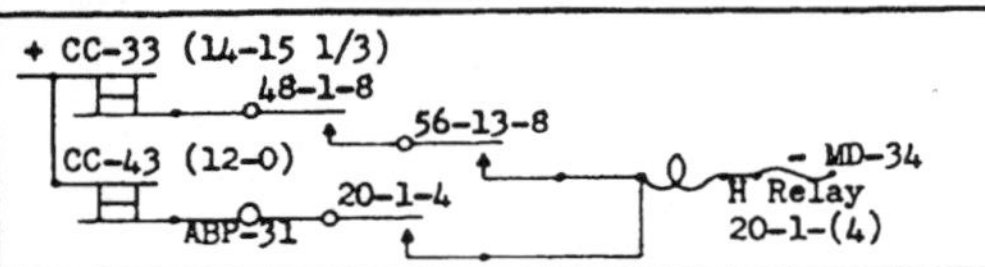

DIVISION CYCLE 15

The quotient reads from the PQ counter to storage through the Q-shift relay, except for column 47 which read through the H relay. The storage counter carry is completed. The sequence counter, cycle counter, 47th column of the PQ counter and MC-DR counters reset. The repeat relay permits the pick up of the start relay. The calculator continues in operation.

Magnet
HD-3 DD-PQ Invert
SC40-4,5,6 Storage Counter In
33 Q Shift
20 H
Storage Counter Magnets
SC40-9 Storage Counter Carry Control
SC40-7,8 Storage Counter Carry
12 A
16 B
48 Sequence Counter Reset
Sequence Counter Magnet
PQ 47th column Counter Magnet
Cycle Counter Magnet
47 MC-DR Reset
HD-5 MC-DR Reset
91 MC-DR Entry Control (1-2)
MC-DR Counter Magnets (1-2)
92 MC-DR Entry Control (3-6)
MC-DR Counter Magnets (3-6)
93 MC-DR Entry Control (4-8)
MC-DR Counter Magnets (4-8)
MC-DR Counter Magnets (5)
MC-DR Counter Magnets (7)
MC-DR Counter Magnets (9)
Seq-27 Repeat
Seq-33 Start
Seq-31 Control
Seq Relays

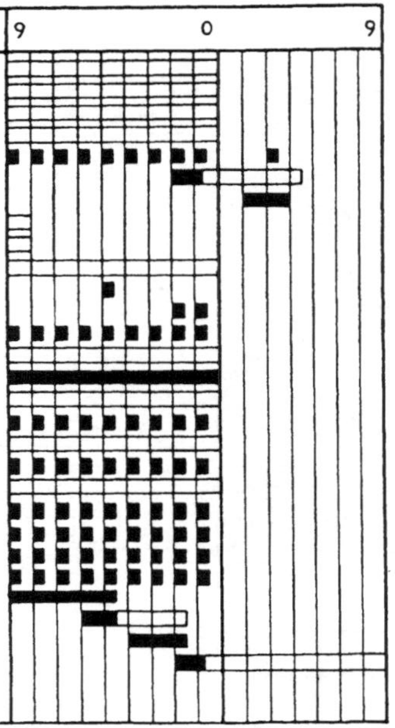

DIVISION CYCLE 15 -continued-

Pick Up Circuit	Magnet	Hold Circuit	Circuit Diagram
CC-1,..,9 HD-3-1,..,9 NC HD-3-10 HD-6-1,..,9 NC PQ Counter RO 33-1-1,.., 33-80-11 Buss SC40-4-1,.., SC40-5-11	Storage Counter Magnet (cols. 1-23)		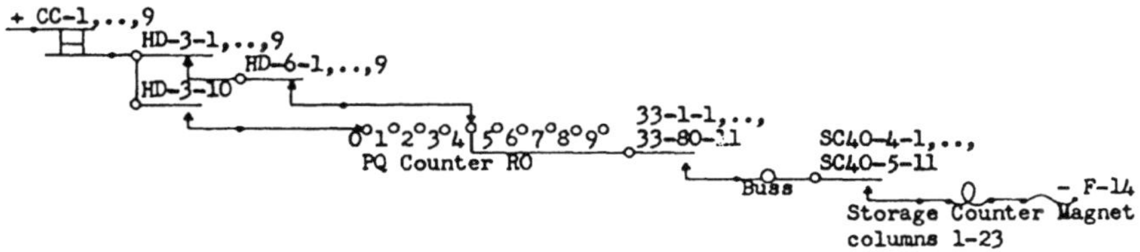
CC-9 (9-9 1/2) HD-3-10 Col.46 zero Col.47 zero or 8 HD-3-11 20-1-1 Buss SC40-5-12	Read 9 from 47th col. of PQ to 24th col. of storage counter		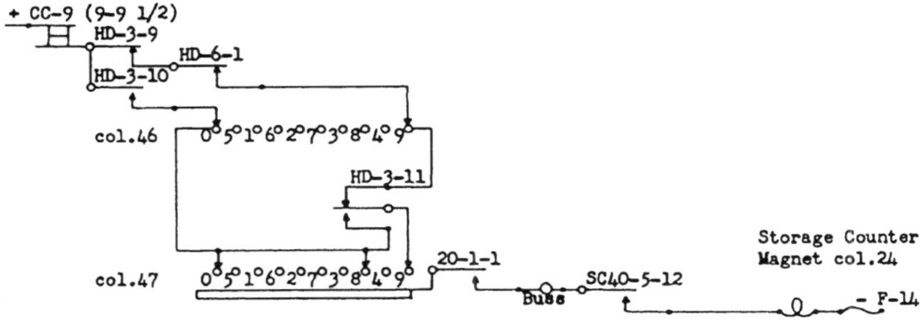
CC-2 (2-2 1/2) 71-1-3 NC PQ 47th column 8 spot RO 20-1-2 CC-1 (1-1 1/2) 71-1-2 NC PQ 47th column 9 spot RO 20-1-2	PQ 47th column Counter Magnet		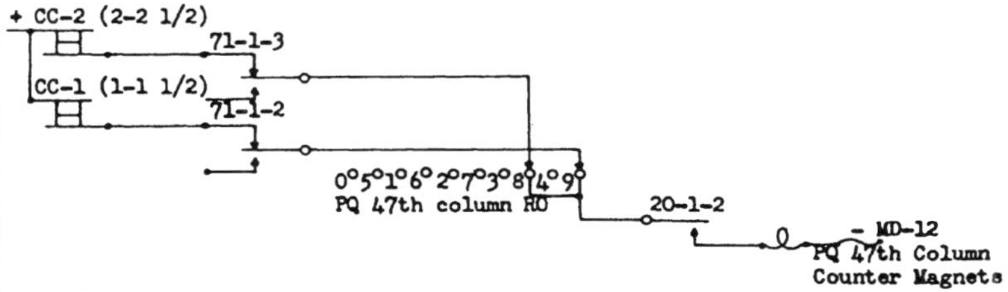

Relay	Row	Contact	Cycle	Function
1-1,..,423-(4) D	1,..,9	1-1,..,46-1	D-6	PU of Q-Control 7-1-(4)
Over Under		1-47-(4)		Does not exist
D-6		2 ≤ k ≤ 9		
		1-(47k-46),..,(47k)-1	D-6	PU of Q-Control 7-k-(4)
		1 ≤ i ≤ 423		
		1-i-3	D-6	Hold
2-1,..,216-(4) D	1,..,9	2-2,.n.,23-1 NC	D-6	PU of Over Under 1-2,.(2n-2).,44-(4)
DR Compare		2-1,.n.,23-2	D-6	PU of Over Under 1-2,.(2n-1).,45-(4)
D-6		2-24-(4)		Does not exist
		2 ≤ k ≤ 9		
		2-(24k-22),.n.,(24k)-1 NC	D-6	PU of Over Under 1-(47k-45),.(2n-k-1).,(47k-1)-(4)
		2-(24k-23),.n.,(24k)-2	D-6	PU of Over Under 1-(47k-46),.(2n-k).,(47k)-(4)
		1 ≤ i ≤ 216		
		2-i-4	D-6	Hold
3-1,..,18-(12) S	1,..,9	3-1-1,..,3-2-11	D-6	PU of DR Compare 2-1,..,23-(4)
3-19,..,24-(12) S	19	2 ≤ k ≤ 9		
3-25-(4) S	21	3-(2k-1)-1,..,3-(2k)-12	D-6	PU of DR Compare 2-(24k-23),..,24k-(4)
Compare In		3-19-1,..,3-20-12	D-6	PU of DD Compare 6-1,..,24-(12)
D-5		3-19-1,..,3-20-12 NC	M-6	Control read-in to PQ ctr magnets
		3-19-1,..,3-20-12 NC	D-7	Control read-in to DD ctr magnets
		3-21-1,..,3-24-9	D-6	PU of DD Compare 6-1,..,24-(12)
		3-21-1,..,3-24-9 NC	M-6	Control read-in to DD ctr magnets
		3-21-1,..,3-24-9 NC	D-6	Control read-in to DD ctr magnets
		3-24-10,12	D-6	PU of Q-Control 7-1,..,9-(4)
			D-12	PU of No-GO 63-1-(4)
		3-24-11; 3-25-1,2	D-5	Hold
4-1,..,27-(12,12,4) S	1,..,9	4-1-1,..,4-2-11	M-6	Control MC-DR times 1 RO to DD ctr magnets
Times Left		4-(3k-2)-1,..,4-(3k-1)-12	M-6	Control MC-DR times k RO to DD ctr magnets
M-5		4-3k-1	M-6	PU of DD Carry Control 27-1-(4)
		4-3k-4	M-5	Hold
5-1,..,27-(12,12,4) S	1,..,9	5-1-1,..,5-2-11	M-6	Control MC-DR times 1 RO to PQ ctr magnets
Times Right			D-6	Control MC-DR times 1 RO to DD ctr magnets
M-5		5-(3k-2)-1,..,5-(3k-1)-12	M-6	Control MC-DR times k RO to PQ ctr magnets
D-6			D-6	
		5-3k-1	M-6	PU of PQ Carry Control 24-1-(4)
			D-7	PU of DD Carry Control 27-1-(4)
				PU of Elusive One 60-1,..,23-(4)
		5-3k-2	D-7	Controls Q Entry into PQ ctr
		5-3k-4	M-5	Hold
			D-6	

Relay	Row	Contact	Cycle	Function
6-1,..,24-(12) D	10	6-1,..,23-1	D-6	PU of Over Under 1-2,.(2n-2).,44-(4) or 1-2,.(2n-1).,45-(4)
DD Compare		6-24-1	D-6	PU of Over Under 1-46-(4)
D-6		6-1,.n.,24-k	D-6	PU of Over Under 1-(47k-46),.(2n-k).,(47k)-(4) or 1-(47k-45),.(2n-k-1).,(47k-1)-(4)
		6-1,..,24-12	D-6	Hold
7-1,..,9-(4) D	10	1 ≤ k ≤ 9		
Q-Control		7-(k)-1	D-6	PU of Times Right 5-(3k-2)-(12); 5-(3k-1)-(12); 5-(3k)-(4)
D-6		7-(k)-2 NC	M-5 D-5	Controls read-in to Cycle ctr
		7-(k)-3	D-6	Hold
8-1-(4) S	10	8-1-1	D-11	PU of F 18-1-(4); G 19-1-(4)
Compare Control		8-1-3,4	D-5	PU of Compare In 3-1,..,24-(12); 3-25-(4)
D-5		8-1-3,4 NC	D-6	PU of MC-DR Invert HD-2-(12)
9-1-(4) D	10	9-1-1	D-14	PU of A 12-1,2-(4); B 16-1-(4)
"9" Relay		9-1-4	D-13	Hold
D-13				
10-1-(4) S	10	10-1-1	- -	Controls read-in to Log Cycle ctr
LE		10-1-2	- -	PU of MC-DR Reset 47-1,..,13-(12) (Log)
		10-1-3	- -	PU of LF 11-1-(6); 11-2-(4)
		10-1-4	- -	Hold
11-1-(6) S	10	11-1-1	- -	PU of LIO In #1 189-1,2,3-(12,12,4)
11-2-(4) S		11-1-2	- -	Hold of LE 10-1-(4); LM 42-1,2,3-(12,12,4)
LF		11-1-3 NC	- -	PU of Intermediate In 50-1,2,3-(12) (Log)
		11-1-4	- -	Hold of LG 201-1-(4)
		11-1-5	- -	PU of Read Control Seq-31-(4) and Clutch Magnet (not used)
		11-1-6	- -	Hold
		11-2-2- NC	- -	PU of Intermediate In 50-1,2,3-(12) (Log)
12-1,2-(4) S	10,11	12-1-1	- -	Controls read-in to Sine Sequence ctr #2
A		12-1,2-2	M-5 D-5	Hold of MP-DIV Control Hold 14-1-(12)
M-10			M-7 D-11	Hold of F 18-1-(4)
D-14		12-1,2-3	M-10 D-14	PU of Read Control Seq-31-(4) and Clutch Magnet
		12-1-4	M-10 D-14	Hold
13-1-(6) S	10	13-1-1	M-5 D-5	Controls read-in to Cycle ctr
MP-DIV Control Pick-Up			D-5	PU of Compare Control 8-1-(4)
M-5 D-5		13-1-2	M-5 D-5	PU of MP-DIV Control Hold 14-1-(12)

Relay	Row	Contact	Cycle	Function
13-1-(6) S	10	13-1-3	M-5	PU of MP-DIV Control Hold 14-1-(12); Column Shift Right
(continued)			D-5	29-1,..,36-(12,12,6)
		13-1-4	D-5	PU of Compare In 3-1,..,24-(12); 3-25-(4)
		13-1-5	- -	PU of XJ 216-1-(6); E Shift 213 and 214 (Exp)
		13-1-6	M-5	Hold
			D-5	
14-1-(12) S	10	14-1-1	M-5	PU of Column Shift Left 21-1,..,36-(12,12,6); Column Shift
MP-DIV Control Hold			D-6	Right 29-1,..,36-(12,12,6)
M-5			M-10	PU of A 12-1-(4); B 16-1-(4)
D-5			D-14	
			M-6	PU of E 17-1-(4)
			D-10	
			M-7	PU of F 18-1-(4)
			D-11	
			M-8	PU of C_2 66-1-(4); D_2 67-1-(4)
		14-1-2	D-7	PU of Compare In 3-1,..,24-(12); 3-25-(4)
			D-6	PU of MC-DR Invert HD-2-(12)
		14-1-3 NC	M-0	Controls read-in to Sequence ctr
			D-0	
		14-1-4 NC	M-0	Controls RO of Sequence ctr
			D-0	
		14-1-5	M-6	Controls read-in to Cycle ctr
			D-7	PU of Compare Control 8-1-(4); Controls read-in to Cycle ctr
		14-1-9	M-6	Hold of PQ 23rd Col 68-1-(4)
		14-1-11	M-5	Hold
			D-5	
15-1-(4) S	10	15-1-1	- -	Controls reset of Sequence ctr to 4 (Exp)
XG		15-1-2 NC	- -	PU of MC-DR Reset 47-1,..,13-(12) (Exp)
		15-1-3,4	- -	Hold
16-1-(4) S	10	16-1-1	M-10	PU of DD-PQ Invert HD-3-(12)
B			D-14	
M-10		16-1-4	M-10	Hold
D-14			D-14	
17-1-(4) D	10	17-1-1	M-7	PU of F 18-1-(4)
E			D-11	
M-6		17-1-2	D-11	PU of F Control 64-1-(4)
D-10		17-1-4	M-6	Hold
			D-10	
18-1-(4) D	10	18-1-1	M-8	Controls Cycle ctr RO A & B mldgs
F		18-1-2	M-8	Controls Cycle ctr RO C & D mldgs
M-7		18-1-4	M-7	Hold
D-11			D-11	

Relay	Row	Contact	Cycle	Function
19-1-(4) D	10	19-1-1 NC	M-5	Controls Cycle ctr RO
G			D-5	
D-11		19-1-4	D-11	Hold
20-1-(4) S	10	20-1-1	D-15	Controls RO of PQ 47th col
H		20-1-2	D-15	Controls reset of PQ 47th col
D-14		20-1-4	D-14	Hold
21-1,..,36-(12,12,6) S	11	1 ≤ k ≤ 11		
Column Shift Left		21-(3k-2)-1,..,21-(3k-1)-12	M-6	Control shift of multiple of MC-DR to cols 2k up of DD
M-5			D-7,8	
D-7		21-34-1,..,21-35-12	- -	Control shift of multiple of MC-DR to cols 0 up of DD
		1 ≤ n ≤ 12		
		21-3n-1	D-7	PU of Elusive One 60-1,..,23-(4)
		21-3n-2	D-7	Controls Q-Entry into PQ ctr
		21-3n-3	D-13	PU of "9" relay 9-1-(4)
		21-3n-5	M-5	Controls MP ctr RO 2nd mldg
		21-3n-6	M-5	Hold
22-1-(12) S	11	22-1-1,..,10	D-2	Control Invert of Q-Shift ctr
Q-Shift Invert		22-1-11	D-1	Hold
D-1				
23-1-(4) S	11	23-1-1	M-1	PU of Intermediate Carry 53-1,2-(12)
Intermediate Carry		23-1-4	M-1	Hold
Control				
M-1				
D-1				
24-1-(4) S	11	24-1-1	M-6	PU of PQ Carry 62-1,..,4-(12)
PQ Carry Control		24-1-4	M-6	Hold
M-6				
25-1-(4) S	11	25-1-1	D-4	PU of Q-Shift Carry 28-1-(4)
Q-Shift Carry Control		25-1-4	D-4	Hold
D-4				
26-1-(4) D	11	26-1-1	M-3	PU of MC-DR Carry 49-1,..,10-(12)
MC-DR Carry Control		26-1-4	M-3	Hold
M-3				
27-1-(4) S	11	27-1-1	M-6	PU of DD Carry 61-1,..,4-(12)
DD Carry Control		27-1-4	M-6	Hold
D-4				

Relay	Row	Contact	Cycle	Function
28-1-(4) S	11	28-1-1,2	D-1,4	Control Q-Shift Carry
Q-Shift Carry				
D-4				
29-1,..,36-(12,12,6) S	12	1 ≤ k ≤ 12		
29-9(2)-(4)	12	29-(3k-2)-1,..,29-(3k-1)-12	M-6	Control Multiple by (2k-1)st col of MP to cols (2k-1) up of PQ or DD
Column Shift Right			D-5	
M-5		29-3k-1	D-7	PU of Elusive One 60-1,..,23-(4)
D-5		29-3k-2	D-7	Controls Q-Entry into PQ ctr
		29-3k-3	D-13	PU of "9" relay 9-1-(4)
		29-9-4	D-11	PU of G 19-1-(4)
		29-3k-5	M-5	Controls MP ctr RO 2nd mldg
		29-3k-6	M-5	Hold
			D-5	
		29-9(2)-1	D-11	PU of G Control 65-1-(4)
30-1-(12) D	12	30-1-1,2 NC	M-5	Hold of MP Cycle Control Hold 37-1,..,26-(4,6 or 12)
C Relay		30-1-3	M-9	PU of DD-PQ Transfer #2 59-1,2-(12); 59-3-(6); MP Reset 40-1,2,3-(12); MC-DR Reset 47-1,..,13-(12); MC-DR Reset HD-5-(12)
M-9				
		30-1-4	- -	Controls RO of Log Cycle ctr
		30-1-5	- -	PU of EIO Reset 218-1,2,3-(12)
		30-1-6	- -	Controls RO of Sine Sequence ctr #1
		30-1-7	- -	PU of Intermediate In 50-1,2,3-(12) (Log)
		30-1-8,9 NC	M-5	Hold of MP Cycle Control Hold 37-1,..,26-(4,6 or 12)
		30-1-10 NC	M-8	PU of C_2 66-1-(4)
		30-1-11	M-9	Hold
31-1-(12) D	12	31-1-1,2 NC	M-5	Hold of MP Cycle Control Hold 37-1,..,26-(4,6 or 12)
D Relay		31-1-3	M-9	PU of DD-PQ Transfer #2 59-1,2-(12); 59-3-(6); MP Reset 40-1,2,3-(12); MC-DR Reset 47-1,..,13-(12); MC-DR Reset HD-5-(12)
M-9				
		31-1-4	- -	Controls RO of Log Cycle ctr
		31-1-5	- -	PU of EIO Reset 218-1,2,3-(12)
		31-1-6	- -	Controls RO of Sine Sequence ctr #1
		31-1-7	- -	PU of Intermediate In 50-1,2,3-(12) (Log)
		31-1-8,9 NC	M-5	Hold of MP Cycle Control Hold 37-1,..,26-(4,6 or 12)
		31-1-10 NC	M-8	PU of D_2 67-1-(4)
		31-1-11	M-9	Hold
32-1-(4) S	12	32-1-1,2	D-4	Control read-in to Q-Shift ctr
Add-22		32-1-3	D-4	PU of Q-Shift Carry Control 25-1-(4)
D-3		32-1-4	D-3	Hold
33-1,..,32-(12) S	13	0 ≤ k ≤ 22		
33-33,..,46-(12) S	14	33-(45-2k)-1,..,33-(46-2k)-12	D-15	Control shift of PQ RO k cols to right
33-47,..,70-(4,6 or 12) S	20	0 ≤ k ≤ 11		
33-71,..,80-(12) S	21	33-(47 + k)-(4,6 or 12)	D-15	Control supply of k nines to left of PQ-RO
Q-Shift				

Relay	Row	Contact	Cycle	Function
(continued)				
33-1,..,32-(12) S		$12 \le k \le 22$		
33-33,..,46-(12) S		33-(35 + 2k)-1,..,	D-15	Control supply of k nines to left of PQ RO
33-47,..,70-(4,6 or 12) S		33-(36 + 2k)-3,5 or 11		
33-71,..,80-(12) S		$0 \le k \le 11$		
Q-Shift		33-(47 + k)-4,6 or 12	D-15	Hold is last point
D-14		$12 \le k \le 22$		
		33-(36 + 2k)-4,6 or 12	D-15	Hold is last point
34-1,2,3-(12) S	14	34-1-1,..,34-2-12	M-11	Control PQ ctr RO
34-4-(4)	14	34-3-1	- -	PU of LIO In #1 192-1,2,3-(12,12,4)
P-Out		34-3-2	- -	PU of Divide 56-1,..,13-(12) (Exp)
M-10		34-3-3 NC	- -	Hold of Tape Selection Relays 183,184,185-1,..,9-(12) (Int)
		34-3-5 NC	- -	Hold of LG 201-1-(4)
		34-3-6	- -	PU of SM-3 83-1,2-(12,4)
		34-3-7 NC	- -	Hold of SM-3 83-1,2-(12,4)
		34-3-8	- -	PU of Read Control Seq-31-(4) and Clutch Magnet (not used)
		34-3-9	M-11	Controls reset of PQ 47 col
		34-3-12; 34-4-4	M-10	Hold
35-1,..,46-(4) S	14	35-45,46-1 NC	M-1	PU of Shift 36-37,38,39-(12,12,4) (No shift)
Shift Pick-Up		35-45-1; 35-43,44-1 NC	D-1	PU of Shift 36-34,35,36-(12,12,4) (Shift 1 col)
D-1		35-45,43-1; 35-41,42-1 NC	D-1	PU of Shift 36-32,33-(12) (Shift 2 cols)
M-1		$3 \le k \le 13$		
		35-45,.(2n + 1).,(47-2k)-1;	D-1	PU of Shift 36-(36-2k),(37-2k)-(12,4,6 or 12) (Shift k cols)
		35-(45-2k),(46-2k)-1 NC		
		$14 \le k \le 22$		
		35-45,.(2n + 1).,(47-2k)-1;	D-1	PU of Shift 36-(23-k)-(4,6 or 12) (Shift k cols)
		35-(45-2k),(46-2k)-1 NC		
		35-n-4	D-1	Hold
36-1,..,39-(4,6 or 12) S	15			Controls shift of k cols to left; last two points read amount of shift to Q-Shift ctr
Shift				
M-1		k = 20,21,22		
D-1		36-(23-k)-1,..,(25-k)	M-2	Hold is last point
		$15 \le k \le 19$	D-2	
		36-(23-k)-1,..,(25-k)	M-2	Hold is 36-(23-k)-11
		k = 14	D-2	
		36-(23-k)-1,..,(25-k)	M-2	Hold is 36-(23-k)-12
		$8 \le k \le 13$	D-2	
		36-(36-2k)-1,..,	M-2	Hold is last point
		36-(37-2k)-(13-k)	D-2	
		$3 \le k \le 7$		
		36-(36-2k)-1,..,	M-2	Hold is 36-(37-2k)-11
		36-(37-2k)-(13-k)	D-2	
		k = 2		
		36-32-1,..,36-33-11	M-2	Hold is 36-33-12
			D-2	

Relay	Row	Contact	Cycle	Function
36-1,..,39-(4,6 or 12) S		k = 1		
(continued)		36-34-1,..,36-35-12	M-2	Hold is 36-36-4
		k = 0	D-2	
		36-37-1,..,36-39-1	M-2	Hold is 36-39-2
			D-2	
37-1,..,26-(4,6 or 12) D	16			A digit in col 1 of MP picks up 37-1,2-(12,4)
MP Cycle Control				A digit in col 3 of MP picks up 37-3,4-(12,4)
M-5		1 ≤ k ≤ 12		A digit in col (2k-1) of MP picks up 37-(k + 2)-(4,6 or 12) in order to read to PQ col (2k-1) and up
		37-1-1	M-5	PU of 29-1,2,3-(12,12,6) Column Shift Right
		37-3-1	M-5	PU of 29-4,5,6-(12,12,6) Column Shift Right
		3 ≤ k ≤ 12		
		37-(k + 2)-1	M-5	PU of 29-(3k-2),(3k-1),(3k)-(12,12,6) Column Shift Right
		37-14-2 NC	M-8	PU of D_2 67-1-(4)
				A digit in col 2 of MP picks up 37-15,16-(12,4)
		2 ≤ k ≤ 11		A digit in col 2k of MP picks up 37-(k + 15)-(4,6 or 12) in order to read to DD col 2k and up
		37-16-1	M-5	PU of 21-1,2,3-(12,12,6) Column Shift Left
		37-(k + 15)-1	M-5	PU of 21-(3k-2),(3k-1),(3k)-(12,12,6) Column Shift Left
		37-26-2 NC	M-8	PU of C_2 66-1-(4)
		37-2,4-3; 37-5,..,10-12; 37-11,12-6; 37-13,14-4; 37-16-3; 37-17,..,22-12; 37-23,24-6; 37-25,26-4	M-5	Hold
38-1,2,3-(12) S	16	38-1-1,..,38-2-1	M-5	PU of Column Shift Right 29-1,..,36-(12,12,6)
Multiply #2			M-8	PU of D_2 67-1-(4)
M-0		38-2-2,..,38-3-1	M-5	PU of Column Shift Left 21-1,..,33-(12,12,6)
			M-8	PU of C_2 66-1-(4)
		38-3-3	M-0	Controls read-in to Sequence ctr
		38-3-5	M-7	PU of F 18-1-(4)
		38-3-6	M-5	Control Cycle ctr RO
		38-3-7	M-6	PU of PQ Carry Control 24-1-(4)
		38-3-8	M-6	PU of DD Carry Control 27-1-(4)
		38-3-11	M-0	Hold
39-1,2,3-(12) S	16	39-1-1,..,39-2-11	M-5	Control read-in to MP ctr and PU of MP Cycle Control 37-1,..,26-(4,6 or 12)
MP In				
M-4		39-2-12	M-5	PU of MD-DIV Control Pick-Up 13-1-(6)
		39-3-1 NC	- -	Hold of X_T Step Control 180-1-(6) (Int)
		39-3-2	- -	PU of Sign Control #1 70-1-(4) (Int)
		39-3-3	- -	PU of SIO Reset 228-1,2,3-(12)
		39-3-4	- -	Controls read-in to Log Cycle ctr
		39-3-5	- -	PU of LF 11-1,2-(6,4)
		39-3-6	- -	Controls reset of X_T ctr (Int)
		39-3-7	- -	Controls read-in to Sine Sequence ctr #1
		39-3-8 NC	- -	Hold of SIO Out #2 Control 237-1-(4)
		39-3-9	- -	PU of Forward Tape Clutch Magnet

Relay	Row	Contact	Cycle	Function
39-1,2,3(12) S		39-3-10	- -	Controls read-in to X_T ctr (Int)
(continued)		39-3-11	M-4	Hold
		39-3-12	- -	PU of EIO 24th Col 9 225-1-6
40-1,2,3-(12) S	16	40-1-1,..,9	M-10	Controls read-in of 10's complements for MP reset
MP Reset		40-2-1,..,40-3-11	M-10	Controls read-in to MP ctr
M-9		40-2-1,..,40-3-11 NC	M-5	Controls read-in to MP ctr
		40-3-12	M-9	Hold
41-1,2-(12) S	16			Controls Sequence ctr RO
Multiply #1		41-1-1	M-0	PU of Intermediate In 50-1,2,3-(12)
M-0		41-1-2	M-0	PU of DD-PQ Reset 58-1,..,8-(12)
		41-1-3	M-1	PU of MC-DR In 43-1,..,10-(12); 43-11,12-(4)
		41-1-4	M-1	PU of Intermediate Invert Control 94-1-(4)
		41-1-5	M-2	PU of First Build Up 44-1,..,5-(12)
		41-1-6	M-2	PU of First and Second Build Up 45-1,..,5-(12)
		41-1-7	M-2	PU of Intermediate Reset 52-1,2,3-(12); HD-4-(12)
		41-1-8	M-3	PU of Intermediate In 50-1,2,3-(12)
		41-1-9	M-3	PU of First and Second Build Up 45-1...,5-(12)
		41-1-10	M-3	PU of Second Build up 46-1,..,5-(12)
		41-1-11	M-4	PU of MP In 39-1,2,3-(12)
		41-1-12	M-4	PU of Intermediate Invert Control 94-1-(4)
		41-2-1	M-5	PU of Intermediate Reset 52-1,2,3-(12); HD-4-(12)
		41-2-2	M-10	PU of Sequence Counter Reset 48-1-(12)
		41-2-3	M-10	PU of P-Out 34-1,2,3-(12); 34-4-(4)
		41-2-4	M-9	PU of MC-DR Reset 47-1,..,13-(12); HD-5-(12)
		41-2-5	M-0	PU of Multiply #2 38-1,2,3-(12)
		41-2-6	M-10	PU of P-Out 34-1,2-(12); 34-4-(4)
		41-2-11	M-9	Hold
42-1,2,3-(12,12,4)	17	42-1-1,..,42-2-3	- -	Controls Sequence ctr RO (Log)
LM		42-2-4	- -	Hold of LE 10-1-(4)
		42-2-5 NC	- -	Controls Sequence ctr reset (Log)
		42-2-6	- -	PU of Intermediate In 50-1,2,3-(12) (Log)
		42-2-7 NC	- -	Controls RO of LIO 23rd col
		42-2-8	- -	PU of Multiply #2 38-1,2,3-(12) (Log)
		42-2-9 NC	- -	PU of Log In #2 190-1,2,3-(12,12,4)
		42-2-10	- -	PU of Log Sine P-Out 72-1,2,3-(12,12,4)
		42-2-11	- -	Hold
		42-2-12	- -	PU of Log Reset 191-1,2,3-(12)
		42-3-2	- -	Controls read-in to Log Cycle ctr
43-1,..,10-(12) S	17	43-1-1,..,43-2-11	M-2	Controls entry into MC-DR (1-2)
43-11-(4) S	16		D-2	
43-12-(4) S	15	43-2-12	M-1	PU of Shift 36-37,38,39-(12,12,4)
MC-DR In			D-1	PU of Shift 36-1,..,39-(4,6 or 12)
M-1		43-3-1,..,43-4-11	M-2	Controls entry into MC-DR (3-6)
D-1				

Relay	Row	Contact	Cycle	Function
(continued)				
43-1,..,10-(12) S		43-4-12	D-2	PU of Q-Shift Elusive One Control 87-1-(4)
43-11-(4) S		43-5-1,..,43-6-11	M-2	Controls entry into MC-DR (5)
43-12-(4) S		43-6-12	M-2	PU of Sign Control #1 70-1-(4)
MC-DR In		43-7-1,..,43-8-11	M-2	Controls entry into MC-DR (7)
M-1		43-9-1,..,43-10-11	M-2	Controls entry into MC-DR (9)
D-1		43-10-12	M-1	Hold
			D-1	
		43-11-1	- -	PU of SIO Out #2 Control 237-1-(4)
		43-11-2	- -	Controls read-in to X_T ctr (Int)
		43-11-3	- -	PU of Forward Tape Clutch Magnet (Int)
		43-11-4	M-2	PU of Sign Control #2 71-1-(4)
		43-12-1	M-1	PU of MC-DR Entry Control (1-2) 91-1,2,3-(12)
		43-12-2	M-1	PU of MC-DR Entry Control (3-6) 92-1,2,3-(12)
		43-12-3,4	M-1	Hold
			D-1	
44-1,..,5-(12) S	17	44-1-1,..,44-2-12	M-3	Control MC-DR times 2 RO to MC-DR (3-6)
First Build Up			D-3	
M-2		44-3-1,..,44-4-12	M-3	Control MC-DR times 2 RO to MC-DR (9)
D-2			D-3	
		44-5-1	M-3	PU of Read Control Seq-31-(4) and Clutch Magnet
			D-3	
		44-5-2	- -	Controls read-in to Log Cycle ctr
		44-5-5	- -	PU of SIO In #2 230-1,2,3-(12,12,4)
		44-5-6	- -	PU of π 278-1,2,3-(12,12,4) (Sine)
		44-5-7	- -	Controls read-in to Sine Sequence ctr #1
		44-5-8	M-2	PU of MC-DR Entry Control (3-6) 92-1,2,3-(12)
			D-2	
		44-5-9	- -	PU of Log Reset 191-1,2,3-(12)
		44-5-11	M-2	Hold
			D-2	
45-1,..,5-(12) S	17	45-1-1,..,45-2-12	M-3,4	Control MC-DR times 2 RO to MC-DR (4-8)
First and Second Build Up			D-3,4	
M-2		45-3-1,..,45-4-12	M-3,4	Control MC-DR times 2 RO to MC-DR (5)
D-2			D-3,4	
		45-5-1	M-3,4	Controls MC-DR Carry Control 26-1-(4)
			D-3,4	
		45-5-2	M-2,3	Controls MC-DR Entry Control (4-8) 93-1,2,3-(12)
			D-2,3	
		45-5-3	- -	Controls read-in to Sine Sequence ctr #2
		45-5-11	M-2	Hold
			D-2	
46-1,..,5-(12) S	17	46-1-1,..,46-2-12	M-4	Control MC-DR times 6 RO to MC-DR (7)
Second Build Up		46-3-1,..,46-4-12	M-4	Control MC-DR times 6 RO to MC-DR (9)
M-3		46-5-1	- -	Controls RO of Log Cycle ctr

Relay	Row	Contact	Cycle	Function
46-1,..,5-(12) S		46-5-2	NR-4	Controls read-in of 1 from Normalizing Register to Intermediate ctr
(continued)				
		46-5-3	- -	Controls RO of Sine Sequence ctr #1
		46-5-4	- -	PU of SIO Out #3 272-1,2,3-(12,12,4)
		46-5-5	- -	Controls entry of 1 into Intermediate ctr 21st col (Exp)
		46-5-11	M-3	Hold
47-1,..,13-(12) S	17,18	47-1-1,..,47-2-11	M-10	Control reset of MC-DR (1-2)
MC-DR Reset		47-2-12	M-10	Controls reset of Cycle ctr
M-9		47-3-1,..,47-4-12	M-10	Control reset of MC-DR (3-6)
D-14		47-5-1,..,47-6-12	M-10	Control reset of MC-DR (4-8)
		47-7-1,..,47-8-12	M-10	Control reset of MC-DR (5)
		47-9-1,..,47-10-12	M-10	Control reset of MC-DR (7)
		47-11-1,..,47-12-12	M-10	Control reset of MC-DR (9)
		47-13-1 NC	M-2	Hold of Sign Control #2 71-1-(4)
		47-13-2	M-9	PU of MC-DR Entry Control (1-2) 91-1,2,3-(12)
		47-13-3	M-9	PU of MC-DR Entry Control (3-6) 92-1,2,3-(12)
		47-13-4	M-9	PU of MC-DR Entry Control (4-8) 93-1,2,3-(12)
		47-13-10,11,12	M-9	Hold
48-1-(12) S	17	48-1-1 NC	M-0	Hold of Multiply #1 41-1,2-(12); Multiply #2 38-1,2,3-(12)
Sequence Counter Reset			D-0	Hold of Divide 56-1,..,13-(12)
M-10			- -	Hold of LM 42-1,2,3-(12,12,4); LE 10-1-(4); LF 11-1,2-(6,4); EX-2 55-1,2,3-(12,12,6); SM-1 81-1,2,3-(12,12,4); IM-1 78-1,2,3-(12,12,4); IM-2 79-1,2-(12,4); SM-5 85-1-(4)
D-14				
		48-1-2	M-11	Controls Sequence ctr reset
		48-1-3	- -	PU of Log In #2 190-1,2,3-(12,12,4)
		48-1-4	- -	PU of EX-2 55-1,2,3-(12,12,6)
		48-1-5	- -	Controls reset of Sine Sequence ctr #1
		48-1-6	M-10	Hold
		48-1-7	- -	PU of Read Control Seq-31-(4) and Clutch Magnet (Int)
		48-1-8	D-14	PU of Q-Shift 33-1,..,80-(4,6 or 12); H 20-1-(4)
49-1,..,10-(12) S	18	49-1-2,..,49-2-12	M-3	Control Carry in MC-DR (3-6)
MC-DR Carry		49-3-2,..,49-4-12	M-3	Control Carry in MC-DR (4-8)
M-3		49-5-2,..,49-6-12	M-3	Control Carry in MC-DR (5)
D-3		49-7-2,..,49-8-12	M-3	Control Carry in MC-DR (7)
		49-9-2,..,49-10-12	M-3	Control Carry in MC-DR (9)
50-1,2,3-(12) S	18	50-1-1,..,50-2-12	M-1	Control entry into Intermediate ctr
Intermediate In		50-3-1	M-1	PU of Intermediate Carry Control 23-1-(4)
M-0		50-3-11	M-0	Hold
D-0				
51-1,2,3-(12) S	18	51-1-1,..,51-2-12	- -	Control RO of Intermediate ctr (Int) (not used in MP-DIV)
Intermediate Out		51-3-1	- -	PU of EIO In 217-1,2,3-(12,12,4)
		51-3-2	- -	PU of IM-3 80-1-(4) (Int)
		51-3-11	- -	Hold

Relay	Row	Contact	Cycle	Function
52-1,2,3-(12) S	18	52-1-1,..,52-2-11	M-3	Control reset of Intermediate ctr cols 1-23
Intermediate Reset		52-2-12	- -	PU of C-6 Step Control 223-1-(4) (Exp)
M-2		52-3-1	- -	PU of C Value to Intermediate Control 90-1-(4) (Int)
D-2		52-3-2	- -	PU of MC-DR Reset Control #2 238-1-(12) (Sine)
		52-3-3	- -	PU of Value Tape Read Clutch Magnet
		52-3-4 NC	- -	Hold of IM-1 78-1,2,3-(12,12,4); IM-2 79-1,2-(12,4)
		52-3-5	M-3	Controls reset of Intermediate ctr 24th col
		52-3-6 NC	M-2	Hold of Sign Control #1 70-1-(4)
		52-3-7	M-3	Controls read-in to PQ 47th col
		52-3-11	M-2	Hold
53-1,2-(12) S	18	53-1-1,..,53-2-12	M-1	Control carry into Intermediate ctr cols 1-24
Intermediate Carry				
M-1				
54-1-(12) S	18	54-1-1,..,5	- -	Control Sequence ctr RO (Exp)
EX-1		54-1-6	- -	PU of Multiply #2 38-1,2,3-(12) (Exp)
		54-1-7	- -	PU of EIO 1-18 Out 219-1,2-(12); EIO In 217-1,2,3-(12,12,4)
		54-1-8	- -	PU of EX-2 55-1,2,3-(12,12,6)
		54-1-9 NC	- -	PU of C-6 Step Control 223-1-(4) (Exp)
		54-1-11	- -	Hold
55-1,2,3-(12,12,6) S	18	55-1-1,..,55-2-3	- -	Control Sequence ctr RO (Exp)
EX-2		55-2-4	- -	PU of Multiply #2 38-1,2,3-(12) (Exp)
		55-2-5	- -	PU of EIO 1-18 Out 219-1,2-(12)
		55-2-6	- -	Hold of EX-1 55-1-(12)
		55-2-6 NC	- -	Hold of XG 15-1-(4)
		55-2-7	- -	PU of C-6 Step Control 223-1-(4) (Exp)
		55-2-8	- -	PU of Intermediate In 50-1,2,3-(12) (Exp)
		55-2-9 NC	- -	Controls reset of Sequence ctr (Exp)
		55-2-10	- -	PU of XG 15-1-(4)
		55-2-11	- -	Hold of RO Control 226-1-(4); XH 220-1-(12)
		55-2-12	- -	Hold
		55-3-1	- -	PU of MC-DR Reset 47-1,..,13-(12) (Exp)
		55-3-2 NC	- -	PU of Read Control Seq-31-(4) and Clutch Magnet
		55-3-3	- -	PU of Exp P-Out 73-1,2-(12)
		55-3-6	- -	Hold
56-1,..,13-(12) S	19	56-1-1,..,56-2-12 NC	M-6	Control Linking of Times Left and Column Shift Left to DD ctr
Divide		56-3-1,..,56-6-10	D-6	Control PU of DD compare 6-1,..,24-(12)
D-0			D-7	Control read-in to DD ctr
			M-6	Control read-in to PQ ctr
		56-7-1,..,56-8-11	D-7	Control Q entry into PQ ctr
		56-9-1,.(2n + 1).,11,.., 56-10-11	D-6	PU of Column Shift Right 29-1,..,36-(12,12,6)
		56-9-2,.(2n).,12,.., 56-10-10	D-8	PU of Column Shift Left 21-1,..,36-(12,12,6)

Relay	Row	Contact	Cycle	Function
56-1,..,13-(12) S (continued)		56-11-1	D-0	PU of Intermediate In 50-1,2,3-(12)
		56-11-2	D-0	PU of DD-PQ Reset 58-1,..,8-(12)
		56-11-3	D-1	Controls RO of Intermediate ctr 24th col 2nd mldg
		56-11-4	D-1	PU of MC-DR In 43-1,..,10-(12); 43-11,12-(4)
		56-11-5	D-1	PU of Q-Shift Invert 22-1-(12)
		56-11-6	D-1	PU of Intermediate Invert Control 94-1-(4)
		56-11-7	D-2	PU of First Build Up 44-1,..,5-(12)
		56-11-8	D-2	PU of First and Second Build Up 45-1,..,5-(12)
		56-11-9	D-2	PU of Intermediate Reset 52-1,2,3-(12); HD-4-(12)
		56-11-10	D-3	PU of Intermediate In 50-1,2,3-(12)
		56-11-11	D-3	PU of First and Second Build Up 46-1,..,5-(12)
		56-12-1	D-3	PU of Add-22 32-1-(4)
		56-12-2	D-4	Controls RO of Intermediate ctr 24th col 2nd mldg
		56-12-3	D-4	PU of DD In 57-1,2,3-(12)
		56-12-4	D-4	PU of Intermediate Invert Control 94-1-(4)
		56-12-5	D-5	PU of Intermediate Reset 52-1,2,3-(12)
		56-12-6	D-14	PU of Sequence ctr Reset 48-1-(12)
		56-12-7	D-14	PU of MC-DR Reset 47-1,..,13-(12); HD-5-(12)
		56-13-1	D-0	Controls read-in to Sequence ctr
		56-13-2	D-5	PU of Compare In 3-1,..,24-(12); 3-25-(4)
			D-6	PU of MC-DR Invert HD-2-(12)
		56-13-3	D-7	PU of Elusive One 60-1,..,23-(4)
		56-13-4	D-7	PU of DD Carry Control 27-1-(4)
		56-13-5	D-13	PU of "9" 9-1-(4)
		56-13-6	D-11	PU of G 19-1-(4)
		56-13-7	- -	Controls RO of Cycle ctr after PU of G relay
		56-13-8	- -	Controls carry from doubling RO of MC-DR (1-2) 23rd col
		56-13-9	D-14	PU of Q-Shift 33-1,..,80-(4,6 or 12); H 20-1-(4)
		56-13-11	D-0	Hold
57-1,2,3-(12) S	19	57-1-1,..,57-2-11	D-5	Control entry into DD ctr
DD In		57-2-12	D-4	PU of Shift 36-1,..,39-(4,6 or 12)
D-4		57-3-1	D-5	PU of Q-Shift Carry Control 25-1-(4)
		57-3-2	M-2	PU of Sign Control #1 70-1-(4)
		57-3-4	D-5	PU of MP-DIV Control Pick-Up 13-1-(6)
		57-3-11	D-4	Hold
58-1,..,8-(12) S	19	58-1-1,..,58-4-10	M-1	Control PQ ctr reset
DD-PQ Reset		58-4-11,12	M-0	Hold
M-0		58-5-1,..,58-8-9	M-1	Control DD ctr reset
D-0		58-8-10,11	D-1	Control Q-Shift reset
		58-8-12	M-0	Hold
59-1,2,3-(12,12,6) S	19	59-1-1,..,59-2-11	M-10	Control DD cols 23-45 transfer to PQ
DD-PQ Transfer #2		59-3-1	M-10	PU of PQ Carry Control 24-1-(4)
M-9		59-3-2	M-10	PU of A 12-1,2-(4); B 16-1-(4)

Relay	Row	Contact	Cycle	Function
59-1,2,3-(12,12,6) S (continued)		59-3-3	M-10	Controls reset of Cycle ctr
		59-3-6	M-9	Hold
60-1,..,23-(4) S	20	60-n-1	D-7	Controls entry of 1 into col n of DD ctr
Elusive One		60-n-2	D-7	Controls prevention of carry to the right in DD ctr
D-7		60-n-4	D-7	Hold
61-1,..,4-(12) S DD Carry M-6 D-7	20	61-1-1,..,61-4-9	M-6	Control DD carry
62-1,..,4-(12) S PQ Carry M-6	20	62-1-1,..,62-4-9	M-6	Control PQ carry
63-1-(4) D	10	63-1-1	D-11	PU of F 18-1-(4); G 19-1-(4)
No Go D-12		63-1-4	D-12	Hold
64-1-(4) S	12	64-1-1	D-11	PU of F 18-1-(4)
F Control D-11		64-1-4	D-11	Hold
65-1-(4) S	12	65-1-1	D-11	PU of G 19-1-(4)
G Control D-11		65-1-4	D-11	Hold
66-1-(4) D	13	66-1-1	M-8	PU of DD-PQ Transfer #1 74-1,2,3-(12,12,4)
C_2 M-8		66-1-4	M-8	Hold
67-1-(4) D	13	67-1-1	M-8	PU of DD-PQ Transfer #1 74-1,2,3-(12,12,4)
D_2 M-8		67-1-4	M-8	Hold
68-1-(4) D	13	68-1-1	M-6	Controls carry to PQ 23rd col
PQ 23rd Column M-6		68-1-4	M-6	Hold
69-1,2-(4) S	14	69-1-1	M-9	PU of C 30-1-(12); D 31-1-(12)
CD Control		69-1-2	M-6	PU of PQ 23rd Column 68-1-(4)
M-9		69-1-3	M-8	Hold of C_2 66-1-(4); D_2 67-1-(4)
		69-1-4	M-9	Hold
		69-2-1,2 NC	M-5	PU of MP-DIV Control Hold 14-1-(12); Column Shift Left 21-1,..,27-(12,12,6); Column Shift Right 29-1,..,27-(12,12,6)
			M-6	PU of E 17-1-(4)
			M-7	PU of F 18-1-(4)
			M-8	PU of C_2 66-1-(4); D_2 67-1-(4)

Relay	Row	Contact	Cycle	Function
70-1-(4) D	19	70-1-1	M-3	Controls read-in to PQ 47th col
Sign Control #1		70-1-2	M-2	PU of Sign Control #2 71-1-(4)
M-2		70-1-4	M-2	Hold
71-1-(4) D	20	71-1-1; 71-1-2,3 NC	M-11	Control reset of PQ 47th col
Sign Control #2		71-1-4	M-2	Hold
M-2				
72-1,2,3-(12,12,4) S	21	72-1-1,..,72-2-12	- -	Control RO of PQ ctr (Log-Sine)
Log Sine P-Out		72-3-4	- -	Hold
73-1,2-(12) S	21	73-1-1,..,73-2-9	- -	Control RO of PQ ctr (Exp)
Exp P-Out		73-2-12	- -	Hold
74-1,2,3-(12,12,4) D	21	74-1-1,..,74-2-10	M-9	Control DD cols 1-22 transfer to PQ
DD-PQ Transfer #1		74-2-11	M-9	PU of CD Control 69-1,2-(4)
M-8		74-3-1	M-9	PU of PQ Carry Control 24-1-(4)
		74-3-4	M-8	Hold
75-1,2,3-(12,12,4) S	21	75-1-1,..,75-2-12	- -	Control read-in of C Value to Intermediate ctr
C Value to Intermediate		75-3-4	- -	Hold
#1				
76-1,2,3-(12,12,4) S	21	76-1-1,..,76-2-12	- -	Control read-in of C Value to Intermediate ctr
C Value to Intermediate		76-3-4	- -	Hold
#2				
77-1,2,3-(12,12,4) S	21	77-1-1,..,77-2-12	- -	Control read-in of C Value to Intermediate ctr
C Value to Intermediate		77-3-4	- -	Hold
#3				
78-1,2,3-(12,12,4) S	21	78-1-1,..,78-2-4	- -	Control RO of Sequence ctr (Int)
IM-1		78-2-5	- -	Controls Forward Tape Clutch Magnet
		78-2-6	- -	Controls read-in to X_T ctr (Int)
		78-2-7	- -	PU of Multiply #2 38-1,2,3-(12) (Int)
		78-2-8 NC	- -	Controls Read Control Seq-31-(4) and Clutch Magnet
		78-2-9	- -	Hold of X_T Step Control 180-1-(6)
		78-2-10	- -	Controls reset of Sequence ctr to 4 (Int)
		78-2-11	- -	Hold; hold of IM-2 79-1,2-(12,4)
		78-2-12	- -	PU of C Value to Intermediate Control 90-1-(4)
		78-3-1	- -	PU of IM-2 79-1,2-(12,4)
		78-3-2	- -	PU of P-Out 34-1,2,4-(12,12,4) (Int)
		78-3-4	- -	Hold
79-1,2-(12,4) D	21	79-1-1,2,3	- -	Control Sequence ctr RO (Int)
IM-2		79-1-4 NC	- -	Controls read-in to X_T ctr
		79-1-5	- -	Controls X_T reset
		79-1-6	- -	PU of MC-DR Reset 47-1,..,13-(12) (Int)

Relay	Row	Contact	Cycle	Function
79-1,2-(12,4) D (continued)		79-1-7	- -	PU of Read Control Seq-31-(4) and Clutch Magnet
		79-1-8	- -	Controls Forward Tape Clutch Magnet
		79-1-9 NC	- -	Hold of X_T Step Control 180-1-(4)
		79-1-10 NC	- -	Controls reset of Sequence ctr to 0 (Int)
		79-1-11 NC	- -	Hold; hold of IM-1 78-1,2,3-(12,12,4)
		79-1-12	- -	PU of IM-3 80-1-(4)
		79-2-1 NC	- -	Hold of Tape Selection Relays 183, 184, 185-1,..,9-(12)
		79-2-4	- -	Hold
80-1-(4) S IM-3	21	80-1-1	- -	Controls Sequence ctr reset (Int)
		80-1-4	- -	Hold
81-1,2,3-(12,12,4) S SM-1	21	81-1-1,..,81-2-3	- -	Control Sequence ctr RO (Sine)
		81-2-4	- -	Hold of SM-1; Multiply #2 38-1,2,3-(12) (Sine)
		81-2-5	- -	PU of MC-DR Reset 47-1,..,13-(12) (Sine)
		81-2-6	- -	PU of Sine Sequence ctr #2 RO Control 237-1-(4)
		81-2-8	- -	PU of Multiply #2 38-1,2,3-(12) (Sine)
		81-2-9 NC	- -	PU of Read Control Seq-31-(4) and Clutch Magnet
		81-2-10	- -	Controls read-in to Sine Sequence ctr #2
		81-2-11 NC	- -	Controls reset of Sine Sequence ctr #2
		81-2-12	- -	Hold
		81-3-1 NC	- -	PU of Read Control Seq-31-(4) and Clutch Magnet
		81-3-2 NC	- -	Controls RO of SIO 24th col
82-1-(12) D SM-2	21	82-1-1 NC	- -	Controls prevention of PU of Intermediate Reset 52-1,2,3-(12) (Sine)
		82-1-2	- -	Controls prevention of PU of Intermediate In 50-1,2,3-(12) (Sine)
		82-1-3	- -	PU of Intermediate In 50-1,2,3-(12) (Sine)
		82-1-4	- -	Controls Sequence ctr reset to 1 (Sine)
		82-1-5	- -	PU of SM-3 83-1,2-(12,4)
		82-1-6 NC	- -	Controls read-in to Sine Sequence ctr #2
		82-1-7 NC	- -	Hold of β, γ and δ 233,234,235-1-(6)
		82-1-8	- -	Hold for .785 236-1,2,3-(12,12,4)
		82-1-9 NC	- -	Controls read-in of sign to PQ 47th col (Sine)
		82-1-11 NC	- -	PU of β, γ and δ 233,234,235-1-(6)
		82-1-12	- -	Hold
83-1,2-(12,4) S SM-3	21	83-1-1 NC	- -	Control prevention of PU of MC-DR Reset 47-1,..,13-(12) (Sine)
		83-1-2	- -	PU of Intermediate In 50-1,2,3-(12) (Sine)
		83-1-3	- -	PU of DD-PQ reset 58-1,..,8-(12) (Sine)
		83-1-4	- -	Controls Sequence ctr reset to 4 (Sine)
		83-1-5	- -	Hold of .785 236-1,2,3-(12,12,4); MC-DR Reset Control #1 239-1-(4); MC-DR Reset Control #2 238-1-(12) (Sine)
		83-1-6 NC	- -	Controls read-in to Sine Sequence ctr #2
		83-1-7	- -	Hold of SM-2 82-1-(12)
		83-1-8	- -	Controls read-in to Sine Sequence ctr #1
		83-1-9	- -	Hold

Relay	Row	Contact	Cycle	Function
83-1,2-(12,4) S		83-1-10	- -	PU of Intermediate In 50-1,2,3-(12) (Sine)
(continued)		83-1-11 NC	- -	PU of β . γ and δ 233,234,235-1-(6)
		83-1-12	- -	Hold
		83-2-1	- -	Hold of β . γ and δ 233,234,235-1-(6); Sine RO Control 240-1-(4)
		83-2-3	- -	PU of SIO Reset 228-1,2,3-(12,12,4)
84-1-(6) S	21	84-1-1 NC	- -	Controls Sequence ctr (Sine)
SM-4		84-1-2 NC	- -	Controls prevention of PU of DD-PQ Reset 58-1,..,8-(12) (Sine)
		84-1-3	- -	PU of π/2 279-1,2,3-(12,12,4)
		84-1-4	- -	PU of SIO Invert 242-1-(12)
		84-1-6	- -	Hold
85-1-(4) D SM-5	21	85-1-1	- -	PU of Log Sine P-Out 72-1,2,3-(12,12,4)
86-1-(4) D	13	86-1-1,2 NC	D-4	Controls addition from Log "N" Switches to Q-Shift ctr
Add-22 Control		86-1-4	- -	Hold
87-1-(4) S	15	87-1-1	D-2	PU of Q-Shift Elusive One 88-1-(4)
Q-Shift Elusive One Control D-2		87-1-4	D-2	Hold
88-1-(4) S Q-Shift Elusive One D-2	15	88-1-1,2	D-2	Control read-in of Elusive One to Q-Shift ctr
89-1-(4) S	19	89-1-1	M-2	PU of Sine Control #1 70-1-(4)
Intermediate 24th col Read-Out Control M-1		89-1-2	- -	Controls RO of Intermediate ctr 24th col
90-1-(4) D	18	90-1-1,2	- -	PU of Intermediate In 50-1,2,3-(12) (Int)
C Value to Intermediate Control		90-1-4	- -	Hold
91-1,2,3-(12) S	1	91-1-1	M-3	Controls circuit to MC-DR col 1 2nd mldg
MC-DR Entry Control		91-1-2,..,91-2-11	M-3	Control circuit to MC-DR col 2-23 3rd mldg
(1-2)		91-3-1	M-3	Controls circuit of 1 impulse to 3rd mldg cols 1-6
M-1		91-3-2	M-3	Controls circuit of 1 impulse to 3rd mldg cols 7-12
		91-3-3	M-3	Controls circuit of 1 impulse to 3rd mldg cols 13-18
		91-3-4	M-3	Controls circuit of 1 impulse to 3rd mldg cols 19-23
		91-3-5	M-3	Controls circuit of 8 impulse to 3rd mldg cols 1-6
		91-3-6	M-3	Controls circuit of 8 impulse to 3rd mldg cols 7-12
		91-3-7	M-3	Controls circuit of 8 impulse to 3rd mldg cols 13-18
		91-3-8	M-3	Controls circuit of 8 impulse to 3rd mldg cols 19-23
		91-3-12	M-1	Hold

Relay	Row	Contact	Cycle	Function
92-1,2,3-(12) S	2	92-1-1	M-3	Controls circuit to MC-DR col 1 2nd mldg
MC-DR Entry Control		92-1-2,..,92-2-12	M-3	Control circuit to MC-DR col 2-24 3rd mldg
(3-6)		92-3-1	M-3	Controls circuit of 1 impulse to 3rd mldg cols 1-6
M-1		92-3-2	M-3	Controls circuit of 1 impulse to 3rd mldg cols 7-12
		92-3-3	M-3	Controls circuit of 1 impulse to 3rd mldg cols 13-18
		92-3-4	M-3	Controls circuit of 1 impulse to 3rd mldg cols 19-24
		92-3-5	M-3	Controls circuit of 8 impulse to 3rd mldg cols 1-6
		92-3-6	M-3	Controls circuit of 8 impulse to 3rd mldg cols 7-12
		92-3-7	M-3	Controls circuit of 8 impulse to 3rd mldg cols 13-18
		92-3-8	M-3	Controls circuit of 8 impulse to 3rd mldg cols 19-24
		92-3-12	M-1	Hold
93-1,2,3-(12) S	3	93-1-1	M-3	Controls circuit to MC-DR col 1 2nd mldg
MC-DR Entry Control		93-1-2,..,93-2-12	M-3	Control circuit to MC-DR col 2-24 3rd mldg
(4-8)		93-3-1	M-3	Controls circuit of 1 impulse to 3rd mldg cols 1-6
M-2		93-3-2	M-3	Controls circuit of 1 impulse to 3rd mldg cols 7-12
		93-3-3	M-3	Controls circuit of 1 impulse to 3rd mldg cols 13-18
		93-3-4	M-3	Controls circuit of 1 impulse to 3rd mldg cols 19-24
		93-3-5	M-3	Controls circuit of 8 impulse to 3rd mldg cols 1-6
		93-3-6	M-3	Controls circuit of 8 impulse to 3rd mldg cols 7-12
		93-3-7	M-3	Controls circuit of 8 impulse to 3rd mldg cols 13-18
		93-3-8	M-3	Controls circuit of 8 impulse to 3rd mldg cols 19-24
		93-3-12	M-1	Hold
94-1-(4) S	21	94-1-1,2	M-1	PU of Intermediate Invert HD-1-(12)
Intermediate Invert		94-1-4	M-1	Hold
Control				
M-1				
95-1-(6) S	18	95-1-1	- -	PU of "9" relay 9-1-(4)
Place Limitation (643)		95-1-6	- -	Hold
96-1-(6) S	18	96-1-1	- -	PU of "9" relay 9-1-(4)
Place Limitation (6431)		96-1-6	- -	Hold
97-1-(6) S	18	97-1-1	- -	PU of "9" relay 9-1-(4)
Place Limitation (6432)		97-1-6	- -	Hold
98-1-(6) S	18	98-1-1	- -	PU of "9" relay 9-1-(4)
Place Limitation (64321)		98-1-6	- -	Hold
99-1,2,3-(12,12,4) S	22	99-1-1,..,99-2-11	- -	Control RO of PQ cols 1-23 to Buss cols 1-23
Special PQ-Out		99-2-12	M-12	Controls reading 9 to Buss col 24 if PQ <0
M-11 (Low order RO)		99-3-1,2	M-11	PU of DD-PQ Invert HD-3-(12); HD-3-(4) wc
		99-3-4	M-11	Hold

Relay	Row	Contact	Cycle	Function
100-1-(4) D Special Sign M-11 (Low order RO)	22	100-1-1,2 100-1-4	M-11 M-11	PU of DD-PQ Invert HD-3-(12); HD-3-(4) wc Hold
101-1,2-(12) S Normalizing Register Read-In Norm. Reg.-2	22	101-1-1,..,101-2-11 101-2-12	NR-2 NR-2	PU of Digit Sensing 102-1,..,23-(4) Hold
102-1,..,23-(4) D Digit Sensing Norm. Reg.-3	22	$1 \leq n \leq 23$ 102-n-1 102-n-4	NR-3 NR-3	PU of Shift Positioning 103-1,..,23-(4) Hold
103-1,..,23-(4) S Shift Positioning Norm. Reg.-3	22	$0 \leq n \leq 22$ 103-(n + 1)-1 103-(n + 1)-2,3 103-(n + 1)-4	NR-3 NR-4 NR-3	Controls reading of 1 to column (n + 1) of Intermediate ctr Controls reading amount of shift n to cols 20 and 21 of Buss Hold
104-1-(4) S Normalizing Register RO Norm. Reg.-4	22	104-1-1,2 104-1-4	NR-4 NR-4	Controls reading of amount of shift to cols 20 and 21 of Buss Hold

HEAVY DUTY RELAYS

HD-1-(12) Intermediate Invert M-1		HD-1-1,..,10 HD-1-12	M-2 M-1	Control inverted RO of Intermediate ctr Hold
HD-2-(12) MC-DR Invert D-6		HD-2-1,..,10 HD-2-11 HD-2-12	D-7 D-11 D-6	Control inverted RO of MC-DR ctrs PU of F 18-1-(4) Hold
HD-3-(12) HD-3-(4) wc DD-PQ Invert M-11		HD-3-1,..,10 HD-3-11 HD-3-12 HD-3-1 wc	M-11 D-15 M-11 M-12	Control inverted RO of DD-PQ ctrs Controls RO of 9 from PQ 47th col if PQ < 0 Hold Controls RO of 9 from PQ 47th col if PQ < 0 (Special RO cols 1-23 of PQ)
HD-4-(12) Intermediate Reset M-2		HD-4-1,..,9	M-3	Control reset of Intermediate ctr
HD-5-(12) MC-DR Reset M-9		HD-5-1,..,9	M-10	Control reset of MC-DR ctrs

Relay	Row	Contact	Cycle	Function
HD-6-(12) DD-PQ Reset M-O		HD-6-1,..,9	M-1	Control reset of DD, PQ and Q-Shift ctrs

SEQUENCE RELAYS

Seq-8-(4) Check Control		Seq-8-1,2 Seq-8-3		PU of Check relay-(4) Hold
Seq-10-(4) Storage RO Minus		Seq-10-1 Seq-10-4		PU of Invert relay-(12) for minus absolute RO Hold
Seq-11-(4) Storage RO Plus		Seq-11-1 Seq-11-4		PU of Invert relay-(12) for plus absolute RO Hold
Seq-27-(4) Repeat		Seq-27-1 Seq-27-2 Seq-27-4		PU of Start Seq-33-(4); Hold of Start Interlock Seq-28-(4) PU of Start Seq-33-(4) Hold
Seq-28-(4) Start Interlock		Seq-28-1 NC Seq-28-4		PU of Start Seq-33-(4) Hold
Seq-29-(12) IVS Invert		Seq-29-1,..,9 Seq-29-12		Control 9's complement for inverted IVS RO Hold
Seq-30-1,2,3-(12,12,4) IVS Out		Seq-30-1-1,..,12 Seq-30-2-1,..,12 Seq-30-3-4		Control RO of IVS cols 1-12 Control RO of IVS cols 13-24 Hold
Seq-31-(4) Read Control		Seq-31-1,2,3,4		Control reading of control tape through reading pins
Seq-32-(4) Stop Control		Seq-32-1,2 NC Seq-32-4		PU of Read Control Seq-31-(4) and Clutch Magnet Hold
Seq-33-(4) Start		Seq-33-1 Seq-33-3 Seq-33-4		PU of Read Control Seq-31-(4) and Clutch Magnet PU of Start Interlock Seq-28-(4) Hold

SWITCH RELAYS

SwA-1,2,3-(12,12,4) Switch A Out		SwA-1-1,..,12 SwA-2-1,..,12 SwA-3-4		Control RO of Switch A cols 1-12 Control RO of Switch A cols 13-24 Hold

Relay	Row	Contact	Cycle	Function
Switch Invert-(12)		Sw Invert-1,..,9 Sw Invert-11		Controls 9's complement for inverted RO Hold

STORAGE COUNTER RELAYS

Relay	Row	Contact	Cycle	Function
SCA-1,2,3-(12,12,4) Storage Counter Out		SCA-1-1,..,12 SCA-2-1,..,12 SCA-3-1 SCA-3-2 SCA-3-3 SCA-3-4		Control RO of cols 1-12 Control RO of cols 13-24 PU of Str Ctr 24th Col Carry (relays 10 and 11) PU of Str Ctr Reset relay-(12) PU of Str Ctr Invert relay-(12) Hold
SCA-4,5,6-(12,12,4) Storage Counter In		SCA-4-1,..,12 SCA-5-1,..,12 SCA-6-1 SCA-6-2 SCA-6-4		Control read-in of cols 1-12 Control read-in of cols 13-24 PU of Str Ctr Carry Control SCA-9-(4) PU of Str Ctr Reset-(12) Hold
SCA-7,8-(12) Storage Counter Carry		SCA-7-1,..,12 SCA-8-1,..,12		Control Carry for cols 1-12 Control Carry for cols 13-24
SCA-9-(4) Storage Counter Carry Control		SCA-9-1 SCA-9-2 SCA-9-4		PU of Str Ctr Carry (relays 7 and 8) PU of Str Ctr 24th Col Carry (relays 10 and 11) Hold
SCA-10-(4) Storage Counter 24th Col Carry (10)		SCA-10-1		Controls end around carry through 10
SCA-11-(4) Storage Counter 24th Col Carry (9)		SCA-11-1 SCA-11-2		Controls end around carry through 9 PU of Str Ctr Invert relay-(12)
SCA-12,13-(4) Storage Counter Carry Booster		SCA-12-2,3 SCA-13-2,3		Control carry booster to col 1 Control carry booster to col 13
Storage Counter Invert-(12)		Invert-1,..,9 Invert-10 NC Invert-12		Control 9's complement for inverted RO NC and Transfer paralleled to "9" spot Hold
Storage Counter Reset-(12)		Reset-1,..,9 Reset-10 Reset-11 NC Reset-12		Control 10's complement for reset of str ctr Controls prevention of carry impulse during reset NC and Transfer paralleled to "9" spot Hold
Sp64-(4) Special 64 In		Sp64-1 Sp64-3 Sp64-4		Hold; PU of Normal Str Ctr In SC64-4,5,6-(12,12,4) PU of Carry Interlock-1-(6) Hold

Relay	Row	Contact	Cycle	Function
Sp65-(4)		Sp65-1		Hold; PU of Normal Str Ctr In SC65-4,5,6-(12,12,4)
Special 65 In		Sp65-3		PU of Carry Interlock-1-(6)
		Sp65-4		Hold
Sp68-(4)		Sp68-1		Hold; PU of Normal Str Ctr In SC68-4,5,6-(12,12,4)
Special 68 In		Sp68-3		PU of Carry Interlock-2-(6)
		Sp68-4		Hold
Sp69-(4)		Sp69-1		Hold; PU of Normal Str Ctr In SC69-4,5,6-(12,12,4)
Special 69 In		Sp69-3		PU of Carry Interlock-2-(6)
		Sp69-4		Hold
Carry Interlock-1-(6)		CI-1-1,3		Control end around carry from col 24 of ctr 65 to col 1 ctr 64
		CI-1-3		Controls carry from col 23 of ctr 65 to col 24 of ctr 64
		CI-1-4		Controls carry from col 23 of ctr 64 to col 1 of ctr 65
		CI-1-5		PU of Carry Control SC64-9-(4) or SC65-9-(4)
		CI-1-6		Hold
Carry Interlock-2-(6)		CI-2-1,2		Control end around carry from col 24 of ctr 69 to col 1 ctr 68
		CI-2-3		Controls carry from col 23 of ctr 69 to col 24 of ctr 68
		CI-2-4		Controls carry from col 23 of ctr 68 to col 1 of ctr 69
		CI-2-5		PU of Carry Control SC68-9-(4) or SC69-9-(4)
		CI-2-6		Hold
Choice-(6)		Choice-1		PU of 24th Col 9 SC70-11-(4)
		Choice-2		PU of Str Ctr Invert-(12)
		Choice-6		Hold; PU of 24th Col 9 SC70-11-(4)
SC71-14-(6)		SC71-14-1		PU of Normal Str Ctr Out SC71-1-(12)
Normal Out Control		SC71-14-2		PU of Normal Str Ctr Out SC71-2-(12)
		SC71-14-3		PU of Normal Str Ctr Out SC71-3-(4)
		SC71-14-6		Hold
SC71-15-(6)		SC71-15-1		PU of Normal Str Ctr Out SC71-2-(12)
Special Out (direct)		SC71-15-2		PU of Normal Str Ctr Out SC71-3-(4)
		SC71-15-6		Hold
SC71-16-(6)		SC71-16-1		PU of Normal Str Ctr In SC71-4-(12)
Normal In Control		SC71-16-2		PU of Normal Str Ctr In SC71-5-(12)
		SC71-16-3		PU of Normal Str Ctr In SC71-6-(4)
		SC71-16-6		Hold
SC71-17-(6)		SC71-17-1		PU of Normal Str Ctr In SC71-5-(12)
Special In (direct)		SC71-17-2		PU of Normal Str Ctr In SC71-6-(4)
		SC71-17-3		PU of Carry Back Control SC71-20-(6)
		SC71-17-6		Hold

Relay	Row	Contact	Cycle	Function
SC71-18-1,2-(12,6) Special Out (shifted)		SC71-18-1-1,..,12		Control RO of ctr 71 cols 13-24 to Buss cols 1-12
		SC71-18-2-1		PU of Normal Str Ctr Out SC71-3-(4)
		SC71-18-2-6		Hold
SC71-19-1,2-(12,6) Special In (shifted)		SC71-19-1-1,..,12		Control read-in to ctr 71 cols 13-24 from Buss cols 1-12
		SC71-19-2-1		PU of Normal Str Ctr In SC71-6-(4)
		SC71-19-2-2		PU of Carry Back Control SC71-20-(6)
		SC71-19-2-6		Hold
SC71-20-(6) Carry Back Control		SC71-20-1		Controls carry back in ctr 71 from col 24 to col 13
		SC71-20-1 NC		Controls carry back in ctr 71 from col 24 to col 1
		SC71-20-6		Hold
Check-(4)		Check-1		PU of Read Control Seq-31-(4) and Clutch Magnet
		Check-4		Hold

CAM CONTACTS

Cam	Make	Break	Function
CC-1	1/16 1	1 5/8	1 impulse control
CC-2	1/16 2	2 5/8	2 impulse control
CC-3	1/16 3	3 5/8	3 impulse control
CC-4	1/16 4	4 5/8	4 impulse control
CC-5	1/16 5	5 5/8	5 impulse control
CC-6	1/16 6	6 5/8	6 impulse control
CC-7	1/16 7	7 5/8	7 impulse control PU of Sign Control #2 71-1-(4)
CC-8	1/16 8	8 5/8	8 impulse control
CC-9	1/16 9	9 5/8	9 impulse control PU of Sign Control #1 70-1-(4)
CC-1,..,9			PU of DD Compare 6-1,..,24-(12) DR Compare 2-1,..,216-(4)
CC-10	0	0 1/2	Controls impulse to Seq Ctr Magnet
CC-12	12	12 1/2	Controls carry impulse
CC-15	15	15 1/2	15 impulse control
CC-16	16	16 1/2	16 impulse control
CC-17	L	L 5/8	CB make 16 points
CC-19	L	L 5/8	CB make 16 points
CC-21	1/16 L	L 1/2	CB break 16 points
CC-23	1/16 L	L 1/2	CB break 16 points
CC-24A	L 1/4	L 7/8	Compare control make
CC-24B	L 1/4	L 7/8	Compare control make
CC-24C	L 1/16	L 3/4	Compare control break
CC-24D	L 1/16	L 3/4	Compare control break

Cam	Make	Break	Function
CC-25	3	14	Hold of PQ 23rd Column 68-1-(4)
CC-26	2	1 1/3	PU of MP-DIV Control Pick-Up 13-1-(6) CD Control 69-1,2-(4)
CC-27	9	12	Hold of DR Compare 2-1,..,120-(4)
CC-28	9	12	Hold of DD Compare 6-1,..,24-(12) DR Compare 2-121,..,216-(4)
CC-29	6	8	Hold of A 12-1,2-(4) B 16-1-(4)
CC-30 (69-1-3 NC)	1/16 3	1	Hold of C_2 66-1-(4) D_2 67-1-(4)
CC-31	12 1/2	9	PU of Times Right 5-1,..,27-(12,12,4) F 18-1-(4) G 19-1-(4)
CC-32 (12-1,2-2 NC)	8 1/2	2	Hold of MP-DIV Control Hold 14-1-(12) F 18-1-(4) G 19-1-(4)
CC-33	14	15 1/3	PU of Shift 36-1,..,39-(4,6 or 12) C 30-1-(12) D 31-1-(12) Q-Shift 33-1,..,80-(4,6 or 12) H 20-1-(4) DD-PQ Invert HD-3-(12); HD-3-(4) wc
CC-34	9	12	Hold of Over Under 1-1,..,235-(4)
CC-35	9	12	Hold of Over Under 1-236,..,423-(4) Digit Sensing 102-1,..,23-(4)
CC-36	12	0	Hold of Column Shift Right 29-1,..,36-(12,12,6) Column Shift Left 21-1,..,36-(12,12,6) Times Right 5-1,..,27-(12,12,4) Times Left 4-1,..,27-(12,12,4) E 17-1-(4)

CAM CONTACTS

Cam	Make	Break	Function
CC-37	11	1/4 12	PU of Q-Control 7-1,..,9-(4) No Go 63-1-(4) Shift Positioning 103-1,..,23-(4)
CC-38	11 1/2	9	Hold of C 30-1-(12) D 31-1-(12) Q-Control 7-1,..,9-(4) No Go 63-1-(4)
CC-39	1/3 15	12	Hold of Compare In 3-1,..,24-(12); 3-25-(4) MC-DR Invert HD-2-(12)
CC-40	1/16 15	9	PU of DD-PQ Transfer #1 74-1,2,3-(12,12,4) DD-PQ Transfer #2 59-1,2,3-(12,12,6) MP Reset 40-1,2,3-(12) MC-DR Reset 47-1,..,13-(12) DD-PQ Invert HD-3-(12); HD-3-(4) wc Compare In 3-1,..,24-(12); 3-25-(4) MC-DR Invert HD-2-(12) Log Sine P-Out 72-1,2,3-(12,12,4) Special Sign 100-1-(4)
CC-41 (30-1-1,2 NC) (30-1-8,9 NC) (31-1-1,2 NC) (31-1-8,9 NC)	12	15	Hold of MP Cycle Control 37-1,..,26-(4,6 or 12)
CC-42	12	1/3 16	Hold of Shift Pick-Up 35-1,..,46-(4)
CC-43	12	0	Hold of Intermediate In 50-1,2,3-(12) DD-PQ Reset 58-1,..,8-(12) Intermediate Invert Control 94-1-(4) Intermediate Invert HD-1-(12) MC-DR In 43-1,..,10-(12); 43-11,12-(4)
CC-43 (continued)			Shift 36-1,..,39-(4,6 or 12) Intermediate Reset 52-1,2,3-(12) Intermediate Reset HD-4-(12) First Build Up 44-1,..,5-(12) First and Second Build Up 45-1,..,5-(12) Second Build Up 46-1,..,5-(12) MP In 39-1,2,3-(12) DD-PQ Transfer #1 74-1,2,3-(12,12,4) DD-PQ Transfer #2 59-1,2,3-(12,12,6) MP Reset 40-1,2,3-(12) MC-DR Reset 47-1,..,13-(12) P-Out 34-1,2,3-(12); 34-4-(4) Sequence Counter Reset 48-1-(12) DD-PQ Invert HD-3-(12); HD-3-(4) wc Q-Shift Invert 22-1-(12) Add-22 32-1-(4) DD In 57-1,2,3-(12) Q-Shift 33-1,..,80-(4,6 or 12) H 20-1-(4) Normalizing Register Read-In 101-1,2-(12) Normalizing Register Read-Out 104-1-(4)
CC-44	2	1 1/3	PU of Intermediate Carry Control 23-1-(4) MC-DR Carry Control 26-1-(4) PQ Carry Control 24-1-(4) DD Carry Control 27-1-(4) Q-Shift Elusive One Control 87-1-(4) Q-Shift Carry Control 25-1-(4) Elusive One 60-1,..,23-(4) F Control 64-1-(4) G Control 65-1-(4) "9" 9-1-(4)
CC-45	1/16 11	13	PU of Intermediate Carry 53-1,2-(12)

CAM CONTACTS

Cam	Make	Break	Function
CC-45 (continued)			MC-DR Carry 49-1,..,10-(12) PQ Carry 62-1,..,4-(12) DD Carry 61-1,..,4-(12) Q-Shift Elusive One 88-1-(4) Q-Shift Carry 28-1-(4)
CC-46	2	13 1/3	Hold of Intermediate Carry Control 23-1-(4) MC-DR Carry Control 26-1-(4) PQ Carry Control 24-1-(4) DD Carry Control 27-1-(4) Q-Shift Elusive One Control 87-1-(4) Q-Shift Carry Control 25-1-(4) Elusive One 60-1,..,23-(4) F Control 64-1-(4) G Control 65-1-(4)
CC-47	3 1/2	16	Hold of MP-DIV Control Pick-Up 13-1-(6) CD Control 69-1,2-(4) Special Sign 100-1-(4)
CC-48	2	4	Hold of "9" 9-1-(4)
CC-49	1	0 1/3	PU of Multiply #2 38-1,2,3-(12)
CC-50 (55-2-6 NC)	1/3 3	16	Hold of XG 15-1-(4) EX-1 54-1-(12)
CC-51	2	1 1/3	PU of LE 10-1-(4) LF 11-1,2-(6,4) XG 15-1-(4) EX-2 55-1,2,3-(12,12,6)
CC-52 (48-1-1 NC)	1/3 3	16	Hold of Multiply #1 41-1,2-(12) Multiply #2 38-1,2,3-(12) Divide 56-1,..,13-(12) LE 10-1-(4) LF 11-1,2-(6,4) LM 42-1,2,3-(12,12,4) EX-2 55-1,2,3-(12,12,6) DM-1 78-1,2,3-(12,12,4) DM-2 79-1,2-(12,4) SM-1 81-1,2,3-(12,12,4) SM-5 85-1-(4) Shift Positioning 103-1,..,23-(4)

Cam	Make	Break	Function
CC-53 (199-1-1 NC)	11	16	Hold of Divide 56-1,..,13-(12)
CC-54	12	12 1/2	Controls impulse to cycle ctr magnet
CC-55	12 1/2	13 2/3	Controls Sequence ctr RO-B PU of Intermediate In 50-1,2,3-(12) First Build Up 44-1,..,5-(12) MP-In 39-1,2,3-(12) Sequence ctr Reset 48-1-(12) Shift Pick-Up 35-1,..,46-(4)
CC-56	12 1/2	13 2/3	Controls Sequence ctr RO-C PU of MC-DR In 43-1,..,10-(12); 43-11,12-(4) First and Second Build Up 45-1,..,5-(12) MC-DR Reset 47-1,..,13-(12) Q-Shift Invert 22-1-(12) DD-In 57-1,2,3-(12)
CC-57	12 1/2	13 2/3	Controls Sequence ctr RO-D PU of DD-PQ Reset 58-1,..,8-(12) Intermediate Invert Control 94-1-(4) Intermediate Reset 52-1,2,3-(12) Second Build Up 46-1,..,5-(12) P-Out 34-1,2,3-(12); 34-4-(4) Add-22 32-1-(4)
CC-58	14	15 1/3	PU of MP-DIV Control Hold 14-1-(12) Column Shift Right 29-1,..,36-(12,12,6) E 17-1-(4) D_2 67-1-(4)
CC-59	14	15 1/3	PU of Column Shift Left 21-1,..,36-(12,12,6) C_2 66-1-(4)
CC-60	6	5 1/3	PU of A 12-1,2-(4) B 16-1-(4) G 19-1-(4)

CAM CONTACTS

Cam	Make	Break	Function
CC-61	12	0	PU of Intermediate Reset HD-4-(12)
CC-62	14	0	PU of DD-PQ Reset HD-6-(12)
CC-63	12	0	PU of MC-DR Reset HD-5-(12)
CC-64	4	12	PU of EIO Reset 218-1,2,3-(12)
CC-65	2	15 3/4	PU and hold of SM-4 84-1-(6)
CC-66	2	1 1/3	PU and hold of SM-3 83-1,2-(12,4) PU of C6-O Step Control 223-1-(4)
CC-67	15	16 1/3	PU of log C values 210-1,..,6-(24,28)
CC-68	14	15 1/3	PU of SIO Out #2 Control 237-1-(4) SIO Reset 228-1,2,3-(12)
CC-69	15	16 1/3	PU of Intermediate Invert HD-1-(12) 1/21! etc 243-1,..,21-(4,6 or 12)
CC-70	8	16	Hold of .785 relay 236-1,2,3-(12,6,4) MC-DR Reset Control #1 239-1-(4) MC-DR Reset Control #2 238-1-(12)
CC-71	14	15 1/3	PU of $\pi/2$ 279-1,2,3-(12,12,4) π 278-1,2,3-(12,12,4) 2 π 280-1,2,3-(12,12,4) SIO Invert 242-1-(12)
CC-72	0 1/2	2	Hold of SM-3 83-1,2-(12,4)
CC-73	14	15 1/3	PU of LM 42-1,2,3-(12,12,4) SIO Out #3 272-1,2,3-(12,12,4)
CC-74 (47-13-1 NC	13 1/2	16	Hold of Sign Control #2 71-1-(4)
CC-75 (52-3-6 NC)	11	8	Hold of Sign Control #1 70-1-(4)

Cam	Make	Break	Function
CC-76	15	16 1/3	PU of MC-DR Entry Control (1-2) 91-1,2,3-(12) MC-DR Entry Control (3-6) 92-1,2,3-(12) MC-DR Entry Control (4-8) 93-1,2,3-(12) EIO In 217-1,2,3-(12,12,4) EIO 1-18 Out 219-1,2-(12)
CC-77	16	0	Hold of MC-DR Entry Control (1-2) 91-1,2,3-(12) MC-DR Entry Control (3-6) 92-1,2,3-(12) MC-DR Entry Control (4-8) 93-1,2,3-(12)
CC-78	15	16	PU of Times Right 5-1,..,27-(12,12,4) Times Left 4-1,..,27-(12,12,4)
CC-79	6	5 1/3	PU of F 18-1-(4)
CC-80	1/16 12	9	Controls impulse to Cycle ctr magnet PU of Compare Control 8-1-(4)

STORAGE CAMS

Cam	Make	Break	Function
SC-1	1	1 1/2	1 impulse control
SC-2	2	2 1/2	2 impulse control
SC-3	3	3 1/2	3 impulse control
SC-4	4	4 1/2	4 impulse control
SC-5	5	5 1/2	5 impulse control
SC-6	6	6 1/2	6 impulse control
SC-7	7	7 1/2	7 impulse control
SC-8	8	8 1/2	8 impulse control
SC-9	9	9 1/2	9 impulse control
SC-10	12	12 1/2	Control carry impulse
SC-11	12	0	Hold of Str Ctr In SCA-1,2,3-(12,12,4) Str Ctr Out SCA-4,5,6-(12,12,4) Check Relay-(4) Invert Relay-(12) Reset Relay-(12) High Accuracy Ctrs Special In Sp64-1-(4) etc. Ctr 71 Normal Out Control SC71-14-(6) Ctr 71 Normal In Control SC71-16-(6) Ctr 71 Special Out (direct) SC71-15-(6) Ctr 71 Special Out (shifted) SC71-18-1,2-(12,6) Ctr 71 Special In (direct) SC71-17-(6) Ctr 71 Special In (shifted) SC71-19-1,2-(12,6) Switch Out SwA-1,2,3-(12,12,4) Switch Invert Relay-(12) PU of Ctr 71 Normal Out SC71-1,2,3-(12,12,6) Ctr 71 Normal In SC71-4,5,6-(12,12,6)

Cam	Make	Break	Function
SC-12	11	14	PU of Carry SCA-7,8-(12) 24th Column Carry SCA-10,11-(4) Check Relay-(4)
SC-13	2	1 1/2	PU of Carry Control SCA-9-(4) High Accuracy Carry Interlock CI-1,2-(6) Ctr 71 Carry Back Control SC71-20-(6)
SC-14	2	14 1/16	Hold of Carry Control SCA-9-(4) High Accuracy Carry Interlock CI-1,2-(6) Ctr 71 Carry Back Control SC71-20-(6)
SC-15	13	15 1/3	PU of 24th Column Carry SCA-10,11-(4) Hold of Choice Relay-(6)
SC-16	14	15 1/3	PU of Reset Relay-(12) Invert Relay-(12) to be used with Choice Counter
SC-17	14	14 1/2	PU of Invert Relay-(12) for minus absolute value RO
SC-18	14	14 1/2	PU of Invert Relay-(12) for plus absolute value RO

MP-DIV RELAYS AND FUSES

Relay No.	Fuse No.	Relay No.	Fuse No.	Relay No.	Fuse No.
1-row 1	23	25	35	64	35
1-row 2	24	26	35	65	35
1-row 3	25	27	35	66	38
1-row 4	26	28	35	67	38
1-row 5	27	29	35	68	38
1-row 6	28	30	35	69	40
1-row 7	29	31	35	70	39
1-row 8	30	32	35	71	38
1-row 9	31	33	38	72	38
2-row 1	14	34-1,2,3	39	73	38
2-row 2	15	34-4	40	74	38
2-row 3	16	35	40	75	38
2-row 4	17	36	41	76	38
2-row 5	18	37	36	77	38
2-row 6	19	38	37	78	38
2-row 7	20	39	37	79	38
2-row 8	21	40	37	80	38
2-row 9	22	41	37	81	38
3-1,..,24	33	42	37	82	38
3-25	38	43-1,..,10	42	83	38
4	32	43-11	36	84	38
5	32	43-12	41	85	38
6	34	44	42	86	38
7	34	45	42	87	41
8	34	46	42	88	41
9	34	47	42	89	39
10	34	48	42	90	43
11	34	49	43	91	32
12-1	34	50	43	92	32
12-2	35	51	43	93	32
13	34	52	43	94	38
14	34	53	43	95	43
15	34	54	43	96	43
16	34	55	43	97	43
17	34	56	44	98	43
18	34	57	39	99	47
19	34	58	39	99A	47
20	34	59	39	Shift Circuit	47
21	35	60	45	Low Order P-Out	47
22	35	61	45	Heavy Duty	46
23	35	62	45		
24	35	63	34		

MP-DIV RELAYS AND FUSES

Fuse No.	Relay No.	Fuse No.	Relay No.
1	Intermediate Counter Magnets	25	1- 3rd row
2	MC-DR Counter Magnets (1-2)	26	1- 4th row
3	MC-DR Counter Magnets (3-6)	27	1- 5th row
4	MC-DR Counter Magnets (4-8)	28	1- 6th row
5	MC-DR Counter Magnets (5)	29	1- 7th row
6	MC-DR Counter Magnets (7)	30	1- 8th row
7	MC-DR Counter Magnets (9)	31	1- 9th row
8	MP Counter Magnets	32	4,5,91,92,93
9	DD Counter Magnets columns 1-24	33	(3-1,..,24)
10	DD Counter Magnets columns 25-45	34	6,7,8,9,10,11,(12-1),13,14,15,16,17,18,19,20,63
11	PQ Counter Magnets columns 1-24	35	(12-2),21,22,23,24,25,26,27,28,29,30,31,32,64,65
12	PQ Counter Magnets columns 25-46 and 47	36	37,(43-11)
13	Q-Shift, Sequence, and Cycle Counter Magnets	37	38,39,40,41,42
14	2- 1st row	38	(3-25),33,66,67,68,71,72,73,74,75,76,77,78,79,80, 81,82,83,84,85,86,94
15	2- 2nd row		
16	2- 3rd row	39	(34-1,2,3),57,58,59,70,89
17	2- 4th row	40	(34-4),35,69
18	2- 5th row	41	36,(43-12),87,88
19	2- 6th row	42	(43-1,..,10),44,45,46,47,48
20	2- 7th row	43	49,50,51,52,53,54,55,90,95,96,97,98
21	2- 8th row	44	56
22	2- 9th row	45	60,61,62
23	1- 1st row	46	Heavy Duty Relays
24	1- 2nd row	47	99,99A,Shift Circuit,Low Order P-Out

INDEX

The references are to pages.

INDEX

INDEX

Made in United States
Orlando, FL
04 November 2026

90200665R00343